FROM REBEL TO RULER

FROM REBEL
to RULER

ONE HUNDRED YEARS *of the*
CHINESE COMMUNIST PARTY

TONY SAICH

THE BELKNAP PRESS *of*
HARVARD UNIVERSITY PRESS

Cambridge, Massachusetts
London, England
2021

Second printing

Library of Congress Cataloging-in-Publication Data

Names: Saich, Tony, author.
Title: From rebel to ruler : one hundred years of the Chinese Communist
    Party / Tony Saich.
Description: Cambridge, Massachusetts : The Belknap Press of Harvard
    University Press, 2021. | Includes bibliographical references and index.
Identifiers: LCCN 2020043104 | ISBN 9780674988118 (cloth)
Subjects: LCSH: Zhongguo gong chan dang—History. |
    Communism—China—History. | China—Politics and government—1912–1949. |
    China—Politics and government—1949–
Classification: LCC JQ1519.A5 S176 2021 | DDC 324.251/075–dc23
LC record available at https://lccn.loc.gov/2020043104

For Junko, Alex, Amanda, Roscoe, and Yasmin,
and my teachers David S. G. Goodman and Stuart R. Schram

Contents

Abbreviations   *ix*

Introduction: Welcome to the Party   1

PART ONE: HOW THE EAST WAS WON

1 The End of the Empire   21
2 Origins, Alliance, and Failure, 1920–1930   38
3 Wanderings in the Wilderness, 1930–1940   77
4 Victories at Last, 1940–1948   115
5 The Chinese Communist Revolution   152

PART TWO: HOW THE EAST IS RULED

6   Consolidating the Revolution, 1948–1956   177
7   Radicalizing the Revolution, 1956–1969   207
8   Charting a Way Forward, 1969–1981   245
9   Reform, Rebellion, and Restoration, 1982–1993   289
10 Renewed Reform and the Roots of Wealth, 1993–2002   325
11 The WTO World and China's Rise, 2002–2012   357
12 Creating the China Dream, 2012–2021   390
    Conclusion: Legacies from the Past, Challenges for the Future   435

Notes   *469*
Acknowledgments   *529*
Illustration Credits   *531*
Index   *533*

Abbreviations

APC	Agricultural Producers' Cooperative
BRI	Belt and Road Initiative
CASS	Chinese Academy of Social Sciences
CC	Central Committee
CCP	Chinese Communist Party
CCRG	Central Cultural Revolution Group
CEC	Central Executive Committee
Comintern	Communist International
CPPCC	Chinese People's Political Consultative Conference
CPSU	Communist Party of the Soviet Union
DPP	Democratic Progressive Party
ECCI	Executive Committee of the Communist International
ERA	Eighth Route Army
GLF	Great Leap Forward
GMD	Guomindang (Nationalist Party)
NFA	New Fourth Army
NGO	nongovernmental organization
NPC	National People's Congress
PLA	People's Liberation Army
Politburo	Political Bureau
PRC	People's Republic of China
SARS	severe acute respiratory syndrome
SASAC	State-owned Assets Supervision and Administration
SOE	state-owned enterprise
USSR	Union of Soviet Socialist Republics
WTO	World Trade Organization

FROM REBEL TO RULER

Introduction

WELCOME TO THE PARTY

⋆

In 1976, when I was studying in China with a group of British exchange students, one of the other foreign students, a pro-Maoist, referred to us as "British empiricists." With no idea what it meant, I took it as a compliment until someone pointed out that the human yo-yo Deng Xiaoping, who had been purged once again, had been denounced by his radical opponents as an "empiricist." Deng was accused of underplaying ideology in favor of "seeking truth from facts"—empiricism! The encounter made me realize the importance of how the Chinese Communist Party (CCP) uses language and ideology not only in daily life but also in factional struggles. Simple slogans point out what is correct behavior and guide how people throughout the system should behave. These slogans were particularly useful when literacy levels were low, because they were easy for the general population to absorb. The CCP's main mouthpiece, the *People's Daily,* used only a limited number of Chinese characters so that its message would reach as many people as possible.

Presiding over Diversity

There is no other political party quite like the CCP. The party's longevity, size, endurance, and ability to overcome seemingly impossible odds make it a very distinct political organization. Yet, it is difficult to define precisely what the CCP is. We can outline its structures and the duties of its members, but we cannot capture its essence this way. The party's sweep and range of control are stunning. There are party branches in almost all of the four million grassroots organizations in China (villages, townships, and urban committees), but reports frequently mention the spreading problems of corruption and unruliness. There are ninety million party members (about one-tenth of China's adult population, and more than the population of Germany), but it has been difficult to get many of the members, especially the wealthy, to pay their dues. What compels people to join the party? Since the CCP is the only game in town, anyone with policy or political or personal aspirations will want to join, thus sucking all the tensions within society into the party. The views of members vary widely. I have met party members who are more Stalinist than Stalin, others who are more conservative than the former British prime minister Margaret Thatcher, and yet others who describe themselves as social democrats or as belonging the democratic faction within the party. Some are among the richest folk in the land, some are true believers, and some are simply trying to advance their own careers. Around one-third of all new party recruits come from college campuses, but a 2014 survey revealed that the younger the applicant, the more likely they were to apply for membership out of self-interest.[1] This diversity within the party explains the CCP's obsession with "unity of thought" and the building or coercing of conformity.

The CCP is an extremely complex organization. At the local level, in the streets and villages, there are subtle interactions between party and society that make clear-cut definitions difficult.[2] Several decades ago, I was in a jeep meandering down a mountain road when I hit a road block. Traffic was being held up while a new bridge was being dedicated in a traditional ceremony. Puzzled, I asked those presiding over the ceremony whether the local party had given permission for the dedication. Baffled looks greeted me until one observer explained that the person in the elaborate robes was the party secretary. It was incumbent on him, as the most important figure in the village, to dedicate the new bridge that would provide a crucial link to the outside world and, the villagers hoped, bring new wealth to the locality. Such events, which occur every day throughout China, cause us to reflect on the relationship between the party and society and between tradition and modernity. Did the party secretary believe that the elaborate dedication would encourage the spirits to ensure that wealth would flow into the village? Did he feel compelled to perform the celebration to retain or build credibility among the locals? Was he bringing the word of the party into the village, or was he bringing local interests and possibly heterodox beliefs into the party? In all of these cases, it was probably both. The traditional ritual contrasted with the construction of the bridge, which represented modernity and integration of the village with the outside world. The bridge was the link to the market that had been the driving force behind the reforms of the 1980s and 1990s.

Even though the CCP has tried to penetrate society more thoroughly than its predecessors, the last seventy years, since it has taken power, have revealed the residual power of local cultures. In the southern province of Guangdong, traditional clan structures play an important role in economic and political life. In villages that I have visited in the province, large lineage halls have been restored or built anew, clearly forming the most important organizing point for political and socioeconomic exchanges. This reemergence of more overt traditional power structures has made implementation of party rule more difficult. In some villages, the party secretary and lineage head are one and the same. In Yantian village in south China, I discovered that every CCP secretary since 1949 had been a member of the same dominant lineage. This included during the period of land reform, when some clan members were executed as landlords, the Great Leap Forward (GLF) of 1958–1960, when communal practices and living were pushed to an extreme, and the period since 1978, as the party has allowed economic reforms. Lineage dominance over local politics is traditional, not Leninist or even class-based. Yantian party secretaries in recent years have proven adept at retaining the full support of the higher-level party authorities while protecting the interests of village members, and in so doing they have acquired considerable wealth for the village. Again, the question arises as to whether the CCP is controlling the local community through the lineage, or the lineage is using the party to protect and promote its own interests, or some combination of the two.

These local identities are reinforced by religious practices and customs. Officially, China is an atheist country, but the CCP has had no choice but to tolerate religious practices as long as they do not challenge state power. The party has adopted a series of secular official celebrations that mark key dates in the history of the revolution or in Communist traditions (such as National Day, October 1, and International Labor Day, May 1), but the most important festivals are derived from Chinese tradition (Chinese New Year, a week in January or February based on the lunar calendar, and Qing Ming, grave-sweeping day in early April) and local customs. Local religious worship and traditional practices have blossomed since the beginning of the reform era, but organized religion that stresses an allegiance beyond the CCP is viewed with suspicion and is usually repressed.

Despite attempts to produce a more monolithic and obedient society, such as the "reeducation" program for those of Islamic culture in the northwest province of Xinjiang, China remains a culturally and linguistically diverse nation. The CCP has fared best when it has accepted this fact and has adapted policy to reflect these variations. Before 1949, the CCP survived where it dealt with local politics and adapted central dictates to suit the local environment. In fact, local Communist Party leaders went even further by using traditional rituals and symbols to attract the residents to their cause and to oppose the traditional powerholders.[3] By contrast, the party was unsuccessful, often with disastrous consequences, when ideology and central dictate dominated and attempts were made to change reality on the ground too quickly or too radically. After 1949, the imposition of an impractical ideological approach to policy led to disaster during the GLF, when tens of millions died from starvation, and later, during the Cultural Revolution (1966–1969), when havoc reigned in urban China in particular and untold numbers were unjustly persecuted.[4] The nation fared better when greater flexibility was permitted to allow for local adaptation, as in the early 1950s and during the reform period since 1978, although Xi Jinping's current centralization of policy-making threatens to challenge this.

From imperial times through the years of the Republic (1912–1949) and into the period of the People's Republic of China (PRC), multiple realities have operated beneath the façade of a unitary nation-state. This makes it dangerous for historians to generalize. CCP policy that might suit the Han heartland can produce unexpected consequences in the border regions or the hinterland. What works in the megacity of Shanghai does not necessarily work in the Yunnan villages along the border with Myanmar. In the policy realm, making a single policy for the whole country is referred to as "cutting with one knife." Topography and climate vary as much across China as across Europe or North America, and living on its land mass are fifty-five recognized national minorities. These minority populations occupy over 60 percent of the total land mass, most of them in strategic border areas, but they account for less than 10 percent of the total population. The periphery has always been important for Chinese security concerns, providing a buffer zone to protect the "Han-core" from potential invaders. Beijing's concern about these areas is heightened by the fact that vital natural resources are also located there. The most recent example of the CCP's concern that these areas might slip out of control is the revelation in 2018 that the party had been supervising a massive program of reeducation in Xinjiang to eradicate Islamic identity, for fear that it might provide an alternative narrative to that of the party-state. The CCP finds any appeal to an alternative narrative of identity problematic and responds with a mixture of repression, suppression of traditional culture, blaming of "outside entities" for stirring up trouble, and hopes that greater investment will "develop" the problem away.

The CCP must rule over this complex environment. When the ruling elite has remained united, it has survived surprisingly well. But when the elite has been divided about the way forward or the tactics to be pursued, crisis has followed. Even though the CCP has existed for one hundred years and ruled for over seventy years, it has not been able to institutionalize its ruling apparatus. This deficit is most apparent with respect to succession. Only once has the party achieved a smooth transfer of power from one generation of leaders to the next. That said, China's institutions have clearly delivered impressive economic growth since 1978, when the limited pro-market reforms were introduced. It remains to be seen whether they will be up to the task of managing China's next phase of development.

All CCP members are supposed to follow certain duties, which sound much like the obligations of many other political parties. The minority should obey the will of the majority, for example; but the problem is that the will of the majority changes as new winners emerge from inner-party struggles. Following an official history can be tricky once "history" changes. Worship of Mao Zedong, which reached its peak during the Cultural Revolution, was encouraged, only to be cast aside following Mao's death and the arrest of his closest supporters. Heroes of the party one day can become villains the next. Liu Shaoqi was one of Mao's most ardent supporters during his rise to power and became China's president in 1959. But during the Cultural Revolution, he was denounced as the "number one person in authority taking the capitalist road," with Deng Xiaoping following as a close second.

Party members are expected to attend regular meetings to hear the party's views on particular topics or, on occasion, even to make self-criticisms about incorrect thoughts or behavior. Such meetings are often perfunctory, with attendees using the opportunity to catch up on local gossip. In the mid-1970s, when my fellow students and I were engaging in manual labor in rural China, we listened to a woman reading the key articles in the CCP's flagship newspaper. It hardly seemed to comprise "political study," but the farmers loved it, as it gave them a rest from backbreaking labor. One party veteran commented to me that it was like going to church in the West. This is not true, however, because no one forces you to go to church, and there are many different faiths that one may choose to follow. By contrast, once you sign up for the CCP, there is only one true faith that you are expected to adhere to.

The overriding conviction of the CCP is that an individual will gain more by entrusting certain choices and freedoms to the collective than she can by acting on her own. This is reflected in the party's frequent use of the term "masses," who are regarded as undifferentiated in their interests. In the reform era, this conviction has come into conflict with the introduction of the market mechanism, in which individual choices, wants, and desires are more important than adherence to a party-prescribed ideology. Citizens rather than masses. Beyond the fact that the state-owned sector is at the core of party patronage and power, this explains the CCP's preference for the state sector and for the collective economy over the private.

Even outside of the party, strict control is exerted over what people can read, see, and enjoy. Although oversight may at times be relaxed, there are rigid limits to what is permissible. Overt opposition to party rule will be crushed, and independent organizations to support labor or other interest groups will be immediately suppressed. There can be only one national labor organization or one women's federation; this restriction creates a silo structure that makes it easier for the party to exert control. Imagine how dreadful it would be for two national philately associations to argue over the value of a stamp. These organizations are supposed to operate like transmission belts, passing down party policy while feeding the members' views back up the system.

On the positive side, this also means that information can be passed up the system to the leadership quite effectively. In the late 1990s, one group comprising senior women from the All-China Women's Federation was deeply concerned about the condition of rural women, especially the growing incidence of female suicide. Forming a nongovernmental organization, they used their "insider" position to gain the attention of senior policymakers. However, the balance is clearly in favor of a top-down approach. Given their population size and the role that official CCP history ascribes to them, it is noteworthy that the one significant group that does not have a national organization is the farmers. The silo structure prevents horizontal coordination or actions that could cut across party authority and undermine the CCP's capacity to exert control. This fear was realized during the massive student-led demonstrations in 1989, when students and workers in Beijing formed independent organizations that bridged the vertical silos. From that moment, their fate was sealed.

The system requires censorship to prevent citizens from accessing information on their own that might conflict with the official narrative. Censorship is extensive, with hierarchical classifications of what can be read at different levels of society and regularly distributed lists indicating phrases that must be avoided and guidelines about how to cover certain events or whether they should be ignored completely. This can produce comical outcomes. For example, it is absolutely forbidden to portray General Secretary Xi Jinping online as Winnie the Pooh. The downside of using language to ensure control is that the regime opens itself up to cynicism, with citizens poking fun at official slogans. Thus, after the implosion of the Soviet Union in 1989, when the party put forward the slogan "Only socialism can save China," the students replied, "Only China can save socialism," while after the 2008–2009 financial crisis, online wags noted, "Only China can save capitalism."

Organization, Formal and Informal

So, what holds the party together? A former secretary of Mao Zedong once told me that a communist party needs only two departments: organization and propaganda. He had headed both. The organization department provides the party with the enormous power of patronage as it places its members in all key posts. The local organization department keeps a dossier, as do workplaces, which records not only one's intimate personal details but also one's political performance. The system of appointments enables the party to remove those deemed undesirable and provides a means to keep people in line. "Correct behavior" is promoted by the propaganda department. The party oversees a vast network of research organizations and training schools to inculcate in members an understanding of and support for central policies. There are almost three thousand party schools spread throughout China. Of course, this strategy does not always work, but it does ensure a near-unanimity of public expression. Expulsion or worse awaits those who do not follow the official view.

During times of change, in particular, this system allows party members to adjust to the "new reality" and know what is expected of them. This was brought home to me when the "Gang of Four" were arrested following Mao Zedong's death in 1976. The "Gang" included Mao's widow and three of her close supporters. Before the arrest, the Chinese media had been full of praise for their views, but their removal brought such coverage to a grinding halt. When, naively, I suggested to one of my Chinese teachers that many members of the media would be purged, she looked at me in surprise and asked, "Why?" They were paid by the party to write what they were told, and they would continue to do so. It was not their fault if the message had changed. Of course, this was not the case for "true believers" throughout the system; they were removed from office, and some of them were executed for their "sins."

Before delving into the history of the party, it is important to outline its key organizational features and explain the language it uses, much of which is jarring to Western ears. Westerners tend to balk at savage denunciations for following or implementing the "incorrect political line," although recent populist trends in the United States and Europe have begun to feature similar abusive rhetoric.

From its earliest days, the CCP adopted a Leninist structure, and, apart from a brief period at the height of the Cultural Revolution, this has remained the dominant organizational form. Although the interpretation of Marxism has been highly flexible, from the late 1920s, democratic centralism has been entrenched as the organizing principle of the party. It enshrined a hierarchical structure of rule that persists to the present day. Democratic centralism is based on three major principles. First, the organizational structure of the party resembles a pyramid, with the individual subordinate to the organization and the minority subordinate to the Central Committee (CC). The second principle is that of collective leadership, which is designed to mitigate the tendency toward a dominant leader that is inherent in such a hierarchical structure. But this has rarely worked. The confusion that can arise between collective leadership and a dominant leader is clearly revealed in the 2017 version of the Party Statutes. One clause notes the need to encourage intra-party democracy and safeguard individual members' rights, but it continues by emphasizing the need to "firmly uphold the authority and centralized, unified leadership of the Central Committee with Comrade Xi Jinping at the core." Only this centralization can ensure the necessary solidarity and unity required to implement party decisions. This mandate sets severe constraints around the third principle, the protection of minority rights and the ability of members to hold views different from those of the party leadership. In principle, individuals can present their views up to and including to the CC, but they must carry out policy while awaiting a decision. In reality, neither party norms nor internal discipline operates in accordance with these strictures. Personal networks and factions run throughout the party. There is a strong tendency toward personal rule, which dominates over institutionalized rule.

This tendency has been embedded in Chinese politics both before and after 1949. The Nationalist Party (also known as Guomindang, GMD, or Kuomintang), with which the CCP alternately vied and allied until the CCP's final victory in 1949, was also organized along Leninist lines. It had been reorganized in this mode by the Bolsheviks in the early 1920s to instill discipline among a motley group of followers of the founder, Sun Yat-sen. As with the CCP, the structure lent itself to the dominance of a powerful individual at the apex, in this case, Chiang Kai-shek, who ruled on Taiwan until his death in 1975. Some claim that in the 1940s CCP leaders promoted Mao Zedong as the supreme leader to counter Chiang's position within the GMD. While the structure has remained the same on the mainland, where the CCP rules, it ended on Taiwan once the island democratized.

The party branch (introduced in 1925) is the foundation of the party at the grassroots level in the workplace and the neighborhood; it leads up through the organization at the local administrative level to the provincial level and then to the center. Grassroots organizations and their reliability have been a constant concern for the party center, not least for the current general secretary, Xi Jinping, who has tried to replace the pursuit of self-interest and local interests with a strengthened loyalty to the party. At the apex of power is the Politburo and its Standing Committee, which in theory are elected by the CCP Central Committee. In practice, CC members are presented with a slate of candidates that has already been thrashed out by the party elite.

In theory, minority rights are to be protected, with debate allowed within the party but not aired in public. In practice, as with the Communist Party of the Soviet Union under Stalin, there is a persistent tendency for the chair or general secretary of the party to dominate the entire apparatus. Before 1949, the stress on organizational stability and adherence to the correct political line went together with the increasing adulation of Mao Zedong and the concentration of power in his hands. While those supporters around him clearly considered "Mao Zedong Thought" to be the pooling of collective wisdom, the personality cult that developed around the "supreme leader" and that contributed to the decimation of the "old party" during the Cultural Revolution clearly originated in pre-1949 leadership practices. Despite continual references to the need for collective leadership, dominance by one person within the party has been a distinctive feature of post-1949 CCP politics. Collective leadership may have gained traction under General Secretary Hu Jintao (2002–2012), who, despite holding the title of general secretary, operated more as the first among equals and sought political consensus. In-dividual dominance and loyalty to the supreme leader were restored as the key test of membership, however, once Xi Jinping consolidated power and was designated as the core of the leadership.

The designation of "core leader" is crucial in CCP parlance, but not all leaders receive such an exalted appellation. Although it has no formal defi-nition or legal standing, "core leader" indicates that the person is more than the first among equals. The concept was resurrected by Deng Xiaoping fol-lowing the traumatic events of the 1989 demonstrations that shook the party to its roots and resulted in the purge of General Secretary Zhao Ziyang, who was deemed to be too sympathetic to the students' demands. To bolster Jiang Zemin, the new general secretary, Deng Xiaoping referred to him as the core of the third generation of leaders—Mao Zedong having been the core of the first generation, and Deng himself the core of the second. Scholars at the Central Party School have noted that the designation "core" in the case of Xi Jinping means that not only does he have the deciding vote if there is a policy deadlock, but he can also initiate policy without engagement by the other senior party leaders.

This tendency to concentrate power is underpinned by the factional struc-ture of the CCP. Although factions are theoretically banned, they have ex-isted from the party's beginnings and have impacted both policy and po-litical outcomes. The party that was formed in the early 1920s from a group centered around Chen Duxiu grew out of the May Fourth study group en-vironment (1915–1919); subsequently, there was a group that coalesced around Wang Ming and those who returned from Moscow in the 1930s and, of course, finally, Mao Zedong built up his own coterie of loyal followers. In 1929, one official in the Jinggangshan Border Region commented, "Party members worship their leader and put their faith in heroes while they ac-cord less recognition to the Party organization."[5]

Personal factions are not necessarily based on policy choices but rather on trust and loyalty that date back years. Many pre- and post-1949 political struggles can be better understood once you know who did what to whom and when. Because individuals depend on personal patronage for career ad-vancement, a cult develops around the faction leader and concentrates power in their hands. Keeping that person in power becomes crucial to maintaining one's own benefits and influence. This dynamic causes political struggle within the party to become intense and highly personal. As Xi Jinping consolidated power, he promoted those who had previously worked with him in the provinces of Fujian and Zhejiang. His two predecessors followed the same practice: Hu Jintao promoted many of those who had worked with him in the Communist Youth League, while Jiang Zemin was viewed as having a Shanghai faction gathered around him.

The supreme leader consolidates their position through promoting and accepting a guiding ideology that the party faithful must follow. Mao Zedong Thought was developed in Yan'an, northwest China, and evolved once power was seized in 1949. After this came Deng Xiaoping Theory, which was intended to guide the period of reform following Mao's death. The achievements of the successor are not meant to eclipse those of the predecessor. Neither of Deng's successors, Jiang Zemin or Hu Jintao, managed to get their names inscribed in the Party Statutes, even though some of their key concepts were included. The strengthened control of Xi Jinping over the party apparatus is evident in the mention of his name in the 2017 Party Statutes, in the phrase "Xi Jinping Thought on Socialism with Chinese Characteristics for a New Era." Use of the term "Thought" places Xi on the same plane as Mao Zedong: Mao guided the CCP to victory, while Xi Jinping provides guidance for the new era of Chinese power. Given the necessity to list the entire sequence of supreme leaders, if the CCP remains in power for another one hundred years, the preamble to the Statutes might be intolerably long.

Ideology, Line, and Infallibility

The language of the CCP can appear harsh and archaic to the foreign ear, but use of the correct language is important for the party to maintain control over its members and society. Words are chosen carefully, and any deviation from a proscribed phrase can spell trouble. But people find inventive ways to get around the prohibition of referring to certain events. Some netizens, for example, refer to June 4, 1989, when martial law troops entered and cleared Tiananmen Square, as May 35.

In early 2009, Chinese cyberspace erupted with news of a lively and tenacious alpaca-like animal that had emerged to battle against encroachment on its habitat in the Gobi Desert. The animal was named the "grass mud horse," which in Chinese is a homophone for a vile obscenity. Its grassland habitat was being invaded by river crabs, a homophone for a party phrase referring to "harmonious society." The clear implication was that online freedom was being curtailed by party intrusion. Sometimes the crabs were said to wear three watches, using a phrase that in Chinese sounds like the Three Represents policy promoted by Jiang Zemin.[6] The play on words caught the censors unawares, and the horse became an instant sensation, with toy horses quickly selling off the store shelves and a children's song about the horse attracting some 1.5 million online listeners. The party disclosed its level of alarm when it announced that such mischief must end, as the issue had been "elevated to a political level." Such events reveal a partially submerged discourse that is at odds with the official discourse. Consequently, the party expends great resources, both material and physical, to scrub the internet clean of such devious posts. Especially notorious are members of the "50-cent party," who are so named for the money they receive for every post they place on the internet that supports party policy.

The new media have also been used for more serious purposes: exposing the government coverup of the spread of SARS in 2002, pushing the authorities to follow up on their alleged culpability for a major high-speed rail crash in 2011, revealing the lavish lifestyles of some corrupt officials, and trying to alert the nation to the dangers of the outbreak of COVID-19 in Wuhan in late 2019. These kinds of exposés run counter to the CCP's traditional management of information. The CCP seeks to channel information flows vertically and, in the same way as with organizations, to limit horizontal flows. Control over information and access are key components of political power. Contrary to President Clinton's assertion that trying to control the internet is like trying to nail Jell-O to a wall, the CCP has proven that it is indeed possible to control the flow of information. Not only has it been remarkably successful in creating the system of online censorship called the Great Firewall, but it has also been able to use social media to promote its own propaganda, both domestically and internationally. Even though Facebook and Twitter are banned in China, the CCP makes effective use of them overseas. In February 2011, when outlining his ideas for strengthening social control, General Secretary Hu Jintao noted that the internet was a major threat to social stability. On taking power, Xi Jinping emphasized that the new social media should be "managed" and used to promote the party's views. For Xi, the internet had become a "major battlefield of public opinion," and thus it was necessary to "construct a powerful internet army" to gain control over it. This control over political discourse and what is permissible to say and write, a kind of soft power with hard characteristics, is combined with strict party discipline and more coercive mechanisms to ensure party control.

The party believes that it possesses the ability not only to correctly interpret the past but also to outline the future, and this belief has led the party
to declare its infallibility. Thus, when mistakes are made, blame must lie
either with members of the party following the incorrect political line and
leading party members astray, or with "outsiders," especially foreigners, med-
dling in party affairs. This results in a particular form of political struggle
featuring the use of accusatory language that has moved beyond even that
of the Communist Party of the Soviet Union under Stalin. Those who run
afoul of the party are denounced as "right opportunists" or "left deviationists"
or, the worst of all sins, "Trotskyites." The terms are not mutually exclusive—it
is possible to be accused of more than one sin.

The most heinous crime is to follow an incorrect political line. The "political line" is a crucial component of the CCP's lexicon and practice of rule.
It is a concise formulation that encapsulates what the party leadership sees
as the core task for party members at a particular moment. Thus it is flexible, changing over time to suit the needs of the present day. When I was a
student at Nanjing University in 1977, the contemporary history course was
titled "The Ten Line Struggles of the CCP" (namely the ten major, historical
struggles within the CCP) and the textbook was designed to follow this
script. The use of "political line" to direct policy and criticize opponents continued not only through the Mao years but also well into the post-1978
reform period. Mao's widow, Jiang Qing, and her closest followers were later
denounced for forming a "counterrevolutionary clique," and for being "anti-
party elements." For her part, Jiang Qing denounced the judge presiding
at her trial as a "fascist." Zhao Ziyang, party leader at the time of the 1989
student-led demonstrations, was accused of the ultimate sin of seeking to
"split the party." Such phrases may sound jarring, but they have helped the
CCP maintain coherence in a dynamic environment, as the party struggled
to take power in 1949 and then to retain control. Adherence to the correct
political line was ensured via campaigns in which all party members, and
often non-party members of the society, were expected to participate.

Inner-party dissent is thus a dangerous game, despite the appeal to democratic centralism and the right of minorities to voice their opinion. One
must not only be careful about comments made in the present but also worry
about words from the past, which can return to haunt one. This happened
to Liu Shaoqi when, during the Cultural Revolution, his views on "How to
Be a Good Communist" (1951) were parsed and said to reveal his inner-
Confucian spirit and anti-party tendencies. Liu himself had warned of this

problem back in March 1937, when he wrote a perceptive text about the problems of debate within the party. Although he was writing about the challenges of working underground in GMD-controlled areas, his critique could be extended to the party as a whole. He noted that it is always better to be "leftist" than "rightist," and that the methods of ideological struggle within the party had become so excessive that "absolutely no freedom of calm discussion" existed. Liu recognized that the party was threatened by new or unorthodox ideas and that the result was meetings to struggle against them. Thus, it was safer to attack the party from the left than from the right. This maxim is still true today. Such a framing of struggle produces a very harsh rhetoric that is part and parcel of CCP discourse.

"Class" and "class struggle" are important in the CCP's lexicon. In good Marxist-Leninist fashion, progress is explained in terms of the class struggle on behalf of the proletariat and their allies. Parties are categorized in terms of their class composition, even if the designations bear little relationship to reality. Before 1949, the CCP defined the composition of the GMD, often erroneously, in class terms. Such definitions provided a guide to action, just as did the classifications of landlord, or rich, middle, or poor peasant. One's classification could mean the difference between life and death. After 1949, Mao Zedong exhorted the party faithful "never to forget class struggle." He denounced the revisionism in Yugoslavia under Tito, and in the Soviet Union under Khrushchev and Brezhnev, that resulted in a "capitalist restoration." Domestically, people at all levels in the CCP could be labeled as "capitalist roaders."

By the 1990s, however, this kind of language appeared more archaic and did not resonate with much of the population, who were enjoying the fruits of the economic reforms and greater personal freedom. Nevertheless, speeches by Xi Jinping are still peppered with such language. In September 2019, addressing students at the Central Party School, Xi used the word "struggle" almost sixty times. One theme that did resonate with the people was the idea that the playing field was not level and those with good connections fared better than others. The 1989 student chants denouncing official corruption won them the support of much of the population in urban China. Thus, in more recent years, the main weapon for inner-party struggle has shifted to accusing opponents of corruption.

Given the self-told history of humiliation at the hands of foreigners, it is not surprising that foreigners are frequently portrayed as seeking to undermine the authority of the CCP, whether be it through transforming the political system to look more like those of the West ("peaceful evolution"), stoking tensions with Taiwan, or encouraging opposition in Hong Kong. As the 2019 Hong Kong demonstrations expanded, it was inevitable that the party would "discover" that Britons and Americans had been stirring up trouble. Reference to this history of humiliation was used to inspire resistance to the economic sanctions imposed by President Trump in 2018–2019; the sanctions were portrayed as just the latest example of a powerful West bullying China to get its way. Similarly, the unrest in Tibet and Xinjiang is not seen as resulting from the CCP's own policies toward the region but rather from the promptings of "foreign elements." Even the premier think tank for the social sciences, the Chinese Academy of Social Sciences, was accused of being "infiltrated by foreign forces" and was said to have engaged in "illegal collusion" at a sensitive time.[7]

This notion of foreign abuse has pervaded society and even the business community. In February 2018, the cochair of the business conglomerate the Hainan Group claimed that investigations into its activities within China came from "reactionary forces from both China and overseas countering China's rise, and are a major conspiracy against the Communist Party Central Committee with Xi Jinping at its core."[8] Apparently, these forces had been indulging in their evil plots for a long time. This tendency to see conspiracy everywhere is a legacy of the prerevolutionary struggle.

These core features of the party developed during a long period of gestation following the CCP's founding in 1921. The early members of the party experienced the collapse of the Chinese imperial system in 1911–1912 and found themselves in uncharted territory as they sought to find solutions that could restore China to its former glory and rightful place in the world. This desire was shared by many of their contemporaries, but ultimately they chose a distinctive path that would provide a holistic solution to the challenges facing China. This path included doses of Leninist organization and Stalinist political methods, combined with selected traditions from China's past. This book seeks to explain how the CCP progressed from extremely unpromising circumstances to gain power and develop into the party that controls the second-largest economy in the world, and how its legacy continues to shape China today.

Before delving into discussion of the principal causes of the Chinese Communist revolution and how the CCP has ruled, let me define how I am using the term "revolution" in this book. First, the focus is on the Chinese

Communist revolution and not on the Chinese revolution in its entirety, which would require an in-depth study of the fall of the imperial system and of the nationalist movement and the GMD. Second, I use an expansive definition of revolution in line with Charles Tilly's notion of a "great revolution" that transforms economic and social structures as well as political institutions.[9] The ultimate outcome of the revolution was a new economic path overseen by an institution radically different from anything that had gone before, which, as in the Soviet Union, sought to transform the nature of the "masses" under its control—yet another attempt to create the "new socialist man/woman." For the Marxist-Leninist–inspired leaders, the utopian revolution was intended to bring power to those oppressed by the old regime and to those who would enjoy greater satisfaction, both material and spiritual, under the new mode of production and its socialist relations. This was a worthy ideal but one, sadly, not achieved by either the Chinese revolution or the Russian revolution.

The period beginning with the disintegration and eventual collapse of the Chinese Empire in 1911 is marked by the search for a suitable state form that could make the nation independent, wealthy, and powerful. However, that search did not end in 1949. In addition to the question of what kind of state system would rule China, there was the associated question of what kind of institutions should preside over the Chinese political system.

The years before 1949 comprised an intense period of learning for the CCP as it adapted Soviet theories, practices, and organization to better suit Chinese realities. This process entailed a shift in emphasis from an urban revolution to a movement based in the countryside, if not a movement of the countryside. The primacy of a Leninist organization was a given, but rule and authority by the charismatic Mao Zedong was slowly grafted atop the Leninist structures. The CCP made good use of alliances, despite a catastrophic disaster in 1927 (when its supposed partner the GMD turned on it and slaughtered hundreds of CCP members), and, positioning itself as a national champion in the fight against the Japanese invaders, kept the movement alive and won new supporters. At crucial moments, the CCP received support from the Soviets, but it was no Soviet clone or baggage-train government like those established in Eastern Europe after World War II. The CCP's own key experiences in the revolutionary struggle were important in shaping not only the institutions that ruled the People's Republic but also the nature and style of PRC politics. These topics are treated in Part 1.

The year 1949 does not represent a clear dividing line in this history, and continuities coexist with change. The search for stability and effective governing institutions did not end in that year. Initially, the CCP oversaw a brief attempt to Sovietize the state, economy, and society while restoring economic stability. This experiment was short lived, taking place before Mao Zedong led the CCP to embark on the economic adventurism of the GLF, followed by the political adventurism of the Cultural Revolution, which almost destroyed the party and devoured some of its most important and influential children. The death of supreme leader Mao in 1976 provided an opportunity for another radical shift in policy direction, following a similar pattern in other authoritarian systems. The CCP refers to the period since 1978 as one of "reform and opening-up," and this has certainly been the case. The reforms, overseen by the new paramount leader, Deng Xiaoping, have changed every aspect of life, while the opening-up has resulted in China becoming a major player on the world stage and a destination for global capital. China is now the world's second largest economy and will eventually become the largest, having witnessed the fastest growth in history. Within a generation, the country went through what has taken other countries centuries to accomplish. The accumulated impacts on the global economy and governance were unimaginable when the CCP took power. How might the PRC use this newfound power, and how will the international community respond? These topics form the content of Part 2.

This book seeks to outline how a group of young men and a few women, who came together in the tumultuous years following the collapse of the empire and World War I, set in motion a movement that would create the most powerful political organization in the world, overseeing an economy that would come to rival that of the United States. It is an extraordinary story of survival, disaster, and resurrection. Given the conditions under which the movement labored, the CCP should never have come to power. The struggle entailed liberating the Chinese people from what the CCP sees as a century of humiliation at the hands of foreigners and domestic exploitation by landlords and comprador bourgeoisie. *From Rebel to Ruler* traces the twists and turns of this history, while drawing lessons from the revolutionary struggle that shaped the patterns and institutions of CCP rule after 1949.

Forty-five years ago, when I was a student in the country, I could not have imagined the changes that China has experienced. If anyone had dared to suggest that it would be possible to pull China out of the morass of the

Cultural Revolution, I would have told them that the idea was crazy. The CCP and the world are now trying to come to terms with the consequences of these changes and what they mean for our collective future. In shifting from a revolutionary party to a ruling party, the CCP has come a long way, but it still faces major challenges to rise out of the ranks of the middle-income countries and to consolidate an institutional framework that will finally deliver the modern state apparatus for which China's leaders have been searching for some one hundred years.

PART ONE

HOW *the* EAST *was* WON

CHAPTER ONE

The End of the Empire

⋆

When thirteen young Chinese men met in the French concession of Shanghai on a hot July day in 1921, they could not have known that the organization they were founding would become the driver of one of the greatest revolutionary upheavals of all time. Less than thirty years later, the CCP had seized power in Beijing, and now, one hundred years later, it is an economic superpower that sends shivers down the spines of many in Washington, who see the country as America's primary rival on the global stage. This book tells the story of how the CCP fought against seemingly insuperable odds to gain power, and how it has survived self-inflicted disasters to maintain that power for seven decades. It is a dramatic story that forms a key part of the global upheavals of the last century. While much of the CCP's energies were absorbed by internal challenges, including civil war and struggle against "class enemies," the party saw itself as participating in a global revolution—initially as part of the Soviet proletarian resistance to imperialism, later as a leader of the nonaligned movement, and finally as a model of development that offered an alternative to the capitalism of the West.

The End of the Old Order: Unity and Diversity

The seemingly innocuous uprising that broke out in Wuchang, Central China, on October 10, 1911, and brought down the Qing dynasty (1644–1912), might look as if it put a sudden end to a long-lived and durable system. However, the system had been in decline for some time. For one thing, it was unable to counter the forces of the West that had burst onto the scene

so aggressively with the First Opium War of 1839–1842. Westernizing influences were not only direct, through military means, but also indirect,
through the penetration of new ideas that led to a questioning of the legitimacy of a system based around the emperor. Despite reformers' best efforts
to update the old to accommodate the new, the old Qing system was rigid
and unable to adapt sufficiently to the new challenges. In addition, domestic
economic pressures were increasing, and they derived from both internal and
external causes.

Traditional Chinese political culture and political arrangements are often
described in broad terms that reduce them to caricatures or clichés that con-
fuse as much as they clarify. Yet, like all such descriptions they contain kernels
of truth. The CCP has adopted many of these broad characterizations—
for instance, in defining China as a unitary entity with one culture, or in
claiming that the imperial legacy and dominant thought system predispose
China, not to democracy, but instead to a hierarchical form of government,
one that can too easily breed authoritarianism. The CCP, of course, uses
more polite phrases, such as "a people's democratic dictatorship" or "socialism
with Chinese characteristics."

Chinese historians and even CCP officials often refer to the longevity of
Chinese civilization, which dates back thousands of years. The CCP came
to power claiming that it represented a radical break with the past and a
new tradition of proletarian internationalism. But as the strength of revolutionary legitimacy has declined, first under Hu Jintao and even more
strongly under Xi Jinping, the CCP has begun to promote itself as the successor to and inheritor of Chinese tradition—including the continuity of
Chinese civilization, the tendency for autocratic rule, the importance of
Confucianism, and the lack of strong civil society organizations to act as
checks or to counter state power. But the reality on the ground, of course, is
always more complex.

It is commonly noted that Chinese state and society were relatively isolated from outside influences, with a self-perpetuating imperial system that
defined and limited the potential for meaningful change. The hierarchical
state system had the emperor at the pinnacle, surrounded by the members
of the court, and underpinned by a group of civil servants highly skilled and
trained in the Chinese classics. The emperor ruled by heavenly decree, but
he could be removed when appropriate signs, such as natural disasters, gave
the people the right to rebel. Rather than leading to fundamental systemic
change, rebellion only replaced one emperor or imperial system with another.

After the devastating Tangshan earthquake of 1976, rumors abounded that the disaster might signal the end of the "new emperor," Mao Zedong. And on September 9, 1976, Mao indeed died, but once again there was no change of system.

The strength of Chinese culture and institutions is demonstrated in the founding of the Qing dynasty (1644–1912). When the Manchus came from the northeast as "barbarian invaders" to found the dynasty, they were forced to accommodate to Chinese culture, adopt traditional Chinese rituals and other forms of legitimation, and use established social structures to ensure effective control over the society they had conquered. This process produced an insularity from alternative modes of thought and an ethnocentrism that the Chinese intelligentsia justified by invoking their unique heritage. Two Chinese words are important for grasping this worldview: *tianxia* and *Zhongguo*. *Tianxia* is literally translated as "the whole world" or "the realm," but the term connotes much more: a world order centered on the emperor and the imperial court, and radiating outward, eventually reaching the "barbarians" beyond the Chinese cultural sphere. To be accepted as new rulers, the Manchus had to acknowledge this cultural core and the essence of established Chinese society. *Zhongguo*, the name for China, literally means "the Middle Kingdom" or perhaps "cultural core." Both concepts express the centrality of Chinese culture, with the emperor at the pinnacle and center of the world order.

In reality, the idea of a unified state that had persisted over the millennia was promoted by the dominant ethnic group, the Han Chinese. Before the Ming dynasty (1368–1644), China probably had been divided for as long as it had been unified, and even the Yuan dynasty (1279–1368) "in many respects had more in common with periods of division than with consolidation."[1] This alternation between division and unity was well ingrained in traditional thought and was recorded in the Chinese classic *The Three Kingdoms*, which describes the fall of the Han dynasty (206 BC–AD 210): "They say the momentum of history is ever thus: the empire, long divided, must unite; long united must divide. Thus, it has ever been."[2]

The notion of continuity was strengthened by and perhaps even derived from the last two dynasties, the Ming and the Qing, which ruled from 1368 until 1912, when the imperial system ended. This was also the period when the empire's spread reached its peak and, with some variation, incorporated the territory over which the CCP claims sovereignty (such as along the border with Mongolia).[3] The seeming unity of the empire was undermined not

only by the increasing aggression of the West but also by growing domestic pressures that placed strains on the system. Beginning in the mid-
1990s there arose a new school of thought known as the New Qing History, which has appealed to newly available materials to question the extent
to which the Manchus absorbed Confucian norms of rule and how much
they had carried with them and perpetuated their Central Asian models.
Importantly, this work reveals a Qing empire that not only covered a territory that was much larger than previously supposed but also possessed
wide-ranging cultural diversity and cultural practices and, importantly, an
increasingly diverse population.[4] Needless to say, this approach has been
criticized by official historians in China because it challenges the party's
narrative.

China is still wrestling with how to rule over a diverse, ethnically mixed
population that does not necessarily accept the dominance of the Han or the
CCP narrative. The challenge for the CCP is that ethnic minorities constitute only about 10 percent of the total population but inhabit 60 percent of
the land mass, much of which is in sensitive border areas (the Guangxi
Zhuang Autonomous Region, Inner Mongolia Autonomous Region, Tibet
Autonomous Region, and Xinjiang Uyghur Autonomous Region). The national language is a recent construct and has priority in schools over the local
languages. About 30 percent of the population speaks a language at home
other than the national language. Although these local languages are referred
to as dialects, they are different languages—in many cases as distinct as
German is from French.

The cultures of the various regions are also quite distinct, and the arrival
of the foreign presence heightened the differences between the open, cosmopolitan south and coastal area and the more bureaucratic northern cultures.
This distinction became more marked as the influence of treaty ports and
foreigners grew in cities such as Shanghai and Guangzhou (Canton), producing urban environments where non-Chinese ideas could spread and be
debated. In contrast, the north and the inland provinces were dominated
by a more traditional agricultural economy and more traditional power
relationships. Early revolutionaries such as Sun Yat-sen, the father of the
nationalist movement, grew up in the more cosmopolitan environment. It
is not surprising that when Deng Xiaoping wanted to kick-start reforms
after 1978, he turned to these coastal areas to set up the first four special
economic zones, which were permitted to bring in foreign investment,

technology, and management techniques.[5] Importantly, these zones were far away from the bureaucratic clutches of the CCP leadership in Beijing.

Problems arise for the CCP among ethnic groups whose cultures and narratives differ from those of traditional China. Tibet and Xinjiang each have an external point of reference—the Dalai Lama for Tibet, and for Xinjiang the old Turkestan empire and now the radical Islamic movements that are active across Central Asia. Both provinces have seen uprisings against CCP/Han rule, and the party has launched various projects to increase the Han population in the areas to make the indigenous population into a minority. During Tibet's failed uprising in 1959, the Dalai Lama fled to India, where he has remained in exile. On the fortieth anniversary of the uprising, in 2008, widespread riots broke out in the capital, Lhasa, and other Tibetan cities, with much of the animosity directed against the Han Chinese who had settled there. As for Xinjiang, the CCP fears that the indigenous population will form links with radical Islamic groups, and in July 2009 the CCP blamed the large-scale unrest on the activities of groups outside of Xinjiang. In 2018 the CCP undertook a major campaign of reeducation, including placing large numbers of locals into camps; earlier it had banned government personnel in Xinjiang from fasting during Ramadan and discouraged beards and veils.

The central government has made heavy economic investments in both regions and has improved transportation links in hopes that improved material wealth might offset the differences in spiritual allegiances. The major Belt and Road Initiative into Pakistan emphasizes routes via Xinjiang, with the hope that this will bring more wealth to the region and reduce regional inequalities. However, it seems unlikely that more investment and economic growth will resolve the fundamental contradictions. Unless there is greater tolerance for religious freedom, the threat of unrest will remain. It is difficult to predict how long the patronizing, paternalistic attitude toward these groups can persist. The paternalistic view that Han culture is superior and that the CCP brings benefit and enlightenment to other ethnic groups in the region seems widely shared among Chinese officials. Even before the 2008 demonstrations in Tibet, the party secretary of the province stated that "the Communist Party is like the parent to the Tibetan people, and it is always considerate about what the children need," noting that the CCP Central Committee is like the "real Buddha for Tibetans."[6] Such comments may go down well in Beijing, but they are not received so well in Lhasa. The CCP has sought to control the narrative of the Tibetan people through patriotic campaigns intended to persuade nuns and monks to accept the CCP narrative.[7] The CCP leadership has sought to eliminate the Dalai Lama's influence in his own succession by organizing training for monks on reincarnation. A senior official involved noted that reincarnation is "never a religious-only issue or a living Buddha's personal right"; instead it must accord with the CCP's strategies and policies within Tibet.[8] Of course, the CCP also seeks to control the international perception of its treatment of the Tibetan people.

This practice is quite distinct from an earlier period when the CCP had to tolerate diversity in order to survive. After 1927 the CCP was banished to the hinterlands and the border regions. How it should deal with the various ethnic groupings presented a major challenge. Different Red Army groups made temporary compromises with a motley assortment of ethnic minorities, bandits, and local power holders. When the Red Army established the Jiangxi Soviet, it absorbed local bandits into their troops; some of these became commanders. Living in potentially hostile environments often meant the sacrifice of principles to ensure survival. At the end of the Long March, Mao Zedong's troops sheltered in northern Shaanxi in an area governed by the Communist guerrilla leader Liu Zhidan. In the late 1920s and the 1930s, Liu had struck alliances with local bandits to build up his strength. One such bandit was his cousin, whose followers formed the backbone of the first guerrilla army in the region. Another bandit leader rose to a senior position within the People's Liberation Army (PLA). Liu Zhidan and the others realized that "only a movement rooted in local ties, bringing together all who could be united with, had any chance of lasting success."[9] Similarly, in 1935 Zhang Guotao (head of the CCP's Fourth Front Army) and a rival of Mao Zedong for CCP leadership, withdrew under pressure from the border areas between Sichuan and Tibet and established the Northwest Federal Government of the Chinese Soviet Republic, promising that the CCP would fight with the minority nationalities (Hui, Mongolians, Tibetans, Miao, and Yi) to help them achieve independence.

Domestic Challenges to Imperial Rule

In addition to the increasing foreign engagement, two other challenges chipped away at Qing rule. First, in the latter half of the eighteenth century, an extensive period of peace, which permitted agricultural improvements and better health care, led to a population explosion. The population more than doubled, from about 150 million in 1700 to 450 million by 1850, with the maximum economic welfare occurring between 1750 and 1775.[10] Second, the Qing now ruled over a more diverse population, living on a larger land mass but without a concomitant increase in state agencies.[11] Local government was very thin, with about 50,000 officials overseeing 450 million people. This put stress on the system and made it more difficult to deal with uprisings, such as the White Lotus Rebellion and the Taiping Rebellion (1850–1864), let alone with the foreign incursions that began with the First Opium War in 1839. One important consequence of this declining state capacity to deal with armed threats was an increase in the power of local militias and the eventual rise of warlords. In its early years the CCP, together with the Guomindang (GMD; the Nationalist Party), had to grapple with a country riven by feuding warlord factions and a roundabout of changes in government. For many young revolutionaries it also led to a deep-seated sense that a military solution was a crucial component for any resolution of China's fate.[12]

The population increase and the strains it caused might have been offset by innovations in science and technology and a parallel industrial revolution. Why this did not occur has been a source of debate and remains a puzzle to this day. Earlier research in the West portrayed a China that passed from economic and scientific progress to stagnation and an absence of inspiration.[13] Confucian thought held merchants in low esteem; the landed gentry saw little incentive to invest in urban industrialization; and the bureaucracy was seen as stifling initiative. Much of the manufacturing that did develop was tightly tied to compradors and foreign businesses. It all amounted to what Mark Elvin called a "high-level equilibrium trap," with China unable to move forward using traditional techniques, yet unable or unwilling to innovate.[14]

This Western research shows that Chinese society changed between the eighth and thirteenth centuries as it underwent an economic revolution, but that progress flattened thereafter. The peasant rebellions produced greater geographical and social mobility, which undermined the traditional system of serfdom. More recent research on the economy suggests that far from being trapped, China had a dynamic and successful economy that was able to feed the growing population and produced various sophisticated institutions, and that, contrary to long-held views, as late as the eighteenth century China was as prosperous as the West.[15] This view remains disputed. Less disputed is the view that in the nineteenth century, economic depression set in, while population growth continued unchallenged.[16] The Qing encouraged growth of the private sector and, in contrast to Europe, had competitive markets for land, labor, and goods.[17] The Qing dynasty took a hands-off approach to the economy and kept taxation rates low, but this limited its ability to invest in necessary public goods and to confront domestic disturbances such as the White Lotus Rebellion (1796–1804) and the increasing penetration of Western powers seeking market access and trade.[18] Some have argued that at least in some areas markets flourished, growth was maintained, and incomes rose right up until the Japanese incursions and the global economic crisis of the 1930s.[19]

Economic decline played into the social unrest, and the cost of putting down these rebellions further undermined state capacity. The most explosive millennial uprising was that of the Taiping, led by the messianic Hong Xiuquan. The movement started in the western province of Guangxi, but in its heyday it undermined the Qing and spread rapidly across China, establishing its capital in Nanjing and ruling over much of China's economic core. The Taiping represented the most extraordinary interaction between China and the West. The established story was that Hong Xiuquan ascended to Heaven in 1837 and was charged by God to rid the earth of those who were leading it astray. On his return to earth, Hong, seeing himself as "God's Chinese son," led a rebellion that killed more than 20 million people, weakened the Qing state, and resulted in the growth of local defense militias.[20] The movement cut to the core the legitimating belief in Confucianism. The adoption of foreign belief systems, grafted onto the traditional nature of peasant rebellions, foreshadowed the intellectual revolution of the twentieth century.[21] Suppression of the movement also brought in foreign troops, which had already brutalized the Qing authorities during the Opium Wars (1839–1842 and 1856–1860).

Confucianism Then and Now

The undermining of Confucianism was traumatic. The Chinese elite had been held together by its manipulation, which in its caricature promoted obedience to the sage-kings, filial piety, and the development of virtue through education—which founded the belief that a system ruled by the educated and the wise would be a good government. At the pinnacle of the system was the emperor, who ruled through the Mandate of Heaven. The process of advancing through the education system and the civil service examinations was grueling, and it severely limited the number of those who could enter the elite. At the same time, it ensured that those who did join the elite were well schooled in the dominant interpretation of Confucianism and were unlikely to use their education to critique the system. It was taught that people were to know their place in the hierarchy, and that the lower orders were to remain subordinate to their superiors. In fact, some of those who rose in rebellion were candidates who had failed the civil service examinations. Hong Xiuquan, the founder of the Taiping Rebellion, failed the examinations four times. He and several other early leaders of the Taiping were outsiders who came from Hakka communities in southern China.

Yet, except for a few dishonorable groups, the examination system was open to all males, no matter their standing. The system appeared to be relatively free from the corruption of paying for a post or using personal connections for advancement, two phenomena that have plagued the CCP system during the post-1978 reform era. In imperial China this openness and apparent lack of corruption created a sense that the system was fair and that wise men could be trusted to govern on behalf of the people and make the best decisions. In reality the system was less meritocratic than it seemed. The process to study and pass the examinations was arduous and required lengthy training in the approved interpretation of the classics. This was very expensive and thus excluded most families from even trying to participate.

Thus, Confucianism reified a hierarchical system that was managed by "good men" (and no women). This clearly meant that Confucianism functioned best when the imperial system was strong and the centralized state was functioning adequately; it fared less well when the state was weakened. In contrast, two other major thought systems, Buddhism and Daoism, were not very effective in terms of managing a hierarchical, disciplined political administration.[22] Confucian edicts went up and down the system reassuring the traditional bureaucracy, but many citizens lived their lives in horizontal networks influenced by Buddhism, or Daoism, or they were embedded in lineage networks. The penetration of Buddhism into China from India shows that the thought system was not sealed to outside influence and, like Marxism in the twentieth century, it found enthusiastic adherents.[23]

Beyond the generalities, it is difficult to define Confucianism precisely. Confucianism covers a wide range of entities from "a narrowly conceived orthodoxy maintained by the cultural elite; a political ideology sustained through civil service examination by autocratic rulers; a philosophical discourse based on the interpretation of a set of classical texts; to a value system supporting patriarchy."[24] Certainly the use that General Secretary Xi Jinping has made of neo-Confucianism, as with his predecessor, Hu Jintao, stresses harmony and order within society so that everyone knows their place. Xi's Confucian revival serves clear contemporary political purposes by drawing a line that links the CCP to China's traditional political culture and reinforces the need for strong hierarchical structures and a bureaucracy staffed by those who are sufficiently enlightened, albeit now with the addition of an understanding of Marxism.

At first sight this revival of Confucianism appears puzzling. The CCP came to power claiming that it represented a radical break with the past and that it would usher in a new proletarian culture. But the Chinese tradition had fled to Taiwan with the GMD. By 1976 the campaign to criticize Lin Biao and Confucius was winding down, with the CCP claiming that the bad, old traditions should be swept away. Fast-forward to September 2014 and we hear Xi Jinping declaring that the CCP is the "successor to and promoter of fine traditional Chinese culture."[25] For the CCP, as for previous dynasties, this approach is intended to strengthen legitimacy by linking the party to a long history, which is often referred to as stretching back 2,000 or 5,000 years. This tracing of historical roots breeds an easy familiarity among the Chinese "masses," who, it is presumed, would not be surprised to find in the pages of the Communist newspaper, the *People's Daily*, events and trends that occurred or developed some 2,000 years earlier but that the party deems to be relevant to contemporary struggles. It is difficult to find a parallel to this in the Western tradition. We do not see US presidents invoking maxims of Plato or Aristotle to jockey with their political rivals. Xi Jinping's interest in Confucianism echoes more closely the ideas of Liu Shaoqi than those of Mao Zedong. Liu was the president of the People's Republic of China (PRC) and second only to Mao until his fall from grace during the Cultural Revolution. Liu Shaoqi's 1951 tract on how to be a good communist—a Confucian framing for the Communist world—called for self-cultivation, but now Marx and Lenin were the masters to be studied.

The adherence to Confucianism as a prerequisite to rule, with the state playing a dominant role in promoting and protecting the official ideology against other contenders, lies behind the notion of the Chinese state as autocratic, articulated most vehemently with the Cold War–era concept of "Oriental despotism." The agricultural demands required major hydraulic systems that could be built and maintained only by a powerful autocratic government.[26] Although one can argue about how autocratic the system was, it is true that there were no organizations that could have rallied alternatives.

The state assumed the role of educator. Even though foreigners in contemporary China might be surprised to see, displayed on buildings or on billboards, poetic couplets expressing love for the CCP and Xi Jinping, or Deng Xiaoping or Mao Zedong, it would not seem strange to Chinese citizens. Such displays are merely a modern manifestation of the couplets that were put up in public places during imperial times. Proper Confucian education would bring out the innate goodness of people and permit them to realize their potential. Of course, goodness was defined by the intelligentsia under the emperor and included those attributes that contributed to the social order and perpetuation of the system. The Qing created a system of district lecturers who were appointed based on their scholarship, age, and worthy character. Twice a month they would expound upon the relevant imperial maxims, and attendance at such lectures was compulsory. Good children would be hailed and rotten elements would be vilified—with their names posted in public places, to remain there until they saw the error of their ways and sought a return to the fold. This practice was adopted by the CCP to promote local or national heroes to be emulated while vilifying persons who were negative examples.

This meant that the state defined an expansive role for itself and that, unlike in the West, its role as moral arbiter was not challenged by other organizations, such as organized religion. As with the hanging of couplets to praise the CCP, Chinese citizens might not have been surprised to recognize the launch of a campaign to "build a spiritual civilization." This system did not expect critical participation from its citizens; instead it required calm obedience, and it did not see the need for a loyal opposition. Dissent would be punished harshly, through banishment or even execution. This established clear boundaries for the role of the intellectual elite: control over information, its dissemination, and learning was portrayed as not only legitimate but also as a worthy objective. For intellectuals who were groomed into this system, the benefits could be great as they became scholar-officials wielding strong political power while enjoying a high social status. In the era of the CCP, these scholars function as "establishment intellectuals."[27]

Given this, it is not surprising that most observers see Chinese society as dominated by the state, with little or no social organization that can serve as a counterbalance. However, the direct penetration of the state at the local level is not overbearing, and this does leave space for temples, lineage, merchant groups, and even secret societies to flourish, but none of these threaten the power of the national state. The network of temples does not form a national organization that can provide an alternative moral center. In the south, in particular, lineage plays an important role in organizing village life and in deciding questions of reciprocity and justice. For example, in Yantian Village in southern China, the Deng lineage traces its roots back to the tenth century, and from imperial times to the present the village has been led by a Deng family member.[28] The merchants' groups did not form the basis for a bourgeoisie as they did in the West, and while some of the associated apparatuses of newspapers and salons developed in cities such as Shanghai, they did not form a bourgeois alternative. For the most part, secret societies, as the names suggest, operated covertly, often as self-help organizations. Perhaps a nascent public sphere, à la Habermas, was emerging in major urban environments toward the end of the Qing and into the Republican period, but it barely consolidated.[29] In total, the various forms of associational life did not pose a threat to the state and did not amount to a civil society as it is commonly conceived.[30]

Interacting with the Outside World

The popular view has been that China was insular and largely ignorant of the outside world until foreigners began to press their interests to open China for trade. For much of history this was true, but there were earlier periods of extensive foreign engagement, such as during the Han (205 BC–AD 220), Tang (AD 618–907), and Song (AD 960–1279) dynasties. Foreign goods found their way across China, and Chinese products found their way across the globe. Yet the Chinese had a remarkable lack of curiosity about the ways and wonders of the world outside of the Middle Kingdom. The Qing dynasty's ability to rule was eroded by its inability to come to terms with foreign powers, but also by domestic and economic turbulence.

In 1557, local officials of the Ming dynasty bequeathed to Portuguese traders the area of Macau, which remained the traders' sole foreign base for the next 300 years. The British were next to arrive, and by 1757 trade was confined to Guangzhou, operating through the Cohong system with thirteen hong (merchants) licensed to deal with the foreigners. Foreigners were denied contacts with officials, and in the period of January to May 1757 they were required to move back to Macau. This was never going to satisfy the foreign traders, especially not the British. Initially the British attempted to establish contacts with the imperial system. In 1793 the British king, George III, sent Earl George McCartney to Beijing to establish relations and to open up trade. For the British it did not go well, but for the empire the process that it set in train would be even worse. To show the fruits of Britain's industrialization, McCartney presented the emperor with gifts, including clocks and watches, scientific instruments, and even a hot air balloon. Some of these trinkets can still be seen today in the Forbidden City. The Qianlong Emperor (1735–1795) was not impressed, and McCartney's failure to kowtow to the emperor in accordance with imperial protocol caused delays in finding a resolution. The emperor's letter that McCartney delivered to George III was clear: "I set no value on objects strange or ingenious, and have no use for your country's manufactures." The British king was instructed to demonstrate his loyalty: by "perpetual submission to our Throne, you may secure peace and prosperity for your country hereafter." The idea of opening a diplomatic mission also received short shrift, as sending a representative was "contrary to all usage of my dynasty and cannot possibly be entertained."[31] Fortunately for Qianlong, he was not around to witness the foreign response to such attitudes that led to the dismemberment of China.

This attitude convinced the British traders that diplomatic engagement to promote their economic interests was not going to be successful and that the use of force was inevitable, even though it took another forty years. This marked the start of what CCP historians and Mao Zedong himself saw as the hundred years of shame and humiliation at the hands of foreigners. This narrative plays a crucial role in the CCP's claims to legitimacy. The immediate catalyst came in 1838, when the Daoguang Emperor (1821–1850) sent commissioner Li Zexu to deal with the foreign trade through Guangzhou. Opium trading was banned, and Li expected foreign compliance in stopping the trade. Instead, in September 1839 the First Opium War was launched, which led to the first of the unequal treaties signed in Nanjing (August 1842), followed by the most-favored-nation clause in 1843 and the Second Opium War (1856–1850). These treaties included heavy indemnities to be paid by China to the British merchants who had been driven out of Guangzhou, the opening up of the treaty ports to include the stationing of British consuls there, contacts with Chinese officials of similar rank, abolition of the Cohongs, and the leasing of Hong Kong Island, and then the Kowloon Peninsula and Stonecutters Island, to Britain. The most-favored-nation clause meant that any special favor granted to a foreign power in one treaty would be granted to all other powers. In 1843 Britain was given full extraterritoriality that exempted its citizens from being subject to local law. Extraterritoriality was not abolished until 1943, when the foreign powers wanted to give a boost to the Nationalists in the struggle against Japan. It was fairly easy to renounce, as the foreigners had been driven out of their most important enclaves.

The defeats for the Chinese Empire did not end with the Opium Wars. In 1884–1885 the empire was defeated by France, and, most traumatically, in 1894–1895 it lost the Sino-Japanese War. This defeat at the hands of the Japanese caused many Chinese intellectuals to become deeply disillusioned with their heritage and led them to look overseas for solutions to China's woes. It also marked the beginning of a more radical turn in intellectual curiosity in China. Defeat "produced an almost traumatic change in the climate of literati opinion."[32] The core problem was identified as the Confucian principles on which the imperial system was based. The regime was losing its intellectual elite as they sought salvation in alternative modes of thought. Yan Fu was the most prominent intellectual to believe that Western power came not only from its weapons and gunboats but also, and more importantly, from its ideas and values. The stage was set for significant soul-searching about how to save China, and as gradual and piecemeal solutions were found wanting, hopeful young intellectuals gravitated to more comprehensive, transformative ideologies.

The empire did try to salvage what it could through moderate experimentation. This began with the Self-Strengthening Movement that dominated in-house reforms until it was exposed as a failure after the Sino-Japanese War. The movement involved a mechanical borrowing of certain aspects of Western advancement, particularly in the military sphere. The attempts were summed up by Zhang Zhidong as "Chinese learning for fundamental values, Western learning for practical application." Unlike Yan Fu later, Zhang did not appreciate that one could not selectively lift out Western technology and machines from the economic, social, and cultural matrix from which they had emerged.

Important attempts at reform from within were also tried during the 1898 Reform Movement, headed by Kang Youwei (1858–1927). Although Kang was born into a prominent scholar-official family, he was opposed to the Shimonoseki Treaty that China had signed following its defeat by the Japanese, and the resistance spawned an energetic outpouring of ideas about reform that were discussed in salons around the country and aired in an increasing number of newspapers. Not surprisingly, Kang and like-minded youths looked to Japan's Meiji reforms for inspiration. The young Guangxu Emperor (1871–1908) was sympathetic and allowed Kang to shake up the system through a series of administrative reforms. There were new ministries for areas such as industry, but Confucianism was not abandoned and in fact it was to be strengthened through a Ministry of Religion. During the Hundred Days of Reform, the examination system was reformed to eliminate the formulaic writing and to include current affairs (these reforms were abolished in 1905). The reform did not last long, as opposition grew, and in September 1898 Empress Dowager Cixi decided to take back power from the young emperor—imprisoning him, ripping up the reform edicts, and purging the reformers, some of whom were executed.

A second response to intrusion was to fall back on China's xenophobic tradition and attempt to completely remove the foreigners. The late Qing was critical of trade, and the increasing dismemberment of China led to the radical Boxer Movement (1899–1901), with violent attacks on foreigners, especially religious representatives, including Chinese Christians. At its most radical stage, the slogan "Wipe out the foreigners!" rang out. By the spring of 1900 the Boxers had advanced on Beijing, putting pressure on the empress dowager and her court to decide whether or not to support them. Eventually, in June, she publicly declared in the name of the Guangxu Emperor the fateful decision that the court would be throwing its weight behind the Boxers. The Western nations formed an alliance with Japan and "liberated" Beijing in August 1900, with Cixi having fled to Xi'an and leaving her people to suffer at the hands of the foreigners. Over 120,000 died during the Boxer Movement, but despite graphic Western accounts of attacks on the foreigners, only about 250 were killed along with about 30,000 Chinese Christians. The remainder were killed by the foreign troops or by Chinese troops that had joined them.[33] Crushed by the foreign troops, the terms of the Boxer Protocol, concluded in 1901, were harsh, and the indemnity to be paid to the foreigners amounted to four times the nation's annual revenue.

Radical uprisings against foreigners or attempts at reform from within gave way to decline, and more young people followed the path of those such as Yan Fu and sought inspiration from thought systems and political processes outside of China. This group included liberals, all manner of anarchists, and eventually Marxists.

Legacies

From this review of the imperial past, what can we discern as legacies that have influenced the CCP?[34] Perhaps most remarkably, given its earlier claims to represent a radical rupture with the past, is its toying with Confucianism and portraying the CCP as the inheritor of China's glorious past. As revolutionary legitimacy declines with each successive generation and with performance legitimacy very fragile, it makes sense to weave in the narrative of inheritance of a continuity that dates back millennia. It is as if the Roman Empire had survived its trials and tribulations and still oversaw politics in Italy today.

Of course, the Communist revolution produced its own cultural traits and patterns of organization and took on a Leninist party structure, but there are some broad general features of CCP behavior that bear comparison with Chinese tradition. These legacies will be explored in greater depth in the Conclusion. First and foremost, the CCP inherited the idea of China as a unitary state that would exist within the most expansive geographic area possible. Except when politically expedient in the pre-1949 period, the CCP has never accepted either federalism or the right of secession. Second, in terms of the notion of the state, since 1949 the party has been the educator and moral conscience of the nation. There is no alternative set of institutions that can provide moral guidance to its citizens on a national basis. The deliberate fusing of the identity of party and state means that undue criticism of the party is portrayed as unpatriotic. Third, this means that the idea of a loyal opposition is an anathema. You are either in or out, and only very rarely somewhere in between. Fourth, there was an easy acceptance of hierarchical rule maintained by a well-heeled army of establishment intellectuals, who explained and promoted the CCP's objectives. The hierarchical structure of the party, despite the party's stress on collective leadership, tended toward one-person rule or dominance over the political system. This tendency was reinforced by the adoption of a Leninist party and its Stalinist variation.

There are two legacies of ambivalence: toward foreigners and toward private enterprise. The CCP came to power claiming that it would set right the injustices of imperialist attacks on China's sovereignty. Of course, initially it formed an alliance with the Soviet Union; after that fell apart, China was alienated not only from the capitalist world but also from the Soviet-led bloc. During the post-1978 period there were massive foreign investments in the Chinese economy and a focus on export-led growth, followed by China's increasing presence on the world stage. But the CCP remains suspicious of foreigners' intentions. Even though the Qing did not prohibit private enterprise, it was not enthusiastic about it. The CCP shares this ambivalence. It essentially wiped out private businesses after 1949, and then in the 1980s began to slowly, and initially grudgingly, allow the development of private enterprises. Now private business plays a major role in the Chinese economy, but the CCP still gives preferential treatment to the state-owned sector where possible and reins in the private sector when it becomes too influential or when it seems to be evading party oversight. Private business does, however, provide a safety valve that the party opens when development runs into difficulty.

One area where the CCP has played a stronger role than the imperial state has been in the oversight of society. Under the emperor the reach of the state more or less stopped at the county level. Under the CCP the state reaches down into the villages of rural China and the streets of urban China. During the Maoist period, three main mechanisms of state control over society were developed. First, the household registration system tied individuals to their places of birth and made mobility extremely difficult. Second, the state supervised citizens through the workplace—the state-owned enterprises in the urban areas and the collectives in the countryside. Third, this type of organization meant that it was relatively easy to maintain individuals' personnel dossiers, which would contain all the crucial information about that person's life. These mechanisms of social control have come under pressure during the reform period, and the CCP has had to seek new forms of collectivity to replace those guaranteed under the Maoist system. The party has tried to use residential collectivities to replace those of the workplace, with local communities taking over the welfare role of the former workplace. These attempts to build a new collectivity are designed to prevent individual interactions with the government.[35] The much-heralded social credit system can be seen as an electronic version of the old paper dossier system.[36] This system was announced by the State Council in June 2014, claiming that it would "allow the trustworthy to roam everywhere under heaven while making it hard for the discredited to take a single step."[37]

CHAPTER TWO

Origins, Alliance, and Failure

1920–1930

★

The 1920s were a tumultuous decade for the CCP. Through collaboration with the GMD, it rose from insignificance to develop into a significant mass party and then was almost completely destroyed. Internal and external factors contributed to its growth, and the fate of the fledgling party was tied not only to its cooperation and rivalry with the Nationalists but also to the internal battles within the Communist Party of the Soviet Union between Stalin and Trotsky. To survive, the CCP learned, it must develop a disciplined organization to replace the loose collection of radical, small study groups that had formed to explore a new path forward. And when the Nationalists turned their military force on them, the leaders of the CCP realized the importance of possessing an independent military force. Finally, Mao Zedong grasped the vital revolutionary potential of the peasantry once mobilized by the party. These factors were important for post-1949 rule.

The CCP emerged from a world in turmoil. Millions had perished in World War I, and out of that war's ashes arose a new Soviet state dedicated to the promotion of global, proletarian revolution. The traditional European powers—Britain, France, and Germany—were weakened after the war. The United States became the most powerful global player, but it did not seem interested in taking on the role of global policeman.

By contrast, the Bolsheviks had no qualms about exporting their revolution beyond their borders. The main revolutionary theater was in the West, yet in the East the potential for revolution was brewing and China was the key country in the struggle between the old and the new. For the Soviets, revolution in China was a crucial link in the chain of their global strategy to resist imperialism. Consequently, they poured significant personnel and material resources into building a Chinese movement for national liberation, including the establishment of a communist party. The ground in China was fertile for sowing the seeds of radical theories such as Marxism.

The collapsed dynastic system had left behind a political and intellectual vacuum. Although the government in Beijing was recognized by other nations, real power rooted with a motley crew of warlords, whose own power was circumscribed by their military strength. Their wars and shifting alliances provided the context within which political groupings had to operate. For young activists, it was a frustrating but exhilarating time as they explored different thought systems that might restore order to the nation. Interest in and sympathy for Marxism grew out of a questioning of China's cultural heritage that was at the core of the May Fourth Movement (1915–1919). Interest in the Bolshevik model intensified following the 1917 Russian Revolution, which offered a possible path forward for the relatively poor and backward Chinese economy. These interests primarily arose among a small intellectual elite who had been active in the study societies that had formed during disillusionment with the chaotic politics of the post-imperial era. However, Marxism was not the predominant intellectual trend. On the left, anarchism exerted greater influence than Marxism, and nascent CCP groups had to struggle against the anarchists to gain a foothold. Liberalism, also inspired by the ideas of John Dewey, captivated some intellectuals.

The fragmented nation allowed space for alternatives to develop, and local environments produced a variety of approaches and policies. First, for the CCP, there was Shanghai, the Paris of the East, an elegant city where foreign concessions afforded protection for radicals to meet and plot their strategies. This was where the CCP was founded and laid out its revolutionary agenda. However, as the 1920s progressed, the Shanghai Municipal Police increased their surveillance of activists in the Shanghai International Settlement, and the party retreated into a clandestine world of secrecy, conspiracy, and fear of betrayal—factors that would shape the future mentality of the CCP. This atmosphere produced a distinctive view of what was necessary to promote revolution as the CCP members worked illegally, scuttling between an array of safe houses.

Second, there was the trading area of Guangzhou (Canton) in southern China. Here the warlord Chen Jiongming and the politician Sun Yat-sen, despite their differences, welcomed the radical thinkers and activists. The

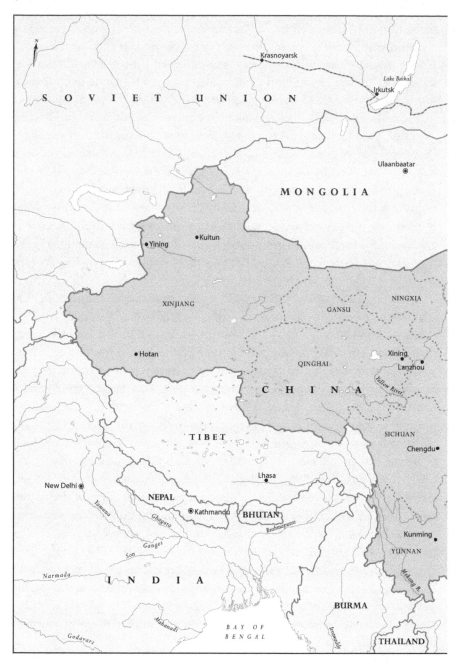

Republican China, 1912–1949

CCP could operate there legally without engaging in clandestine maneuvers. Sun Yat-sen was the founder and head of the GMD and was recognized by those on the left as the leader of the revolutionary movement. The relationship between the CCP and the GMD would define China's history not only in the 1920s but also in much of the period that followed.

Third, there was the area that straddled the Hunan-Jiangxi border, with its history of rebellion and activism. The warlord who controlled most of Hunan tolerated the Communists and claimed to be a socialist. This allowed pro-labor activism, and three key CCP leaders—Mao Zedong, Liu Shaoqi, and Li Lisan—cut their revolutionary teeth there.[1] The three were leaders of the local labor resistance among the coal miners and railway workers in the town of Anyuan. During the 1920s, this area formed a crucial training base for the CCP. In addition to labor activism, peasant associations were established, and after the CCP's catastrophic defeat in 1927, many joined the new Red Army.[2] It became known as "China's little Moscow," and at it is peak one-fifth of its 80,000 inhabitants were CCP members.

These brief vignettes of different revolutionary experiences reveal the complexity of the CCP revolution from its outset. The revolution looked different depending on where one stood, and this dictated different approaches to strategy and tactics. No matter how forcefully Moscow or the Party Center tried to impose uniformity, local demands and conditions could always produce different responses. There was a world of difference between operating illegally in the North and operating openly in the South. These different environments shaped the perception of how cooperation with the Nationalists should be carried out.

Throughout the 1920s these circumstances complicated the CCP's ability to take advantage of opportunities as they arose. The revolution not only looked different, but was also a very different experience, for those in the GMD-protected areas of southern China than it was for those working in the semiclandestine conditions of Shanghai. By the late 1920s Mao Zedong was relatively free of Soviet influences, allowing him greater freedom to develop an alternative approach to revolution that was based in the countryside and supported by armed force.

Laying the Groundwork for a Party

It was a once-popular myth that the CCP was either a Soviet creation from its origins or emerged organically from domestic trends.[3] The reality is more nuanced. Outcomes depended on complex relations among local innovation, intricate relationships between local actors, and the promptings of Soviet agents not only from the Communist International (Comintern) but also from the Soviet Foreign Ministry and the International Labour Organization. For example, Soviet influence was evident with the formation of the Communist groups in Beijing, Guangzhou, and Shanghai; more indigenous factors were important in Changsha and Wuhan; and a lively group of Communists came together in Chongqing with no apparent contact with the Soviets or the other Communists in China. No account of the CCP's origins can ignore these realities. That said, the Soviets did play a crucial role in the CCP's early years, providing financial and organizational support. Yet there were serious divisions among the various Soviet agencies as well as within the same organization.

Had there not been fertile ground on which the Bolshevik seeds could be sown, the efforts by Soviet Russia might have come to nothing. An intellectual quest for alternatives following the collapse of the imperial system, combined with frustration from post-imperial politics, provided opportunity. The quest for alternatives was boosted by the intellectual experimentation and discovery that took place during the May Fourth Movement, which took its name from the more limited nationalist demonstrations of 1919. The demonstrations were sparked by the disclosure that the Versailles Treaty of 1919 had ceded control of the German concession of Shandong to Japan instead of returning it to China. The shock of this revelation was made all the worse when it became known that Britain, France, and Italy had secretly agreed to this during the war.

Of deeper importance were the attacks on Chinese tradition that had been brewing among radical intellectuals, with slogans that advocated bringing down the "old Confucian shop." The wide-ranging critiques led to a questioning of many traditional practices of authority and behavior, including sexual mores and gender roles that would shape the thinking of early Communist sympathizers. Some of the early Communist leaders embraced feminism and advocated liberation from the repressive institutions of household, clan, and religion.[4] These impulses were repressed as the CCP became more involved in military conflicts with the Nationalists and the Japanese.

Following the collapse of the Qing dynasty, initial experimentation with a republican system ended in failure and frustration. The pull of tradition was too strong, and the natural heir, Yuan Shikai, assumed increasing powers, culminating in his declaring himself emperor in December 1915. His death in

June 1916 prevented further embarrassment but left behind chaos and confusion as military leaders throughout China vied for power, thus ushering in the warlord period. Then began an elaborate merry-go-round of different groups trying to wrest power in Beijing, the internationally recognized capital.

In addition to the actions by Soviet agents, four major changes took place that supported the establishment of a Communist party. First, there was a growing acceptance that Marxism could provide a solution to the dilemmas faced by China. Marxism gradually came to replace anarchism and more moderate forms of socialism among those on the radical left. Second, the intellectuals who formed the Marxist study groups came out of their ivory towers, where they had merely published papers and discussed theories, to become activists. Third, members of the study groups had come together through personal relationships, a fact that frustrated the Comintern advisers as they tried to build loyalty to the organization rather than to a particular individual, region, or educational institution. Those who had cut their radical teeth debating within these intimate groups resisted the tighter institutional structure of a Leninist party. Fourth, there was a gradual acceptance by some that a Leninist form of organization was needed by China to unite internally and to resist external pressures. These four themes would dominate CCP work throughout the 1920s and even beyond.

For our story, most important was the growing influence of Marxism as an integrated system of thought and a guide to action among a small group of intellectuals. The attraction of Marxism when combined with the organizational power of Leninism appeared to provide a pathway to redemption that neither anarchism nor liberalism could offer. Leninism's appeal was heightened by its linking China's struggle for national salvation with global liberation from the forces of imperialism, casting China as a key component in an international movement for emancipation. That said, it is debatable how sophisticated the understanding of Marxism and Leninism was among the early CCP members. For those who stuck with the party after its establishment, they were Bolsheviks before they were Marxists. Much has been made of Mao Zedong's adaptation of Marxism to China's conditions (the Sinification of Marxism), but from the beginning the young intellectuals interpreted Marxism in terms of their own intellectual heritage. In its Leninist form, Marxism offered a pathway to the wealth and power they yearned for. While acceptance of the Leninist form of the party was indisputable, CCP members were skilled at selectively adapting those elements of the ideology that suited their circumstances, while rejecting others.[5]

Although Mao Zedong claimed that Marxism entered China from Russia, intellectuals in Japan were the prime source for the radical ideas within East Asia. Many early works were translated from Japanese by Chinese who had studied there. The fascination with Japan grew as young Chinese tried to come to terms with their nation's traumatic defeat in the Sino-Japanese War (1894–1895), which had been fought primarily over supremacy in Korea. Searching for the key to Japan's success led to an interest in the Meiji Restoration and resulted in travel to Japan, where some discovered radical ideas.

By 1919 Marxist and socialist thought were gaining traction among the radical intellectual elite, and Leninism's attractiveness was increased by the victory of the Russian Revolution and the actions of Soviet agents. Articles published in *New Youth*, which would become the major CCP magazine and *The Communist* (a journal established in November 1920) shifted from translations of Japanese theoretical works to works written in English that were more focused on action rather than on theory: how to confront imperialism and how to carry out a socialist revolution. This shift in emphasis created divisions within the radical camp and brought about a clear split between those attracted to anarchism and those who were striving to understand the Bolshevik revolution and the Leninist organizational form. The two key figures in the early Communist movement, Chen Duxiu and Li Dazhao, readily adopted the ideas of Marxism and Leninist organization.[6]

The shift was rapid as young people experimented with different ideas. In this context, Chen and Li were important as elder statesmen of the leftist intellectual arena. Their prestige drew in acquaintances and former and current students to the small radical movement. Enthusiasm for Soviet Russia was strengthened by the Karakhan Declaration, which appeared to renounce all former czarist territorial claims in China, thus distinguishing the new Soviet regime from the other foreign powers. The declaration was passed on July 25, 1919, and was published in March 1920. It renounced the unequal treaties with Russia and promised the return of the Chinese Eastern Railway without requiring any compensation from China. This crucial artery became a focal point of subsequent disagreement as the Soviets backed away from this agreement. When the declaration was published in the Soviet press, the rejection of compensation was excluded, and in late 1922, when the Soviet foreign affairs representative, Adolf Joffe, was confronted about the claim, he denied that any such offer had ever been made. The following year, Karakhan himself, after whom the declaration was named, denied making such a generous offer.[7]

Soviet Creation or Chinese Invention

For as long as the Soviet Union existed, official historians dueled with those in China about the origins of the CCP. Selected and abridged documents were released to argue their respective cases. Not surprisingly, Chinese historians stressed and continue to stress the indigenous sources of the party's origins. Historians promulgated the phrase "Chen [Duxiu] in the South and Li [Dazhao] in the North" to explain the roots of the small groups that came together to form the CCP, with the two most influential early Communists using their contacts to develop the early groups.[8] With the opening of the Comintern China archives, we can now reach a more accurate assessment. Reality was more complex, but Soviet engagement was crucial.

Although Chen and Li were key figures laying the theoretical foundations for the party, it was a Russian, Grigori Voitinsky, and a Dutchman, Henk Sneevliet (alias Maring),[9] who brought to China concepts of Leninist organization. Crucially, Sneevliet devised the specific Communist tactic of collaborating with the Nationalists to expand the CCP's influence.

Voitinsky was not the first to visit China with a mission to assess its revolutionary potential, but his mission, which arrived in April 1920, was the most crucial.[10] He traveled as a journalist, a common cover for Soviet agents working overseas and one later also adopted by the CCP. With the groundwork laid for more direct engagement and the growing sense among a small group that China's salvation was linked to the global need for emancipation from imperialism, Voitinsky had raw material with which to work. Assigned for Comintern work in the East, he had crucial influence on CCP policy throughout the 1920s and was the Comintern representative in China when Chiang Kai-shek struck in 1927.

Voitinsky's mission was to scope out leaders of the revolutionary movement and bring together those in North China who professed anarchist and Communist views. Initially he was not tasked with founding a party, but he quickly shifted his views to realign them with those of the Comintern to push for a more orthodox party rather than an assembly of radical elements. Voitinsky undertook three tasks that established the foundation for the CCP: he met with notable figures among the radicals and reported their views back to the Comintern,[11] he promoted materials on the Bolshevik movement, and most importantly, he engaged in organizational work to plant the seeds of the notion of forming a Communist party by establishing the Shanghai Revolutionary Bureau as the core of the party. The bureau was composed of five members, including himself and Chen Duxiu, and three departments: pub-lication, information and agitation, and organization; there was a sub-bureau in Guangzhou. In all probability, "The Manifesto of the CCP" (November 1920) was published by the bureau, well before there was an actual CCP. The manifesto proposed a radical, orthodox view of the party's objectives but exhibited little feeling for the realities of China. Common ownership was proposed, private property was to be abolished, as was the state (reflecting the influence of anarchism), and society was to be classless. Class struggle led by the CCP would defeat capitalism and, via the dictatorship of the proletariat, would lead to a society governed by a soviet.

Voitinsky left China in January 1921, but his short visit yielded important progress. The foundations for the Communist Party had been put in place and the idea of a national congress was floated. In Shanghai, Voitinsky had nurtured a small but strong nucleus of comrades and tutored them on the importance of organization and propaganda when developing a revolu-tionary party. Organization and propaganda would remain core elements of CCP work, albeit with varying degrees of success and intensity. The impor-tance of Voitinsky as a catalyst is revealed by the fact that following his de-parture, momentum stalled due to time pressures, inadequate resources, and internal squabbles about the nature of the party. The arrival of his replace-ments, Henk Sneevliet, on behalf of the Comintern, and Vladimir Nikolsky, sent by the Far Eastern Secretariat to oversee the First National Congress of the CCP, got work moving again. The two played major roles during the congress, drawing up plans and covering the expenses, and Sneevliet was in-strumental in shaping the first period of cooperation with the GMD.[12]

The First Party Congress: Going It Alone?

The congress, which convened in Shanghai from July 23 to August 5, 1921, marked a crucial milestone. Thirteen Chinese delegates, joined by Nikolsky and Sneevliet, represented small groups in Shanghai, Beijing, Wuhan, Changsha/Hunan, Guangzhou, Ji'nan, and those Chinese studying in Japan. The thirteen delegates, chaired by Zhang Guotao, a later rival to Mao Ze-dong for party leadership, represented a grand total of 53 members. In se-cret, they gathered at a member's house in the French concession on Rue Wantz (now 76 Xingye Road). Indicating the precarious nature of under-ground work, the meeting was interrupted by a mysterious figure who entered the house, thus causing the meeting to adjourn and subsequently retreat to

South Lake in nearby Jiaxing, Zhejiang province. The congress elected a provisional Central Executive Bureau—Chen Duxiu (secretary), Zhang Guotao (organization), and Li Da (propaganda)—to liaise with the regional branches.

At the time, the congress was not regarded as a big deal. The two most important figures in the Communist movement, Chen Duxiu and Li Dazhao, did not attend, and Sneevliet dismissed its significance. The spirited and animated debates focused on the nature and role of the party, and whether it should join with other social forces. The fluidity of the views of the founders is reflected in the fact that of the thirteen delegates, only three attended the Second Congress and only two were still members in 1949.

The participants divided into two main camps. The majority continued the harsh rhetoric and exclusionist stance of the November 1920 manifesto. They called for the overthrow of the capitalists by the revolutionary army of the proletariat and they were hostile to any form of collaboration with other groups, especially the "yellow intellectual class." Members were to shun joining the National Parliament. Soviets would form the main organizing principle within the party, operating as a secretive entity along hierarchical lines. The minority rejected such activism and wanted to take a more academic approach, sensing that it was too soon to become involved in the labor movement. The best strategy was to equip the intellectual elite with an understanding of Marxism, and only then could workers be organized and their class consciousness raised. This measured approach would permit more time to reflect on the comparative values of Bolshevism and German Social Democracy. Rather than a tight Bolshevik organization, the minority preferred a looser organization that would recruit students, intellectuals, and all who believed in and were willing to promote Marxism. The revolution would be a long process, and participation in a "bourgeois" government was perfectly acceptable. This approach was rejected, with the final decision barring CCP members from holding posts as government officials or as parliamentary representatives.

Sneevliet sought to persuade participants that it was essential for the small party to ally with the national revolutionary movement, best represented by the GMD. Driven by his practical experience in the Dutch colony, he drew on the decisions of the Comintern's Second Congress, held in July–August 1920. The theses adopted contained contradictions that would lead the CCP down the road to calamity in 1927. The important role of the movement in the East was to overthrow imperialism as an integral component of the global proletarian struggle. Lenin emphasized that it was necessary to enter into a temporary alliance with bourgeois democracy, while maintaining the independence of the proletarian movement. Meanwhile, temporarily, the bourgeoisie would lead the revolutionary movement. When operationalized, this approach was a continual source of contention not only within the Comintern but also within the CCP. The key questions were: How much independence should the labor movement enjoy? How could the party prevent proletarian interests from becoming subsumed under those of the bourgeoisie? and How temporary was temporary?

Despite the stress on struggle and action, one of the most effective areas of Communist work was education—setting up workers' clubs and schools for workers and their families. This is hardly surprising, given that most of the early party members were drawn from the intelligentsia and education was their trade. In addition, the role of a teacher held a venerable place in the Confucian tradition, and while teachers impressed local workers, they also used this traditional access to inculcate Marxist ideas and proletarian consciousness. The pioneer was Luo Zhanglong, who oversaw a workers' school on the important Beijing-Hankou Railway line.[13] Others were impressed, and future CCP leader Li Lisan learned from Luo Zhanglong and set up a school in Anyuan. The Communist-run school system in Anyuan was crucial to local CCP success in recruiting members and sympathizers. By 1925 there were seven schools under the auspices of the Communist-run workers' club, where 1,500 workers and 2,000 children were studying.[14]

Conflicting Views in the Alliance

Sneevliet's proposal for cooperation was bitterly contested and open to different interpretations, which had significant strategic consequences. The key question was who the alliance should be formed with. Soviet agents sought cooperation with a variety of individuals, not only Sun Yat-sen, the leader of the GMD, but also Chen Jiongming, the powerful warlord in Guangdong, and Wu Peifu, the power in the North. Some in Moscow saw Chen Jiongming and Wu Peifu as better options. The comrades in Guangzhou favored cooperation with Chen Jiongming rather than Sun Yat-sen. Those CCP members such as Zhang Guotao who worked with the labor movement were opposed to CCP members joining the GMD as individuals to form a bloc within. Key disputes centered on the level of cooperation and whether it was possible to build a mass Communist party. Given the slaughter when the CCP was defeated in 1927, one can point to the inherent contradiction in the Comintern's policy, but in 1920 it was not obvious and most delegates to the Comintern's Second Congress were far more interested in developments in the West than in wrestling with any contradictions. For Sneevliet, Voitinsky, Mikhail Borodin (Sneevliet's Bolshevik party successor in China), and the Chinese comrades, the issue of how to operationalize the seemingly simple formula within China's complex reality would lead to continual conflicts about the way forward.

Sneevliet created the tactic of a bloc within the GMD, with all CCP members joining the GMD as individuals. Sneevliet's extended trip to southern China during the winter of 1921–1922 impressed upon him the potential for a successful national revolution. He traveled during the great Hong Kong seaman's strike, which resulted in victory for the workers and significant wage increases. Sneevliet contrasted the GMD engagement favorably with the lack of activity by the CCP and their stumbling efforts at labor organization in the North. Reporting his views to the Comintern in July 1922, he claimed that the CCP had no significant proletarian base, not even in Shanghai, and he saw little chance for the development of a revolutionary socialist movement. On other occasions, he even noted that the Communist Party had been born too early by foreign means. Sneevliet's positive view of the GMD and the weakness of the CCP was shared by others.[15] To head off criticism of cooperation with a bourgeois party, Sneevliet claimed that it was not a party but rather a four-group bloc, comprising the intelligentsia, the emigrants living in other colonial countries, the soldiers in the army of the southern government, and the workers. This loose coalition meant that the CCP could work within the GMD openly and disseminate socialist propaganda while building up its strength among the working class.

Sneevliet returned from his trip to the South convinced of the correctness of his vision for China's future, but he found himself opposed, both within China by Chen Duxiu and Zhang Guotao and in Moscow by key Comintern leaders, including Voitinsky, who had received reports painting a more negative picture of the GMD and of its leader Sun Yat-sen.[16] Before reporting to Moscow, Sneevliet shared his views with his Chinese comrades, who did not receive them well. Chen Duxiu complained that outside of Guangzhou, the GMD was regarded as a "political party scrambling for power and profit" and that the comrades from Guangdong, Beijing, Shanghai, Changsha, and Wuhan who had met to discuss cooperation had unanimously rejected Sneevliet's ideas. Chen Duxiu asked Voitinsky to present the Chinese views to the Executive Committee of the Communist International (ECCI), should it discuss Sneevliet's ideas.[17] While Chen reluctantly fell in line with Sneevliet's approach, others dug in. Sneevliet returned to China from Moscow and used his prestige, together with Comintern support, to push CCP members to accept the tactic of forming a bloc within the GMD instead of working alongside as a bloc without. This rapprochement paved the way for the groundbreaking Sun-Joffe Statement of January 26, 1923, which authorized collaboration between the GMD and Soviet Russia. For Sun, it meant that his movement could receive Soviet financial support. Joffe, the key Soviet envoy to China, had requested that the Soviets provide two million gold rubles in financial support, and on March 8, 1923, the Politburo (Political Bureau) of the Russian Communist Party (Bolshevik) approved the request.

The Third Party Congress: Let's Collaborate, Perhaps

While momentum was moving forward in China, opposition was growing in Moscow, providing support to those in the CCP who were still uncomfortable with the idea of a bloc within. Cooperation again proved controversial at the Third Party Congress, which met June 12–20, 1923. In addition, measures were proposed to create a more orthodox Leninist party structure. The Central Executive Committee (CEC) was asserted to be the most powerful organization and was granted the task of enforcing congress decisions and examining and deciding on the policies and actions of the party. Anarchism was to be combatted and the party was to operate under "centralized and iron-like laws." Such statements had little practical effect. Opposition to the form of cooperation with the GMD persisted, and the party once again fell into disarray.

The situation was so dire that Chen Duxiu tendered his resignation as party leader. He had attempted to be loyal to Moscow while trying to deal with the reality on the ground, but obedience to the Comintern was paramount, as the party was not viable without Soviet financial support. Between October 1921 and January 1922, of the 17,500 yuan spent, 16,555 yuan had come from the ECCI.[18]

Before the Third Congress convened, any optimism that CCP members might have felt was extinguished by the crushing of the northern railway workers' February 1923 strike. The sobering defeat revealed that the CCP had not developed strength within the working class, and it led CCP members to be more sympathetic to the idea of working with the GMD. Before the strike, CCP engagement in labor activity had been rising. Of particular note was the successful, peaceful miners' strike in Anyuan, Jiangxi province, which resulted in not only economic gains for the workers but also official recognition and support for the Communist-controlled labor organization. The action had been led by three future CCP leaders: Liu Shaoqi, Li Lisan, and Mao Zedong. Li Lisan raised the slogan "Once beasts of burden, now we will be men," which appealed to the pervasive calls at the time for human dignity.[19]

These successes provided support to those in the CCP and in Moscow who thought that a mass Communist party could be developed based on the proletariat. CCP strength was in the North, among the railway workers and the miners of Hubei and Hunan, not in Shanghai where workers' organizations were underdeveloped. In fact, in the fall of 1922 the Labor Secretariat had moved from Shanghai to Beijing. Naively, the CCP leadership thought this would bring the movement under the protection of sympathetic warlord Wu Peifu. It is true that the number of strikes had been rising, but for the most part they were focused on material issues and did not raise class consciousness. To rectify this, at a January 1923 meeting it was decided that future political struggles should be waged based on opposition to imperialism and warlordism and in defense of the right to strike.[20] The increasing activism made Wu Peifu realize that the workers' actions might threaten the vital Beijing-Hankou Railway. The tense standoff along the railway was broken in the early hours of February 7, when troops under Wu Peifu broke up the strike, killing ten workers and wounding thirty. The severed head of one of the strike leaders was hung on a bamboo pole to instill fear in the hearts of others. This was merely the first of a series of betrayals that followed the CCP's placement of trust in sympathetic collaborators.

The idea that the working class could provide a base upon which the CCP could build the revolution had been dispelled, and pessimism prevailed. The CCP lost around 90 percent of its support, and only in Hunan did the labor unions escape persecution. The ensuing terror led the CCP to be more sympathetic toward the GMD and toward the possibility of building a revolutionary base in the South. The CCP moved its headquarters via Shanghai to Guangzhou, where it could operate in the open.

The massacre provided a somber backdrop as the party met in Guangzhou to hold its Third Congress. Yet the defeat did not quell the disputes over the nature of collaboration with the GMD. The basis for the discussions at the

The author with Luo Zhanglong, leader of the February 1923 Railway Workers' strike, in 1988.

congress was the Comintern's January 1923 resolution, agreed upon in Moscow by Voitinsky and Sneevliet and under Bukharin's promptings.[21] The message was clear: the CCP had to cooperate with the GMD. The weakness of the labor movement meant that a national revolution was the priority, and therefore CCP members would remain in the GMD. Yet room for disagreement persisted, as the CCP had to organize the workers, enlighten them, and create professional unions. This would provide the basis for a strong, mass Communist party. Confusingly, this work was to be conducted independently, but, at the same time, it was not to disturb the national revolutionary movement. The CCP was not to become entirely entangled within the GMD and was not to "furl its own banner."[22]

Based on the Comintern's January 1923 resolution, Chen Duxiu, supported by Sneevliet, presented a set of ideas to the congress that called on the CCP to keep the GMD on the revolutionary road and to create within the GMD a left wing of workers and peasants. The CCP was to continue to organize the workers, but CCP interests would rest mainly with the national movement. Zhang Guotao took special exception, accusing Sneevliet of trying to liquidate the CCP. Sneevliet criticized Zhang for his leftist tendencies and his illusions that a rapid development of a mass workers' party was possible.

Zhang Guotao raised three issues: Did the GMD represent the national movement? Would it be possible to reorganize the GMD? and Was there an alternative to this mode of cooperation to promote the revolution? He feared that if all CCP members were to join the GMD, then CCP interests would be ignored unless the GMD were to be reorganized—which he did not think was possible.[23] In Zhang's view, the CCP's key task was to build the labor movement, and not to support the GMD in the North where it was weak. Sneevliet defended his and Chen's views and claimed that the only question to be debated concerned implementation, not the principle of whether or not to join the GMD. He argued that an independent labor movement was not possible and that Chen Duxiu's ideas provided the only correct guidance on how to collaborate with the GMD. The ensuing vote was close (21 to 16), indicating substantial opposition to this form of collaboration. However, the result of the votes for the new CEC revealed a decline in personal support for Zhang Guotao, as he received only 6 out of a possible 40 votes, whereas support for Chen Duxiu was unanimous. At its first meeting after the congress, the CEC elected a five-person Central Bureau, with Chen Duxiu as chair, Mao Zedong as secretary, Luo Zhanglong a labor activist, and Sneevliet's German interpreter as party accountant.

The congress manifesto stressed the need to rally around the GMD as the central force in the national revolution. The weakness of the working class ruled out the possibility of developing a mass Communist party. Within the GMD, CCP members were to attract radical elements who would then help to expand the party. Progress was not smooth, however, and the resolution was barely implemented. The Central Bureau moved back to Shanghai as it felt that the party could not achieve much with Sun Yat-sen remaining in the South. The CCP wanted to develop new organizations or bring about radical change within the GMD and create a new national party. The one region that was positive about cooperation with the GMD was Guangzhou. The Comintern and Bolshevik emissary Borodin had arrived there in early October 1923 to replace Sneevliet as Stalin's man in China. The shift from the globe-trotting Dutchman to the Bolshevik party man signified the emergence of Russian national interests at the expense of proletarian, world revolution.

Alliance Fuels the Growth of the CCP

There is no doubt that the united front with the GMD initially was beneficial to the CCP. Membership grew from just under 1,000 in January 1924 to almost 55,000 by April 1927. However, from the beginning the policy was fraught with tensions over maintaining CCP integrity and supporting growth of the GMD. Disagreements continued about the role of the labor movement, the degree of CCP autonomy, and to what extent the CCP should build its own strength in those areas where the GMD was not strong. The CCP's capacity to act independently of Soviet advice was limited by the general esteem for Moscow's agents—and their financial support, without which the CCP would not have been able to operate. Problematically, there was no unanimity in Moscow about the relationship between the GMD and the CCP and the balance between promoting the national revolution and the development of a mass Communist party. Resolutions often embodied contradictory views, allowing the comrades in China to pick and choose whichever approach they favored. This uncertainty led to a series of CCP resolutions that sought to define the nature of the GMD: at times it was viewed as homogeneous, while on other occasions it was said to comprise a left and right wing, or a left, right, and center. The different analyses of the nature of the GMD and the potential for promoting the national revolution can be clearly seen in the differences in the approaches of those working in Guangzhou and those working in Shanghai. The trajectory of the revolution looked very different for those working clandestinely out of safe houses in urban, foreign-dominated Shanghai compared to those who were operating under the security umbrella of the GMD military, where the CCP could openly mobilize. Borodin even went so far as to state that there were "two lines" in the Chinese revolution.[24]

The CCP's success during the first years of cooperation set the stage for its later repression. It must have been obvious to all involved that, sooner or later, the interests of the national revolution led by the bourgeoisie and those of the proletarian revolution led by a party promoting the interests of the workers and peasants would clash. Stalin anticipated that, when the time was ripe, the Nationalists would be squeezed dry like a lemon and tossed aside. Yet, beginning from the slaughter of the CCP sympathizers in Shanghai in April 1927, it was the CCP that was squeezed so hard that it barely survived. Divisions within the GMD and the concentration of military power in the hands of Chiang Kai-shek sealed the CCP's fate.

In addition to the unresolved challenge of cooperation, there were also organizational problems. Throughout the period, the CCP adopted various resolutions to tighten up the organization and to shift it away from the small-group mentality, which had been crucial to its origins, to become a disciplined Bolshevik machine. To dilute the influence of the intellectual elite within the party, more workers and peasants were recruited and membership criteria were relaxed. Workers were not expected to understand the intricacies of Marxism, but they were seen as natural fodder for the CCP. Class consciousness and loyalty to the party were sufficient. The influx of new members, in turn, led to a new set of problems as complaints began to spread that many members lacked both theoretical sophistication and practical experience. Slowly but surely, in a country that was overwhelmingly rural, the realization dawned that the peasantry had a role to play as members of the revolutionary fold. One such early theoretical advocate was Chen Duxiu, while Peng Pai began rural organization in South China even before Mao Zedong championed a focus on the peasantry.

Under Borodin's guidance the reorganization of the GMD along Leninist lines went well. Financial support from Soviet Russia helped, but both as a Russian and as a party member, Borodin enjoyed a higher status than his predecessor, Sneevliet. With Sun Yat-sen's willing support, the reorganization culminated in January 1924 with the First National Congress of the GMD. The Congress Manifesto fell in line with the Comintern's view that stressed the anti-imperialist and anti-warlord nature of the current struggle, calling for far-reaching economic, political, and social reforms. Communists were well represented in the GMD leading bodies. Three Communists were elected to the twenty-four-person CEC and headed the organization and the peasant bureau. The policy of cooperation seemed to be working.

This did not appease everyone in the CCP or the Comintern. Voitinsky remained concerned about the capabilities of the GMD in general and about Sun Yat-sen in particular. Yet the initial responses were positive. In November 1923 the CCP CEC adopted its most positive view of the relationship, calling on all those who had not yet joined the GMD to sign up and help the GMD form organizations in places where it did not yet have any. The focus of work was the nationalist movement, with labor, peasant, student, and women's work all subordinated to meeting this goal. The strategy of subversion from within was clearly established. The CCP was to maintain its secret organizations within the GMD party branches, but it was to seek a central position within the GMD.

Yet vacillation continued, and even Borodin discovered how frustrating it could be to work with Sun Yat-sen. In February 1924, Borodin criticized Sun's utopianism and neglect of the mass movement when speaking about the organizational and ideological confusion within the GMD.[25] Suspicion about the true nature of the GMD was quickly revived, and the CCP remained aware that a majority in the right wing of the GMD remained opposed to CCP entry into the party. Thus, in May 1924 an enlarged meeting of the CCP CEC shifted the emphasis of its work by defining a friendly left wing and a more hostile right wing within the GMD; no longer was it a homogeneous organization. The meeting defined the CCP as the "left," setting the stage for a struggle with the GMD right. However, the CCP did not wish to push things too far, rejecting an open struggle in favor of criticism in the press that would keep the GMD on the correct revolutionary path. In late July the party published this new analysis in a secret circular, calling for strengthening the left and hinting that perhaps a new GMD could be formed. The analysis was based on Borodin's view that there were three groups attending the First Congress of the GMD: a right of thirty to forty people, an extreme left of about the same number, and a center (the majority), control over which was the object of struggle: Sun's task was to hold this party together.[26]

A Rising Tide for Labor

The bullish attitude toward progress was reflected at the CCP's Fourth Congress, held in Shanghai on January 11–22, 1925. This was compounded by the sense that serious divisions were weakening the grip of the warlords. In early 1925 the GMD broke with the northern warlord Duan Qirui, leading to differences over whether Sun Yat-sen should engage with Beijing. The Party Center wanted Sun to stay in Guangzhou to consolidate the gains there, while Borodin and the Guangzhou comrades felt that going to Beijing would help bring the movement to the national stage. Further, the Guangzhou group correctly sensed that the mass movement was on the rise and that it would be possible to work within the labor movement more effectively. This appealed to the sentiments of the key Comintern figure, Voitinsky, who not only attended the Fourth Congress but also had a major influence on the congress documents, which reflected his emphasis on the need to independently step up work in the labor movement.[27]

The congress embodied this spirit as it prepared for the rising tide of labor activism. The Fourth Congress resolution depicted the period of warlord-dominated politics as coming to an end, providing an opportunity to expand the movement, as witnessed by demands for a National Assembly that had "spread all over the country like a surging wave." The labor movement was defined as the "foundation of the nationalist movement." In a fateful turn of phrase, the CCP was to benefit from a closer relationship with the Comintern, "the supreme commander of the world revolution." Importantly, in the review of work on the nationalist movement, the congress acknowledged both leftist and rightist mistakes but saw the latter as the most dangerous. Its dangerous tendencies included ignoring CCP work by focusing too much on building up the GMD, aiding the entire GMD rather than exploiting the differences between the left and the right, and downplaying the role of class struggle. The national revolution was not to be characterized as representing the interests of the bourgeoisie. Leftist mistakes included excluding classes other than the proletariat.

Now the GMD was seen as comprising not two but three groups. In addition to the left and the right, there was a center composed of "those revolutionary elements among the petty bourgeois intellectual class." Though small in number, the group occupied leading positions in the GMD. Work in the GMD was to reject class conciliation, stress class struggle, expand the left, and support the center when it clearly opposed the right.[28]

The party was correct about a rising tide in the labor movement, and this led the CCP to believe even more strongly that the working class could shoulder the responsibility of the revolution. The congress saw the movement entering a new phase that would provide opportunities for the national revolution to expand, but it was critical of the Guangzhou comrades for allowing this work to overshadow the independence of labor. Consequently, the CCP's main task was to organize labor unions and spread propaganda that had a class perspective. Workplace branches were the key to carrying out party policy. This approach left the party well positioned to take advantage of the next tide of activism. It was not long in coming.

Sun Yat-sen died on March 12, 1925, and as talks collapsed in Beijing, the upsurge in nationalism culminated in the May Thirtieth Movement. It was especially strong in Shanghai, where the party was able to capitalize and expand its influence.[29] The movement began quietly in February with a strike at a Japanese-owned textile mill in Shanghai, but it escalated dramatically on May 15 when one of the strikers was killed by a factory guard and a number of others were wounded. Injuries and arrests spread across Shanghai, and on May 28 the CCP, together with other organizations, coordinated demonstrations that would take place on May 30. Reacting to this threat, the International Settlement Police fired on the demonstrators, wounding many and killing ten. To try to take control of the movement, on June 1 the CCP set up the General Labor Union, headed by labor activist Li Lisan. Li, a future CCP leader, had already spearheaded the successful September 1922 Anyuan miners' strike. As the movement rumbled on into July, it did not lead to the expected revolutionary outcome, and by mid-September the General Labor Union was closed down and the CCP was driven underground.

A major problem was maintaining funding and relief for the strikers, which progressively diminished the longer the strike went on. Most of the support came not from the Soviets via organizations in China but rather from patriotic citizens and the General Chamber of Commerce. This indicates that support was inspired by nationalist outrage rather than by socialist solidarity. The movement did spread to other cities, most notably with the Hong Kong–Guangzhou strike, which lasted from June 1925 until October 1926. Thus, Communist influence spread as membership grew, but it sent warning signs to opponents within the GMD. One clear indication of what was to come was the crushing of China's "Little Moscow," when the local elite launched an all-out military attack on the Anyuan Workers' Club and its associated schools. Three workers were killed, some 10,000 were dismissed from work, and 2,000 were sent home to their native villages.[30]

Despite this setback, enthusiasm and a bullish attitude permeated an enlarged meeting of the CCP Central Executive Committee in Beijing in September–October 1925, which concluded that the working class had clearly demonstrated its leading role in the national revolution. However, the meeting warned that a balance had to be struck between promoting the workers' economic demands and engaging in political struggle, which was not to be forgotten. Indeed, the party in Anyuan was criticized for not conducting sufficient political work and for not preparing a secret organization to withstand attack and establish a foundation for a Bolshevik mass party.[31] However, the bravest and most loyal workers, armed in groups of 10 or 100 under a military committee, were set up under the CEC. The CCP was articulating its shift from an open, educational role to an emphasis on military and class struggle.

Party numbers were clearly expanding and this required attention. The strike led to a significant change in the composition of the party. In May 1925, of the 297 members, 57.3 percent were defined as working class; by September 1925, of the 1,080 members, 78.5 percent were defined as working class.[32] The task of the CCP was to accelerate its transformation from a small group to a centralized mass party. This meant that membership criteria were relaxed even further. For example, the probation period for workers and peasants was reduced to one month, while intellectuals still had to wait three months, although even this was a reduction from the previous six-month probation period. Workers did not have to understand Marxism—as long as they displayed class consciousness and loyalty to the party, they could be admitted.

Organizationally, the CCP had already adopted new statutes at the Fourth Congress, in January 1925, with organization designated as the most important issue for the survival and development of the party. As before, the hope was that this would help the party break away from its mentality of operating as small propaganda groups. The statutes adopted what would become and remain to this day the most important organizing principle of the party: the branch as the fundamental building block. Formerly a cell required five members, but the new branches only required three members. The idea behind this was to shift the party from being area-based to being based on occupation to help strengthen party work among the proletariat.

By the time of the enlarged meeting of the CCP CEC, the growing importance of the peasantry was recognized. To mark this, the workers' and peasants' committee was divided into two committees, although the peasants' committee was actually established in November 1926, with Mao Zedong as secretary. The meeting called for a military committee, and the following month Zhou Enlai, China's future premier, was named as its head. Following continual promptings from the Comintern, a serious organization was coming into being, with its leaders trying to break with old traditions to create a centralized Leninist party. This attention to organization was strengthened by the return of Chinese students from Moscow. The moves to centralize and unify party organization soon faced stress from the challenges of developing a mass party while maintaining cooperation with the GMD and the challenges of increasing pressure from the GMD right.

Tensions within the party had already surfaced at an October 1925 meeting when the Shanghai Party Center criticized the approach to work in Guangzhou. Naturally, work in Guangzhou was acknowledged as important for the national revolution, but the comrades there were criticized for not expanding the ranks of the CCP during the "revolutionary upsurge." Their tendency to work as individuals among the workers, peasants, and soldiers rather than making clear their party affiliation meant that people did not understand that the CCP was distinct from the GMD. The party simply appeared to be a "shadow" wearing a GMD mask. The most important task now was to rapidly expand the CCP, with the aid of a commissar sent from the Center to improve organizational work. While Borodin in the South was establishing a strategy to gain power within the GMD, Voitinsky and Chen Duxiu in Shanghai were thinking of a weaker bond and the possible development of independent CCP power. The earlier assessment that there was a center in the GMD was rejected, with the CCP now recognizing only a left wing and a right wing. The strategy was to help the left and to fight the right. The previous classification of the leaders of the GMD as the center had led CCP members to ignore the party's own positions and simply become members of the GMD left, giving the false impression that the GMD left was synonymous with Communist.[33]

Warning Signs Flashing

The shifting strategy was becoming embroiled in debates in Moscow and in divisions within the GMD. Under Borodin's direction, actions in Guangzhou seemed to move beyond Stalin's intention to operate within the GMD while not neglecting CCP work for the subsequent opportunity to develop the revolution. Those in Shanghai under Chen and Voitinsky were beginning to think about the possibility of independent CCP activity outside of the framework of cooperation with the GMD. This approach would be developed further by Leon Trotsky and the opposition in Moscow as they struggled against Stalin. Indeed, Chen Duxiu was later a leader of the Trotskyite movement in China.

The increasing influence of the CCP had an impact on the thinking of its opponents within the nationalist movement, but the warning signs were initially ignored. Although it is true that the left strengthened its position after Sun Yat-sen's death, other events had more serious repercussions. In August 1925 one of the most influential figures on the left, who was sympathetic to the Communists, was assassinated, and in late November 1925 a group of opponents met in the Western Hills just outside of Beijing. The group called for the expulsion of Borodin from Guangzhou and even the expulsion of the Communists from the GMD. Earlier in August an influential GMD theorist had correctly anticipated the CCP strategy of infiltration and called for GMD organization to be strengthened to resist CCP influence.

The warning signs were again missed and discounted further by the successful, from the CCP's viewpoint, convocation of the Second Congress of the GMD in January 1926. The meeting reinforced the GMD left and the idea of cooperation with the CCP. CCP members occupied three of the nine positions on the GMD Standing Committee. The CCP responded enthusiastically in February 1926, presuming that left-wing control of the GMD was a reality. As the meeting was convening, Stalin was consolidating his views and his position in opposition to Trotsky.[34] In April 1925 Voitinsky had already sent an optimistic account to Moscow, cautioning that Stalin was building his views based on reports from Borodin. He described the CCP as developing its own strong independent organization, while enjoying freedom in the GMD.[35] Subsequent developments confirmed Voitinsky's views.

Despite Voitinsky's concerns, the February meeting swung support behind those in Guangzhou, helped by Chen Duxiu's absence due to illness. The increasing isolation of the proletariat after the high point of the May Thirtieth Movement meant that Shanghai was no longer seen as the hub of the revolution, and the importance of GMD work in Guangzhou assumed greater importance. Whether to move the Party Center to Guangzhou or to Beijing was discussed, with a preference for Beijing so that work could take on a national character. The impending Northern Expedition by GMD troops, launched in July 1926 to unify China, was regarded as a crucial vehicle to expand the influence of the national revolution and thus it was to be supported. With the working class taking a backseat, the role of the peasantry was accorded greater importance. With the bourgeoisie showing its true colors, it was now patently obvious that only an alliance of workers and peasants could bring about the success of the national revolution. Voitinsky now bought into the view of the left's dominance within the GMD, and he reported to the Comintern that the CCP was directing the GMD, which actually was a "popular democratic party."[36]

The next warning sign came soon after the meeting on March 20, when Chiang Kai-shek declared martial law following the Zhongshan Incident, claiming that the Communists had used the Zhongshan gunboat to kidnap him. It is unlikely that there was any such plot, but Chiang exploited this story to appeal to the GMD right and to reduce the influence of the Communists before the Northern Expedition set out. Soviet advisers and a number of Communists were placed under house arrest. Borodin, on his return to Guangzhou from Russia on April 29, 1925, negotiated their release, but he had to make some serious concessions—including abandoning separate CCP organizations in the GMD, supplying a list of all CCP members in the GMD, no longer serving as a bureau chief, and restricting CCP membership on executive committees to no more than one-third of the total members. Finally, Borodin was forced to support the Northern Expedition, something he had previously opposed. In return, Chiang would restrain the GMD right. In fact, Chiang was limited in what he could do, as he was still dependent on Soviet financial support and materials. Thus, Chiang made it clear that his actions were not directed against the Soviets. The Soviet advisers and the CCP members may have been encouraged to accept a short-term retreat because they had the impression that many of Chiang's colleagues did not agree with his actions.

Chiang's actions heightened the divisions within the CCP and Moscow about the nature of the relationship. Publicly, following Comintern advice, the CCP accepted the various measures passed by the GMD CEC. But beneath the surface, responses differed. The Guangzhou comrades favored a tough response against Chiang by attempting to take over the GMD from within. Chen Duxiu, not for the first time, contemplated withdrawal, perhaps prompted by Voitinsky, who had suggested it in April 1926.[37] In June 1926 a compromise was reached within the CCP in favor of a bloc without to replace the bloc within, a suggestion rejected by the Comintern.[38] Reports from the Soviet advisers working in Guangzhou placed blame on their own failings and those of the CCP members who only paid attention to their own organization and did not try to build up the GMD left.[39]

Only one week before the Zhongshan Incident of March 13, the Sixth Plenum of the ECCI had decided that the collaboration should be maintained, and it praised the government in Guangzhou as the model for a future China. While critical of any attempt to dissolve the Communists into the GMD, the plenum warned of the leftist mistake of believing that the revolutionary-democratic stage could be skipped in favor of immediately implementing proletarian dictatorship and ignoring the peasantry, "the most important and decisive factor of the national-liberation movement."[40] Given this, it is not surprising that the Comintern sought to play down the significance of the Zhongshan Incident. At the plenum, the suggestion for a bloc without was rejected.[41] The differences over collaboration now played directly into the disputes between Stalin and Trotsky, and the alternative approach was again definitively rebuffed by the Soviet Politburo.[42]

That some within the GMD were concerned about the role of the CCP and the intended Bolshevization of the national movement did not go unnoticed by the Soviet advisers, including Borodin, who noted that there were some who genuinely feared that the CCP might take over the party.[43] However, given that Trotsky was beginning to think that a bloc without might be more acceptable, Stalin insisted that the policy remain. Even Voitinsky fell in line and must have baffled Chen Duxiu by insisting that any notion within the CCP about leaving the alliance should be resisted. The CCP was to remain in the alliance, but it was to work to expand the GMD left.[44] His knuckles having been rapped, Chen told CCP members to pursue an approach along the lines laid out by Sneevliet, which, of course, he had earlier opposed.

Thus, cooperation continued, though the idea that the CCP might seize power through a mass movement was dropped. Meeting in Shanghai in July 1926, the CCP CEC adopted more moderate motions and even the bourgeoisie was depicted as an important part of the movement, having demonstrated "a capacity for leadership." The Northern Expedition was referred to as a "defensive war" against hostile forces in Hunan and Guangdong rather than as a "real revolutionary" action.[45] The CCP accepted the views of the Soviet advisers that the fault rested with the Communists themselves and their overzealous efforts to take over the GMD from within, a clear criticism of the Guangzhou comrades. Yet again the nature of the GMD was redefined, now as consisting of four blocs: the reactionary right, the new right composed of the reform movement of the bourgeoisie (including Chiang Kai-shek), the left composed of the resistance movement of the middle and small merchants, and the workers and peasants represented by the Communists.

Criticism of those in Guangzhou was clear, and Shanghai was restored to its place as the "heart of the nation's anti-imperialist movement." Despite all that had happened earlier, there was still a belief that a genuine Communist Party could be created in Shanghai, and the party committee was instructed to concentrate on local movements to win over the middle and petty bourgeois masses. Not surprisingly, Borodin disagreed, refusing to accept that Shanghai could become the revolutionary base because he believed that the imperialists were too heavily entrenched there. Compromise was inevitable unless open conflict were to break out. As a result, Borodin proposed establishing bases elsewhere and strengthening work in the Northeast, where the power of the imperialists was weaker and where the Soviet Union could more readily provide support.

While those in Guangzhou thought that the national revolution had almost run its course, meaning it was time to launch the proletarian movement, Chen Duxiu felt that the task was far from over as two-thirds of the country was still under the control of the warlord cliques. To support his view, Chen presented his interpretation of Sun Yat-sen's legacy, which has remained the CCP's standard interpretation to this day, as consisting of three fundamental policies: allying with Soviet Russia, allying with the CCP, and supporting the workers and peasants. Further, he accused Borodin and the others of suffering from a "left sickness." Chen was clearly learning from the Soviets the language of how inner-party struggles should be waged. Even though Chen Duxiu supported Stalin and the Comintern's approach, within a year he would be denounced as a "right opportunist" for pursuing these same policies. The Comintern's Seventh Plenum, held in November–December 1926, deemed that continued cooperation with the GMD left was necessary to complete the national revolution and that the CCP was to take control of the social revolution.

The CCP found itself between a rock and a hard place, fighting off attacks from the GMD right while wrestling with how to move forward with rural mobilization without alienating important groups. For a brief period the balancing seemed to work. In December 1926 the GMD CEC moved the seat of its government to Wuhan rather than to Nanchang, where Chiang Kai-shek was based. Chiang's legitimacy was challenged further in March 1927, when he was placed under the leadership of a revived Military Council and the post of CEC chair was abolished and replaced by a seven-person Presidium of the Political Council. Wang Jingwei, the leader of the GMD left, emerged as the temporary winner of these measures, and the Communists took over the posts in charge of labor and agriculture. The highpoint of collaboration culminated on April 5, 1927, when Wang Jingwei and Chen Duxiu issued a joint statement confirming GMD leadership in the national revolution, with the CCP having no intention to overthrow it—proletarian revolution was not part of the program. Things did not end well for Wang.

The Northern Expedition was pushing forward, and in Shanghai a general strike was called on March 21. This was the "third armed uprising" organized by the CCP. The first two (in October 1926 and February 1927) had been crushed within a day. By the time of the third strike, the CCP had learned that military training was essential and that they could not rely on itinerant and unemployed workers; instead they had to use factory workers who might exhibit greater loyalty. By the time the Northern Expeditionary Forces arrived, the city, except for the International Settlement and the

GMD sympathizers turn on the CCP, Shanghai, April 1927.

French Concession, was under the control of armed militias.[46] On top of this, on March 26 troops loyal to Chiang Kai-shek entered the city. In a clear warning sign, Chiang withheld recognition of the provisional municipal government that had been established on March 29. Energized, the Soviet Politburo pushed for a more aggressive approach, calling for the GMD right to be excluded and removed from leadership positions. Receiving reports that Chiang was engaging in a coup, the Soviets called for resistance and the militias were instructed not to hand over their weapons.[47] The euphoria was short-lived. On April 12, Chiang Kai-shek's troops set about eliminating all Communists in the areas under his control. Although as a result he was expelled from the GMD, with the left-wing government in Wuhan displaying sympathy for those in Shanghai, it was too little too late. Chiang set up his own government, with its capital in Nanjing. The earlier warning signs either had not been taken seriously enough or had simply been ignored. The White Terror was brutal. Martial law was declared in Guangzhou on April 15, and a call was issued for all Communists in the area to be arrested.[48] In Beijing, the party had been broken earlier, on April 6, when warlord troops entered the Soviet embassy, seized documents, and arrested suspected Communists. Among those caught up in the swoop was Li Dazhao, who was executed on April 28.

Heads in the Sand: From Worse to Worst

Bizarrely, this repression did not mark the end of attempts to collaborate with the GMD. At the Fifth Congress of the CCP, which ran from April 27 to May 9, 1927, members tried to make sense of what had happened and where the party should go next. It was a traumatic period that led to more failures for the party, rendering it ineffective in the cities, almost destroying the party, and driving the remnants of the party into inhospitable areas where it was more difficult for Chiang Kai-shek's forces and his partners to pursue it. Ever the optimists, the CCP claimed that Chiang's betrayal had brought the revolution to a new stage, and the delegates discussed how to move ahead with the peasant movement without disrupting cooperation. Clearly, the bourgeoisie had betrayed the revolution, and while membership was now smaller, quality was higher! In the CCP's analysis, the four-class bloc was replaced by a united front of workers, peasants, and the petty bourgeoisie. From the defeat of the militia in Shanghai, the party drew the lesson that it should strengthen work in the military. Those bourgeois elements who remained had to be watched carefully and expelled if they exhibited counterrevolutionary tendencies. Stalin and his supporters in Moscow shared this enthusiasm. In May 1927 the ECCI agreed with the CCP's assessment that the break with Chiang was positive, and it called for a continuation of the alliance, within which the rural revolution would take center stage.[49]

Amazingly, Chen Duxiu told the party to prepare to seize power as it was no longer an opposition party but instead would lead the revolution.[50] They were to create a "revolutionary democratic regime" in GMD-controlled areas, albeit an objective that was still far off. Overestimating the revolutionary potential had become endemic in the CCP, and much of this was prompted by directives from Moscow. Apart from any other reason to follow Moscow's advice, the CCP remained totally reliant on the Soviets for financial support. In addition to the funding sent to China, by 1930 the Soviets had spent five million rubles on training Chinese comrades at the Communist University of the Toilers of the East. Although the CCP might have opposed specific Comintern agents, they would never oppose the power center in Moscow.[51]

In terms of the labor movement, the debacle was given a positive spin: the rise in revolutionary activity among the proletariat was said to have caused the bourgeoisie to betray the revolution. As a result, the party set the optimistic objective of pursuing nationalization and worker participation in management to hit back at the bourgeoisie. How on earth they intended to carry this out was unclear. What was important was that now that the revolution was in abeyance in the urban areas, the treatment of the peasantry had become even more important for the future of the revolution. However, the need to continue the alliance with the GMD meant policy would err on the side of caution. Previous rural policy was denounced for being too rightist, but policy was still to move from rent reduction to land confiscation, with protections for small landlords. The proposal to confiscate all land was rebuffed, as was the moderate proposal that only land belonging to the enemies of the GMD should be confiscated.

Despite previous rhetoric and measures directed to the need for better organization, Chen Duxiu declared that this was the worst component of party work. The small-group mentality had never been overcome and the splintering of the party meant that unless this mentality was changed, the CCP would never amount to more than a group of provincial parties. To improve the situation, a Politburo replaced the CEC, and the Central Committee (CC) was to be expanded. For training, Chen suggested setting up a party school. Following the congress, the new Politburo promulgated new statutes. They spelled out in more detail the organizational structure of the party and, for the first time, asserted that democratic centralism was the guiding principle of the entire party. Further, the party set up a Standing Committee to oversee day-to-day work and a central supervisory committee to oversee party discipline. Now, on paper at least, the CCP was looking like a true Leninist party. The next step would be the use of "line struggle" and ideology to resolve disputes within the party. This would not be long in coming.

Despite the enthusiasm, disasters continued. Even the left-wing GMD government in Wuhan became frustrated with CCP activities among the peasantry, blaming the CCP for what it viewed as the movement's excesses. At the same time, many peasants were frustrated by what they saw as CCP attempts to rein in their actions and leave them at the mercy of vengeful warlords and even GMD troops. Repression of the Communists continued, and the events of the summer of 1927 made a mockery of the continued alliance with the GMD. Among the notable disasters was the Horse Day Massacre on May 21 in Changsha when Communist-led mass organizations were crushed by the local GMD garrison commander. The masochistic tendencies of the CCP to preserve the alliance with the GMD is revealed in a joint

CCP-GMD investigation, which concluded that misguided leaders had caused the peasants to break loose from control and to unleash a reign of terror.

This gesture and similar ones—such as acknowledging the leadership of the GMD in the national revolution, the Communists giving up government posts, and requiring mass organizations to submit to GMD leadership—did little to allay concerns within the GMD about the true intentions of the CCP. This was not helped when, in early June 1927, the newly dispatched Comintern envoy, M. N. Roy, showed the leader of the GMD in Wuhan, Wang Jingwei, the contents of a telegram from Stalin that clearly laid out the strategy. The Communists were to reorganize the left, expel the reactionary leaders such as those who maintained contact with Chiang Kai-shek, and then prepare concrete steps for a revolutionary army. This was all to take place under the Nationalist Party leadership. New leaders were to be drawn into the party from the workers and peasants to replace the old GMD leaders who were "vacillating and compromising."[52]

Not surprisingly this did not go down well with Wang Jingwei, and things rapidly collapsed. By the end of June the workers' militias were being disarmed, the trade unions were shut down, and the Communists were arrested. The Soviet envoys, Borodin and Roy, fled Wuhan, and on July 15 the Political Affairs Committee of the Wuhan GMD announced an end to cooperation. Following this, on August 1 the Communists launched the Nanchang Uprising, and on August 5 Wang Jingwei launched a major purge of Communist activists.

In the middle of this debacle, on July 12 Chen Duxiu resigned from his post following Comintern instructions and a new five-person provisional Standing Committee of the Politburo was selected. On the following day, the Standing Committee issued its criticism of the Wuhan government. Clearly, the Comintern and Stalin were not going to take the blame for the disasters of 1927. Stalin placed the blame on Borodin, Roy, and the Chinese leadership. Chen Duxiu and the leadership were blamed for their "right opportunism," even though on at least three occasions Chen had called for changing the nature of the alliance. It was not until September 1927 that Stalin accepted that the future struggle would be led by the CCP.[53]

The common assessment has been to dub the disaster as Stalin's failure in China, a view strongly supported by the Trotskyites. But within the Comintern or the Bolshevik party, was there a credible alternative? This is highly unlikely, given not only the politics within the Soviet party but also the tardiness with which the opposition formulated its critique of Stalin's approach.

By the time the opposition was able to articulate an alternative, they could not get their views known or debated because Stalin and his supporters had such strong control over the party apparatus and its publication outlets.

Only after the alliance had begun to collapse did the opposition pull its views together. Trotsky wrote, falsely, in 1931 that "the entrance of the Communist Party into the Kuomintang [GMD] was a mistake from the very beginning." His contemporaneous writings show that he fully supported the basic principles of the united front as outlined in 1922 and only in April 1926 did he begin to oppose the dominant view, probably sparked by the March 1926 Zhongshan Incident.[54] However, it was not until June 1927 that Trotsky was able to persuade his fellow oppositionists that the alliance had run its course. It was clearly a case of too little too late. At a time when an alternative might have made a difference, there was no effective tactic to pursue. By late June it was unlikely that the logistics and support could have been put in place, or that the Comintern workers in China and the CCP leadership could have been brought on board to prevent the GMD left wing from turning on them.

The CCP remained optimistic, and it spent the final years of the 1920s looking for signs of a revival of revolutionary potential, yet all attempts at insurrection were defeated. The first assessment of what had gone wrong was conducted at an emergency conference convened in Hankou on August 7 by the newly arrived Comintern agent, Vissarion Lominadze. The new strategy finally marked the end of cooperation. The previous leadership was blamed and criticized for opportunism in dealing with both the GMD and the mass movement and for failing to carry out Comintern policies effectively. Yet cooperation was still to be sought, when possible, with elements of the GMD left wing. This token gesture has often been ascribed to the need to protect Stalin, but there was a basis in China's reality. Not all those in the GMD were happy with the actions of Chiang Kai-shek and Wang Jingwei, and there were deep personal ties that overrode immediate political loyalties. For example, Song Qingling, Sun Yat-sen's widow, became a counterpoint to her sister, who was married to Chiang Kai-shek, and some in the GMD later became CCP military leaders. For the party as a whole, the CCP was to prepare for life underground by forging "strong, secret organizations."

Insurrections: Another Policy Failure

Far from licking their wounds and retreating, the new party leader, Qu Qiubai, proposed a series of insurrections to initiate a peasant uprising. This approach followed the failed Nanchang Uprising and laid the groundwork for the Autumn Harvest Uprising. The emergency conference held on August 7, 1927, is perhaps most noteworthy for Mao Zedong's famous dictum "Political power grows out of the barrel of a gun."

As with the Nanchang Uprising, the Autumn Harvest Uprising ended in failure. The plan was to launch the movement based on peasant associations in four southern provinces (Hunan, Hubei, Guangdong, and Jiangxi), with the goal of redistributing the land of the larger landlords. Not surprisingly, only in Hunan, where Mao Zedong was in the lead, did the uprising make any headway, but even there it was defeated, and Mao and the Hunan Front Committee decided not to follow the orders of the Party Center to attack the provincial capital of Changsha; instead they decided to pull back to the remote mountain refuge of Jinggangshan.

Again, such failures did not dampen enthusiasm, and in November 1927 the provisional Politburo adopted a more radical policy for work in both the urban and the rural areas. The CCP announced a definitive break with the GMD, which would hold for the next decade. All landlords were to be attacked, no matter how much land they held, and in the cities workers were to seize power at their workplaces. Nationwide insurrections were to be promoted, and the leaders of the failed Nanchang and Autumn Harvest Uprisings, including Mao Zedong, were criticized for lacking determination and "strong revolutionary will."

The only place in China where such demands bore any resemblance to reality was in Guangzhou, where after some initial success the Guangzhou Commune was crushed in December 1929. The Comintern representative had promoted the uprising, but it led to the loss of some 5,000 Communists. Although CCP military leaders, Ye Ting and Ye Jianying, had opposed the uprising, they were blamed for its failure. In disgust, Ye Ting left China for Europe, not to return for a decade. Those who survived were ordered to retreat to the mountain areas. The policies pursued under the latest iteration of Comintern agents and CCP leader Qu Qiubai did result in destroying any remaining links with the urban proletariat, but the surviving troops retreated to a number of rural enclaves where they could survive.

Once again, a new strategy was required, and it was outlined at the Sixth Party Congress, held in Moscow from June 18 to July 11, 1928. In assessing the past, the congress used Stalinist parlance to criticize both Chen Duxiu's "opportunist right deviation" and Qu Qiubai's "putchist left deviation."[55] At least the party had learned how to deflect blame onto individuals and how to conduct inner-party struggle. Now the revolution was between two waves, defined as "bourgeois democratic under the leadership of the proletariat," keeping the door open for future uprisings. This created uncertainty, because "new waves" were difficult to detect and the leadership was always on the lookout for their imminent arrival. In practice, this encouraged rash action in support of perceived revolutionary stirrings. Recapturing the urban areas was a priority, but the revolutionary role of the peasantry was stressed—under the leadership of the proletariat, of course. Poor peasants were to provide the movement's backbone, engaging in guerrilla warfare.

When they returned to China, the leadership found a better situation than they had left behind. There was a modest recovery in the cities and steady growth in the soviet areas and the Red Army. Mao Zedong and Zhu De controlled a base on the Jiangxi-Hunan border, and other Communists controlled bases on the Hubei-Henan-Anhui border, in east Hunan, and in northwest Jiangxi.

Given its perennial optimism, it is not surprising that the CCP leadership soon saw heightened revolutionary potential. Under the leadership of Li Lisan, by June 1929 policy became more radical following the ECCI's claims that signs of the new revolutionary wave were clearly visible and that a rightist trend should be jettisoned.[56] At its June 1929 plenum, the CCP accepted this judgment but was cautious about when the next wave might arrive.

An October 26, 1929, missive from the Comintern pushed the CCP to pursue a more radical approach and finally in June 1930 caution was cast aside with the party announcing that a new revolutionary high tide had arrived and that the party should give up its "petty bourgeois vacillations." A cautious approach, defined as rightism, was confirmed as the major danger. The challenge for the CCP leadership was to find and catch the revolutionary tide. Despite the Comintern's stress on promoting political strikes and preparing for armed insurrection, this was not viable in urban China. Consequently, the party turned to the soviets in the countryside to provide support to regain control of the cities. The June 1930 plenum set out concrete plans to launch a revolutionary upsurge and to capture the central city of Wuhan as part of the seizure of one or more provinces. The strength of Comintern support was unclear, and appeals for Soviet aid were ignored.

On July 27 Peng Dehuai's troops took Changsha, but they were forced to retreat after only seven days, weakening Li Lisan's position. It is quite possible that Li did not know what was happening in Changsha at the time, and at two Politburo meetings, on August 1 and 3, he rejected Comintern concerns and announced that the nationwide revolutionary upsurge was indeed nigh. He then called for the whole party to prepare for an immediate revolution.

The failure was followed by harsh condemnation and further reorganization of the leadership. In August 1930, Moscow sent former leader Qu Qiubai and Zhou Enlai back to China to moderate the policies, but not yet to repudiate them entirely. However, an October letter from the ECCI to the CCP stated that Li's mistakes were indeed those of line rather than tactics and denounced him as anti-Comintern and a "semi-Trotskyite" for his suggestion that actions in China could set off a final, global class war. Comintern influence over the CCP was strengthened by the students returning from Moscow, such as Wang Ming, who would aspire to assume to the leadership. Yet another new Comintern representative, Pavel Mif, under the auspices of the Far Eastern Bureau (FEB) of the Comintern, took almost complete control of the party in late 1930 and early 1931.[57]

The following period marked the high point of Comintern influence as Mif was ordered to organize the CCP's Fourth Plenum, which met in Shanghai on January 7, 1931. Li Lisan was harshly condemned for ignoring the Comintern's policy, resulting in havoc within the party. The Comintern wanted to replace the leadership with younger members who were supportive of the Comintern, but the FEB was cautious, favoring a combination of long-term members who had returned from Moscow, such as Liu Shaoqi, Zhang Guotao, and Zhou Enlai, together with more recent trainees such as Wang Ming. The group that was most obviously excluded from the leadership consisted of those who were running the soviet areas. However, the FEB did see their work as important and set up a CCP Central Committee Bureau for the Central Soviet District, headed by Zhou Enlai, as well as Central Committee bureaus in other areas. In the spring of 1931 the FEB sent more than 60 percent of those working in the Shanghai party organs to the soviet areas, marking the decline of Shanghai's leadership role. In so doing, it eroded the influence of the FEB, and by the summer of 1931 FEB work had effectively stopped.[58] Comintern influence over the CCP would never again be as strong.

Mao Zedong Discovers the Power of the Peasantry

When disaster struck in Shanghai and Wuhan, Mao Zedong was pursuing a different approach based on the Comintern and the party's view of the revolutionary role of the peasantry. Initially the CCP as an organization showed little interest in the role of the peasantry, and it was not until the Party's Fourth Congress, in January 1925, that it began to pay attention. This was driven by the growth of the peasant movement in the areas under GMD control. The congress criticized the GMD for using the peasantry for its own ends, only organizing them where it needed them for support and not providing them with sufficient protection. However, the congress provided little guidance in terms of what should be done.

The founder of the CCP peasant movement was Peng Pai, who in fall 1922 formed the first peasant association in Haifeng County, in southeast Guangdong. It advocated rent reductions and boycotts of landlords, and provided social relief. When cooperation with the GMD was launched, Peng Pai served as the secretary of the Peasant Bureau and he established the Guangzhou Peasant Training Institute, where Mao Zedong honed his skills. After the failure of the Nanchang Uprising, Peng returned to Haifeng and established the CCP's first soviet government of Hai-Lu-Feng Workers and Peasants.[59] It was crushed in August 1929, but the experience suggested an approach of territorial control backed by armed force, which Mao would champion.

After the party had become radicalized, it turned back to moderation in terms of policy for the rural areas, especially after July 1926. Mao rejected the retreat to moderation. Unlike the Party Center, in his February 1927 report on the peasant movement in Hunan, Mao claimed that any excesses were essential to overcome the power of the gentry in the countryside.[60] Mao paid lip service to the proletariat, but in his report the role of the proletariat is insignificant compared with the potential of the peasantry. In Hunan many of the peasant associations that Mao championed were headed by former Anyuan workers, who had been sent back to their native village following the September 1925 crackdown. At the time of the report, Mao had not linked the power of the peasantry to the establishment of territorial bases and military force; this would come following the defeat at the end of 1927.

Party weakness in the peasant movement was highlighted in a July 1926 report on the peasant movement in Guangdong that pointed out that there were 800,000 peasants in associations but only 600 party members stretched across twenty counties. The phenomenon of counting big numbers and equating them with CCP strength had been present in a report from Chen Duxiu in January 1925, in which Chen announced that some 10 million people were in peasant associations. In reality, given that the peasant associations were in South China, what really held them together was GMD military power; and once the GMD turned on the CCP and its allies, the peasant associations unraveled. The post-1927 policies of using peasant mobilization to regain a foothold in the cities led to further deterioration of the peasant organizations. However, the move to the more inhospitable areas did lead to the consolidation of the rural bases, defended by military force.

Following the defeats of 1927–1928, Mao retreated to the countryside in the Jinggangshan region, in southwest Jiangxi province, where his small number of troops comprised a mixture of outcasts who were poorly trained.[61] Importantly, in April 1928 Mao linked up with Zhu De's forces to try to expand the base area to cover the Hunan-Jiangxi-Guangdong border region. Mao was appointed secretary of the Hunan-Jiangxi Special Border Area Committee, and in November 1928 he was appointed secretary of the Front Committee, directly under the Jiangxi Party Committee. Before the years of what is referred to as the Jiangxi Soviet (1931–1934), Mao could experiment with policy that would be later codified in the soviet. Initial policy was radical, with all land to be turned over to the Border Area Soviet Government and then divided on a per capita basis to those who supported the regime. This did not go down well, and many peasants bridled at the radicalism; as a result, production dropped and much of the small-scale trading ground to a halt. Thereafter, an increasing militarization of society created uneasy relations between the Red Army and the local population. This caused Mao and his followers to abandon Jinggangshan at the end of 1928 as supplies ran out and the number of troops dropped from 18,000 to about 6,000. As a result, in January 1929 Mao and Zhu decided to move their troops to southern Jiangxi. Policy became more moderate, with only public land and that of the landlords to be confiscated for redistribution. Mao found favor with Moscow. While criticizing the Party Center, the Comintern highly praised the work of Mao and Zhu De, and the FEB viewed them as the most effective Chinese comrades.

Mao rejected the pessimism of the Party Center. He might not have been aware of Soviet support, given his remoteness, his moves, and the slowness of communications, but he did adopt a more aggressive stance. On January 5, 1930, he wrote to Lin Biao, a future military leader, that he did not share the pessimism of Lin and the Party Center. His letter had an evocative title: "A Single Spark Can Start a Prairie Fire." He criticized Lin for thinking that the revolutionary high tide was still remote, and he favored mobile warfare to extend political influence. A proper understanding of the current stage of the revolution would enable Lin to "understand that the development of the

Red Army, guerrilla forces, and the soviet regions is the highest form of peasant struggle" in semi-colonial countries. Mao wrote that his policies, together with those of like-minded colleagues, in setting up the base areas and "systematically setting up political power, and by promoting and expanding this power emphasizing the coordination and organization among the Red Army, the guerrilla forces, and the broad peasant masses, training in the struggle, the pursuance of the rural revolution and the expansion of armed organizations" was the "only way to build the confidence of the masses toward the nationwide revolution."[62] Clearly, Mao was beginning to stake out his own approach to the revolution. Mao's actions were based, not on instructions from the Party Center or from the Comintern, but instead on his own assessment of the realities on the ground. He would now try to develop his strength and his ideas in the sanctuary of the Jiangxi Soviet.

Although the decade ended with a series of disasters, the period established enduring legacies: the structure of a Leninist party, the use of ideology and political line in inner-party struggle, and the experiment of forming a united front with other political and social forces. More importantly, Mao Zedong experimented with combining the revolutionary potential of the peasantry with military strength.

CHAPTER THREE

Wanderings in the Wilderness

1930–1940

☆

Defeat in the cities and the failure of the various uprisings should have spelled doom for the CCP. The remnants of the party were reduced to hiding in safe houses in Shanghai and other cities or seeking refuge in the remote Chinese countryside. Yet CCP members showed considerable resilience even after they were forced to abandon their main base in the Jiangxi Soviet and embark on what became known as the Long March. However, beneath this broad canvas, they gained important experience that would serve the party well in the future. In Jiangxi the CCP experienced governing in all its complexities. On the Long March, Mao Zedong began his climb to the pinnacle of power within the CCP, pushing aside the old Shanghai leadership and outmaneuvering Zhang Guotao, who oversaw a stronger military force, and Wang Ming, who had returned from Moscow possessing a stronger theoretical armory. Last but not least, the Japanese incursions into China saved the CCP from destruction by the GMD and allowed it time and space to recuperate in the remote northwest.

Life in the base areas, was not easy and compromises had to be made with local populations and activists. The leaders in the rural bases shared a different perspective on tactics and policy from those in the Shanghai Party Center. There were two fundamental questions to be answered. The first was how to use the Red Army. Should it simply defend the base areas and provide security for the local population, or should it provide the shock troops to carry out the ambitious policies of the Party Center to capture one or more major urban centers? This was related, of course, to the other key question:

What was the purpose of the base areas? For those who saw them as transitory stations serving as launchpads for recapturing power in the cities, clearly their role was to provide resources and sustenance to the Red Army, which could drift in and out. For others, including most of the indigenous Communists, the bases were mini-states to be consolidated and to provide a developmental model superior to the corrupt nationalist regime with its capital in Nanjing.[1]

Settling in the Wilderness: The Jiangxi Soviet

Mao Zedong's experiences in Jinggangshan in the late 1920s helped shape his ideas during the era of the Jiangxi Soviet. However, he did not have consistent involvement in decision making—he took spells of sick leave and was sidelined by representatives of the CC from Shanghai. The fact that Mao was sidelined as the base area unraveled during 1934 was to his advantage in later political struggles, allowing him to claim that he was not involved in the military decisions that failed to defend the base from GMD attacks. Subsequently Mao attacked the policies to promote his own views and to begin his ascent to power within the party.

Mao's thoughts on how to use the military and the bases did not appear out of thin air; they were developed as a product of the environment in which his troops found themselves after the retreat from the Autumn Harvest Uprising. As in other base areas in Central China, such as the Hubei-Henan-Anhui (E-Yu-Wan) and the Hunan–West Hubei (Xiang-E-Xi) Soviets, local Communists and Party Center representatives opposed Mao's evolving ideas. His rural investigations convinced him of the radical potential of the peasantry and their willingness to be mobilized if the local bullies were to be removed and the land redistributed. All the same, radical proposals for land confiscation created serious divisions within the base areas. The February 1930 Land Law promoted the equal division of the land, using phrases such as "drawing on the fat to compensate for the lean." Many of the original founders of the rural strongholds were bandits or former schoolteachers, embedded within the communities, and some of them resisted this approach. Many were disturbed at the unnecessary stripping of property from the locals, especially those who were not considered rapacious landlords. They also feared that radical actions would undermine support from wealthier peasants, who might turn against the CCP and be unwilling to supply necessary logistical support. Discussions bogged down in arguments about who was a rich peasant or a middle peasant, who should be appeased, and who should have their land confiscated. These local debates were linked to the politics at the Party Center, where the CC in Shanghai and those running the base areas fought over how radical the policy should be. The debates sharpened after Bukharin, head of the Comintern, was dismissed for his so-called rich-peasant line—his support for a moderate policy toward wealthy peasants and achieving socialism "at a snail's pace."

In Jiangxi, the first clear example of the extreme difference in views between the local party officials and Mao Zedong and the Red Army forces appeared at the end of 1930 and in early 1931 with the Futian Incident.[2] Conflicts arose with the Party Center after the arrival of its emissary, Xiang Ying, from Shanghai. This distilled the struggle for supremacy between the rural-based and the urban-based wings of the party.[3]

In December 1930, Mao drafted his views on how the base area should resist GMD encroachment, following the suppression campaigns launched by GMD leader Chiang Kai-shek. Soviet territory was not sacrosanct and could be abandoned to lure the enemy in deep where Communist forces enjoyed advantages and could pick them off. This meant that mobile rather than positional warfare was to be the main form of fighting. Reality dictated this approach, but it diverged significantly from the aggressive posture of Li Lisan, and even after Li's rashness had been denounced, Mao clashed with his successors.

The possibility of giving up territory within the base, combined with the land policy, which some local Communists denounced as egalitarianism, caused dissension and intensified local opposition. Toward the end of 1930, opponents were attacked as members of a secret organization, the A.B. League, which, it was claimed, sought to undermine the revolution by engaging in "liquidationism."[4] The claim was that in 1927 the so-called league had struggled with the CCP for control within Jiangxi and had infiltrated the local party and the Red Army. In early November 1930 a large-scale movement was launched to clean out the Red Army forces of presumed A.B. League members, with about half of the 4,000 members investigated and some executed.[5] This caused the Twentieth Red Army, which had suffered from the purges, to march into the town of Donggu and release a group of Communists who had been arrested by one of Mao's associates. Mutual recriminations followed, and the Jiangxi leadership under Mao stepped up measures to root out "counterrevolutionaries." The rebels in the Twentieth Red Army called on Red Army colleagues to resist Mao and his authoritarian colleagues, claiming that Mao intended to arrest the likes of the respected Red Army leaders Zhu De and Peng Dehuai. The rebels were massacred, and the purges continued; by the spring of 1932, more than 90 percent of the officials in southwest Jiangxi had been killed, arrested, or put out of office.[6] Rebels' claims that other Red Army leaders had been arrested were untrue, and it is not at all certain that the league had actually infiltrated the base area and the Red Army. Most importantly, this episode was an important triumph by outsiders over the original founders of the base.

While these events were taking place, two other trends were developing that would have a vital impact on life within the Jiangxi Soviet: one threatened its entire existence, and the other affected power within the party apparatus. The first was the series of five suppression campaigns launched by Chiang Kai-shek and troops nominally loyal to him that would eventually cause the abandonment of the soviet. In November 1930, Chiang emerged victorious from his battles with the warlords in North China, allowing him to turn his attention to the Communists in Central China. The first campaign, led by the Jiangxi Provincial Army, began at the end of December but was beaten back by the Red Army—as was the second campaign, launched in May 1931. These victories were seen as vindication of the strategy of luring the enemy in deep to destroy it. Having consolidated power within the Red Army, Mao Zedong turned to purge the opponents within the base area. In June 1931, Mao suggested moving his troops to remote areas to prevent Chiang Kai-shek from pursuing them, hoping that Chiang might turn his attention to fighting his opponents in the South. While still pursuing perceived enemies within the base area, Mao proposed that a replacement be found before removing any leader of the resistance, even if the replacement was from the discredited A.B. League.

The second level of friction was between the emerging leadership in the base area and the emissaries sent from the CC in Shanghai. Following the party's Third Plenum, which was held in September 1930, the comrades in Shanghai sought to exert more oversight over base-area work, sending Xiang Ying, who arrived at the base area by year's end. The Party Center established a Central Bureau of the Soviet Areas under the Central Military Commission. The purpose of these organs was to control political and military affairs, and to this end the Mao-dominated General Front Committee was abolished on January 15. Nominally, the Central Bureau was headed by Zhou Enlai, who remained in Shanghai, meaning that the real head was Xiang Ying, who was in charge of the new Central Military Commission. This placed Xiang in a difficult position, faced with trying to understand an operational environment with which he had no experience and having to reconcile the conflicts between the group around Mao Zedong and those denounced as "counterrevolutionaries." Shortly after his arrival, Xiang tried to reach a compromise: accepting Mao's assessment that the Futian Incident had been counterrevolutionary, but judging that the repression had been too harsh.

In early 1931 the Comintern recommended that the Party Center move from Shanghai to Jiangxi, thus intensifying its direct control. The Fourth Plenum, in January 1931, appointed yet another new leadership promoted by Comintern agent Pavel Mif. These new leaders were a group of student returnees from Moscow gathered around Wang Ming. Their mission was to get the revolution back on track. The plenum proposed that Zhou Enlai and other veteran revolutionaries move to the soviet areas. The Party Center's ability to lead the movement effectively was undermined not only by the reality that the revolution's soul was now firmly lodged in the countryside but also by the unraveling of the Shanghai organization. In April 1931 the head of the CCP's security services was caught by GMD agents, and he gave up crucial information that led to the arrest and execution of thousands of CCP members and sympathizers, including the party's general secretary. This delivered the final blow to Shanghai as the revolutionary epicenter, and members who remained there could do little more than be a funnel for information from the Comintern. Even so, it was not until early 1933 that Bo Gu, now general secretary, and the other leaders moved to the Jiangxi Soviet.

In April 1931 the first delegation of the Party Center arrived to outline the spirit of the Fourth Plenum; three members remained behind to join the Central Bureau. Surprisingly, their first action was to criticize, not Mao Zedong, but Xiang Ying for his weak handling of the Futian Incident, denouncing his rightist tendency in not recognizing a counterrevolutionary rebellion when he saw one. Mao's position was briefly enhanced as he replaced Xiang as acting secretary of the Central Soviet Bureau. Sympathy for Mao did not last long, as the three members discovered that real power had rested not with Xiang but with Mao. As a result, in November 1931 the verdict on the Futian Incident was revised again, now highlighting Mao's harsh repression rather than the "crimes" of the rebels. It made little difference, as by this time most of the officer corps of the Twentieth Red Army had been arrested or executed, as had many of the original founders of the base area.

This maneuvering about interpretation reveals the slowly changing relationship between Mao and the representatives of the Party Center. Mao was removed from direct involvement in party and army affairs and put to work in the government apparatus. In retrospect, this served Mao well in two ways. First, it took him out of the key decision-making apparatus as the military situation declined before the final evacuation. Second, it gave him a chance to oversee very practical logistical questions about running a government and ensuring the supply of essential goods. This experience served him well later on in the Shaanxi-Gansu-Ningxia (Shaan-Gan-Ning) Border Region.

Beyond the Jiangxi Soviet

Similar trends were witnessed in other wilderness locations, such as the Hubei-Henan-Anhui and the Hunan–West Hubei Soviets. The relatively small size of the former—just three Red Army divisions of 2,000 soldiers—meant that it did not attract the same level of attention from the leadership, especially from Li Lisan. They were not instructed to attack the major cities, and this allowed the local leadership to expand its numbers to about 6,000 soldiers. The leadership of the Hubei-Henan-Anhui Soviet resisted the first two GMD suppression campaigns and grew Red Army strength further to about 15,000. Now the Party Center began to show interest, and in April 1931 it sent Zhang Guotao and two other colleagues to oversee work. In May, Zhang announced the Hubei-Henan-Anhui Sub-Bureau of the CCP CC. The old leadership structure was abolished, with instructions for the new leaders to carry out the policies of the Fourth Plenum.

In July 1931 the Jiangxi leadership was surprised by the speed with which Chiang Kai-shek launched the third suppression campaign. The area was again saved by distraction when Wang Jingwei and others allied with the warlords in the southern provinces of Guangdong and Guangxi to try to establish an alternative government to challenge Nanjing. In September 1931 they marched north to Hunan to take on Chiang, causing him to withdraw his forces from the suppression campaign. Although Chiang beat off the challenges, he was unable to resume his assaults on the Jiangxi Soviet until August 1932. Japanese intrusions into Manchuria and probes around Shanghai caused further distraction, and a truce was not reached until May 1933.

These developments enabled the Hubei-Henan-Anhui Soviet to expand further, but, as elsewhere, disputes arose over military tactics between the local Fourth Front Army and the CCP Sub-Bureau. The local leader was removed as political commissar and replaced by Party Center emissary Chen Changhao, who launched a major movement to overcome counterrevolution. Dog-eat-dog fights within the CCP were becoming commonplace as the struggles between local revolutionaries and "professional revolutionaries" from outside intensified. The claim was that an uprising had been planned for September 1931, and, as in Jiangxi, the supposed leaders were accused of belonging to the A.B. League or other opposition groups. Again, evidence for the accusations is scant.

Unlike Hubei-Henan-Anhui, the Hunan–West Hubei Soviet was affected by Li Lisan's insurrectionist policies. In April 1931 a new leadership arrived and began to find fault with the local party. Former labor activist Deng Zhongxia, now the political commissar of the Third Front Army, was criticized for following Li Lisan's policy. However, this did not preclude expansion, and by early 1932 the soviet had grown to cover about twenty counties with a Red Army of about 15,000 soldiers.

With the fourth suppression campaign, Chiang Kai-shek shifted tactics and decided first to attack the Hubei-Henan-Anhui and Hunan–West Hubei Soviets and to follow this with an attack on the Jiangxi Central Soviet. He had about half a million troops at his disposal. Hubei-Henan-Anhui used the same tactics as before, and while both the GMD and the Fourth Front Army suffered similarly, the latter could not afford such losses and fled from the base—to settle in north Sichuan. After three months of wandering, its forces were reduced to just 15,000. In this new home, on December 29, 1932, the Sichuan-Shaanxi Base Area was established under Zhang Guotao. The central party leadership was not happy with the move but left Zhang in charge. The Third Front Army in Hunan–West Hubei fared no better and in October 1932 left to move north. After two months it was able to return to the Hunan-Hubei border, where a base area had been established in the late 1920s. Thanks to former connections, this gave them a brief respite, but they had to leave again in June 1933. The area was too barren and too exhausted to provide support. Eventually, in January 1934, the army settled in northeast Guizhou, but only 3,000 troops remained.

The Demise of Shanghai as a Revolutionary Center

The party in Shanghai found itself in an urban wilderness following the 1927 defeat. Although it was nominally in charge of the revolution and always eager to see a new high tide on the horizon, beyond its liaison function with the Comintern it was slowly losing its relevance and was alienating its support among those who remained working underground.[7] The blows to the party continued unabated, and even the International Settlements declared enough was enough and no longer provided safe havens. The crackdown also disrupted the critical source of funding from the Comintern. The class-based politics of the Party Center endangered the grassroots members by encouraging strikes, demonstrations, and other activities that did not bring the new high tide of revolution but instead exposed participants to arrest and execution. As the squeeze started on the base areas, the atmosphere in Shanghai intensified with GMD calls to confess one's crimes and to give up comrades in return for a pardon. In April 1931 a major blow was delivered when the head of CCP security was apprehended in Hankou while masquerading as a magician and was given the choice of death or becoming a turncoat. He chose the latter.[8] This was devastating as he provided the names and addresses of key leaders and the storage locations for information and materials. One arrest led to another, with many of those caught also turning in others. Key leaders such as Zhou Enlai and Bo Gu escaped only because the CCP had its own person inside the GMD Special Services Bureau. When he got wind of an impending arrest, he sent his son-in-law to tip them off. Many others were not so lucky. Neither was the head of the CCP security force. Zhou Enlai ordered retribution by killing any members of his family that the CCP could lay its hands on, including his wife, in-laws, and brother-in-law.[9]

When Zhou Enlai left Shanghai by January 1933, no members of the central leadership were left in the city, and a White Area CC Bureau was set up to provide leadership. As betrayals continued, the departure of the Soviet-trained leaders offered those few remaining Communists a chance to rethink their role in the revolution.[10] The Party Center, with its ideological disposition, revolutionary optimism, and desire to follow the Comintern, established party policies that were inappropriate for the time and place. The politics of class and reliance on the urban proletariat were no longer meaningful, if they had ever been. Japanese actions in Manchuria in 1931 and Japanese bombing of Shanghai in January 1932 changed sentiment in the city and led to an increase in patriotism and anti-Japanese feelings. With the old leadership in place, the CCP was unable to take advantage of this by forming new cross-class alliances and engaging with the patriotic movement. Once it left for the Jiangxi Soviet, the local party was able to adopt approaches that would enable it to survive and connect to the rising anti-Japanese sentiment, connections that would prove very beneficial by the mid-1930s.

The Highs and Lows of the Jiangxi Soviet

The central government in Jiangxi survived longer than the other centers, including Shanghai, and even gave itself the trappings of a state to rival that of the GMD. However, it was finally defeated by the overwhelming firepower of the GMD, arguments over tactics, and internal divisions. In December 1931, Zhou Enlai arrived in the soviet and took over as head of the CC Bureau. Zhou saw value in not alienating Mao Zedong, but he did follow the Comintern's insistence in late 1931 that developments were positive, allowing for a "popular revolution to overthrow the GMD" and a "national revolutionary war to oppose Japanese imperialists and all other imperialists."[11] As usual, the Shanghai leadership absorbed the enthusiasm, and on January 9, 1932, it issued a resolution urging an "initial victory in one or more provinces." This created disputes in the soviet between Zhou Enlai and the comrades from Shanghai, who ordered an attack on Ganzhou, the largest city in southern Jiangxi. Mao Zedong and Zhu De opposed the idea to no avail, and on January 10 an attack order was issued. Mao took one of his strategic sick leaves.

Despite mustering 30,000 soldiers, the attack was a disaster, and an entire division was lost. In March 1932, following four assaults, the troops were forced to withdraw. Although it was bad for the Red Army, the defeat was positive for Mao, with Xiang Ying forced to ask Mao to return from recuperation. The CCP leadership still searched for other cities to capture, but Mao studiously avoided any such instructions and pursued his own circuitous path, avoiding attacks on key cities. Ignoring reality, the CCP leadership concluded that failure was the result, not of a misguided strategy, but of the tendency to hold back, as exhibited by Mao. In early May, Zhou Enlai sent the CC a telegram strongly critical of Mao, complaining about his opportunism and his disobedience with respect to CC and Comintern directives, and calling for his mistakes to be struggled against.[12]

Despite this, Mao still enjoyed considerable support, and on August 8, 1932, he was appointed political commissar of the First Front Army. However, this did not end the criticism of Mao, and in October 1932 virtually all of the leadership present criticized Mao's arrogance toward the party leadership and his autocratic control over the Red Army—a somewhat prescient analysis, given later developments. The Politburo demanded that he return to work. But Mao claimed he was suffering from tuberculosis, and he did not return to government work until early 1933, when he was posted to the rear. Until the breaks in the Long March in late 1934 and early 1935, Mao only had intermittent involvement with the defense of the soviet. This served him well once the recriminations began. The First Front Army was brought under closer party control with a collective leadership that included Zhou Enlai and Zhu De.

As the GMD began the fourth and fifth suppression campaigns, conflict over military strategy intensified. In January 1933 General Secretary Bo Gu and the remainder of the Party Center leadership arrived in Ruijin, the soviet's capital, and continued with their optimistic view supporting a more aggressive military policy and demanding that the Red Army seize the city of Nanfeng. Now it was Zhou Enlai, as political commissar of the First Front Army, who found himself on the front lines pitted against those in the rear who were urging the Red Army forward. His pleas for withdrawal fell on deaf ears and the attack ended in defeat and retreat.

Just before Zhou Enlai's arrival, the much-delayed First All-China Soviet Congress was held in Ruijin on November 7–20, 1931. The congress had all the trappings to rival that of the GMD government. With the consolidation and expansion of the bases in Central China, the congress set out separate national governing and military structures. Zhu De was appointed chair of the newly established Central Military Commission, meaning that Mao Zedong lost direct control over the military, but he was appointed to the newly created position of chair of the soviet government. The congress adopted two major documents—a Constitution and a Land Law.[13] The Constitution provided the soviet with the trappings of a national state, describing it as a "democratic dictatorship of the proletariat and the peasantry," Lenin's 1905 formulation. The peasantry was all around, but it was hard to find the proletariat in the soviet, with the workers being primarily artisans, handicraft workers, and farm laborers. Despite this, the Constitution acknowledged that only the proletariat could lead the broad masses to socialism and thus they were given extra representation in the elections within the soviet. The Constitution began with bold claims that the tasks could be achieved only following the "overthrow of the rule of imperialism and the GMD and the establishment of the Soviet Republic throughout all China." Organizationally, when the congress was not in session, power was vested in the All-China CEC of the Soviets, which would appoint a Council of People's Commissars to conduct all business and promulgate decrees and laws. Considering the CCP's later insistence on the indivisibility of sovereignty, the Constitution recognized the right of self-determination for the national minorities and their right to "complete separation from China and the formation of an independent state for each national minority." They could join the Union of Chinese Soviets or could secede and form their own state as they saw fit.

The Land Law was more moderate than prior practice but did call for the confiscation of land belonging to "feudal lords and landlords, militarists and village bosses, gentry and other big private landowners." There would be no compensation The major change was to appease the middle peasants who had found previous practices disadvantageous, especially the ban on the sale of property. Bowing to their pressure, the law stated that they could be exempt from the program of land distribution if the majority were in support. Land nationalization was dropped, and collectivization was not mentioned, even though Li Lisan had pushed this in May 1930. The draft prepared by the Party Center did include the possibility of "voluntary collectivization."[14] The finalized law called for special treatment for Red Army soldiers, who would be given a plot of land, which the government would take care of in their absence. Given the concern that the previous egalitarian distribution had caused, the law trod carefully. Although this was the "most thorough" way to destroy "all feudal agrarian relations and the shackles of private ownership of land by the landlords," the policy was not to be carried out by force and it had to be explained clearly and fully to the peasantry. In another show of concern for local sensibilities, land belonging to religious institutions and temples could be turned over only if the peasants agreed of their own free will "so that their religious feelings would not be offended."

Despite these positive expressions, the movement was still riven by divisions over tactics and pressure from without by the squeeze that the GMD applied. In February 1933 the fourth suppression campaign began, but it was swiftly rebuffed and by March it was called off. The fact that it was held off by more traditional military engagement without yielding territory and engaging the enemy outside of the soviet gave the Party Center confidence in its tactics.

However, the Tanggu Truce with the Japanese (May 1933) allowed Chiang Kai-shek to deploy the full force of his military might against the soviet. He assumed personal command of the 500,000 troops that began a new campaign in October. More importantly, Chiang had learned from previous campaigns that as the troops advanced, they should build blockhouses that covered strategic points and lay highways to link the blockhouses, connecting them to the reserve forces waiting in the rear. There was to be no precipitate rush forward, but instead a slow, measured tightening of the cordon around the soviet. Rebellion again frustrated Chiang's plans, but this time not for long.

This more coherent strategy was developed just as the CCP split over tactics and policy radicalization within the soviet. Bo Gu had arrived in January 1933 with other leaders, followed in late September 1933 by a new military adviser, Otto Braun. Together they oversaw the defense of the soviet. As when other leaders had arrived from outside, Bo Gu began with a campaign to consolidate his position, this time against what was called the Luo Ming line. From March 1932, Luo Ming had been acting secretary of the Fujian CCP Committee. His writings revealed how the GMD attacks had caused panic and fatigue in West Fujian. What upset the central leadership most was Luo's accusation that the Red Army needed to adopt a flexible approach that could adapt to different conditions in varied environments rather than assume a one-size-fits-all approach. Luo's support for Mao Zedong's approach angered Bo Gu, and clearly he was an easy surrogate for an attack on Mao. On February 15, 1933, the campaign against Luo began in earnest with the adoption of a resolution.[15] The resolution went so far as to declare that the group was "openly advocating the abolition of the party and the revolutionary unity of the masses." The call went out for Luo Ming to be immediately removed from his post, and the Central Bureau was to send delegates to oversee a meeting of the provincial party congress to ensure that the errors were clearly understood and properly corrected. The Fujian Provincial Committee was in "a very grave condition," and under Luo Ming a "small group of comrades" were following the path of opportunism and were "pessimistic and defeatist," cowering in the face of the enemy. The Center presented Luo's views as criticism of the party strategy as a whole, whereas in reality he was simply arguing from the perspective of his own jurisdiction. Many of those criticized were close to Mao Zedong or shared his views, including Mao's brother and Deng Xiaoping.

The second major movement that Bo Gu launched was the Land Investigation Movement, beginning on June 1. To complete Mao's humiliation, Bo Gu put him in charge of a movement to correct his own previous policy. The movement ran through 1933 and into 1934 with the intention of using the question of land to create a favorable atmosphere to serve political and military purposes. However, the movement fluctuated in terms of targets, and this must have confused the peasants rather than helping to win their enthusiastic support. Excesses caused retrenchment and a turn to a milder or anti-leftist policy. From June to September, policy was tough, with many middle peasants reclassified as landlords—whereas from October to December many landlords were reclassified as middle peasants. Then in January and February 1934, the rich peasants were attacked. The merry-go-round might have continued had it not been for the deteriorating military situation.

Chiang Kai-shek's fifth suppression campaign was interrupted by a rebellion that broke out among GMD allied troops in Fujian, causing him to set aside attempts to crush the Communists.[16] The rebellion collapsed in December as loyal GMD troops drove into the region. This bought the CCP time but not much else, as it failed to persuade more GMD leaders and troops to abandon Chiang and focus on the struggle against Japan.

The CCP did use the respite to convene two meetings that celebrated their successes but reflected the ongoing power struggle within the party, the army, and the government.[17] First, the Fifth Plenum of the Sixth Central Committee met in Ruijin on January 15–18, 1934. Amazingly, given the CCP's situation and the dangers it faced, Bo Gu's report informed the attendees that the revolutionary situation in China and abroad was excellent, and he reaffirmed that the policies of the Comintern and the CCP were infallible. In what was clearly a slap at Mao Zedong, he noted that the main task for the party was to oppose the "right opportunists" who refused to see this excellent situation. Before the end of the year, the soviet would be abandoned. This was a classic example of what Mao denounced as "bookism": fine, empty words that bore no relationship to reality.

Even more surprising, given the campaigns waged by Chiang Kai-shek and the disagreements over tactics, there was no report on military affairs. Perhaps it was simply because there were such differences among Mao, his supporters, and the Party Center under Bo Gu and Otto Braun that no report could be drafted. Even though he did not attend the plenum, Mao was elevated to full Politburo membership—but not to the more important newly established Secretariat. Secretariat membership was dominated by the returned students under the leadership of Bo Gu. This was with the full support and even the insistence of Moscow.

Mao did attend the Second All-China Soviet Congress, which was held from January 22 to February 1, 1934. No expense was spared in showcasing the soviet as a national regime. A large auditorium was built, and a military parade was organized, complete with a full gunfire salute. Far from seeing itself under threat, trying desperately to string together small, fragile soviets, the congress portrayed the soviet as a formal state to rival the GMD. The government roster even included the post of commissar for foreign affairs. The scattered soviets were to be designated as provinces, even if their size hardly merited such a designation. In reality, they were small islands of rebellion in a sea controlled by the GMD. Mao addressed the congress on behalf of the CEC and as chairman of the Council of People's Commissars, although he was soon replaced as chair by Zhang Wentian, another returned student.

Wanderings: The Long March

The two meetings offered no solutions for dealing with the suppression campaigns, which resumed soon thereafter. The Party Center continued with positional defense to hold off the GMD troops. Adherence to the military strategy and opposition to Mao Zedong's flexible tactics were reinforced by the arrival, in October 1933, of Otto Braun, who seemed to despise Mao just as much as Bo Gu did. He took over defense of the soviet with what Mao later denounced as a "pure defensive line," a tactic that Braun referred to as "short, swift thrusts." By April 1934 the GMD was approaching a key town only twenty miles to the north of the soviet capital. Braun and Bo Gu saw the town's defense as a crucial and decisive battle, during which Bo replaced Zhou Enlai as political commissar. The swift thrusts were meant to disrupt the GMD before it could bring up reinforcements, but in a short two weeks the Red Army was defeated and lost one-fifth of its troops. During May and June the GMD penetrated farther into the soviet, and it became clear that Braun's strategy could not save it. Defense from inside the base had failed. In July and August, two Red Army detachments were sent to the "white areas"—areas that were not under the control of the CCP—to try to draw the enemy out of the soviet, but both were defeated and the pressure was not relieved.

Braun's tactics were failing, and another solution would have to be found. In September 1934, too late to help, Wang Ming and the Chinese delegation to the Comintern called for the Party Center to adopt Zhu De and Mao's strategy of operating in guerrilla detachments. The advice fell on deaf ears for Braun and Bo Gu.[18] The idea of leaving the base had been floated as early as 1931, but the most important decision was taken by the CC Secretariat in May 1934.[19] The decision was kept under tight wraps, but the Comintern was informed and on June 8 it sent its approval but called the retreat a temporary measure. The three-person group of Bo Gu, Zhou Enlai, and Otto Braun worked out the details, which were then agreed upon by the Politburo Standing Committee, with senior military leaders informed only on a need-to-know basis. By late August the rest of the Politburo was informed, along with the Military Council. The only remaining question was whether the bulk of the troops were to break out or whether a smaller group should do so, indicating that the intention was to return. Similarly, there were questions about who should remain and who should leave.

The decision to retreat was made public in an article with the splendidly misleading title "All for the Defense of the Soviet" (September 29, 1934). In true CCP tradition, the piece put a positive spin on the disaster, but it did contain an opening salvo criticizing Braun's strategy. The author, returned student Zhang Wentian, proposed that it was entirely possible to surrender a particular soviet in order to ensure victory for the soviet movement throughout the whole country. The battles during the previous year had "attested to the truth" that "the political power of the worker-peasant soviet is an invincible and unconquerable force" and that the spread of the soviet throughout the country could not be stopped, no matter what mechanism was used. The article highlighted the retreat of the Hubei-Henan-Anhui Soviet where the "transfer" of troops had permitted a partial victory. Tactics had to be adapted to fit the realities that the Red Army was facing. To persist with an offense strategy that was based on a presumption that revolution would be continually victorious was to adopt "abstract formulas" or "dogmatic prescriptions" that impeded useful action. Those who clung to the idea of defending the soviets from within their own territory were denounced as opportunists and dogmatists.

In October the GMD pushed forward, closing off the CCP's options, and the decision was taken to make a "strategic transfer." Later this would be repackaged as the Long March. The main force of the Red Army, some 86,000 soldiers, broke through the GMD blockade and headed west toward southern Hunan. Another 15,000 and 10,000 sick or wounded remained behind under the command of Chen Yi and Xiang Ying.[20] After meeting little resistance, the retreating troops ran out of luck while trying to cross the Xiang River in northwest Guangxi province. GMD troops caught up with them, and by the time the Red Army moved on from the Xiang River, it had lost perhaps half of its troops and a considerable amount of its equipment.

The Red Army was now truly in the wilderness, having left the soviet with no clear destination in mind. Those left behind were always on the move,

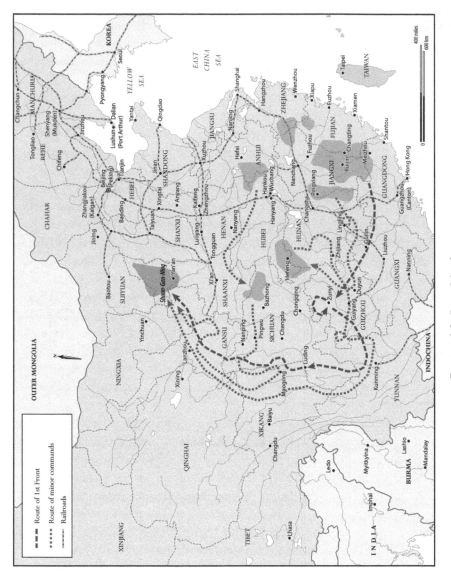

Routes of the Long March, 1934–1935.

and the CCP in urban China was shattered and attempting to avoid extinction. The troops could have headed for central Hunan, the Guangxi-Hunan border, to find other troops, or to circle around and try to return. Quickly, the chasing GMD troops sealed off their options.

The 86,000 soldiers who set out on the Long March were supported by about 10,000 administrative personnel and thousands of civilian porters. They mainly moved at night, carrying their materials on their backs or pulling horse-drawn carts. By the time they arrived in Wuqizhen in northern Shaanxi, only 5 to 10 percent of those who had started on the march had made it to the end. They had traveled 4,000 to 6,000 miles, crossed twenty-four rivers and eighteen mountain ranges, and endured harassment and occasional bombardment from enemy troops. Disease, hunger, and desertion reduced their numbers, causing as many, if not more, casualties as had been caused by combat. In fact, there was not one Long March but several, as the defeated troops in the south sought refuge in both the west and the north of the country.

The marches took the CCP through some of the most inhospitable land in Guizhou, Sichuan, and Yunnan provinces, and the marchers had to make accommodations to win support from the local populations. The CCP should never have survived, but Chiang Kai-shek and the GMD exerted little effective control over much of the area and many nominal allies were really warlords who were more interested in protecting their own strength than in hunting down the Communists. One anecdote from the family of a former relative in Sichuan, a local warlord, illustrates the point. He received telegraphic instructions from Chiang to seek out the Communists in his area and destroy them. When he found them, he saw a pathetic group of stragglers whom he could not imagine causing any future harm. In addition, he discovered that one person in the group, Deng Xiaoping, was from his home area. He decided to let them pass through if they promised not to make any trouble, and the warlord telegraphed Chiang to inform him that the problem had been taken care of.

Subsequently, the Long March became one of the most important foundational myths in CCP history, and its spirit is still evoked to this day when the party wants to mobilize the people in times of difficulty. But at the time the Long March did not seem so heroic, and some have actually questioned the truth of some of its alleged major incidents, such as the crossing of the Luding Bridge over the Dadu River, in Sichuan province. CCP historians recount that a small group crossed the bridge while facing gunfire

Mao on the Long March.

and a superior force, and secured the bridgehead, enabling the main force to cross in safety. Films and posters have been produced to showcase the heroism. Based on the accounts given by survivors and locals, some have questioned this heroic tale and have suggested that the crossing was considerably less challenging than it is portrayed as having been.[21]

One reason for the official praise of the Long March is that historians regard it as a key step in Mao Zedong's rise to power within the CCP. During some of the forty-four rest days, an important meeting was held at Zunyi in January 1935 that facilitated Mao's ascent. The second important political event during the Long March was the increasing tension between Mao Zedong and his troops, on the one side, and those under the command of Zhang Guotao, who had fled the Hubei-Henan-Anhui Soviet, on the other.

In Zunyi, in northern Guizhou province, the depleted forces found time to rest as the leadership convened an enlarged meeting of the Politburo on January 15–18, 1935. The weakly defended town had been captured during the previous week. The leaders clearly needed to discuss the current situation, what should be done, and where the Red Army should go, but they ended up engaging in a major review of previous policies. The meeting marked an important shift in the leadership of the party and its approach to survival. Most of the civilian and military leaders were present, together with Comintern adviser Otto Braun. Mao Zedong had clearly been preparing for the meeting in advance, and he was able to convince two key members of the returned students' group, Zhang Wentian and Wang Jiaxiang, to support his views. However, the main report at the meeting was delivered by Bo Gu in his capacity as party leader, and Zhou Enlai delivered a supplementary report. A bitter debate ensued, and then Mao delivered a long speech that contained his opening salvo criticizing the military line but not, as some have suggested, the political line. Seeing that Mao enjoyed the support of Zhang Wentian and Wang Jiaxiang, Bo Gu and Otto Braun must have realized that they were on the losing side. This point was brought home when Zhang Wentian oversaw the drafting of two formal documents summing up the experiences of the fifth suppression campaign.[22]

Whereas the first, longer document summarizes in broad terms the decisions at the meeting, the shorter version, which was presumably only for internal dissemination, names names. The shorter version was sent by telegram to the leaders of the Red Army in other areas, including Zhang Guotao and Xiang Ying. It incorporated a compromise, not refuting the general political line but placing the failure to defend the soviet squarely on the shoulders of Bo Gu and Otto Braun for their rejection of mobile warfare and for supporting a "pure positional defense." They should have sought out the enemy's weak points and amassed superior forces to destroy them—that is, they should have followed Mao's strategy. In the future, tactics were to be more flexible, allowing for rest while waiting for suitable circumstances to allow for a counterattack. Adding insult to injury, Braun's "rude method of leadership" in the Military Council was criticized, and "Comrade Bo Gu" was to "bear most of the blame" for the poor decisions of the Military Council. Although this was not assessed as a mistake of a political line, it did constitute "serious partial political mistakes." The document concludes with the normal upbeat assessment that any setback was temporary and that current circumstances were still favorable for the creation of a new soviet.

For Mao Zedong, this marked a significant political victory, even though he was still not yet the dominant figure. He was promoted to the new five-person Standing Committee (Secretariat) and he would serve on the three-person Military Leadership Group as Zhou Enlai's chief assistant. He thus had the right to comment on all political and military matters at the highest level. Immediately following the meeting, Zhang Wentian replaced General Secretary Bo Gu, who was forced to step down.

Thus, the period of the Central Soviets ended. Bo Gu and his supporters, who had returned from Moscow or who had been working in Moscow, had followed ideological doctrines to disparage those in the soviets, but they lacked practical experience of operating on the ground. With internal divisions, external pressures from the GMD pushed the soviet over the edge. The way was now open for a new strategy, but it had not yet been resolved which direction the armies would head.

Two Tigers Fight: Mao Zedong Confronts Zhang Guotao

With their spirits lifted, what remained of the First Front Army decided to leave northern Guizhou, cross to the north of the Yangzi River, and set up a new base in southern Sichuan. This might allow them to link up with Zhang Guotao's troops in northwest Sichuan. For the First Front Army to achieve its objective, it sought help not only from Zhang Guotao and the Fourth Front Army but also from the joint forces of the Second and Sixth Army Corps that were roaming along the Hunan-Sichuan border. With this initial decision, the First Front Army made two mistakes. First, in underestimating the strength of the GMD troops in the region, it suffered a major defeat at the hands of the GMD troops in Sichuan. Second, it overestimated the willingness of Zhang Guotao and other army corps to make sacrifices on their behalf. The Party Center requested Zhang's help by engaging the GMD troops in Sichuan. Not surprisingly, Zhang chose to ignore this as, essentially, he was being asked to sacrifice his own troops for the sake of the Party Center. Instead of moving south as requested, he moved north to begin the Southern Shaanxi Campaign, which lasted until early March 1935. Finally, in late March when his progress was blocked, Zhang turned his Fourth Front Army in the requested direction, but by this time Mao's forces had already moved on.

Within the party, Zhang Guotao was a more formidable foe than Bo Gu and the Moscow returnees. He had a strong revolutionary pedigree, having chaired the First Party Congress; he had engaged in the early labor movement; and he had overseen his own administration in the Hubei-Henan-Anhui Soviet. Clearly, he did not think much of Mao: in his view, Mao's thinking was "sometimes quite bizarre, and he would make mythic utterances. He lacked the ability to organize and was reluctant to make precise calculations when dealing with difficult matters. Sometimes his ideas were not clearly expressed, and he often defended his 'opinions of a genius' in an emotional mood."[23]

Obviously, Zhang underestimated Mao's ability and skill in inner-party struggle. While the disputes between the two men appeared to be over military strategy, they were really over who would control the party. Zhang's forces were roughly four times the size of the forces that had survived the flight from the Jiangxi Soviet. Zhang, who had not attended the Zunyi meeting, did not feel bound by the decisions taken there, and a clash was inevitable. Despite his more formidable army, Zhang did not command the political positions that Mao and his supporters held, and this put him on the defensive.

Defeat by the Sichuan Army meant that the First Front Army had to abandon its original plan to move to Sichuan, and it spent the next three months wandering in Guizhou and Yunnan provinces, harassed by enemy troops. Militarily, the new leadership was not faring much better than the old leadership, but in late April the First Front Army was able to enter southwest Sichuan. From there it pushed on north to try to establish contact with Zhang's Fourth Front Army. By early June 1935 Zhang had moved to west Sichuan and then on to the Sichuan-Tibet border, where he set up the Special Committee of the CCP and announced the establishment of the Northwest Federal Government of the Chinese Soviet Republic. In mid-June, almost by accident, the two armies met, but at a June 14 rally to celebrate the event, the tensions between Zhang and Mao Zedong were evident. One of them had to be vanquished.

The troops were together for three months, and Mao outmaneuvered Zhang at a series of meeting. Their first dispute focused on which direction the Red Army should head. Zhang wanted to head east, but the Party Center settled on moving north. The dispute rumbled on to the Shawo Conference of August 5–6, 1935, with Mao wanting to use his political majority to force Zhang to agree to move north, whereas Zhang wanted to exploit the defeat of the First Front Army in Jiangxi to restructure the leadership of the Party Center. Zhang Wentian, now a close associate of Mao, had drafted the resolution before the meeting, and it is not surprising that, on balance, it favored Mao. This set off a bitter fight, and before a final version of the resolution was distributed, Zhang's criticisms of the Jiangxi Soviet were rejected, the personal criticisms were removed, and a decision was taken to march north to establish a base on the Sichuan-Shaanxi-Gansu border. Although

Zhang's name was not mentioned, the resolution criticized "a very small number of comrades in the Red Army" who felt that the political line was wrong—no prizes for guessing who this was. New appointments, however, recognized the strength of Zhang Guotao's forces, and he was confirmed as political commissar of the Red Army, with Zhu De as commander in chief.

Following the meeting, the troops split into two groups for the move north. The Left Route Army comprised the General Headquarters and included Zhu De and Zhang Guotao. The Right Route Army, composed of the Front Headquarters, took with it Zhang Guotao's two most senior military commanders. Relations did not improve, and on August 24 the CC sent a telegram to Zhang requesting that he link up with the Right Route Army, but on September 3 Zhang declined. The call was repeated but was again rejected, with Zhang agreeing to link up but insisting that they should come to him and continue south. The situation went downhill fast and there were rumors of possible combat, something blocked by one of Zhang's commanders, with the Right Route Army claiming that it was unthinkable for one Red Army to fight another. On September 10, at a meeting that Zhang Guotao did not attend, Mao Zedong obtained agreement for an immediate move north.

Sensing his advantage, Mao delivered a report to the CC that was critical of Zhang. Thereafter a decision was circulated to CC members accusing Zhang of opportunism and splitting the Red Army, thus indicating his warlord tendencies. These warlord tendencies were revealed by the fact that Zhang did not believe that the Communist Party leadership was the primary condition for the "Red Army to become an invincible iron Red Army." As in the 1920s, Zhang was accused of forming his own small group in opposition to the Party Center. Tracing errors in the present to actions in the past would become a common practice in CCP history when denouncing opponents.

The two armies split, with the First and Third Armies heading north, eventually arriving in northern Shaanxi, and Zhang turning south, reaching the Sichuan-Tibet border, where he would spend the winter of 1935–1936. Not to be outdone in the rhetoric, on September 13–14 Zhang Guotao convened his own conference, at which he flung the label "right opportunism" at Mao, Zhou Enlai, Zhang Wentian, and Bo Gu. For Zhang Guotao, the other four's move north was simply "flightism and defeatism." Raising the stakes even higher, in early October Zhang challenged the Party Center by establishing a new central party apparatus. He passed a resolution not only to dismiss the four from their posts but also to expel them from the party and have them arrested. On December 5, feeling secure as he was perched in his base on the border, Zhang informed the First Front Army that he represented the Party Center and that they should stop using the "false title of Party Center" and rename themselves as the CCP Northern Bureau. The First and Fourth Front Armies would be renamed the Northern Route Army. The "real" Party Center hit back, replying on January 22, 1936, that Zhang had "alienated himself from the party and the Chinese revolution" and that he had to give up his opposition. The September 1935 decision criticizing Zhang was disseminated within the party at large.

It is impossible to know how this standoff might have played out and whether Zhang Guotao could have emerged as the dominant figure within the party. Fate resolved the issue. The Party Center survived as it settled into its new base in the Shaanxi region, whereas Zhang's troops were defeated in February 1936 by the GMD Central Army and Zhang was pushed farther west to even more inhospitable land. There on the Tibet border, he found an area inhabited by nomadic groups. Zhang's Fourth Front Army was joined by other Communist troops searching for a home. Reunion provided some cheer to Zhang and his demoralized group, but it also led him to tone down his criticism of the First Front Army, even acknowledging that they had made some progress in north Shaanxi. Zhang dropped his self-anointed titles, claiming that relations had improved because of agreement with the Comintern's instructions about the need to promote the national revolution. However, Zhang was not going to cede authority to the group around Mao, claiming that both groups had agreed, first, not to use the title "Party Center" and, second, to let the CCP mission to the Comintern temporarily take over the functions of the Party Center. The group in Shaanxi would be named the Northern Bureau and Zhang's group would be named the Northwest Bureau. Having accepted the shift to promoting the anti-Japanese struggle earlier than those in Shaanxi, Zhang claimed to be the faithful follower of the Comintern.[24] This would have placed power in the hands of Wang Ming, whom Mao Zedong viewed as the next obstacle to his consolidation of power.

The reunion led to the decision to rejoin the Party Center, and in early July all reunited in north Shaanxi. The end was near for Zhang Guotao, and in early 1937 criticism intensified, with the Politburo deeming his mistakes to be those of "the entire 'political line.'" Zhang fled Yan'an, joining the GMD in April 1938. In May, Zhang penned an open statement criticizing the CCP and the cruelty of the inner-party struggle, something in which he had earlier enthusiastically participated. Last but not least, Zhang felt that the CCP was hypocritical because of its revival of collaboration with the GMD, which he saw as not genuine.

Emerging from the Wilderness

Three challenges awaited the Party Center once it completed its wanderings. The first was to integrate effectively into the base area in the Northwest and resolve the power relationships with the forces already in residence. The second was to decide how to respond to the rising resentment against the Japanese incursions and what kind of relationship the CCP could form with the other forces in society inside and outside of the base area. Third, Mao Zedong and his supporters differed from those aligned with Wang Ming regarding cooperation with the GMD. This was inextricably linked with the struggle for supremacy between Mao and the returned students, led by Wang Ming. Two developments helped the CCP emerge from the wilderness: the second phase of collaboration with the Nationalists and the respite that the Japanese invasion of 1937 brought with it.

It was only by accident that the Red Army troops discovered that a base area existed some 250 miles away. The CCP discovered this from GMD newspapers they found in a post office that they had just captured.[25] This ended the roaming, but it took a while for the Party Center to settle into its new surroundings. There were about 1.5 million people living in a region scarred by deep ravines that cut through the hills. The soil was soft loess, and many of the CCP inhabitants, including Mao Zedong, dug themselves, or had dug for them, caves to live in. The caves looked out on a barren landscape that had been devastated by a mix of fighting, banditry, and natural calamities that had caused famine and disease. Yet it was here in such unpromising circumstances that Mao consolidated his power and built up an apparatus, both civilian and military, that would serve the CCP well during the civil war. Between 1937 and 1945, the number of troops across North China grew from about 30,000 to about 1 million.[26]

For all who went there, it was a groundbreaking moment in their lives—heralding a rupture with the past, and providing hope that a new beginning might offer redemption. Yan'an, the eventual capital, became the party's spiritual home.[27] Social groups responded differently to the tough physical environment. Soldiers back from skirmishes found it tranquil and calm, a "peaceful paradise," and they were puzzled by the behavior of the intellectuals. By contrast, the intellectuals who came from the cities complained about the harshness of the physical conditions and the daily chores and struggles.[28]

The Party Center's main objectives upon arrival were twofold: to take control of the base and to secure the region. To meet the first objective, it had to deal with the complicated politics within the region, and for the second it had to break the loyalty to Chiang Kai-shek of the Northeast Army and the Northwest Army under Yang Hucheng. The latter would end an immediate threat to the Red Army and drive a wedge between it and Chiang's more loyal troops.

Before the Party Center arrived, the rivalries in north Shaanxi between local revolutionaries and emissaries from the Center mirrored those earlier in the Jiangxi and the Hubei-Henan-Anhui Soviets. The local leader was Liu Zhidan, and his swashbuckling style had brought him into conflict with the two representatives sent to the area by the Party Center.[29] The early 1930s was marked by intense fighting and resulted in CCP fratricide. As elsewhere, the two representatives waved the wand of ideological correctness to battle Liu Zhidan. Yet realities on the ground and the need to survive in a complex environment meant that compromise was the order of the day. Land reform was moderate, and deals were cut with bandits, some of whom became recruits.

Liu Zhidan and his colleague Gao Gang were locals and commanded respect as much through acquaintance and relations as through adherence to ideological belief and the CCP's mission. Liu was a member of the important secret society, the Gelaohui (the Brothers' and Elders' Society), and he used his relations to help establish the base. Before the emissaries arrived, adaptation and personal relations had been critical. Even after Mao Zedong and his troops arrived, the Gelaohui was formally recognized, and in August 1936 the soviet government convened a meeting of more than eighty grand masters to explain CCP policy and to promote resistance to Japan. Thus, although the Center's emissaries were granted senior positions befitting their status, they lacked real power. They used their authority within the party to attack Liu and Gao, to renounce their guerrilla tactics, and to denounce the base for its "Shaoshan line" (mountainism)—the tendency to use guerrilla tactics and to avoid coming down from the mountains to engage in battle.

By all accounts, Liu Zhidan was a feisty character who informed the intruders, "You come from Beiping [Beijing]. Why then did you not build the base in Beiping? . . . Moreover, Mao built a base in the Jinggangshan, why then can't we build a base in the Shaanxi mountains? Shanghai is a nice place. Xi'an is also a friendly place. Why don't you build a base there?"[30] Such ridicule was unacceptable, and in the summer and autumn of 1935 tensions increased as the locals were excluded from the senior leadership. One month before the main Red Army arrived, the Twenty-Fifth Army under Xu Haidong arrived and supported the Center's emissaries in arresting and killing several local cadres, one of whom was reportedly boiled alive. The emissaries took the senior positions in the party apparatus, and the military was placed under Xu Haidong's command. Liu Zhidan was arrested and tortured as a "confess your crimes" campaign unfolded; one hundred or so of his followers were also arrested, including Gao Gang. One survivor of the events estimated that about 300 were killed, with the dead buried in a large hole.[31]

The arrival of the Long March veterans changed the equation on the ground. Mao Zedong was informed of the situation by a relative of Liu Zhidan, and an investigation by Zhou Enlai, Liu's old colleague from days at the military academy in Guangdong, vindicated him. While Liu and his supporters were released, the emissaries were not punished, presumably to facilitate an end to the in-fighting. The coalition of interests between Liu Zhidan and Mao Zedong was short-lived. As with his predecessors, Mao found Liu too independent. The challenge of how to deal with him was resolved only when he died in a battle during the Eastern Punitive Expedition in 1936. Not only was a rival removed, but Mao was also able to present him as a revolutionary martyr.[32] As we shall see in Chapter 6, Gao Gang initially thrived as one of Mao's strongest supporters before he was judged to have pushed too hard for power and cast aside in the 1950s.

Renewed Collaboration: Old Friends and Enemies

Although the formal second united front with the GMD was only launched on September 22, 1937, following the aggression of the Japanese during the Marco Polo Bridge Incident of July 7 and the Hongqiao Airport Incident of August 9, ever since the early 1930s there had been inklings of a shift in the CCP's approach to cross-class collaboration. These shifts had domestic and international origins. On September 18, 1931, the Japanese Kwantung Army fabricated a bombing incident to claim that it needed to conduct a military coup for protection, leading to Japanese annexation of the Northeast in

February 1932 and the attacks on Shanghai, which were not terminated until the unsatisfactory Tanggu Truce of May 31, 1933. The Party Center denounced the truce as treasonous and clear capitulation. The Chinese armies were forced to retreat to Hebei, leaving the land north of the Great Wall under the control of the Japanese Imperial Army.

The increasing Japanese aggression and the full-scale war that broke out in 1937 significantly changed the environment for the CCP. The conflict saved the party from being extinguished by Chiang Kai-shek's forces, allowed the Red Army to penetrate behind Japanese lines while holding most troops back from direct conflict, and allowed the CCP propaganda machine to portray the CCP as true patriots resisting Japan, as opposed to Chiang's ineffective attempts at resistance. The CCP's approach was aided by Chiang's belief that the internal threat had to be eradicated before the external one could be quashed. In January 1937 Chiang wrote in his diary: "The greatest danger is not the Japanese, but most of all communist expansion everywhere."[33] He may have been correct, but such sentiment was seriously out of touch with the national mood. The December 9, 1935, movement, dealt with below, showed that significant numbers of patriotic, educated youths placed a priority on supporting resistance to Japan. The Japanese aggression would affect politics at the Party Center and the lives of those left behind in Shanghai and in Jiangxi.

In January 1933 the situation in Manchuria had already caused the CCP to suggest a policy shift for local members. The CC declared that it was permissible to collaborate with the "national bourgeoisie," provided that a solid united front from below could be assured, with proletarian leadership over the resistance. This policy almost certainly originated with Wang Ming.[34] The most important strategic shift again came from Moscow following the Comintern's Seventh Congress of July–August 1935. The growing anxiety about German and Japanese intentions led the congress to call for a united front of all elements, classes, and nations in the fight against fascism. In the name of the CCP and the Chinese soviet government, Moscow sent the "August 1 Declaration" to members in China. Stalin and Georgi Dimitrov, who led the Comintern from 1934 to 1943, approved it, highlighting its importance, but Wang Ming claimed to have drafted it while convalescing from illness.

The declaration marked the shift from civil war to a new phase of collaboration, shifting the emphasis of the 1933 letter to a united front from above rather than from below. The "scum" and "traitors" such as Chiang Kai-shek were denounced for not resisting Japan: they had "the face of a man but the heart of a beast." All should "resist Japan to save the nation," and it was even possible to work with the GMD if it stopped its attacks and focused on resisting Japan, no matter what other differences there might be. The CCP proposed a ten-point program to expel the Japanese, which could form the basis for a government of national defense. The program included not only resistance to Japan but also the introduction of significant social reforms and the adoption of a democratic system.[35] It took a while for the declaration to reach the CCP leadership—by the latter stages of the Long March, contact with Moscow had been severed.

Exactly when the CCP received the news from Moscow about the policy shift is unclear. Radio contact was restored in late June–July 1935, and in November a representative from the CCP delegation to the Comintern arrived in the Northwest and briefed the in-country leadership. By October 1935 the Party Center certainly knew of the intent, as it issued a secret letter informing members that their task was to "oppose Japan and condemn Chiang." The armies of the CCP were now in the Northwest, where they could fight the Japanese, whereas Chiang used his planes "to spread poisonous gas" on China's only resistance fighters—the Red Army. In December 1935 Mao Zedong oversaw an enlarged Politburo meeting that conceded that Japanese actions had created a new revolutionary situation. The meeting called for combining the civil war with the national struggle against Japan. This meant that the main tasks for the next year were to build up the strength of the Red Army and to shift to guerrilla warfare. The soviet areas were to be expanded in Shaanxi to the east and Suiyuan to the north. The hope was that the base areas would be able to link up with the Soviet Union so that the two armies could work together to resist the Japanese. The political resolution called for as broad a front as possible to fight the Japanese and Chiang Kai-shek. Reflecting this conciliatory approach, the name of the Worker and Peasant Republic was changed to the People's Soviet Republic. To encourage unity and participation, policy was moderated: the property of rich peasants would not be confiscated, rich peasants would enjoy the same rights as others, and investment by entrepreneurs was welcomed. Those who were dogmatic in their approach and did not respond flexibly to the changing circumstances were criticized.

With the focus for 1936 on consolidation of the base area, the Party Center explored whether an alliance might be possible with the GMD-affiliated troops of Zhang Xueliang and Yang Hucheng. On January 25 the Red Army issued a letter to the soldiers of the Northeast Army recalling the repression that the people of the Northeast had suffered under the Japanese and reminding them that the army was being treated unjustly by the GMD government. The letter called for a truce so that the two armies could struggle together against the Japanese. During the early part of 1936 the CCP probed contacts, and on April 9 Zhou Enlai traveled to Yan'an (then named Fushi) for a secret meeting with Zhang Xueliang. The two agreed to stop the fighting and open up trade.

The CCP wooed Zhang Xueliang and the Northeast Army by emphasizing patriotism and dropping the slogans of class struggle. However, a key directive of June 20 outlined the same strategy for cooperation that it had used with the GMD in the 1920s: negotiate with senior leaders of the Northeast Army and praise their patriotism, while agitating among the rank and file and setting up secret party organizations.

Comintern criticism pushed the CCP toward reconciliation with Chiang Kai-shek. On July 23, 1936, a meeting of the ECCI acknowledged the courageous fight against Chiang's troops but claimed this was politically immature, with CCP policy lagging a few years behind the times. Greater efforts were needed to bring Chiang into the anti-Japanese struggle. On August 15, Moscow followed up with a telegram to the CCP to press home its views. As far as the ECCI was concerned, Chiang Kai-shek could not be placed on the same level as the Japanese and it was essential to engage Chiang's army, or the majority of his army, in an agreement. To move forward, Moscow advocated establishing a unified Chinese Democratic Republic with an All-China National Assembly forming a government of national defense. The various CCP-controlled areas would become part of the new setup. They could advocate forming soviets as democratic organs in the Republic to consolidate their position until the final victory of soviet power. Contacts with Zhang Xueliang were to be maintained, although he was not to be seen as a trusted ally, to enable propaganda for the anti-Japan united front to be pursued among his troops and officer corps. The telegram concluded by calling on the CCP and the Red Army to send a proposal to initiate collaboration and demanding a detailed response.[36]

The CCP's policy adjustments convinced Zhang Xueliang that Chiang Kai-shek had to seek accommodation with the Communists. On August 25, 1936, an open letter from the CCP commended Chiang for his opposition to Japan's encroachments and even referred to him as "Generalissimo." Most importantly, on September 17 the Politburo issued a resolution suggesting an agreement with Chiang. Aware that this could create confusion within the ranks, the call for the GMD to join the united front was combined with a statement that criticism would continue, with the ultimate objective remaining the building of a socialist state. The rising tide of patriotism would push the GMD to join the united front under a "democratic republic." This form of government would be more progressive in terms of democracy than that practiced either in the soviets or by the Nanjing government. It would not only mobilize the nation against the Japanese but also ultimately deliver socialism.

Zhang Xueliang was faced with a dilemma and remained frustrated that Chiang placed priority on first crushing the internal threat. Thus, while visiting Xi'an to oversee the campaign, Zhang and Yang Hucheng kidnapped Chiang. On hearing gunfire, Chiang, in his pajamas, bolted, leaving his false teeth behind in his bedroom, which contemporary guides at the site will gleefully show you. The kidnapping created a dilemma not only for Chiang Kai-shek but also for Stalin and the CCP. Totally unforeseen by the CCP, it reduced the threat of GMD attacks but posed the problem of what to do about Chiang.

Initially Mao Zedong was jubilant at the news and the CCP wanted a public tribunal; some even suggested that Chiang be executed. For Chiang, his seizure caused him to recalculate the priority of removing the Communists as a precursor to resisting Japanese aggression. Chiang wanted assurances that the soviets would provide support in the event of war.[37] Stalin clearly saw Chiang Kai-shek as the key leader of any movement to resist Japan, and his telegram to the CCP leadership (it was sent on December 17, but it might not have been deciphered until December 20) made his views clear that there should be a united front under Chiang.[38] Stalin's implicit support—and the apparent promise to allow Chiang Kai-shek's son, who had been held effectively hostage in Moscow since 1925, to return to China—seemed to convince Chiang that Soviet support would be forthcoming. On December 16, 1936, Chiang wrote in his diary, "My heart was at ease as the Soviet Union could not endorse their rebellious conduct and the Soviet Union never took Zhang [Xueliang] seriously."[39]

Chiang was released on December 25 but still called for tight constraints on CCP political and military activities should collaboration progress. Resolution marked the beginning of the shift from civil war to the War of Resistance. The outcome did not end well for Zhang Xueliang, who was arrested after accompanying Chiang back to Nanjing and remained under house arrest until 1990. The Northeast Army was disbanded, allowing the CCP to fan out and occupy Yan'an, a much larger city that would be its capital for the next decade—a symbolic icon in the history of the party. With the immediate threat removed, the Red Army spread its control close to the major city of Xi'an and the party established secret branches in dozens of counties throughout the region.

On February 10, 1937, the CCP CC called for a new period of cooperation with the GMD, offering a few concessions in return for opposition to Japan and the establishment of a democratic government. Negotiations faltered over control of the military and the role of the border regions. Japanese aggression in the Marco Polo Incident in Beijing on July 7, and the Hongqiao Airport Incident on August 9, created a dilemma for Chiang Kai-shek. It was increasingly evident that he would have to act militarily, as room for a negotiated settlement with the Japanese had disappeared. Given the material weakness of the Nationalist forces, support from the Soviet Union was crucial, and this would require a political settlement with the CCP. This caused Chiang to drop his resistance to Mao Zedong's demands and permitted the CCP to keep its territorial bases, renamed as border regions. Similarly, Chiang accepted Communist forces as members of the Nationalist army, and on August 21, 1937, the Red Army was renamed the Eighth Route Army (ERA), and in November the guerrilla forces that remained in Central China were renamed the New Fourth Army. On September 22, cooperation was formally recognized as both parties issued their own statements. The Soviet Union did provide Chiang Kai-shek with significant aid for the first four years of the war.

One unexpected impact in the border region was a shift in the relationship between the local CCP and the Gelaohui. With a broader alliance now established and the border region secure, support from the relationship was less important. Some worried about the Gelaohui's influence and whether it had infiltrated CCP power structures. Collegiality was further undermined when Zhou Enlai's entourage was attacked in May 1937 on its way to Xi'an for negotiations, with nine killed. This led to moves to suppress bandit groups and criticism of the Gelaohui for its backward and feudal ways. However, perhaps because of its deep roots, the Gelaohui was not suppressed and was even a participant in local government once elections were carried out in the border region.

Revival in Shanghai

The new accommodations affected the work of the party in other regions and led to conflicts over how to operate within the new united front. This challenge became integral to the power struggle within the CCP between Wang Ming, the returned students, and Mao Zedong and his supporters. The resolution of this struggle not only would decide the soul of the CCP but also would have major consequences both for the party's independence and for how China would be ruled after 1949.

In Shanghai, while the party was reeling from the brutality of the "white terror," local residents were becoming increasingly angered by Japanese aggression, which strengthened their patriotic sentiment. The GMD pulled together the National Salvation Association for Resistance to Japan.[40] Anti-Japanese boycotts were launched, thus heightening tensions and conflicts with the roughly 30,000 Japanese living in Shanghai. At the end of January 1932, armed conflicts broke out between the Chinese Nineteenth Route Army and a group of Japanese marines; outnumbered, the Japanese troops resorted to artillery fire and bombing. Chinese troops pulled back on March 5, and on May 5 a peace agreement was signed. The devastation was extensive, and the agreement offended Chinese national pride. Some 10,000 to 20,000 civilians had died as well as about 4,000 Chinese soldiers; 769 Japanese had died. Among other measures, the agreement forced Chinese troops to stay outside of a 30-kilometer radius of Shanghai.

The anti-Japanese sentiment allowed the CCP to reengage in political life. With its links to the working class shredded, it set up Red Mass Leagues to engage with a broader swathe of the Shanghai population, covering both labor and cultural work.[41] Even though this marked a shift in work, it did not shake the legacies of the central leadership—therefore it failed. Increased activism with the general public exposed clandestine CCP members, which in turn led to greater repression. However, it provided an important learning experience for developing a different approach in Shanghai. By 1935 the few who remained had lost all contact with the central party leadership, reconsidered their strategy, and returned to covert work.

The August 1935 Comintern instructions had supported Shanghai CCP members in engaging fully with other classes and groups to oppose Japan and, initially, Chiang Kai-shek. This helped the local party put "long-term revolutionary objectives on the back burner in favor of short-term patriotic ones by incorporating themselves into the city's growing number of patriotic organizations."[42] Perceiving correctly that Chiang Kai-shek's priority was to eradicate the Communists before engaging the Japanese, patriotic sentiments linked with anti-Chiang sentiments. The anti-Japanese student demonstrations in Beijing on December 9 and 16, 1935, echoed in Shanghai among the remaining CCP members who continued their work of forming broader patriotic coalitions. On December 21, under the leadership of a group of intellectuals gathered around the editor of a popular journal, the Shanghai National Salvation Association was formed. Its various petitions and documents called for an end to capitulation to Japan, an end to civil war, and united resistance against Japan. This last call, on July 15, 1936, was swiftly endorsed by Mao Zedong. For his part, Chiang Kai-shek was never comfortable with the organization, seeing it as infiltrated by the Communists, which was true even if the organization as a whole was not controlled by the CCP.

In June 1937 the Party Center made a more assertive effort to engage with the work in Shanghai. The launch of the Japanese campaign increased the resistance movement, but the Japanese occupation of Shanghai made overt activities too dangerous. Following the shift in focus proposed by Mao Zedong, work to build links for national resistance continued, but the building of independent strength among the population was considered even more important.

Whither the United Front? Mao Zedong and Wang Ming Clash

For Mao Zedong, the main issue in the new relationship with the GMD was to preserve the strength of the Communist troops. The War of Resistance was now a reality, but Mao was concerned that rash, showcase actions would lead to the waste of soldiers' lives at the hands of the better-armed and better-trained Japanese troops. An enlarged Politburo meeting in Luochuan on August 22–25, 1937, supported Mao's views over those of Zhu De and Peng Dehuai, who favored more active engagement, whereas Zhou Enlai was concerned that a lack of action might dissipate the national credibility that the CCP had built up.[43] Mao favored the dispersal of troops, with only the CCP itself deciding on troop movements. As the ERA set off for the front, it seems that general principles about self-preservation and expansion were agreed upon. This did not mean avoiding conflict but instead engaging where victory could be ensured. In September and October, the troops engaged in some one hundred battles and defeated roughly 10,000 Japanese troops. Such victories were popular with the Chinese population, but Mao continued to warn his military commanders to be careful about risking their troops. He still preferred guerrilla tactics to protect troop strength.

The issue of intense engagement became part of Mao's struggle with Wang Ming. By November 1937 Mao was already concerned that the GMD would not be able to lead the War of Resistance, and he warned of right opportunism—subjugating too much to the GMD. On November 29 Wang Ming, whom Mao would later accuse of being the chief right opportunist, arrived in Yan'an, together with seven members of the CCP mission to the Comintern. The group included those who would eventually become Mao's stalwarts—Kang Sheng, who would oversee the security apparatus, and Chen Yun, who would become an important economic planner. Although Mao greeted Wang's arrival as "a blessing from the sky," the warmth did not last for long.[44]

At a Politburo meeting of December 9–14, 1937, Wang Ming established his credibility in the party by delivering a keynote speech, while Mao sat in silence. As with other new arrivals who had little practical experience, Wang sought to use his theoretical sophistication and study in Moscow to exert authority. For Wang, policy was to place "everything through the united front," which he saw as the best method to develop the CCP as a credible national force outside of the base areas. The alliance was to be a long-term strategy that would bring together other societal forces and continue into a phase of national reconstruction. Wang did agree with Mao that the ERA should maintain its independence, but the general thrust of his views clearly conflicted with Mao's.

Wang's warm welcome but politically weak position was revealed in the organizational changes that were made at the Politburo meeting. A twenty-five-person committee was established to prepare for the Seventh Party Congress as soon as possible, although it did not convene until 1945; Mao was chair, with Wang as secretary. At the Comintern's request, the post of general secretary was abolished to encourage collective leadership, with a new Secretariat established, comprised of the former general secretary, Zhang Wentian, plus Mao, Chen Yun, and Kang Sheng. Crucially, Mao retained his position as chair of the Military Council.

Wang Ming was at the forefront of the collaboration with the GMD, and together with Zhou Enlai and Bo Gu he went to Wuhan to take up his position as secretary of the CCP Yangzi Bureau. On the one hand, this made him responsible for the success of the collaboration, while, on the other hand, it moved him away from the center of power in Yan'an. The environment in Wuhan was, of course, quite different from that in Yan'an. His approach was successful initially in expanding Communist influence in the more open, legal environment.

In early March 1938 the differing views were aired at a Politburo meeting. A stalemate and Mao Zedong's opposition meant that no formal resolution was issued but a written version of Wang's report was widely distributed.[45] For Wang, the united front was to be consolidated into a "national revolutionary alliance," which would be similar to the ill-fated first united front or would be a confederation within which each party would enjoy political and organizational independence. He called for the creation of a national assembly to facilitate consultation with other parties, and he proposed legalization and development of mass organizations. As opposed to Mao's support for guerrilla warfare, he proposed mobile warfare as the primary form of combat, which would be coordinated with positional warfare.

Military strategy was crucial and became even more so when the key city of Xuzhou fell and Japanese forces threatened Wuhan. Throughout April and May, Mao continued to stress guerrilla warfare where conditions were favorable, and the development of bases. The ERA was to conduct mobile warfare only when conditions were favorable. Further instructions marginalized the work in Wuhan. On May 14 the New Fourth Army and the Yangzi Bureau were instructed to move work to the rural areas to set up guerrilla forces, and on May 22 the party branches in Hebei, Hunan, and Wuhan were told that after the fall of Xuzhou, they were also to focus on the creation of guerrilla bases in the countryside. Students, workers, and other revolutionaries were to return to their home villages to aid in this work.

By contrast, Wang Ming was fixated on the defense of Wuhan and, while acknowledging that the city might fall, he cited Madrid during the Spanish Civil War as an example of heroic defense. Together with Zhou Enlai and Bo Gu, he believed that the GMD could lead a massive mobilization of the citizens to fight the Japanese with mobile warfare outside of Wuhan. The ERA was expected to work behind Japanese lines to destroy supply lines. The GMD became very suspicious of this mobilization, and on August 5 it placed restrictions on the mass organizations, with the GMD secret police keeping a close eye on CCP activities. The strategy of working legally within the GMD to expand CCP influence was unraveling when a mortal blow was delivered on October 25, 1938, when Wuhan fell to the Japanese.

Mao and his supporters moved quickly to push home their advantage within the party by convening the Sixth Plenum of the Sixth Central Committee from September 29 to November 6, 1938. Despite the failure to defend Wuhan, positive news arrived from Moscow. Comintern head Dimitrov acknowledged Mao Zedong's leadership of the CCP: the political line was correct, and guerrilla warfare was the best military strategy. In July, Wang Jiaxiang, acting head of the CCP delegation to the Comintern, was so informed, and he returned to China and on September 14 reported this information to the Politburo. Upon hearing this news, Mao decided to convene the plenum.[46]

Any sense of harmony was short-lived. By the end of the plenum Wuhan had fallen, and before Mao had delivered his concluding speech, Wang Ming departed to attend the National Political Consultative Assembly, which was held from October 28 to November 6. Wang clearly believed that he had reached some kind of compromise with Mao. He obviously had not studied Mao's skill with political intrigue. Mao had claimed that he still saw value in continuing the united front, and he praised both the GMD and Chiang Kai-shek, even ceding primacy to the GMD. He portrayed cooperation as long-term, as he predicted a glorious future for all who were engaged in the united front. Instead of socialism, a new democratic republic based on Sun Yat-sen's "three principles of the people" was on the agenda. The CCP would retain its independence, but class struggle would not be allowed to impede the interests of national resistance. Wang Ming supported the approach, but once he departed, Mao delivered a report with a very different tone. He criticized Wang's slogan of "everything through the united front" as well as the GMD for not allowing the united front to adopt an appropriate organizational form. GMD approval for action was not always necessary. Mao directed his ire at Wang's approach of using legal means to develop the party, claiming that Wang had mistaken the direction of the flow of the revolution by thinking that it could progress from the cities to the countryside.

At this stage the party at large was not to be informed about the tensions, and the political resolution adopted did not include harsh public condemnation of Wang. However, on November 9 Wang's institutional base, the Yangzi Bureau, was abolished and was split into the Southern Bureau and the Central Plains Bureau, both headed by Mao supporters—Zhou Enlai and Liu Shaoqi, respectively. Mao's earlier alliance with Zhang Wentian had allowed him to defeat Bo Gu, but as this alliance weakened, the alliance between Mao and Liu Shaoqi was strengthened. The reorganization of the central party apparatus also placed more power in Mao's hands. While the Polit-buro was to meet at least once every three months, the Central Secretariat was to take on an increasingly powerful role, handling the day-to-day af-fairs of the CC and carrying out its policies. Crucially, the Secretariat was to convene Politburo meetings and prepare their agenda. This meant that the Secretariat controlled the flow of information and what should be dis-cussed. Even more important was the decision that if a new emergency arose when the Politburo was not in session and could not be convened immedi ately, the Secretariat could issue decisions in the name of the CC and only subsequently receive approval from the Politburo. The person who controlled the Secretariat as general secretary would be in an extremely powerful posi-tion. (It was no accident that in the Soviet Union, Stalin was the general secretary.) Mao replaced Zhang Wentian as general secretary.

With Wang Ming's organizational base destroyed, Mao set about at-tacking Wang's claims to superior theoretical knowledge. Mao announced that there was no such thing as abstract Marxism—instead it had to be adapted to local conditions and rendered in a form that people could easily understand and respond to.[47] To make the party his own, Mao had to pro-vide its ideological foundations and construct a history of the Chinese revo-lution that placed not only the CCP but also himself at the core. He com-pleted this over the next few years in Yan'an, using Wang Ming as his whipping boy representing incorrect theory and revolutionary practice. Wang stood for the antithesis of all that Mao proposed and that, in Mao's view, revolutionary success demanded.

Before Mao could take care of this task, the CCP had to deal with the mounting tensions in the cooperation with the GMD, which by 1941 led to the effective, if not actual, demise of the collaboration. After the plenum in 1939, relations began to deteriorate, and as Communist forces expanded their influence, there occurred a series of conflicts with the GMD troops in December 1939 into March 1940, and in January 1941. The CCP referred to these as the "first and second anti-Communist upsurges." The conflicts con-vinced Mao that it was all the more necessary to be cautious in working with the GMD, while promoting a broader alliance to isolate Chiang Kai-shek. Beyond these domestic challenges, the changing international environment required attention as Europe descended into warfare that would consume the globe.

To present a more attractive face to the public, the CCP moderated its economic policies in the areas under its control and developed mechanisms for power sharing, while still ensuring that it would retain ultimate control. Mao had to provide an alternative to the approaches advocated by Wang Ming and the GMD. He put this forward in his work "On New Democracy" (January 1940). The moderation of economic policy was due to the economic pressure that the Shaanxi-Gansu-Ningxia Border Region came under in the early 1940s because of the Nationalist blockades and cuts in Nationalist subsidies. The last challenge faced by the CCP was the fear that the GMD, or some of its members, might seek rapprochement with the Japanese. Indeed, this soon occurred. Wang Jingwei was swayed by the peace terms outlined in Fumimaro Konoe's "new order for East Asia" (November 3, 1938) and went over to the Japanese side. The terms were rejected by Chiang Kai-shek, and on January 1, 1939, Wang was expelled from the GMD. Temporarily, this shored up CCP support for Chiang and the CCP denounced Wang. Again, this confidence in Chiang was short-lived. In comments to the Fifth Plenum of the GMD, held January 21–30, 1939, Chiang indicated that the fight against Japan was simply intended to restore circumstances to the way they had been previous to July 1937. Did this mean that Chiang was willing to accept the Japanese occupation of Manchuria? This was certainly the CCP's interpretation, which continued support for Chiang's commitment to resist Japan but called for a critical response to his position with respect to Manchuria. Such criticism was to be phrased carefully so that the majority of the people would be convinced of the CCP's position.

What the CCP was not aware of was the decision of the GMD plenum to step up measures to curb CCP activities.[48] With conflicts increasing, financial and logistical support to the Shaanxi-Gansu-Ningxia Border Region was cut off in October. Troops loyal to Chiang Kai-shek advanced to the border region, leading to numerous clashes in December. The increasing squeeze convinced the CCP leadership that it must put forward its own clear vision for the future, one that would be compelling to a broad section of the Chinese population who were patriotic and frustrated by the GMD's inability to push back the Japanese. This would be developed within the Shaanxi-Gansu-Ningxia Border Region during the following years.

The decade had been turbulent, but finally the CCP had found a new home where it could develop policies and institutions to guide post-1949 rule. The importance of military control was confirmed, as was the need for a disciplined party.

CHAPTER FOUR

Victories at Last

1940–1948

✭

From 1940 on, despite unpromising conditions and setbacks, the CCP was victorious in three important areas. First, it built a coherent party apparatus that not only would promote the struggle against Japan but also would offer a viable organizational alternative to the GMD. This entailed rallying around Mao Zedong as the core leader, underpinned by a narrative of struggle designed to place Mao and the party at the center of the Chinese revolution. Large numbers of recruits were making their way to the city of Yan'an, but many individuals who wished to fight against Japan knew little about the CCP, its beliefs, and its ultimate objectives. Some embodied the intellectual legacy of the May Fourth Movement of 1915–1919, and they were pressured to accept the party's new orthodoxy. Second, the invasion by Japanese troops saved the CCP from the continued repression by the GMD, and then Japan's defeat opened a path to power. Third, against long odds the CCP was victorious in the civil war against the GMD, which was complicit in its own destruction on the mainland. Victory led to a first phase in the consolidation of power that was marked by the continuation of radical land reform and the adoption of the Soviet model.

A Fragile Alliance

The collaboration between the CCP and the GMD was unstable from the beginning, and whenever the opportunity presented itself, the GMD would increase pressure. In 1939 it strengthened the blockade of the

Shaanxi-Gansu-Ningxia Border Region, opposed the expansion of Communist troops in Central China where the New Fourth Army (NFA) was active, and cracked down on activities of Communist organizations in the areas controlled by the GMD. Subsequently with the changing international situation, the GMD moderated its attacks on the Communists, and in March 1940 it halted the attacks. As a result the CCP continued to reaffirm the necessity of the united front and warned of the leftist dangers posed by those who wanted to weaken it. However, again this atmosphere would not last for long, and by the beginning of 1941 the united front was effectively dead following the Southern Anhui Incident, when, after the Jiangxi Soviet evacuation, the troops of the NFA that had remained behind were decimated by GMD troops. This marked the culmination of tensions that had been building up with the revived cooperation.

When the main Red Army forces moved out of Jiangxi, they left behind some 42,000 troops in Central and South China and virtually all their civilian followers.[1] In addition to simple survival, their job was to harass the GMD troops and to keep alive the flickering flame of the revolution in South China. By the spring of 1935, radio contact with those on the Long March had been lost, and it was only in late 1937 that contact with the Party Center was restored. Following the departure of the main Red Army, for the next three years the troops left behind lived in terrible conditions on mountaintops and other inhospitable areas, scattered across various base areas. Rather than rely on class mobilization or the land policies operating in Shaanxi-Gansu-Ningxia Border Region, they used traditional networks, such as clans, lineages, and old friendships, to win support. The pressure to survive led them to eschew ideological categories and to try to localize the revolution whenever and wherever possible. On the whole, apart from West Fujian, the most successful bases were led by locals, who were able to deflect or avoid central interference. This led to a very different political culture, with a "strong 'feudal' flavor of communism," which "contrasted markedly with the bureaucratic-centralist character of the party in the north."[2] One important lesson from the experiences of those left behind was that if the party managed to sink roots, it would be difficult to entirely eliminate them—even after defeat, traces would remain. The CCP was not a monolithic entity but instead displayed a variety of responses to local conditions that shaped the relationship to the community within which it was embedded.

It must have come as a shock to many of these soldiers when they heard of Chiang Kai-shek's release after he was kidnapped in Xi'an and as policy moved toward finalizing a new collaboration with the enemy that had hounded them during the previous three years. In August 1937, during a final round of negotiations—with Chiang Kai-shek desperate for Soviet aid—the GMD agreed to the Communist suggestion that the guerrilla fighters in the south be reorganized and join the fight behind Japanese lines. In October the NFA was formed from about 12,000 soldiers operating in south Jiangsu, south Anhui, and north Jiangxi to south of the Yangzi River, and in northeast Hubei and north Anhui to the north of the river.[3] This was a shrewd move, because during the following eight years the number of troops expanded to several hundred thousand and they would play an important role in the civil war.[4] The dramatic change in their physical environment was extraordinary. They had to adapt not only to different techniques for fighting but also to a different socioeconomic environment. Now as the troops were coming down from the mountains, they had to fight across one of the most developed regions of China. Unlike in the north where the ERA could control the entire area of operations, the NFA could not exert complete control and had to coexist with other political and military forces. It established its headquarters in Wuhan on December 25, 1937, bringing Xiang Ying back into contact with his old associate Wang Ming. In January 1938, Wang Ming's Yangzi Bureau established the Southeastern Bureau headed by Xiang Ying, who was given the task of leading NFA work.

Given the new circumstances, conflicts arose over the deployment of these troops. Should the priority be engagement with the Japanese or protection of CCP members? And who should have ultimate control, the Party Center or the local commanders? In late 1937 Mao Zedong requested that two-fifths of the troops remain in the base areas, although in southwest Fujian and south Zhejiang they should all remain. Xiang Ying more or less agreed, informing the Politburo that one-third of the troops should remain behind. However, Xiang Ying quickly changed his mind, leaving behind very few because he wanted the troops to be at the front where they would be under his command.[5] The party saw the Yangzi Delta as fertile ground for party expansion, and through 1939 clashes in the rear increased. By early 1939 the Party Center decided that it was not useful to expand the bases in Jiangsu south of the Yangzi, and it called on the NFA to move north into central China. A January 1940 directive reconfirmed this, demanding that the NFA cross to the north bank of the river, an appeal repeated in February and March.[6] The Party Center saw the Yangzi River as a natural barrier, with the Communist troops to the north in a possible standoff with Chiang Kai-shek.

In May 1940 Mao Zedong was still pressuring the NFA to expand its sphere of influence, despite ongoing talks with the GMD to try to reduce tensions and clashes. Xiang Ying was uncomfortable with this approach and offered to resign.[7] Nevertheless, by October 1940 the NFA occupied all of Jiangsu north of the Yangzi and east of the Grand Canal as well as large areas of Anhui and Hubei and smaller areas south of the Yangzi.

Chiang Kai-shek was not pleased and sought to frustrate this expansion. He had already been restricting the growth of Shaanxi-Gansu-Ningxia Border Region, and now he sought to push all Communist troops to the north of the Yellow River. Resolving this standoff required complicated negotiations. Talks began in June and focused on the size of the Communist forces and the zones in which they could operate. The GMD held to the view that Communist troops should move north of the Yellow River, but declared that the area in southwest Shanxi should be excluded from Communist influence. Subsequently the GMD hardened its stance, intending to restrict the number of counties in the Shaanxi-Gansu-Ningxia Border Region to eighteen rather than the twenty-one proposed by the CCP; it instructed that the number of CCP forces should be reduced dramatically, from 500,000 to 100,000, and that all Communist forces should move north of the Yellow River within one month. This would have meant that the Communists would give up their bases in Henan and Shandong, which were south of the Yellow River. The problem was that precisely these two bases had been identified in the January 1940 directive as presenting the best opportunities for Communist expansion.

The concession that the Party Center proposed was to move its troops from south Jiangsu and Anhui—that is, south of the Yangzi River. It feared that agreeing to GMD terms might trap the Communist troops between the Yellow River and the GMD and the Japanese armies. Disagreement over the move north continued, and Zhu De and Xiang Ying, among others, rejected the GMD demand to make the move within one month to meet the deadline of November 9, 1940. Their rejection noted the support that Communist troops had been providing to the war effort, including the "100 Regiments Campaign," which lasted from August to December 1940.[8] Many expressed strong resistance to moving from Central China because it would mean leaving the places where "their ancestral tombs, land, property, houses, parents, and wives are. They cannot bear the thought of exposing them to the brutality, slaughter, and lust of the enemy."[9] They claimed to have abided by Chiang Kai-shek's principles and feared the consequences of suddenly being ordered to move north. Clearly, the response fell on deaf ears. On December 9 Chiang repeated the demand that, by year's end, these troops should move out of south Anhui and south Jiangsu. The ERA was expected to be north of the Yellow River by this time, to be followed by the NFA one month later.

On December 25, 1940, Mao Zedong ordered Xiang Ying to begin an immediate evacuation, but Ye Ting's and Xiang Ying's forces did not begin the move until January 4. Disaster was about to strike. When they did start their move, they were harassed by GMD troops and forced to move southwest to regroup. Nationalist forces surrounded them and some 9,000 NFA troops were killed or arrested. Ye Ting was arrested on January 13 while trying to negotiate a settlement, and several weeks later Xiang Ying was killed by a turncoat within his own troops.

All sides tried to put their own spin on the event, with each side blaming the other for the clash and the outcome. The GMD claimed that the NFA had been insubordinate and had engaged in unlawful expansion, and that therefore on January 17 it had called for the army to be disbanded. CCP liaison offices in a number of Nationalist-controlled cities were closed, and direct contacts between Chongqing, the GMD capital, and Yan'an were scrapped.

The CCP publicly claimed that it had been following orders, but while moving north to link up with the ERA, the NFA had been ambushed by GMD troops. This provided a public propaganda windfall, with the CCP seeking to win sympathy and to discredit the GMD in general and Chiang in particular. Mao Zedong claimed the incident was a premeditated act by "pro-Japanese conspirators" and those of the "diehard Communist faction" who had not renounced their anti-Communist prejudice, placing this above the national interest. He called for punishment of those involved in the plot, the release of captives, compensation for the wounded and for the families of those killed, the removal of pro-Japanese elements, and an end to the blockades in Northwest China. For Mao, it raised the possibility of a return to civil war.[10]

A single event can serve multiple purposes, and the Communist message varied depending on the audience. An internal party directive carried the same basic message but drew a sharper line, naming names in the GMD who were pro-Japanese "capitulationist elements" who had cooperated with the pro-American and pro-British elements under Chiang Kai-shek. The event was also used by Mao Zedong to advance his struggle with Wang Ming by criticizing right opportunism in the party. Given its sensitive nature, this decision was for the eyes of senior party members only and was not to be distributed under any circumstances to the public at large. In January 1941 the Party Center issued a decision on Xiang Ying's mistakes, claiming that ever since September 1937 Xiang had committed right opportunist errors in the work of the united front. He was criticized for not recognizing the need for CCP independence. This was, of course, an attack on Wang Ming. Any potential future conflict was ended on March 14, 1941, when one of his own staff killed Xiang.[11] On January 20 the leadership of the NFA was reorganized, with Chen Yi, who was much closer to Mao, appointed temporary commander. By March 1941, pressure on the Communists eased again and they declared that the "second anti-Communist onslaught" had ended, the first having ended in the winter of 1939–1940.

Dramatic Changes in the Global Order

While these events were unfolding, dramatic changes were taking place internationally that affected domestic developments. In an attempt to protect its own national interests, the CCP faithfully followed the twists and turns of Soviet policy as the threat of war and actual war heightened in the West and the East. Throughout 1939 and for most of 1940, the CCP portrayed the war in Europe as simply a war between bourgeois and fascist nations. Criticism of Great Britain, the United States, and France continued, and the CCP tried to focus on making sure that the GMD did not reach any form of appeasement with the Japanese. The fear that the GMD would do this was not unrealistic. In December 1938 senior GMD leader Wang Jingwei split with Chiang Kai-shek and, in Nanjing, announced his pro-Japanese regime. Further, some of those very close to Chiang were thought to harbor pro-Japanese sentiments. For the most part, criticism focused, not on Chiang directly, but on those around him.

The Nazi-Soviet Nonaggression Pact of August 23, 1939, caused shock waves, but the CCP supported it as a sign of Soviet prowess in international politics. Three events of 1941 brought major changes to the global environment and the situation on the ground for the CCP: First, even more surprisingly, the CCP supported the Soviet-Japan Neutrality Pact, which was signed on

April 13, 1941. Second, Germany invaded Soviet Russia on June 22; and third, on December 7 the Japanese attacked Pearl Harbor. The new alliances created by these events would endure until the end of the war. The CCP now welcomed the previously denounced "imperialist nations" of Great Britain and the United States to join the struggle against fascism in the West and the East. This ended the fear that the East might witness the same kind of appeasement as that exhibited by Neville Chamberlain when he concluded the agreement with Germany in September 1938, declaring "Peace for our time."

The CCP heralded the Soviet-Japan Neutrality Pact as yet another victory in the Soviet Union's peace policy. In a twist of logic, the CCP claimed that the pact did not compromise Soviet support for China's war effort, a view not shared by Chiang Kai-shek. By 1940 the relationship between Chiang and the Soviets had already soured. Over the winter of 1939–1940, the Soviet Union invaded Finland, prompting a swift response from Great Britain and France, which sponsored a motion to expel the Soviet Union from the League of Nations. China, a member of the League Council, refused to use its veto power, much to the anger of the Soviets. This effectively ended its relationship with the Soviets during the war with Japan.[12]

For the CCP, the pact meant that it was up to China to recover all Chinese territory south of the Yalu River. This put the CCP in the difficult position of defending a policy that was not helpful in pursuit of the nationalist agenda in the war against Japan. In this context, the German invasion of the Soviet Union on June 22, 1941, provided relief. The Soviet Union was no longer sitting above the fray of a capitalist war. Instead, it was now leading the fight against fascism. The world had changed, and the capitalist powers of Great Britain and America were viewed as part of the global united front against fascism.

The sudden Japanese attack on Pearl Harbor brought the United States into the war and aided CCP calls to develop the united front. The CCP dropped the view that it would recover the territories on its own. On December 9, 1941, the CCP called for the establishment of an anti-Japanese and antifascist front in the Pacific to include all governments and peoples opposed to Japan. The United States and Great Britain were now allies and destined to play an important role in reunifying China and eradicating the Japanese menace. All party members were instructed to cooperate, and a left deviation (going it alone and promoting independent activities) was to be avoided at all costs.[13]

Broadening the Party's Appeal

To counter GMD rule and win support from independent elements, it was necessary for the CCP to present a compelling vision of China's future that would guarantee it a place in the post-conflict world. Mao Zedong expressed his own vision in two important articles—"Introduction to *The Communist*" (October 1939) and "New Democratic Politics and New Democratic Culture" (January 1940).[14] The former was intended for CCP members, while the latter was for public consumption, presenting a palatable vision about what it would mean for the broader public. "New Democratic Politics" skirts the question of Communist party leadership, while the "Introduction" simply assumes that CCP members understand that the party will exert hegemony. The "Introduction" began the process of promoting the Maoist interpretation of history, marking the Zunyi meeting of January 1935 as the key moment when the party took the Bolshevik road and laying the foundation for the united front against Japan. This was a swipe against Wang Ming and the other returned students, as previously the claim was that Bolshevization had been ushered in at the Fourth Plenum, in January 1931, when Comintern envoy Pavel Mif had moved in his protégés. In 1945 that plenum would be entirely discredited.

In the "Introduction," Mao put forward the "three magic weapons" that would bring victory for the CCP—the united front, armed struggle, and party building. For the united front, the policy was unity and struggle, maintaining the alliance with the national bourgeoisie, and thus avoiding left opportunism. Any struggle was to be conducted in a peaceful and bloodless manner, while the party strengthened itself to avoid falling prey to those who sought to suppress it. This would avoid right opportunism: party members would remain in the united front but retain the prospect of future revolutionary action against the bourgeoisie. Mao now informed party members that the history of the CCP was one of armed struggle in the form of a peasant war employing guerrilla warfare. Party building was crucial and would be the key focus between 1941 and 1944 during the Rectification Campaign of 1942–1944. A shared understanding of the CCP's eighteen-year history was a crucial component of unity. Yet Mao was cautious about his criticism of the early 1930s. This was prudent, because during that time policy had been driven by the Comintern. Although its direct influence over the CCP was declining, the Comintern still carried weight in the Chinese Communist movement.

Given its audience, the essay "New Democratic Politics" was more conciliatory but reflected a significant shift in Mao's views since the October 1938 Sixth Plenum. For the first time, the CCP put forward its claim to lead the revolution. The bourgeoisie's dualism combined revolutionary characteristics with compromise. The tendency toward compromise meant that the proletariat would have to take on a leadership role in the struggle against imperialism and feudalism. Initially there would be a revolutionary democratic dictatorship of several classes, with the non-proletarian classes gradually being transformed during a second stage as the new democratic revolution moved on to the socialist stage. Although Mao was vague about when the transition would occur, the first stage would be lengthy, and he criticized as leftists those who thought that socialism could be embarked upon before the new democratic revolution was completed. Shortly after the CCP took power, Mao ignored his own advice and, in the mid-1950s, accelerated the process.

Given the forecast of a lengthy transition period, a moderate economic policy was proposed. Private capitalist production was permitted if it did not dominate the "livelihood of the people on a national scale." In the rural areas, the previously derided rich peasant economy was promoted, with only the land of the big landlords ripe for confiscation and redistribution. Taken as a whole, the program assured the party faithful that the ultimate goal of socialism was not forgotten, but in the interim the GMD should be isolated by offering intermediate elements a stake in the CCP's world.

It was important to have such a guideline because not only in the Shaanxi-Gansu-Ningxia Border Region but also in other border regions, the CCP was consolidating power. In early 1940 the most important other base areas were Shanxi-Chahar-Hebei (Jin-Cha-Ji), Shanxi-Hebei-Shandong-Henan (Jin-Ji-Yu-Lu), Shanxi-Suiyuan (Jin-Sui), and Shandong.[15] These bases were situated in poor, remote areas that straddled provincial boundaries where it was more difficult for the GMD troops to penetrate. On the whole, geography was more important to the survival of a base area than its socioeconomic structure.[16] Life in these other border regions was quite distinct from that in Shaanxi-Gansu-Ningxia, which was beyond the reach of the Japanese attacks and was home to the Party Center.

The Shaanxi-Gansu-Ningxia Border Region was established earlier than the others, with the consequence that it was almost entirely consolidated, whereas survival elsewhere was precarious, always vulnerable to Japanese attack. Consequently, policy was more flexible and accommodating to prevent local landlords and others from turning against the Communists to support either the GMD or even the Japanese. As the Party Center began to pull together its administrative and economic policies, the Shanxi-Chahar-Hebei Border Region served as a model and received Mao's seal of approval.[17] On March 6, 1940, Mao put forward the "three-thirds" system of political power that had been developed in the Shanxi-Chahar-Hebei Border Region. The Communists were to be restricted to one-third of positions in all political organs, with nonparty left-wing progressives occupying another third. This left the final third for intermediate elements who were neither left nor right.[18]

The best articulation of this approach was provided by the leader of the Shanxi-Chahar-Hebei Border Region, Peng Zhen, in a report to the Politburo in September 1941.[19] Policies such as rent and interest reductions and popular elections enabled the party to embed itself in local society and enhance its influence. Peng was aware that the CCP had to construct a system of political power that enabled it to retain control in a decentralized and fragmented environment. The trick was to destroy the old power structures without alienating the traditional elite. The answer was to set up a system of village councils to select local administrative officials through an indirect system that would prevent the traditional elite from ensuring their own automatic election to leadership positions. To be successful, they would have to seek alliances with others under a system whereby the CCP would have an automatic one-third representation. For its part, CCP members had to be well drilled and disciplined and had to work to expand party organization in the villages. However, Peng Zhen called for flexibility in implementation, and he even suggested that should the CCP gain more than one-third of the seats, some could resign. This did occur during the first round of elections in May and June 1942, when about one hundred CCP members withdrew to ensure that the three-thirds balance was maintained.[20]

Concessions for the traditional elite were outlined in the CCP Northern Bureau's document "The Double Ten Policy" (published August 13, 1940). Only the land and property of the worst traitors would be confiscated, with others allowed to keep their land and even to receive rent. Policies included an eight-hour workday, low rents, and a progressive tax system. For the elite, rent strikes were forbidden and payment was to be enforced. The policy was formalized in the Shaanxi-Gansu-Ningxia Border Region in May 1941 and formed the basis for policy in all other regions. It was an encapsulation of "power management" whereby threats from the local elite were neutralized by means of their cooptation into the power structure.[21]

Economic Hardship and Policy Response

Although the worst of the conflicts with the GMD moderated after the January 1941 crushing of the NFA, the GMD did not release its grip on the Shaanxi-Gansu-Ningxia Border Region. Prior to this, from August 20 to December 5, 1940, the ERA launched its largest and longest offensive during the anti-Japanese war, the 100 Regiments' Campaign. This was launched by Peng Dehuai in an attempt to break the tightening control of the Japanese troops, but Peng had acted without the approval of the Central Military Commission or Mao Zedong. The intention was to help link Shaanxi-Gansu-Ningxia with Shanxi-Chahar-Hebei. Following initial success, by late October the Communist attacks were faltering and a major Japanese backlash took place in North China from 1941 to 1944. In July 1941 General Okamura Yasuji launched wide-ranging search-and-destroy missions, labeled the "three-all"—that is, kill all, burn all, and loot all—not only against the Communist forces but also against the local population. The pressure on the border region intensified, even if pressure from the GMD was receding.

Prior to the squeeze by the Japanese forces, pressure from the GMD had increased and support for the border region had ended. Even before the financial support was terminated, inflation in the GMD areas had become a problem, with the result that by 1940 the money received from the GMD had only one-seventh of its original value.[22] Until 1941 the Nationalists had subsidized the Shaanxi-Gansu-Ningxia Border Region to the tune of around 1.2 million yuan per year for government expenses and 6 million yuan per year for military expenses. In 1939 these Nationalist subsidies accounted for 89.66 percent of the entire border region budget; in 1940, the year when the Communists complained about the withholding of funds by the GMD, the subsidies still accounted for 73.5 percent.[23] In 1941, the first year without GMD support, the budget ran a deficit of 15 million yuan. Fortunately, however, Stalin authorized monthly support of $300,000 per month, almost 1 million yuan.[24] Bad harvests increased the economic damage. As a result, what had cost 500 yuan in 1940 cost 2,200 yuan in 1941.[25] In 1941 the commodities index in Yan'an rose four times, and in 1942 it rose fourteen times.

Beyond these immediate problems, there was an inherent weakness in the economy of the border region.[26] The CCP had failed to establish a firm financial footing, relying heavily on confiscation of the property of the enemy forces to supplement the outside help. GMD support had meant that the party only had to tax the rich peasants. The economic blockade forced the

CCP to increase taxation, but there were limits and the amount levied did not compensate for the lost revenue. By 1943 the shortfall in budgetary needs was almost one-third.

In addition to the pressure from the Japanese and the GMD, a large number of refugees and others had come to Yan'an. Not only did this increase the problems of feeding everyone and supplying sufficient goods, but it also meant that the region was filling up with a heterogeneous group of individuals who were more attracted by resistance to Japan than to the principles of the Communist Party. To deal with these challenges, the CCP launched a three-pronged strategy: first, simplify administration and train troops to defend the region; second, piece together a viable economic strategy; and third, unify the party to lead the border region and to provide leadership for a strong fighting unit.

To deal with these challenges, the party initiated a series of mobilization campaigns, which would become a hallmark of CCP policy implementation. The hope was that the enthusiasm of the local population would overcome objective barriers blocking successful economic development.[27] These campaigns comprised what came to be known as the "Yan'an spirit" and they are credited with turning the economy around. Appeals to the Yan'an spirit are frequently heard when the party finds itself confronted by seemingly insurmountable problems, and campaign-style policy implementation formed a core component of Mao Zedong's supposed voluntarism. When mobilized, the people, or the masses in Maoist terminology, could pull themselves up by their bootstraps by engaging in a patriotic and noble vocation. The production and self-sufficiency campaign became a core element in the legend of Yan'an. While this contains a kernel of truth, the reality was very different.

The policy of "Crack Troops and Simple Administration" had the dual objectives of reducing the size of the government bureaucracy and the regular military organizations while improving their overall quality. The approach was adopted by the border region in November 1941, and beginning in December 1941 it was promoted more broadly. Two major problems in the administrative structure were identified: too many people and organizations at the top, and too few people and organizations of sufficient quality at the lower levels. This led to good policies being carried out only with some reservations or not being implemented properly. The culture of the guerrilla party weighed on the nature of administration, meaning that rules and systems were not fully systematized. A well-functioning, lean administrative system was viewed as essential to effective promotion of the War of Resistance. Well-educated and competent senior officials were to be transferred to work at lower levels. Later this would become a common Maoist practice. Military officials deemed to be surplus were transferred to engage in production as part of the attempts to achieve self-sufficiency. Central government officials who were deemed superfluous were sent for education, while those at the lower levels were to work in production. Reducing the numbers did not prove simple; in December 1941 there had been 7,900 officials working in the government at all levels, but this number had risen to 8,200 by early 1943.[28] The number of officials, students, and others consuming "government grain" without engaging in production placed further pressures on the economy.

Before 1942 Mao Zedong had not presented his views on the economy, but economic pressures required that he present a clear strategy. The production campaign began together with a more moderate economic policy, as it became clear that private enterprises and more productive peasants were necessary. Turning to the private sector for help when the economy faced problems has been a common tactic for the CCP. Once the economy revives, preference is again given to the collective and state sectors. The more relaxed economic policy contrasted sharply with the harsher climate for party members once the Rectification Campaign began in earnest in 1942. The move to unify the party under Mao's leadership and Mao Zedong Thought was not meant to spill over and hurt the economy.

On January 28, 1942, the Politburo issued a decision on land policy that was intended to have a broad appeal to all classes.[29] The peasants were described as the "basic strength" of the resistance, most landlords were described as anti-Japanese, and even some members of the gentry were thought to be sufficiently enlightened to be in favor of democratic reforms. Landlords were guaranteed any outstanding money once rent and interest reductions had been completed. The capitalist mode of production was given a positive vote as "the most progressive method" in China, and the bourgeoisie, especially the petty and national bourgeoisie, were viewed as relatively progressive. This decision provided something for everyone in the border region.

In December 1942 Mao Zedong presented the leadership's thinking about economic policy to a conference of senior officials of the Northeast Bureau; the conference ran from October 1942 into January 1943.[30] The report pulled together the experiences in economic work and how policy might deal with the economic stresses faced by the border region. The proposals followed the approach of the January 1942 decision to engage as broad a coalition as possible to develop the economy. Improving living standards was crucial to retaining support, and in turn this would help with the War of Resistance. Although this was not stated, the view was that, over the longer term, policy would tie the fate of the local elite and the general population to that of the CCP, and this might encourage them to fight harder to defend themselves against the GMD.

The private sector, agriculture, handicrafts, and commercial businesses were essential to improving living standards and moving the economy. Rich peasants were encouraged by the criticism of previous leftist deviations, so that this crucial group could produce without fear of being labeled enemies. Productivity was vital, thus a certain level of exploitation was acceptable in the mixed economy. To improve efficiency, mutual-aid teams were promoted to help with contracting and labor exchange. As with the initial policy after 1949, these mutual-aid teams built on traditional patterns of cooperation, such as the pooling of labor for planting and the gathering of crops at harvest time. Participation was voluntary, but the party clearly sought to encourage this and to develop the teams as longer-term solutions to inefficiencies.

Peng Zhen's September 1941 report had highlighted this approach. For Peng, the experience of the Shanxi-Chahar-Hebei Border Region revealed that the only correct policy was to unleash the initiative and spontaneity of small producers and entrepreneurs. There had to be tangible benefits to keep all onboard. Peng noted, "If it gives milk, it is mother." Private management was at the core, and except for the armaments industry, state-owned industry would play only a very small role. Peng ridiculed the idea that Soviet-style planning was appropriate in the border region, and he claimed that building a large number of state-owned enterprises was akin to building a "skyscraper on shifting sands" or "painting a cake to prevent hunger." He did, however, agree with Mao on the role of the collectives, which he described as an "economic pillar" to "smash the manipulation of speculative merchants." This would ensure party control.

Thus, to help ensure that the market would function efficiently, consumer and producer cooperatives were promoted. The model Mao Zedong proposed was the Southern District Cooperative, which was owned and controlled by peasant shareholders. This allowed the cooperatives to serve as a go-between for the government and the peasants, and it would ensure that the peasants implemented government policy. The last crucial plank of economic policy was the demand that party, army, and government agencies become as self-sufficient as feasible through their operation of agricultural, industrial, and commercial undertakings. Mao indicated that the best exemplars of this were the army, and in particular the 359th Brigade under Wang Zhen, who would later become vice president of China, and Nanniwan Farm, south of Yan'an. With agriculture as its base, the farm had diversified to develop industry, handicrafts, transport, and commercial outlets.

The drive improved the economic situation, but in 1943 the budget deficit was only reduced by 20 percent. What helped resolve the problem was the production of opium and its export from the border region.[31] However, the party was strict in controlling its use within the border region and did abandon production once the crisis had passed. Opium production was seen as a necessary evil to help the border region and the revolution survive. Perhaps not surprisingly, one of the principal investors was none other than Wang Zhen's model 359th Brigade.[32] In terms of finances, in 1943 the official deficit would have been twice as large without the opium revenue. For 1944 and 1945, when opium revenue is included, the deficits turned into account surpluses. Even as early as 1942, profits from opium production constituted 40.9 percent of revenue. Thus, beyond the mythic stories of the Yan'an spirit, there is a hard, cold reality that whatever was necessary would be done to ensure survival.

Unifying the Party under Mao Zedong

The third challenge was to build a coherent party uniting the heterodox elements who had come to the border region. This process was intimately bound to Mao Zedong's consolidation of power as the undisputed leader of the CCP. It did not simply entail the removal of other contenders for power—Zhang Guotao had already been expelled from the party, and Wang Ming's influence had been reduced. Building allegiance to Mao required accepting a party history that placed Mao at its core. Once rival narratives had been squashed, getting Mao's worldview accepted was relatively easy, as the "storm membership drives" meant that over 90 percent of party members were new recruits. Among these, maybe two-thirds were illiterate; the others were well-educated. The illiterate would acquire literacy by learning the correct history. All would have been ignorant about the struggles that had taken place through the 1920s and the 1930s. The outcome was the Sinification of Marxism, which marked the end of the legacy of the May Fourth intellectual trends within the party. Those who joined the party had to be brought to heel.

The new orthodoxy situated Mao as the central player in the Chinese revolution, which in turn put him in an unchallengeable position of leadership. Seen as having correctly analyzed the past, he would be given authority to make the correct decisions for the present and the future. In this endeavor, he was supported enthusiastically by other key leaders. Having allied with Zhang Wentian to overcome Bo Gu, the returned students, and Wang Jiaxiang, to hammer the final nail in Wang Ming's political coffin, he found enthusiastic support from Liu Shaoqi to confirm his preeminence. For his supporters, Mao Zedong Thought was a collective endeavor rather than the ideas of a single individual. Mao clearly did not share this view, but after his death the collective nature of the ideology was stressed to prevent de-Maoification, akin to de-Stalinization, which could undermine party legitimacy. Mao was both the Lenin and the Stalin of the CCP, and thus there was no one else to fall back on.

To meet this objective, Yan'an became a study community, in which forty-four educational institutions were established. This amazed the resident Comintern representative, Vladimirov, who was perplexed by the intensity of the Rectification Campaign during the height of military conflict and economic hardship.[33] The study movement was to bring unity not only to those in the Shaanxi-Gansu-Ningxia Border Region but ultimately across all the Communist-held areas. It was a process of peaceful proselytizing that also contained a hard edge—those who did not accept the new narrative would be subjected to harsh struggle to bring them into line, in a process of criticism and self-criticism that would become a hallmark of CCP politics.

To start the movement, Mao Zedong and his supporters were more explicit in their criticism of the supposed leftist line of the early 1930s. This attack was directed against Wang Ming and the returned students to ensure that ideology as a guide to action was based firmly on Chinese realities rather than on the notebooks of Marx and Lenin or decisions made in Moscow. Who better to formulate this ideology than the person who had never set foot outside the country but had spent the last twenty years fighting for the revolution in the Chinese countryside? On the day before his birthday, December 25, 1940, Mao criticized the early policy approach in Jiangxi as "all struggle and no alliance." Of course, this assessment was made at a time when policy in Shaanxi-Gansu-Ningxia was moderating. Policy toward the landlords, rich peasants, and capitalists had been misguided, power had been unduly monopolized, and intellectuals had been attacked. This latter point was a bit ironic, given what was about to happen to independent, critical intellectuals in Yan'an.[34] "Intellectual" is a term frequently used by the CCP. In reality, there were very few in Yan'an who could be considered genuine intellectuals.

Presenting Wang Ming's position as a mistake of line faced opposition and spurred Mao to launch a program of study for senior officials based on a carefully chosen collection of party documents and speeches. In May 1941 Mao told senior officials that the party still suffered from "very great shortcomings" that had to be dealt with, requiring the study of current affairs, history, and the practical application of Marxism-Leninism in revolutionary work.[35] Practical application of ideology posed the greatest challenge, especially for the returned students and middle and senior officials, because they might interpret work subjectively. There was continued opposition to revising historical judgments, which delayed publication of the speech until March 27, 1942.

However, a process had been set in motion. To commemorate the founding of the CCP, on July 1, 1941, the CC called for strengthening, unifying, and centralizing the party to overcome fragmentation when the Center met resistance and personal loyalties remained strong. This caused the "development of a petty bourgeois individualistic ideology." Without discipline, victory could not be obtained, and decisions and resolutions had to be implemented properly, in a timely manner.

The Rectification Campaign that followed would change the party forever. Normally dated as beginning in February 1942 with a major speech by Mao, an enlarged meeting of the Politburo that began on September 10, 1941, introduced the rolling momentum. The meeting began with detailed discussions about how to link Marxism-Leninism with the Chinese situation and how to correctly interpret party history for the period 1927–1937. In Mao's view, although corrections were made at Zunyi in January 1935, subjectivism in ideological work had persisted. For Mao, three factors caused this subjectivism: leftism in the Chinese tradition;[36] the influence of foreign traditions from Russians, such as Bukharin and Zinoviev; and the petty bourgeois nature of China. Looking ahead, it was necessary to recognize the seriousness of the problem, clarify the differences between genuine Marxism and dogmatic Marxism, expose those whose theory was divorced from practice, and deal with sectarianism. Tightening the noose around Mao's opponents, the meeting made two decisions concerning the early 1930s, even though they were not publicized at the time. First, from the Fourth Plenum of January 1931 until September 1931, serious mistakes had been made, but the political line was basically correct. Second, from September 18, 1931, until the Zunyi conference, the line pursued by the Party Center was incorrect, but this was corrected after the Zunyi meeting. The Fourth Plenum was not yet criticized directly, but this would come in 1945, when a formal resolution on party history was adopted.

The broadening of the campaign was signaled by two major speeches by Mao Zedong, on February 1 and 8. The speeches outlined the three problems within the party—subjectivism, sectarianism, and formalism.[37] Mao's target was two problematic groups in Yan'an—the returned students, who had remained faithful to Wang Ming, and the group of intellectuals who had come to Yan'an but had not been engaged in the party's revolutionary struggle. The campaign would instill Mao's vision as that of the party as a whole and would end intellectual diversity within the movement. The role of party intellectuals was made clear: they were not to provide an independent critique of policy and practice; instead they were to serve as cheerleaders for the party, faithfully proselytizing its views.

Mao had developed a great ability as a storyteller, and many who had been in Yan'an felt that his speeches encapsulated their own individual experiences and placed them in a broader, more meaningful context. Those in Yan'an felt they were riding an important wave of history. The stories Mao told nested inside one another. There was the story of the long arc, which was the loss of sovereignty at the hands of the imperialists after the Opium Wars, and the exploitation of the peasantry through the feudal system. The intermediate story told party members of the chaos that followed and focused on who would be the rightful inheritor of Sun Yat-sen's legacy: Mao Zedong or Chiang Kai-shek. It narrowed down to the immediate struggle within the CCP over what was the correct political line. This brought the grand scheme of history down to Yan'an and the centrality of Mao.[38] Mao rendered the big picture specific: "In virtually every essay, Mao deals in some fashion with large themes in the context of specific events. He is good at making connections between abstract thought and empirical knowledge. . . . Mao had an extraordinary ability to think on several levels at once, and could grasp the central issues and the large concern."[39]

The two February speeches attacked dogmatism and sectarianism, respectively. On February 1, Mao criticized Wang Ming indirectly, noting that it would be irresponsible to call oneself a Marxist if one had only studied the Marxist classics and had not used them to understand the concrete realities of China. This speech contained Mao's famous sentence

"The arrow of Marxism-Leninism must be used to hit the target of the Chinese revolution."

On February 8 the attack on Wang Ming became even clearer as Mao dealt with the challenge of formalism as a consequence of subjectivism and sectarianism. Especially pernicious was foreign formalism—that is, recycling foreign tracts—and despite calls for its eradication at the Sixth Plenum in 1938, "some comrades" were still advocating both "foreign formalism" and "dogmatism." No naming of names yet, but no prizes for guessing the target.

Mao attacked anyone who placed their individual interests above those of the party, of course as defined by Mao. Instead, it was vital that personal interests were subjugated to the interests of the party to ensure unity of action. For Mao, the party needed democracy but centralism was even more important. However, Mao was careful to make sure that the movement did not slip out of his control, leading to the kind of party fratricide that had occurred earlier. In another analogy that would become a key component of Maoism, although often breached, the process was to be like a doctor curing a disease. The intention was not to let the patient die but instead to cure the symptoms to allow the party member to continue to work as a good and faithful comrade.

The details for the study process were impressive, with a General Committee, headed by Mao and with Kang Sheng as his deputy, guiding and overseeing groups in each department and workplace. Work hours were reduced, with mornings in Yan'an set aside for study. Kang's appointment formed the link to what would become the Rescue Campaign. Dressed in his austere black garb with his black Alsatian dog and riding a black horse throughout Yan'an, Kang oversaw secret-service operations, but now he was also in charge of the daily operations of the study program. He liked to pursue guilt by association and declared that leniency had its limits. In August 1941 Kang had been appointed head of the Cadre Investigation Commission, which vetted political attitudes. With Kang involved in rectification and cadre investigation, the two movements would be brought together in the 1943 Rescue Campaign.

An End to Independent Intellectual Inquiry

A key element of party consolidation was to outline the correct role for intellectuals who were party members. Mao outlined the principles in May 1942, and they have remained constant to the present day. He was responding to

the independence of some, and the critical thinking that was imbued with
the ideals and cosmopolitanism of the May Fourth Movement of 1915–1919.
Many intellectuals clearly misinterpreted the purpose of rectification and
took it as an opportunity to criticize the inequalities and unfairness they had
observed in Yan'an. They would not be the last to misunderstand the limits
of tolerance that the party was willing to permit.

The writer Ding Ling incurred Mao's wrath for criticizing male sexism
in the border region, for which she was dismissed from her position as
editor of the arts column of the CCP's main newspaper, *Liberation Daily*.
Ai Qing made his famous comment that he could not describe "ringworms
as flowers." Ding Ling's fellow editor of the art column, Liu Xuewei, wrote
about how coarse, dull, and inferior revolutionary literature was. Freedom
of thought should be the basis of "New Democracy." But the main focus of
CCP criticism was reserved for Wang Shiwei, who exposed what he
viewed as the problems with the ruling elite in Yan'an. He was especially
vexed by the inequalities perpetuated by the Yan'an leadership, which were
diminishing the enthusiasm of youth in the border region.[40] Wang Shiwei
was committed to the CCP's drive for national salvation and felt that exposing the defects would help the Rectification Movement. But like the
others, he wanted more independence and the ability to criticize abuses of
power.

Although Wang believed the world of Yan'an was superior to the world
outside of it, he believed that this should not be used as an excuse to prevent
criticism. He was especially vexed by the system of rankings that divided
clothing into three grades and food into five. This created resentment as well
as embedded inequalities, as those more senior had better access not only to
material goods but also to gossip and secrets about what was happening in
border region politics. Wang called for the leaders to share the day-to-day
life and tribulations of the ordinary folk as this would create an "iron-like
unity" and a more "profound love."

As would happen again in the mid-1950s and subsequently, these intellectuals were looking for more openness than the party leadership was willing
to allow. With these writers' views appearing in the flagship newspaper and
on posters, they had to be nipped in the bud before such ideas spread beyond the border region. The party apparatus swiftly turned its fire on the
intellectuals, attacking their petty bourgeois mentality; with the notable
exception of Wang Shiwei, most recanted. Colleagues Ding Ling and Ai
Qing even denounced Wang Shiwei during his subsequent interrogation.

Despite this, Wang Shiwei's influence ran deep, and in April 1945 Mao Zedong admitted that he projected a powerful voice in Yan'an.

Putting an end to Wang Shiwei's influence entailed a twofold process, the methods of which would become a common part of Maoist political practice. The first step was to clearly establish the correct relationship of art and literature to political power. The second was to break Wang Shiwei and turn his supporters against him. Mao outlined the correct role for art and literature in the revolution in his two speeches to the Yan'an Forum on Literature and Art on May 2 and 23, 1942.[41] Literature and art could not exist independently of politics, and the idea of art for art's sake that could transcend class or party was a fantasy. There was no such thing as abstract love, freedom, truth, or human nature, and literature and art had to serve the revolutionary tasks as established by the party. Those who believed otherwise suffered from bourgeois influences, and all art forms belonged to particular classes at a particular time. Far from obscuring class differences by concentrating on supposed universal qualities, literature should reflect class differences. Thus, CCP literature and art was to be primarily for the workers, peasants, and soldiers, and only secondarily for the petty bourgeoisie. Works should attest to the glory of the border region and not expose its darker sides. Any shortcomings would be dealt with by the party itself. Fire should be directed at the Japanese and the areas under GMD control. Given the mass line that linked the masses to the leadership, any attack on the party elite was an attack on the masses. There was no way that Mao would cede to the artists and Wang Shiwei the right to look after the revolution's soul while the politicians looked after the material needs and wants. More than three decades later, reflecting on his role in the attacks on Wang Shiwei, journalist Wen Jize stated, "It is possible that Wang Shiwei spoke the truth, but to speak the truth at that time was not helpful to the Communist Party."[42] Seventy years later General Secretary Xi Jinping confirmed the correctness of Mao's view, and stated that his approach still guided policy toward literature and the arts.

The second step was to launch struggle sessions to discredit Wang Shiwei and destroy his credibility in what would become the prototype for criticism of intellectuals. Once private attempts to rein in Wang failed, a public criticism session began, lasting from May 27 until June 11, 1942. The process of struggle was described in articles in *Liberation Daily* published on June 28 and 29, indicating that the party saw this as an ideal process.[43] Many of Wang's former colleagues confessed that they had exhibited an extreme democratic attitude, which required self-criticism. If they thought this would convince Wang to return to the correct path, they were mistaken. Wang was accused of being anti-party and holding the views of a Trotskyite. Further, Wang thought that Stalin was not "lovable," that the Comintern was responsible for the failure of 1927, and that the accusation that Zinoviev, former head of the Comintern who was executed in 1936 at Stalin's behest, was a traitor should be taken with a pinch of salt. Clearly, these were serious crimes. Wang was said to have slandered party leaders by leveling accusations of corruption against them, disrupting party unity.

Wang's mistakes were deemed not only ideological but also political. His final humiliation came when his former colleague, Ding Ling, emerged to criticize him: "We tried everything to pull him out of his latrine but he wanted to drag us down with him. . . . Wang Shiwei has one last chance to climb out of his counter-revolutionary latrine."[44]

His former colleagues demanded that he be expelled from the party, and he was expelled. The warnings about the limits to intellectual independence were clear, and liberalism was to be totally and resolutely opposed. The coup de grâce was delivered in a stinging attack by Mao Zedong's close associate and secretary, Chen Boda. It was not enough to criticize contemporary views; one also had to show that evil intent had always been present. This form of attack would be a feature of future campaigns in the People's Republic of China, and Chen Boda would be a major activist during the Cultural Revolution. He again made the link to the Trotskyites, claiming that it was a strain that was "anti-masses, anti-nation, counterrevolutionary, and anti-Marxist, and one which serves the ruling class, the Japanese imperialists, and the international fascists." Personally, Wang was as "great as a 'leech,'" which hides in the water with the intention to get into their skin and suck their blood." In his finishing blow, Chen Boda declared that "sometimes, such insects grow out of the 'Wild Lily.'"[45]

All Hail to the Chief: The Seventh Party Congress

With the ground carefully laid, the party leadership rallied around Mao's supremacy atop the hierarchy. This rallying process began with expressions of loyalty in the form of personal confessions about previous mistakes, stressing the wisdom and correct line of Mao Zedong as opposed to those of Li Lisan and Wang Ming. This included Zhou Enlai, who declared that Mao was the first to recognize the revolution as a revolutionary peasant movement. The fact that the party had not followed Mao's views at the Sixth Party Congress was its "misfortune."[46]

The big prize was acceptance of Mao's rectitude by Bo Gu and Wang Ming. It was more easily obtained from the former than from the latter. Bo Gu folded at a Politburo meeting on November 13, 1943, acknowledging his erroneous military plans for the Long March. He did not acknowledge a political line mistake, but he accepted that Mao had saved the movement at Zunyi in January 1935. At the Seventh Party Congress, in 1945, Bo Gu went further, claiming that Mao's two pet peeves—dogmatism and sectarianism—had come together at the time of the Fourth Plenum. Of course, this was precisely the time when Bo Gu and Wang Ming had consolidated their power. Contrary to his previous mea culpa, Bo Gu now stated that he did not realize his mistakes at the Zunyi meeting and he had persisted in following a mistaken line until the end of the year.

Wang Ming was a tougher nut to crack, and by his own account he never accepted the party history according to the words of Chairman Mao.[47] Yet he did write a letter accepting the Maoist resolution on party history in which he had recognized errors and admitted that his classic work *The Struggle for the Further Bolshevization of the Party* contained leftist errors.[48] Later he dismissed this confession as a tactical move he made so that he could live to fight Mao another day. That day would never come, and he lived out his days in the Soviet Union, writing tracts criticizing Mao, his deviations, and his dominance of the party.[49]

To reinforce obedience in the party at large, Kang Sheng, ably supported by Chen Boda, oversaw the Rescue Campaign. People would be arrested and interrogated for having uttered casual phrases and mere suggestions. The presumption was guilt before innocence. Many of those who had come from the outside were presumed to be GMD spies. One interviewee told me, "So many were arrested that the caves could not hold them all."[50] The objective was to root out these spies and to rescue those who had strayed from the correct line by having them confess their sins. Before the campaign could proceed too far in setting Communist against Communist, Mao reined it in, but it did preview the kind of attacks that would become a feature of post-1949 Maoist political practice. At the time, those under investigation did not immediately see the implications. Speaking with Li Rui, who was arrested during the campaign and would later be a secretary to Mao and even later a bitter critic, saw it as fully justified. He noted that the party was at war and there were indeed spies at work in Yan'an. The fact that Li Rui was released after investigation revealed to him that the process was fair.[51] However, for others the campaign came as a shock, and in hindsight they saw it as a dress rehearsal for the Cultural Revolution.

For Kang Sheng, rectification had exposed counterrevolutionaries, such as Wang Shiwei, nestling within the party and refusing to recant. Kang saw rectification as "curing the sickness to save the patient." The act of repentance allowed the cleansing of the soul, and the catharsis prevented one from being "cheated into serving the enemy." Confession allowed the slate to be wiped clean and the party could rejoice in another soul saved. Yet there was also a warning, as Kang stated that for those who did not confess, there was a limit to leniency.[52]

The new orthodoxy was explained to the party leadership at the Northwest Bureau Conference, then to the broader ranks of the party at two important party meetings spanning May 1944 to April 1945, and then codified with the adoption of the "Resolution on Party History." In addressing the conference, Gao Gang outlined an analysis of the history of the border region in the same terms as Mao's critique of Wang Ming. Gao claimed that the former leaders of the border region had committed left deviation errors before 1935 and then right opportunism after the united front policies were adopted. This analysis would be expanded to party history as a whole in the "Resolution on Party History."[53]

The pressure continued with the strengthening of the centralized party leadership at the Politburo meeting of March 16–20. The Secretariat was subordinated to the Politburo, which was to lead party work when the CC was not in session. However, the Secretariat was to carry out the day-to-day work of the Politburo and could make decisions on problems that might arise, as long as their decisions did not run counter to Politburo policy. Mao Zedong was to chair the Secretariat, with Liu Shaoqi as one of the members. The chair was granted final decision-making power on items discussed; Mao was also appointed chair of the Politburo. His and his supporters' power was enhanced further by the formation of a Propaganda Committee, with Mao as secretary, and an Organization Committee, headed by Liu Shaoqi. The committees were stacked with Mao supporters, with the one exception of Bo Gu, but he had already recanted. Organizationally, Mao was now in a very powerful position, enjoying the backing of the Northwest Party apparatus and the party's white areas, as represented by the prominence of Liu Shaoqi and Ren Bishi.

Many accepted Mao's ascendancy as a necessary counterweight to the promotion of Chiang Kai-shek as the Nationalist leader, and it was eased by the abolition of the Comintern in May 1943. Stalin made this decision as a conciliatory gesture to his allies in the fight against fascism, but for the CCP it clearly marked its independence. This did not mean that Soviet support and advice could be ignored, and direct Soviet influence would not be truly eradicated until the end of the CCP's first decade in power. Nevertheless, abolition of the Comintern did nothing to harm Mao's dominance within the CCP.

The decision to dissolve the Comintern undercut any last hope that Wang Ming might have had of challenging Mao. It will come as no surprise that the dissolution was welcomed, allowing local Communist parties to have a stronger national character. A leading center was deemed unnecessary, and in any case on May 26 the CC claimed that the Comintern had not interfered in the domestic affairs of the CCP since 1935, basically since the Zunyi Conference. The CCP could now focus more firmly on its target—the Chinese revolution. There were ramifications. Some asked why China needed a Communist Party if there was no longer a Comintern. By February 1943 the German attack on the Soviet Union had been repulsed and the view grew that the war would eventually be won by the Allies. This would be significant for the Pacific War generally and the war in China more specifically. The key question became who would rule a postwar China: Chiang Kai-shek with his *China's Destiny* (published March 10, 1943)? Or Mao Zedong and the Communists? Or some combination of both?

The buildup to what became the cult of Mao began in earnest on the twenty-second anniversary of the founding of the CCP and it was championed in a glowing article written by Liu Shaoqi—which was sad, given that he would be the highest-profile victim of the Mao cult during the Cultural Revolution. Liu slammed the "false Marxists" and tied this to the tendency to only "learn the lessons of the revolutionary experience of comparatively distant foreign countries." The list was long, including Chen Duxiu and the Chinese Trotskyites, followers of the Li Lisan line and the left opportunism of the civil war period, and dogmatism—although no names were mentioned, it was clear who was being referred to. Instead of these erroneous tendencies, the focus should be on China's own revolutionary experiences, so ably guided by Mao Zedong. All members had to understand the history of the two-line struggles within the party, and all had to "diligently study and master Comrade Mao Zedong's doctrines of the Chinese revolution and other subjects. They should arm themselves with Comrade Mao Zedong's thought and use Mao Zedong's system of thought to liquidate Menshevik thought in the party."[54]

Spanning eight meetings, from May 21, 1944, to April 20, 1945, the Seventh Plenum of the Sixth CC laid the groundwork for the Seventh Party Congress and adopted two key resolutions. The first recognized that the core of the revolution might shift back to the urban areas, and the second was the long-prepared resolution on party history.[55] On June 5, 1944, the CC established a fourteen-person urban work committee, instructing it to take over leadership in the large cities and along communication lines to expel the Japanese. This work was to link the base areas to the urban masses preparing for armed insurrection. By the end of 1944 or early 1945, "outstanding achievements" were expected. In September 1944, work in the urban areas was placed on an equal footing with that in the border regions, with urban work departments established at all levels above the local party committees. Despite its years in the rural wilderness, the party had not forgotten its proletarian roots.

The "Resolution on Party History," published on April 20, 1945, finally named names and clearly laid out the Maoist party history. It covered only the period up until the Zunyi meeting, identifying three left lines between 1927 and the Zunyi meeting, with a heavy emphasis on the third such line that was in operation from the Fourth Plenum (January 1931) and reached a peak at the Fifth Plenum (January 1934). The resolution noted: "During the withdrawal from Jiangxi and during the Long March the error of flightism was committed under the 'left' line. The leaders of this 'left' line were the two dogmatists, Comrades Wang Ming and Bo Gu."[56] In a clear sign of his capitulation, Bo Gu was even a member of the drafting committee, while Wang Ming, who was sick, just sent a letter of approval. The two were accused of underestimating the role of the peasantry and ranking attacks on the bourgeoisie, including the petty bourgeoisie, on the same level as the struggle against imperialism and feudalism. The military line was criticized for its focus on positional warfare rather than guerrilla warfare. For the political future, the resolution cemented the relationship between Mao Zedong and Liu Shaoqi, who had made similar criticisms some eight years earlier concerning work in the white areas. Liu would become Mao's biggest cheerleader. The groundwork was prepared for approval by a full party congress. In 1951 an official history was published for the consumption of the population at large.

The increasing realization that the Allies would win the war also formed the background to the Seventh Party Congress, which ran from April 23, 1945, into June of that month. The savage Operation Ichigo launched by the Japanese in April 1944 in a desperate attempt to clear a land route from Korea all the way south to Hanoi, had exhausted Japanese capacity by the end of the year. The Japanese troops were increasingly distracted by their need to deploy forces elsewhere in the Pacific to counter the US troop advance. In the West, Italy was already out of the war and Germany, despite fierce resistance, was in retreat. Could a coalition between the GMD and the CCP really come about? Or would they talk while also preparing for civil war?

As early as January 1944 Mao Zedong suggested resuming talks between the CCP and the GMD. In May there were meaningful contacts in Xi'an, but they faltered over a range of disagreements. The possibility of collapse alarmed the United States, and it persuaded Chiang Kai-shek to allow an observers' group, the "Dixie mission," to visit Yan'an. The mission's charge was to review the possibility of coordinating military activities, and on the whole the mission was impressed with what it saw in Yan'an. This positive view starkly contrasted with some CCP members' critical views on the corruption and inefficiencies in the GMD areas.

The CCP certainly saw the value of making a good impression, and in August 1944 it sent a directive on how to deal with diplomatic work. This directive lies at the heart of its international united front work that has since remained reasonably constant for those times when China is seeking to engage in a broader coalition. The directive acknowledged that because of the party's relative isolation, diplomacy was the least developed area of work. The domestic united front of the previous eight years was evaluated positively, leading the party to see even greater benefits in a successful international united front. Military cooperation would lead to cultural and finally political and economic cooperation. To present a positive contrast to the GMD-controlled areas, reports and dispatches were not to be censored or seized. With respect to religion, the separation of church and state was to be observed, if the priests did not oppose CCP leadership. "National self-respect and self-confidence" were to be strengthened but not to the extent of encouraging xenophobia and keeping out foreigners. The directive stated clearly that anything revealed should be true, while "things that cannot be revealed should be concealed. We should refuse to respond to or provide things that concern state secrets and inner-party secrets. Things that are not convenient to answer should be avoided or evaded."

Finally, any activities or discussions with foreigners could only proceed after the CC had approved.[57]

President Roosevelt sent General Patrick J. Hurley as his personal envoy to breathe life into the negotiations between the GMD and the CCP. While visiting Yan'an, Hurley on November 10 signed an agreement with Mao Zedong that he hoped would be supported by the GMD. The GMD did not sign, and on November 22 the GMD issued its own three-point agreement. If nothing else, the two documents clarified differences between the GMD and the CCP. The CCP proposed a coalition government composed of a broad base of all anti-Japanese parties and organizations, with the same being true for the reorganization of the Military Council. The CCP requested that the GMD recognize it as an equal. This was totally unacceptable to the GMD, calling for the CCP to be subjugated to the GMD, with its troops under the National Government controlled by the Military Council.

Despite the seeming impasse, on February 3, 1945, Zhou Enlai reached an agreement to convene a political consultative conference to discuss establishing a constitutional government, develop a common political program, unify military forces, and set up a system for other parties to join the National Government. Yet both sides remained suspicious of each other, and before Zhou left Chongqing, on February 15, he stated that he did not want to place CCP troops under effective GMD control through the Military Council nor did he accept the one-party dictatorship of the GMD, stressing that a coalition administration should be formed as a precursor to a democratic government. Chiang welcomed the CCP and other parties to participate in the National Government, but made it clear that ultimate decision-making power would reside with the GMD until a people's congress had been convened to launch a constitutional government. The CCP saw this simply as a way to perpetuate GMD rule. Considering their recently revived interest in international work, Zhou Enlai proposed, together with Dong Biwu, who had attended the First Party Congress, and Bo Gu, that they attend the San Francisco Conference in April so that China's views would not be expressed solely by the GMD. Dong Biwu did attend the conference, Zhou did not.

The Seventh Party Congress was held against the background of Mao's supremacy in the CCP and rivalry for postwar leadership. Mao's two reports to the congress displayed different messages for different audiences. The public report, "On Coalition Government," sought to bring together representatives of all groups and parties to set up a provisional coalition govern-

*Mao's supremacy within the CCP was evident at the Seventh Party
Congress, in Yan'an, 1945.*

ment. This would be followed by convocation of a national assembly and a
democratic coalition government. Mao rejected the GMD plan to first convene a national assembly as simply a ruse to maintain its power. The report
was intended to undermine the legitimacy of the GMD by attacking its conduct during the war and its pattern of rule in the areas under its control.
Mao contrasted this with rule in the Communist-held areas. For the future,
he proposed at a minimum a program of New Democracy as conditions did
not yet exist for socialism. Although socialism and communism would be
far in the future, this new democratic state would be led by the working class.
On the whole, moderation was the name of the game as reflected in the moderate land policy. Sun Yat-sen's policy of giving land to the tillers was put on
a back burner, and to keep the landlords on the side of the CCP, policy was
to practice only reductions in rent and interest.[58]

For the party faithful, Mao drew a tougher line.[59] He recognized that even
though GMD power might be waning, in certain respects, especially in international affairs, the GMD was more influential than the CCP. The program of New Democracy would enhance CCP prestige at the expense of the
GMD and would portray the CCP as the true inheritor of Sun Yat-sen's
legacy. By not mentioning communism in the public report, Mao hoped to
avoid attracting unwarranted and harmful criticism. Although Mao criticized the CCP for forgetting the peasantry in 1927, he stressed that it was
still a proletarian party and that it would not be Marxist to sit in the villages and simply rely on the peasantry. The cities were to become the center
of activity, and the party would commit a large force to develop work there.

The new statutes, the first since 1928, adopted by the congress displayed the preeminence of Mao Zedong, as did Liu Shaoqi's report on the changes in the statutes.[60] The statutes included Mao Zedong's ideas among the guiding principles for party work, together with Marxism-Leninism. Liu praised Mao's thought as the "most important historical characteristic of our current revision"; it was "communism and Marxism" as applied to China. Claiming a wider applicability, Liu stated that it was the "development of Marxism with respect to the national-democratic revolution in the colonial, semi-colonial and semi-feudal countries of the present period." Mao was clearly the worthy successor to Lenin! If this was not enough praise, Liu claimed that "our Comrade Mao Zedong is not only the greatest revolutionary and statesman in Chinese history but also the greatest theoretician and scientist." Mao's thoughts and speeches were turned into volumes of selected works to become required reading for all party members.

By mid-1945 the CCP had built the foundations for a strong, centralized, unified party focused around the ideas and persona of Mao Zedong. The Rectification Campaign had inculcated these values, with punishment in the Rescue Campaign for those who resisted. Abstract theory from abroad was now rendered in a form that seemed applicable to Chinese conditions to provide a guide to action for party members scattered across a range of environments. Mao had unprecedented power—this was beneficial for the next stage of the struggle, but it would come back to haunt the party once it took power. The party seemed well equipped to deal with the peace that was expected to follow the war. However, that they would win victory during the civil war that soon followed appeared far from certain.

The Slide into Civil War

Anyone looking at the situation in 1945 would have been amazed to discover that the GMD squandered its advantages and the seemingly weak CCP emerged victorious. Further, the GMD had the benefit of a set of external relationships with the United States and initially even with the Soviet Union, whereas the CCP was on the back foot seeking to emerge from its mountain strongholds and urban hiding places. However, the GMD had been brutalized by the War of Resistance, and its prewar elite had divided over resistance, accommodation, or appeasement to the Japanese invaders. Subsequently these divides were difficult to bridge. The civil war contained two stories: First, how did the decisions taken by the GMD leadership undermine its seeming advantages? Second, how did the CCP retain sufficient support to survive the GMD attacks and then grow in strength to launch its own offensives as the GMD weakened?[61] Some writers have focused on the degradation of the GMD's institutions and the toll the war had taken, which made it incapable of embarking on postwar reconstruction.[62] But it was still the GMD's victory to lose, and with a series of grave errors it frittered away its chances for victory. In addition, the CCP, which had shrewdly protected its resources during the war, was able to exploit the Japanese defeat and withdrawal to expand its influence, first in Northeast China and then throughout the North.[63]

As World War II drew to a close, the interests of the United States and the Soviet Union coincided to try to bring about cooperation between the CCP and the GMD. Concerted efforts were made and agreements were even reached, but the decades of mistrust meant that the CCP and GMD, although negotiating publicly, were both engaged in trying to gain territory on the ground and undermine the other. As a result of the Yalta Conference, held on February 4–11, 1945, the Soviet Union made a secret agreement to join the war against Japan two months after the German surrender. This would give the Soviets the dominant position in Manchuria, a development that would be crucial to a CCP victory. Just two days after the United States dropped the atomic bomb on Hiroshima, the Soviets declared war on Japan, and on August 10 the Japanese indicated their willingness to surrender. This marked the onset of the fight for control of China's Northeast.

The Soviets' first move was to conclude a Sino-Soviet Treaty with the Nationalists, on August 14. At that time Soviet interests coincided with those of the United States as both sought to broker a peace between the two sides, resulting in Chiang Kai-shek's invitation to Mao Zedong to go to Chongqing for discussions. Mao remained in Chongqing for almost two months. Despite the negotiations, the CCP responded to the dramatically changed circumstances by calling for the concentration of troops to force the surrender of the Japanese armies—or to wipe them out if they resisted. At the same time, both large and small towns and communication lines were to be seized. Subsequently CCP troops were to brace themselves for a GMD assault and thus mobilize to deal with a potential civil war. Publicly they moderated their criticism of Chiang and the United States. The leadership recognized that the struggle was shifting to the urban areas, and it again called for a significant number of CCP officials to move to the cities.

Stalin's primary motive was to ensure that sooner rather than later US troops would vacate China and Korea, and this would be more likely if the

CCP and GMD could reach an accommodation. The Sino-Soviet Treaty recognized Chiang Kai-shek as the leader of China, proposed joint Sino-Soviet control of the Chinese Eastern Railway, with eventual return of the railway to Chinese ownership, and independence for Outer Mongolia following a referendum. Soviet Russia was expected to stop aiding the CCP. Protocols to the treaty allowed the Soviets to keep a naval base at Port Arthur (Lüshun) for thirty years and to control the port at Dalian. With respect to the crucial area of Manchuria, the Soviets agreed to pull out their troops three months after the Japanese surrender (mid-November), but they did not actually leave until May 1946. While Nationalist troops raced to control the Northeast, aided by the United States, the extra time gave the CCP an opportunity to infiltrate farther into the region.

Stalin did not want to risk these potential gains should civil war break out, especially because the GMD appeared to be the dominant force. Indeed, once civil war did commence in the second half of 1946, the CCP lost about half of the territory it controlled. Unintentionally, Stalin's policy ultimately undermined the peace process, not because of his grand strategy to bring the CCP to power but because of the timing of the withdrawal of Soviet troops from Manchuria. Stalin wanted to avoid possible conflict with the United States and prevent a unified China from allying with the United States. To achieve these objectives, he had to have the CCP negotiate with the GMD and offer concessions. He did not achieve these objectives.[64] Thus, he urged Mao Zedong to negotiate with Chiang Kai-shek to avoid open conflict, and to consolidate troops in the countryside rather than in the major cities.[65] Given Stalin's insistence, Mao felt that he had no choice but to go to Chongqing, but this did not produce a very conducive frame of mind for negotiations. The day before he left Chongqing to return to Yan'an, the GMD Ministry of Information on October 10 drafted a summary of the discussions to be issued on the following day.

The agreement was worthless. Both sides rushed to gain the advantage in the areas they occupied when Japan surrendered. Not surprisingly, this led to numerous clashes, and the GMD asked the Soviets to delay their withdrawal to allow more time for GMD troops to reach the Northeast. As Mao was negotiating in Chongqing, it was becoming clear that the Northeast was crucial to CCP plans.[66] Publicly the CCP accepted the Soviet demands. On August 29 a CC directive noted that the Soviet Union would not be in a position to help the party because of its desire to maintain peace in the East and because of the terms of the Sino-Soviet Treaty. But the directive went on to say that the delay in the Soviet withdrawal gave the CCP a wonderful opportunity to gain the upper hand in the three northeastern provinces. Any actions were to be kept secret, and instead of taking over the main cities, troops were to focus on the small towns and on the vast expanses of the countryside where the Soviet troops were not active. Despite Moscow's warnings, cadres did infiltrate the larger cities.[67] Control would come later.

In mid-September 1945, the Politburo decided to set up a Northeast Bureau, with Peng Zhen as its secretary, and on September 19 the Communist bureaus were informed that the strategy was to expand in the North while defending the South. Following Mao Zedong's October agreement to pull out from the South, the Northeast acquired even greater importance. China looked as if it might split into a North controlled by the Communists and a South controlled by the Nationalists. Had Chiang Kai-shek not made the error of consolidating the gains of late 1946 and early 1947 and trying to keep Manchuria after it was clearly lost, this might have been the outcome.[68]

The Soviet order to evacuate the cities incensed Peng Zhen, who could not believe that one Red Army might use force to drive out the troops of another Red Army.[69] However, with the Soviets expressing their support for the GMD in the Northeast, the Northeast Bureau did, on November 20, call for the withdrawal from the major cities to be orderly. No property was to be destroyed, and good relations with the local people were to be maintained. Propaganda work was to stress the need for a peaceful resolution to the conflicts, and democratic self-rule was to be instituted. The CCP explained that the struggle was between the United States and Chiang Kai-shek versus the Soviet Union and the Chinese people. This necessitated a tactical retreat for the Soviet Union to regain the initiative. CCP officials and organizations that were publicly known were to withdraw swiftly to the rural areas. Such actions were to counter the diplomatic offensive by the United States and Chiang and to frustrate the "treacherous intervention" of the United States.[70] In late December the CC and Mao followed up with a call to set up long-term bases in the Northeast, a process that might take three to four years. These were to be situated away from the major cities and the communication lines. The groundwork was to be laid in 1946. The party hoped to retain mass support by campaigning for rent reduction and promoting production. Traitors were to be dealt with mercilessly.

Despite the stated intentions, realities on the ground painted a different picture. Soviet views soon shifted and facilitated CCP infiltration, promising large quantities of arms and equipment. As the relationship with the

United States deteriorated, the Soviets became more hesitant about the GMD taking over the Northeast.[71] On September 5, 1945, the Soviets and the CCP had already agreed that once the Soviet troops had withdrawn, how the Chinese forces would enter the Northeast would be up to them. In early October the Soviet Red Army actually encouraged the CCP to deploy 300,000 troops to prevent entry into Manchuria from the south. By the end of the month the Soviets were urging the CCP to move ahead quickly, promising that they would hand over to the CCP all factories and equipment that had not been shipped back to the Soviet Union.[72]

With the situation threatening to spiral out of control, the United States increased efforts, led by General George Marshall, to broker a peace. A ceasefire agreement was reached and was to come into effect on January 13, 1946. Large-scale troop reductions were called for. As a result, Lin Biao, who oversaw the troops in the Northeast, was instructed to halt the civil war. The CCP's priority was to obtain legal recognition, although it knew that this would be difficult to achieve. Consequently, it was important to consolidate military strength and the base areas. On February 1, 1946, the CC reinforced the peace message that the most important struggle at the time was a parliamentary one.[73]

Things unraveled quickly, and in March 1946 the right wing of the GMD pushed through changes to the January agreement, placing curbs on provincial autonomy and pulling back from a cabinet government in favor of presidential rule. The joint veto power of the CCP and the Democratic League in the putative State Council was revoked. The League had been set up in 1941 by democratic groups to offer an alternative to the CCP and the GMD. The CCP and the Democratic League then refused to participate, and in November 1946 the GMD unilaterally convened the National Assembly. Despite further attempts by General Marshall to bring about a ceasefire, once the ceasefire ended at the end of June, the GMD began its all-out offensive and in July the CCP began to criticize US policy and demand that the United States withdraw.

During the first year of conflict, the war went badly for the CCP and it was forced to retreat from many of the areas that it had occupied. In the Northeast, all of the cities under its control were lost, except for Harbin, and on October 10, 1946, Zhangjiakou (Kalgan) fell. During the last half of 1946, the CCP lost a significant amount of territory and was driven out of 165 towns.[74] Morale was low and many troops deserted. The Nationalists convened the National Assembly on November 15 without Communist participation, prompting Zhou Enlai to leave Chongqing for Yan'an. The losses did not end, and in the winter of 1946–1947 most of the Shanxi-Hebei-Shandong-Henan base area was lost, and Yan'an itself was taken over in March 1947.

As a consequence of the losses, the CCP leadership made a decision that would have important consequences post-1949. They divided the leadership into two groups, with a front-line committee headed by Mao Zedong, Zhou Enlai, and Ren Bishi, which was to remain in north Shaanxi to lead the struggle for national liberation. The other group would be a work committee headed by Liu Shaoqi and Zhu De, which moved to Shanxi-Chahar-Hebei and set up shop in the village of Xibaipo (Pingshan county). On April 9, 1947, it was decided that the CC and the General Headquarters of the People's Liberation Army (PLA; formerly the Red Army, renamed in July 1946) would remain in Shaanxi-Gansu-Ningxia. For the remainder of this period until 1949, Mao was more heavily involved in the war effort, and Liu Shaoqi became the key person directing administrative issues. Ultimately their different experiences would lead them to clash over the nature of the transition to socialism.

By May 1947 the GMD was overextended and had trouble getting reinforcements, so their attacks abated. Mao foresaw this in October 1946, claiming that it was "bound to be the direct cause of our victory and Chiang Kai-shek's defeat."[75] He maintained this upbeat assessment, and in the summer of 1947 the war did indeed begin to turn in favor of the CCP. The GMD's attempts to retake Harbin and Manchuria were thwarted by Lin Biao's hit-and-run raids across the Sungari River. In May, Lin launched his fifth attack on the Nationalist forces with a five-week siege of Sibinggai. The Communists suffered significant losses, and by the end of June the siege was lifted but the pendulum was moving in Lin's direction. By November 1947, Communist forces had succeeded in isolating the major cities in central and south Manchuria and in cutting communication links with North China. Troops in Central and South China took Shijiazhuang, enabling the merger of the Shanxi-Chahar-Hebei base with the Shanxi-Hebei-Shandong-Henan base.

This progress enabled Mao to draft a CC directive, dated September 1, 1947, to analyze the war and the strategy for the next year. Strategic withdrawal was no longer necessary; instead a nationwide counteroffensive would be launched in the GMD-held areas. Operationally, the approach of concentrating overwhelming force to destroy the enemy remained the same. To retain support within the base areas, Mao stressed the importance of land reform and linked it with victory in the civil war.[76]

Two major campaigns effectively sealed the fate of the GMD: the Liao-Shen Campaign, from September 9 to November 2, 1948, and the Huai-Hai Campaign, from November 6, 1948, to January 10, 1949.[77] Lin Biao pressed the CCP advantage with a mixture of brutality and intelligent tactics. The GMD was left with only a few pockets of resistance in the Northeast around key cities, the most important of which were Changchun and Shenyang. In April 1948, Lin Biao began a five-month siege of the key Northeast city of Changchun, where about 500,000 civilians were seeking refuge. The strategy was to starve the GMD troops into surrender, turning Changchun into a "city of death" and not letting anyone escape. Perhaps as many as 160,000 people perished.[78] A ten-month siege was laid against Shenyang, a key city in the Northeast, and despite a strong defense it fell on November 1. With the fall of the Northeast, Chiang Kai-shek lost some 400,000 of his best troops and the CCP was in control of the rich region.

The Huai-Hai Campaign, which was fought in Shandong, Jiangsu, Anhui, and Henan, was the largest military engagement after the end of the War of Resistance. It began with attacks on Xuzhou, which was seen as the gateway to the Nationalist capital of Nanjing. Beaten back by the Communist forces, the troops retreated within the city and were reliant on air drops for provisions.[79] Frustrated in their attempts to break out, the commander of the GMD troops surrendered to the Communist forces on January 10, 1949. Beijing fell on January 31. The commander of the GMD troops in Beijing, when faced with a forty-day siege, perhaps thinking of the siege of Shenyang, surrendered to the Communists and his 240,000-strong force was absorbed into the PLA. In fact, by late 1948 almost one-half of the PLA regulars had been fighting against them earlier.[80]

On January 14, shortly after the culmination of the Huai-Hai Campaign, the CCP put forward eight conditions for the surrender of the GMD. Before the CCP issued its demands, Stalin had sent a telegram to Mao Zedong suggesting how he should respond to rumored GMD peace proposals and stating that Mao's proposed visit to Moscow should be postponed. Mao rejected the idea of talks and went so far as to suggest how the Soviet Union might respond to calls for mediation.[81] Given the CCP's dominance and expectation of victory, the proposals were tough. The GMD government was expected to turn its powers over to a democratic coalition government that would be formed by the political consultative conference. War criminals were to be punished and the land system was to be reformed. Chiang Kai-shek's rejection of the terms was irrelevant, and he stepped down, handing over the negotiations to the vice president. The negotiations went nowhere, and when the deadline passed on April 20 with a GMD rejection of the CCP terms, the PLA began to cross the Yangzi. Nanjing fell on April 23. Shanghai fell on May 25. The CCP now turned its attention to preparing for rule.

CHAPTER FIVE

The Chinese Communist Revolution

✫

The CCP's rise to power was the most significant revolutionary movement of the twentieth century. In its scale and impact it eclipses other revolutionary movements of that century, such as those of Vietnam and Cuba, and although the Russian Revolution had the impact, it did not cover such an extensive historical period. The Chinese Communist revolution should be seen in the context of the revolutionary upheavals of the twentieth century. Although it had its own dynamics, the CCP saw itself as part of the global revolutions that swept the world after World War I—as a key component of the proletarian uprising against the capitalist West. The fact that the complexity of the revolution spanned such a lengthy period and involved so many actors makes it more difficult to characterize and explain than any of the other major revolutions. Thus, not surprisingly, there are varying interpretations of what led to the success of the revolution and of the legacies its struggles bequeathed to post-1949 rule. This chapter looks at competing but often complementary explanations for the CCP victory.

In his work on the Russian Revolution, Richard Pipes raised three "whys," the first two of which, as rephrased for China, are relevant for our study of the Chinese revolution: Pipes's first two questions regarding Russia were: Why did tsarism fall? Why did Bolshevism triumph?[1] In the preceding chapters we have considered the first of the two questions, recast for the Chinese context, in depth, and I will synthesize the main points below but, for the most part, here we will concentrate on the second question: Why did the Communists triumph? This has long been debated by historians and social scientists who have looked for deep, structural causes for the victory. However, such analyses operate at a relatively abstract level.[2] Those looking for an answer based on a detailed study of the revolution have disagreed about the primary causes.

The first generation of writings concentrated on the political dimension, focusing on why the CCP won the struggle with the GMD. These explanations range from the preeminence of Nationalist appeal during the war against the Japanese to social mobilization to the power of organization.[3] Similarly, the degree of Soviet dominance was debated, with scholars such as Benjamin Schwartz and Stuart Schram highlighting the indigenous roots of the Chinese revolution and the Sinification of Marxism that took place under Mao Zedong.[4]

The next generation of scholarship focuses on the social and economic dimensions of the revolution and begins to point the way to pre- and post-1949 continuities.[5] Other studies show the complexity of the pre-1949 revolutionary experience and how the local environment affected the outcomes and led to different policy approaches.[6] The socioeconomic and cultural dimensions were as important as the military struggle for theorizing about the revolution. In terms of both the economic and the social revolution, the year 1949 was clearly not a divide—as we shall see, the economic and political policies experimented with before 1949 were pursued earnestly after 1949.

Finally, there was the cultural discourse aspect of the revolution.[7] The narrative framing of Chinese history was crucial to Mao Zedong's ascent to power. Attempts to transform culture and the citizens' essence continued after 1949, with the anti-rightist campaign of the 1950s and the Cultural Revolution of the 1960s and into the 1970s. But reality is more complex than any unidimensional explanation can illuminate. Yes, resistance to Japan was important, certainly in the CCP's self-told narrative, but so was luck and Soviet intervention at crucial moments. Luck is not a very scientific term, but without it the CCP would have been swept away.

John Dunn has written: "At the center of every revolution . . . is an intense and deadly struggle for power (personal and impersonal, imaginative and economic, organizational and coercive): an internecine war à l'outrance between enemies whose allegiance can never be confidently predicted and for control that can never be conclusively secured."[8] This captures well the complexity and the sweep of the Chinese Communist revolution, with not only the bitter struggles for power between the Chinese and the Japanese and between the CCP and the GMD but also the vicious fights for power within the CCP itself. The CCP and the GMD underwent periods of alliance and civil war that divided families and those committed to different visions of China's future.

Given the grand scale of the revolution, it has influenced not only those inspired by Maoism to copy its methods but also the intellectual elite in cities like Paris, practical revolutionaries in Latin America and Southeast and East Asia, and comparative theorists.[9] The attraction of grand theory is not surprising. Four structural factors characterize revolutionary movements: weak states, conflicting elites, rapid population growth, and erratic international intervention.[10] As we saw in Chapter 1, these broad structural factors played a role in the collapse of the Qing dynasty and the emergence of the revolutionary movements. The Taiping Rebellion (1850–1864) from within and the Opium Wars (1839–1842 and 1856–1860) from without weakened the Qing state at a crucial time. This led to a rise in localism, as the state's capacity to manage defense and provide sufficient public goods for its people declined. The Chinese state was seeking to rule over its largest geographical expanse in history, with a rising population but without increasing state capacity.

Defeat in the Sino-Japanese War (1894–1895) was traumatic and a turning point for many of China's elite as they sought alternatives—first to save the dynasty and then to explore alternatives to replace it. Clearly, the rules of the game no longer held. This search for new rules gave rise to reforms from within, such as the "Self-strengthening Movement" (1861–1895) and the "Hundred Days Reform" (1898), and those searching for new alternatives—such as Hu Shi, who sought salvation through liberalism; Sun Yat-sen, who hoped to find redemption through anti-imperialism and his "three people's principles" (nationalism, rights of the people, and livelihood of the people); and Teng Jie, who believed that the führer principle would provide the leadership necessary—and those, such as Chen Duxiu and Li Dazhao, who ultimately turned to Marxism to save China.

During the period of calm under the Ming (1368–1644) and the early part of the Qing, the Chinese population more than doubled without any accompanying growth in state capacity. This does not seem to have been destabilizing, but it may have contributed to the rebellions that started to break out as it became ever more problematic for the peasants to carve out a livelihood.[11] Crucially, the arrival of the foreigners who wanted to force open the China market seriously undermined the ability of the Qing to function. The opening to foreigners also brought in different ideas about how the state could be organized and how the economy should function. With these four conditions present, we see that "a revolutionary ideology emerges, combining elements of nationalism and utopianism, plus whatever indigenous widespread beliefs that can be used to oppose the ideology that supports the current regime."[12]

Theda Skocpol's structural analysis of major revolutions covers the incapacity of the old regime to deal with new challenges, resulting in rebellions, especially of the peasantry, and attempts by the "mass-mobilizing political leaderships to consolidate revolutionary state power."[13] Barrington Moore similarly focuses on how conflicts between a rural class base and the state can result in the establishment of a revolutionary regime.[14]

In addition to these structural factors, we need to bring agency more sharply back into the revolutionary picture. The revolution was conducted by men and women who suffered extraordinary hardships, with many falling by the wayside. For those who stuck with the revolution, their desperation, lack of alternatives, and belief in a viable alternative played important roles. The rituals and symbols that inspired individual party members to struggle on against seemingly impossible odds must be explored. In particular, once Mao Zedong consolidated his power in the 1940s in Yan'an, his power of narrative played a vital role in creating a commitment to the revolutionary cause, when objective circumstances might have appeared bleak even to the most optimistic of revolutionaries. Mao's ability to tell a broad story of China's humiliation and its redemption under the CCP linked individual life histories to the majestic sweep of the revolution. In Yan'an, the CCP began to develop the symbols of its revolution, which combined with organization and not a little coercion to build strong loyalties.[15] It is important to understand how the CCP interpreted the revolution and how this interpretation was received by its members and the broader society.

Although much recent research has tended to disaggregate the party in the revolutionary struggle, we need to understand what bound the individuals together and produced a coherent identity for those living and working in extremely different environments. This research turns away from the major theories and common structural features that encapsulate the majestic sweep of the revolution to provide us with intimate portraits of how the party operated in a variety of landscapes. Most importantly, this work confirms the view that the outcome was not the result of one cause, but was instead the coming together of several factors that produced the uniqueness of the Chinese Communist revolution.

Was the Chinese Revolution a Creation of Soviet Russia?

The release in the 1990s of a treasure trove of Comintern documents on the Chinese revolution has provided us with a much more nuanced view of Soviet involvement. The post-1949 Sino-Soviet alliance, the heightened atmosphere of the Cold War, and the installation of the baggage-train governments in Eastern Europe led many to assume that the CCP was a product of Moscow and that Comintern influence was crucial in the pre-1949 period.[16] The tendency to ignore the indigenous elements of the Chinese revolutionary experience was exacerbated by the attacks on those Americans who had served in China in the pre-1949 period and who had developed a more sympathetic view of the CCP.

Against this backdrop, Benjamin Schwartz's work stands out for its sophistication. Schwartz acknowledges the CCP's debt to the Soviets in terms of ideology and organization, but he also stresses the important contributions made by Mao Zedong and his closest comrades.[17] These contributions became increasingly important when the Communists were driven out of the cities after 1927 and when they pursued their revolution in the rural base areas, defended by their own military forces. Communications with Moscow became increasingly difficult, and those who had returned from Moscow, such as Wang Ming, found it difficult to gain traction in the movement by relying solely on their "superior" theoretical knowledge.

This notwithstanding, the Comintern and Soviet Russia played a crucial role in the Chinese revolution, in the founding of the party, in convincing the CCP to join an alliance with the GMD in the early 1920s and the late 1930s, at crucial moments during the civil war (1945–1949), and in providing a model for post-1949 development.

At one level, it is obvious that the Soviet Union was crucial for the establishment of the CCP. The Bolshevik revolution revealed to many young would-be activists that there was a viable alternative to resist the capitalist nations and their intrusion into China. It is not surprising that the success of the Bolsheviks led to inquiries about their ideology and the kind of organization that ruled over the country.[18] On the Soviet side, China was seen as an important cog in the wheel of resistance to Western powers and it was believed that the promotion of revolution in the East might provide the breakthrough that had been lost with the floundering of the revolutionary movements in Western Europe. The nature of the Sino-Soviet relationship has been clouded by official historians on both sides. Naturally, official Chinese historians stress the indigenous nature of the revolution, whereas their Soviet counterparts, making selective use of closed archival materials, stress the importance and indispensability of Soviet engagement.

The idea that the CCP was nothing more than a Soviet creation is effectively punctured by Hans van de Ven, whose work shows the variety of early organizations, including one in Sichuan that appears to have had no contact whatsoever with outside agents.[19] Yet from the very beginning of the new Soviet state, its emissaries the Comintern, the Foreign Ministry, and the International Labor Organization alike—sought out those who were attracted to total solutions to China's predicament. The mission of Grigori Voitinsky (April 1920) was crucial to pulling groups together to form a Communist Party, and Henk Sneevliet (1921–1924) was the driving force for collaboration between the Communists and the Nationalists, but the groundwork had been established by earlier explorers searching for progressive elements in China.[20] Although it might be true that the CCP could have developed independently of Moscow, materials now available show that it would not have been established so early and would not have been able to continue without Soviet financial, logistical, and organizational support. Of the 17,500 yuan spent by the CCP between October 1921 and January 1922, the Comintern had provided 16,555 yuan. In 1923 the Comintern earmarked 12,000 gold rubles for the CCP, but in May 1923 the Comintern promised 2 million yuan for Sun Yat-sen. The original small groups that provided the nucleus for the formal party came together in various ways, some with heavy Comintern guidance (in Beijing, Shanghai, and Guangzhou), some prompted by individuals (from Hunan) who had been radicalized overseas, and some (from Nanjing and Chongqing) who had no discernible Soviet connections

The policy of cooperation with the GMD was driven by Moscow. Even when the alliance appeared to be falling apart, Stalin insisted on keeping it going, thus contributing to the disaster of 1927 when the GMD turned on its Communist partners. This formed a key element in Russia's own "who lost China debate," as it occurred during the intensified struggle between Stalin and Trotsky for the soul of the Bolshevik party. Supporters of Trotsky blamed Soviet strategy, and more particularly Stalin, for the 1927 defeat of the revolution, a view shared by other scholars.[21] These accounts blamed Stalin for insisting that the CCP remain in the alliance after the use of infiltration to expand CCP power had passed. Trotsky himself stated that Stalin's policy had been wrong ever since 1924, and in 1931 he said that the strategy had been a mistake from the very beginning. Yet Trotsky did not have an alternative plan until it was too late. It was not until late June 1927 that Trotsky and his supporters called for withdrawal and the establishment of soviets.[22]

Mao Zedong gave positive assessments of Comintern policy up until 1927 and, indeed, there was much to be positive about. Voitinsky pulled together the scattered study groups to form the seeds of a Bolshevik party, and following Sneevliet's and Borodin's promptings, the united front with the Nationalists protected the fledgling movement and allowed it to grow significantly during the 1920s. The CCP developed wider connections within the radical movement and among labor in the major urban areas. Party membership rose from just under 1,000 in January 1924 to about 50,000 in April 1927. Traction was gained in the southern labor and peasant movements as leaders began to understand the importance of organization. Clearly, "the CCP's dramatic wartime revival would not have been possible without the stature it had acquired during the National Revolution of the 1920s."[23]

Although contacts became more sporadic as the CCP retreated to the rural areas, Soviet policy was once again decisive in the mid-1930s as it called for a second period of collaboration with the Nationalists. With Soviet Russia's concern about the rise of Germany and Japan, the Comintern's Seventh Congress, in July–August 1935, called for all elements, classes, and nations to come together in a united front in the fight against fascism. This found favor with the evolution of thinking within the CCP when it was considering its response to the Japanese occupation of Manchuria. When the CCP rhetoric against the Nationalists softened, the kidnapping of Chiang Kai-shek in December 1936 and his negotiated release under Soviet promptings marked a shift toward a second period of alliance.

Some writers have suggested that Mao Zedong was not supported by the Comintern, which preferred one of the returned Bolsheviks, Wang Ming. In fact, the Soviets were not opposed to Mao and they recognized the credibility he had within the party in China. Certainly, Wang's theoretical prowess and close relations with Moscow provided him with credibility, but he could never effectively challenge Mao, nor, most importantly, did Moscow push him to do so. In fact, at the Seventh Party Congress, in 1945, Mao acknowledged Comintern support in resolving the leadership issue within the party.[24] Thus, Mao was not categorically opposed to the Comintern, nor was the Comintern against Mao. In addition to the progressive role the Comintern played in the 1920s, from mid-1935 until its dissolution in 1943 Mao positively appraised Comintern advice.

The third important element in Soviet engagement came after the dissolution of the Comintern in the postwar period and during the civil war. With the defeat of Nazi Germany and the surrender of the Japanese, first and foremost the Soviet Union sought to protect its national interest. Thus, much to the consternation of the CCP, on August 14, 1945, the Soviet Union signed the Sino-Soviet Treaty with the Nationalist government. But the delay in evacuating its troops out of Manchuria allowed the CCP to infiltrate the countryside and smaller towns while sending its cadres into the larger cities. This was carried out in secrecy so as not to draw unwanted attention and, presumably, not to upset the Soviets. Indeed, the Soviets had told the CCP to evacuate the major cities in Manchuria, including Shenyang.

Finally, the Soviet experience was crucial to the CCP as it took power. With no other model to follow, it was inevitable that the CCP would look to the Soviet Union for guidance and start to create a Soviet-style economy and, by extension, a Soviet-style society. The CCP's base-area experiences declined in importance as full-scale warfare began and preparations for rule were made. Although much writing has focused on the return of Wang Ming and his challenge to Mao's leadership in Yan'an, others who returned with Wang had a more lasting influence on the CCP in terms of economic and party organization. Kang Sheng was well versed in the dark arts of Stalinist inner-party struggle, Chen Yun influenced economic policy, and Ren Bishi played a role in party organization. During the Rectification Campaign, important Bolshevik works were key study materials for party members, and Mao Zedong was a big fan of Stalin's *Short History*. Much of the planning for the institutions of the new state was left to others, such as Liu Shaoqi and Ren Bishi, who maintained close contacts with the Soviets and drew up plans clearly modeled on the Soviet experience of economic development and social transformation.

Was Victory the Consequence of Nationalist Resistance to Japan?

The Japanese invasion of China and the war after 1937 were crucial to the survival of the CCP and its ultimate victory, but not because a wave of peasant nationalism swept the party to power. The impact of peasant nationalism was considerable but more diffuse than a mono-causal explanation might suggest. Chalmers Johnson's pathbreaking book *Peasant Nationalism and Communist Power* (1962) seeks to link the success of the Chinese revolution, and that of the former Yugoslavia, to the rise of a national consciousness among the peasantry. The development of the idea of a nation lifted peasants' eyes beyond their local environment to see China as an entity to be defended. The CCP was able to capitalize on the rise of spontaneous organizations of resistance by being better nationalists than the GMD, the Nationalist Party. As a result, the peasantry associated the fight against foreign oppression with the CCP's leadership.

The CCP has effectively presented this narrative in its propaganda both before and after 1949. Its vivid portrayals of the CCP leading the Chinese people to victory remain as strong today as they were in the past. In 2014 the National People's Congress created two new days of observance: Victory Day on September 3, marking the Japanese surrender, and December 13 marking Japan's massacre of Chinese citizens in Nanjing. General Secretary Xi Jinping, in attending the first Victory Day celebrations with other Politburo members, commented on the patriotism of the Chinese people, who under CCP leadership had defeated the invaders.[25]

Johnson strengthens his argument by pointing out that the Communists were unsuccessful in their attempts to create radical social transformation in the early 1930s. The importance of the Japanese invasion for the CCP victory was enthusiastically endorsed by Mao Zedong when he met Japanese visitors.

Johnson's view has been rightly criticized for the mono-causal nature of his account. Conditions varied from one base area to the next, and the large-scale mobilization that would have been necessary could not have been maintained over such a long period. However, local discontent rarely escalates to a national scale, and "local self-defense is indeed a far cry from revolutionary action."[26] Most importantly, the CCP was not the main force fighting the Japanese, something that even mainland historians have come to recognize. It was the GMD forces and the Chinese people who suffered from the brunt of the Japanese attacks. The initial major conflicts were in South China and were fought by the GMD without any CCP support. In fact, CCP forces engaged in few armed conflicts, preferring guerrilla attacks and sabotage missions, which militarily were irritating but not crucial. In January 1940 Zhou Enlai informed Stalin that even though more than one million Chinese people had died thus far at the hands of the Japanese, only

30,000 were from the ERA and 1,000 were from the NFA.[27] Zhou also acknowledged the leadership role of Chiang Kai-shek in the fight. At least one-third of the CCP forces remained in the base areas and did not engage directly with the Japanese.[28]

So how did the Japanese invasion help the CCP? It certainly saved the party from extinction. The CCP was in a pitiful state. There were the reduced numbers who had survived the Long March and found their way to join up with the guerrilla forces in northern Shaanxi, and others were scattered throughout a few other small base areas. The tightening GMD blockade and military pressure were slowly but surely strangling the life out of the Communist movement. The war relieved GMD pressure and enabled the CCP to better position itself for the inevitable civil war with the GMD, protecting its own forces while those of the GMD suffered heavy losses. Chiang Kai-shek recognized the inevitability of conflict between the two parties, but his dedication to eradicate the Communists while resisting the Japanese undermined his credibility as a patriot and turned key commanders against him. Chiang's approach provided the CCP with a massive propaganda coup as CCP members extolled their patriotism and willingness to place the highest priority on defending the nation. The CCP was able to expand its armies and membership. The war weakened and divided China, but "the road to victory for the Chinese Communist Party in 1949 lay within the devastated landscape of China created by the years of war with Japan."[29]

During the initial phase of the conflict, Communist troops were able to establish footholds behind Japanese lines as Japanese troops were concentrated in the major cities and along communication routes. In April 1944 the huge Japanese Ichigo offensive drove back the Nationalist troops, whose retreat allowed the CCP to move troops into the vacated areas in North and Central China. Consequently, by the summer of 1945 the CCP had a strong foothold in North China that encompassed roughly one-quarter of the Chinese population.[30]

Thus, despite the valid criticisms of Johnson's thesis, the Japanese invasion, while not guaranteeing CCP victory, did lay some foundation for success in the civil war. It allowed the CCP and its military to expand significantly. The war left China weak and divided, and it forced a cruel halt to the modernization that had been under way under the GMD. Finally, although the GMD had borne the brunt of the fighting, Chiang Kai-shek's credibility as the leader of national salvation was critically tarnished by the perception that his primary objective was to defeat the Communists.

Did the Socioeconomic Policies Rally Support?

In the base areas under its control, the CCP could introduce progressive policies that might mobilize support from the peasantry. Again, we see a more complex picture than rural reform causing poor peasants to rally under the banner of the party. We have to be mindful of the different time periods and the different areas to which we are referring, as conditions varied significantly, and even within the primary base area, Shaanxi-Gansu-Ningxia, there was variation among different counties. Indeed, contrary to the standard picture, after 1937 the rural elite were more readily attracted to the CCP program of resistance than were the poorer peasants.[31] However, agency was important and the CCP worked hard to build support and to create a movement that was reflective of its self-description as favoring the poorer peasantry over the traditional local elite.

A common argument in the literature is that the peasantry are the key players in the revolutionary movements. This seems to derive from an almost romantic attachment to the idea of an oppressed class instilling its values into a movement that redresses past wrongs and seeks to create a new moral authority.[32] In reality, the CCP had to work hard, not just to win the support of the peasantry, especially the poor peasantry, but also to then keep the peasantry on its side.

Lucien Bianco combines the thesis of the importance of the Japanese invasion with an emphasis on the social and economic programs of the CCP. The national problem was a catalyst, but "at the very heart of the 'national' stage of the revolution lay the social problem" and "it was through Communism that nationalism triumphed."[33] The social program was certainly important, and in Shaanxi-Gansu-Ningxia the party launched an extensive program of rent and interest reduction. Importantly, compared to other areas under CCP control this region was less affected by the Japanese attacks and the GMD blockade, which gave it more breathing space to experiment. Even more important was the reduction of taxes, which was more readily accepted and represented the peasants' opposition to the local state rather than to their immediate landlord, even if he was present. Taxes were the most pressing issue, and low tenancy rates meant that many peasants did not pay rent.[34] Mark Selden is the strongest proponent of the idea that the program for socioeconomic transformation was the basis for the Communists' ultimate success. There is much truth to this, but the experience in Shaanxi-Gansu-Ningxia also contained the seeds of "destructive forms of fundamentalism resting on party claims to exercise a monopoly on morality and truth."[35]

Much research shows just how difficult it was for the party to mobilize societal support. Building and maintaining the support of workers and peasants, the supposed social base of the party, was sufficiently difficult that the question is not so much why the CCP was successful as how on earth it managed to gain state power when faced by such significant challenges. The revolution was not the result of inevitable structural factors that combined "revolutionary preconditions" with "revolutionary consciousness."[36] It was a political process that required hard work, dedication, and not a little luck along the way. Where the CCP was successful and able to lay down roots was where it handled micropolitics well; it tended to be less successful when it tried to change local realities too quickly and to impose an ideologically determined set of programs.

The CCP had difficulty establishing an effective connection with both the working class and the peasantry. The CCP's initial policies followed orthodox Bolshevik lines, organizing the proletariat to use strikes and industrial actions to engineer a social revolution that would bring the party to power. In the 1920s the party found this difficult even in the major urban centers such as Beijing and Shanghai. The lack of party members in Shanghai was particularly acute; few had experience in the labor movement, and they faced competition for workers' loyalty from local place associations, such as the Green and Red Gangs and even the YMCA. In Guangzhou, the GMD and the anarchists were more influential. The situation was miserable enough that in May 1924 the Shanghai Party Committee summed up its achievements as "nil."[37]

Things improved with the May Thirtieth Movement (1925) and with the success of the Northern Expedition, but the continuing shortage of members with experience in the labor movement led the CCP to adopt a strategy of trying to take over the movement from the top down. The failure to build grassroots support diminished the party's ability to maintain momentum among the working class, and party leaders admitted that their role had been limited even in the May Thirtieth Movement. Yet some in the party did come to think that the rise in nationalist sentiment combined with the anti-imperialist thrust could lead to a revolution led by the CCP. This enthusiasm was reflected in the May 1926 statement by Chen Duxiu that the party sat astride 1.25 million workers, based on the number of workers in organizations who attended the Third Labor Congress. In reality the CCP had not constructed a mighty "colossus but rather a Buddha that turned out to have feet of clay."[38] The proletariat did not come to the party's aid in enough strength to stop the April 1927 onslaught from Chiang Kai-shek's supporters.

The defeat of the CCP in 1927 meant that the initial strategy lay in tatters, and although underground work continued, the CCP had no truly effective connection with the proletariat until it took power in the Northeast in the late 1940s, some years before seizing national power in 1949. The party did not abandon its rhetoric about the proletariat and its leading role, but in those conditions it did claim that it was acting on behalf of the proletariat without the inconvenience of having to deal with it. As soon as conditions permitted, the party reasserted the primacy of work in the cities over that in the countryside, where it had been based since 1927. As early as May–June 1944, CCP leadership highlighted this emphasis.[39]

CCP engagement with the peasantry was even more complex than work in urban areas, and gaining traction was no easier than it had been in urban China. Initially the peasantry had not figured in CCP thinking, but as the Northern Expedition advanced, large areas came under the control of the GMD-CCP alliance. The experience of working with the peasantry was especially fruitful and strong in the provinces of Hubei, Hunan, Guangdong, and Jiangxi. CCP members did play an active role in the mobilization and organization of the peasants through the peasant associations.[40] The head and secretary of the Guangdong Central Peasant Department were both Communists, and all the training was overseen by the Communists. This was a formative experience for the CCP: "The Communists and the Guomindang left believed a new rural politics centering on the peasant association would finally replace the old politics dominated by the gentry, landlords, and local militia."[41]

As in urban China, the protection of the GMD forces enabled the CCP to extend its influence. Once the right wing of the GMD became concerned about the increasing Communist influence, it moved to suppress the CCP and the peasant associations. With little alternative, the CCP retreated to the wilderness and, after a brief period of radical policy implementation in the Jiangxi Soviet (1931–1934), the CCP found itself in control of the base areas, such as Shanxi-Chahar-Hebei and Shaanxi-Gansu-Ningxia. Here they wrestled with local politics and developed policies that would not compromise their principles without driving potentially hostile groups into the opposition camp.

This was a learning experience for the CCP, and initial support came not from the poor peasantry but instead from the elite and from itinerant folk, local hoodlums, and bandits who had little to lose. The older generation seemed nervous about the new masters, but the CCP did attract some of the village youth as well as those who were single. This left the party in the tricky situation of "trying to initiate a peasant movement without peasants."[42] The actions by the peasants were mainly defensive and displayed neither class consciousness nor nationalist sentiment that could mobilize them against the Japanese invaders.[43] With this as the background, the CCP should be congratulated for having not only survived but also eventually thrived in its remote rural bases.

Continued military control of the rural areas was crucial. This gave the party time to experiment with policies and also forced the local elite to either acquiesce or actively support the party. Military conquest was the first step in CCP rule, either where it established local military superiority over the GMD around Wuhan from 1928 to 1934 or in the North and Northeast from 1937 when the GMD withdrew in the face of the Japanese onslaught. In the Northeast, in particular, the Japanese destroyed the local elite who were facilitating Communist penetration.[44]

On taking control of an area, the CCP had to show that it was different from the other warlords or bandit groups, and this entailed carrying out a social revolution. CCP documents are full of attempts to classify the villages in terms of class categories and to devise policies on this basis. Who were the landlords? How much land did one need to be a rich peasant? Whose land should be confiscated? How much should rent be reduced? The introduction of class into rural life was new and not well understood or well received; most of the countryside was organized around traditional groupings—clans, lineages, and divisions by age and gender. In some of the barren northwest of Shaanxi, the problem was not landlords, if they actually existed, but the struggle against harsh nature and the bugbear of taxes.

In Chen Kaige's 1984 movie *Yellow Earth*, there are no rapacious landlords exploiting the peasantry and the only visible presence of the CCP is a member of the Propaganda Department of the ERA who had come from Yan'an to the GMD-dominated area of northern Shaanxi to collect peasant songs. The movie punctures the myth of the CCP reorganizing the countryside to resist not only the landlords but also the Japanese. It does not give much credence to the notion that the CCP was able to help the local peasants. As the film ends, the peasants perform a rain dance in the hope of obtaining relief from the drought that is destroying their crops.

The policies pursued after 1937 reduced the role of class definitions that in the radical early 1930s had alienated the local elite. Most importantly, the earlier approach created problems for the group that the CCP classified as middle peasants. Policy in Shaanxi-Gansu-Ningxia now focused on tax and rent reduction rather than on land redistribution. As noted, the earliest supporters were not downtrodden peasants but instead other displaced rural groups, such as students, rural schoolteachers, roving bandit groups, and secret societies. In this base area, the earliest support came from those who had lost their land because of nonpayment of taxes or loans. The widespread anger over taxes that was directed against the local authorities, not the landlords, provided support for the Communist guerrillas to establish their base in the early 1930s.[45]

These attempts at local accommodation could lead to unexpected outcomes and a different gloss being put on the proposed policies. When the CCP's Third Army arrived in northern Guizhou in January 1934, revolutionary propaganda was dropped so that the local peasants would not become alienated. Seeking an identity with the "celestial soldiers," CCP cadres described the local peasants' attacks on excessive taxes and fees as simply a form of primitive revolutionary struggle. They then linked this to the broader objectives of the CCP. The recurrent defeats of these local celestial soldiers, despite their heroic struggles, were portrayed as deriving from their having a narrow focus with no plan to overthrow the reactionary GMD. Without this and an organization beyond the "celestial temple" that could represent the workers, peasants, and the poor, they could never throw off the burdens from which they suffered.[46] Accommodating the secret societies did not always work out well. In Shanghai in the 1920s the CCP attempted to collaborate with the secret societies, but this contributed to the 1927 disaster when the most powerful group, the Green Gang, sided with the GMD to crush the labor groups associated with the CCP.

When the party felt more secure in a base area, the tendency was to return to more radical policies, often inspired by the peasants themselves, who, once mobilized, would often move beyond the party's intentions. This occurred in the Jiangxi Soviet and again during the civil war of 1945–1949. For

example, in May 1946 CCP land policy took a radical turn when land confiscation replaced the moderate policy of rent and interest reduction.
Equal distribution of land threatened to undermine the party's relations with
the middle peasants, and the radical upsurge grew out of hand. Not surprisingly, this was not well received by the local elite. The paramount focus of
the CCP at this time was the war effort, and the CCP leaders feared that
such a radical upsurge would undermine their capacity to defeat the GMD.
Of particular concern was the reclassification of the middle peasantry in the
newly liberated areas as rich peasants, which entailed confiscation of their
property. This necessitated a slowing down of the land reform in 1947–1948.
But it also foreshadowed the brutality of land reform after 1949, as peasants
took revenge on the local elite. In addition, it foreshadowed the CCP's willingness to push ahead with radical social reform once it felt its power was
more secure. This would have disastrous consequences for the peasantry
after 1949.

Over time the CCP in the base areas did recreate itself to reflect a more
balanced membership, recruiting poorer peasants as it drove out the rural
elite and bandit elements. True, support had always been conditional, but
hard work had created a party that was more in line with the image the CCP
sought to portray. To remain in power, a mass party rooted among the poor
peasantry was not necessary. What was more important was the acquiescence
of key groups to CCP control. This could be underscored by serving the material interests of specific groups while coercing those who did not comply.

Dedication and hard work on behalf of those who did commit to joining
the revolution was crucial. Furthermore, organizational discipline also played
an important role. On top of this, the Japanese invasion and the GMD withdrawal caused the breakdown of the traditional power structures, and for
many there appeared to be no viable alternative to the CCP. The GMD was
portrayed as ineffective at best and corrupt at worst, and the appellation of
Chiang Kai-shek as "General Cash My Check" was emblematic. The liberals seemed to have no answer that could deal with the traumatic events
that were consuming China.

The Power of Organization and Ideology?

"A Communist Party only needs two departments: organization and propaganda. I should know as I have headed both," said Li Rui, a former secretary to Mao Zedong.[47] Although the CCP was decimated in 1927, it had

adopted the principles of a Leninist organization, and loyalty to the party and the correct political line began to jostle with personal relations as the fundamental organizing principle.[48] The contours of a traditional Leninist party were ingrained fairly swiftly in CCP documents, although often breached in practice. Despite the commitment to collective leadership, the structure led to a hierarchical order. After 1935 Mao Zedong slowly gained more power, culminating in his control of the party in Yan'an during the Rectification Campaign. This planted the seeds for the cult of personality that reached its zenith during the Cultural Revolution.

The idea of a modern mass party was alien to traditional Chinese culture, and early contacts relied much more on personal networks, a feature that has survived in varying degrees up to the present. However, within Chinese tradition there is a culture of adherence to the idealistic belief system of Confucianism, which organized relationships in the world and one's place within the world. For our purposes, the important question is what roles ideology and organization played in helping the CCP come to power. The ideological direction changed frequently during the pre-1949 period, but the Leninist organizational structure ensured that most party members followed the prevailing party line. This gave the CCP a discipline and an ability to act in unity, something that its opponents did not have. This is not to say there was no struggle, but those who lost out were cast aside for their deviation from the policies of the party leadership. Thus, accusations of being a right opportunist, left adventurist, and so forth abound in CCP literature and speeches. Increasingly, the use of ideology after 1927 as a political weapon became an important component in the armory of inner-party struggle.

It is true that we should not fetishize the party.[49] And blind obedience to the party led to disaster as well as to success both before and after 1949. For example, during the Great Leap Forward, party policy provided coherence and guidance to a very disparate group of followers looking for salvation. Loyalty to the organization as a whole, or more correctly loyalty to the party leadership, was intended to pull together work in the diverse environments. Loyalty was to transcend a particular region or individual, although eventually loyalty was to the supreme commander Mao Zedong. The role of ideology was to give common purpose to action and to allow individuals to commit to the superior wisdom of the party elite, whose role was to define the bigger trends in history that mere mortals could not divine by themselves.

Although acquiescence by the general public might have been enough, this was not enough for the party activists. The necessary commitment and direction were provided by the imposition of ideology and organization: "The organization could transform all these disparate local experiences into a national goal; its ideology could give the experiment a greater importance and dignity for participants than mere survival. The presence of a resilient, disciplined revolutionary organization performed the crucial function of retaining the loyalty of the activists who might have otherwise deserted the cause."[50]

The challenge was particularly acute as the party in the Shaanxi-Gansu-Ningxia Border Region began to expand after the war with Japan began in earnest. During this period, significant numbers of people, including many intellectuals, fled to Yan'an not because they were necessarily attracted to communism but because they were patriotic and wanted to resist Japan, or because they simply had nowhere else to go. The party also expanded through the "storm membership drives." Of the students at the party's premier ideological training institute, 82 percent were classified as urban intellectuals, and 74 percent had joined the party after 1937.[51]

For Mao and his colleagues, it became more pressing to provide a framework for the actions of these individuals and to view their own objectives as part of a grander scheme. In Yan'an, Mao presented an "entire cosmology that summed up all of human history on a cosmopolitan, supra-natural basis."[52] This Sinification of Marxism was enforced among party members through the Rectification Campaign. Mao's narrative was compelling, linking the long arc of China's humiliation through the redemption of the struggle against the Japanese and the GMD and within the CCP that led inevitably to Mao's own leadership. Many of those with whom I spoke about their experiences in Yan'an remarked that on hearing Mao's telling of the revolution, they could identify their own individual fates. This enabled them to understand that what had befallen them was not a random act but part of a larger working-out of history that would lead to individual redemption and national salvation: "In a movement weaned on the notion of ideological correctness, the apparent correlation between party successes and Mao's ideas was powerful persuasion indeed."[53]

Given the parlous situation in which the CCP found itself in the early 1940s, it is remarkable that so much time was dedicated to study. The study had two primary purposes: to ensure loyalty that placed Mao Zedong at the Center, and to mobilize party members to accept the truth as laid down by Mao and his closest advisers. The endgame was to eradicate alternative interpretations and discourse within the party. Thus, despite seeing the study campaign as a way to end struggle within the party and some of the fratricide that had occurred, it also led to a bitter end for those who refused to go along with the new orthodoxy.

The unification of the party under the banner of Mao's leadership placed it in a strong position to exploit circumstances after Japan's surrender. Victory was by no means certain, and for a while defeat in the civil war looked just as plausible. In achieving victory, the CCP was aided by the lack of alternatives or the incompetence of rivals and luck, or what many people prefer to refer to as contingencies.

Incompetence or the Failure of Alternatives?

Much early writing has stressed the failures of the GMD not only to mount effective resistance to the Japanese invasion but also to develop a credible social base and effective institutions. More recent writing has been kinder to the GMD, accepting that it took the brunt of the fighting against the Japanese, which severely weakened its capacity to confront the Communist forces. Even in 1945, CCP victory was by no means assured; had several of the battles turned out differently, the GMD might have emerged victorious. Further, the GMD's attempts to build a modern state were rudely interrupted by the onset of war, and the toll of fighting a war seriously undermined its capacity to build an effective set of institutions. When Japanese troops invaded the lower Yangzi region, the GMD lost the support of the emerging middle-class business community. Those who did not flee inland with the GMD had to compromise with the Japanese or the pro-Japanese Wang Jingwei regime based in Nanjing.[54] The loss of the eastern urban centers deprived the GMD of financial resources, and it was never able to develop policies and structures that could mobilize resources effectively from the countryside.

It is important to note that the GMD copied the Leninist form of political organization and led a revolutionary movement in the 1920s that was committed to national liberation. Thus, the answer to why it was less successful than the CCP must lie elsewhere.[55] Those sympathetic to the GMD have pointed to the difficulties of genuine unification after 1927, when the GMD was nominally in charge of the whole country. The GMD decade, 1927–1937, did not develop durable governing institutions and social policies that could engender support to see them through the tough times after the beginning of the war with Japan. Not only was there an internal threat from the CCP, which was the most important issue for Chiang Kai-shek, but also there were divisions within the movement and between the Center and the localities. Within the GMD, there were challenges from Hu Hanmin on the right and Wang Jingwei on the left. The de facto independence of many areas, a legacy of the warlord period, meant that Chiang was reliant on these local leaders to do his bidding. They often set about serving themselves rather than the nominal national leader, and they extracted high "fees" from local society. This rendered it difficult to find the necessary financial resources and bodies to fill the armed forces after the first engagements with Japan. After Chiang's most loyal troops received a heavy battering, this problem became acute. The engagement of the old warlords and others associated with the pre-GMD administrations caused some of the young, new recruits to doubt the GMD's commitment to genuine reform.[56]

Although the GMD had adopted a Leninist form of party organization, it was inefficient, certainly in comparison with the organizational strength the CCP had developed in Yan'an. Unlike the CCP, the GMD did not have effective supervision over the government apparatus. This caused Chiang Kai-shek to rely on the military and mobilization through the creation of alternative organizations, such as the Blue Shirts (a quasi-fascist group organized in 1932) and the Youth Corps (which was organized in 1938 and clashed with many of the traditional power holders). The New Life Movement, launched in 1934, was designed to bring about rural reconstruction through a fusion of neo-Confucianism and fascism. However, as Chiang bemoaned, after 1927 the GMD armies had abandoned the political commissar system, which could have ensured discipline and obedience. Chiang himself was scathing about his own political and military institutions, but he seemed powerless to effectuate change.[57]

Despite victory in 1927, the GMD was unable to develop a mass base of support. As the right wing of the party came to dominate, the mobilization of peasants and workers that had been effective during the 1920s, and especially during the Northern Expedition, was terminated. The peasant associations were closed, the sympathetic workers were crushed in Shanghai, and attempts were launched to eradicate the Communists. This made it difficult to carry out the much-needed social reforms because it was all too easy for opponents to paint them as Communist-inspired. Although the Communists found a way to deal with the challenges of rent reduction and taxes and moderate land reform, this was more difficult for the GMD. The real power of policy implementation resided with the local elite, and implementation by the GMD would have alienated the local elite, as their position was often tied to control over rural resources.

With a lack of cohesion and with fragmentation, the GMD bureaucracy was notoriously corrupt and inefficient. Common to other such systems, as with the CCP after 1949, the information passed up the system was inaccurate and self-serving. If the reports of the successes against the Communists had been true, the CCP would have been eradicated many times over. The bureaucracy became an end in itself, and the GMD, in seeking to create a modern state, equated modernization with bureaucracy in its worst form.[58]

Chiang's assessment that the first priority should be to defeat the Communists made it difficult for him to place himself at the head of the national movement and cost him important support within his own party and troops.[59] Had it not been for the Japanese invasion, Chiang might well have succeeded in his objective of destroying the Communists; Japanese aggression certainly saved the CCP and weakened Chiang's moral authority, even though he took on the key role of defending the nation.[60] Bad luck, if that is what one can call it, struck again after the end of the war with Japan. Manchuria could have provided the GMD with a strong industrial base, financial resources, weapons, and other matériel that could have been taken from the Japanese. However, the Soviet Union took away key industrial plants and eventually allowed the CCP to move into the Northeast and take possession of the confiscated military matériel. This was not helped by Chiang's later poor choice to continue fighting in the Northeast after the Communists became dominant.[61]

Thus, Chiang relied on his inefficient military to maintain power, and this alienated the urban intellectuals who might have been drawn to an alternative to communism. Liberalism did witness a flowering during the May Fourth period of 1915–1919 and later, but it never seemed to address the dire situation in which China found itself, and slowly but surely people were pulled toward more total solutions. During the May Fourth period, liberalism found proponents, such as Hu Shi, a disciple of John Dewey, who sought to combine Western traditions with the idea of unleashing individual power and energies to restore the integrity of the Chinese nation. Hu Shi debated the early CCP leader Li Dazhao regarding the way forward. Rejecting the Bolshevik total solution, Hu wrote about the need for "more study of problems, less talk of isms." He rejected the all-embracing solutions proposed by the radicals, as he felt that China's problems stemmed from many different causes. For Hu, the adoption of such all-embracing ideologies would lead to disaster.[62] Any doctrine had to be based on an in-depth analysis of specific practical problems. Li Dazhao, by contrast, did not see the study of specific problems as incompatible with a specific doctrine. Moreover, what the nation needed was a political transformation to precede any effective solution to the social problems that engulfed China. The question came down to whether China's problems should be solved through political revolution or through slow, evolutionary change.[63] Although Hu had shared the enthusiasm for the Russian February revolution, he did not support the Bolsheviks and he did not share the Communists' view of the dangers of imperialism, seeing less sinister motives in foreign engagement in China. As time for reform ran out by "inches and drops," the activists were attracted to the more inclusive solutions proposed by the Nationalists and the Communists. Liberalism continued to attract some intellectuals but it was ineffective in providing political solutions. The proposals by those such as Carsun Chang (Zhang Junmai) for constitutional democracy, as an alternative to the more radical theories, failed to gain traction. There was not a sufficiently independent middle class or merchant class that might have supported a different path forward, and the civil war and the Japanese invasion effectively negated any gradual solution.

Contingencies?

Grand structural explanations notwithstanding, to be successful all revolutions need luck. Certainly this was the case for the CCP. There were numerous occasions when the CCP came close to perishing, and without the Japanese aggression, it is quite possible that the GMD annihilation campaigns that were encircling and squeezing the northern Shaanxi base area would have been successful. The flight from the Jiangxi Soviet, on what later became known as the Long March, is full of examples of fortuitous turns of events and bravery saving the army from losses. As they wandered aimlessly, pursued by GMD forces and local troops loyal to Chiang Kai-shek, the Communists on the Long March were surprised to discover that there was a Communist stronghold in northern Shaanxi, only about 250 miles from where they were situated. In 1935, just as Mao Zedong was contemplating moving there, the area had almost been wiped out, but the arrival of Mao's troops saved the day.[64] The precarious nature of existence in all the base areas is well reflected in all accounts about them.

After the CCP arrived in northern Shaanxi, fortune again saved it from possible extinction when, in December 1936, Chiang Kai-shek was kidnapped, which resulted in the GMD abandoning its attacks on the CCP in favor of resisting Japan. Chiang's temporary jailer, Zhang Xueliang, was unaware that his actions were unnecessary because secret negotiations were already under way for collaboration between the Communists and the Nationalists.

As we have seen, the CCP was aided by the mistakes and incompetence of the GMD, which left the door open for the CCP to survive and thrive. This was evident during the first period of the civil war, when the GMD could have maintained control. Chiang's decision to focus on the Northeast, where the Communist forces had infiltrated, was misguided; he neglected consolidating his position and instead continued the struggle for too long when it was clear that the Communists had gained the upper hand. The collapse of the GMD troops in the Northeast caused the loss of almost 140,000 of its best troops. Similarly, crucial mistakes were made during the Huai-Hai battle in late 1948.[65]

Obviously, luck alone does not explain the CCP victory. The party was flexible and adaptable in its learning process, enabling it to keep moving forward and to modify its policies to deal with variations over time and space. The party learned that to survive after 1927, it would have to have its own military force, and this would be essential to guarantee continued control over areas where it could experiment with policy. After the failure of the Jiangxi Soviet, the CCP learned that the imposition of inappropriate policies derived from ideological dictates had to be tempered by accommodation to local realities; the CCP had to be good at micropolitics. In Shaanxi-Gansu-Ningxia, Mao Zedong realized the importance of a unified, disciplined party. The movement needed coherence to bind together the diverse individuals working across very different terrains. The CCP learned the power of narrative in binding millions of individual stories into the broad canvas of China's struggle for redemption and salvation. However, this new narrative and orthodoxy contained a dark side. It was intended to eradicate alternatives to the "correct" interpretations of the CCP and it went hand in hand with the rise of Mao Zedong as the predominant arbiter of the Chinese revolution and the architect of its future.

PART TWO

HOW *the* EAST *is* RULED

CHAPTER SIX

Consolidating the Revolution

1948–1956

When Mao Zedong told the Chinese people that they had stood up, they did so to look upon a country that was economically distressed, overwhelmingly rural, and with considerable opposition to CCP rule.[1] The economy had been devastated by the incessant conflict from the late 1920s up to 1949, and inflation was rampant. Pockets of resistance remained from troops loyal to the GMD, and there was armed resistance from Tibetans, who did not want to be incorporated into the People's Republic of China (PRC). In the South, in particular, there was suspicion of the CCP and its ultimate objectives. So what the CCP did manage to achieve in the first several years was remarkable. With the exception of the foreign enclaves of Hong Kong and Macau and the GMD stronghold of Taiwan, the country was unified. With respect to the economy, inflation was brought under control, land reform was completed, and stable economic growth was achieved.

Not surprisingly, this period is remembered fondly by many elderly CCP members as a golden age, preceding the tumultuous years of later Maoist radicalism.[2] Yet how stable was the situation and how great was the cost of reunification and pacification? Only a few years later, the stability and progress that many expected was blown away as the CCP led the people through a series of disastrous movements that fractured the ruling elite, caused social dislocation, turned family members against one another, and created famine on a massive scale, with political campaigns that eventually culminated in the Cultural Revolution. Even in the early 1950s, tensions were not far below the surface as the party laid out a clear strategy for the transition to socialism. That the transition came more rapidly than many expected was the only surprise. In the 1980s some CCP members sought to push the timing of the golden age back to the period of New Democracy that preceded the 1949 victory. They viewed as a great mistake the abandonment of the more moderate politics and the inclusive nature of the united front that accompanied CCP rule in many of the areas it controlled.[3] The crucial question after 1949 was whose interests the new regime would serve—those of the social forces that brought the party to power (primarily the peasantry)? Or of those in whose name the party was brought to power (the proletariat)? Or of the party's own bureaucratic structures and personnel?

Two sets of policy debates dominated the 1950s. The first set has been common to all Soviet systems that sought to refine the constraints of the economic model. The second set concerned the relevance of the Soviet model to the specific situation in China. Did the Soviet approach to development require incremental changes or a wholesale rethinking of the model?

Any socialist framework limits the possibility for change, with policy debate shuffling along a continuum of alternatives.[4] The framework essentially is characterized by a centrally planned economy with dominant, if not total, social ownership of the means of production and overseen by a hierarchical, highly centralized political power structure concentrated within a one-party state ruling over an atomized civil society, which is weak and ineffective in terms of exerting restraint. Fundamental change is possible only once these pillars are weakened.

The persistence of these features ensures that debate revolves around a limited number of core questions. In the economy, what is the relationship between the party and government and the state-owned sector, and can the collective and private sectors play a supplemental role? If so, to what extent? What is the most appropriate relationship between consumption and accumulation? Is there a role for foreign trade, especially trade with capitalist countries? Should managers and workers be incentivized to work by material incentives or by moral exhortation and social recognition?

With respect to management and administration, there have been different views about the role of directive planning and the use of economic incentives to guide the behavior of economic actors. For the production units, debates have focused on how much autonomy they should be allowed and in which functional areas. Should they be responsible for their own profits and losses? As China questioned the viability of the Soviet model, one important question was whether economic decision-making resides with the center, with the local administrative units, or with the enterprises themselves.

The most important debate in the political realm was over the correct relationship between the party secretaries in enterprises and other workplaces and the authority of the managers. How much control should party secretaries exert in the workplace? Should their work be limited to ideology and propaganda and to ensuring that in broad outline the political line is followed? In the universities and research institutes, how much intellectual freedom should be permitted? Finally, there were questions about the role of civil society and its organizations. Could civil society even exist within socialism? If so, should it take on social tasks on behalf of the state? How should it be regulated to ensure that civil organizations do not stray from party policy?

Preparation for Rule

The CCP began preparations for the post-liberation state before the seizure of power. As it became more confident that it would win the civil war, the CCP began to summarize the recent past and its plans for the future. Mao Zedong had been consumed with war planning, but as the CCP moved to take power, his health was not good. Further, shortly after announcing the establishment of the PRC, Mao spent two months in Moscow, from December 1949 into February 1950. At that time the Soviet Union was the only effective model for how to shape the new state. The experiences in the base areas were important, but these were primarily rural areas rather than the major cities that the CCP would eventually control. Industrialization along the lines of Stalin's Soviet Union became the priority. There was a shortage not only of experience but also of skilled personnel, resulting in the retention of many of those who had worked for the Nationalists. Further, the CCP could not afford to alienate the business community.

To provide assistance, a huge influx of Soviet advisers arrived in China to work in all sectors. Overseeing the creation of the new state were Liu Shaoqi, Ren Bishi, and Zhou Enlai.[5] Liu would expand the state model he had developed in North China; Ren was well trained by the Soviets and understood their organizational practices; and Zhou was the chief diplomat who would handle united front affairs and international relations, along with intelligence gathering. None of them, however, shared to the same degree Mao Zedong's voluntarism and willingness to take on seemingly insurmountable obstacles in unorthodox ways. In the early 1950s it seemed as if China would settle down into an essentially Soviet-style state, with some variation, given the overwhelming importance of the rural population. The search for a suitable state form that had consumed China since the end of the Qing dynasty appeared to be resolved. This was not to be the case, however, as some in the Chinese leadership began to question the consequences of the Soviet model for Chinese conditions.

In September 1948 the Politburo met to tighten up organization as the party anticipated victory. They met at Xibaipo, in western Hebei province, in what was the largest gathering of party leaders since the end of the war with Japan. At the time, however, Mao did not predict victory for another five years. The party repeated its call for a political consultative conference that would be held in the liberated areas and attended by nonparty democrats, the democratic parties, and various people's organizations to establish the provisional government of the PRC.[6] This continued the approach of wooing those who were disillusioned with the GMD and presenting the CCP as nothing to be afraid of.

The key problem to be addressed was centralizing party organization, which had suffered from significant dislocation because of the war years. Although a certain degree of local autonomy was important, discipline had suffered with problems of "anarchy, localism, and guerrillaism." For Mao, this meant that the necessary powers should be concentrated in the hands of the CC and its organs. This would facilitate the shift from guerrilla warfare to regular warfare. The shift in the focus of party work from the rural areas to the cities would contribute to centralization.

Resolutions were passed that sought to tighten the party's organizational structure. The Politburo resolved that party meetings would be convened properly in line with the stipulations in the statutes. On paper, at least, the CCP was sounding like a regular Marxist-Leninist party, and Mao even signed on to restoring rule by party committees.[7] Congresses and conferences were to be held regularly, and party committees were to be strengthened to counteract the tendency toward one-person rule. Important matters had to be decided collectively, not by individuals. In a statement that stretched reality somewhat, the resolution claimed that "Marxist-Leninist revolutionary theories and democratic centralism have served as the basis for the CCP from the day it was established."[8]

By January 1949 the Politburo predicted that victory was close at hand and would be achieved in 1949 or 1950. The Politburo called for the creation of an air force and a navy to protect the coasts and rivers. However, as the armies were taking over increasing amounts of territory, the Politburo warned against complacency, and in the South for the next three to five years it called for a moderate policy of rent and interest reduction rather than land redistribution. In 1949 it called for a political consultative conference to be convened, the announcement of the establishment of the PRC, and the establishment of the central government.

It was not the rural areas but instead the Northeast that served as the model for the occupation of the cities. The framework was pulled together at a city work conference that ran from late July until August 31, 1948. The principal future task was to develop the state sector of the economy, which was strongest in the Northeast. With "feudalism and bureaucratic capitalism" completely destroyed, the party described an economy composed of five elements: the state sector, the cooperative economy, the national capitalist economy, the private capitalist economy, and the small-scale commodity economy. With its socialist character, the state sector would forge an economic alliance between the urban proletariat and the rural peasants to protect the interests of the proletariat. The lack of experience in managing a modern economy was a major problem, but this could be addressed by studying management and bringing the sector under the control of a unified plan. Plans incorporated Mao's ideas about the role of the cooperatives as a way for the state to link up with the large number of small producers. However, participation was to be voluntary and beneficial to those who joined. The cooperative economy would be led by the proletariat, and in a clear indication of what was to come after 1949, collectivization and cooperativization were presented as key to preparing the countryside for the introduction of socialism. Private capital was not to be frightened away, but it could not be allowed to develop unfettered and thus it had to be kept in check. The form of state capitalism developed in the Northeast would integrate the private economy, thus avoiding the anarchy and panic of a capitalist economy.[9] This important framework outlined policy for the post-1949 regime: collectivization in the countryside and tying private capital to the state, or to the interests of the party. The policy would facilitate a smooth transfer to "socialism without bloodshed." Clearly, all economic activity was to serve the interests of the state; the private economy would be allowed only insofar as it met this objective.

In March 1949 the Second Plenum of the Seventh CC furthered preparation for rule, confirming that it was time to convene a political consultative conference and to form a democratic coalition government. Importantly, the plenum did not propose a state form of the dictatorship of the proletariat; instead, in keeping with the idea of the united front, it adopted the slightly less ferocious term "people's democratic dictatorship." Work was to focus on the cities. In contrast to the strategy since 1927, surrounding the cities from the countryside was to be replaced in the South by the PLA first occupying the cities and then moving to the countryside.

Confirming his growing importance in the transition, Liu Shaoqi delivered the key report to the plenum. For the most part he focused on the work for the cities, with the exception of acknowledging mistakes in recent rural work, mistakes for which he himself was primarily responsible. Liu outlined the problem of engaging the private sector and helping to restore healthy production. If owners of important private enterprises proved difficult, cadres or military representatives were to be sent in to supervise them. Indeed, as the PLA moved to conquer the South, the first manifestation of the CCP came in the form of those wearing military uniforms.

With rules for the party strengthened, priorities for urban work outlined, and policies for the economy clarified, it remained for the party to outline the new state form that would govern China. On June 30, 1949, to mark the twenty-eighth anniversary of the party's founding, Mao Zedong published "On the People's Democratic Dictatorship," which outlined a four-class united front: the working class, the peasantry, the urban petty bourgeoisie, and the national bourgeoisie. The working class assumed leadership, which in practice meant the CCP as the vanguard of the proletariat. Unlike the move toward a more highly centralized political power, the description of the four classes made more sense for the economy. To get the war-torn economy back on track, support for what the CCP described as the national bourgeoisie was essential. Capitalism would be regulated but not destroyed, and the national bourgeoisie had to be educated to understand when the time was ripe to "realize socialism, that is, to nationalize private enterprise." Internationally, Mao put forward the notion of "leaning toward one side," making China a part of the "anti-imperialist front headed by the USSR."[10]

The cities in the South continued to fall to the PLA—Nanjing in April, Shanghai and Wuhan in May, and Guangzhou in October. On December 10, 1949, Chiang Kai-shek retreated to Taiwan, where he ruled until his death in 1975. The CCP had laid out clearly what people could expect after the CCP took power: rural land would be collectivized, private capital would eventually be squeezed out, the state sector of the economy would be preserved and developed, and institutions of the state and mass organizations would be under the leadership of the proletariat.

In September 1949 the Chinese People's Political Consultative Conference (CPPCC) met in Beijing to proclaim the establishment of the PRC. The authority of the CPPCC was a concrete manifestation of the politics of the united front and the CCP's initial commitment to New Democracy and to a gradual phase of transition. Many members of the CPPCC were non-Communists, but they were figures of influence within society and special ists and experts upon whom the party would rely. However, the CPPCC's most urgent task was to oversee its replacement as the nation's most important government agency. The meeting of the CPPCC elected the Central People's Government Council and the Government Administration Council, the forerunner of the State Council, and it approved the Common Program and the Organic Law that outlined the organizational principles of the new state structure.

In 1954 the National People's Congress (NPC) met and took over the powers from the CPPCC to become the highest organ of state power. The new State Constitution armed the NPC with a formidable array of powers, but in reality, the agenda was not set by the NPC. Major decisions and appointments were to be made by the party, and usually ratified by the CC and then passed on to the NPC for its "consideration." The 1954 meeting placed most municipalities under the leadership of provinces, with the exception of the three major cities of Beijing, Shanghai, and Tianjin. A second autonomous region was set up for Xinjiang, and preparations began for the creation of an autonomous region for Tibet (only realized in 1965).[11] In 1958 Ningxia and Guangxi were added. The State Council was established as the executive organ of the NPC, made up of various ministers and overseen by a premier—the position held by Zhou Enlai from 1954 until his death in 1976.

By and large, this has remained the administrative system ever since, with people's congresses and people's political consultative conferences operating at all levels of government (national, provincial, county and district, township and town). The CPPCC has continued as an advisory body, but it became insignificant as the Mao years rolled on. The congress and its agencies at the local level were subject to dual rule: from the higher level of government and the government—that is, party—administration at the same level.

During these first few years there were important domestic and international developments. Domestically, land reform was completed, progressive social legislation was passed, but major campaigns were launched to control opposition and root out corruption.[12] Externally, the CCP signed the Treaty of Friendship, Alliance, and Mutual Assistance with the Soviet Union and entered the Korean War. The early period, 1949–1952, was billed as years for creating stability and consolidation. An administrative framework was established along Soviet lines, with party penetration of the state. An important component of this system was the use of revolutionary terror against enemies of the state to ensure compliance by the broader population to the norms and objectives of their new rulers. This was revealed most obviously with the nationwide extension of land reform, the Campaign to Suppress Counterrevolutionaries (1950–1953), and the Three-Anti and Five-Anti Campaigns (1951–1953).[13] The harshness of the campaigns was heightened by China's engagement in the war on the Korean peninsula. The repression of undesirables who stood in the way of revolutionary consolidation was accompanied by paternalism toward key constituencies (peasants, workers, and party bureaucrats) to mobilize their support.[14]

Land Reform: Destroying the Old?

Land reform was crucial to party survival before 1949 and for the consolidation of power after 1949. Mao Zedong saw land policy as integrally linked to success in the civil war and the initial post-1949 period. However, the "land to the tiller" policy in the base areas was soon abandoned in favor of collectivization. Before 1949, policy varied contingent on the situation at the time and the balance between the power of the Communists and the need for support from different social forces.

On May 4, 1946, the CC announced a more radical turn in policy. A directive drafted by Liu Shaoqi moved policy from rent and interest reduction to attempts to realize Sun Yat-sen's dream of land to the tiller.[15] The claim was that the party was responding to actions on the ground, where the masses had been spontaneously seizing the land of landlords. In some places the policy of equal distribution of land was limiting all people, including landlords, to a mere three mu of land, barely enough to survive on. How widespread this was is unclear, but it seems to have been based primarily on experiences in the North and Northeast.[16] Although party members had previously been hesitant to radicalize policy, now they were told to support the peasants' "reasonable demands" and endorse land transfers where they had already occurred. The party leadership did not want to be seen as lagging behind the peasant masses, especially at a time when they were suffering in the civil war. Policy intent was to tie the peasantry to the fortunes of the CCP—if the party were to be driven out, the peasants would face severe retribution from the returning elite. Yet there was a degree of moderation, with middle peasants protected and rich peasants coming under pressure to give up their land only when other peasants demanded it. Gentry and landlords who were sympathetic to the Communist cause were to be treated carefully, and to protect commercial activity, their commercial enterprises were not to be confiscated. Even the unrepentant, collaborators, evil gentry, and local despots were to be guaranteed enough land to survive. This courtesy would not extend to those who had committed "heinous crimes," who were to be executed after a trial. This was a modified form of the rural united front.

Given its importance, the land question was discussed extensively at the National Land Conference, which was held in Xibaipo from July 17 to September 13, 1947. Over time, and from place to place, policy had vacillated between rightist and leftist deviations. Bad weather also had an impact on the rural areas. For example, in Yan'an by late 1946, some 40,000 people were short of food; by April 1947 that number had increased to 400,000.[17] The situation was similar in other bases. In some cases, peasants were unable to till the land because they were required to support the Communists. With the increasing number of mouths to feed in the bases and the heavy administrative toll, extractions by the Communists were reaching a precarious level. Consolidating land reform to ensure support was deemed essential.

Considering the wartime situation, the Xibaipo conference was a major affair, attended by about 1,000 delegates who exchanged views about land reform to date. To ensure conformity, the meeting adopted the "Outline Land Law of China" on October 10, 1947.[18] Despite spending most of the previous two decades working in the white areas, Liu Shaoqi emerged as the key figure overseeing land reform, delivering a major report and a summary. In Liu's analysis, land reform had been thorough only in Shanxi-Hebei-Shandong-Henan and the northern Jiangsu bases. Work in other bases such as Shanxi-Chahar-Hebei had been held up by bureaucratism. The peasants desired land and democratic freedoms, which the CCP defined as a basic guarantee for consolidating land reform. For Liu, although rightist mistakes (being too lenient) had been corrected, now the problem was leftism, whereby local officials used their unlimited power to force the peasants to attend meetings and to beat and kill landlords.[19]

In Liu Shaoqi's view, a major part of the problem was that in many counties, leadership was in the hands of landlords and rich peasants. At the village level, middle peasants dominated, and the poor peasants who had formed the majority in the earlier years of the War of Resistance were now a minority. Thus, the formerly heralded three-thirds policy, which was intended to give the former elite a stake in the new future, acted as a brake on the radicalization of land policy. Corruption of the system ran deep, with many veteran cadres succumbing to temptation by marrying the daughters of landlords. To investigate, higher levels would send in work teams, a method that would be commonly used in the future. Often they snuck into the villages secretly, because once they became known, they were lied to by local officials. Power transformation in the villages was to be carried out by creating poor peasant leagues and peasant associations, with village officials subject to annual elections to keep them in line.

At the core of the Land Law was the equal distribution of land among all villagers, regardless of age or sex. Confiscation included not only land but also homes and all movable property. The poor peasant leagues and peasant associations oversaw this process, with arbitration decided by newly established people's courts. What was proposed was nothing short of a new socioeconomic revolution. Extending the policy to the various base areas unleashed turmoil that challenged party power. The party was trapped between dealing with the enormous social dislocation and fighting the escalating war.

As the CCP took over new areas, the problems became worse. The party identified a causal relationship between land reform and support for the war, but it clearly overestimated the relationship. In December 1947 Mao warned about repeating the mistakes of 1931–1934 when the ultra-left policy had resulted in the landlords receiving no land. The interests of the middle peasant were to be protected. The expansion of the party, which had grown from tens of thousands in 1937 to 2.7 million in 1947, exacerbated the problem. Inevitably, landlords, rich peasants, and other "riffraff" had joined the party and taken up leadership positions, so it was necessary to educate and reorganize the party ranks.[20]

Through 1948, attempts were made to moderate land reform, and reports indicated that some peasants had been incorrectly classified as landlords or rich peasants and that some industrial and commercial enterprises had been encroached upon. With new areas falling under CCP control, the party was trying to balance policy that had been developed in the old base areas with the challenges that arose in the newly liberated areas. To prevent the ultra-

left policies of 1931–1934 from resurfacing to undermine support, Mao outlined a threefold categorization of the liberated areas, each of which would
require a different policy. In the areas that had been held from before the
Japanese surrender, land redistribution was already completed and thus
nothing more needed to be done. In the areas that had been liberated during
the period from the Japanese surrender to September 1947, the Land Law
was to be fully implemented. The poor peasant leagues would form the leadership core. In the recently liberated areas, the Land Law was to be imple
mented in two stages: First, the rich peasants were to be neutralized, with
only the landlords coming under attack; this would be a two-year process.
Second, land rented out by the rich peasants was to be redistributed, together
with their surplus land and some of their other property; this was to take
one year.[21]

A directive issued by the CC on May 25, 1948, reined in land policy more
effectively. The directive, drafted by Mao, outlined three necessary conditions that had to be satisfied before land reform could be designated as a task
for 1948. All enemy troops had to have been wiped out and the situation
stabilized, and a majority of the basic masses had to be pushing for land reform. but they could not be left to spontaneous actions. Rather, this work
had to be overseen by adequately trained cadres. Consequently, land reform
was not to be undertaken in a number of areas.

Thus, pre-1949 land reform had a checkered history, as the leadership
wrestled with policy responses in the changing environment and the need
to ensure that vital support was not alienated during the civil war. Once they
achieved nationwide victory, these constraints were removed and a maximum
program of land reform could be pursued without fear that the old elite would
desert the revolution and go over to the side of the Nationalists. Even if they
wanted to, there was now nowhere for them to go. For many, peace and stability overrode concerns they may have had about living under the CCP.

Land reform was a crucial component in the destruction of the old state
and in laying the foundations for a new set of power relations that would
enable the party to penetrate more deeply into the countryside than during
any previous regime,. Land reform could not be scrapped immediately in
favor of a rapid move to socialist agriculture. The party leadership was wary
of following the Soviet mistake of promoting a premature rush to rural collectives before winning support from the peasants. Last but not least, the
party did not have sufficient numbers of qualified administrative and technical cadres to effectively manage a collective rural economy. The party ended

the land reform campaign by appointing local people who had cooperated during the campaign and would be loyal to the party leadership at the next higher level. Initially the vast majority of peasants benefited from the reward of new land and this strengthened their support for the CCP. Policy emphasized caution and persuasion, with most excesses coming from below rather than from above.[22] This would change.

A new Land Law of June 28, 1950, pulled together prior legislation and practices.[23] Reporting on the law, Liu Shaoqi stated that "chaotic conditions must not be allowed to occur" and that under CCP guidance the law should be carried out in a "planned, orderly way."[24] To help local officials weave their way through the rural complexities, a fivefold categorization based on property relations was proposed: landlords, rich, middle, and poor peasants, and farm laborers. Redistribution to the laborers and the poor peasants was to be carried out without alienating the rich and middle peasants. The category of middle peasant was the vaguest, but a middle peasant essentially worked the land without engaging in exploitation. The land worked on did not necessarily belong to the peasant, a distinction that would be important subsequently. The land of the landlords was requisitioned and redistributed, with the blow softened for those who had supported the revolution. The land of the rich and middle peasants, including the prosperous middle peasants, was to be protected. Defending a possible attack on a rich peasant line, as Stalin had accused Bukharin in the 1930s, Liu noted that the situation had changed from pre-1949, with the emphasis now on production; furthermore, there was nowhere they could escape to. With military service and corvée labor no longer necessary, and a reduced burden of public grain delivery, peasant life would improve. Peasant associations would be dominated by poor peasants and farm laborers, and more women would be encouraged to participate.

Although Liu Shaoqi predicted that the process would take up to three years, the bulk of land reform was completed in the eighteen months after the 1950 harvest. Several hundred million mu of land were redistributed among some 300 million peasants, giving them each an average of 2 to 3 mu.[25] There was considerable variation among regions, and some areas, such as Tibet, where Beijing had signed a short-lived agreement promising national regional autonomy, did not undergo land reform at all during this phase. In such areas, party power was weak or nonexistent, and the central leadership did not want to alienate the traditional religious elite in the sensitive border areas.

The process was far from peaceful and did not always follow the measured approach outlined by Liu; indeed, violence or the threat of violence was integral to land reform.[26] A peaceful, negotiated approach, as in Japan, Korea, or Taiwan, was not useful to the CCP. Chinese policy toward the rural areas was a classic example of "cutting with one knife"—the application of a class-based analysis of the social structures in the countryside that barely fit the reality on the ground. Much of the countryside did not have a system of recognizable landlords, and the countryside was not feudal in a traditional sense. Wheat farming in the North was very different from rice farming in the South or the much more commercial farming along the fertile Yangzi valley, to say nothing of the nomad areas in the Far West and the Northwest.

In Yantian, southern China, not too far from the border with Hong Kong, lineage was far more important in village life than class-based divisions. If there was struggle, it was between the lineage and outsiders. Nonetheless, land was redistributed and landlords were executed, even though they were all members of the same lineage. Land reform did not begin until after the spring of 1952 with the assignment of class categories, and then work teams were dispatched to ensure that class status had been assessed correctly and redistribution had been carried out accordingly. Of the 784 households, home to 3,054 villagers, eighteen households were classified as landlords and sixteen as rich peasants. Even though this accounted for only 5 percent of the village population, they owned 96.4 percent of the paddy. Landlords held an average of 202 mu, rich peasants held 44.6 mu, and the other categories held only 0.35 mu per household. With redistribution, the work team held a mass rally to denounce the landlords and to ensure obedience; two landlords were executed on the spot. A later review discovered that some of the middle peasants were incorrectly classified as rich peasants.[27]

The variation from region to region made the situation difficult, and actions were often arbitrary such as when some local officials were expected to punish landlords and take their land. It was even more difficult for those officials transferred from the North to the South, where they were wholly unfamiliar with farming practices and social structures. It was not surprising that the so-called liberating potential of land reform was resisted vigorously in some of these areas. Hubei, Guizhou, and even Hunan, Mao Zedong's home province, put up resistance. The main focal point of dissent seemed to be grain procurement by the new state.[28] The party, of course, saw all resistance as counterrevolutionary reaction against the party and its policies.

There were also local leaders who did not pursue the reorganization of the countryside with sufficient ardor. Some chose to spend their time working on their newly acquired land, and some even employed labor. Such rightist tendencies provoked radical actions from the party.[29] Estimates of violence vary and it is difficult to provide an exact number. Up to 800,000 landlords were killed in the campaign of 1950–1952; many more were beaten, tortured, or humiliated in public demonstrations in front of the villagers. If one includes the period from 1946, when land reform began in earnest, the total would be much higher.[30]

Land use was now in the hands of the peasants, but it would not remain that way for long. The CCP was not going to tolerate household-based farming indefinitely, as it ran counter to Stalin's view that collectivization was a key component of socialism. By 1953, with economic revival under way, China's leadership returned to the task of building socialism and viewed a rural system based on private farming and markets as anachronistic. The small size of the farms rendered it difficult to use the land efficiently to produce the necessary surplus for the cities and the industrial enterprises. Mechanization would be difficult on such small tracts of land. According to the Soviet model, to be modern was to be urban and industrialized. Gradualism, if one can refer to land reform in this way, was soon abandoned in favor of collectivization and the curtailment of small-scale rural markets.

Campaigns to Consolidate Political Power

The new regime was impacted by the international environment not only by "leaning to one side" but also by the Korean conflict, which had major consequences for policy. Before the outbreak of the Korean War, Mao Zedong advocated moderation and caution so that the CCP would not lose support as it moved to consolidate power. The focus of attack was on the remaining Nationalist forces, the secret agents, bandits, and landlords. Sovereignty was to be restored by liberating Tibet and Taiwan, while the struggle against the imperialist forces was to continue.[31] War changed the situation dramatically and the party launched a series of tough campaigns to eradicate enemies both real and imagined. The campaigns were successful in rallying support behind the party, or at least ensuring that people were aware of the consequences if they stepped out of line. The landlords were dealt with by land reform, counterrevolutionaries were attacked in a campaign to suppress them, corrupt officials were attacked in the Three-Anti Campaign, private entrepreneurs in the Five-Anti Campaign, and independent intellectuals in a broad thought-reform campaign.

After taking power, the CCP proposed leniency for those who came forward and acknowledged their previous affiliations with the GMD or with other groups that had struggled against the CCP. Concern about resistance was justified. In March 1950 the CCP Southwest Bureau reported that there were 104 bandit groups active in Sichuan, Xikang, Yunnan, and Guizhou, with 60,000 active members, and it warned that this activism could spread.[32] In the summer of 1950 some 1,400 cadres and 700 troops were killed in Guangxi, the province next to the Vietnam border.[33] On October 10, 1950, the CC issued its "Double Ten" directive to respond to these challenges and the Campaign to Suppress Counterrevolutionaries was formally launched.[34] With some leaders, such as Liu Shaoqi and Peng Zhen, pushing for a harsher crackdown, the directive sought a middle path. "Excessive lenience" was rejected in favor of "combining suppression and lenience." Major criminals were to be executed, and others were to be imprisoned, but the majority were to be placed under house arrest. Torture was not permitted, and before sentencing, written proof was to be furnished. As late as December 1950, Mao Zedong reiterated the need for caution because persecution that was too aggressive might undermine support.

The Korean War shifted the focus dramatically. Forced to fulfill quotas for executions and arrests, local officials pulled out their files on those who had voluntarily come forward. By mid-January 1951, Mao was promoting a more aggressive approach, calling for large-scale executions where bandits and secret agents were rampant, and he started establishing quotas, while calling for more executions in Shanghai and Nanjing.[35] To guide punishments, a wide range of counterrevolutionary crimes were listed on the front page of the *People's Daily*.[36] This led to the harshest phase of the campaign— in the spring and summer of 1951. In Guizhou, all eighty-one county magistrates who had been in position at the end of GMD rule were executed, and nearly all of the old township heads around Chengdu were labeled counterrevolutionaries and executed.[37]

The CCP deemed the campaign a success. Together with land reform, it had quelled resistance and mobilized mass support. But this came at a cost. Exact figures for how many died in the campaign are difficult to come by. In 1957 Mao Zedong claimed that 700,000 had been executed.[38] Bo Yibo, a close associate of Liu Shaoqi and a vice premier, suggested a figure of two million, which might be more accurate.[39] In May 1952 the CCP sought to moderate the campaign to limit executions. It introduced the concept of a two-year suspended death sentence to allow the accused time to ruminate on their crimes, repent, and show loyalty to the CCP. This became a core feature of the CCP punishment system.

The Three-Anti Campaign, which ran from November 1951 to June 1952 and merged then with the Five-Anti Campaign, was targeted against the abuse of official positions to engage in corruption, waste, and bureaucratism.[40] The Three-Anti Campaign had the dual function of ensuring the loyalty of officials in the new China, many of whom had served the old regime, and of promoting production. As with most policies pursued in urban China, the campaign originated in the Northeast. In May 1951 Gao Gang launched a movement to "increase production and reduce expenditure," and in November Mao Zedong, when reporting to the CC, criticized "embezzlement and degeneration" and he approved the report calling for expenditures to be reduced and production to be increased by reducing corruption, waste, and bureaucratization.[41]

After the CCP took power, collusion between party and government officials and those seeking the spoils of victory was seen to be rife and had to be curtailed to maintain the momentum of the revolution. In his love of tiger analogies, Mao announced that "big tigers" were those who had embezzled over 10,000 yuan, while "little tigers" had embezzled only 1,000.[42] Bo Yibo found that there were 100,000 "tigers" in East China; in the Northwest 340,000 cases of corruption were uncovered, even though Xi Zhongxun, a vice premier and Xi Jinping's father, thought that there actually may have been three times this number. In October 1952 it was announced that some 1.2 million people had embezzled 600 million yuan.[43] Interestingly, only 200,000 of this group were party members, meaning either that the campaign was directed at holdovers from the old regime or that party members protected one another and blamed the old officials for the problems, or both.

The Five-Anti Campaign that eventually merged with the Three-Anti Campaign made it clear to businesspeople that there would be limits to their acceptability in the new China. The campaign sought to prevent private businesspeople from violating regulations and colluding with local officials. Party members found it useful to focus on the old capitalists rather than themselves. The five targets were to reduce bribery, tax evasion, theft of state property, theft of economic information, and cheating on government contracts. The campaign was overseen by the newly established Federation of Industry and Commerce, which all entrepreneurs had to join. Many of the private entrepreneurs had been persuaded to stay or return by promises that their business activities would be accepted under the terms of New Democracy.[44] Seeking to curry favor with the party, workers denounced not only the entrepreneurs but also other businesspeople. Some even denounced family members who were seen as possibly carrying out betrayal. The campaign led to a dramatic spike in suicides and was the beginning of the end for the capitalist class in China. Official reporting noted that within a two-month period in Shanghai, 644 people had committed suicide.[45] The fines that were levied also came in handy to contribute to the war effort in Korea.

The campaigns spread far and wide across urban China and included thought reform for the intellectuals and urban intelligentsia, reeducation for commercial sex workers as the party moved to close down the brothels, squeezing out the foreign communities in China, and the nationalization of foreign institutions, such as China's most prestigious hospital—the Peking Union Medical College, which had been built and funded by the Rockefellers. Religion came in for special criticism, as priests and nuns were driven out. Not only did foreign religion come under attack but also many secret societies and local religious practices were denounced as evil cults. The campaign against "all secret societies and superstitions" preceded the Campaign for the Suppression of Counterrevolutionaries and similarly started in the consolidated area of North China. A particular target was the influential Unity Sect, whose membership included 200,000 people in Tianjin and 15 percent of the population of Beijing, including 1,100 members of the Public Security Bureau. The sect combined various religious streams: Buddhism, Taoism, Confucianism, Christianity, and Islam.[46] The CCP took similar action in the 1990s with its repression of the Falun Gong religious movement.

Social Reforms: Constructing the New?

In addition to these campaigns to break up traditional elites and to create the new Maoist person, there was important social legislation, such as the Marriage Law and the creation of institutions that would become mainstays of party-state control over society. The Marriage Law, passed on May 1, 1950, reflected the ethos of the May Fourth period, which opposed traditional practices such as arranged marriages, having concubines, and the prevention of divorce. The new law provided a civil registry for marriages and raised the marrying age to twenty for men and eighteen for women. Divorce was tolerated for marriages that dated from the old era, but it became more difficult for those who married after 1949. The party had presented its new policy as enabling marriage based on equality and thus was concerned that divorce did not become a common feature of the new China. Political labels did, however, play an important role in the choice of partner, as no one would want to marry a person with a bad class label.[47]

An important mechanism for party rule over society was reinforcement of the cellular and hierarchical structure of society. Trade unions, student associations, and women's organizations were strengthened to provide sectoral representation, which did not allow for horizontal connections across society or across different administrative jurisdictions. The existence of an official trade union negated any reason to set up an alternative union, and the party suppressed radical activists who pushed for workers' rights that might undermine the CCP's focus on production.[48] Such structural social organizations were referred to as transmission belts in Leninist parlance, but the main direction of communication was from top to bottom, with less capacity for members to influence national policy. The workers learned that their role as masters of the country was subject to party guidance and leadership.

The cellular nature of Chinese society was reinforced by two institutions—household registration and the workplace system that restricted labor mobility. Both were distinct from Soviet practices. These two institutions defined interactions between state and society during the early years of the PRC, and when collectivization was completed in the countryside, the workplace became central to the lives of virtually all those living in China. Household registration privileged urban over rural society and ensured that state resources were channeled primarily to the cities, with substantial amounts of the rural surplus transferred to urban industry, the military, and other priority projects of the party. For the individual, place of birth decisively determined one's life chances, and there were severe restrictions on mobility. For the party-state, this enabled low levels of urbanization and easy monitoring of citizens.

With millions of refugees having fled the land for the cities during the years of war and turmoil, the registration system played a key role in reducing the numbers in urban China. The program was successful because for the most part it was voluntary and the state offered land or cash as an incentive to return to the countryside. Not all returned voluntarily. Many commercial sex workers, beggars, vagrants, and other undesirables were sent back to the countryside irrespective of their wishes. The government did not make it clear that in the future the cities would be closed off to the rural population. However, in 1955 and 1958 new regulations were issued that created a permanent household registration system for the cities and the countryside. The new regulations made it nearly impossible to move legally not only from the countryside to the cities but also between cities and from village to village. This system "established and reified a permanent spatial hierarchy of positions that were transmitted across generations."[49] The one exception was during the Great Leap Forward, when the famine drove many off the land, some 62.5 million in 1958 alone.[50]

The dominance of the workplace in urban China led to "Communist neo-traditionalism" in factory life, a core component of the social foundation of the Chinese Communist political order.[51] Through this system the CCP made use of material incentives and other benefits to create a network of supporters through personal ties, which created a clientelist pattern of authority. Over time this evolved into a system of personal rule, which resulted in a divided workforce. It was reinforced by the increasing dominance of state-owned enterprises in the urban, industrial system.

Leaning to One Side and the Korean Conflict

Given the pre-1949 struggle, it was inevitable that the CCP would choose a close alliance with the Soviet Union, which had significant implications for China's long-term development strategy. In June 1949 Mao Zedong highlighted the policy of leaning to one side that entailed learning from the Soviet Union; anyone who thought differently was naive.[52] Toward the end of 1952, the importance of this alliance became apparent as the party began to think about shifting its focus from recovery to development—which would require increased centralization and conscious adoption of Soviet development practices. With the benefit of hindsight, problems with the Soviet model seem obvious, but at the time it was a logical choice. It was the only socialist model for building a modern state and socializing the economy, and it appeared to be successful. Central planning seemed to offer an effective way to unite the fragmented economy and distribute scarce resources rationally and effectively. Centralization implied one nation unified under CCP rule. Economic centralization paralleled the increasing political centralization that victory in the civil war and the campaigns of the early 1950s had consolidated. Furthermore, China required considerable financial and technical aid, and given the contemporary environment, even more so after the Korean War began, the Soviet Union was their only option.[53]

After seizing power in Beijing, Mao Zedong undertook his first foreign trip to spend two months in Moscow, from December 16, 1949, to February 17, 1950. His main purpose was to sign the Treaty of Friendship, Alliance, and Mutual Assistance. This had been delayed several times and, as a result, he first sent Liu Shaoqi, together with Gao Gang, who was the head of the party in the Northeast, and Wang Jiaxiang. Their negotiations in Moscow paved the way for adoption of the treaty, which was signed during Mao's visit.[54] Liu was asked to secure a $300 million loan and push for Soviet advisers and support for the PLA in Xinjiang, and he presented a major report to Stalin and the Soviet Politburo on the Chinese revolution and its policies.[55]

Although Mao got most of what he wanted, he was frustrated during his visit by being kept waiting and not being accorded sufficient respect. His three main objectives were to seek Soviet security and protection against the United States, to be reassured that there would be Soviet assistance as outlined in the talks between Stalin and Liu Shaoqi, and to kill off the lingering treaty that Stalin had agreed to with Chiang Kai-shek in 1945.[56] The new treaty, which was signed on February 14, 1950, recognized the PRC, thus ending recognition of the Republic of China, and gave China its $300 million in loans (which were used up by 1953), a security guarantee, support to help develop the air force and long-range artillery, and the return of sovereignty over the Chinese Eastern Railway, Dalian, and Lüshun.

The outbreak of conflict on the Korean peninsula was a world-changing event. The origins of the war have been much debated, obscured by access to only partial information. Before the establishment of the Democratic People's Republic of Korea in September 1948, China had been using the territory as a base for operations in Manchuria and to deal with the Soviet Union.[57] Mao supported the Soviet presence in Korea but thought that over time, as the PRC settled down, China would take on greater responsibility for Korea's defense. The Chinese leadership was worried about the possibility that Kim Il-sung, Korea's leader, would try to reunify Korea by force and might push the Soviets to support this. Indeed, from 1948 into 1950, Kim bombarded Moscow with almost fifty telegrams expressing enthusiasm for reunification.[58]

It is surprising that Stalin never mentioned to Mao Zedong in February 1950 that he was also making plans with Kim. Given that Stalin had already turned down Mao's request for assistance for Taiwan, he may have considered it inopportune, and there was always the possibility that Mao might have rejected the idea.[59] China's leaders thought that Stalin shared their view, but Mao Zedong was shocked when Kim went to Beijing on May 13, 1950, to announce that he had Soviet support for a push south. Requesting confirmation, Mao received a reply stating that any decision should be taken jointly by the Koreans and the Chinese and that, if there were disagreement, any resolution should be postponed. However, Mao was also informed that Stalin agreed with the Koreans that they should begin reunification. Left with little choice, Mao confirmed his support.[60] Stalin had already shifted his initial stance to not challenge the United States on the Korean peninsula, but no one really expected that the United States would intervene in the conflict. Mao had commented that they should not be afraid, as "the Americans will not enter a third world war over such a small territory."[61] It was a fateful, incorrect assessment by all concerned.

The Chinese leadership still seemed surprised by the notification that an attack was to take place on June 25, and while offering support, it did not think its own troops would enter the conflict. When the Soviet Union withdrew from the United Nations Security Council deliberations, the council voted, with only Yugoslavia abstaining, to send UN forces to Korea. The US response was unexpected. US troops landed at Inchon and drove the North Korean forces back toward the Yalu River and the Chinese border. On October 1, Stalin informed the Chinese that without their support, the Korean resistance would collapse. Despite reservations, including those of Mao himself, the view that Chinese intervention was inevitable eventually won out, and on October 18, the order was sent for the Chinese People's Volunteer Army under Peng Dehuai to engage and support the Koreans. After Stalin died, peace negotiations could be pursued, and on July 27, 1953, a ceasefire was signed. The war had been brutal. Some 152,000 Chinese soldiers had been killed and a further 230,000 wounded; North Korea lost 520,000 troops, South Korea 415,000, and the United States 142,000.[62] The Soviet Union lost only 299 troops. The cost for China was enormous, and a serious set back to its ability to invest in the future, making it even more reliant on Soviet support. At the end of the three years, Korea was still divided along its prewar border.

China's Golden Age?

With internal opposition effectively curtailed, land reform completed, the urban population warned about future behavior, and the Korean conflict ending, the leadership turned its attention to completing the goals of the revolution. Whether or not these early years were a golden age depended on where one viewed the situation from. The domestic wars had ended and this held out hope that a period of stability and tranquility might follow. The poorer farmers had access to land that they had never had before. Many workers had guarantees that they did not have before, although activists' wings had been clipped. The party leadership and most of those who had fought their way out of the base areas and down from the North had their wishes fulfilled with a unified China, free of colonial dominance. The view looked very different, though, for the old elite in the countryside, and patriotic capitalists thought they saw signs that the united front might be shorter-lived than they had been led to expect. For intellectuals and scientists, it was clear that they had to follow the new orthodoxy of the CCP and the Soviets.[63] Writers and performers had to take Mao Zedong's Yan'an Talks on Literature and Art to heart: they were to be uncritical promoters of the party, not critical voices about the Chinese state and society. Many of those who had benefited or had been left unharmed by this first phase would be shaken by the turn of events in the following years as the revolution radicalized. The period also saw the first major post-1949 political purge.

In June 1953 Mao Zedong outlined the path forward for the economy and society with the policy statement "General Line for the Transition Period." This projected that the country's industrialization and socialist transformation of agriculture, handicrafts, and capitalist industry and commerce would be accomplished over a "relatively long period of time."[64] "Gradually" and "relatively long" were the key words here—the estimate was that this would take ten to fifteen years—but in fact it took only three years. At a meeting of the Central Secretariat in September 1952, the transition had already been approved and preparations made.[65] The approach was approved by the February 1954 CC plenary meeting. And in case anyone had missed it, the new State Constitution of September 20, 1954, stated that the "necessary conditions have been created for the planned economic construction and gradual transition to socialism." In October 1953 the First Five-Year Plan was effectively launched. Although it was not formally ratified until 1955, it covered the temporary economic programs of 1951–1954.

China was to become a Soviet-style economy and society; thus, it would encounter many of the problems that had already surfaced in the Soviet Union and those with which the new satellite countries of Eastern Europe were beginning to wrestle. The Soviet model emphasized the productive forces; this meant that investment focused on infrastructure and heavy industry, and social spending and consumer demand were ignored. The service sector was poor to nonexistent.[66] Private enterprise was to be eradicated, and the urban economy would be based on the state-owned sector. This concentration allowed investments and pricing to be controlled by the central plan. Agriculture was to serve industry, and prices were to be set artificially low to keep down food prices in the cities, which in turn meant that wages were to be held down. Collectivization also made it easier for the national government to extract produce from the countryside and channel resources to the urban areas where industrialization could advance. Common prosperity was delayed until a later stage of economic development.[67]

Initially the application of Soviet planning appeared successful, and the necessary infrastructure for heavy industry developed rapidly. This was not surprising, as 88 percent of state capital investment was in heavy industry: 649 major industrial enterprises were to be built, of which 472 were to be situated in the interior provinces of China. Of these, 156 were to be constructed using Soviet advice and equipment. Industrial production was growing at 18 percent per annum, well above the target of 14.7 percent. Not surprisingly, agricultural growth lagged at 4.5 percent, but that was very respectable by global standards. However, some doubted that agriculture would be able to support the projected urban growth and the ambitious plans for industrial expansion. The leadership became convinced that the collectivization of agriculture had to be promoted; the only question was, how quickly?

When the plan to collectivize agriculture was launched, the Chinese economy was relatively weak compared with that of the Soviet Union. In 1952, Soviet output per capita was about four times that of China, and Chinese agricultural output was only one-fifth that in the Soviet Union. The result was that less could be extracted from the countryside to fuel the programs for industrial development. By 1956, Chinese repayments of Soviet loans began to exceed the value of new monetary aid, meaning that the Chinese leadership would have to devise policies to more effectively generate investment capital.[68] Agricultural production had to be increased and farming made more efficient, both of which were unlikely given the small scale of household-based farming. The stage was set for the eradication of private enterprise in the cities and the end of the first phase of land reform in the countryside. Chinese society began to exhibit key features of the Soviet Union, and the tensions in the model soon became apparent.

Although national capitalists were initially encouraged to lay the foundations for a modern economic structure, they would have no opportunity to benefit from it. The mixed economy functioned, but the state made sure that it alone had the ability to coordinate economic activity. Once bound into state patronage, the national capitalists were ripe for elimination. The approach taken allowed the party to transform the mixed economy to its own advantage without creating a major disruption in production and distribution. The state controlled both ends of the production process, controlling the inputs and raw materials that the enterprises needed through allocation by the national ministries and then placing orders with the private entrepreneurs for processed and manufactured goods. This bound the privately controlled companies into state patronage, and the CCP began to promote the creation of joint state-private enterprises. Unable to compete with the state sector and lacking sufficient capital to replace their outdated machinery, many entrepreneurs acquiesced. The push reached a peak in 1954 with the program to buy out private owners, who were paid interest on their shares at a rate determined by the state. The policy proved to be very beneficial for the party, as even in 1952 industrial production was restored to its highest pre-1949 levels.

The neglect of consumption as a driving force for the economy meant that not only conspicuous consumption but also all consumption had to be carefully controlled. Austerity was a core component of the development strategy, and it was achieved through three mechanisms: ideological exhortation, restricting high incomes, and rationing. These went hand in hand with an egalitarian distribution policy and elevating the interests of the collective above those of the individual. Workers were exhorted to work hard today for a brighter future tomorrow. Rewards for good work were not monetary bonuses but instead red flags and public recognition at meetings. A system of ration coupons for virtually all goods was established in 1955, paired with frustrating long queues and a scarcity of goods to purchase. A friend of mine brought up under socialism would automatically join any queue, noting that if there was a queue, there must be something good at the end of it.

Basic ration coupons were issued for rice or grain, cloth, cooking oil, and so forth. There were also industrial ration coupons for higher-grade goods, such as bicycles, although there was also a waiting list for such products. This was the source of petty corruption and favoritism, as local officials controlled who came where on the list. The system of rationing reinforced the lack of mobility, as the use of ration coupons was tied to the place of issue. This meant that most people could consume only what was available in their local jurisdiction. The policy of self-reliance was not only for production but also for consumption, which was linked to local production. Given the technical backwardness of China and the concentration of large-scale industry in a few coastal cities and the Northeast, geographical self-reliance could only work if consumption was restricted to a few basic commodities. This privileged areas such as Shanghai that could produce more goods of higher quality. Its "flying pigeon" bicycle was a much-coveted item.[69]

In the countryside, the shift from family-based farming was implemented quickly. With the move to socialism, a rural sector based on private farming was anachronistic. For Soviet- inspired planners, bigger was better and swift growth was more important than the quality of production. Gradualism was abolished, and although cooperativization began relatively slowly, by 1955–1956 the crash program of communization gathered pace. The shift away from land reform went through four distinct stages: mutual-aid teams (1952–1954); lower-stage agricultural producers' cooperatives (APCs, 1954–1955); higher-stage APCs (1956–1957); and people's communes (1958–1959).

The transition began slowly with the formation of mutual-aid teams that shared seasonal work and other chores. This built on traditional practices, with five to eight households combining their labor in busy seasons. Even though labor was pooled, animals, tools, and land were still in the hands of the individual households. In the village of Yantian, less than six months after the poor peasants had received their land the CC issued two documents, in February and December 1953, that confirmed the an initial three-stage transition. This move surprised villagers; they felt that even if there were problems with household farming, there had been little time for such problems to be uncovered. However, the program for mutual-aid teams was carried out through the summer of 1953 and temporary collaborations soon turned into permanent entities; in less than one year, 556 households (74 percent of the total) had formed teams.[70]

The next step was to move to the lower-stage APCs. Each of these cooperatives grouped together roughly 30 households, including not only labor but also property, land, farm implements, and draft animals. The peasants received income proportional to the size of the shares of property that they contributed. In Yantian the process began in October 1954 with the formation of the Nanxi lower-stage APC, with 168 households. This was unusual and was on the scale of the higher-stage APCs that would follow in 1956 as policy became more radical. Following Mao's report "On the Question of

Agricultural Cooperativization" (July 31, 1955) outlining the necessity of lower-stage APCs, while still noting that they were voluntary, three more were formed. This time they were formed under the guidance of a work team sent by a higher-level administration. By the end of 1955, as a result, 548 households (71 percent of the total) had formed lower-stage APCs. In Yantian, as elsewhere in rural China, the peasants lost out to a party system that sought to penetrate society to undermine tradition and to break up social structures so as to exert greater control over the lineage. Relations that extended outside the village, which were once mediated by the market and travel, were attenuated by statist restrictions.[71] The peasants of Yantian were not happy that their land was taken away, but far worse was yet to come.

By 1955 the large military forces that had been needed for the civil war and the Korean conflict had been demobilized. Many of the troops had come from rural areas, and significant numbers of former soldiers could be placed in the newly formed collectives, providing leadership for the local areas while helping to resolve the problem of employment for demobilized soldiers.

The speed of the transition concerned some in the CCP leadership, who were worried that it could cause disruption and even opposition. Through the summer and fall of 1955, not only in Yantian but nationwide, the formation of APCs moved swiftly, which created a sense of euphoria among the leadership. However, the transition was accompanied by peasant dissatisfaction, as voluntary became compulsory. Reports spread of peasants slaughtering their livestock and destroying their agricultural assets. In addition, a bad flood led to the government levying a tax of 5 billion jin.[72] This led to calls in January and February 1955 to consolidate the progress to date. Interestingly, it was Mao Zedong who proposed an approach more moderate than that of Deng Zihui, who oversaw the program in his position as vice premier responsible for agriculture. Whereas Deng Zihui had called for 50 percent of peasants to be in APCs by the end of 1955, Mao cautioned that one-third would be better.[73] In provinces such as Zhejiang and Hebei, the number of APCs was reduced and work in the Northeast was brought to a halt; across the nation the number was reduced from 670,000 to 650,000. However, in a sudden about-turn following a trip to the South in April 6–22, Mao decided to step up the pace. He felt that the situation was better than he had expected and the problem was that some local officials were holding back.

Mao criticized Deng Zihui and warned him not to repeat earlier mistakes. In July he upped the stakes, declaring, "Some of our comrades, tottering along like a woman with bound feet, are complaining all the time, 'You're going too fast, much too fast.' Too much carping, unwarranted complaints, boundless anxiety and countless taboos—all this they take as the right policy to guide the socialist mass movement in the rural areas."[74] Mao used a typical approach to promote his agenda by circumventing other central leaders, delivering the speech to local leaders to ensure that the movement would accelerate. In October 1955 at an Enlarged Plenum of the Seventh CC, Mao told those assembled that leaders in the CC Rural Work Department, espe cially Deng Zihui, had made mistakes that were right deviationist and empiricist. He added with the following flourish: "It is also wrong to say that 'no co-operatives can be set up with junks and animal-drawn carts.' As we see it now, the millions of working people engaged in junk or animal-drawn cart transport should also be organized into co-operatives."[75] The stage was set for the next radical phase.

The PRC's First Major Political Purge: Exit Gao Gang

Despite debates over the speed of the transition, throughout this period the leadership remained reasonably united, with the exception of the purges of Gao Gang and Rao Shushi, the leaders in the Northeast. In February 1954 the CC charged Gao with having attempted to set up an independent kingdom in the Northeast and, even more amazingly, having schemed to seize state power.[76] Gao had been a key figure in the Shaanxi-Gansu-Ningxia Border Region and had been praised by Mao for his work there. Subsequently he had been transferred to Manchuria to oversee the construction of Communist power. This was the first area consolidated by the Communists, and it was the industrial heartland where the Soviet model of development made the most sense. In addition, Gao was known to enjoy a close relationship with the Soviet Union and was a great admirer of its achievements.

Starting in 1949, Gao Gang had been providing information to Stalin on the Chinese leadership, especially about Liu Shaoqi, whom he described as being rightist and "overestimating the Chinese bourgeoisie." For good measure, he threw in criticism of other leaders, such as Zhou Enlai and Bo Yibo. Stalin rejected Gao's assessment and said that Liu Shaoqi had been correct on the question of including the democratic parties in China. Apparently Gao had also mentioned the anti-Soviet and "right Trotskyite" tendencies of Mao Zedong! Despite Gao's high regard for the Soviet Union, he himself was not held in high regard by Stalin. When Stalin and Gao met with

Liu Shaoqi in Moscow in 1949, Stalin cut off Gao, who was making some extravagant proposals calling him "Comrade Zhang Zuolin"—the name of Manchurian warlord who had ruled the Northeast until 1928. Presumably Stalin alerted Mao to Gao's attitude and handed over to him various reports and materials that had originated with Gao via Russian interlocutors.[77]

In late 1952 and early 1953, as the leadership began to think about moving on from recovery, a number of leaders were transferred to the capital. Gao Gang was appointed head of the State Planning Commission, a very powerful position, and Rao Shushi was moved from East China to head the Organization Department, another very powerful party organ. The main reason for their removal was Mao's suspicion of subordinates who might pose a challenge and factional strife between those who had worked in the white areas and the Red Army leaders.[78] Liu Shaoqi, of course, had built his credibility based on his work in the occupied areas. Although Liu was clearly number two in the hierarchy, he had differed with Mao over the speed of the transition to socialism. In discussions with Gao, it seems that Mao suggested his dissatisfaction with Liu and Zhou Enlai. Gao possibly saw this as an opportunity to challenge Liu. In terms of policy, Gao was in favor of a more rapid transition, the swift elimination of the bourgeoisie, and pursuit of the Soviet model.

Consequently, at the National Conference on Finance and Economic Work in mid-June to mid-August 1953, Gao Gang criticized a close associate of Liu, Minister of Finance Bo Yibo, who had put forward favorable tax concessions for the remaining capitalists. Mao shared Gao's view, but did not see Bo's mistake as being too egregious. During the National Organization Work Conference in September–October, Rao Shushi criticized another Liu Shaoqi associate, An Ziwen, for the slate of candidates he put forward for the new Politburo leadership, a slate that was said to favor leaders from the white areas. The final straw came when Mao called for Liu Shaoqi to take over during his absence in December. As a counter, Gao Gang suggested rotating the deputy for Mao. It seems that Gao also sounded out other colleagues about replacing Liu, and this news filtered back to Mao. At the end of December, Mao criticized Gao's underground activities and left Liu to run the February 1954 Fourth Plenum, which criticized Gao and Rao.

Zhou Enlai summarized Gao's mistakes, prompting Gao to attempt suicide. His first attempt failed; his second attempt, in August 1954, succeeded. Gao was only too aware of the fate of those who crossed Mao. It is unclear why a public denunciation was slow in coming, perhaps because of the need to maintain the veneer of unity or perhaps because Gao had deeper support within the party. It was not until March 1955 that Gao and Rao were expelled from the party, in Gao's case posthumously, and a short resolution was promulgated. Deng Xiaoping reported to the March 1955 National Party Conference providing far more detail on the accusations against the two.[79]

The purge revealed three things about the political process within the CCP. First, Mao was clearly the central figure, with colleagues jockeying for favor in "politics at Mao's court." Second, it was very dangerous to try to second-guess Mao, who could shift his views quickly, and one should not be seen to be making a grab for power. Third, there were dangers in being seen as an heir-apparent. This fate would befall Liu Shaoqi later and then Lin Biao during the Cultural Revolution.[80] While support for the Soviets may not have been the core reason for the purge, the removal of Gao and Rao did coincide with a wider debate about the suitability of the Soviet model for China. In March 1955 the Campaign to Wipe out Hidden Counterrevolutionaries was launched to remove any remaining supporters and to reassert Mao's and his allies' control over the economic and political bureaucracies, which had increased in power once the First Five-Year Plan was launched. The path was opened for a shift in development strategy.

The economic problems that had developed in the Soviet Union also emerged in China. Overly concentrating on heavy industry at the expense of other sectors had led to bottlenecks in the system and imbalances. For citizens it meant continued austerity, and for the peasants it meant greater extractions. The obsession with heavy industry, growth rates, and gross output figures meant that quality was neglected, and no one thought about whether anyone would actually buy what was produced. Incentive structures were weak, and clearly no amount of awarding red flags could raise workers' and management's enthusiasm. Gradually, rates of return on capital investments declined along with labor productivity. Consumption was repressed so that funds could be dedicated for capital construction.

Applying the Soviet model meant adopting Soviet management techniques and accepting that Chinese society would look more like a Soviet-style clone. The Soviet model of hierarchical control might have had a superficial resonance with ideas of order in traditional China, but it conflicted with some of the practices the CCP had developed in the base areas before 1949. For Mao, it was unacceptable that the development of a Soviet-style society would create two new elites. First, there was the new technocratic elite of managers and economic professionals who were needed to make and implement the plans. Second, a new elite of party professionals was developed. The managerial modernizers were beginning to take over from the revolutionary modernizers. For Mao, the path to socialism was as important as the final goal, and any backsliding might lead to the restoration of capitalism. Mao Zedong had certainly learned from Stalin that violent conflict was necessary to bring about social change and that class struggle persisted under socialism.[81] The party needed to push ahead swiftly to secure the goal of socialism. The stage was set for debate about the way forward.

CHAPTER SEVEN

Radicalizing the Revolution

1956–1969

*

By 1956 the CCP was facing the challenges of ruling the country, which required skills different from those that had brought it to power. Initially the CCP sought to apply the Soviet model of development as it claimed power in the cities, which the party had vacated some two decades earlier. This meant reliance on more methodical, planned approaches to policy making and implementation rather than reliance on mass mobilization, which had been a key feature of the leadership that had emerged under Mao Zedong in the border region. This created tensions within the leadership between those, such as Liu Shaoqi, who wanted to continue in a more measured way, and those who were impatient to push ahead as swiftly as possible to reach the end goal of the revolution. For the former group of "managerial modernizers," the end result was equally important but the means to achieve it was less so. A dictum attributed to Deng Xiaoping—"It doesn't matter whether a cat is white or black, as long as it catches mice, it is a good cat"—expresses this view. For Mao, a "revolutionary modernizer," the means to the end were as important as the end itself. Indeed, unless revolutionary pressure and means were retained throughout the transition, the revolution could be derailed and revisionism could triumph.[1] Mao came to see overcoming class enemies rather than bureaucratic inertia as the key to progress, exhibiting his intellectual indebtedness to Stalin. The future challenge was how to use the skills and militant practices that the CCP had used for "state-breaking" to serve "state-making."[2]

Reviewing their years in power, the Chinese leadership could feel satisfied with their achievements. Enemies had been eradicated, foreigners driven away, cooperativization completed, private entrepreneurs squeezed out, the Soviet model of development introduced, intellectuals brought to submission, and promotion of Soviet science was under way. Within a mere two years, though, the Chinese leadership embarked on a tough campaign against intellectuals, peasants were herded into communes, and the radical economic strategy of the Great Leap Forward (GLF) was launched. The disastrous consequences led not only to a massive famine but also to serious divisions in the leadership regarding the future. How did it come to this?[3]

Clearly, Mao Zedong's desire for a rapid transition played a significant role, but so did important external factors and unexpected domestic developments. The Chinese response to de-Stalinization and the unrest in the Eastern bloc, especially Hungary, led first to an outpouring of critical views followed by a harsh crackdown. Domestically, moderation was quickly followed by a rapid pace of transition. The impressive growth rates in the economy did not convince the leadership that the best way forward to pull China out of its economic backwardness would be to continue with narrow Soviet-style planning. The key challenge was how to boost agricultural production to a level adequate to provide for the growing urban sector. Mao rejected mechanization of the agricultural sector in favor of exploiting traditional farming techniques combined with swift changes in land ownership and accelerated industrial production.

Debating Economic Strategy and Leadership

The CCP did not launch the Great Leap Forward until 1958, but there had been earlier signs of concern regarding economic strategy, and the years 1955–1957 were crucial for the looming radical departure. With respect to the economy, the main debates revolved around the speed of development, the relationship of the socialization of agriculture to technical transformation, and whether the economic system should be decentralized and, if so, how? In 1955 Mao's criticisms accelerated the process of collectivization, and after a brief hiatus it would speed up again. Politically, questions revolved around how to respond to de-Stalinization—should the party open up to criticism from without, should the party take care of its own, should critics be silenced altogether, and were class enemies still at work in China?

In early 1956, economic policy moderated, continuing until the Third Plenum of the Eighth Party Congress in September–October 1957. Mass mobilization in the countryside settled down and caution was the name of the game, with leaders such as Zhou Enlai, Bo Yibo, and Chen Yun trying to reduce investment levels, often over the desires of local officials.[4] By the spring of 1956, the strain of too-rapid growth caused both shortages and waste. The projections for the Second Five-Year Plan were adjudged to be realistic and did not require adjustment. By May 1956 the mood of caution was reinforced as criticism of rightism and conservatism declined.

Liu Shaoqi dominated the Eighth Party Congress, which was held September 15–27, 1956, with Mao Zedong playing a limited role. Liu's report and Zhou Enlai's report reflected the calmer approach, but called for a "comparatively high" pace of development.[5] Liu sought to steer a middle path, with development unfolding "step-by-step" over a "fairly long period," and he criticized both those who were satisfied with achievements to date (rightists) and those who thought socialism could be achieved overnight (leftism).[6] The First Five-Year Plan was hailed as a success, and there were preparations for the Second Five-Year Plan to begin in 1958. To meet consumer demand, more emphasis was placed on light industry, but agriculture remained the lowest priority. The plan remained within the Soviet playbook, with the fundamental premise that socialist transformation required a developed industrial base.

Khrushchev's secret speech denouncing Stalin, in February 1956, had an impact on the Eighth Party Congress. The CCP stressed collective leadership and downplayed the notion of the cult of the individual. The euphoric praise that Liu had showered on Mao at the Seventh Party Congress in 1945 was absent, and mention of Mao Zedong Thought was dropped from the new Party Statutes. Such modesty disappeared in early 1957 when Mao returned to his theme of "more, faster, better, and more economical" growth.

Khrushchev's denunciation of Stalin at the Soviet Twentieth Party Congress on February 25, 1956, created consternation and confusion among the CCP leadership. As with economic policy, the initial response was to usher in a moderate atmosphere in the political realm, but as with the economy, moderation was soon jettisoned. However, Mao was not willing to go as far as Khrushchev's negative appraisal of Stalin, claiming that Stalin's contributions outweighed his mistakes,[7] an assessment that the post-Mao leadership would later make about Mao's contributions. Too negative an assessment would reflect badly on Mao, who had overridden concerns about the pace of collectivization in 1955 and was clearly more than *primus inter pares*. Further, high Stalinism had greatly impacted Mao's thinking in the 1930s.

Criticism did cause Mao to think about leadership, and the 1956 uprising in Hungary led him to reconsider the relationship between the party and urban society. In November 1956 the Soviet Union sent in troops to crush protestors in Budapest, but Mao blamed party leaders in Hungary for being divorced from the people. In "On the Ten Major Relationships," Mao outlined his view of leadership, and his comments on May 2, 1957, set forth the idea "Let a hundred flowers bloom, let a hundred schools contend."[8] Mao suggested that a balance needed to be struck between democracy and centralism when dealing with other political parties and society. The mass line would ensure that the leaders were not divorced from the led. The response seemed to imply that the principles of New Democracy were still valid. He noted that "it's perhaps better to have several parties," and he called for "long-term coexistence and mutual supervision" between party members and those who were not party members. He even mused on the prospect that one day neither the Communist Party nor the democratic parties would exist—"It will be very pleasant." Although it was the task of the party to hasten this extinction as well as the dictatorship of the proletariat, at the current stage it was necessary to strengthen the party and the dictatorship. Signaling future developments, Mao warned that "because classes and class struggle still exist in China, there is bound to be opposition in one form or another." However, there were to be no executions.

Flowers Blooming, Contending, and Wilting

The new five-year plan required continued input from scientists and intellectuals. In January 1956, intellectuals were informed that they had much to offer and could contribute even more if the constraints were relaxed a little.[9] In March, Liu Shaoqi used the phrase "Let one hundred flowers bloom," and by May, Mao's speech brought these in-house discussions into the public domain. Mao called for mobilizing all positive elements, but he made a clear distinction between those who were considered to be "among the people"—who enjoyed freedom of expression—and counterrevolutionaries. On February 27, 1957, Mao emphasized this distinction.[10]

Those critical of Mao Zedong view the hundred flowers motif as merely a cynical ploy to draw out regime critics and then punish them. More likely, Mao thought that the party bureaucracy had become increasingly conservative and institutionalized and thus needed shaking up by outside critics. Further, Mao must have concluded that the intelligentsia had learned their limits from previous campaigns and now basically supported the revolution so they would provide constructive criticism. This view was not accepted by all, with Liu Shaoqi and Peng Zhen preferring to keep criticisms in-house rather than airing them in public. Once the movement began, Peng used his position as mayor of Beijing to control the capital's press and related departments to hold back criticism.[11] Deng Xiaoping supported Mao in the view that there were no systemic problems and the party would only have to deal with the old bugbears of bureaucratism and dogmatism.[12]

The response from society was tepid—which was not surprising, given the experience of the first few years of campaigns in the PRC. Fresh in the minds of many was the 1955 campaign against Hu Feng and his "counterrevolutionary clique."[13] Hu had been critical of Mao's overly political views on literature and art. Consequently, Hu and his close associates were arrested and a nationwide campaign against them was launched. Hu was sentenced to imprisonment for speaking out; and he was not released until late 1965.[14] More than 2,000 writers and editors were investigated, 92 were imprisoned, and many more were dismissed from their posts.

Mao's February 1957 speech marked a brief high point in the blooming and contending. He was explicit about the viability and necessity of external criticism to prevent the leaders from becoming aloof. Mao distinguished between contradictions that needed to be dealt with by the dictatorship of the proletariat (antagonistic contradictions) and those that could be aired, discussed, and resolved peacefully (nonantagonistic contradictions). For Mao, Marxism was a scientific truth and therefore the party should not fear criticism—Marxism would be worthless if it could be overthrown by mere criticism: "Fighting against wrong ideas is like being vaccinated."

This apparent green light did unleash criticism, not as a "gentle breeze of a fine rain" but instead as an unexpected torrent. Criticism ranged far and wide, airing not only personal grievances but even calling into question the legitimacy of the party and the revolution itself. Some called for a reevaluation of the case of Hu Feng. Shockingly, complaints were raised not only by opponents of communism but also by people who assessed the system on its own terms and found it wanting. Seeing no immediate crackdown, the critics became braver and more expansive in their analyses, and a number of independent organizations were established.[15]

This unexpected outpouring lasted only five weeks before the crackdown occurred and the Anti-Rightist Campaign was launched. Mao Zedong, shocked by the virulent attacks, stayed in bed, immobilized and sick, while plotting his revenge.[16] The beginning of the end was signaled with a *People's Daily* editorial on June 8, 1957, that denounced the rightists who had abused this glimpse of freedom to attack the party and socialism. Class struggle was not extinct and was manifested in the ideological sphere. A series of *People's Daily* articles pressed home the message that things had gotten out of hand and the movement would be reined in. On June 19, when Mao's February speech "On the Correct Handling of Contradictions among the People" was published officially, it was considerably revised to be less accommodating to open criticism. In addition to reducing numbers about how many people had been put to death in the campaigns against counterrevolutionaries (700,000 to 780,000), the speech established clear limits to the realms of the permissible. Mao warned against excessive criticism, and recognition of continuing class struggle was inserted into the document. Importantly, the section criticizing Stalin for failing to distinguish between contradictions among the people and those with the enemy was deleted.

The retreat represented a significant setback for Mao, but it did not end his enthusiasm for making use of the masses to work around the party to promote his own agenda. The events convinced Deng Xiaoping and Liu Shaoqi that movements should be controlled and conducted in an orderly top-down manner to prevent them from getting out of hand. In his role as head of the Central Secretariat, Deng Xiaoping was put in charge of cleaning things up, as was Peng Zhen, who had been cautious about the movement from the beginning.[17] The subsequent chaos of the Cultural Revolution, which led to the death of Liu, confirmed Deng Xiaoping's view, and consequently Deng set careful limits to post–Cultural Revolution criticism of both Mao and the political system.

The impact was swift. Of the 500,000 to 600,000 people who were investigated, most lost their jobs, the more unfortunate were sent to labor camps, and thousands, seeing the writing on the wall, committed suicide. Contrary to Mao's earlier statement that no one should be executed, those who were now judged to be counterrevolutionaries were indeed executed, including workers who had organized strikes and students who had led violent protests. Resistance convinced the party leadership to move more quickly to complete the task of building socialism. The socialization drive of the new party-state had run against the material interests of the two core classes of workers and peasants. Evidence shows that in the winter of 1956–1957, peasant abandonment of the cooperatives was extensive and growing. It was dubbed a "small typhoon."[18] The new working class had issues with the socialization of industry. By early 1957, reforms had led to a decline in real income for workers and a loss of input into decision making, leading to an increase in strike activity in Shanghai and other industrial centers.[19] Protesters were rejecting the process of socialization for economic reasons, but the ultimate consequences could become political. This shook the party leadership's confidence in the resilience of the revolution and provided further justification for the Anti-Rightist Campaign and the need to press on rapidly to complete the transition to socialism.

Leaping into the Unknown Socialist Future

Radicalization in the political realm went hand in hand with growing economic radicalization, which would culminate in the GLF. The moderation of the Eighth Party Congress had dissipated in early 1957 as Mao Zedong returned to his theme of developing "more, faster, better, and more economically." The signs had been there earlier in 1956, when Mao, in his Twelve-Year Plan for Agriculture, proposed that socialization of the countryside was a prerequisite for a rapid increase in production; socialization would precede technical transformation.

Mao was not the first to articulate an alternative to the Soviet planning model. Chen Yun, the key economic figure in the early 1950s, began to rethink his support for a full system of Soviet planning.[20] Chen had overseen the revival of the Chinese economy and had fully supported the structure and aims of the First Five-Year Plan. While his ideas remained within the realms of central planning, he suggested modifications, similar to experiments elsewhere in the Soviet bloc. Chen was vehemently opposed to political campaigns interfering with economic production, and hence he had been wary of the impact of the Five-Anti Campaign on the economic front. He supported the promotion of collective agriculture, but he warned that the transition should not go too quickly. His speech to the Eighth Party Congress outlined an approach that would give greater play to the market. Individual production units would be allowed greater freedoms to purchase inputs and sell their products on the market, and demand could have a greater role in determining prices. Different forms of ownership would be permitted, thus decentralizing power with the individual units enjoying greater authority. Although rejected at the time, Chen's policies, together with his policies for an agricultural recovery after the GLF, formed the starting point for the post-Mao reforms in the late 1970s and early 1980s.

By the party's Third Plenum, which was held from September 20 to October 9, 1957, Mao had clearly rejected the moderate policies of the Eighth Party Congress and was pushing for a major shift in strategy that would pave the way for the GLF.[21] For Mao, greater reliance on the market and material incentives would encourage the growth of "spontaneous capitalist tendencies." Decentralization was needed not for individual production units but for administrative jurisdictions. This would allow greater flexibility but ensure that mobilization campaigns could boost production.

Mao articulated his economic preferences in a number of speeches, such as "On the Ten Major Relationships," and in his *Critique of Soviet Economics.*[22] The Third Plenum heralded a clear break with previous policy and a push forward for rural policy. The most important shift was not economic but instead political. Having had time to reflect on the outpourings of the Hundred Flowers and the events in Eastern Europe, Mao declared that the challenge was the conflicting interests of the proletariat and the bourgeoisie. Class struggle was alive and well and had to be pursued. Mao complained that his views expressed in the Forty Articles (the ambitious Twelve-Year Program) and his slogan of "more, faster, better, and more economical" had been "blown away."[23] The stage was set for the radicalization of both the political and the economic agendas.

Mao's professed starting point was that the peasantry should not be exploited to build the socialist state—a rightist deviation committed by Stalin. Of course, with the GLF and the rush to form communes, the peasants were exploited for the sake of the crash program of transition and industrialization. Modernization and socialization of the Chinese countryside could not be completed in a gradual manner because the scale of the farming units had to be larger in order to create demand for tractors and other machinery. Peasant plots were simply too small. Chen Yun agreed, but he disagreed about the speed of transition. Simple machinery and other inputs could be produced by small-scale rural industry in enterprises run by brigades or communes. Light industry and agriculture were not to be neglected in favor of what could only be a short-term acceleration of the heavy industrial sector.

Mao's more voluntaristic approach to development relied on the human will to drive progress forward and overcome objective laws that constrained faster development. He stressed the revolutionary potential of the transition to socialism rather than the evolutionary, mechanical potential. He rejected the idea that socialism was an independent mode of production; socialism was a transitional form between capitalism and communism, and thus it contained elements of both. The Soviet Union's view that socialism was free of contradictions was wrong. Socialism in China was riven by contradictions between the economic base and the superstructure, and between the productive forces and the relations of production. Thus, class struggle continued to exist, a perspective that supported Mao's idea of permanent revolution that would prevent institutionalization and bureaucratization. Continuing or new contradictions would be resolved through a series of qualitative changes as part of the process of realizing the development goals.

Despite the pullback from the GLF, these ideas underpinned Mao's rationale for launching the Great Proletarian Cultural Revolution. The thinking dictated concrete policy preferences, such as intellectual workers and officials engaging in manual labor, restrictions on material incentives, workers' control in production units (in name rather than in practice), and curtailing the use of private plots in the countryside to snip off the "tails of capitalism."

In the countryside the changes were devastating as the peasants were moved swiftly from the cooperatives to the communes, the crucial institutional innovation of the GLF. From 1956 to 1957, the peasants had been shifted from the lower-stage APCs to the higher-stage APCs, and before the changes had settled down, the communes were being promoted. The 750,000 higher-stage APCs were collapsed into 24,000 people's communes. Cash income was replaced by a system of work points, given for each day of labor. At the end of the year, grain and any cash were doled out according to the work points earned. Men received more points than women for the same work. The communes functioned as the key political units in the countryside, responsible not only for agriculture but also for industrial work, trade, education, military affairs, health, village administration, and social welfare. This created a three-level structure in the countryside, which remained until the 1980s when the communes were reorganized into counties. Under the commune were the brigades (the old higher-stage APCs) and the production teams (the old lower-stage APCs), which functioned as the basic accounting unit. Those who wished to move more swiftly to the socialist nirvana pushed to lift the basic accounting unit from the team to the brigade, bigger clearly being not only better but also more socialist.

In March 1958 a CCP CC work conference made the decision to merge the APCs into larger units, with Mao criticizing those who opposed moving ahead rapidly. "Rash advance" was Marxist, not foolhardy. On the defensive, Zhou Enlai referred to Mao as "the representative of truth." Policy radicalized swiftly: in May the Second Session of the Eighth CCP Congress

Work on the commune.

adopted the slogan "more, faster, better, and more economical results"; on May 29 the *People's Daily* emphasized that "speed was the soul of the Great Leap"; on August 29 the Politburo agreed that communes were the "best organizational form for the construction of socialism and the gradual transition to communism." The problem was that the transition was not gradual and the nationwide chase to establish communes was on.

An integral part of the GLF strategy was "walking on two legs"—the dual use of modern, large-scale, capital-intensive methods of production in tandem with traditional small-scale methods. The rural areas were to provide for themselves what they needed, and they were to seek external help only when this was not possible. This policy of self-reliance was a strategy for geographical decentralization and the dispersion of economic activities. Local inputs were used to produce for local use. For the national economy, self-reliance was a caution against overreliance on foreign trade and investment. To the extent that the strategy mobilized local resources that would not have been exploited otherwise, it could further economic development. However, for much of the country it diverted resources to less-efficient use. The most no-

Backyard steel furnaces were a hallmark of the Great Leap Forward.

torious example was the backyard steel furnaces that produced a huge volume of steel from pots and pans and whatever else people could lay their hands on, much of it useless.

Returning from his November 1957 trip to Moscow, Mao Zedong was sufficiently enthused by Khrushchev's lavish claims that he too wanted to set his own ambitious targets. The intention was to enable China to catch up with and surpass the United Kingdom in the production of steel and other products within fifteen years. During the high tide of the commune period, Yantian village participated actively in the steel-making campaign. In the winter of 1958 Yantian villagers designed and built a blast furnace on a nearby mountain. The villagers were "encouraged" to contribute their old iron farm tools and household pots and pans. Iron ore was collected from the nearby mountains. To fuel the furnace, some 1,000 lychee and longan trees were cut down to produce thirty tons of scrap steel. The product was useless, and making it had destroyed many valuable trees. Another key feature of the movement was communal kitchens. To release more labor for agricultural production, Yantian built ten public canteens to feed between 100 and 600 people. However, after only half a year, supply problems led to food rationing. The grain ration, mainly for rice, was set at 0.1 to 0.15 kilograms per person per day. Starvation combined with the exhaustion from the heavy labor of deep plowing caused many to die of hunger and disease.[24]

What made the Great Leap Forward so devastating was not only Mao's fallacious economic thinking but also the campaigning approach to implementation: "The Leap would have failed to spur economic growth; the politics of the Leap turned it into a disaster."[25] Mao Zedong now owned economic policy decision-making, and he overrode the planners, relying on provincial party leaders to realize his ambitions. Local officials were whipped into an enthusiasm to set and pursue production targets that were increasingly ridiculous and impossible to fulfill. The association of caution with rightism or even class sabotage meant that constructive criticism was impossible. Revealing just how party officials suspended their belief, one senior party member told me that when he went to the countryside for inspection, he thought the swollen bellies of the children were due to an abundance of food, not disease and malnutrition.

The GLF rendered central planning impossible. Local variation and changes would have required continual revisions as localities kept adjusting what they deemed possible. The enthusiasm generated for production resulted in fake reporting, which contributed to setting incorrect targets in the plans for the following year. The fear of being denounced as a class enemy meant that those who did not believe what they were seeing, hearing, or reading did not dare to speak up. The plans for 1959 were based on false estimates of agricultural output for 1958, although it had been a good year. Grain production in 1957 was about 195 million tons, yet incredibly the target for 1958 was set at 375 million tons, later revised down to 270 million tons.

The radicalization of rural policy would also end autonomy for Tibet. Land reform and collectivization had not been implemented in Tibet during the 1950s, but this would end and would be part of the causes for the 1959 uprising that resulted in the flight of the Dalai Lama to India. In 1958, in the neighboring province of Qinghai, which had a significant Tibetan population, the local leadership undertook a program to turn the traditional system of grassland livestock grazing into settled farming to meet targets for agricultural self-sufficiency. The policy was a disaster and contributed to the 1958 uprising by the local Tibetan community.[26] Some survivors fled over the border into Tibet and were involved in the larger 1959 Tibetan uprising. The March 1959 uprising was sparked by the rumor that there was a plan to kidnap the Dalai Lama, but it expressed a deeper frustration with CCP rule and policy choices. Although the uprising was crushed in a few weeks, the enmity felt by many Tibetans toward the CCP remains to this day.

By April 1958 the Party Center was receiving reports of food shortages and even riots, and certainly by the beginning of 1959 it was aware that food shortages were occurring nationwide.[27] Despite calls to take a more pragmatic approach, the momentum was difficult to stop. In 1959 production in all sectors began to fall. In industry, much of what was being produced fell below basic quality requirements. Mao Zedong would not accept responsibility for the problems with strategy; in his view the fault lay with implementation. Even more incredibly, as officials sought to shift blame down the system, claims were made that there was adequate grain but it was being hoarded. As a result, a campaign was launched to deal with "false reporting and grain hoarding."

Serious reconsideration and opposition to the GLF erupted at the Lushan Plenum, which ran from July 2 to August 1, 1959.[28] The main critic was Minister of Defense Peng Dehuai, who based his concerns on investigations he had carried out in late 1958.[29] He pulled together the criticisms of Mao and the GLF in his "Letter of Opinion."[30] Implementation was too fast, exaggerated production figures were making planning impossible, and the creation of communes was condemned. Rubbing salt into the wounds, Peng criticized not only implementation but also the "petty bourgeois fanaticism" of the GLF that had severely hampered democracy within the party and its relationship to the masses. Mao was never going to accept a colleague telling him about policy for the countryside or about the party's relationship to the people. Mao did accept some blame for the excesses, especially the backyard steel furnaces and the speed of setting up the communes, but he was not willing to abandon the whole. He advised "some other comrades" not to waver "at this crucial time." Effectively, Mao demanded that the party choose between himself and Peng, claiming that he would go back to the peasants and lead them to overthrow the government if his ideas were rejected: "If those of you in the Liberation Army won't follow me, then I will go and find a Red Army, and organize another Liberation Army. But I think the Liberation Army would follow me."[31]

For the post-Mao leadership, the plenum marked an important turning point in the history of the People's Republic of China, ending any pretense of democracy in the party. Mao's position was later criticized, and the Third Plenum of the Eleventh Central Committee, held in December 1978, posthumously rehabilitated Peng Dehuai. The post-Mao leadership traced a line from this event to the rise of the "Gang of Four" in the Cultural Revolution. Ultimately the 1981 "Resolution on Party History" absolved Peng and claimed that Mao "erred in initiating criticism of Comrade Peng Dehuai" and in launching a party-wide struggle against right opportunism. The assessment came two decades too late.

At the time, however, there was nothing to stop Mao, and even those who may have agreed with Peng's criticism did not dare to speak up, and some even joined the criticism. At the CC plenum that followed immediately after Lushan, on August 2–16, Mao pressed home his attack and denounced Peng for leading an anti-party clique, and he criticized the attacks on the GLF as a manifestation of right-wing opportunism. Mao portrayed the debates as a fundamental struggle between two lines. Deriding his critics, he said, "When they say they want freedom of expression, what they want is freedom to destroy the General Line with their speech, and freedom to criticize the General Line."[32] The criticism of Peng and those associated with him intensified.

The consequence was that rather than focus on a course correction, the party was dragged off into a new anti-rightist movement, and the numbers of those dying from starvation rose. In March 1960 an enlarged Politburo meeting called for extending communal kitchens and communes to the cities, while calling for upholding the "Three Red Banners." The Three Red Banners had become a brief encapsulation of the GLF: the General Line for socialist construction, the GLF, and the people's communes. It was not until June that Mao began to call for quality over quantity in steel production and suggested lowering production targets.

Even to this day, the party finds it impossible to accept full responsibility for the disaster of the GLF. The closest the leadership ever came was in January 1961 at the Seven Thousand Cadres Conference when Liu Shaoqi took a stand against Mao in light of the disastrous outcomes of the Great Leap Forward. This could not have endeared Liu to Mao, who exacted his revenge just a few years later and the judgment was reversed. The problems were blamed primarily on the "three years of national disasters" and compounded by the withdrawal of Soviet aid and advisers. In a common CCP assessment, only 30 percent could be attributed to policy mistakes, not the 70 percent claimed by Liu.

The impact on the economy was enormous. Agricultural production suffered a major setback, and industry didn't recover until 1964.[33] Assessments of how many died vary, with the highest around 30 million. As a part of the revisionist history under Xi Jinping, some neo-Maoists have sought to minimize the number of deaths, producing a number in the low millions.[34] Certainly, a higher figure is more plausible. Later, new figures were released showing that the crude death rate between 1957 and 1960 increased 2.5 times, infant mortality doubled, and the population declined by more than 10 million.[35] Mao Zedong had no choice but to pull back after he hounded Peng Dehuai. But after having made it clear that he dominated the party, he did abandon his principle that the General Line was correct and that opposition was a sign of class struggle. During a brief interregnum, others struggled to restore the economy, but class struggle as a slogan would roar back to prominence during the Cultural Revolution.

The End of an Imperfect Relationship

Just as the Chinese leadership was dealing with the fallout for the domestic economy, it was struck by the blow of the Soviet Union pulling out its advisers and aid. Although tensions had always existed in the relationship, the Soviet Union had been instrumental in the development of the CCP. Following its pre-1949 support, post-1949 party, state and economic policy drew on the Soviet experience. However, following Stalin's death, Khrushchev's secret speech, and the uprisings in Poland and Hungary, tensions slowly came to the boil.[36] Mao had felt slighted for not receiving the respect he felt he deserved on his first visit to Moscow. On his second visit, in November 1957, he came away unimpressed with Khrushchev as the leader of the socialist camp; in turn, the Soviet leaders were alarmed by many of Mao's comments. The subsequent split had major ramifications not only for global alignments but also for China's domestic politics. Ironically, given that part of the criticism of Khrushchev was that he was reluctant to challenge US imperialism in a nuclear age, the split eventually led to rapprochement with the United States. Domestically, the line of criticism that the Soviet party had been taken over by revisionists working on behalf of the bourgeoisie justified Mao's attacks on his own party during the Cultural Revolution.

After 1949 the relationship between the two Communist giants proceeded relatively smoothly, and it was only after 1957 that the relationship began to deteriorate. Although the Soviet Union may not have sent the 10,000 advisers that is often quoted, it did play a significant role in China's development, one that increased after Stalin's death.[37] What seems to have sown the seeds of the later disintegration of the relationship were the events at the November 1957 Moscow Conference of World Communist and Workers' Parties.[38] Mao Zedong played an important role in preparations for the conference, and CCP leaders had originally proposed the meeting and the "Peace Manifesto," which was adopted. Clearly the Chinese saw themselves as an equal with the Soviet Union now that Stalin had died, and this represented a high point of cooperation.

After the meeting the relationship deteriorated, with both sides accusing the other of betraying the spirit of the agreements, and with the Soviets alarmed by Mao's fiery rhetoric. The conference appeared to start well, with Mao arguing that the Soviet Union, not China, was still the leader of the socialist camp, but he clearly felt that he was now the senior citizen in terms of analyzing the international situation and even in terms of domestic developments. Mao's speech on November 18, 1957, contained a number of memorable assertions.[39] He began with a claim that all could sign on to: "The East wind is prevailing over the West wind" and that while "our skies are all bright," those of the West are "darkened by clouds." Mao asserted that if the USSR could overtake the United States in steel production within fifteen years, then China could catch up with and overtake Great Britain within the same time period, thus presaging his GLF claims.

Two of Mao's cavalier comments were disturbing, especially his view of the consequences of atomic warfare: If half the world population were killed, imperialism would be destroyed and the remaining population would become socialist; and in any case, after some years the original global population would be restored. Reflecting his voluntaristic approach to development, he noted that the decisive factor in any struggle was first of all the desire of the people. Second, Mao commented on internal affairs in the Soviet Union, applauding Khrushchev for his removal of Stalin's foreign minister, Vyacheslav Molotov, noting that it was an antagonistic struggle between two lines. He reasserted his firm beliefs not only that contradictions exist under socialism but also that socialism "teemed with contradictions."

The launch of the GLF as a development strategy was in complete contradiction to the post-Stalin methodological Soviet approach. Further, the Chinese bombardment of Guomindang-held Jinmen island in the summer of 1958 disturbed the Soviet leadership. As a result, in June 1959 the USSR rescinded its prior promise of October 1957 to deliver a prototype A-bomb to China. Nuclear help was a sticking point in the relationship, with China pushing for greater help and the Soviet Union resisting. In fact, Stalin's approach had been to offer China the protection of a nuclear umbrella but not to help it develop a nuclear program. During his 1954 visit to China, Khrushchev offered help for peaceful nuclear development, and in the following year he offered help for both peaceful and weapons development. However, by August 1960 all nuclear advisers had returned to the Soviet Union.[40] The Soviet withdrawal left many projects half-finished, putting pressure on Chinese scientists and engineers to pick up the slack.[41]

The definitive break came in July 1963 when the differences in ideology and perspectives on world politics were made clear for all to see.[42] The CCP announced that world peace could only be attained through armed struggle, and it rejected calls for universal disarmament as naive. Further, class struggle and the dictatorship of the proletariat would continue long after a Communist state had been created, and concepts such as the Soviet principle of "parties of the whole people" were denounced as bourgeois. The CCP claimed that rejection of the personality cult was merely a tactic to force parties to change their leadership.

On July 14 the Soviets denounced the "slanderous and groundless attacks" on its party congress resolutions. The Chinese defense of the personality cult was perplexing because it was clearly a petty bourgeois theory. As far as the Soviets were concerned, the existence of nuclear weapons had created a "radical, qualitative change" in the nature of war. The initialing of the partial test-ban treaty between the USSR and the United States only confirmed the Chinese view that the Soviets were heading down a revisionist path. In response the CCP issued the "nine polemics," the most dramatic of which was the last one, which denounced Khrushchev's "phony communism" and enunciated what it meant for the world.[43] The document attacked the leadership of the Communist Party of the Soviet Union, while laying the ideological groundwork for Mao's attacks on his own party, which would follow just two years later. The policies pursued by the "revisionist Khrushchev clique," such as the use of material incentives and permitting high salaries, were attacks by the bourgeoisie on the proletariat. Clearly, the Soviet bourgeoisie had purged genuine Communists and taken control of the party. Sadly, "the first socialist country in the world . . . is now facing an unprecedented danger of capitalist restoration."[44] The challenge for the CCP was to ensure that China did not follow the same path and to train a new generation of "revolutionary successors." The global and the domestic were now linked.

Retreat from the Great Leap Forward

In 1960 the party focused on reviving agricultural production. A series of decisions rolled back the worst excesses of the GLF's high tide: collective farms were reduced in size, greater guarantees were to be provided for the peasants, the use of private plots was tolerated, and the fever pitch and stress of the transition to socialism were reduced. This work was overseen by Liu Shaoqi, Zhou Enlai, and Deng Xiaoping; Mao Zedong was conspicuously absent from detailed economic work, and in April 1959 he had passed on his position as president to Liu. Mao had supposedly retired to the second front, but he remained engaged and approved the policy moves. Even if he was ambivalent about the measures, he tried not to lose sight of his ultimate goal of rural transformation. He was more than happy to criticize those on the first front, such as Deng Xiaoping and Peng Zhen, if they acted without his approval.[45]

The decisions contained sufficient ambiguity that local leaders were left with flexibility of interpretation.[46] The brigade was guaranteed to be the key unit for five years, peasants were to be allowed private plots, and the communal mess halls were not to be expanded. However, the economic situation was still described as good and the communes and the Great Leap were praised. At the end of August, Li Fuchun, who was chair of the State Planning Commission, and Zhou Enlai put forward the slogan of "adjustment, consolidation, replenishment, and enhancement," and on November 3, 1964, the party issued directives that sought to rein in leftist excesses by emphasizing the three levels of ownership, with production teams as the basic accounting unit. Communal kitchens were retained.[47] Confiscated property was to be returned or compensation was to be provided at fair value. The party approved the initiatives in January 1961, but Mao himself realized that these did not go far enough and he directed his staff to undertake rural investigations to begin work on what would become the Sixty Articles on Agriculture. These measures were approved at a CC work conference, held from May 21 to June 12, 1961, that liberalized rural policy even further, including eliminating the communal kitchens. There were three principles: "From each according to his ability, to each according to his work"; "More pay for more work"; and "He who does not work does not eat."[48] The articles rolled back some of the egalitarian redistribution between richer brigades and poorer brigades that had occurred during the earlier phase of communization. The production team was to guarantee production, labor, and costs, with any surplus production providing a reward for the team. Up to 5 percent of the land was for families to produce vegetables or to raise livestock; this was later extended to 7 percent.

While these high-level discussions were taking place, local experiments were under way that would place the household at the center of farming. In the more permissive atmosphere, the party secretary of Anhui promoted "responsibility fields" to stave off starvation among the peasants.[49] Output quotas were fixed for each piece of land and responsibilities were contracted to individuals. By the fall of 1961, the system had been adopted by 85.4 percent of brigades and teams in the province and 20 percent of the brigades and teams nationwide. In fact, many peasants, when given the opportunity, rejected the collective structures. After the famine, when local leaders and peasants sought any strategy for survival, they chose non-sanctioned ones, especially the method of contracting production to the household.[50] Mao was willing to decentralize some powers to the production team, but a retreat to empowering the household was unacceptable to him. The peasants did not agree, and they continued the practice even after a crackdown began in November 1961 to eliminate household farming, calling it "spontaneous capitalist tendencies of the peasantry." As late as May 1962, a household-based system of responsibility had been adopted by 20 percent of all rural households; by the summer of 1962 the total reached 30 percent. If this trend continued, it would deliver a severe blow to the Party Center's view of the transition to socialism. Once Mao reasserted himself in the political process, the Anhui party secretary was denounced as a "capitalist roader."

Adjustment policies shifted the economic priority to agriculture rather than light industry, with the formerly privileged heavy-industry sector placed last. Thus, in pulling back from the Great Leap strategy, the Chinese leadership did not return to the original Soviet model, and a lower growth rate for industry was anticipated than that proposed in either the First Five-Year Plan or during the GLF. The proposal associated with Chen Yun for agriculture was the "three freedoms and one guarantee"—freedom to sell over-quota production, free plots, and free markets, with a guaranteed production quota—which was the starting point for the post-Mao reforms. The communes were reduced in size but increased in number from 24,000 to 75,000. The three-tier structure of commune, brigade, and team was confirmed, with the team as the basic accounting unit. The size of the team was decreased to only thirty to forty households. The team was now the most important unit in the countryside, making final decisions on both the production of goods and the distribution of income.

In the industrial sector, financial retrenchment was introduced to rationalize production. Capital construction investment was reduced by 80 percent, causing thousands of construction projects to be scrapped or stopped. To increase production, material incentives were reintroduced and managers were given greater freedoms to run their enterprises. Surplus laborers, totaling some 20 million, were shipped back to the countryside. To prevent their return to the cities, the urban areas were sealed off by tightening the household registration system. To buy loyalty for those workers who remained, workplaces set up systems for cradle-to-grave welfare.

The recovery program was successful, and between 1962 and 1966, from an admittedly low base, growth averaged 15 percent per annum. Although Mao had been willing to go along with some policy modification, he upheld his general principles for the correct transition to socialism. By 1964 Mao and his supporters clearly felt that recovery had been completed and that many of the earlier maladies had reappeared. The urban-rural differential had increased and again skilled workers and technocrats were privileged, leading to the recurrence of social tensions. There was agreement on the priority given to agriculture, but specific policies were disputed, especially the enhanced role of the household. Disagreements focused on the nature of the legacy of the GLF. Mao was not willing to see all the GLF policies abandoned in favor of those that were less concerned about the means to achieve socialism. The battle lines were beginning to be drawn.

Whither the Revolution?

The first indication of Mao's growing impatience was revealed during the discussions at the Seven Thousand Cadres Conference, which ran from January 11 to February 7, 1962.[51] The meeting was called to sum up the lessons from the GLF and to "unify thought" so that the party could move forward. Liu Shaoqi and General Secretary Deng Xiaoping were tasked with overseeing preparation of the meeting's report, which, unusually, at Mao's behest was not discussed first by the Politburo to suggest revisions. The report was presented directly to the participants for discussion. At Mao Zedong's request, Liu delivered an oral report that, despite beginning with the obligatory praise of Mao, continued by laying much of the blame on the Chairman's strategy rather than simply poor implementation. Liu analyzed the drastic decline in agricultural and industrial production. Rather than claiming it as his own view, Liu carefully noted that peasants in Hunan apportioned the blame as three parts a natural disaster and seven parts manmade. This was a direct challenge to Mao's preferred depiction of nine fingers being good and only one bad. When challenged by Mao, Liu claimed that "in some places the shortcomings and errors comprise more than three fingers."[52]

Liu Shaoqi also questioned the Three Red Banners and withheld unreserved praise, viewing them as experiments that had to be tested in practice to see if they were correct. Although the General Line was correct, there had been too much emphasis on quantity over quality. Liu adjudged that the fault lay with the Party Center. Mao's fervent supporter was Lin Biao, now minister of defense, who praised the Three Red Banners and blamed natural calamities for the disaster. Lin would become Mao's designated successor, a fateful anointment for him. Amazingly, Lin claimed that if the leadership had listened to Mao and had followed his directives, the party would be facing fewer difficulties.[53] Lin was supported by Zhou Enlai. Not surprisingly, Mao loved Lin's defense of the General Line and his approach to socialist transition.

When Mao addressed the meeting on January 30, he did not talk about the Great Leap; instead he focused on the importance of democratic centralism, democracy, and the mass line. He felt that they had been abandoned during the period of retrenchment. Unless the party paid attention to this, China would run the risk of becoming like Yugoslavia: "a country that is effectively capitalist. Our proletarian dictatorship will be transformed into a bourgeois dictatorship, and what is more, into a reactionary fascist style of dictatorship."[54] It was no surprise that Mao disagreed with Liu's comment that the Three Red Banners had to be tested in practice. The conference ended with apparent tensions but the participants did confirm the policy of "adjustment, consolidation, replenishment, and enhancement" as well as the positive role of the Three Red Banners. The earlier decision about Peng Dehuai that had been taken at Lushan was upheld.

Unaware of the depth of Mao's resistance, Liu Shaoqi felt that he had a green light to push ahead with measures to revive the economy. But it soon became apparent that adjustment would not be enough. Liu Shaoqi, Deng Xiaoping, and Zhou Enlai traveled to Wuhan to report to Mao, who agreed with the suggestions for reviving the economy, but Mao cautioned that the picture was not as uniformly bleak as that painted by Liu and the others.

Undaunted, Liu pushed ahead with a plan for restructuring at a CC work conference held May 7–11, 1962, and he saw a far bleaker picture than Mao saw. After Mao returned to Beijing in July, his frustration boiled over in a private discussion with Liu. Liu stood his ground, stating, "History will record the role you and I played in the starvation of so many people, and the cannibalism will also be memorialized." Clearly concerned about his legacy and perhaps mindful of what happened to Stalin's reputation after his death, Mao commented, "The Three Red Banners have been refuted, the land has been divided up, and you did nothing? What will happen after I die?"[55] Liu assured Mao that he would not suffer the same fate as Stalin, the communal kitchens would be disbanded but not the communes, and exaggerated targets would not be set. If Liu thought that this settled things, he was seriously mistaken.

In late September 1962, at the Tenth Plenum of the Eighth CC, Mao returned to the theme of class struggle, which was crucial in setting the CCP on the road to the Cultural Revolution. Mao had already set the tone on August 6, when he unexpectedly delivered a speech on class and rejected the dark picture of China that others were painting. On September 24, answering his own question as to whether classes and class struggle existed in socialist countries, he pointed out: "We can now confirm that classes do exist in socialist countries and that class struggle undoubtedly exists."[56] Again Mao's whipping boy was Yugoslavia, which was clearly ruled by "reactionary nationalist elements" who were facilitating the shift from a socialist country to a revisionist country. Mao's insistence on the continuation of class struggle did not predict the massive upheavals that would occur a few years later, as he claimed that those who admitted their mistakes and reformed would be welcomed back into the fold. Class struggle was not to interfere with economic work but was to proceed simultaneously, and it would not be placed in a "very prominent position." Mistakes were still "contradictions among the people." Mao did state that the trend of reversing verdicts of those deemed guilty was incorrect.

Following the plenum, the Socialist Education Campaign of 1962–1965 was launched, targeting corruption and abuse of power in the countryside.[57] This supported Mao's analysis that the problems derived from implementation rather than from the General Line. The problems were caused by class enemies who had seized power at the grassroots in the countryside.[58] Liu Shaoqi quickly signed on to the notion that rural problems derived from class struggle, thus driving the campaign forward.

The campaign started slowly and was not launched nationwide until May 1963. The objective was to eradicate the "spontaneous tendencies toward capitalism," which were caused by the policies of economic retrenchment and cadre corruption that had arisen because of the increasing bureaucratization of the party. To investigate the corruption and collusion by officials with rich peasants, poor and lower-middle peasant organizations were formed. The model for people to aspire to was the PLA, not the party, which was now led by Mao's biggest booster, Lin Biao. The military was seen to embody the correct virtues of selflessness and collective endeavor. A campaign was launched to study a PLA soldier, Lei Feng, who had kept a diary of his good deeds on behalf of others. The message was clear: citizens should be loyal, unquestioning, and obey the party without reservation. Sadly, the obedient Lei Feng died when a utility pole fell on his head.

All the leadership signed on to the objectives, but views differed about the methods to be pursued. Liu Shaoqi and Deng Xiaoping feared that the movement might run out of control and derail the revival of the economy. To prevent this, it was crucial for the party to oversee the movement, with teams from higher levels rectifying the errors of lower levels. Thus, the work of the peasant associations was taken over by work teams sent in to lead and coordinate the movement. Their work was to be carried out in secrecy, infiltrating the villages and exposing the corrupt officials. Liu and Deng narrowed the scope of the movement by issuing two documents in September 1963 and September 1964. The spirit of these documents departed significantly from the radical thrust of the original May 1963 document. This is not to say that Liu was not harsh in his pursuit of corruption, and he did extend the movement into the urban areas. It is possible that as many as five million party members were punished, with some 77,000 hounded to death. This was the most vicious purge in PRC history to date.

Mao was not satisfied, and by the end of 1964 he had strong reservations about the way Liu was managing the campaign. The differences within the leadership were shifting from nonantagonistic to antagonistic contradictions. Having criticized Liu's approach in December, by January 1965 Mao had made the decision that Liu had to be removed.[59] That month a Central Work Conference issued a new document mapping out how the movement would proceed. This signaled a dramatic change in the targets of the campaign. The logic proceeded from the premise that the struggle between socialism and capitalism existed within the party itself, and not only at the local levels. Consequently the principal target was now "people in positions of authority in the party who take the capitalist road." Some of these people were even working in CC departments.[60] The role of the work teams was undermined in favor of the masses exercising supervision. The peasant associations were authorized to seize power temporarily if the local administration had been usurped by capitalist elements. In line with this broadening of the scope of the campaign, the "Four Cleans," which had applied to cleaning up specific irregularities, were redefined as "clean politics, clean economics, clean organization, and clean ideology."

Mao was convinced that the source of the troubles lay in the heart of the party, thus drawing the battle lines for the Cultural Revolution. In fact, in many organizations the lines were already drawn as conflicts during the Cultural Revolution replayed those that had been carried out during the Socialist Education Movement. Imposition of the movement at Peking University provides a splendid example. In July 1964, Kang Sheng sent in a work team that found that the party secretary and vice party secretary had taken the capitalist road, and struggle sessions commenced against them. Beijing party secretary Peng Zhen and Deng Xiaoping felt that the attacks were extreme, and in March 1965 Deng called for rectification of the university and the work team. The original leadership was restored, and Kang Sheng and the radical elements at the university were criticized.[61] One of these was the party branch secretary of the philosophy department, Nie Yuanzi. The following year, she would take her revenge.

Rule through Chaos: The Cultural Revolution

The temporary emphasis on the economy required reengagement with the technicians, planners. and intellectuals who had been hammered since the mid-1950s. The expanded social space did not give rise to the kind of open critiques that were witnessed during the Hundred Flowers Movement. However, it did allow space for a number of publications in the cultural realm that criticized by allusion. In his September 1962 plenary speech, Mao Zedong had already warned about this trend: "Writing novels is popular these days, isn't it? The use of novels for anti-party activity is a great invention. Anyone wanting to overthrow a political régime must create public opinion and do some preparatory ideological work."[62] In July 1964, speaking with his nephew Mao Yuanxin, Mao suggested that the Ministry of Culture was in the hands of revisionists, and he noted that "the cinema and the theater are entirely in their service, and not in the service of the majority of the people. Who do you say is exercising leadership? To study Marxism-Leninism is to study class struggle."[63] Writers were forewarned, and the spark for the Cultural Revolution did indeed come from the unexpected field of literary criticism.

Peng Zhen was one of the very few leaders who did not support the GLF strategy, and under his tutelage as Beijing party secretary a group of writers enjoyed greater freedom to write satirical, if not counterrevolutionary, pieces. The most important were the pieces written by Deng Tuo (who had been dismissed as editor of the *People's Daily* in the late 1950s)—first in his "Evening Chats at Yanshan," and then together with Wu Han, vice mayor of Beijing, and Liao Mosha in the series "Notes from Three Family Village."[64] The piece that proved incendiary was Wu Han's historical play *Hai Rui Dismissed from Office,* which told the story of a sixteenth-century court official who was unjustly dismissed from office due to his support of the peasantry. Not surprisingly, the play was seen as covert criticism of Mao Zedong for his dismissal of Peng Dehuai.

Following a January 1965 work conference, Mao established a five-person Cultural Revolution Group, under Peng Zhen's leadership, to investigate the Socialist Education Movement and to conduct a Cultural Revolution. The first salvo came from a Shanghai literary critic, Yao Wenyuan, who published a criticism of Wu Han's play in the local newspaper. Four years earlier Mao had praised the play and its author Wu Han, but now it served the purpose of undermining Peng Zhen, the first major target en route to the removal of Liu Shaoqi.

Peng Zhen, in his role as the head of the Cultural Revolution Group, sought to limit the extent of the damage. In 1966, in Mao's absence, the Cultural Revolution Group's February Outline Report was approved by the Politburo. Despite criticizing Wu Han for adopting a "bourgeois worldview of history," the report sought to limit the polemics to the academic sphere, and it criticized Yao Wenyuan for seeking to turn the issue into a question of politics. In the cultural sphere, less emphasis was to be placed on class struggle; there should be greater toleration of diverse ideas within the party, but a rectification campaign was still necessary. It was a "strategy of defense by definition."[65] This approach ran counter to Mao's view and contributed to his belief that Peng had to be removed.

At the same time as Peng Zhen was seeking to limit expansion of the movement, the Shanghai group around Zhang Chunqiao, Yao Wenyuan, Jiang Qing, and Lin Biao in the PLA was gearing up for further attacks.[66]

Jiang and Lin used the PLA to turn up the heat, with the army newspaper starting to publish more radical critiques that called for a campaign against bourgeois ideology. These pieces made it clear that debate should not be restricted to the academic and cultural spheres. This was precisely the criticism of the post-Mao leadership that claimed that Yao Wenyuan's original article set the precedent for fabricating charges against innocent people and, far from being the "prelude to the Cultural Revolution," was "nothing but a shocking frame-up that initiated the campaign of persecution against the academic and cultural circles."[67]

The Cultural Revolution is the most complicated and misinterpreted event in the history of the PRC.[68] Understanding it is not helped by simplistic explanations that it was a two-line struggle between the correct road to socialist nirvana and a route backward through revisionism to a capitalist restoration.[69] Why would Mao Zedong seek to tear down the party apparatus that he headed, and cast aside those with whom he had worked for many years, or even decades in some cases? With the benefit of hindsight, the warning signs were there earlier, but it is clear that Mao's original objectives were only vaguely formulated and he changed his views and tactics as unexpected consequences arose from his actions. The removal of Khrushchev in October 1964, combined with Mao's sense that revisionism was under way in China, reinforced his view that a radical shake-up was necessary. Was the real problem class enemies or the "tenacity of bureaucratic hierarchies"? As Andrew Walder presciently argues, in reality Mao was in many ways a "reactionary who clung to Stalinist doctrines long after their time."[70]

Mao was the product of a movement that was violent and marked by secret betrayal and plotting. Did he see in Liu Shaoqi a person who enjoyed his own independent revolutionary trajectory and was more of a party animal than Mao, or China's Khrushchev, waiting to remove Mao for his excesses conducted during the GLF? We will never know, but Mao made it clear that, as far as he was concerned, the bureaucracy had to be shaken up and a new generation of genuine Marxist-Leninists had to be trained to ensure continuation of the revolution. In the ninth polemic against the Soviet Union, Mao wrote: "In the final analysis, the question of training successors for the revolutionary cause of the proletariat is one of whether or not there will be people who can carry on the Marxist-Leninist revolutionary cause started by the older generation of proletarian revolutionaries." It was a matter of life or death for the party and nation whether the "emergence of Khrushchev revisionism" could be prevented.[71]

The emerging power structure brought together members of the military who, under Lin Biao's leadership, were seen as faithful supporters, veteran cadres devoted to Mao and his goals, and new blood from the rebels who were schooled by the "storm." Mao thought that the new generation had to undergo a baptism of fire analogous to that which had brought the CCP to power in 1949. This not only would keep the revolutionary fires burning but it would also give the younger generation a sense of the revolutionary enthusiasm that Mao had enjoyed as a young man. To achieve this latter objective, Mao not only attacked from above but also mobilized from below via the Red Guard movement, which would dispose of the old guard who was deemed revisionist. The Red Guards were difficult to control and led Mao to adapt tactics as events unfolded in unpredictable ways, eventually by 1969 calling for a return to order. Overlaying all this was loyalty to Mao himself. Zhou Enlai commented early in the Cultural Revolution, "With a single stroke of the pen, all your past achievements will be cancelled out, should you fail the final test of loyalty."[72] The first objective, to remove his perceived opponent at the apex of power, was carefully conceived and carried out; the second, seizure from below, was chaotic and led to intolerable levels of violence.

What the Cultural Revolution did deliver was a shattered social fabric, with students turning on their teachers and fellow classmates, children encouraged to denounce their parents, workmates fighting one another, leading to ridicule and disrespect of authority in all its forms with the exception of the holy writ of Mao. The movement exposed many of the social tensions that had built up under CCP rule, revealed the frustration of many with the bureaucracy, and allowed people to seek revenge on those who had attacked them during previous movements, such as the Socialist Education Movement. For a brief period even the leading role of the party was called into question as existing institutions collapsed. A new organ, the Revolutionary Committee, was called into being to fill the power vacuum, and at the center, to keep the country functioning, a set of temporary organizations was established, such as the Central Cultural Revolution Group (CCRG) in May 1966 and the Working Group of the Central Military Commission. The CCRG effectively took over the work of the Central Committee and replaced the original five-person Cultural Revolution group that had been established under Peng Zhen's leadership.

Mao Zedong's opportunity to remove Beijing party secretary Peng Zhen came when Liu Shaoqi was out of the country on a tour of South Asia from

Victims of the Cultural Revolution were often subjected to violence and mass denunciation.

March 26 to April 19, 1966.[73] Mao's faithful disciples Kang Sheng and Chen Boda attacked Peng and criticized the February Outline Report at an April meeting of the Central Secretariat. Developments unfolded rapidly; the Secretariat established a small group, which became the CCRG, to draft documents. At an expanded session of the Politburo held May 4–16, Kang Sheng relayed that Mao had been dissatisfied since the Tenth Plenum, in September 1962, and especially with Peng Zhen and Minister of Culture Lu Dingyi since November 1965. Unbelievably, on May 18 Lin Biao accused Peng Zhen and others of "plotting a coup," and the ever-faithful Zhou Enlai announced they had "taken the capitalist road."[74]

Peng's denunciation as a member of a four-person anti-party group was the final piece in Mao's preparation to remove party leaders at all levels who were deemed to be taking the "capitalist road."[75] Lin Biao was in charge of the military; Mao's wife Jiang Qing, Kang Sheng, Chen Boda, and the group in Shanghai were lording over the cultural field; Zhou Enlai was managing the State Council, insofar as it still existed; and Wang Dongxing, the head of the elite security detail, was in charge of the General Office of the Central Committee. So Mao had control over the key organs of party-state power. Yet he still unleashed what became an uncontrollable mass movement to attack the party.

The activist phase of the Cultural Revolution was unleashed after the CC release of Mao's "May 16 Circular."[76] The document marked a shift in the battle from the academic to the political sphere. It denounced the February Outline Report and absolved Kang Sheng of blame by claiming that Peng Zhen had worked behind his back. Distribution of the February Outline Report was stopped, Peng Zhen was criticized, and the original five-person Cultural Revolution Group was dissolved. The kick came at the end, claiming that the targets were "representatives of the bourgeoisie who sneaked into the party, the government, the army, and various cultural circles" and who were "a bunch of counterrevolutionary revisionists." These people resembled Khrushchev, who would seek to seize political power and "turn the dictatorship of the proletariat into a dictatorship of the bourgeoisie." Party committees at all levels were to pay attention to this challenge.

Clarifying the targets, on May 21 Zhou Enlai noted, "The stress will be on the inside and at the top."[77] Things unfolded quickly in Beijing and in the central organs. In June, Peng Zhen and the heads of propaganda and cultural affairs were removed from their posts. By July all ten vice mayors of the Beijing municipal government had been purged and eighty-one department directors or vice directors had been imprisoned.[78] Exit for some was suicide. However, the brutality and venality of the movement was only just beginning.

By the end of May a new leadership organization had been set up to oversee the movement, the CCRG. Originating with a small group of those faithful to Mao, including Chen Boda and Kang Sheng, both of whom were prominent figures in the Yan'an Rectification Campaign, and Jiang Qing, Mao's wife, it grew into a large, unwieldy, sprawling organization—a fractious group driven by members with large egos who often clashed. By all accounts, Chen and Kang could barely abide one another. As early as January 1967

more than half of the original nineteen members and advisers had been removed or sidelined.[79] With this dysfunctional group at the center, and lower-
level resistance or confusion about what the objectives were, Mao turned
elsewhere to look for support. Lin Biao ensured military loyalty, and this
seemed to be the obvious choice as the meltdown in the party and civilian
apparatus was unfolding. But Mao first turned to the college, high school,
and middle-school students throughout the country to pursue his radical
agenda.

On May 25, 1966, Nie Yuanzi came roaring back when, together with six
colleagues at Peking University, she put up a big-character poster denouncing
the university leadership as revisionists connected to an anti-party clique in
Beijing.[80] Through the poster, the group sought revenge for their treatment
during the Socialist Education Movement and they renewed the attack on
the party leadership of Peking University, denouncing the leadership's
"Khrushchev-type revisionism." With Mao's support, the poster unleashed
the student Red Guard Movement, even though none of the authors were
students. Furthermore, there is evidence that Kang Sheng actively encouraged Nie and her colleagues, even though neither he nor the others had a
very high opinion of her. Nie had joined the party in 1938 in Yan'an, and
Kang is reported to have said of her: "I've known since back in Yan'an that
Nie Yuanzi is not a very good person. But now we will support her, even if
she is a fucking turtle's egg."[81] Quite an assessment coming from one such
as Kang. On Mao's instruction, the poster was reprinted in the *People's Daily*
and commended for its revolutionary Marxist-Leninist nature. This signaled
support from the highest levels for an assault on the education system, and
the student Red Guard organizations duly obliged.

On the understanding that the movement would not interfere with production and that stability would be retained, Liu Shaoqi and Deng Xiaoping
ordered work teams to enter the universities. Throughout June and July 1966,
different factions within the Red Guards clashed, and they also fought
against the work teams, which they viewed as trying to control them. Indeed, Mao made the same claim, using the role of the work teams to criticize Liu and Deng. On July 21, speaking with central leaders, Mao noted
his dissatisfaction: "There were even some which suppressed the student
movement. Who is it who suppressed the student movement? Only the Beiyang warlords. It is anti-Marxist for communists to fear the student movement." He made it clear that such people were following a bourgeois line to
serve the bourgeoisie.[82] He then took advantage of a series of meetings of

party leaders on July 24–26 to condemn the "fifty days" of control by the work teams and demanded their withdrawal. Mao accused them of suppressing the masses, and on July 28 the Beijing Party Committee ordered the withdrawal of the work teams, leaving leadership on the campuses to mass organizations elected by the revolutionary teachers and students.[83]

On August 5 Mao Zedong scribbled his own big-character poster, calling on people to "bombard the headquarters." He praised the poster by Nie and her colleagues as well as the *People's Daily* commentary and claimed that a "white terror" had been imposed by those who "have puffed up the arrogance of the bourgeoisie and deflated the morale of the proletariat. How poisonous!"[84] This was penned during the Eleventh Plenum of the Eighth CC of August 1–12, which adopted the "Sixteen Points" outlining the objectives of the Cultural Revolution. People were instructed to not fear disturbances and to trust the masses; clearly, this was no longer only a question of culture. The document asked the classic question: "Who are our enemies? Who are our friends? This is a question of the first importance for the revolution and it is likewise a question of the first importance for the Great Cultural Revolution." "The main target of the present movement is those within the Party who are in authority and are taking the capitalist road."[85] On the final day of the plenum, Lin Biao was anointed Mao's chosen successor and named the only vice chair of the party.

Cultural nihilism was not forgotten, with the call to destroy the "four olds" (the old ideas, culture, customs, and habits of the exploiting classes). This led to a massive fiesta of destruction of cultural relics and books by rampaging Red Guard groups fanning out across the country. If the highest levels of the party were infected, they clearly could not be relied on to supervise purification at the lower levels, and thus the masses had to liberate themselves. Attempts to restrain the attacks called for the use of reason rather than force and to distinguish clearly between contradictions among the people and contradictions with the enemy. This had little impact on the student groups that launched a "red terror," as officials and others were dragged out for public humiliation, some were beaten to death, others were crippled or chose suicide, and houses of identified enemies of socialism were ransacked. In Beijing alone, during the months of August and September, 33,695 homes were looted by Red Guards, while in Shanghai 84,222 homes of "bourgeois" families were ransacked.[86]

Two major features of this period were the flood of students coming to Beijing from outlying areas to attend the mass rallies in hopes of seeing the

Enthusiastic Red Guards wait to greet Chairman Mao.

"revered Chairman Mao" and the student treks around the country to visit revolutionary sites and recreate parts of the legendary Long March. By the time the last rally was held on November 26, some twelve million Red Guards had seen Mao.[87] One purpose of the massive rallies was to usher people through Beijing as swiftly as possible. The transportation systems were swamped and the pressure on the infrastructure in Beijing was huge. There was even difficulty in providing food for the visitors. The poor hygiene and the throngs of people moving around the country led to the spread of disease. Some 160,000 people died from meningitis.[88]

The students were very effective as destructive revolutionary weapons, but they exacerbated the chaos and clearly were not going to usher in a new revolutionary order. The movement was becoming increasingly unruly and disorganized, leading to attempts to reassert control, which ultimately required rebuilding the party and state structure. However, having been summoned up, the students were not to be wished away so easily. Many opposed a system that they felt was essentially the same as the one that they had sought to bring down. One enthusiastic participant later came to reflect that Mao was correct that class struggle existed but it was between the CCP and the ordinary Chinese people.[89] A more stable form of organization than the mass organizations formed from below was necessary to replace the old system. This would take a while, but it would entail a significant role for the PLA and for those cadres who had survived the initial onslaughts.

An October work conference turned the screws tighter on Liu Shaoqi and Deng Xiaoping. Chen Boda spoke about the two lines in the Cultural Revolution and called for the majority to unite. On October 23, Liu and Deng made self-criticisms but Liu's self-criticism was far more muted than Deng's, who acknowledged that his actions had represented a "bourgeois reactionary erroneous line." Whether these developments were meant to be kept within the party or not was moot, as on October 21, a poster at Peking University had already attacked Liu Shaoqi as China's Khrushchev.[90] On October 25 Mao made a mild but pointed self-criticism. While acknowledging that it had been his idea to divide the leadership into two lines, with himself in the second line, Mao used this to state that he had put too much trust in others and that mistakes had been made. He asked, "Why was the criticism of Wu Han initiated not in Beijing but in Shanghai? Because there was nobody to do it in Beijing. Now the problem of Beijing has been solved." Furthermore, he accepted responsibility for the havoc that was created nationwide after he had approved of Nie Yuanzi's poster and written his own message "Bombard the Headquarters." Yet having noted that the democratic revolution lasted twenty-eight years, a mere five months was too short for people to understand the movement's importance. He concluded by offering a ray of hope for Liu and Deng: "Nor can we put all the blame on Comrade Liu Shaoqi and Comrade Xiaoping. They have some responsibility, but so has the Center. The Center has not run things properly."[91] Such generosity of spirit would not last long.

Toward the end of 1966 and into January 1967, the movement to seize power from local party organizations was launched. The leaders in those areas that were not faithful to Mao were to be replaced. The experience of Shanghai was the first to gain nationwide prominence, marking a notable shift, as workers had initially been discouraged from forming rebel groups to prevent production from being disrupted. In early December, workers were encouraged to establish revolutionary organs in their spare time. For Wang Hongwen, a young Shanghai worker, it would become a full-time occupation that would set him on the road to national power.

On November 6, Wang had assumed the position of commander of the Shanghai Workers' Revolutionary Headquarters, an organ that was not recognized by the Shanghai party apparatus. With Mao's approval, Zhang Chunqiao intervened, blaming the party organization and supporting the new organ.[92]

On January 6, the Shanghai party secretary was denounced at a mass rally, and on February 5, Zhang Chunqiao announced the establishment of a new organ of power: the Shanghai People's Commune. Zhang Chunqiao was the head, Yao Wenyuan first vice chair, and Wang Hongwen principal deputy. Together with Jiang Qing, they formed the radical group that later would be denounced as the "Gang of Four." That this process was completed without a major civil disturbance and disruption of the local economy provided evidence that a power seizure could be beneficial. Despite its revolutionary-sounding credentials, the commune was rejected as a potential nationwide model. During meetings with Zhang Chunqiao and Yao Wenyuan in February, Mao rejected the commune in favor of three-way alliances. He suggested that the commune be converted into a "revolutionary committee or a city committee or a city people's committee."[93]

The preferred model for the future was the revolutionary committee, the first of which had just been established on January 31, 1967, in the northeast province of Heilongjiang.[94] The need for a semblance of control was reflected by promotion of the "supervision formula" rather than "seizure and control," which gave the center far more control over who and what should replace the overthrown administrations. The provisional organs of power would now be established through an exchange of views and consultations among leading members of the revolutionary mass organizations, leading members of the local PLA units, and revolutionary leading cadres of the existing party and state organs—the "three-in-one" combination. This was an attempt to bring the victorious groups under one roof. The model was not immediately accepted and the struggle continued before the last revolutionary committee was established in Xinjiang in September 1967. Initially the formation of the committees did not quell the violence, as one of their first tasks was to "cleanse the class ranks."[95]

The intention was to remove anyone opposed to this new unity, beginning in Shanghai in late 1967 before extending across the country. The Central Case Examination Group, established in 1966, was to draw up cases against purged national officials. The investigations snagged some one million people.[96] Perhaps between 600,000 and 800,000 died, around half of all deaths from unnatural causes during the Cultural Revolution.[97] The cleansing wound down through the winter of 1968–1969.

The movement was especially brutal in the south and southwest of China, and even included accounts of cannibalism in two counties in Guangxi and Yunnan provinces.[98] Guangxi had been the scene of ferocious fighting during the high tide of the Cultural Revolution, and it took attempts by central leaders, such as Zhou Enlai and Kang Sheng, to calm down the situation. In Bingyuan county, 3,861 people were executed and thrown into mass graves within one ten-day period in 1968.[99]

Enter the Army

The PLA was crucial to the restoration of order and construction of the revolutionary committees. With the party and state machinery in disarray and the mass organizations clearly incapable of bringing about unity, the military was the only functioning national organization. Thus, by default, the job of restoring order fell to the army, and on January 23, 1967, the central authorities directed the PLA to "resolutely support the left."[100] A few days later, the order went out that military installations should not be attacked while order was being restored, the arbitrary ransacking of homes should cease, and people should not resolve "contradictions among the people" using methods designed to deal with the enemy.[101]

Despite Lin Biao's pledge of loyalty to Mao, local commanders had to make difficult choices, and the military was far from united. When faced with the task of mediating between the contending groups, they often chose to side with the familiar local bureaucrats rather than the more unruly "revolutionary rebels." Mao Zedong's ambivalence did not help the situation, but he did see the need to halt the anarchic and ultra-leftist trends unleashed by the movement to "seize power from below."

Resistance to army control was strong in some areas, and by the summer of 1967 China was in danger of disintegrating into multiple civil wars. Factories, schools, and administrations were divided as groups jostled for power in the new structure. Even Mao was moved to say that China had descended into a state of "all-round civil war."[102] The greatest threat came during the Wuhan Incident in July 1967.[103] The Wuhan regional commander had moved to reassert order and to get work moving again, but clashes effectively paralyzed the city. The rebel groups were pushed to the verge of defeat by a group called the "Million Heroes," but this did not sit well with the CCRG, which ordered the commander to put a halt to any further attacks. The CCRG sent emissaries Wang Li and Xie Fuzhi to support the rebels against the "Million Heroes."[104] As a result, on July 20 they broke into the compound where Wang and Xie were staying, beat them up, and kidnapped Wang. On July 22, Wang was released and returned to Beijing to a hero's welcome. By contrast, the local commander was summoned to Beijing and accused of having attempted a coup d'état. On July 27 the Center issued an open letter calling for the masses to struggle against the Wuhan Military Region and the Million Heroes. The violence resumed and during the following months more than 184,000 alleged members of the Million Heroes in Hubei province were beaten or killed, and in Wuhan itself 66,000 were wounded and more than 600 were killed.[105] "Arm the Left" became a common refrain, and the violence spread across virtually all cities as the undefinable left directly challenged the credentials of many military leaders.

This rising violence even disconcerted Mao, and by the end of August he was trying to restrain the chaos. The demise of those denounced as the ultra-left was signaled with the public disgrace of Wang Li and a number of other CCRG members. Blame was placed on a group referred to as the "May 16 Corps," who had taken their name from the 1966 radical document. Both Jiang Qing and Chen Boda appeared less in public, and together with Zhang Chunqiao they pulled back from their support for the rebel groups challenging the military commanders.[106] On September 5 a directive was issued on how to deal with the situation, ordering the PLA to restore order and to use force when necessary. The demand for order was clear, but the left would enjoy one last upsurge. From May to July, violence spiked again, but this marked the death throes of the ultra-left. On July 28, 1968, Mao Zedong told the Shanghai Red Guards that they had let him down and had "disappointed the workers, peasants and army men of China."[107]

For the most part, by September 1967 it was recognized that the PLA was the key to enforcing order through the establishment of revolutionary committees. Not all authority was bourgeois and the push continued to set up the committees. This placed the military in a dominant position, heading twenty of the twenty-nine provincial revolutionary committees that had been formed by September 1968. The same dominance was true for those committees below the provincial level. The revolutionary rebels had little voice on the newly established organs. Many were frustrated with what the imposition of order from above meant and with the backroom deals that put the new revolutionary committees together.

The rebels' frustration was best expressed in the Shenwulian manifesto entitled "Whither China."[108] The manifesto was by a loosely formed organization in Hunan drawn from those who were disillusioned with the progress of the Cultural Revolution. They criticized the "red capitalist class" and preferred the people's commune to the revolutionary committee. For them, Zhou Enlai was the chief representative of this class. They praised the fact that in January 1967 key figures in the national leadership and in the Hunan provincial leadership had been swept aside. Among those mentioned was Hua Guofeng, who would emerge as Mao's immediate successor as chair of the CCP after Mao's death. They complained that Hua had returned with unlimited power in the spring, and again in the fall, and some referred to Hua as the "butcher of Hunan." For them, "the revolutionary committee's road of bourgeois reformism is a dead end," while "the China of tomorrow will be the world of the 'Commune.'"[109]

Hua Guofeng denounced their reactionary ideas as "counterrevolution in action." He found support in Beijing not only from Zhou Enlai but also, more surprisingly, from members of the CCRG (Jiang Qing, Chen Boda, and Kang Sheng) as they walked back their more radical views to align with Mao's demands for order. Mao himself weighed in when meeting with Beijing Red Guards in July 1968, referring to the "Shengwulian-style hodgepodge" and then criticizing their approach when visiting Hunan in June 1969.[110] By February 1968 the group had effectively been destroyed and on April 8 the Hunan Provincial Revolutionary Committee was formally recognized by Beijing.

The October 1968 CC Plenum maintained the momentum toward reconstruction. Zhou Enlai announced that preparations for the Ninth Party Congress would begin, together with adopting new party statutes and investigation of errant leading CC members. The plenum communiqué congratulated the party and Mao on the correctness of the Cultural Revolution and its progress. It reaffirmed Mao's big-character poster and the correct decisions of the Eleventh Plenum.[111] The plenum accepted the seventy-four-page indictment of Liu Shaoqi that had been prepared by the Central Case Examination Group, with full supporting evidence to prove that he was the "number one party person in authority taking the capitalist road, is a renegade, traitor and scab hiding in the Party and is a lackey of imperialism, modern revisionism and the Guomindang reactionaries who has committed innumerable crimes." Not bad for a lifelong CCP member. This exposure was declared a major victory for Mao's thought and the Cultural Revolution. As a result, a unanimous resolution was adopted to expel Liu Shaoqi from the party once and for all. People throughout the country were called on to eradicate his counterrevolutionary ideas and those of "the handful of other top party persons in authority taking the capitalist road." Deng Xiaoping was not named in the communiqué nor was he expelled from the party, permitting Mao to recall him in 1973.

The year 1969 marked a time for consolidation, and the Ninth Party Congress, held in April 1969, was hailed as a "congress of unity and a congress of victory." Yet it was difficult to see what the victors had won for themselves. There were deep scars and divisions, the healing and resolution of which would dominate politics for the next decade. At the Center, there was tension between old-timers, such as Zhou Enlai, and the new entrants into national politics, such as Jiang Qing, Zhang Chunqiao, and Wang Hongwen. The military was in a dominant position, but was bruised and battered from its attempts to restore order. Although Lin Biao sat almost at the pinnacle of the power elite, many of those beneath him were frustrated with having been thrown into local politics with little direction or protection from Lin himself. The revolutionary masses had been disarmed and their organizations dismembered, with many sent down to labor in the countryside or to work in the factories. Their eyes having been opened to the vicious world of CCP politics, many became disillusioned or cynical. On their travels around the country, they had seen a world that did not fit the party's propaganda. A set of purged and humiliated officials bided their time for a possible return to power and revenge on those who had humiliated them.

CHAPTER EIGHT

Charting a Way Forward

1969–1981

★

In certain ways China in 1969 was back where it had started in 1949. The CCP was no closer to having determined the suitable state form to make China wealthy and powerful. What was to be the relationship between the state and the people? What was the most suitable economic model? The Cultural Revolution had done nothing to resolve policy differences and had only created new challenges. Now there was the issue of what kind of Communist Party Mao Zedong and the leadership imagined would rule China. Importantly, what was the appropriate role of the PLA, which had emerged as the dominant institution at the end of these chaotic years? Challenges abounded in the international space, with the Vietnam War at one border, continued tensions with India, and conflicts with the Soviet Union on another border.

To restore some semblance of order, certain steps were necessary. These steps were complicated by the desire of Mao and those in the CCRG not to entirely lose the gains and momentum of the radical phase. The first step was to establish a new administrative structure with the revolutionary committees. The violence had resulted in military dominance throughout the political system. Second, the ultra-left had to be defanged, including the radical students summoned up by Mao to overthrow the reactionary powerholders. Universities were closed and many urban youths were sent down to the countryside to do manual labor; a smaller number were sent to work in urban factories. In late July, Red Guard leaders such as Nie Yuanzi and Kuai Dafu, arriving a little late because of the fighting at Tsinghua

University, were summoned to the Great Hall of the People to receive a dressing down from Mao, who was flanked by Jiang Qing, Lin Biao, and Zhou Enlai, among others. Clearly, their services in making revolution were no longer needed.

In addition to the students being sent down to labor in the countryside as educated youth, many officials and academics were also sent down to May Seventh Cadre Schools.[1] The ostensible reason was to learn from the peasants, but it was also important to clear out the cities to help restore order and rebuild the administrative apparatus with those loyal to the revolution. Further, with the universities closed, it was useful to park the students and faculty somewhere. For many, it reinforced just how much the Chinese countryside differed from the idyllic portraits in most propaganda. Relations between urbanites and their rural teachers were not always smooth, with the townies seen as outsiders. One woman in a cadre school recounts the following encounter: "Countless mounds of sweet potatoes that we had planted were dug up and stolen in a single night. . . . What the peasants said was: 'You buy your food every day, so why do you have to plant your own crops?' They dug up all the saplings we planted, then turned around and sold them in the marketplace." She concludes that the peasants considered the officials to be part of, not "us," but "them"—just "ill-clad, well-fed people with wristwatches."[2]

The third step was to build a new unity for the remaining party members and the public to rally around. The process began with yet another vicious campaign for cleansing the ranks to remove those individuals who were not on board with the new agenda of reconstruction. In many workplaces and localities, this provided yet another chance to inflict revenge on those who previously had been persecutors. Accompanying this, the propaganda apparatus went into overdrive to promote a cult around Chairman Mao. Badges were proudly worn, and rituals abounded honoring the Chairman for his wisdom and seeking his guidance. The key feature of the lovefest was the "three loyalties and the four loves" (loyalty to Chairman Mao, Mao Zedong Thought, and Chairman Mao's proletarian revolutionary line; love for Chairman Mao, the Communist party, Mao Zedong Thought, and Chairman Mao's proletarian revolutionary line).

A Congress of Unity and Victory?

The Ninth Party Congress, held on April 1–14, 1969, was the watershed in the process of party reconstruction and was hailed by Mao and his followers as a congress of "unity and victory." This designation proved to be far from the truth. The congress followed the harsh "cleansing of the ranks" movement, but friction continued between the acceptable left, the military, and the civilian cadres who had hung on or thrived.

The congress was notable for a number of features: the installation of Lin Biao as Mao's official successor; reconfirmation of Liu Shaoqi's disgrace; new statutes that restored Mao Zedong Thought to pride of place; and ratification of a new central leadership that would take over control from the ad hoc CCRG. Lin Biao delivered the political report, a fitting gesture given his elevated position. Yet he had not studied or even read the report before delivering it, and its writing and revisions had been subject to intrigue before the congress.[3] The report claimed that the Cultural Revolution had "tremendously strengthened our party"—having shattered the "bourgeois headquarters" and smashed the "plot to restore capitalism"—and it contained a lengthy diatribe against Liu Shaoqi.[4] Liu's evil was traced all the way back to the 1920s. Domestic revisionism was linked with the international struggle: "From Khrushchev to Brezhnev and company, they are all persons in power taking the capitalist road" who turned the Soviet Union into "a dark fascist state under the dictatorship of the bourgeoisie." Perhaps signaling future shifts, while denouncing both Soviet revisionism and US imperialism— "the most ferocious enemy of the people of the whole world"—the report noted that the United States was going progressively downhill.[5]

The new statutes were pithy and radical, containing a preamble and only twelve articles. They confirmed the principles of democratic centralism, with a structure that returned the Standing Committee of the Politburo to the apex of power. In form, if not in content, the emerging party structure resembled the structure that existed before the Cultural Revolution. Indeed, in September 1969, the CCRG ceded its powers and operations to the new Politburo, with Zhou Enlai overseeing most of the meetings. The statutes stated that the CCP program was to completely overthrow the bourgeoisie and replace its dictatorship with that of the proletariat. Lin Biao was named Mao's "closest comrade-in-arms and successor," and Mao Zedong Thought restored to dominate along with Marxism-Leninism.

Immediately following the congress, a new leadership was elected, confirming that the army was not only "the main component of the state" but also of the party. By the time of the congress, the chairs of twenty of the twenty-nine provincial revolutionary committees had a military affiliation.[6] As provincial party committees were reformed during 1970 and 1971, military figures took on key roles.[7] Thirty-five percent of the new CC members were from the military, whereas the new Politburo reflected the tripartite division, with members drawn from the military, the cadres who survived, and the new more radical blood. Of the twenty-one members, eight could be counted as part of the radical camp, with Zhou Enlai as a possible wavering ninth. The military members were complex, comprising old military leaders and regional military commanders who were not in the radical camp and not clear supporters of Lin Biao. Those who had risen together with Lin were drawn from the centrally directed units, such as the air force and the navy, and previously they had not been used to enjoying such high political positions. One of the older retained cadres was none other than Dong Biwu, who had been together with Mao at the First Party Congress. The five-person Politburo Standing Committee reflected those who had benefited from and strongly supported the Cultural Revolution: Mao Zedong (chair), Lin Biao (vice chair), Zhou Enlai, Chen Boda, and Kang Sheng. By September 1976 all of them would be purged or dead. Although she was not on the Standing Committee, Mao's wife Jiang Qing was the clear leader of the radical group, with its power base in Shanghai and its support in Beijing from the minister of public security.

Exit the Ultra-Left and Lin Biao

If the twists and turns of the Cultural Revolution had not been confusing enough, events took an even more bizarre turn after the congress. Within two years, two of the brightest stars, Chen Boda and Lin Biao, were in disgrace. With reconstruction on the agenda, Zhou Enlai and the veteran cadres played a more prominent role, and one of the first groups to be nullified were the "ultra-leftists," identified with Chen Boda. Chen had become wary of Jiang Qing and had clashed with Zhang Chunqiao; as a result, he began to detach himself from the CCRG and align himself more closely with Lin Biao. Matters came to a head at a plenum held in late August 1970 at Lushan. Clearly, Lushan was not a good place for those Mao saw as a rival. This meeting would prove to be no different.

Whether the position of head of state should be reinstituted in the new State Constitution created divisions and raised suspicions. In bouts of modesty, Mao refused the honor, as did Lin Biao when Mao suggested that he should take the position. On August 22, the day before the plenum, Mao called for unity but was angered when Chen Boda and Lin again raised the issue of head of state. In his anger, Mao declared, "Whoever wants to be state chairman can do it, but I won't," and he proceeded to criticize Lin.[8] It is unclear why Lin Biao continued to raise the idea. Did Lin think that Mao was displaying false modesty, or did he simply misread the Chairman's mood? Or was the Chairman setting Lin up for a fall?

At the plenum, however, the furor focused on how to characterize Mao's thought, and especially his "genius."[9] Lin spoke first, praising Mao's genius, and discussions of the speech supported Lin's view, while suggesting that some were opposed to Mao's genius. In addition, the idea of state chairman was floated again. Although not named, Chen Boda and Lin had Zhang Chunqiao in their sights for criticism. Supporters of Zhang suggested to Mao that some people were stirring up trouble. Mao took their side and criticized Chen Boda and others for breaching the Ninth Party Congress agreement to promote unity, not division. The fact that Chen's criticism of Zhang was supported by some CC members may have convinced Mao that the real intent was to roll back the gains of the Cultural Revolution.[10]

Chen Boda, who had drafted so much of Mao's radical works and had directed venom against Mao's opponents, now found himself the victim of such attacks. He was denounced as a "sham Marxist," stripped of all his posts, and vilified first within the party and then through public criticism. In an open letter of August 31, Mao discussed his criticism of Chen and his faulty ideas of genius, claiming that Chen wanted to recognize Mao's genius in order to take on the chairmanship of state.[11] Interestingly, Mao noted that Lin Biao agreed completely with this assessment. Conforming to the norms of denunciation, deceit had to be traced back in time, something difficult to show for the Yan'an period, and thus Chen was accused of siding with Peng Dehuai in the 1959 Lushan attacks on Mao over the Great Leap Forward. In truly impressive fashion and in a manner that only Communist rhetoric can claim, in the summer of 1972 Chen Boda was labeled a "Guomindang anti-Communist element, Trotskyite, renegade, special agent, and revisionist, guilty of the most heinous crimes."[12]

Lin Biao was not attacked yet, but it was the beginning of the end. With Chen removed and the ultra-left criticized in a campaign that ran well into 1971, the next target was to reduce military influence in the political system, especially those at the Center who were enjoying new powers. The events surrounding Lin's death while reportedly fleeing to the Soviet Union after an attempted coup d'état require the reader to suspend belief. There is no evidence that Lin plotted to assassinate Mao or that he actively sought to replace Mao; but such actions might have been contemplated by his wife, Ye Qun, who had worked hard to mobilize support for her husband and their son, Lin Liguo.[13] The Lin Biao who emerges from the accounts is a man who is sickly and passive, and not willing to rouse himself even when he was made aware that Mao would purge him.

The supposed plotters compiled the "571 Plan," a homophone that in Chinese sounds like "armed uprising." The plan included an assessment of a military that was far from united. Mao was referred to as B-52, while the plotters considered all kinds of ways to remove him, including flame-throwers, bombing his special train, and using rocket guns. The picture painted of Mao was quite accurate and must have had some party members nodding in agreement. He was described as paranoid and a sadist who had handed a final death sentence to all those whom he initially supported: "Those who are his guests today will be his prisoners tomorrow." Of course, the plotters were denounced as seeking to restore the landlord bourgeois class and to "capitulate to the Soviet revisionist social-imperialism."[14] Lin was also accused of trying to blow up the Chairman's train near Shanghai before his fatal flight to Mongolia where his plane crashed, killing all onboard, including Lin, his wife, and son.

The news must have come as a devastating shock to the political elite and Mao himself, who fell very sick as he wrestled with the consequences.[15] Slowly the news was disseminated throughout the party, first via a top-secret missive on September 18 to senior officials. On September 24, the four generals closest to Lin were dismissed from their posts, and then the news spread further. To give credence to Mao's ability to detect the evil intent of these individuals with whom he had worked closely, there was put into circulation a letter that Mao had sent to Jiang Qing on July 8, 1966, which raised criticisms about Lin Biao and his poor understanding of Marxist theory. This was difficult for some to swallow and marked a break in their understanding of the Cultural Revolution.

Although the stories are highly improbable explanations as to why the closest comrade-in-arms lay dead in a field in Mongolia, there were reasons for the split. There had been a need to reduce military influence in the political system and to reduce the power the PLA might wield at a time of high tension with the Soviet Union. Although there is no clear evidence that Lin Biao was opposed to a possible rapprochement with the United States, the tensions with the Soviet Union may have influenced Mao's thinking. When the leadership gathered for the Ninth Party Congress, a major conflict with the Soviet Union was well within the realms of possibility. In the summer of 1968 the Soviet Union had sent troops into Czechoslovakia to overthrow the government and crush the demonstrators. The Brezhnev Doctrine asserted that the Soviet Union had the right to remove any government that deviated from Communist principles—as defined by the Soviet Union, of course. This disturbed the Chinese leadership, which began to refer to the "social imperialism" of the Soviet leadership. The situation deteriorated even further with the March 1969 clashes at Zhenbao Island on the Ussuri (Wu suli) River. The CCP rallied support by claiming that this was Soviet aggression, but it now seems clear that the conflict had been set in train by the Chinese side.[16] This provides a different spin to the earlier idea that Soviet aggression had opened a pathway for an improvement in Sino-US relations.

Tensions and clashes continued beyond the congress, talks on the border situation did not go well, and Beijing was spooked by rumors of a strategic strike on its nuclear capabilities.[17] In response, seemingly within his rights as head of the military, Lin Biao ordered aircraft around Beijing to be dispersed on September 30, and on October 20 he called for the leadership to disperse. What was most controversial was Lin's issuing, on October 17, a six-point directive regarding strengthening defense to counter a surprise attack. The following day Lin's chief of staff distributed the directive to the military regions, the air and naval forces, and the Beijing garrison, packaged as "Vice-Chairman Lin's First Verbal Order." The entire military was placed on combat readiness in case of Soviet aggression. Mao was angered by the directive and called for it to be burned. Perhaps this brought home to Mao just how quickly the military could be mobilized and, given its dominance in the political system, this could be interpreted as a threat to Mao's position.

In response, Mao turned to the ideas of some of the old-time generals who did not see either the Soviets or the Americans as a major threat. Given the domestic situation and his desire to reduce military influence and the perceived threat from the Soviet Union, Mao took the extraordinary initiative to improve relations with the United States.[18] Luck was on his side, as President Nixon and Secretary of State Henry Kissinger were seeking alliances outside of the European sphere to counteract the Soviets. In October 1969, Nixon approached Pakistan's leadership, which enjoyed good relations with China, to facilitate contacts. In May 1971 Nixon sent a secret message to Zhou Enlai that he would be willing to travel to Beijing if Kissinger went first and an appropriate framework was established.[19] Eventually, in February 1972, Nixon visited the ailing Mao in Beijing, by which time Lin Biao was dead. During the meeting with Nixon, Mao claimed that Lin had opposed the meeting and had tried to flee to the Soviet Union.[20] That Lin had a view contrary to that of Mao seems highly unlikely. The most tangible and far-reaching outcome of this détente was the vote on October 25, 1971, supported by the United States, for the PRC to take up the China seat on the UN Security Council and for the Republic of China to be removed.

If the PLA had been united, it would have been extremely difficult, if not impossible, to remove Lin Biao. The two most important divisions were between the regional commanders and the leaders of the centrally directed units and between those favoring a professional, military role for the PLA and those like Lin, who favored a political role. This political role had been approved by Mao ever since the removal of Peng Dehuai in 1959. As Lin Biao came under increasing pressure, the powerful regional commanders in the Politburo could have offered support, but they opted not to and, consequently, they retained their positions. Their reluctance to support Lin can be traced to their experiences in the Cultural Revolution when Lin became increasingly identified with the left, with which they had clashed when trying to restore order. Lin's inactivity in supporting his colleagues stood in marked contrast with the efforts by Zhou Enlai, and isolated him from the regional command. Those who favored a more professional military sought withdrawal from political work and may well have harbored grudges against the central military leaders for not protecting them from the Red Guards. Lin Biao could not assure Mao and the civilian leaders that the military would withdraw from politics in an orderly fashion, meaning that he was isolated and satisfying none of the groups, thus facilitating the ease with which he and his supporters could be removed.

What Kind of Party-State Should Rule?

Following Lin Biao's death, the leadership stressed once more that the party controls the gun, with the CCP, rather than the army, taking on the mantle of national unity. Initially Lin was criticized as an ultra-leftist, a behind-the-scenes leader of a "May 16 corps." Whether such a group actually existed or not is debatable. The description of Lin Biao and Chen Boda as leftists provided an important part of the answer to the question of who would fill the ranks of the party leadership as the military was withdrawn. It would not be the Cultural Revolution radicals but instead many of those who had previously been disgraced. A related question was whether the masses should enjoy greater accountability with a mobilization work style or should revert to an idealized form of the pre–Cultural Revolution party, exercising leadership as an organizational decision-making body. The left favored promoting those who had been tempered in the storms of the previous years: this included those referred to as revolutionary cadres, such as future party leader Hua Guofeng in Hunan, and those who had risen to prominence as a result of the Cultural Revolution. Wang Hongwen, who rose like a helicopter through the Shanghai radical movement, is the best example of the latter. Wang was a member of the new CC and would rise further to become a member of the Politburo Standing Committee at the Tenth Party Congress, held on August 24–28, 1973. The radicals enjoyed strongholds in Shanghai and in the fields of propaganda and education, with a strong presence at the Center among those gathered around Jiang Qing. Tensions grew as more familiar faces returned to the political scene.

Not surprisingly, Zhou Enlai oversaw the task of vetting the officials who might return to work, and in March 1972 he submitted to Mao a list of some 400 senior officials for his approval, which was duly given.[21] The rehabilitation of significant figures was made at Mao's instigation, with Zhou, as always, carrying out the Chairman's wishes. Thus, the bulk of the new cadres were not new at all but were those who had been attacked or purged during the Cultural Revolution. The most notable was Deng Xiaoping, the man who had been the "number two person in authority taking the capitalist road." Mao harbored a softer spot for Deng than for the others, and Deng was certainly helped by his self-criticisms that acknowledged the error of his ways. In April 1973, at a reception for Cambodian military officials, Deng was introduced by Zhou Enlai as a vice premier of the State Council.

The period leading up to the Tenth Party Congress emitted mixed signals. At one level, the return of so many veteran officials was accompanied by a more relaxed atmosphere as people digested what had happened. A range of underground literature wrestled with the personal and societal consequences of the tumultuous upheavals.[22] These writings and the manifesto of the Shengwulian group, mentioned in Chapter 7, revealed that, far from enforcing conformity within Chinese society and blind allegiance to Chairman Mao, there was considerable diversity, and different groups and people experienced this high point of Maoism in different ways.

The most coherent alternative critique of the political system came on November 10, 1974, when a group of writers posted their Li-Yi-Zhe manifesto on the streets of Guangzhou, although it had been in gestation for at least a year.[23] Although initially the writers were arrested, their views reflected some of the ideas that would appear in later official documents that were critical of the practice of rule during the Cultural Revolution. The authors had become disillusioned by the events that had unfolded, and their manifesto contained a mix of the aspirations of the movement's original intent and criticism of the outcomes. The criticism centered on what they termed the "Lin Biao system," which they denounced as fascist. Despite his death, the system had not died with him. The manifesto called for "socialist democracy and legality," a slogan of the post-Mao leadership, to replace the new "feudalistic social-fascist dictatorship." The authors agreed with the argument that special privileges had formed the basis for a new bourgeois class, but they were more tolerant of different perspectives and were opposed to the violence that had become part and parcel of the struggle. They claimed that "the theory of genius" had eliminated 800 million brains, but people were not allowed to ask why. They enjoyed some degree of official support—when the authors were rehabilitated in 1979, CCP official organs, including the *People's Daily*, praised the manifesto.

As people were coming up for air with the more relaxed atmosphere, another trend was developing in the buildup to the congress. Some were concerned about the return of so many purged officials, worrying that their intent was to roll back the gains of the Cultural Revolution. By late November and early December 1972, a focal point of difference was how to assess Lin Biao. Zhou Enlai wanted to maintain the view that his actions were ultra-leftist, as this supported the return of officials who had been disparaged during the Cultural Revolution. By contrast, Zhang Chunqiao questioned this and, together with Jiang Qing, said that Lin's ultra-right tendencies should be the focus: Jiang considered his actions "left in form but right in essence."[24] Before a December 17 meeting with Zhou Enlai, Zhang Chunqiao, and Yao Wenyuan, Mao had not taken a clear stance, but now he told them that Lin Biao's actions were indeed those of the ultra-right, not the ultra-left. Although it still took some time for this revised assessment to make its way through the system, Mao was clearly concerned about a rollback of the gains of the Cultural Revolution. These tensions played out at the Tenth Party Congress.

The congress was not one for new initiatives. Instead it offered correctives to the events of the past four years and delivered a formal assessment of Lin Biao. Much-needed new statutes were adopted to replace the existing ones, which had still noted that Lin was Mao's chosen successor. The sooner the new statutes could be passed, the better for Mao. Finally, a new leadership was elected that showed a clear representation of those who supported Mao and the aims of the Cultural Revolution.

Zhou Enlai's political report displayed for all to see the reputed behind-the-scenes maneuvers of Lin and his followers.[25] The task was to defend the line of the Ninth Party Congress while criticizing Lin Biao. Thus, Zhou declared that the congress represented a great victory for the line of the Ninth Party Congress, while Lin was denounced by name as a "bourgeois careerist, conspirator, and double-dealer," and, importantly, Zhou noted that Lin had continually "committed right opportunist errors." The report claimed that the Ninth Congress report had been drafted by Lin and Chen Boda and had emphasized the need to develop production, thus sneaking in the "same revisionist trash that Liu Shaoqi and Chen Boda had smuggled into the resolution of the Eighth Congress." Zhou indicated this was not the end of the matter but only the beginning of a stepped-up, concerted effort to thoroughly weed out the Lin Biao "revisionist clique" and its "poisonous influences in China."

The rapidly rising star Wang Hongwen delivered the report on the revisions to the statutes, although Yao Wenyuan had drafted his report, with Zhang Chunqiao overseeing the revisions. Given the more radical tenor of this group, the new statutes defended the Cultural Revolution and incorporated key concepts from it. The now embarrassing mention of Lin Biao was excised, while confirming the correct line of the Ninth Congress.[26] The statutes comprised a mix of traditional party norms combined with elements derived from the experience of the Cultural Revolution. Democratic centralism remained the key organizing principle, and it was stressed that the "party must exercise leadership in everything," and all organizations, including the PLA and the revolutionary mass organizations, had to accept the party's centralized leadership. However, the statutes noted that "revolutions like this will have to be carried out many times in the future," while Wang added that every seven or eight years "monsters and demons will jump out themselves." Other new elements included the need to criticize revisionism, to support the "revolutionary spirit of daring to go against the tide," and to train millions of successors.

A clear majority of the new leadership would support Mao and presumably protect the gains of the Cultural Revolution. Interestingly, even though Mao had decided to bring Deng Xiaoping back in April 1973 after his three and a half years working in a tractor factory in Jiangxi province, he was not elevated to the Politburo. PLA representation on the new CC dropped by almost one-half, while about forty full members, including Deng Xiaoping and Chen Yun, were appointed from among those who had been purged during the Cultural Revolution. The Standing Committee was expanded from five to nine members, with an overwhelming majority supportive of Mao and only Zhou Enlai and Ye Jianying likely to support the returnees. Even the venerable Dong Biwu was retained! Mao had learned his lesson about identifying a successor, and five chairmen were named, including Mao as chair, Zhou as first vice chair, and Wang Hongwen as second vice chair. One could argue that tacitly Wang was named as Mao's successor and this should have given comfort to the radicals in the leadership.

Rivalry over the future direction continued and again attacks on Lin Biao were used to push the agenda of the remaining radicals against the returnees. Over the summer and into the fall, the campaign against Lin Biao was linked to a campaign against Confucius, and this morphed into the Campaign to Criticize Lin Biao and Confucius. While there were social objectives to the criticisms of Confucianism that were designed to break down the remaining influence of superstition and traditional thinking, the main objective was clearly political. The intention was to protect the "newborn things" of the Cultural Revolution against those who were pushing to return to earlier practices. The archaic nature of the campaign left many confused. In 1977 at Nanjing University, Chinese students complained bitterly about their earlier visits to the countryside to promote the campaign. The peasants shouted at them for wasting their time, talking about irrelevant topics, and in tears they returned to their campus.[27]

On February 2, 1974, the political situation heated up further when the *People's Daily* called on people to "dare to go against the tide and advance into the teeth of storms" and a campaign of mass criticism was unfurled. The targets were becoming clear: Zhou Enlai and those who had returned to positions of power and sought his protection. However, the continuing campaigns and the calls to go against the tide were affecting the economy. In 1974–1976 industrial production stagnated. The poor development in 1974 was linked to worker unrest, arising from the movement to "criticize Lin Biao and Confucius." On July 1 a CC circular noted the problems with production in many key sectors, including iron and steel, the chemical industry, and cement. The problems derived not only from factors such as poor coal production and transportation bottlenecks but also from factional struggles within the factories. Consequently, the circular called for calm, and the workers were asked to stop criticizing economic policy and making work claims, and instead to concentrate on production and, ironically, criticizing Lin Biao and Confucius.[28] Although the situation improved somewhat through 1974, in some cities, such as in Hangzhou, order was not restored until the summer of 1975 following the purge of leading officials and the dispatch of troops.[29]

With Zhou Enlai's health deteriorating, Mao Zedong decided to place Deng Xiaoping in charge of the economy in preparation for the Fourth NPC. However, Mao did not want to focus exclusively on the economy at the expense of the revolutionary agenda. As a result, in the fall of 1974 he issued three directives: to achieve calm and unity within the army and party; to "study theory and oppose revisionism"; and to promote economic development. The relationship among these three became the core of the disagreements between Deng Xiaoping and the radicals. The radicals complained that Deng simply focused on the economy while ignoring politics.

Against this background, the Fourth NPC convened in Beijing on January 13–17, 1975, and one last attempt was made to put together a policy and leadership coalition that could work together to ensure economic growth and revolutionary momentum. Neither objective lasted for long. Zhou Enlai came off his sickbed to deliver the report outlining the "four modernizations" (agriculture, industry, national defense, and science and technology), a program that he had first presented in 1964. He proposed a two-stage program: the first objective would be to build an "independent and relatively comprehensive industrial and economic system" by 1980, and the second objective would be to bring the national economy to the front ranks of the world by the year 2000. He painted a glowing picture of the economy, including a positive assessment of the role of the people's communes. The report was laced with praise for the Cultural Revolution and the revolutionary objectives of recent years.[30]

The new Constitution was a lean affair in comparison with the 1954 Constitution, with just thirty articles instead of 106. It encapsulated the radical approach of the period since 1954, and consequently it was also the shortest-lived Constitution, replaced in 1978. Given the trials and tribulations over the question of head of state that had devoured Lin Biao and Chen Boda, the post of head of state and the position of vice president were deleted. Zhang Chunqiao noted that this would help strengthen the centralized leadership of the party over the state apparatus.[31] The Constitution warned of the dangers of capitalist restoration and of aggression by imperialism (the United States) and social-imperialism (the Soviet Union), and it called for the exercise of all-round dictatorship over the bourgeoisie in the superstructure, including all spheres of culture. Importantly, leadership of the party over the state sector was confirmed, through which the working class would exercise its leadership. One interesting legacy from the struggles of the Cultural Revolution was the inclusion of the "new forms of carrying on socialist revolution": "speaking out freely, airing views fully, holding great debates, and writing big-character posters."

The new posts for Deng Xiaoping and Zhang Chunqiao reflected an attempt to balance the returnees and the radicals in order to retain the gains of the Cultural Revolution while at the same time generating economic growth. Deng and Jiang Qing had been in conflict earlier, but then they clashed at a Politburo meeting on October 17, 1974. Wang Hongwen was asked to fly to Changsha to meet with Mao, but he did not receive the reply he expected when he was told to unite with Deng and to be wary of Jiang. Mao also informed Wang that Deng should be made a vice chair of the party, vice chair of the Central Military Commission, and PLA chief of staff. To provide balance, Zhang Chunqiao was to be head of the General Political Department and the second-ranking vice premier.[32] This clearly tilted the balance of power in Deng's favor. The most disappointed must have been Wang Hongwen, as it confirmed that Mao did not see him as an heir apparent.

The Coalition Falls Apart

The brokered coalition was too fragile to survive and began to fall apart very shortly after the congress. Two developments hastened the disintegration. First, the poor health of the old guard brought the question of succession to the fore. In December 1975 Kang Sheng died, and Zhou Enlai, Zhu De, and Mao would die in January, July, and September 1976, respectively. As the rumors of the illness of the leaders circulated, others began to plot a world without them and tried to strengthen their own positions.

The second development was the drafting of concrete economic plans for implementation in 1976, and this pushed to the fore the differing approaches to economic strategy. While Deng and his supporters set about outlining their policies for economic growth, the group later to be denounced as the "Gang of Four" launched a series of theoretical campaigns directed against those who were "whittling away" the gains of the Cultural Revolution.

During the summer of 1975, Deng worked with the recently established State Council think tank to produce three important policy documents.[33] Even though Deng produced the documents, his opponents controlled the propaganda and publishing sectors.[34] The documents were denounced as "poisonous weeds" by his opponents, but later they were heralded as "fragrant flowers." The first document covered industrial development (the Twenty Points), outlining the measures necessary to fulfill the Ten-Year Plan for Industry. The proposal was for industrial systems that would have their own special characteristics and strive for basic autonomy in core goods. Agricultural production had to be increased before the industrial sector could expand sufficiently, and the industrial sector was to provide support to agriculture. Deng was willing to export China's raw materials to generate income to import the machinery needed to develop manufacturing. At the same time, he was willing to use material incentives. These points were seized upon by his opponents, who accused him of being a traitor if he was willing to export China's natural resources, and they dismissed his ideas on the use of material incentives to get the economy moving.

The second document covered scientific research and was a critique of what had occurred in the education and scientific realms. The scientific community, with the exception of the nuclear program, had been devastated during the Cultural Revolution. The revitalized Academy of Sciences was placed under the leadership of Hu Yaobang, a future CCP general secretary. It called for better training, raising education standards, and bringing China up to world scientific standards by the year 2000. The report even noted that learning from foreigners could be beneficial, although not everything from abroad was good. Clearly, more emphasis was to be placed on the "expert" in Mao's formulation of being both red and expert.

The third document covered work for the party and the nation. Although it used Mao's thinking, the way it was put together would anger those closest to Mao and Mao himself. The ultimate goal of revolution was to increase social production, and for this "stability and unity" were crucial for economic growth. On October 20, 1975, when Mao saw the draft, he was angry that his views had been distorted to place undue emphasis on economic work over theory and struggle. The documents were not released formally at this time, but the contents became widely known as they were distributed as study materials for criticism. Over 81 million copies were distributed for criticism.[35] The "Gang of Four" distributed the documents, and supporters of Deng also distributed them—almost verbatim, with a few lines attached pointing out what terrible revisionist theories they were.[36]

Within a month after the Fourth NPC concluded in January 1975, the campaigns began with the call to "study well the theory of the dictatorship of the proletariat."[37] This was the start of a number of campaigns to undermine Zhou Enlai and Deng Xiaoping and remove them from the political scene. The rationale was pulled together from four comments by Mao that warned of the need to restrict bourgeois rights under the dictatorship of the proletariat to prevent revisionism. The theoretical journals covered the movement, but throughout 1975, economic practice leaned more heavily to the policies of the Fourth NPC, with the result that a large gap was opening up between theory and practice, reflecting the different spheres of influence between those around Deng and those around the "Gang of Four."

Building on Mao's comments and those made earlier on the existence of classes under socialism, the two main theorists of the group, Zhang Chunqiao and Yao Wenyuan, sought to explain how these classes and class struggle could continue to exist in a socialist society after the means of production had been socialized. Their theory was used to justify the attack on the veteran cadres. Although the phrase "continuing the revolution" had been put forward at the Ninth Party Congress, it was Mao's "important instructions" on theory from February 1975 that provided the impetus. Mao noted that the unequal wage system and other inequalities could be restricted by the dictatorship of the proletariat but could not be eliminated.[38] This justified moves to restrict bourgeois rights. Together with the persistence of capitalist factors, such as commodities and differential wages, they provided the material basis for the reproduction of capitalism and the source of power for a new bourgeoisie to emerge and prosper.[39] The division of labor created an intellectual aristocracy that ruled over the production units, denying workers access to real power. While the most blatant inequalities—between capitalist and worker, and between landlord and peasant—had been eradicated, other inequalities based on relative skills, strengths, or occupations still existed. Privileged groups would seek to perpetuate their vested interests and not accept the move toward communism. Zhang Chunqiao held the view that even an enterprise that was owned by the whole people could, in practice, be capitalist if its leadership followed a bourgeois line. To prevent this capitalist restoration, it was necessary to enforce the "dictatorship of the proletariat."[40] Deng's promotion of material incentives and the four modernizations provided precisely this kind of basis for a capitalist restoration. The radicals were critical of the policy of "all-round adjustment" and of Deng's empiricism. In one of their more memorable phrases, they claimed they would rather have a "late socialist train" than a "capitalist train that ran on time."

The next campaign, launched in the fall of 1975, derived from the Chinese classical story "The Water Margin." This was a tale of the derring-do of a band of rebels opposed to the imperial court. One of the leaders, Song Jiang, who was formerly praised by Jiang Qing, was criticized in the campaign for his capitulation to the emperor to advance his own interests, thus subverting the cause of the rebels. While it gave Chinese people the chance to read something other than dire political propaganda, its political message was clear. Zhou Enlai—actually Deng Xiaoping, given Zhou's health—was overseeing class capitulation domestically and internationally by playing down the role of class struggle and calling for greater involvement in the world economic system to promote the four modernizations.

By early November 1975, Mao came to see Deng's policy of all-round adjustment for the economy as undermining the gains of the Cultural Revolution. Even though Mao's mental faculties may have remained strong, he suffered from a number of physical complaints and his contacts with the outside world were limited. Much of his information was brokered by his nephew, Mao Yuanxin, who had been brought down to Beijing from Liaoning province to serve as Mao's go-between.[41] At this stage Mao still held out hope that Deng could see the error of his ways, but in 1976 Mao concluded that Deng could not be trusted to retain the gains of the Cultural Revolution.

As happened during the launch of the Cultural Revolution, the first attacks took place at the universities, with Deng as a target of criticism. As early as August 1975, criticism of education policy was posted at Beijing's Tsinghua University, and in November the minister of education, Zhou Rongxin, was attacked in wall posters at Tsinghua and Beijing Universities; some of the posters included criticism of Deng. These moves were coordinated with the growing criticism of Deng at the political center. On November 26 a central document claimed that unnamed people concerned with education had as their true target the Cultural Revolution. On December 20, at Mao's instigation, the Politburo was asked to issue a resolution confirming the value of the Cultural Revolution. Deng was forced to chair the meeting but no such resolution was issued. Throughout December and during the first few weeks of 1976, the Politburo was meeting almost daily to criticize Deng at meetings that Deng himself chaired.

The New Year's Day editorials in the CCP's main newspapers prepared the public, emphasizing the positive role of the Cultural Revolution, particularly the reforms in education. The editorials linked the attempt to reverse educational policy with the "right deviationist wind to reverse correct verdicts," which was being promoted by "representatives of the bourgeoisie" who stood in opposition to the proletariat. Yet the editorials made it clear that this was not to herald the unleashing of the kind of forces that rose up in the universities to launch the Cultural Revolution. Rather, the movement was to proceed through reeducation under party supervision. Significantly, Mao issued a new comment: "Stability and unity do not mean writing off class struggle: class struggle is the key link and everything else hinges on it." Subsequently Deng was charged with not appreciating this comment and with placing unity, development, and class struggle on the same level, instead of prioritizing class struggle.

On January 8, 1976, Zhou Enlai died of cancer, and on January 15 Deng delivered the eulogy, only to be removed as the senior vice premier a few days later. To the surprise of outsiders, Hua Guofeng was announced as acting premier. This shocked Zhang Chunqiao and the others because it signaled that Mao did not trust them to run the country in a manner that would safeguard the gains of the Cultural Revolution and develop the economy. In fact, Mao had criticized them several times between July 1974 and September 1975. At the last Politburo meeting he chaired, on May 5, 1975, Mao criticized them for being empiricists and not having adequate Marxism-Leninism, and with respect to factionalism, he told them not to behave like a "Gang of Four." This appellation was important for the post-Mao leadership when it justified their arrest. Responding, Jiang Qing offered a self-criticism in which she admitted that factionalism was serious and there actually existed a "Gang of Four." For his part, Zhang Chunqiao swore to avoid forming a "Gang of Four." During the next three months they even went so far as to avoid one another's company in order not to give the wrong impression.[42]

After Deng was passed over for the post of premier, the campaign against him picked up steam, and by mid-February, with Mao's full support, that "unrepentant capitalist roader" was under attack. The *People's Daily* continued Mao's warning that the bourgeoisie was "right in the Communist Party" and thus the "capitalist roaders" were "still on the capitalist road."[43] For those who missed the message, on March 23 the target was made even clearer in a published comment by Mao: "This person does not grasp class struggle; he has never referred to this key link. Still his theme of 'white cat, black cat,' making no distinction between imperialism and Marxism."[44]

Mao and the "Gang of Four" seriously overestimated the Chinese people's appetite for yet another political campaign, especially one targeted at the legacy of Zhou Enlai and Deng's policies for the future. Universities again took the lead, but this time they supported Deng. In March 1976, Nanjing University became a focal point of the resistance, and after an oblique but unmistakable criticism of Zhou Enlai was published, hundreds of thousands came out to protest.[45]

In April 1976 the resistance climaxed with clashes in Tiananmen Square, where up to two million people gathered in protest. This provided the pretext for stripping Deng of all his official posts, but, significantly, again he was not dismissed from the party. The Qingming Festival, on April 4, is the traditional day for visiting and sweeping the graves of ancestors. In the lead-up to the festival, citizens had been placing wreaths, posters, and manifestos around the square in memory of Zhou Enlai. But during the night, the square was cleared, causing huge numbers to come out on April 5, and leading to conflicts and rioting. The militia and armed troops broke up the crowds; the head of the Beijing Revolutionary Committee denounced the protests as counterrevolutionary. After the later fall of the "Gang of Four," the incident was described as "completely revolutionary" and held up as a symbol of the masses' disapproval of the practices of the past few years. At the time, a very different view was taken, and on April 7, with Mao's approval, the Politburo met to dismiss Deng from his posts and to appoint Hua Guofeng as first vice chair of the CC and premier.

The campaign's clear target was now Deng, and the "Gang of Four" appeared to be in firm control as they mobilized the media to deepen their attacks. Deng's removal did not signal the end of the attacks, however, and in August 1976 moves to target other rehabilitated cadres intensified. Late in the month the *People's Daily* called for an intensification of the struggle against capitalist roaders and drew attention to those who had been "unmasked and criticized before" but who still wanted to "reverse verdicts."[46] At the same time, some of the provincial newspapers were carrying articles on the need for unity and promotion of production. This view was supported not only by those who feared for their own positions but probably also by Hua Guofeng, who had benefited from the Cultural Revolution but did not share the radicalism of the "Gang of Four." Following their arrest, the "Gang" was faced with evidence that they had criticized Hua for his revisionist and "capitulationist" tendencies.[47]

Death Sparks a Radical Shift

The question of succession became all the more acute with further attacks on June 26 and September 2, as Mao Zedong's health rapidly deteriorated after a heart attack on May 11 had left him bedridden. He died on September 9—and not for the first time, the death of a supreme leader opened the way for political change. On September 9 in Tiananmen Square there was a somber atmosphere as the loudspeakers began to broadcast that everyone should return to their units for a very important broadcast that would be announced at 4 p.m.[48] It was clear what would be announced and, indeed, instead of the usual sign-off after all of Mao's titles "Long Live Chairman Mao, Eternal Life," the sign-off was "Remain Immortal." The words were followed by wailing, not so much out of sorrow but more out of fear about what would come next. Indeed, as he lay in state, an atmosphere of uncertainty dominated the next few days. His memorial was held on September 18.

Scheming over the future began almost immediately, and at the memorial service it was apparent for those with a keen eye for obscure Chinese phraseology. For their legacy, the "Gang of Four" had put forward the phrase

At Mao Zedong's funeral the original lineup of party officials shows gaps where the images of the "Gang of Four" were subsequently deleted.

An anti-"Gang of Four" poster, "Smashed by the Monkey King."

"act according to the principles laid down" as Mao's last words, and this was used to portray themselves as Mao's chosen successors.[49] Their supporters at Tsinghua and Peking Universities said this meant carrying on the struggle against the capitalist roaders and intensifying the criticism of Deng. Although the phrase was used at every provincial memorial meeting, Hua Guofeng excluded it from his eulogy. One wonders what the provincial leaders must have thought when they looked at the newspapers the next morning.

Although there is no evidence that the "Gang of Four" was seeking to seize power, Hua Guofeng and his allies were taking no chances. As early as September 11, Hua had already secured the support of veterans Li Xiannian, Ye Jianying, and Wang Dongxing to resolve the issue. Wang's support was critical because he was head of the 8341 Special Regiment that provided protection to the senior leaders, and he had been very close to Mao. At the end of September the group discussed whether the "Gang" could be dismissed

An anti–"Gang of Four" poster, "Crushed by the Workers."

by a Politburo vote but there were concerns that this might prove difficult to get through the CC. Consequently the "Gang" were arrested in the evening of October 6 as they arrived to attend a fake meeting of the Standing Committee. For good measure, Mao's nephew, Mao Yuanxin, was also taken. Thus, the post-Mao era that was committed to restore an orderly process and to promote socialist legality began with a good old-fashioned coup.

The extreme sensitivity of the arrest meant that the Chinese people were not informed of the arrest until October 18. Prior to that, posters were put up around Beijing announcing "Smash the anti-party Gang of Four clique," but it wasn't clear to the public what this meant. The British Embassy was informed, and through this the *Daily Telegraph* broke the news internationally.[50]

"Spontaneous" anti-"Gang of Four" demonstrations.

By October 22 Chinese students knew what had happened, and in the university area of Beijing there were so many celebrations that the stores sold out of alcohol. Somewhat chaotic demonstrations began in the center of Beijing and, unlike previously, people were happy to have foreigners join and take photos. As they marched across Tiananmen, the elite 8341 Special Regiment was greeted as heroes. Gradually the demonstrations became more organized, culminating on October 24 with a mass rally in the square. At the rally it was announced that Hua Guofeng had been appointed to the concurrent posts of chair of the CCP CC and chair of the Central Military Commission.

"Spontaneous" anti-"Gang of Four" demonstrations.

The turmoil unleashed by the Cultural Revolution was at an end, even though the new leadership predicted more such movements to come. The post-Mao leadership was harsh in its assessment of the previous ten years but tried to dissociate Mao from the "Gang of Four," Lin Biao, and the worst aspects of the Cultural Revolution—not something that was readily believed.[51] The Cultural Revolution was "responsible for the most severe setback and the heaviest losses suffered by the party, the state, and the people since the founding of the People's Republic. It had been initiated and led by Comrade Mao Zedong."[52]

Legacies of the Cultural Revolution

By the time the "Gang of Four" was arrested, the Chinese political and economic systems were beset with major problems. A host of new problems confronted the leadership, and the challenges that had faced the party when Mao launched the Cultural Revolution had not been resolved. The political system had become completely reliant on the supreme leader to adjudicate, and there was little trust within society for the institutions of party and state, given the attacks launched on them over the previous years. The fabric of society had been torn apart by the continual campaigns and by the pressures to denounce friends and relatives. In many workplaces people had to labor alongside those who had attacked them in a previous movement. Many young people who had been led to believe that they were important actors ended up being sent down to the countryside to labor, leading to widespread cynicism about the political process. Although the economy might not have been in crisis, it was in poor shape and a major overhaul was necessary.

Mao had not left his successors a clear blueprint of the kind of organizational system he preferred, and he had been ambivalent regarding questions of organization.[53] It was difficult to separate the party as an institution from the individuals who were being purged and criticized, and this undermined the prestige of the party and raised the question of legitimacy. When Mao was alive, this was resolved by the cult of the individual. With Mao gone, could the party be restored as a source of authority and legitimacy and not simply an organization that employed the coercive apparatus of the state?

The "Gang of Four" and its supporters struggled to devise new organizations that could combine the more traditional concepts of a Leninist party with ideas spread during the Cultural Revolution. Yet they failed to break with the structural and normative logic of a Leninist-Stalinist structure and they could not provide an alternative that would have satisfied the rebels' desire for more authority to be transferred to the masses. Eventually they used hierarchical means to bring about democracy and invoked obedience to the Chairman to encourage initiative.[54] The inability to develop alternatives and the weakness of support for the "Gang" within society and even within the senior leadership meant that they invoked Mao as their source of legitimacy.

Neither Mao nor his supporters had been willing to accept a plurality of views within society. Mao's 1942 speech in Yan'an on the role of art and literature had already made this clear, and it was demonstrated again with the Anti-Rightist Campaign that followed the brief Hundred Flowers Campaign in the mid-1950s. Individuals were expected to display loyalty to the Chairman; the problem being, of course, that this "loyalty" was simply blind obedience. The realities of the Maoist experiments—the GLF and the Cultural Revolution—diverged radically from their stated intents. Initially both movements appeared to provide new means for participation, but the Cultural Revolution led to an unexpected, spontaneous mass participation that went far beyond anything seen in any other Leninist system. For some, it had a liberating effect as the Chinese people enjoyed an unprecedented opportunity to attack their "bureaucratic leaders," read classified materials that revealed the shenanigans of their top leaders, and to openly express their views. These allowed dissenting critiques to appear, such as the Li Yizhe poster of 1974, and they laid the basis for the short-lived Democracy Wall Movement of 1978–1979.

The type of mass mobilization that was unleashed could not be regularized and was not beneficial. During the GLF, it did not bring about the promised economic breakthrough, and planning and economic coordination were rendered almost impossible, resulting in economic dislocation and widespread famine. During the Cultural Revolution, this contributed to the temporary destruction of the old party elite, but it could not contribute to building a suitable organizational form to aid the process of economic modernization. Indeed, it was a major hindrance to that process. Maintaining legitimacy in the eyes of the people was a significant difficulty that neither Mao Zedong nor the "Gang of Four" nor Hua Guofeng could resolve.

Problems abounded in the economic sphere. The post-Mao leadership denounced the Cultural Revolution as "ten lost years," but this was a political rather than an economic judgment. Even though the economy was not in crisis, a major structural overhaul was necessary. In 1975 the gross value of agricultural output was 35.7 percent higher than it had been in 1966. Total value of industrial and agricultural output grew 9.6 percent in 1966–1970 and 7.8 percent in 1970–1975. With the exception of labor productivity in state-owned enterprises, the figures were not too bad. Labor productivity rose 2.5 percent in 1966–1970 and then declined by 0.3 percent in the subsequent period. In comparison with other large economies, such as India and Indonesia, China was performing better, but it was far behind the best-performing economies in East Asia, such as South Korea, Japan, and even Taiwan.[55]

The distribution of income and quality-of-life indicators stood up reasonably well in comparison to other countries in the region. However, the apparently low level of inequality was aided by the repression of consumption and the rationing of goods, which led to privileged access for those with connections and power. It also masked significant inequality between urban and rural China. Some 200 million people suffered from chronic malnutrition at the time of Mao's death.[56] Other indicators showed progress despite the massive upheavals and the starvation of the GLF. For example, average life expectancy had risen, from 40 years, to 64 years in 1976, and infant mortality had dropped from 175 per thousand births to 45 per thousand births since 1949.

Yet aggregate figures mask the increasing problems and structural imbalances in the Chinese economy. Most importantly, after the economy began to recover in the early 1970s as the more radical phase of the Cultural Revolution was reined in, the growth rate again began to decline. In 1976, it was approaching crisis proportions, as the average growth rate in national income dropped 2.3 percent and the growth of total production, at 1.7 percent, was below the rate of population growth.[57] It is important to keep in mind that as a result of Mao's rejection of birth-control measures in the 1950s, the population had almost doubled from 582 million in 1949 to 932 million.

The poor growth can be partly attributed to the terrible Tangshan earthquake of July 1976, which killed more than 250,000 people and caused some 10 billion yuan of economic losses. An equally, or perhaps an even more, plausible explanation is the political paralysis that seized China's economic decision-making in these years. In fact, the response to the earthquake immediately became a political issue. Hua Guofeng refused international assistance and argued that his governmental response to the disaster bolstered his credentials for leadership, and the "Gang of Four" complained that rescue efforts should not detract from the movement to criticize Deng Xiaoping.[58]

The economic downturn contributed to dissatisfaction with the already widespread stagnating living conditions. The government's consistent overconcentration on accumulation to the neglect of consumption meant that rationing, queueing, and hours spent on tedious housework were daily fare for most. Even if there had been more to buy, few could afford it. In 1977 the average wage of state employees was 5.5 percent lower than it had been in 1957, and that of industrial workers was 8.4 percent lower. Part of this decline was due to the addition to the workforce of many younger workers who received lower pay. Given the anti-bureaucratic rhetoric of the Maoist era, it is interesting that the average wage for government employees was almost the same in 1977 as it was in 1957. By 1976 many of China's citizens had had enough of tightening their belts for the seemingly empty promise of reaching a Communist nirvana in the distant future.

At the time of Mao's death, China's bureaucracy was ill-qualified by age and level of education to administer the kinds of programs that were needed to move the country forward. The Cultural Revolution had exacerbated this by creating intense factional conflict among the population. Many intellectuals who had been denounced as the "stinking ninth category" were alienated and disillusioned, urban youth had witnessed the disintegration and repression of the Red Guard movement and many had been sent down to the countryside, while urban workers had not seen significant increases in living standards. Peasants had seen their land taken away and had been herded into collective agriculture, which many abandoned whenever the opportunity presented itself.

Perhaps the best adjudication of the Mao years was provided by Chen Yun, his longtime collaborator: "Had Chairman Mao died in 1956, there would have been no doubt that he was a great leader in the proletarian revolutionary movement of the world. Had he died in 1966, his meritorious achievements would have been somewhat tarnished but still very good. Since he actually died in 1976, there is nothing we can do about it."[59]

Hua Guofeng Struggles with the Legacy

The challenge of dealing with these legacies fell first to Mao's anointed successor, Hua Guofeng, who had to use the flag of Maoism to find a new course. His tricky task was to rebuild trust in the broken administrative system without undermining all the gains of the Cultural Revolution. He tied his legitimacy closely to being the rightful heir to Mao, retaining certain ideas along with all their ambiguities, while pushing ahead for change. He saw the party as a vehicle for mobilization to carry out political and economic campaigns to meet ambitious economic targets, something with which Deng Xiaoping would agree. However, Hua found himself tied to the pledge that there would be more Cultural Revolutions in the future and that the masses should continue to monitor abuses by party cadres. As a result, suspicion of the party persisted and Hua moved toward developing a new personality cult to bolster his position and legitimacy.

Hua Guofeng's replacement by Deng Xiaoping as the paramount leader confirms our emphasis throughout this work that the CCP structure tends toward one-person dominance. In his work with Warren Sun on the initial post-Mao phase, Frederick Teiwes consistently emphasizes the lack of policy disputes between Hua Guofeng and Deng Xiaoping.[60] There was a general understanding that reform was necessary, and the policies initially pursued under Hua were based on those proposed by Deng in 1975–1976.[61] However, Hua Guofeng had to negotiate a very difficult legacy that subsequently made him vulnerable to criticism. It was impossible for a party novice such as Hua, who had joined the party in 1938, to resist pressure from party heavyweights such as Deng Xiaoping and Chen Yun. The fact that Hua was consistently reelected subsequently to the CC reflected high support for his having orchestrated the arrest of the "Gang of Four," his not having vigorously opposed Deng's return, and his having launched significant reforms to begin the move away from Mao Zedong's legacy.

To strengthen his legitimacy, Hua oversaw the building of a mausoleum to house Mao Zedong's stuffed body, took over the editing of volume 5 of Mao's works, and even adopted Mao's hairstyle. His portrait was displayed next to Mao's in Tiananmen Square. A widely distributed poster showed an avuncular Mao sitting with Hua and saying, "With you in charge, I am at ease." Significantly, Hua was associated with the group promoting the slogan of the Two Whatevers: "Whatever Chairman Mao decided upon, we shall resolutely defend; whatever directives Chairman Mao issued, we should steadfastly obey."[62] Not a good approach when the times were clearly calling for a change in strategy to repair the disasters that Mao had loosed on the country. This is not to say that Hua did not move policy forward in his brief time in charge, and the Mao he sought to promote was less radical than the Mao of the Cultural Revolution. Volume 5 of Mao's works end in 1957, and the most important speech included is his balanced "Ten Major Relationships." This notwithstanding, Hua was constrained and vulnerable to criticism, once the policies came under greater scrutiny.

Hua and the initial post-Mao leadership favored a quick-fix approach for the economy, setting ambitious planning targets and selectively importing high-level technology to transform the economy. The approach owed much to the alternative policy proposals put forward by Deng Xiaoping in 1975–1976. Deng's discredited "Twenty Points on Industry" formed the basis for the "Thirty Articles" adopted in April 1978. They reaffirmed that industry must serve the development of agriculture, and they established a set of sectoral priorities: extractive industries, transport and communications, light industry and handicrafts, and consumer goods. The development of

Mao confers legitimacy on Hua Guofeng by informing him that "With you in charge, I am at ease."

energy sources was dealt with separately. However, when the policies did not produce the expected boost, it was Hua, rather than Deng, who was blamed.

Clearly there was pressure from the leadership to show results, but society also expected the quality of life to improve as quickly as possible. During 1977, as rumors swirled about the possible return of Deng, two things were always mentioned: that Deng would raise living standards and that he would reunite families who had been separated by the Cultural Revolution. The basis for the economic new leap was the 1976–1985 Ten-Year Plan that was presented to the Fifth NPC in February–March 1978, based on earlier documents drafted under Deng's tutelage. The plan also bore resemblances to Mao's Twelve-Year Plan of the mid-1950s that had preceded the GLF. On April 4, 1977, the *People's Daily* had already called for a new leap forward, a point reiterated at the Eleventh Party Congress of August 1977 with the call to follow the general line of the leap: "going all out, aiming high to achieve greater, faster, better, and more economical results in building socialism."[63]

Enthusiasm was boosted by seemingly good economic results through 1977. A total of 120 large-scale projects were scheduled for completion by 1985 and an almost 150 percent increase in steel production was called for. The previous sectoral policy was reversed, emphasizing the development of heavy industry rather than agriculture, although grain production was to be increased by 40 percent. Hua and Deng shared Mao's obsession with steel and grain as indicators of national strength, and the massive Daqing oil field and the model commune of Dazhai, which had emphasized self-reliance to overcome physical constraints, were held up as worthy of study and emulation. Unlike the "Gang of Four's" criticism of foreign trade, foreign trade was welcomed by the post-Mao leadership and this was reinforced by the many study trips that various leaders took overseas that confirmed just how far China had fallen behind other nations. The budget set aside for importing advanced technology was raised progressively, eventually amounting to $80 billion.

Unfortunately this enthusiastic strategy compounded the problems. The high quantity of imported technology—the "Great Leap Westward" as some have dubbed it—completely overwhelmed China's export capabilities needed to balance the books and its domestic capacity to absorb it. Stories abounded of machinery not being repaired because not enough technicians were familiar with the technology. Much of the machinery the technicians were accustomed to working on consisted of outdated Eastern European models. There was the infamous case of the ultra-modern Wuhan steel plant that would have required, it was claimed, more electricity to keep it running than to supply the needs of the entire city. The trade deficit with capitalist countries grew from $1.2 billion in 1977 to $4.5 billion in 1979.

While these ambitious plans were being put together, Deng Xiaoping returned to work and was fully supportive. Immediately after the arrest of the "Gang of Four," Deng had expressed his support for Hua Guofeng, claiming Hua was the "the most appropriate successor to Chairman Mao."[64] Resistance to Deng's return was signaled by the Beijing party chief, Wu De, at the rally held on October 24, 1976, to commemorate the arrest of the "Gang of Four," noting that the movement to criticize Deng would continue.[65] Hua spoke in a similar vein, even though his language was somewhat milder.[66] Although Deng enjoyed strong support from many of the old-timers, his return was fiercely resisted by those such as Wu De and Mao's bodyguard Wang Dongxing. Nevertheless, in July 1977 Deng was restored to all his posts as a vice chair of the CCP, a member of the Politburo Standing Committee, vice premier, vice chair of the Central Military Commission, and PLA chief of staff. This decision had been taken as early as January 1977, but arrangements did not begin until May.

No matter how hard Hua and Deng may have tried to cooperate, there was no room in the Chinese political leadership for two dominant figures. Deng enjoyed far higher prestige within the party than Hua, and sooner or later Hua would have to cede his preeminent position to Deng. Whether he agreed or not, Hua's implied association with those opposed to Deng's return and his need to defend some legacies of the Cultural Revolution, while trying to shift policy in practice, rendered him vulnerable. Too far-reaching criticism of the "Gang of Four" and the Cultural Revolution would inevitably place the blame on Mao, which would be a problem for Hua as his legitimacy was derived from his anointment by Mao. Conversely, it was extremely difficult to agree to Deng's return without raising questions about Mao's image and his decision making late in life. Hua would cede power gracefully without setting off the kind of vicious power struggle that marked previous CCP power shifts.

Hua Guofeng's political dilemma was expressed clearly in his report to the Eleventh Party Congress, held on August 12–18, 1977. He announced the end of the eleven-year Cultural Revolution and designated the "Gang of Four" as ultra-right counterrevolutionaries, representing the eleventh line struggle in CCP history. Much of Hua's report outlined the crimes of the "Gang," while explaining that Mao had been fully aware of their activities and had provided warnings. However, there had been positive consequences as well. Hua affirmed that "political revolutions in the nature of the Cultural Revolution will take place many times in the future," and he reaffirmed the theory of continuing revolution, claims that were repeated in the new statutes. However, he weaved in the more moderate Mao, pointing out that Mao had declared that over 95 percent of the cadres and people should be united together. But Liu Shaoqi was still viewed as an "absolutely unrepentant capitalist roader," and the Cultural Revolution was described as a "momentous innovation which will shine with increasing splendor with the passage of time." It was not long, though, before it was denounced as the worst mistake the party and Mao had ever made. Clearly this was the public position of most of the leadership, and the same sentiments were echoed by Ye

Jianying in his report on the revisions to the Party Statutes. Deng, in his brief concluding comments, mentioned class struggle, but he suggested a very different approach, not mentioning continuing the revolution or the need for future political revolutions but stressing the need to adhere to the "practice of seeking truth from facts."[67]

"Seeking truth from facts" was promoted in May 1978 and provided the more pragmatic leaders with a theoretical basis for criticizing those who sought to preserve what remained of the innovations of the Cultural Revolution.[68] This reinforced Deng's critique of those who adhered slavishly to Mao's thoughts and recited Mao's words mechanically, thus appearing as "false Marxists." In June a "special correspondent" argued in the *People's Daily* that Mao's canon would be updated periodically in light of the new situation.[69] The pressure was on. Those who clung to the Two Whatevers became known as the "whatever faction." Hua seems to have tried to steer a middle course, but in the post–Cultural Revolution cleanup there was no space for a middle way.[70]

Deng Xiaoping Breaks with the Legacy

The Third Plenum of the Eleventh CC, held on December 18–22, 1978, marked a decisive shift in party work, beginning a reevaluation of PRC history and eroding the fragile post-Mao policy consensus. At a preparatory CC work conference, rather than focusing only on the economy, Chen Yun called for verdicts to be reversed on key figures purged during the Cultural Revolution, such as Peng Zhen and Peng Dehuai, although not yet Liu Shaoqi. Chen declared that the 1976 Tiananmen Incident was revolutionary, blamed Kang Sheng for much of the chaos of the Cultural Revolution, and criticized Wang Dongxing for his affiliation with the "Gang of Four." Wang Dongxing and three of his close associates made self-criticisms at the end of the meeting.[71]

By the time of the Third Plenum, Deng had formed a close alliance with Chen Yun; not only did they agree on the need for a reversal of verdicts, but Deng also came to appreciate Chen's concerns about the speed of economic development. In this sense, the initial victory at the plenum was Chen's rather than Deng's. This contradicts most official histories that ascribe the policies almost exclusively to Deng. Deng's usurping of credit for the original reform program and its subsequent radicalization angered Chen, and he would ultimately become one of the brakes on Deng Xiaoping's exhortation to speed ahead. On a number of occasions Chen upbraided Deng for ignoring the opinions of others, thus defying the principle of collective leadership that Chen claimed had been restored at the plenum.[72]

The plenum placed the highest priority on economic work, while superficially urging China to forget the past, look to the future, and concentrate on socialist modernization now that the campaign against the "Gang of Four" had been successfully completed.[73] However, far from forgetting the past, the plenum led to a review of the entire history of the PRC. For example, Peng Dehuai, now deceased, was rehabilitated, opening the way for criticism of the adventurism of the GLF. Others still living, such as Bo Yibo, Peng Zhen, were rehabilitated, as was the deceased Liu Shaoqi. The path was opened for an examination of Mao's role. The plenum communiqué stated: "It would not be Marxist to demand that a revolutionary leader be free of all shortcomings and mistakes and errors. It would also not conform to Comrade Mao Zedong's consistent evaluation of himself."[74] The message was clear; within limits, it was permissible to criticize Mao, and the reassessment of history could go back in time to before the Cultural Revolution and include the Great Leap Forward.

In his speech of October 1979 commemorating the thirtieth anniversary of the founding of the PRC, Ye Jianying referred to the three leftist errors that had occurred during the late 1950s: the broadening of the scope of struggle against the rightists in 1957; the rashness of the 1958 economic program; and the inept conduct of the inner-party struggle in 1959. The unwinding of Mao's radical path was under way, with a reevaluation of the Cultural Revolution to follow in June 1981.

The new leadership reflected Deng's increasing influence with supporters, such as Chen Yun and also Hu Yaobang, who was now promoted to the Politburo. Hu would replace Hua as party chairman in 1981. He was appointed to run the Department of Propaganda, giving Deng and his supporters greater control over the media, and another Deng associate was appointed to head the Organization Department, a crucial division that oversaw all senior appointments.[75] Chen Yun was placed in charge of the new supervisory organization, the Central Discipline Inspection Commission, which oversaw exposure of those remaining ultra-leftists and others deemed undesirable to the new leadership. Wang Dongxing lost his job in charge of the palace guard and as head of the General Office. Elite politics was certainly looking more favorable for Deng.

In terms of the economy, the plenum ratified a policy to encourage agricultural production by substantially increasing procurement prices and modernizing agriculture through brigade and team investments. The plenum embodied a strong sentiment for reform but lacked specifics.[76] Through 1979 specific measures were introduced to raise procurement prices. Although this was good for the farmers, it contributed to a growing budget deficit as the regime did not want to pass on the increases to the urban sector, leading to over 1 billion yuan in state subsidies. Policy was relaxed to allow different regions to make use of the "law of comparative advantage." Private plots, a scourge for the radicals, were deemed important for agricultural growth and for raising farmers' incomes. To allow the peasants to sell their products, including their above-quota grain, private markets were tolerated. Policy was firmly based on the collective as the core, reflecting Chen Yun's earlier ideas. Experimentation with these reforms was promoted by Hua Guofeng rather than by Deng, given Hua's more extensive experience with the rural sector, but this would not count for anything as the political tides rolled in against him.[77]

The massive levels of state subsidies were unsustainable over the long term. The Chinese leadership faced the same dilemma as it had in the mid-1950s: How could productivity be boosted without increasing state spending? This time the answer was radically different and instead of pushing ahead with collectivization, the collectives were gradually pared down. The shift was away from production quotas for the collective to focus on the household as the basis for production, referred to as a "production responsibility system." Actually, the farmers themselves pushed reform, often without official sanction. Their abandonment of the collective, although opposed by many local cadres, received tacit support from the pro-reform officials.[78] This did not include Deng Xiaoping, who shared the broad support for collective agriculture among the party leadership. As late as 1981, Deng was noncommittal as to whether or not the practice was positive. However, two close associates of Deng's—Wan Li in Anhui and Zhao Ziyang in Sichuan, a city that for centuries had been an exporter of rice but now had no recourse but to import it—were important for promoting the policy. A popular saying involved a play on Zhao's name: "If you want to eat, look for Ziyang" (*yao chifan, zhao ziyang*).

Following the plenum, those who had been rehabilitated and supported Deng, Chen Yun, and Bo Yibo began to criticize the ambitious economic plans, warning of "economic rashness": the need to comply with "objective economic laws" was emphasized. In June–July 1979, these warnings were heeded when the Ten-Year Plan was postponed and then, one year later, when it was abandoned altogether. This was replaced by a three-year period of "readjusting, restructuring, consolidating, and improving the national economy." Economic priorities were reordered, with heavy industry relegated to the bottom of the pile behind agriculture and light industry. The main focus was on fixing targets for the agricultural sector. Rather than leading the economy, heavy industry was to receive only those funds necessary for it to adapt to the demands of the other sectors.

As the reform program evolved, liberalization of previous economic and political practices was at the core.[79] Economic policy revolved around the introduction of market influences to modify the inefficiencies of allocation and distribution that had been part and parcel of the central planning system. To take better advantage market levers, localities were given greater powers of decision making. This was particularly the case for production units. They were given greater say over what and how much to produce and where to sell their products. At the core of this system was the contract, which was expected to govern economic activity. Material incentives were the major motivating force for labor, and the socialist principle of "to each according to her/his work" was to be applied firmly. Egalitarianism was attacked as a dangerous idea that curtailed economic growth. The domestic reforms were accompanied by an unprecedented opening to the outside world in the search of export markets, new technology, foreign investment, and higher-quality consumer goods. Mao must have been turning over in his mausoleum!

The reorganization of the political elite continued. At the Fifth Plenum, held on February 23–29, 1980, Liu Shaoqi's reputation was restored and the various negative labels attached to him were lifted. Significantly, the four "whateverist" members of the Politburo, including Wang Dongxing and Wu De, were asked to resign from their posts. Deng's close associates, Hu Yaobang and Zhao Ziyang, major players during the following decade of reforms, were promoted to the Politburo Standing Committee. In an important organizational change, the Central Secretariat was restored, with Hu Yaobang as general secretary. The restoration of the Central Secretariat allowed for working around Hua Guofeng, and indeed, Hu Yaobang replaced Hua Guofang as party chairman in 1981. Reflecting the more sober atmosphere, the CC recommended deleting from the statutes the phrase that citizens "have the right to speak out freely, air their views fully, hold great debates, and write big-character posters."

The dismantling of the Cultural Revolution was completed in June 1981 following the trial of the "Gang of Four" (which ended in January 1981) and adoption of the "Resolution on Party History." Together with the remaining ten members of what was now referred to as the "Lin Biao and Jiang Qing counterrevolutionary clique," they were found guilty on all counts. The demarcation of the "Gang of Four" as ultra-right was dropped, allowing for a reevaluation of many of the Cultural Revolution innovations. Jiang Qing and Zhang Chunqiao were sentenced to death with a two-year reprieve, Wang Hongwen was sentenced to life imprisonment, Yao Wenyuan was sentenced to twenty years, Chen Boda eighteen years, and the followers of Lin Biao received a variety of punishments.[80] They were accused of persecuting senior officials, especially Deng Xiaoping and Liu Shaoqi, and of causing the deaths of 34,800 people and the severe mistreatment of a further 726,000 people. While Zhang Chunqiao sat in silence and the others looked contrite, Jiang Qing, befitting her former role as an actress in Shanghai, responded with numerous outbursts, the most memorable being "I was the Chairman's dog. Whoever the Chairman said to bite, I bit."

Hua Guofeng's position was progressively undermined. At a November 1980 Politburo meeting, he made a provisional self-criticism, accepting his errors during the previous three years: persisting in a left line, especially in the economic field, promoting the Two Whatevers, resisting a reversal of the verdict on the Tiananmen Incident, and resisting the return of Deng Xiaoping.[81] Hua requested that he be relieved from all his positions, something that was duly granted at the following plenum. The appearance of playing by the rules was important to the leadership.

The Sixth Plenum of the Eleventh CC, which met on June 27–29, 1981, made a number of important personnel changes, but most importantly it adopted the "Resolution on Party History," which outlined the latest assessment of the Cultural Revolution and Mao's role in instigating it. To allow him a modicum of self-respect, Hua Guofeng was retained as a vice chair of the CC but his name was placed last on the list of the seven members of the Politburo Standing Committee. He was replaced as party chairman by Hu Yaobang, Deng Xiaoping's first chosen successor.[82] Deng proved to be no better than Mao at picking a successor, as he eventually lost his first two choices, first Hu Yaobang and then Zhao Ziyang. Despite taking the post,

Hu Yaobang dutifully deferred to Deng as the most important figure within the party.

The resolution denounced the Cultural Revolution as "responsible for the most severe setback and the heaviest losses" since 1949 and noted: "It was initiated and led by Comrade Mao Zedong." Still, it divorced Mao's errors from the scheming of Lin Biao and the "Gang of Four" and noted that the errors were those of a "great proletarian revolutionary" with his "merits primary and his errors secondary." Earlier drafts of the resolution apparently had been harsher, noting "serious mistakes" and even "crimes."[83] The period after 1956 was also criticized, but the errors of the Anti-Rightist Campaign and the GLF were deemed those of both Mao and the collective leadership. Nevertheless, Mao was singled out for his mistake in criticizing Peng Dehuai in 1959.

The resolution exacted revenge for Deng's second dismissal in 1976, noting that Mao did not accept the "systematic correction" of the Cultural Revolution offered by Deng, which triggered his downfall, the movement to criticize him, and the Tiananmen Incident. Hua Guofeng received praise for removing the "Gang of Four," but he was criticized for his leadership thereafter and the development of his own personality cult. The ship was finally righted, with the convening of the Third Plenum in December 1978.[84]

Defining the Limits of the Permissible

The trauma of the Cultural Revolution and the failings it revealed about the political system caused many people—not only the general public but also some within the party establishment who had suffered during the movement—to believe that deep changes might be needed. Although the general consensus of the leadership was that the problems stemmed from Mao's departure from the path developed by the mid-1950s, and all that was necessary was a return to the mores and practices of those years, others asked whether deeper reforms were necessary. The years 1978–1980 witnessed a range of suggestions for political reform, and in August 1980 Deng Xiaoping appeared to sanction change when he stated that people's democracy should be developed to the fullest possible extent. For Deng, it was important for the Chinese people truly to enjoy the power of supervision over the state and its actors in a variety of effective ways. In particular, the people were to "truly enjoy the right to manage state affairs and particularly state organs at the grass-roots level and to run enterprises and institutions."[85]

Deng's 1980 speech was not published officially until 1983 but it was known to senior leaders and did lead to a number of interesting reform proposals. The fact that it was republished in June 1987 is indicative that Deng wanted to keep his reform options open, even though by late 1986 serious divisions within the party had been exposed about what was acceptable. The impetus to think about further reforms had come from society during the Democracy Movement of 1978–1979.

With the right to post big character posters enshrined in the Constitution and the verdict reversed on the Tiananmen Incident in November 1978, posters began to go up along a wall to the west of the Forbidden City in the heart of Beijing. It would become a major focal point of curiosity and interest in the coming months.[86] The wall was the symbol of a society coming back to life after the Cultural Revolution, and the period saw the release of many political, literary, and visual works that had circulated underground during the lost decade.[87] Many of the initial Democracy Wall posters supported Deng's position and criticized his perceived opponents who had resisted his return and the reevaluation of the Tiananmen Incident. Thus far so good, and Deng seemed supportive. Although he was concerned about the criticism of Mao, he still declared that the posters were a good thing.[88]

Despite this and unbeknownst to those on the streets, Deng had already established boundaries to what would be permissible both within and outside the party.[89] As the posters grew more critical of the entire system, the senior leadership became less sympathetic to the movement. Some posters began to question Mao's political judgment given his close relationship to the "Gang of Four," and one poster in particular raised tricky questions: How could Lin Biao have reached power without Mao's support? Did he not know that Jiang Qing and Zhang Chunqiao were traitors? And how could have the campaign against Deng been launched without Mao's knowledge?[90] By December, posters became more critical of the system and the movement spread to other cities, such as Shanghai and Guangzhou, while Deng himself also began to face criticism.

The most famous wall poster was put up on December 5 by a young electrician from the Beijing Zoo, Wei Jingsheng, who had been sent down to work in an urban factory. His poster, titled "The Fifth Modernization," presented the most coherent appeal for democracy and critique of the current leadership. He wrote: "After the arrest of the Gang of Four, the people eagerly hoped that Vice Chairman Deng Xiaoping, who might possibly 'restore capitalism,' would rise up again like a magnificent banner. Finally, he

"The Chinese People Shackled," a poster on the
Democracy Wall.

did regain his position in the central leadership. How excited people felt! How inspired they were! But alas, the old political system so despised by the people remains unchanged."

Wei Jingsheng saw the Cultural Revolution as the first time that people had flexed their muscles, but they did not know how to proceed and democracy was not their goal. They were bought off by "bribes, deception, division, slander, or violent suppression." With their "blind faith" in "ambitious dictators," they became the "tools and sacrificial lambs of tyrants and potential tyrants." In contrast, the situation became different and the people found "their true leader: the banner of democracy."[91] Although Deng and other leaders such as Hu Yaobang tried to accommodate the protests, eventually the level of criticism became intolerable. On March 25, 1979, Wei Jingsheng followed up with an even harsher critique, asking "Do We Want a Democracy or a New Dictatorship?" For Wei, Deng was moving toward becoming a "dictatorial fascist." As a result, Wei was arrested and in mid-October he was sentenced to fifteen years in prison. He was arrested again in 1994, and in 1997 he was sent into exile in the United States.

Deng and the more conservative minded members of the leadership had the chaos of the Cultural Revolution fresh in their minds, and their concerns were heightened by some of the ideas circulating among the senior leaders in the party. These ideas were expressed at the 1979 Theory Conference, with a range of views being floated by key intellectuals, such as Li Honglin, Su Shaozhi, Yan Jiaqi, and Yu Guangyuan.[92] The meeting was chaired by Hu Yaobang, and during the first session many strong reform ideas were debated. When the meeting began, Deng was visiting the United States, but on his return he was briefed by the conservative Hu Qiaomu, who complained forcefully about the nature of the debates.

Under pressure, Deng had to establish a position that would unify the party. Unsettled by the depth of criticism from within and without, Deng's desire for order was heightened by China's mid-February invasion of Vietnam. His March 30 speech to the conference established the "four cardinal principles," which indicated there were clear limits to the permissible and suggested a range of obligations for those engaged in discussions about political reform. All things had to adhere to the principles of upholding the socialist party, the people's democratic dictatorship, the leadership of the CCP, and Mao Zedong Thought and Marxism-Leninism.[93] Clearly, party dictatorship was paramount. In addition to the need to maintain control, political reform was to be subordinate to the demands of economic regeneration. The only changes that would be permitted were those that burnished the wheels of economic modernization. The essential challenge was to determine how far could control be relaxed to promote the necessary inputs for economic development without threatening party dominance. Party leaders were still haunted by the experience of the Hundred Flowers Campaign and the Cultural Revolution, and this made them wary of activities that were not under party oversight. Deng, of course, had been instrumental in overseeing the Anti-Rightist Campaign that followed the Hundred Flowers Campaign. For these leaders, change was to be brought about by a step-by-step revolution from above. The party leadership would define what was acceptable, ensuring stability and not allowing the reforms to degenerate into chaos. During the summer of 1980, the destabilizing workers' strikes in Poland increased the CCP leadership's desire to maintain control.

Despite the setting of limits, the most dramatic reform suggestions came in October 1980 from Liao Gailong, a former political secretary to Zhu De. For Liao, democracy was not merely a means but it was also an end—"our ultimate end." He wrote that people wanted not only affluence but also "freedom, extensive freedom, as well as a high degree of democracy."[94] Liao wanted to remove the "rubber-stamp" label from the NPC by reducing the number of delegates and splitting it into two chambers to supervise the work of the State Council and to balance one another. Deputies to the first chamber would be elected on a territorial basis and those in the second chamber would be representatives of different social groupings. Trade unions and student organizations were to represent their members. Local government was to be strengthened at the expense of the central government, an independent judiciary was to be set up devoid of party influence, and the media were to be let off the leash. None of these ideas came to fruition, which frustrated many intellectuals and students.[95]

This is not to say that nothing happened: new Party Statutes and a State Constitution were adopted to more clearly delineate the division between party and government, the bureaucracy was trimmed, and some steps were taken to promote more citizen participation.[96] Measures were introduced to strengthen the electoral process: electors were to supervise and recall deputies, within limits elections were to be more competitive with more candidates than places available, and there was to be a loosening of the regulations for nominating candidates. Direct elections were introduced for the people's congresses, up to and including the county level. This measure had first been proposed by Zhou Enlai in 1957. Electoral enthusiasm even seized the official press, with claims that at some time in the future, county elections could "lay a solid and reliable foundation for direct or even national elections."[97]

However, when candidates who were not supported by the party proved very popular, authorities intervened.[98] Deng Xiaoping's speech in March 1980 enabled the more cautious or conservative leaders to begin a pushback against the far-reaching reform ideas and to end the participation that was taking place on the streets of some major cities. The fear of disorder rang loud in their ears and they wished to return to what they saw as the orderly leadership of the party over state and society that had existed in the early to mid-

1950s. In the 1980s, this would be marked by a series of campaigns to "oppose bourgeois liberalization."[99]

Dealing with the Devil: Relations with the United States

In addition to Mao's death and the arrest of the "Gang of Four," the second major game changer was the normalization of relations with the United States, which was formalized on January 1, 1979. It had taken a long time between Kissinger's secret diplomacy, Nixon's first visit, and Carter signing off, but it marked a new era for China's reform and global politics. As we have seen, in the 1970s Mao Zedong had identified the Soviet Union as the greater threat and had approved a move to open relations with the United States. The "Shanghai Communiqué" (February 28, 1972) accepted the one-China policy, while not making a judgment on what the one China might be. The communiqué agreed that US troops on Taiwan would be scaled back and that economic and cultural contacts between Taiwan and the mainland would be expanded. Trade expansion followed, as did limited military collaboration against Soviet actions in countries such as Angola and Mozambique after they achieved independence from Portugal in the mid-1970s. Perhaps the most significant impact for the United States was that it helped ease the country out of the war in Vietnam. With China now cozying up to the United States, Vietnam was left exposed and this accelerated the move to settle the conflict.[100]

The formal announcement of the establishment of diplomatic relations between China and the United States terminated official US relations with Taiwan. Embassies in Beijing and Washington were established, a bilateral trade agreement was signed, and limited arms sales began. In December 1978 President Carter had already announced the withdrawal of all US troops from Taiwan and the termination of the Mutual Defense Treaty. In its stead, the Taiwan Relations Act provided a continued legal framework for commercial and other relations without diplomatic recognition. At the end of January, Deng Xiaoping visited the United States to promote the relationship and to end the "period of unpleasantness between us for 30 years."[101] Deng's US hosts were concerned about the vehemence of his anti-Soviet views, especially as the Carter administration was pursuing a treaty to limit strategic weapons, and they were also worried that they might be embarrassed by a Chinese invasion of Vietnam during the visit. Showing diplomatic politeness, Deng waited until his return to China to invade Vietnam

Deng Xiaoping on his historic trip to America.

(which happened on February 17, 1979), and his anti-Soviet rhetoric played better to the incoming Reagan administration in the 1980s.

Unlike the domestic program of reforms, which suffered from ups and downs in the 1980s, the Sino-US relationship proceeded smoothly. Many Americans believing that the reform path might make China become more like the United States—until the events of June 1989 delivered a rude awakening. Deng's visit also played into domestic politics. There was a debate about what should be shown on Chinese television about Deng's trip, with some wishing to censor the shots of the affluence of American society that would highlight China's backwardness. Those around Deng pushed ahead with images of wealth and luxury in the United States to shock the Chinese into realizing how necessary reforms were to stop China from falling further behind.[102]

CHAPTER NINE

Reform, Rebellion, and Restoration

1982–1993

☆

During the 1980s China made considerable economic progress, accompanied by greater relaxation in the social sphere. Despite this, conservative economic leaders fretted about policy moving too rapidly and causing instability, whereas conservative moral guardians launched periodic movements against spiritual pollution and bourgeois liberalization to ensure the purity of the revolution. The 1980s saw the purge of Deng Xiaoping's first two chosen successors, culminating in the massive student-led demonstrations of 1989 that shook the leadership to its core. Until 1986 Deng was reasonably successful in preventing leadership divisions from destabilizing the system, and the limited political reforms aided his attempts to get the Chinese system moving again. His new team of Hu Yaobang as party general secretary and Zhao Ziyang as premier seemed in tune with his reform objectives, and with Hua Guofeng removed from any influence, the way seemed open for Deng to push ahead. It turned out to be a much more complicated decade than anyone could have imagined. Yet, given the breadth and depth of change—with decollectivization, opening to foreign investment, removing and reducing the influence of the veteran revolutionaries, reviving the private economy, and developing close relations with Japan—for a while the system held together remarkably well.

Bicycles parked in Beijing, 1980s.

Party Critics of Reform

Deng Xiaoping was happy to announce that in 1982 China was in the midst of "an administrative revolution," with policies to reduce the size of the bureaucracy, eliminate functional overlap, prevent a concentration of power, and to recruit new and better-qualified party members. He declared that the Twelfth Party Congress, held on September 1–11, 1982, was the most important since 1945, when the road had been established for the Communist victory in 1949. Restructuring continued in the first half of the 1980s, but there was resistance to any major structural overhaul of the political system. All agreed on the party's leading position and balked at any notion of a curtailment in its power. This did leave space, however, for disagreement on crucial questions of reform. In 1980 and 1981 it was already apparent that opposition was building, and three main groups of critics had emerged: those concerned about the impact of the reforms on China's social fabric, those worried about the rapid changes in the economic structure and the speed of growth, and some in the military who were concerned about the undermining of Mao's prestige. These groups would come together to stall the progress of the reforms and to promote the dismissal of Hu Yaobang and Zhao Ziyang, but they were never able to roll back the reforms for any length of time, not even following the violent suppression of the 1989 people's movement.

A group of party leaders, including Deng Liqun (not a relative of Deng Xiaoping), Hu Qiaomu, a close associate of Mao Zedong's, Peng Zhen, and even Chen Yun became concerned that liberalization might damage China's social fabric. They argued that the party must exert its leading role in the ideological sphere and that socialism had a spiritual as well as a material goal. Only the party could define these goals and how they should be met. Picking up on Deng's March 1980 speech on the four cardinal principles, at the CC work conference in mid-December Chen Yun put forward the slogan "Oppose bourgeois liberalization" to accompany his critique of economic policy.[1] As before, criticism began in the cultural sphere. Chen's group was offended by satirical plays and works that poked fun at the party. One such piece was *What If I Were Real*, a play similar to Gogol's *The Inspector General*. During its initial run, the audience was told that the start of the show would be delayed because of the late arrival of an official—not an uncommon occurrence in China. As the wait was extended, the audience began to speculate on just how senior the person was to hold up the start for so long. The con man eventually arrived and the show began.[2]

The main focus of the group's ire was the screenplay *Bitter Love* by Bai Hua. It tells the tale of disillusionment of a young Chinese intellectual who returns to China after 1949 only to be persecuted during the Cultural Revolution for his bourgeois revisionism. The persecution continues as the play unfolds and he comes to question his faith, claiming his love is unrequited, and his daughter asks him whether his country loves him, despite his continued love for China. Public criticism began on April 20, 1981, with a commentary in the *Liberation Army Daily* claiming that Bai Hua was opposing the four cardinal principles with his distortion of patriotism. If left un-checked, such thinking could undermine political stability and unity. At the end of March 1981 Deng had already signaled his support, calling for the military to take the lead in criticism, and he complained that Bai Hua's play "vilified the party."[3] Hu Yaobang, known to hold more liberal views, was dragged into the criticism. However, the campaign was reined in by the end of the summer, as Deng began to worry that it would affect the reforms. It did, nevertheless, have an impact on the decisions of the Twelfth Party Congress when Hu Yaobang, in his role as general secretary, announced a reversal in the listing of the party's tasks—placing the building of a spiri-tual civilization ahead of democratization—and thus making the building of spiritual civilization a prerequisite for democratization. This paved the way for subsequent campaigns against spiritual civilization and bourgeois liber-alization in 1983, 1987, and 1989–1990.

The conservative defenders of morals also saw the open-door policy as a vector for moral corruption, and despite Deng's adage that a few flies would come in if you open the door, the views of the conservatives were accepted by October 1983. An official decision on party consolidation accepted the correctness of the open-door policy, but noted the increased "corrosive in-fluence of decadent bourgeois ideology and remnant feudal ideas."[4] One year earlier, at the Twelfth Party Congress, when announcing the program for party consolidation and rectification of party style, Hu Yaobang had not mentioned the "open door" as a source of problems.

The group concerned about the direction of the economic reforms included Chen Yun and some of the more traditional planners. They recognized the need for change, but they were concerned about the destabilizing effects of promoting marketization too far and too fast. Chen's memorable analogy was that the economy should resemble a bird in a cage. One could make the cage larger, but if the bars were to be removed entirely, the bird would fly away. Ironically, it was the periodic checks on inflation and restoring balance that allowed Deng to accelerate growth. If there was one thing in addition to the primacy of the party that Deng shared with Mao Zedong, it was that faster was always better. In March 1983 Chen Yun criticized Hu Yaobang for his encouragement of local officials who promoted rapid local growth and who developed their communities without paying due consideration to the na-tion's overall economic health. Premier Zhao Ziyang shared this critique of Hu's rashness, as did staunch defenders of planning and of the state-owned sector, who periodically criticized the growth of the private sector. These critics refused to redefine property rights, in order to protect the state's priv-ileged position. Chen Yun argued that some of the smaller township and village enterprises that were springing up were wasting resources and con-suming materials needed by the state-owned sector—which in turn eroded the profitability of the state-operated enterprises (SOEs), making it more dif-ficult for them to provide for their retirees.[5] The First Plenum of the Thir-teenth CC, on November 2, 1987, decided that Deng would remain the ulti-mate authority but Chen Yun would be consulted on economic affairs. Growth of the private sector and the rise of market forces were viewed as major sources of the corruption that had developed in the reform program.[6] This is not to say that Deng and other reform leaders were not concerned about corruption, but they may have disagreed on the causes.

The third group was composed of some military officers who had been closely associated with Mao Zedong and were disturbed by the attacks on his legacy. They agreed with those who attacked the spiritual pollution that was infesting Chinese society. In February 1981 the PLA dusted off the model soldier Lei Feng for emulation, and on April 26, 1981, the military's *Liberation Army Daily* warned that contrary to what liberals might think, anti-rightism was just as dangerous as anti-leftism. The military was active in the campaign against Bai Hua and his play *Bitter Love*. In terms of de-fending Mao, the most surprising article warned of becoming too extreme when criticizing Mao, and it called for all patriots to forgive his mistakes and treat him with love and respect.[7] The article was surprising because the author had spent twenty years in prison for his association with Peng De-huai at Lushan in 1959. Criticism was also raised about the decline in the military's prestige and the inadequate military budgets. Among the rank and file, peasant recruits saw new opportunities in the countryside. The impact of the responsibility system in agriculture provided new avenues to make money, causing the government to introduce a conscription law in 1984.

These were some of the challenges facing Deng Xiaoping during the first half of the 1980s. In addition, the leadership had to manage the rising ex-pectations of the urban populations, who were getting a taste of the new free-doms but looked jealously at what they mistakenly saw as the new wealth produced in the countryside. Until the end of 1986 Deng and his supporters managed to handle the conflicting interests and pressures, but thereafter various factors combined to bring the CCP its deepest crisis since the Cul-tural Revolution. This time the attack on the party and its institutions was not launched from the top—it came from below as the urban population, led by the students, pushed for more radical change. It would ultimately end in bloodshed and repression.

Mixed Signals

It is difficult to know what to make of the Twelfth Party Congress, as it is peppered with mixed signals: Which had primacy, economic development or ideology? Rejuvenating the leadership or retaining the old guard? Deng and Hu Yaobang tried to strike a balance between the more conservative and the liberal groups within the leadership. In their speeches Deng and Hu both stressed that the development of a "socialist spiritual civilization" was the necessary platform upon which to build the economy. Some in the leadership clearly felt that guidance had to be provided to remedy the lack of faith that resulted from the Cultural Revolution. Hu stated that the most important task was to "push forward the socialist modernization of China's economy," but he also noted that a "high level of socialist spiritual civilization" was a "strategic principle for building socialism."[8] Deng pushed for opening up China, but he warned of the dangers of "decadent ideas" and visions of a "bourgeois lifestyle" penetrating the country.[9]

The congress adopted new statutes and began the process of rejuvenating the party ranks. Ye Jianying and Chen Yun both spoke of the need to bring in younger leaders. Therefore, the statutes introduced a new Central Advisory Commission, which elderly leaders were encouraged to join in order to free up places on the CC for those who might be more in tune with the needs of the modern world. Conspicuously, neither Ye nor Chen availed themselves of this opportunity. The incentive for Central Advisory Commission members was that they would retain their influence and be able to continue to participate in important meetings. Billed as temporary, the commission threatened to become permanent and began to provide an institutional base for conservative criticisms of the reform program. This tendency became even more marked after 1987, when Chen Yun took over as chair of the commission following his retirement from the Politburo Standing Committee. The commission would be disbanded in 1992 when the party again tried to rebuild its credibility following the trauma of 1989.

The new Party Statutes contained a number of significant amendments to deal with the overconcentration of power. Most importantly, the post of chairman of the CC was replaced by that of general secretary. The claim was that this would prevent erratic and individualistic decision-making because the general secretary would merely convene meetings but would not preside over them. Apparently the Chinese had not looked too closely at the experience of General Secretary Stalin in the Soviet Union. The statutes expressly forbade "all forms of personality cult" and the use of public office for private gain. Framing and false accusations were also outlawed, and the duties of party members were made more onerous.[10]

The attempt to rebuild institutional structures continued with the adoption of a new State Constitution at the Fifth Session of the Fifth NPC on December 4, 1982.[11] As with the Party Statutes, the State Constitution, modeled after the Constitution of 1954, eliminated the experiments of the mid-1950s onward. The state was now defined as "a socialist state under the people's democratic dictatorship" rather than the fiercer sounding "socialist state of the dictatorship of the proletariat." However, the waters were muddied by the statement in the preamble that the people's democratic dictatorship is, in essence, the dictatorship of the proletariat, thus equating the two terms! The resurrection of the people's congress system was incorporated in the Constitution. In 1978 the revolutionary committees had been restricted to levels of government and no longer operated factories and schools, and in 1979 they had been abolished altogether.

The new Constitution hid the power of the party in the state sector, unlike the Constitutions adopted in 1975 and 1978 in which party control was explicit. The reference to the party as the core of leadership was dropped, as was the claim that it was the duty of citizens to support the party. Now citizens were asked merely to abide by the Constitution and the law. However, the party's leading role was acknowledged in the four cardinal principles. In the future, the premier was to be appointed based on nomination by the president rather than by the CC. Given the dislocation caused by the Cultural Revolution, greater attention was paid to the rights and duties of citizens, with additional provisions on the inviolability of the home, protection of freedom, privacy of correspondence, and the right of citizens to criticize state organs and functionaries. But now gone were the rights to criticize allowed during the Cultural Revolution—such as the right to speak out freely, debate, write big-character posters, and to strike. The removal of the right to strike was presumably a response to the events in Poland. A weak defense argued that the management reforms had rendered such actions unnecessary and that "striking is not only disadvantageous to the state, but also harmful to the interests of the workers."[12]

The orderly process envisaged by the new Party Statutes and the State Constitution did not prevent tensions from rising within the party about the way forward, including the question of how far and how fast the economic reforms should proceed, and what role socialist spiritual civilization should play in guiding not only the reforms but also the morals of society. Until 1986, despite the campaigns of 1983 and 1985, the tensions had been controlled and the focus remained on the economy. Further, Deng was successful in continuing the restructuring of the military and party leaderships. Following the establishment of the Central Advisory Commission and the establishment of such commissions throughout the administrative system, the military leadership was restructured. Its direct political influence was reduced, and many elderly officers were replaced by a younger generation more in line with the idea of a less political, more professional military. In December 1984 forty senior officers of the PLA General Staff retired, the largest such retirement ever; in January 1985 budget cutbacks were announced; and in April 1985 Hu Yaobang announced that troop levels would be cut by 25 percent—about one million personnel. PLA political influence was weakened through two other important measures. In June 1985 Deng Xiaoping reorganized the regional military command structure to break up the powerful regional ties. Such reshufflings occur only rarely and mark a leader's attempt to assert authority, as Mao did in 1973 to remove the influence of Lin Biao.

In September 1985 a series of party meetings, including a special party conference, carried out a similar shake-up of the party leadership. One consequence was a sharp reduction in military representation on the Politburo. Ten members resigned, of whom six were from the military, and none were replaced by military figures. The military did resist replacing Deng Xiaoping by Hu Yaobang, probably encouraged by Deng himself as chair of the Central Military Commission. Although willing to accept Deng's authority, they were unwilling to accept his protégé, clearly reducing Hu Yaobang's prestige and preventing him from cementing an alliance with the reformers in the military. Acceptance and control of the military is a key to power in China, and all leaders have sought to head the Central Military Commission. Deng had the same problem when he was unable to place his second chosen successor, Zhao Ziyang, as head of the commission. This was a serious blow to the pragmatic reformers and presaged future events in 1989 when the military would be called in to save the party.

Six newcomers were named to the Politburo, including Li Peng, the adopted son of Zhou Enlai, as a possible successor to Zhao as premier, and

Hu Qili, as a possible successor to Hu Yaobang as general secretary. The Politburo Standing Committee was divided equally between liberal and conservative reformers, Deng being the decisive figure. However, key conservative figures, such as Chen Yun, Peng Zhen, and Hu Qiaomu, remained on the Politburo. Younger, more-qualified people were brought onto the CC: of the sixty-four new members, 76 percent were college-educated and their average age was just over fifty.

Despite this progress, the question of political reform was becoming a seriously divisive issue within the political leadership, and this became openly apparent in the summer of 1986. In the spring and summer, critical intellectuals within the party tried to push forward political reforms along the lines of those raised at the end of the 1970s and in early 1980s. A number of daring notions were put forward by influential party figures. A deputy editor of the *People's Daily* raised discussion of socialist humanism, which meant that "all-round dictatorship" should be discarded, as should the cult of personality. Others debated whether alienation could exist in socialist society.[13] Deng Xiaoping came to see this as a challenge to party hegemony, and by September 1983 he concluded that party control should be tightened. This led to the campaign to quash spiritual pollution. The campaign was not pursued vigorously and it soon wound down amid fears that it might have a negative impact on reviving economy.[14] Yet by the end of the decade such views had been soundly rejected, and Hu Yaobang, who was thought to be sympathetic, had been dismissed from his position as general secretary.

The first years of reform had been a boon to China's farmers due to the dismantling of the collective structures and the return to household-based farming. These were the heady days of the so-called 10,000-yuan households, when farmers close to the urban markets were able to boost their incomes. Many in urban China were under the impression that all those in rural China were moving ahead economically, while those in urban China remained stuck. However, by the end of 1984 the rapid pace of economic growth had slowed down and, ironically, the next phase of the reforms adversely affected the farmers' income. This was exacerbated as the one-time boost from the dismantling of the communes and other incentives were wearing off.

With grain yields declining and state subsidies spiraling to keep costs down for the urban sector, Chen Yun proposed calling a halt to the second phase of the reforms. Many farmers had turned away from grain production because it was not profitable and lucrative alternatives had been developing, but now they were forced to return to grain production. They resented this assault on their new-won freedoms, as stringent grain-production quotas were reintroduced and moves to dismantle the state monopoly over distribution were effectively abandoned. Farmers were forced to sell to state agencies at below-market prices. Further, many farmers had already left the land to work in the cities or in the more lucrative jobs in the rapidly growing rural industrial sector, which by 1984 was producing almost 25 percent of industrial output.

Concurrently, problems were arising in the industrial sector as policy moved toward a market-influenced economy. Just as the reforms in the agricultural sector were tapering off following the initial shot in the arm, the leadership turned its attention to the urban industrial sector. This sector was obviously unable to effectively meet the demands of the increasingly commercialized, decentralized agricultural sector. Success in the rural sector led to the decision in October 1984 to adopt similar measures in the urban sector.[15] The decision, noting that the current structure of the urban economy hindered development, offered a more comprehensive outline for the future than the previous piecemeal reform experiments. The key was to make enterprises more responsible economically through the introduction of a system of enterprise profit retention. Managers were given greater decision-making autonomy, including over the hiring and firing workers. State subsidies were to be phased out and cautious support was given for small-scale private businesses. Chinese industrial policy was moving in the direction of Hungary's market socialism.

The new incentive system for enterprises, together with the lifting of price controls, led to a major overheating of the economy by late 1984 and early 1985, which resulted in a surge in inflation in 1985. As a result, the Seventh Five-Year Plan for 1986–1990, unveiled by Premier Zhao Ziyang in April 1986, struck a note of caution, emphasizing the need for balanced growth. Growth rates were to be lowered, but they still were predicted to be at a healthy clip of 7.5 percent per annum. The slower growth rate was to avert strain on the economy and to facilitate the reforms. Zhao's concerns focused on the twin problems of the slow pace of implementing the industrial reforms and the decline in grain production. In fact, Zhao and the party leadership came under pressure from delegates from grain-producing provinces to increase government investment in the sector and to pay more attention to grain production. In a major break from past practice, the plan suggested shifting from mandatory targets to using guidance planning for production figures. This was sensible, given that, historically, most plans had never delivered the specified targets. For Zhao, the plan provided a solid basis for the continuation of the reforms: industrial reform would continue to encourage enterprises to be genuinely responsible for profits and losses. Under the socialist commodity market, Zhao proposed a further extension of market measures and the establishment of a new form of macro-management, with the state gradually moving from direct to indirect control of enterprise management.

Despite this restatement of the reform objectives, opposition was coming together and differences about ideology and political reform provided the catalyst for removing Hu Yaobang. In July 1985 conservative ideologue Deng Liqun was replaced as minister of propaganda by a close associate of Hu Yaobang. The following eighteen months saw yet another twist in the turns of liberal push and conservative backlash. Again, there was an upsurge in critical articles and explorations of subjects such as alienation and Marxist humanism. The wings of the intellectual community fluttered again, with the most remarkable work by Liu Binyan, who challenged the nature of loyalty to the party. Should one blindly follow party orders as a sign of loyalty, or was there a higher loyalty to serve the ideals for which the party was established?[16] A popular slogan argued that economic reform required political reform. It seemed that the push to put political reform back on the agenda was supported by Deng Xiaoping, with a five-person discussion group set up to review the options.[17]

The renewed thrust of liberal articles in the official press, combined with strong proposals for political reform, drew the ire of the more conservative reformers. In summer 1986, at a leadership retreat in the seaside resort of Beidaihe, some leaders argued that, for the most part, the current political system was suited to the needs of economic development, but that too much reform could lead to the negation of party leadership and could undermine the four cardinal principles. To prevent this, they proposed a strict set of obligations for those who were debating political reform. A key figure in this resistance was Politburo member Peng Zhen, who warned against those who yearned for bourgeois democracy "as if the moonlight of capitalist society was brighter than our socialist sun."[18]

These differences caused an expected decision on political reform to be postponed until the Thirteenth Party Congress in October 1987.[19] Instead the September 1986 party gathering returned to the theme of ideological and cultural work, ignoring any mention of political reform. Successful economic construction could be achieved only if a socialist spiritual civilization was constructed.[20] Now Deng threw his weight behind the criticism, reminding the leadership that bourgeois liberalization was indeed a threat.

Some were clearly uneasy with Hu Yaobang's leadership style and his tendency to go off script and improvise. The opportunity to remove Hu as general secretary was provided by the student demonstrations that festered beginning in the summer of 1986 and grew in intensity by late 1986. In December, protests began not in Beijing but in Hefei, Anhui province, because official interference had prevented students from standing in a local election. The demonstrations spread rapidly and combined a mix of student grievances over living and study conditions and broader concerns over stalled political reform. For the most part the students expressed their support for Deng and Hu, and very few raised criticisms about the nature of one-party rule. Their complaints found little resonance within society, as much of the population considered the students to be a relatively privileged and pampered group. The turning point in official tolerance came when students in Beijing defied a government ban and held a New Year's Day demonstration in Tiananmen Square; thirty-three students were arrested.[21] The criticisms by intellectuals and discussions about alienation and humanism, although disconcerting, had been dealt with relatively lightly, especially in comparison with what would come after. On the streets, activism was another matter entirely. Further outrage followed when students burned copies of the *Beijing Daily*.

Pressure on Hu Yaobang increased, and on December 27 a group of party elders visited Deng Xiaoping to request Hu's dismissal.[22] Deng took up their complaints, and on December 28 he blamed the student demonstrations on those who did not stand firmly against bourgeois liberalization.[23] Deng went on to criticize ideas such as the separation of powers and to point out that even when China arrested Wei Jingsheng, there had not been any foreign outcry, and he praised the Polish authorities for their handling of Solidarity in 1981. Ominously he noted that one should not only talk about using dictatorial means but one should also be ready to "actually use them."[24]

The writing was on the wall for Hu and the liberal reformers. On January 6, 1987, the *People's Daily* ran a tough editorial criticizing those who were concerned about leftist thinking but who ignored bourgeois liberalization. The article called for them to wake up as this was poisoning the young and disrupting reform and opening. The situation could no longer be ignored. On January 16 Hu was removed from his post after he refused to resign. He was formally criticized for resisting the entirely correct policy to fight against spiritual pollution and bourgeois liberalization, fighting only against the left but never against the right, letting the economy run out of control, and often acting without authorization. His laxness facilitated the environment that had led to the student demonstrations.[25] In a sign that the leadership had learned from the past, Hu retained his seat on the Politburo and the dispute was not raised as a struggle between two lines. The lesson was not learned for long, however. In a sign of things to come, the document relaying Hu's dismissal noted that elder leaders such as Deng, Chen Yun, and Li Xiannian should supervise the new leaders as long as their health permitted.

The campaign against bourgeois liberalization that was launched after Hu's ouster was short-lived because Deng and Hu's replacement as general secretary, Zhao Ziyang, feared that it might disrupt the economy. Despite this, Hu's removal did have an effect. The manner of his removal—the avoidance of formal procedures, the launch of an old-style political campaign, and the expulsion of three prominent, critical intellectuals from the party—showed that the old guard still possessed the power to block what they did not like and that Deng was willing to go along with them on issues of ideology and to repress political activities that took place outside of party control. This point would be reinforced emphatically in 1989. The dismissals shook the faith of some party reformers and many students who disagreed with Deng Xiaoping's top-down approach. This opened up the path for even more radical demands for change.

Differences emerged about how to move forward. Pragmatic reformers around Zhao began to outline a rationale for an elitist approach to top-down reforms. In 1986, articles appeared supporting neo-authoritarianism, and by late 1988 the theory had become an important justification for keeping a firm hold on power as the reforms began to falter. A strong central power was necessary to push through tough reforms and to prepare the ground for democracy.[26]

By contrast, other party intellectuals were pushing for more radical reforms based on institutional changes. These reforms included improving the representativeness of the people's congress system, granting delegates immunity during debates, and reducing party interference in government organizations and society at large. They argued that the freedoms of speech, assembly, and the press should be expanded, that the party should become more accountable to outside organizations, and that democracy within the party should be enhanced, including allowing for the existence of factions. These factions might then form the basis for the emergence of a multiparty system. In the view of Su Shaozhi, director of the CASS Institute of Marxism-

Leninism and Mao Zedong Thought, the party should take seriously its role as a vanguard. Vanguards comprised only a small number of people who set broad outlines and did not need to dominate all aspects of state and society.[27]

Despite Hu Yaobang's removal, the political reform agenda was pushed ahead at the Thirteenth Party Congress, held on October 25–November 1, 1987, by the new general secretary, Zhao Ziyang. Zhao announced that the CC had decided that "it was high time to put political reform on the agenda of the whole party."[28] He traced problems in the political system to the legacy of both feudalism and the party's own experiences during the revolution, such that the current structures failed to "suit economic, political, and cultural modernization under peacetime conditions or the development of a socialist commodity economy." There was some compromise, but on crucial questions Zhao came down on the side of the reformers. Thus, he reiterated the compromise agreed upon with the conservative reformers that it was necessary to uphold the four cardinal principles while also pursuing reform and opening-up to the outside world. This was the compromise that Zhao had put forward in May 1987 to try to halt the leftist backlash that was threatening the reform program.[29]

Zhao then went on to announce the most radical document on political reform ever put forward by the Chinese leadership.[30] The first five sections of the report dealt with reform; the conservative demand for building a spiritual civilization came last on the list of tasks. Most importantly, Zhao confirmed that China was at the initial stage of socialism, a stage that would last for about 100 years.[31] This was meant to remove ideological objection to reform experimentation, whereas the major task was to improve material standards and not to wage class struggle. As China was entering uncharted waters, theory was to be defined as policy developed, thus freeing China's decision makers from the restraints of Maoist dogma. Zhao also announced a new party line of "one center and two basic points": the center being economic development with adherence to the four cardinal principles, and reform and opening-up being the two points. This formulation tried to bridge the divide between the preferences of the liberal reformers and those of the conservative reformers.

Political reform was reaffirmed as indispensable if economic reform was to continue. Even though detail was missing, Zhao called for a redistribution of power both horizontally to state organs at the same level and vertically to party and state organs lower down the administrative hierarchy. The idea of separation of party and state was to be promoted aggressively, and the holding of multiple positions across party and state was to be curtailed. The most important measure put forward was the abolition of leading party groups in units of state administration and the elimination of groups that overlapped in their functions. Previously it was normal practice for party members in state administrative organizations, including research entities, to hold caucus meetings to discuss policy, and over time they had become increasingly powerful. The groups were established by the party committee at the next highest level and were answerable to that committee. The abolition of these groups was interpreted by scholars as a major weakening of party power within the research organizations.[32] Zhao warned that the party must not become an executor entrapped in the mundane technicalities of daily command.[33] The importance of political reform was implicitly recognized by dropping the four modernizations, which had an exclusively economic focus.

The party was to pull back from day-to-day management of enterprises, and in April 1989 the Seventh NPC adopted the Enterprise Law, which limited the scope of party work. The measures were intended, not to grant institutions and enterprises autonomy, but instead to provide a clearer differentiation of roles and to extricate the party from direct administration, while retaining political leadership over major issues. It was not the role of the party secretary to decide how many lavatories should be in a factory and where they should be situated.

With respect to the economy, Zhao attacked the two traditional shibboleths of state socialism: central planning and state ownership. The report proposed a dramatic reduction in the role of the plan in directing the economy, opening up the way for further development of the non-state sectors of the economy. Moving beyond previous practices, Zhao advocated the use of commodity markets not only for consumer goods and the means of production but also for "funds, labor services, technology, information, and real estate." In what must have been sacrilege to some, he announced that no longer would the only source of income be "distribution according to work." In the future, interest would be available for those who purchased bonds, shareholders would receive dividends, and enterprise managers would be rewarded for the risks they carried. Last but not least, the owners of private enterprises who had a workforce would receive some income that did not come from their own labor. Deflecting criticism that these were capitalist mechanisms, Zhao simply stated that such mechanisms were "not particular to capitalism."

However, the report was not a complete sweep for the more liberal reformers, and there were compromises on certain economic questions dear to the hearts of the conservative reformers. The Maoist obsession with grain production was not eliminated entirely, as Zhao made a commitment to major increases in grain production over the next decade. More significantly, the report was cautious on the vital topic of price reform. It was obvious that to be successful, the industrial-reform program required thoroughgoing reform of the pricing and subsidy systems. These systems were a source of the growing corruption. Yet each time this issue was placed on the agenda, rapid retreat followed in the face of the subsequent inflation.

The congress approved a new leadership that ushered out the Long March generation and brought in a younger, more educated group of successors. Reflecting the more democratic atmosphere, the elections for the CC were competitive, with 5 percent more candidates than places to be filled. This resulted in one significant, unexpected outcome. Hu Yaobang's nemesis, Deng Liqun, had been slated to take over the seat vacated on the Politburo by another conservative ideologue. However, he was not elected to the CC. Only ten of the twenty Politburo members were reelected, with Zhao the only member remaining from the prior Standing Committee. The lineup of the new Standing Committee was the subject of vigorous debate. Quite amazingly, Deng revealed the members to Henry Kissinger during his summer visit; naturally they were not revealed to the Chinese people.

Organizationally, the position of the Standing Committee of the Politburo as the preeminent body was confirmed by a downgrading of the Secretariat—it was reduced in size, and its members were to be nominated by the Standing Committee. This prevented the Secretariat from becoming an alternative power base. Unfortunately for Zhao, two other institutions retained considerable influence, and both were beyond his control. The first was the military and, as with Hu Yaobang, Zhao was not given the position of the head of the Central Military Commission; instead the position was retained by the trusted Deng Xiaoping. The second was the Central Advisory Commission, which was now headed by conservative reformer Chen Yun and ably supported by Bo Yibo. These two organizations would play a key role in the decision to implement martial law in 1989 and the removal of Zhao as a result of the demonstrations. One final decision, not made public at the time, that would prove crucial in 1989 was that on all political issues, the Standing Committee would consult with Deng and on all economic matters the Standing Committee would consult with Chen. That Deng had the authority to convene Standing Committee meetings was revealed by Zhao Ziyang in his meeting with Gorbachev on May 16, 1989. Deng was infuriated that this authority was revealed to Gorbachev. Chen Yun's role was not revealed.

The appointment of the two heads of the commissions revealed how practical concerns overruled party rules. According to the 1982 Constitution, the heads of the Advisory and Central Military Commissions should be members of the Politburo Standing Committee as part of the efforts to institutionalize leadership in the party and to break away from the dominant system of personalized rule. This attempt clearly failed, but presumably Deng preferred to face criticism for yet again rewriting the rule book rather than to have his critic Chen Yun still on the Standing Committee. Given the ages of Deng and Chen, it would have made the policy of introducing younger faces appear as utterly ridiculous.

Following the congress, the economy faltered and inflation took off as the government experimented with price reform. Initially it looked as though, with Deng's support, the party might stay the course, but by the summer of 1988, following the problems that resulted from removing price controls, Deng started to back away and to shift the blame for the problems to Zhao. Zhao tried to use his position as general secretary to limit the ability of the more conservative premier, Li Peng, to delay more radical reforms. Having previously been critical of Hu Yaobang's attempts when he was general secretary to influence Zhao's work as premier on questions such as the speed of growth and enterprise policy, Zhao now found himself in the same position. Zhao's speeches stressed the need to keep up the pace of reform, while the newly confirmed premier, Li Peng, focused on stabilization and caution, not mentioning price reforms and calling to increase grain production.[34]

Zhao's ability to argue for economic reform was weakened by the fact that he was outside of the State Council network, even though he claimed that Deng insisted he should continue to run the crucial Central Economic and Finance Leading Group because Li Peng was less familiar with the pressing economic issues.[35] The reality was that Zhao was slowly losing his grip on power as he came under increasing criticism during the winter of 1988–1989. Deng Xiaoping backed away from his promotion of faster reform and especially price deregulation, leaving Zhao to take the blame and increasing Zhao's isolation. By September 1988 Zhao was making a self-criticism, having earlier offered to resign. Decision making on the economy had shifted to Li Peng and the State Council and away from Zhao and his supporters.[36]

Reform in Crisis

The economic situation increased the general disgruntlement among the urban population, while many of the reform-minded intellectuals became frustrated at what they saw as a lack of progress on the political front. The façade of unity began to crack under the strain of managing conflicting views about the way forward and it was blown apart by serious differences about how to deal with the massive student-led demonstrations that erupted throughout China in the spring of 1989. The catalyst for the widespread disruption was the sudden rise in inflation starting in 1988—the worst inflation in the history of the PRC.[37] The spontaneous demonstrations that filled Beijing streets for some seven weeks and that spread to other cities confronted the party with its most serious challenge, exposing a high level of frustration with the reforms and revealing deep divisions within the CCP leadership about China's future development.[38]

Unlike the 1986 demonstrations, the 1989 movement found support and resonance within society at large, especially because of the accusations of official corruption and criticisms of the behavior of the children of senior officials. Both white-collar and blue-collar workers saw their livelihoods undermined by inflation as they grew unsure about the future. Talk of price reform and the removal of subsidies created a sense of unease, as did the plans to privatize housing and remove rental subsidies. The workers were effectively being offered a questionable deal to trade in their secure, subsidy-supported, low-wage life for a riskier, contract-based system that might bring higher wages and rewards but might also mean rising costs and unemployment. With no social security system in place, it was a worrying gamble. In the spring and summer of 1989, it did not appear to be a risk worth taking.

Some intellectuals were breaking away from the traditional system of regime patronage, thus beginning a new round of independent activity.[39] Especially disconcerting for the leadership was the petition movement, begun by an open letter by astrophysicist Fang Lizhi to Deng Xiaoping, calling for the release of political prisoners, especially Wei Jingsheng. Fang Lizhi had been a driving force behind the student activism that launched the demonstrations in Anhui in 1986 and he had already been expelled from the party. Deng had denounced him by name, saying that he could not understand how a party member could call for a multiparty system.[40] On January 28 Fang Lizhi joined with others to form a "new enlightenment salon," which together with its journal provided important venues for the promotion of unorthodox ideas.

But it was the students who were the first to move. Less tied into the system of patronage and not constrained by the structure of the traditional workplace, they were more able to mobilize, especially because key university campuses were concentrated in northwest Beijing. On-campus lectures and democratic salons provided students with a chance to both hear and discuss unorthodox viewpoints. These included the democratic salon organized by Wang Dan and the Olympic Science Academy organized by Shen Tong at Peking University, and the Confucius Study Society organized by Wu'er Kaixi at Beijing Normal University. Shen Tong's Academy was strongly influenced by the writings of Karl Popper, the vehemently antitotalitarian philosopher. Popper's ideas concerning the conditions under which free, open, and rational discussion can take place provided Shen Tong and his group with a philosophical rationale for their attacks on authoritarian one-party rule.[41] Not surprisingly, these three young men became key leaders of the student movement. Indeed, the three of them had already been planning political activities for the anniversary of the May Fourth Movement before events overtook such planning with Hu Yaobang's death, April 15, 1989, following his second heart attack, which provided the spark that ignited these smoldering embers. The rumor, later dismissed, that his first heart attack had come during an argument with Bo Yibo at a Politburo meeting to discuss education only served to further inflame passions.

On the evening of April 16 some 300 students from Peking University arrived at Tiananmen Square to lay wreaths in memory of Hu Yaobang. The numbers began to swell; students felt a sense of injustice because of their treatment by the authorities. The students' resolve was strengthened following the tough *People's Daily* editorial on April 26 that condemned the students' actions as a planned conspiracy that constituted turmoil directed against the party. The editorial was based on Deng Xiaoping's assessment in discussions several days earlier.[42] The reaction was massive—Beijing's largest spontaneous demonstration since the founding of the PRC. Despite official warnings that force would be employed to halt the protests, some 50,000 to 100,000 students broke through a series of police cordons to flood onto Tiananmen Square. Importantly, the demonstrations showed that there was a substantial reservoir of support for the students among the Beijing population. Up to one million residents lined the students' route, encouraging them on their way and providing them with food and drink.

What the leadership found most threatening was when the students moved to organize themselves independently of the official student bodies. On

April 18, students at Peking University set up the first autonomous organization, and on April 26 the Beijing Students' Autonomous Federation was formally launched. The formation of the Workers' Autonomous Federation combined with the independent intellectual activism conjured up visions of a Polish-style crisis. However, the students kept their distance from the workers' movement. With the huge demonstrations on May 15–18, it was clear that key elements of the party and the state apparatus were siding with the demonstrators. Even some members of *People's Daily* marched with a banner proclaiming "The People's Daily Tells Lies," perhaps one of its more truthful proclamations.

Despite the harsh April 26 editorial, the leadership was divided over how to respond. Zhao Ziyang was on a week-long visit to North Korea when the editorial was published, and on his return he rejected it, calling for retraction or modification as part of a process to resolve the issue peacefully. Deng refused to meet Zhao after his return to Beijing. The slowness and incoherence of the party response was not only because of divisions but also because the entire leadership was taken back by the scale of the demonstrations. The forthcoming visit of the Soviet president, Gorbachev, meant that the eyes of the world's media were on Beijing. Zhao mistakenly believed he had gained Deng's support for a more conciliatory approach, and in two key speeches he was accommodating and sympathetic to some of the student demands. This led the demonstrators to believe that there was support at the highest levels, but the conservative leaders supported by Deng decided the only route was repression. The key questions were when and how.

The student capture of the moral high ground was reinforced by the launch of a hunger strike on May 13. The students' perception that they were morally correct made it very difficult for the authorities to reach agreement with them. The strength of the students' opinions impeded Zhao Ziyang's attempts to reach a compromise through negotiation. For example, the hunger strikers rejected out of hand Zhao's appeal on May 17 for them to end their fast in return for promises that there would be no retribution and that their grievances would be seriously discussed. Having gained momentum, it was difficult for the students to pursue any course other than one that would result in conflict. The movement took on a life of its own and moved toward a critique of the state itself. Among many students and citizens, the general view that came to prevail was that if the state could not see the necessity to

Student hunger strikers in 1989.

redress the just grievances, then there must be something fundamentally wrong with the state itself. Student leaders themselves could not control the movement, with the hunger strikers and those coming in from out of town vetoing attempts at compromise. Violent suppression was difficult against a group that was demonstrating peacefully, singing the *Internationale,* and calling for support of the Communist Party and for further reforms and opening-up. However, engaging in serious dialogue with the students would mean recognition of autonomous organizations in society, which was anathema to orthodox party members.

Unbeknown to those on the square, politics at the Center was shifting dramatically against them. It would have been awkward to send in troops to impose martial law when Gorbachev was in Beijing. As soon as Gorbachev departed, in the evening of May 17, Deng convened an enlarged Politburo meeting at his home that decided to impose martial law, over Zhao's objections.[43] On May 19 Zhao made an appearance on the square, asking the students for forgiveness, saying that he had come too late. Li Peng declared martial law as of May 21, and on May 24 another enlarged Politburo meeting dismissed Zhao from the Politburo Standing Committee for opposing the April 26 editorial. Initially martial law troops were unarmed, and because of their massive sympathy for the students, Beijing citizens blocked the army's attempts to regain the square. However, preparations were already under way for a tough response.

During the night of June 3–4, troops advanced on the square and by morning had cleared it of all the remaining protestors, and the Goddess of Democracy statue, which had been erected on May 30, was toppled. There was some dissent within the military, but not enough to cause Deng and the others any concern.[44] The final assault on the square was violent, with troops opening fire on unarmed demonstrators and citizens. Once the square was sealed, the military was careful to ensure that no one died at the symbolic heart of Beijing. Early in the morning of June 4, an exit was negotiated for the remaining protestors. The troops who carried out the action were well drilled, but they were soon replaced by less-disciplined troops, many of whom looked like fresh-faced recruits from the countryside. A group of them were clearly awed to see a blonde foreign woman coming up to them to shout abuse and the political commissars behind them kept barking instructions to keep their eyes front ahead and not to engage. Once anyone wavered, they were yanked from the ranks and replaced.

The Goddess of Democracy faces Mao's portrait in Tiananmen Square, 1989.

Conservative Backlash

Conservative reformers saw suppression as a way to subdue the rising tide of dissent and as a way to remove Zhao Ziyang from his post as general secretary, thus paving the way for a major attack on the economic and political reform programs. These leaders were aware that the economic reforms and the breakdown of traditional techniques of control provided a structural basis for the emergence of new socioeconomic forces that were difficult to accommodate within an orthodox Leninist structure. In launching the repression of June 3–4, they counted on the psychological exhaustion among the people to undermine the emotional foundation of the protest movement. Deng Xiaoping never doubted that he had made the correct decision.[45]

Subsequent events revealed both the capacity of the conservative reformers to frustrate measures they opposed *and* their inability to roll back the momentum of the economic reforms for any length of time. The argument of Chen Yun and others was that adjustment was needed to calm the overheating of the economy that had followed the lifting of price controls in the summer of 1988. Chen had consistently been a moderating influence on Deng's exuberance for rapid economic growth. Decision-making power was now back in the hands of the veterans. The conservative reformers had two main objectives. First, they strengthened the program of economic austerity, in order to reduce the size of the "birdcage" that Chen Yun favored and restore the role of the plan. Second, they sought to tighten political control over society, combined with a major political campaign, in order to eradicate once and for all the pernicious influences of bourgeois liberalization. Deng was an enthusiastic promoter of the second objective, but he worried that a program of economic austerity would roll back his program of reform and opening. To reemphasize his support for party control, in August 1989 the *People's Daily* carried a speech that Deng had made thirty-two years earlier, in which he had argued that too much democracy was undesirable for China, making it clear that the party would retain its paramount position. The proposals of the Thirteenth Party Congress in1987 to separate party from government and to reduce the party's overbearing role were swiftly dropped.

On June 9 Deng Xiaoping offered his congratulations to the martial law troops and delivered his verdict that his basic policies were correct and that the problem was "basically a confrontation between the four cardinal principles and bourgeois liberalization."[46] For Deng it was a "storm that was bound to happen sooner or later" and luckily the old comrades were still around to resolve it successfully. An enlarged Politburo meeting on June 19–21 reached a basic agreement on what had happened and why. Three things are noteworthy. First, the meeting was dominated by party elders, who stressed that the need for ideological discipline was more important than economic reform. Second, unable to accept responsibility for the underlying causes of the protests, the veterans resorted to claims that they were the fault of an "extremely small group of people," who had stubbornly promoted "bourgeois liberalization." Of course, they claimed that these counterrevolutionary elements had linked up with "hostile foreign forces." Third, all participants were required to display their obedience to and faith in Deng's judgment. Hu Qili, the leader most sympathetic to Zhao Ziyang, had to confess how poor his political judgment had been and how "inadequate was my comprehension of the truth." A major challenge was to protect Deng, because he had originally supported and proposed Zhao's policies. An old Yan'anite, Wang Zhen, made a spirited attempt at this by claiming that Zhao's approach to "reform and opening" was leading China down the capitalist road and would have destroyed Deng's socialist path.[47]

The decisions were rolled out at the Fourth Plenum of the Thirteenth CC, held on June 23–24, 1989. The communiqué reaffirmed the April 26 editorial and, as usual, blame was placed on a "very small number of people" who had taken advantage of the student unrest to stir up "planned, organized and premeditated turmoil," which later developed into a "counterrevolutionary rebellion in Beijing" to overthrow the CCP. Li Peng reported that Zhao had made some contributions in economic development but that he had fallen well short of the requirements in the political and ideological spheres. Zhao's passive attitude to opposing bourgeois liberalization and to upholding the four cardinal principles meant that he bore "unshirkable responsibility" for the turmoil. His actions had sought to split the party.[48] Zhao accepted blame for certain mistakes and the suggestion that he be removed as general secretary, but he rejected the accusations that he had supported the disturbances and that he had split the party. He defended his approach of mediation and guidance to resolve the demonstrations, but he accepted that he had been lax in confronting bourgeois liberalization.[49]

To the surprise of many outsiders, the party secretary of Shanghai, Jiang Zemin, was promoted to replace Zhao, rather than either anyone from Beijing municipality or anyone working at the Party Center. This decision had already been taken earlier, but it was decided to withhold an announcement until the Fourth Plenum to observe niceties. Deng Xiaoping signaled that Jiang should form the core of the new leadership, but this was contested by others who suggested either another candidate or that Jiang and Li Peng together should be designated as the core.[50] However, the fact that Jiang was not involved in the crackdown in Beijing and had handled the 1986 and 1989 demonstrations in Shanghai effectively and with no bloodshed won the day. Once more the party system was unable to deal with a leadership transfer in line with its professed norms. In terms of institutionalization, the manner of Zhao's purge and Jiang's ascent revealed how little progress had been made. The crucial decisions were made by a cabal of veteran revolutionaries at Deng's home and then sent to party functionaries for official transmittal.

Although both Deng's June 9 speech and the plenum communiqué stressed policy continuity, both the ideological mistakes and also the economic policies came under attack. The renewed energy to combat bourgeois liberalization in the summer of 1989 was matched by calls to strengthen the party's leading role throughout the political system. The need to uphold the four cardinal principles figured prominently in the press, giving conservative reformers the right to criticize anything they disapproved of.[51] The tightening of control was clear with respect to the intellectual community, many of whom were driven into exile or silenced. The conservative head of the propaganda system informed intellectuals that it was wrong for them to consider themselves the "most advanced and outstanding of the working class."[52]

General Secretary Jiang Zemin presented an ambiguous message when commemorating the May Fourth Movement (of 1919) in 1990, acknowledging that the vast majority of intellectuals were patriotic and that the growth of heterodox ideas within society was the fault of the party.[53] He signaled greater party guidance over the youth—a patronizing attitude that was reflected in the revival of the requirement that students study various model heroes such as Lei Feng, with Jiang, Li Peng, and Yang Shangkun all signing inscriptions to learn from the obedient soldier. Patriotic education would be strengthened. With respect to the media, Jiang asserted that all journalists had to follow the line set by the CC, and that those who deviated and promoted unorthodox ideas would be punished.[54] On National Day 1989, rather than offering an olive branch to society, Jiang indicated that the tough line would continue. He called for vigilance against efforts by the West to subvert the Chinese government and institute capitalism, and for vigorous suppression of dissent, support for economic retrenchment, and a more forceful role for central planning.[55]

Despite the harsher rhetoric, the party tried to give the impression that it was responding to some of the demonstrators' demands. It launched a widely trumpeted campaign against official speculation and corruption, and the Politburo adopted a seven-point program to deal with corruption. The program advocated shutting down enterprises that had possibly engaged in corrupt activities, preventing the children of senior officials from engaging in commercial activities, and limiting the perks derived from official positions—such as lavish entertainment allowances, international travel, supplies of scarce goods, and cruising around in imported cars.[56] Most of these measures went out the window once China returned to breakneck development in the mid-1990s. On November 9, 1989, one of the main demands of the demonstrators was met when Deng Xiaoping stepped down from his final official position as chair of the CCP Central Military Commission, something that, in mid-June, he had already told CC members he intended to do.

What wounded Deng were the attacks on his economic reforms. While he shared the harsher view of political and ideological matters, he sought to preserve and protect the economic program. The supporters of economic caution pointed to the fact that the post-1989 policies had curbed excessive economic growth and calmed the inflation that had rocked urban China. In 1989, GNP growth was only 4 percent, the lowest growth rate in the post-Mao era. Inflation was clocked at 17.4 percent for the year, but by year's end it had moderated to just 3 to 4 percent. Critics also took the opportunity to attack the collective and private sectors, and what must have most irked Deng was the criticism of the coastal policy of export-led growth.

Yet signs were emerging that austerity might push the economy into recession, and this was not helped by the foreign sanctions imposed in response to the harsh crackdown on the demonstrators. In October 1989 industrial output fell on a month-to-month basis for the first time in a decade; from January through March 1990, industrial output recorded no growth. The collective sector fared even worse; by September 1989, growth of monthly output had dropped from 16.6 percent to 0.6 percent. The slowdown meant that many factories lay idle, and in the first two months of 1990 alone some 1.5 million urban residents lost their jobs. The tightening austerity program was reaching its limits and was not dealing with, and was sometimes exacerbating, the fundamental structural problems in the Chinese economy.

The severity of the economic downturn was unexpected and created concern about social instability, leading to the quiet introduction of measures to ease the austerity despite resistance from fiscal conservatives. Although Zhao was under house arrest, where he would remain until his death on January 17, 2005, the policies associated with his period of rule were gradually reinstated or had simply continued without any publicity. The positive role of the private and collective sectors was recognized and the strategy of coastal development and the special economic zones was also reaffirmed. In February 1990 Li Peng visited the main zone of Shenzhen and spoke positively of its establishment and role.[57] Government policy also returned to the question of prices and subsidies. In April 1991 the sharpest price increases in about twenty-five years were introduced for staple foods, with the price for high-quality rice rising 75 percent and wheat prices rising 55 percent. In April 1992 the price of rice increased a further 40 percent.

When the CCP celebrated its seventieth anniversary on July 1, 1991, a dramatic shift in policy direction appeared to be highly unlikely. Jiang Zemin, reaffirming the hard line, claimed that class struggle would continue for a considerable period of time in some parts of China. This contrasted with the approach that had dominated since 1978, when the party called a halt to extensive class warfare and put an emphasis on economic modernization. The demonstrations and the prevalence of bourgeois ideas had clearly called for a rethink. The party congratulated itself for quelling the dangers from within, and for not having suffered the fate of those East European countries where communism had dramatically collapsed, and for not having to deal with the sorts of profound changes that were shaking up Gorbachev's Soviet Union. Regarding these challenges, Jiang noted: "We Chinese Communists are convinced the temporary difficulties and setbacks recently experienced by socialism in its march forward cannot and will not ever prevent us from continuing to develop." With respect to the West, policy was to remain focused on resisting the capitalists' attempts to transform China through "peaceful evolution."[58]

Deng Travels South to Revive Economic Reform

By the time of the Fourteenth Party Congress, held on October 12–18, 1992, a dramatic swing in policy was under way that unleashed fast-paced economic change. It was a difficult time. It was the first congress to be held since the 1989 demonstrations, the purge of Zhao Ziyang, the collapse of Communist rule in Eastern Europe and the Soviet Union, and the disintegration of the Communist Party of the Soviet Union (CPSU). There was also some urgency felt because it would be the last congress at which many of the elders would be able to exert any real influence. The stakes were high.

The prime mover for change was Deng Xiaoping, and three factors affected his thinking. First, the failure of the hard-liners' coup in the Soviet Union in August 1991, and the resultant collapse of the CPSU, erased any sense of complacency the leadership might have felt. Second, the economic austerity program was not improving people's livelihoods, and unless the citizens' material needs were satisfied, there could arise another crisis of legitimacy. Third, there was a growing gap between life on the streets and party rhetoric, which showed a leadership out of touch with the desires of its people.

While publicly the CCP claimed that events in the USSR were the USSR's own internal matter, China's internal publications displayed alarm and fear about possible consequences for China.[59] Even before the coup, internal reports had been harshly critical of Gorbachev, placing the blame for the collapse of communism in Eastern Europe squarely on his shoulders. Some accounts even referred to him as a traitor. These reports were even more critical of his successor, President Boris Yeltsin, and when Jiang Zemin visited Moscow in May 1991, he declined to meet with him. Reformer Yeltsin's assumption of power in December 1991 was a nightmare come true for the conservative reformers.

It seems that China had quietly been cultivating ties with the more conservative members of the Soviet military and was in favor of Gorbachev's possible removal, or at least moderation of his policies. On the day Gorbachev was arrested, a document was circulated to midlevel and senior officials in the CCP under the title "A Victory for the Soviet People Is a Victory for the Chinese People." Gorbachev was condemned and the leaders of the coup in Moscow were praised for returning the USSR to the path of socialism. The speed with which the document was produced suggests the CCP had some forewarning.[60] The coup lasted only three days before collapsing.

In China, different groups used the coup's failure to strengthen their own position. Conservatives congratulated themselves on their actions in 1989 and renewed calls to tighten ideological work. The differences among the elite are best reflected in a piece by the *People's Daily* editor, installed after June 4, and a piece sponsored by a group around Chen Yuan, the son of Chen Yun. Speaking to his staff, the editor claimed that Gorbachev's decision to dissolve the CPSU amounted to the most traitorous act in the history of world communism. Gorbachev's problems had started with his criticism of Stalin and had caused confusion among the Soviet people. Unlike the Chinese leadership, he made the mistake of dispensing with class struggle and adopting the approach of social democracy rather than communism. Nor was the writer impressed with the plotters, who should have taken a leaf out of the CCP's playbook when it arrested the "Gang of Four" in 1976: no advance warning, no escape, and no communications with the outside world. Not grabbing Yeltsin showed the plotters to be "immature proletarian politicians." In such situations, law and the constitution meant nothing—a troubling observation.[61] The editor used the failure of the coup to justify China's policies, calling for proletarian dictatorship to be strengthened, ideological pluralism to be resisted, and the state-run economy to dominate over the private economy.

Others recognized the need for change if the CCP was to avoid the fate of the CPSU. It was a watershed moment in debates between those who favored ideological and economic orthodoxy and those who wanted to explore authoritarian rule combined with a more deregulated, market-oriented economy. The children of some of the elders argued for a measured, rather than hard-line, response. Their analysis pushed for a middle way that would avoid both radical and delayed reform to avoid the fate of the former Soviet Union. They viewed themselves as neoconservatives and patriotic modernizers in a line of descent from those of the late nineteenth century.

In a seminal piece, they put forward the view that China had to move on from the methods that had been used to gain power, and that the party had to transition from a revolutionary organization to a ruling organization. Class struggle should be downgraded along with the use of populist measures and mass campaigns to implement policy. The participation of intellectuals was crucial and they should not be treated as class enemies. The way forward was a carefully guided economic reform under an authoritarian political structure that would prevent the possibility of social dislocation leading to chaos and upheaval. It was a neoconservative agenda.[62] This approach distinguished them from "traditional diehard conservative forces," as they would adopt whatever was useful in both the traditional and the present order and they would gradually, when appropriate, introduce some elements from the West. However, they rejected large-scale privatization and the use of shares and the stock market, as this would not be beneficial to the state sector, even though it might be used for smaller enterprises. With the demise of the USSR, the CCP could now focus on the distinctively Chinese character of its own revolution and stress the particularities of China to persuade people that "only socialism can save China."[63]

Deng Xiaoping was stung by a *People's Daily* article of September 1, 1991, which was interpreted as an attack on his economic reform program.[64] Deng accepted the approach that, at least for the short term, the party's legitimacy to rule would be tied to its ability to deliver the economic goods. Deng and his supporters recognized that the party had to position itself at the forefront of the reform effort or risk being passed by. Instead of economic policy being made by default or incrementally through struggles with differing views, a clear statement of intent and direction was needed. The pending Fourteenth Party Congress increased the pressure for the differences to be resolved and clarity to be offered.

Deng began to move. First, on September 15, 1991, he warned Jiang Zemin and PRC president Yang Shangkun of the dangers of anti-reform leftism. He feared that the events in the USSR had caused a resurgence of the left in China, which might damage economic progress. Second, Yang Shangkun's speech to mark the eightieth anniversary of the 1911 Revolution was the first public indication of a shift in the reform effort.[65] Although Yang paid much attention to Taiwan and reunification, more important was the significance of his assertion that the core of all work was promotion of the economy. Yang claimed that the party's attention had never shifted from this central task, a clear blow to those in the party who emphasized class struggle.

Third, Deng's "family tour" of South China in January and February 1992 provided a strong statement of intent.[66] Deng exhibited the impatience of someone who felt thwarted and had one last chance to make sure that reform proceeded according to what he felt was necessary for China. His comments during the trip were to the point and were wrapped up in a more careful version that was distributed as Central Document No. 2 (1992). Given the forthright ideas expressed, Deng's opponents tried to prevent their distribution and only acquiesced once some of the general criticisms and negative evaluations of specific individuals among the party leadership were toned down.[67] Deng defended policy since the Third Plenum and the Thirteenth Party Congress, and stated categorically that this line should be adhered to for a hundred years "with no vacillation." He called for boldness and that "we must not be like women with bound feet." He reaffirmed the view that capitalist methods could be used under socialism and that such an approach did not amount to walking the capitalist road. While acknowledging rightism, he noted "it is the left tendencies that have the deepest roots." To be leftist appeared to make one more revolutionary and this had created "dire consequences" in the past. Last but not least, he called for action rather than sitting around talking in meetings with speeches that were too long and boring. Formalism was to be opposed.[68]

While the essence of Deng's approach was adopted in the work report delivered by Jiang Zemin to the Fourteenth Party Congress, the strength of Deng's argument and the possible consequences that might flow from not pursuing rapid economic reform were either watered down or excluded.[69] Central Document No. 2 noted that if the economic reforms were reversed, the support of the people would be lost and the party "could be overthrown at any time." In Deng's view, without the reforms the party would not have survived 1989. Nevertheless, the attempts to revive faster reforms were opposed and there was no press coverage or film footage of the Deng's southern tour presented publicly for several weeks. It was not until March 31, 1992, that the *People's Daily* published a detailed account of Deng's trip.

Li Peng's March 1992 work report amounted to "soft resistance."[70] Somewhat cautiously, Li followed the economic views but diverged significantly on the political views. This was even more unusual as the Politburo had already accepted Deng's new assessment.[71] Jiang Zemin had even submitted a self-criticism. Li dropped the view that leftism was currently the greatest danger and generally echoed language more closely associated with the orthodox party leaders. Moreover, Li did not promise that the political line would remain unchanged for a hundred years, but chose to say that China would become a "powerful, socialist country standing firm as a rock in the East."[72] The economic concerns reflected those of Chen Yun. The report called for a slower economic growth rate of around 6 percent, as opposed to Deng's 10 percent or even higher, and it was much more guarded in its praise of stock markets and the non-state sector of the economy. After the NPC meeting, Deng found a new champion for the economic reforms in Vice Premier Zhu Rongji, who had been moved to the Center from Shanghai. In spring 1991 Deng had picked Zhu to deal with the problem of the loss-making SOEs, and he had come to be a fan of Shanghai's new stock market. Deng praised Zhu as "one of the few cadres who really understands how the economy works," and in June Zhu was appointed to head the State Council's newly created Economic and Trade Office. This new office was to take over certain functions from the more conservative State Planning Commission to push ahead with the reforms of the SOEs, joint ventures, stock companies, and foreign trade.[73]

Chen Yun made use of his institutional power base within the Central Advisory Commission to resist. In the summer of 1990, he had already clashed with Deng, suggesting that Deng's first two choices for general secretary had been weak on opposing bourgeois liberalization, thus creating the conditions for the corruption that had been a key theme in the 1989 demonstrations. On August 24, 1992, he launched a ten-point critique of Deng's economic project that warned against pushing for a too-high growth rate, because unless conditions were ripe, such a pursuit could be destructive. He criticized the tendency to see progress solely in terms of absolute numbers, such as the growth rate. Although not opposed to the expansion of stocks and shares, he cautioned that a sound legal framework was a prerequisite. Turning the tables on Deng with his own interpretation of leftism, Chen viewed the tendency to rush headlong into opening stock markets as a sign of the kind of leftism that had often damaged the party in the past. He was cautious of using Western capital, as it would have political consequences. Perhaps he was influenced by the international response to the suppression of the 1989 demonstrations.[74] Thus, Chen offered conditional support but was not fully onboard with the correctness of the formulation of China as a socialist market economy.

The battle lines had been drawn, but Jiang Zemin's work report to the Fourteenth Party Congress tended to favor Deng's view, while walking a fine line between the different approaches. He did call for rapid economic reform, but he did not use Deng's colorful phrases or warning about the consequences of not doing so. Deng's call for 10 percent growth was rejected, as was Li Peng's suggestion of 6 percent growth, and instead a compromise figure of 8 to 9 percent was decided upon.[75] The work report was notable for three key features: the praise showered on Deng as the architect of the reforms, the wide range of reforms proposed under the formulation "socialist market economy," and the absence of serious discussion of political reform. Deng was "the chief architect of our socialist reform" and was credited with developing the "theory of socialism with Chinese characteristics."[76] This was written into the new Party Statutes, but Deng's name was not appended. China was in the primary stage of socialism, which would last for a hundred years. China was entering another great revolution, equivalent in importance to the "New Democratic Revolution" led by Mao. Whereas Mao knew how to bring classes together to liberate China, Deng's contribution was to put together a new coalition to modernize China's backward economy.

A socialist market economy legitimized the market playing a greater role than at any time previously, with the state only providing macro-level control. However, much of the work report reads like a tortuous compromise between the advocates of central planning and those favoring further opening and reform. For the SOEs, the report called for stricter delineation between government administration and enterprise management, but it did not call for the withdrawal of the party. In fact, quite the opposite; Jiang called for the party to form the political nucleus of the SOEs, a point that was added to the statutes. Party dominance at all levels was emphasized, and there was no mention of abolishing party cells in government organizations. Party unity was a major theme as there was concern that further reforms might cause instability. A strengthening of the people's democratic dictatorship was called for so that hostile forces could be dealt with severely. The party was still responding to the events of 1989, which were now called a counterrevolutionary rebellion, and the Fourth Plenum held just before the congress upheld the judgment on Zhao Ziyang, calling this an end to the investigation.[77]

The new leadership, on balance, favored Deng, as did the increase of provincial representation, as provincial leaders were more likely to be interested in economic results. The congress and its First Plenum approved the new leadership, which tilted the balance in Deng's favor. Of the formal delegates, just over 70 percent came from provincial delegations and five of the twenty-five Politburo members were provincial leaders. This important role of provincial leaders has continued to the present. An emerging norm for senior leadership is to have spent time in the provinces, preferably shared between work in a developed eastern area and in one of the poorer provinces. Civilian control of the military was reaffirmed as Jiang Zemin, unlike Hu Yaobang and Zhao Ziyang, was confirmed as the chair of the Central Military Commission. Given the criticism from the children of senior officials, it is not surprising that none of them were selected to be members of the CC. The basis for the new leadership reflected a compromise struck between Deng and Chen Yun that the so-called Jiang-Li axis not be disturbed.[78] Jiang had done enough to retain Deng's trust. In addition to his March 1992 self-criticism immediately after Deng's "family trip" to the south, in which he noted that he had not done enough to promote reform or oppose leftism, in mid-May he publicly supported Deng's view that elements of capitalism could be relevant under socialism, and on June 9 he made a pilgrimage to the Central Party School to express his complete support for Deng's policies.

One person who did not make the Standing Committee was Tian Jiyun, the scourge of the conservatives. His ridicule of their economic approach made him unacceptable. He gave a very lively speech to the Central Party School in late April 1992 in which he reiterated support for Deng's southern tour, but then went on to suggest that perhaps the leftists in the party might want to set up their own special economic zones. There, salaries and the prices of goods would be low, queuing and rationing would be commonplace, there would be no foreign investment, foreigners would be excluded, and no one would be able to travel abroad. In late May 1992 bootleg tapes of the speech were one of the hottest items for sale. By contrast, there was the unexpected promotion of Hu Jintao, who would eventually take over from Jiang as general secretary. It seems that he was Deng's choice, but was supported by different factions in the party and had shown his mettle during the crackdown on demonstrations in Tibet in 1988–1989, when he was party secretary there.

Removing an obstacle to reforms, the congress confirmed the abolition of the Central Advisory Commission, which had become the institutional base for Chen Yun's sniping at Deng Xiaoping. It had been created in 1982 as a temporary expedient to deal with the question of retirement. If it had not been abolished ten years later, it might have become a permanent feature of the political landscape. This removed the formal regulations that allowed members of the commission to attend Politburo and CC meetings.

The Eighth NPC, in March 1993, endorsed Deng's approach to economic reform. Although Li Peng's report held to the projection of 8 to 9 percent growth, actual growth was around 14 percent. Importantly, Li endorsed Deng's view that the central task was economic development, and the socialist market economy was enshrined in the revised Constitution, as was the idea of China being at the primary stage of socialism. Jiang Zemin replaced Yang Shangkun as president, ending the experiment in which the top posts in the nation were held by different people. From this time on, the same person headed the holy trinity of party, army, and state, with one brief exception. The heads of the three nonparty bodies, the president, the chair of the NPC, and the chair of the CPPCC were all members of the Politburo Standing Committee. This is now common practice.

By 1993 it appeared that the party had recovered from the trauma of 1989 and that economic reform and experimentation were at the forefront of the policy agenda. With his reforms safe, Deng Xiaoping for the most part withdrew from public life, leaving policy implementation to the new leadership.

The next phase of the reforms would present new challenges. Many of the easy parts had been completed, and restructuring would affect key sources of party power, such as the SOEs. The wounds within society were not entirely healed, and study of the model soldier Lei Feng had little appeal for a new generation that was becoming more acquainted with the world outside and that would enjoy the economic fruits of reform. The need to fall back on a mini-cult of Deng to generate legitimacy for the reforms, while politically expedient, showed how little progress had been made with the institutionalization of policy making. Rather than coming to grips with the changes in society, the proposals were for authoritarian rule, with a more market-influenced economy operating under centralized political control. The tensions under this model were forgotten for much of the next decade as many focused on taking advantage of the new economic opportunities.

CHAPTER TEN

Renewed Reform and the Roots of Wealth

1993–2002

☆

The second half of the 1990s laid the foundation for unprecedented wealth, which in turn created the basis for even more spectacular growth after China joined the World Trade Organization (WTO) in 2001. The leadership under Jiang Zemin, Li Peng, and Zhu Rongji (who succeeded Li as premier in 1998) wrestled with Deng Xiaoping's legacies. The economy took off but risked once again running out of control in a boom-bust cycle. Zhu recognized that the problems were not cyclical but rather structural, and that they required a fundamental shift in approach. Given the entrenchment of vested interests that resisted structural reforms, Jiang and Zhu sought to use the external discipline of the WTO to force through domestic reforms. However, carrying out SOE restructuring without causing social instability required boosting alternative employment sources and creating a rudimentary welfare state to support those threatened with unemployment. Restructuring the working class was a gamble that could have undermined the authority of the CCP. CCP control was weakened by the rush to get rich, with many placing a priority on their own interests over those of state and society. Control over society began to slip, and heterodox ideas again permeated the intellectual sphere. By the latter half of the decade, Jiang Zemin realized the need to revitalize party control to prevent political decay.

Wrestling with a Red-Hot Economy

Whereas Deng Xiaoping's interventions saved the reform program, both the economy and the society were in danger of exhausting party control and oversight. The economic boom was fueled by investment and growth of the non-state sector, the real estate sector, and foreign investment in manufacturing. In Beijing, more of the old city was lost to real estate speculation than had been destroyed in any previous decade, including during the periods of the Japanese invasion and the civil war. Cities all over China became building sites. The joke among foreigners was that the national bird of China was the crane. There was a sense within society that military units, police forces, and government institutions were all profiting from the development opportunities.

Growth boomed but so did inflation, which according to official figures rose from 13 percent in 1993 to just over 20 percent in 1994 and most probably 30 percent in the major cities. The task of dealing with the challenge fell to the new vice premier, Zhu Rongji, who effectively took over economic policy making from Li Peng. Zhu was a no-nonsense character who had been punished during the Anti-Rightist Campaign of the 1950s. He was willing to make tough decisions that went against vested interests, and when he became premier in 1998, he made it clear that he would only serve one term. Zhu's economic remedy and his measures to set up an effective revenue-sharing system between the Center and the provinces stabilized the economic and political environments. At the time, success did not seem so certain and Zhu was criticized by the left for his excessive use of privatization and by the right for not moving fast enough with marketization to remove the inconsistencies that fueled corruption.[1]

During 1993 and 1994, policy measures attempted to calm growth and prevent the rising inflation from leading to social unrest. Memories remained of the high inflation in late 1988, which formed the backdrop to the unrest of 1989. Attempted retrenchment did not work. GDP growth for 1993 was 13.4 percent—well above the projected 9 percent, and in 1994, it accelerated even further. Another dangerous stop-and-go cycle was brewing, therefore a group of economists, recognizing that the problems were structural and not cyclical, gathered around Zhu Rongji. Consequently, the Center had to strengthen oversight and establish a clear strategy, leading the reform process rather than playing catch-up with the twists and turns of development. The Center unveiled the most far-reaching policies to enable the economy to "grow out of the plan."[2] But the plan's grip proved difficult to escape from entirely. Zhu's power temporarily was curbed as Li Peng reasserted his role over economic policy making, and another Jiang Zemin associate was placed in charge of SOE reform.

During the initial period under Zhu's guidance, in November 1993, a set of industrial reforms was put forward, together with a plan for the division of taxes between the Center and the provinces. Both sets of policies shared the premise that decentralization had gone too far, causing the Center to lose control over key macroeconomic levers and therefore necessitating careful recentralization. The central government had significant trouble securing a solid and predictable financial base. Zhu and his supporters decided that, rather than responding to developments, a comprehensive statement of reform intent was necessary. Overheating, runaway inflation, and local initiative had spun out of control to the detriment of macroeconomic stability. The reform agenda of the 1980s had been completed, producing strong growth, but now the leadership had to deal with the new and outstanding policy challenges: SOE restructuring, impediments to rural-to-urban labor flows, reform of the banking system, and the integration of the domestic economy with the global economy.[3] This was no easy matter and Zhu had to restate the objectives even more forcefully in 1997–1998.

The Third Plenum of the Fourteenth CC, held on November 11–14, 1993, outlined the establishment of a socialist market system, announced a reversal of the de facto economic decentralization, and proposed an extensive role for the market combined with modernization of the enterprise system.[4] For the restructuring to be successful without causing social unrest, it was necessary to provide social welfare support to those workers who would be released from the SOE sector. To create a modern enterprise system, property rights had to be defined clearly, with individual enterprises taking responsibility for profits and losses and with bankruptcy as a real option. Of course, this had already been proposed in 1984, but the bankruptcy law passed in 1986 had proved to be ineffective. Most importantly, for the first time it was stressed that economic reform required an effective financial system, necessitating overhaul of the taxation, banking, and monetary systems. The People's Bank of China was to function as a central bank, operating monetary policy independently, and extricating itself from local politics by permitting the head office to take regulatory responsibility of the size of loans. Neither of these objectives was met fully.

Bargaining between the provinces and the Center over the division of revenue had become a major feature of politics prior to 1993. Before the NPC session, there was the unseemly sight of central officials traveling to the rich provinces, such as Guangdong, to try to extract more revenue. Guangdong was the major beneficiary of the reforms, enabling it to take advantage of its proximity to Hong Kong and to draw in its capital and manufacturing.[5]

The fiscal system before the 1993–1994 reforms gave local governments a powerful incentive to accelerate economic growth while limiting the Center's ability to benefit from the expansion.[6] The system was a self-financing regime for the Center and the provinces, with the provinces collecting and spending up to 70 percent of budgetary revenue. This trend led to a cottage industry of analyses debating whether China's unitary state would disintegrate or, at least, whether there would be an unhealthy rise in the power of the regions.[7] Reforms stabilized the fiscal relationship and guaranteed the Center a fair share of the economic growth, while ending the bargaining and arm-twisting that had become a key feature of relations between the Center and the provinces. The intent was to strengthen the Center's fiscal capacity by raising the budget-to-GDP ratio and the ratio of centrally collected revenue to total budget revenue. The Center's share of state revenue was to be raised to a minimum of 60 percent, with 40 percent dedicated to central expenditures and 20 percent for transfer grants to local governments. The increase was necessary to fund the new social welfare programs. The tax-sharing system was formalized in the Budget Law, which became effective on January 1, 1995. The division of spending responsibilities between the Center and the provinces was delineated clearly, as was the division of taxes and how the collection of central and local taxes would be administered. The new system did raise revenue as a whole and improved the central share, although it never reached 60 percent. But it did have a dramatic impact on the ability of local governments to finance public goods. Over 80 percent of government expenditures—an extremely high percentage—were covered by local governments. This contributed to the inequalities, with large discrepancies in welfare provision depending on the relative wealth of the region. Whether rich or poor, urban or rural, the localities were required to derive their own sources of revenue to cover centrally mandated obligations for welfare. Revenue mobilization dominated other distribution and growth objectives, often causing the localities to ignore central government policies. Initially these new problems had not been anticipated.[8]

The economy did not cool down, nor did the SOEs behave in a more economically rational manner. At the end of 1994, inflation was still above 20 percent, the localities were pushing ahead with rapid growth-generating policies, with almost half of the SOEs losing money and 80 percent of SOE income dedicated to serving debts they had accrued.[9] A further tightening of the screws was necessary along with a serious shake-out of the SOE sector. By the end of 1997, annual growth had slowed to 8.8 percent and inflation had declined to 0.8 percent. The economy may not yet have landed softly, but time had been bought for policies to be applied to end the vicious stop-and-go cycle.

Jiang Zemin Takes Command

For many, Jiang Zemin had seemed to be a stopgap leader sent to Beijing due to the fallout from 1989: a buffoonish figure who liked to cite from American and Western classics and to burst into song. However, he was a shrewd politician, adept at maneuvering his way through the bureaucratic apparatus. One seasoned Russian diplomat told me how much Jiang reminded him of Brezhnev, not in the sense of causing economic stagnation but in terms of his understanding of how the rules of the Leninist-party game were to be played. As Deng Xiaoping withdrew from the political scene and his health began to fail, Jiang consolidated his own power.

At the CC's 1994 plenum, Jiang devoted his attention to the party and to a reassertion of control, perhaps at Deng's suggestion, and he basically ignored the economy.[10] By the mid-1990s there was a general sense that not only the economy but also society and even the party were slipping out of control. The plenum emphasized the party's leading role and the principle of democratic centralism, going even further to emphasize the need for a core within the leadership. Jiang Zemin would be the core of the third generation of leaders, following Mao Zedong as the core of the first generation and Deng Xiaoping as the core of the second. Boosting what would become known as the "Shanghai clique," close associates of Jiang were promoted to leadership positions.

The tax-sharing scheme was used to rein in the provinces, and the centralization of leadership around Jiang was to rein in the wayward society and party members. The poor quality of grassroots organizations was criticized and ideological work was to be enhanced. The perennial challenge of dealing with corruption was highlighted, and the need to ensure that party members acted with integrity was stressed. During the summer of 1993, an anticorruption campaign was launched, but during the winter after the Fourth Plenum, corruption roared back with a vengeance. Accusations of corruption would become the weapon of choice to remove rivals. Criticizing pursuit of the wrong political line had become discredited because of the twists and turns of the Cultural Revolution. The pursuit of corrupt behavior fused political intrigue at the apex with attempts to create popular support from below.

Beijing party secretary Chen Xitong had served as mayor during the 1989 demonstrations, sending Deng Xiaoping alarmist accounts of the students' activities. Given the outcome, Chen may have thought that he, rather than Jiang Zemin, deserved to be general secretary. He was the one clear rival to Jiang's position as the core of the third generation. Jiang's corruption campaign zeroed in on Beijing municipality, resulting in dozens being detained, including those working closely with Chen Xitong. In April 1995 the city's vice mayor, Wang Baosen, committed suicide under strange circumstances, and rumors spread in Beijing that Wang must have been very skilled to be able to commit suicide by shooting himself in the back! As the events unraveled, by the end of the month Chen was removed from office; in September 1996 he was dismissed from his posts, and in 1998 he was sentenced to eighteen years in prison.

The CC's Fifth Plenum, held on September 25–28, 1995, not only confirmed Chen's dismissal because of his "dissolute and extravagant lifestyle" but also outlined the new five-year economic plan. The meeting furthered Jiang's rise as he marked out a course that moved closer to the left in terms of limiting what could be tolerated. Leading up to the plenum, the old left, gathered around the irrepressible Deng Liqun, had launched a series of critiques of reform in what were referred to as the "10,000 Character Manifestos." The manifestos revived familiar themes about the rise of bourgeois liberalization, the infection that private enterprise would bring to the socialist body, and the loss of sovereignty wrought by foreign engagement. There were also warnings about the existence of a Chinese Gorbachev—a not too subtle reference to Zhu Rongji and his policies of economic reform that would weaken the SOE socialist heartland.

Reining in an Unruly Society

Jiang Zemin was not going to be upstaged by these critiques, and in a number of speeches he signaled that although control over society would be tightened, preserving the momentum for the economic reforms would be upheld.

In October 1995 he delivered a speech entitled "More Talk about Politics," which clearly outlined this new approach. Consequently, through 1996 and beyond, tougher measures were introduced to deal with the unruly society. Challenges were seen as originating from independent organizing, including underground labor and religious associations, a revival of the critical arts and publishing, stirrings among the ethnic communities in China's border regions, and the spread of the internet. During the next several years the CCP took on each of these challenges to reassert control. The only question was whether traditional control mechanisms would prove as effective in a society on the move and enjoying the fruits of economic success.

Early in the decade democratic activists had been marginalized with the development of an intellectual discourse that was largely independent of politics—that is, a "genuinely societal discourse."[11] Many who had been attracted to the democratic ethos of the 1980s supported the regime's call for stability to ensure the maintenance of economic growth. The view that only the party stood between society and chaos was promoted in the official media, and the fate of the Soviet Union was used to legitimize CCP rule. Articles recounted how formerly privileged Soviet academics were reduced to trying to scrape together a living amid the ashes of the former Soviet state—selling off precious books and heirlooms to make ends meet. Such activities were buttressed by a newfound nationalism.

In the 1980s there had been a close relationship between the reformers in the party and the intellectuals who critiqued the system. But during the 1990s the situation was quite different, with a wider variation of views within intellectual circles. Some sought fame and fortune; some others took up the causes of the "vulnerable groups."[12] Writers such as Wang Shuo were irreverent, seeking heroes not from among the pantheons of the party greats but rather from the underside of Chinese society. One of Wang Shuo's characters comments: "That's right, enjoy yourself, that will really piss them off."[13] Although the CCP informed the people that "women hold up half the sky," Shanghai writer Wen Hui announced that women "have much more freedom than women fifty years ago, better looks than those of thirty years ago, and a greater variety of orgasms than women ten years ago."[14]

Wang Xiaobo was one of the first truly independent writers to focus on the vulnerable groups in society. His 1992 work, *The Golden Age*, pokes fun at all forms of authority while trying to give voice to the disadvantaged. Wang sees these groups as the "silent majority of society."[15] Concern for the vulnerable populations was not found only in literature. Others organized to provide practical help to achieve the rights guaranteed to them in Chinese law. Such organizations included legal clinics based near the universities that sought to help victims of domestic violence and migrant workers who were cheated out of their wages, hotlines for those contemplating suicide, and support networks for people living with HIV/AIDS. Attention to women's rights was boosted by the United Nations Nongovernmental Forum on Women, held in Beijing in September 1995. The forum brought Chinese activists into contact with international colleagues and sensitized them to a range of issues. In the buildup to the forum, women's nongovernmental organizations (NGOs) were allowed to form in China, in part because only NGOs could participate in the forum. After the forum, the space for such organizations began to close down.

However, by the middle of the decade, political activism was restored. At the time the leadership was more concerned about the larger potential threat of labor activism, as the SOE reforms had led to large-scale layoffs in the Northeast and in Sichuan, where the SOEs played a dominant role. Again the CCP leadership was confronted with the possibility of a movement like Poland's Solidarity. In a dangerous move, Jiang Zemin and his supporters decided to cut the umbilical cord that tied the interests of the working class to the CCP. Although the official figure for unemployment in 1996 was only 3 percent, more reliable calculations range from about 12 percent to the World Bank's estimate of 20 percent.[16] The official figures do not include those who had not registered as unemployed, including the large number of laid-off workers on the books of the still-functioning SOEs. If one adds underemployment, the figure is likely much higher. Given the situation, local authorities were very successful at restraining unrest, and the inability of workers to ensure independent representation moderated the possibility of strikes.[17] A popular phrase in the Northeast was "yellowing," the color leaves turn before they fall off the trees.[18]

However, one major strike did show the CCP leadership the potential of worker unrest. In late July 1997 about 100,000 workers in the city of Mianyang, Sichuan province, protested, fueled by their perception that local officials had been siphoning off funds that were meant to cushion the blow of redundancy by providing worker support and retraining.[19] In what became the mode for the CCP tough response, nine protest leaders were arrested and any potential organization was immediately crushed. At the same time, subsidies and "policy loans" were issued to try to reverse the losses in key industries.

Unrest also occurred in the sensitive border provinces of Tibet and Xinjiang, where tensions have festered, with occasional explosions, up to the present. The most serious was in Yining, western Xinjiang, where two days of anti-Chinese demonstrations led to rioting. Perceived anti-Muslim actions by the local authorities sparked the unrest, but the initial peaceful demonstrations were met with tear gas and water cannons. On the following day, violence broke out and nine were killed and another 200 were injured. Public sentencing rallies were held, with three sentenced to death. In response, the provincial party secretary called for stepping up the fight against separatism. While not as dramatic, ninety-six people were detained in Tibet, and the patriotic education campaign that had been launched in 1996 was intensified.[20]

Although worker and rural unrest was kept under control, the CCP leadership became concerned about the renewed political activity. As is often the case after a party congress, activism increased through the fall of 1997 and the spring of 1998, as a "Beijing Spring" movement began to blossom. However, it very soon froze over. A few optimistic pro-reform tracts were published, the most notable of which was the book *Crossing Swords* by two senior figures at the *People's Daily*. The book takes up the fight against the leftist manifestos and notes how the reforms and Deng Xiaoping's 1992 southern trip had removed the cult of personality and the cult of the planned economy. The Fifteenth Party Congress had now removed the cult of ownership.[21]

In a direct challenge to CCP rule, activists throughout China formed the China Democracy Party. For a brief period it appeared that its activities might be tolerated, but in November 1998 its key members were arrested and other members were periodically picked up and harassed. In another event that was considered a threat, a spiritual movement, the Falun Gong, was banned. This followed the incident in April 1999 when thousands of Falun Gong supporters surrounded the party's central headquarters in Beijing, waking central leaders to the potential of faith-based movements to inspire loyalty.[22] In October an anti-cult law was passed to legalize the repression of such groups.

Jiang Zemin's hardening attitude toward dissent and unapproved publications was signaled in an October 1996 speech in which he returned to the theme of building a socialist spiritual civilization, claiming that this objective would not be sacrificed in the search for short-term economic achievements. Control was to be strengthened over the press and publishing, and the guardians of ideology would shape propaganda and public opinion. These calls featured prominently in the official press during the first months of 1997. They were followed by concrete measures. In late August the Ministry of Culture issued new regulations to cleanse the performing arts and banned "vulgar content." Foreigners were prohibited from producing or funding theatrical works, but they could invest in building theaters and other physical infrastructure. Imaginative movie makers found it difficult to make new films or to get them shown in China, where a chill wind was blowing. Other measures included a crackdown on underground churches, a process for registering religious organizations, the reregistering of publications combined with more serious efforts to ban unacceptable publications and to control content, a new law that set tougher limits on the activities of social organizations and tightened control over their operations, and new restrictions on research collaboration with foreigners in the social sciences.

A new challenge was how to deal with the spread of the internet. The CCP did not want to negate the economic and scientific benefits of the internet, but it wanted to control unwanted political messages or social practices. The Chinese authorities began a continual cat-and-mouse game by requiring users to register and by blocking those sites that were considered undesirable. US president Bill Clinton was not impressed with the attempts to control the new media, and on March 8, 2000, he wished the leaders good luck, saying, "That's sort of like trying to nail Jell-O to the wall." Yet China has been far more successful at controlling access, promoting its own messages, and dominating online debate than anyone could have imagined. Having established his credentials with the left, Jiang Zemin created space to push ahead with the economic reform program.

Maintaining Economic Reform: The Fifteenth Party Congress

Jiang Zemin recognized that most people were primarily concerned about their livelihoods, and therefore nationalism and legitimacy were increasingly predicated on the CCP's ability to deliver the economic goods. At the time of the October 1996 plenum, in preparation for the 1997 Fifteenth Party Congress, supporters of Jiang published "Heart to Heart Talks with the General Secretary." The materials placed a much more positive spin on the need for reform and opening up the economy, in response to the attacks from the left. Unlike the leftists, who blamed Gorbachev and his reforms for the collapse of the Soviet Union, Jiang and his supporters claimed that it was Brezhnev and his lack of reforms that had caused the stagnation that had led to collapse. To avoid the same fate, it was necessary for China to push ahead. The work advanced the process of drawing on Chinese tradition to legitimize CCP rule.[23] The approach highlighted themes that would be taken up at the Fifteenth Party Congress and the following session of the NPC.

Jiang also tried to restore credibility with establishment intellectuals when he visited Peking University on May 4, 1998, to celebrate the centennial anniversary of its establishment. By all accounts Jiang was very relaxed, enjoying his interactions with faculty and students. It was a risky gamble given that Peking University had been at the epicenter of the 1989 demonstrations. Jiang also showed that he was a smart politician, noting that "although Tsinghua University is our present, Peking University is our future."[24] The attitudes of graduates, students, and faculty were revealed at the main celebration in the Great Hall of the People. When Premier Li Peng came onto the stage, the applause was lukewarm, but the deposed university president was greeted with thunderous applause.[25]

Amid the debates—about reform, about tensions over the question of Taiwan, and about the return of Chinese sovereignty over Hong Kong— Deng Xiaoping died, February 1997. Zhao Ziyang was refused permission to attend his funeral. The Fifteenth Party Congress was the first since the beginning of the reforms that did not have Deng's presence overseeing the proceedings. It was Jiang's chance to place his stamp on the CCP's future as the core of the third generation. In fact, Jiang had been strengthening his position in the several years running up to the congress, while wrapping himself in the mantle of Deng's legacy.

The Fifteenth Party Congress, held on September 15–18, 1997, and the National People's Congress held in March of 1998 clarified the policy approach of the Jiang administration.[26] There were six clear components: commitment to high economic growth to ensure social stability; commitment to a mixed economy; substantial restructuring of the SOE sector; strengthened CCP control; a quickened pace of integration into the global economy; and good relations with the United States, while also responding to the rising nationalist sentiment.

Jiang's report drew its legitimacy from Deng Xiaoping, who received fulsome praise.[27] Deng's theory of "building socialism with Chinese characteristics" was taken as the guiding light for development in the twenty-first century, and Deng's theory was added to the statutes behind Marxism-Leninism and Mao Zedong Thought. This ensured that a more pragmatic approach to economic reform could be pursued, with other work being subordinate to the central task of economic development. This was under-pinned on the political front by the judgment that although the party had to remain vigilant against the right, the biggest threat came from the left. Per-haps more surprisingly, the slogan "primary stage of socialism" was revived to allow continued experimentation over several generations. The theory had been put forward by Zhao Ziyang in 1987, but its revival did Zhao little good as he remained under house arrest.

Policy innovation was necessary for the SOE sector. By the time of the congress, it was even more apparent that the sector was a drag on the overall economy. The World Bank suggested that perhaps less than 10 percent of the 100,000 SOEs were viable. In 1995 SOEs absorbed 60 percent of na-tional investment and received subsidies amounting to one-third of the na-tional budget, and net credit to the SOEs amounted to over 12 percent of GDP. Importantly, 50 to 75 percent of household savings, mediated and di-rected by state banks, went to finance SOE operations. In 1996 half of the SOEs were losing money, and in the first quarter of 1996 the sector had slipped into the red for the first time since the founding of the PRC.[28] The net deficit was some $850 million. China was clearly nearing a situation where government resources would be insufficient to pay depositors and bondholders if the SOEs were unable to service their bad debts. These prob-lems were compounded by the high welfare costs the SOEs carried. In 1995 the cost of social insurance and welfare funds as a percentage of the total wage bill rose from 13.7 percent to 34 percent.[29] Not surprisingly, bankrupt-cies rose 260 percent in 1996, leading to rising unemployment.

Jiang announced that a shareholding scheme would be adopted, with 1,000 of the largest enterprises reinvigorated in hopes that they would behave like the *chaebols* in South Korea.[30] Other enterprises were to be reorganized through a mixture of mergers, leasing, contracting, joint stock partnerships, or sales. This was referred to as "grasping the large and releasing the small" (adopted in 1996). Given the contentious nature of this policy innovation, Jiang expanded the definition of the state sector to include the collective en-terprises, stating: "Even if the state-owned sector accounts for a smaller proportion of the economy, this will not affect the socialist nature of our economy." Jiang acknowledged the hardships this might bring for some workers, so he called for strengthening job training, pensions, and insurance systems. In March the new premier, Zhu Rongji, added more detail, claiming that the problem would be resolved during a three-year period. However, the Chinese leadership is still dealing with this challenge today.

What was missing from the congress was any serious consideration of political reform. When addressing the topic, Jiang rejected any idea of copying Western ways, such as having multiparty electoral competition or interest-group pluralism, and he reaffirmed the need for the press to toe the party line and extoll the party's virtues. Even though in his speech Jiang mentioned the word "democracy" thirty-two times, the stress was on cooperation with China's other political parties but under the leadership of the CCP.

In the leadership stakes, Jiang was able to outmaneuver Qiao Shi, a potential rival who headed the NPC and may have felt that he was worthier of leadership than Jiang. In a deft maneuver, Jiang suggested that the demands to rejuvenate the leadership be heeded and that all those over seventy years of age should retire, starting with himself. In what was clearly a choreographed move, one of the remaining party elders noted that rejuvenation should be combined with stability and continuity. Given that Jiang was scheduled to undertake a state visit to the United States after the congress, the party elder suggested that Jiang should remain but the others should step down. Qiao was left with no alternative but to step down. Jiang was supported by Li Peng, who coveted taking over Qiao's position as head of the NPC once he had stepped down as premier.[31] The only other person over the age of seventy not to retire was dear old Hua Guofeng.

At the March 1998 NPC meeting, Premier Zhu Rongji expanded on the economic reform proposals, and Hu Jintao, Jiang's expected successor, was appointed to the important position of vice president. Zhu first announced an overhaul of the banking system with the reorganization of the local branches of the People's Bank along regional lines. The intent was to reduce political interference in lending decisions by influential provincial party secretaries. Zhu announced that the "power of provincial governors and mayors to command local bank presidents is abolished as of 1998."[32] Further, he announced an integrated set of five significant reform measures. The first decision was to set up a nationwide grain market to ease pressures on the country's reserves. Government subsidies to the sector were reduced, shifting the CCP away from the Maoist obsession with grain. Second, the regulatory functions of the Central Bank were stepped up as part of the overhaul of the financial system to reduce both waste and duplicate capital investments. Commercial banks were to be let off the leash and allowed to make their own decisions.

Third, reforms were introduced to reduce the welfare burden on enterprises. The economic reforms dramatically shook up welfare provision, but it took the leadership some time to come to this realization.[33] The most dramatic impacts were in the countryside and among the rural migrants, but the Jiang-Zhu leadership focused on the fraying urban welfare system as it sought to push ahead with the reform of the SOEs. The increasingly market-influenced economy exposed the high cost of welfare that enterprises carried, and it was clear that many were struggling to cover these costs. The policy shift resulted in the layoff of some 50 million industrial workers and the end of what is referred to as the "iron-rice bowl."[34]

Premier Zhu announced the end of the enterprise-based, cradle-to-grave care that the Chinese industrial working class and government employees had come to expect. Policy sought greater individual responsibility through contributions to pensions, medical and other insurance, and the privatization of workplace housing stock. Those living in enterprise housing were allowed to purchase their homes at a discounted rate, while those who did not purchase their homes were subject to a rise in rent up to 15 percent of their family income. The new approach had three objectives: to reduce the welfare costs of the SOEs and redistribute them across enterprises and to individuals working in other ownership categories; to provide equal rights and levels of protection across all ownership categories; and to establish links between the contributions individuals made to their own benefits and what they actually received. The leadership feared the SOE restructuring would create a systemic threat, so it moved swiftly to put these systems in place.

The welfare reforms were an attempt by the authoritarian regime to shore up support for its core constituencies during a period of rapid change. It was no longer possible to protect the industrial working class from the consequences of reform, so the next best option was to put in place minimum support schemes to cushion the blow. Through the 1990s the government strengthened initiatives or reaffirmed benefits for those groups that provided the base of regime support: bureaucrats and those working in the formal sector of the economy (the traditional working class). Health care reforms were introduced in 1994, and they were drafted into a new comprehensive scheme that became operational by the end of 1999; a new pension system for enterprise workers was drawn together in 1997; and a scheme for minimum subsistence relief was established at the end of 1999. These measures reflected the pro-urban, coastal, and elitist thrust of policy throughout the 1990s, and they involved transferring primary responsibility for social welfare from the workplace to the local governments. However, these initial reforms left most people in rural China and those working in the informal sector to their own devices, a challenge that the next generation of leaders, Hu Jintao and Wen Jiabao, would wrestle with.

Fourth on the reform docket was dealing with a major cause of the unrest in the countryside: the excessive levying of fees and taxes by local governments. As a result, the tax system was to be rationalized to mitigate the effects of the local government squeeze.

Finally, an associate of Zhu presented a major plan to overhaul government administration, reducing the number of ministries from forty to twenty nine. One important component was the abolition of some industrial ministries that oversaw the SOEs, thus breaking the link between the individual enterprises and the powerful bureaucrats at the Center. This resulted in large-scale layoffs in central government employment, totaling some 33,000 workers and contributing further to the dismantling of cradle-to-grave care. Many were being left in a world of uncertainty where they were being asked to trade in their secure but low-wage, benefit- supported lives for a riskier, potentially better-rewarded future. Many were unwilling to take the risk.

Wrestling with the Consequences of Reform

As 1998 progressed, the reform momentum ran into headwinds that slowed progress. The layoffs created instability and caused concern and moderation. In addition to the layoffs of SOEs and government workers—perhaps four million throughout the system—there were the 500,000 members of the military cut by Jiang Zemin's policy, and perhaps as many as ten million workers in township and village enterprises who had become redundant because of technological advances and capital-intensive investment.[35] It is not surprising that unemployment hit its highest rate since 1949.[36] The insecurity this induced was enhanced by worries about an economic slowdown. During 1998–1999 the economy was slipping into a period of deflation, with prices dropping by 2.6 percent and growth at 7.8 percent. The Asian financial crisis that began in 1997 did not have a direct impact on China: capital controls and healthy foreign exchange reserves provided protection. However, it did provide a warning to the leadership about the pitfalls of rapid liberalization of the financial sector. There was another warning in the sudden fall of Indonesian strongman Suharto, followed by the rapid systemic collapse. In Chinese eyes, here was a leader who had overseen a lengthy period of economic growth, who was secure in power and was supported by the military and the security apparatus, and yet he was swiftly swept aside by street demonstrations that surfaced due to decades of frustration. The parallels set off alarm bells.

Further, the system was buffeted by corruption and smuggling scandals. These were linked to the theme of economic security, which came to dominate many articles and speeches as the year progressed. In 2000 the campaign against corruption continued, with 23,000 cases under investigation and the execution of a number of senior officials, including a former vice chair of the NPC. Military involvement in corruption, especially the smuggling of oil, was concerning particularly because these activities could undermine combat readiness. The depth of corruption was highlighted by the smuggling scandal at the Yuanhua Group based in the open city of Xiamen. The case implicated many local officials, PLA intelligence officials, and by association Jia Qinglin, a close ally of Jiang Zemin. The smuggling included firearms, vehicles, crude oil, and electrical items, amounting to at least 80 billion yuan. The involvement of Jiang's associate made investigation tricky—it took the Politburo three years to authorize action, and apparently even then it moved only after Zhu Rongji threatened, in the summer of 1999, to resign. Eventually eighty-four people were arrested, and eleven were sentenced to death, by which time Jia was safely ensconced in Beijing as party secretary. Premier Zhu had been sufficiently shocked that he stated on television that the ringleader, who had fled overseas, "should be killed three times over."[37] The levels of corruption and PLA engagement did, however, push Jiang Zemin to decree that the military should withdraw from business activities. Some engaged in a shell game of hiding their activities, but on the whole this move was more successful than many had predicted.

Overshadowing these troubles and the future of economic development had been the big question of whether or not China would enter the WTO. Supporters saw this as a natural step in China's integration into the global economy and as a way to apply pressure for domestic economic reforms; opponents were worried about the potential loss of sovereignty and possible job losses.

Concern about these factors led to a cautious approach to the speed of reform. Reform without losers was turning into reform with multiple constituencies who, if not losing, were not benefiting as well as the rich coastal elite and the new rich, most of whom had strong party connections. Beginning at the end of 1998 the government launched a massive public building and infrastructure program to maintain a growth rate of 7 to 8 percent. The Ministry of Finance issued several rounds of government bonds, totaling

401.5 billion yuan for bank recapitalization, in order to stimulate infrastructure investment. Further, to deal with the debts that had accumulated in the commercial banking sector, asset management committees were set up to liquidate the bad loans and to provide a fresh start. Like during other times of stress, the government turned to the private sector to support the flagging economy. In 1999 the private sector was producing over 90 percent of new employment and 80 percent of growth.

The Third Plenum of the Fifteenth CC, held on October 12–14, 1998, focused attention on the rural sector, but the adopted decision was also concerned with keeping up economic growth by pushing for greater investment in the rural areas and beginning to deal with the regional inequalities that had spread during the 1990s. During the boom years of the early 1990s, little attention had been paid to redistribution, the general belief being that high levels of economic growth would lift all boats and resolve all problems; this is another example of a failed trickle-down theory. By the end of the 1990s it was clear that not all had benefited equally from the reforms and that inequality and differential access to services had become a major problem. After narrowing in the 1980s, the urban-rural divide was increasing. By the mid-1990s the ratio of urban to rural income had risen to about 2.38:1. Other indicators revealed a similar story. Access to health and education services that were widely available in the 1980s had become more dependent on income by the 1990s. In 1998, in high-income areas 22.2 percent of persons were covered by cooperative medical facilities, but in the poorer regions only 1 to 3 percent were covered.

Other initiatives tried to wrestle with this problem. The grandest was the "Develop the West" program launched by Jiang Zemin in late 1999 and confirmed at the Tenth NPC in March 2003. The program included twelve provinces, with policy relying on state-led infrastructure investment combined with political persuasion and arm twisting of the more developed provinces to shift investment to the interior provinces. The NPC meeting of March 2000 had already announced the shift in the focus of economic construction away from the coast and to the western regions. Per capita GDP in the west was only about 60 percent of that in the east. In Premier Zhu's view, this was to be a long-term situation, lasting for several generations. In 2000 some $6 billion was set aside for investment, and Zhu headed a leading group to oversee the work. In reality, state commitments were limited, with most of the projects already scheduled, allowing many provinces to shift the costs to the central government from the provincial budgets. Many analysts saw the program as serving political purposes rather than serving genuine developmental needs, and the excluded provinces expressed their resentment.

The leadership did begin to pay attention to the dire situation of rural health care. In December 1996 a national conference sought to fix the broken system. The change of tone at the meeting was remarkable. Rather than describing China's health-care system as a model for other developing countries, participants expressed concern about its collapse. To redress the situation, the government declared that it would increase spending, from 2 percent to 5 percent of the national budget, something that was not achieved. Preventive health was to be revived, public hygiene awareness was to be raised through public education, and village doctors were to receive a pay increase to bring their pay in line with that of government officials, and to put an end to doctors' increasing their income by accepting kickbacks and overprescribing drugs. Most important was the revival of the cooperative medical system, which had been severely damaged by the withdrawal of state funding. These were all initiatives that Jiang's and Zhu's successors would build upon as the challenge of social equity loomed ever larger.

Consequently, when Jiang Zemin celebrated the twentieth anniversary of reform in December 1998, he was not as enthusiastic in his praise as he might have been. He ignored calls for more rapid economic reforms, and political reform did not even merit consideration. He pursued a cautious approach, with tight political control legitimated by a strident nationalism. Rumors circulated in Beijing that, under pressure from Li Peng, Jiang announced that political reform would not be discussed for two to three years. His speech made it clear that radical ideas of Western-inspired models of economic and political reform were not for China. Instead he focused on the need to maintain stability and to immediately crack down on any potential unrest, and he emphasized Deng Xiaoping's four cardinal principles. Basically, the bold reforms would be moderated to allow people to adjust to their consequences. Commemorating the anniversary of reform was tricky because so much of what had transpired had been overseen by the disgraced Hu Yaobang and Zhao Ziyang, with the result that the key figures who had inspired the reforms were not mentioned. One other example is Du Runsheng, who had been the key figure promoting the rural reforms of the 1980s. Jiang refused to acknowledge Du, in part because of his closeness to Zhao, and as a result some of his juniors held a celebration for him in a private courtyard at Peking University. However, it was not too long before WTO membership and the direction of reform were back on the policy agenda.

Sovereignty: Hong Kong, Taiwan,
the United States, and the WTO

Jiang Zemin had to navigate a difficult legacy in the international arena, especially in dealing with the fallout from the repression of the 1989 demonstrations and the collapse of the Soviet Union. The end of the US-Soviet superpower rivalry meant that the CCP had to reconfigure its international position without the room for maneuver that the Cold War had offered. It was a struggle to adjust to the new world order, especially because of the way CCP leaders were accustomed to analyzing global politics—in terms, that is, of an overarching framework based on ideological premises that provided structure for policy and relationships. The CCP had settled into a foreign policy premised on the notion that international politics would be dominated by the existence of a bipolar relationship between the two superpowers. This allowed China space to play one off the other and to create more room for itself in international affairs. With this balance gone, CCP leaders felt vulnerable and marginalized in world affairs. However, as we saw in Chapter 9, it did allow China to develop policy in terms of its own national interest without having to consider the great-powers balance.

The changing environment brought to the fore latent tensions in China's relations with the United States and—combined with the West's reaction to the military crackdown in Tiananmen Square in 1989—introduced greater uncertainty into the relationship. President George W. Bush was personally invested in maintaining a smooth relationship with China and chose not to maximize pressure on China. Bush's national security adviser traveled to Beijing and met with Deng on July 2, 1989. Instead of being contrite, Deng aggressively asserted that it was up to the United States to repair their relationship because the United States had been a principal inspiration for the counterrevolutionary rebellion of 1989. By and large, President Bush obliged.[38] Further, many Chinese believed the United States had become arrogant because it was the only remaining superpower. The honeymoon period of the 1980s ended abruptly, and issues about which the United States and the West had been quiet—such as rights abuses—became the focus of extensive media and political attention.

Throughout his tenure as general secretary, Jiang Zemin had to navigate the rise in nationalist sentiment, not repressing it but also not letting it slip out of control. Following 1989, patriotic education was promoted, especially for students. Inevitably, the targets of criticism were Japan and the United

States. Apart from the seesawing in the relationship with the United States, there were also tensions with Taiwan as the CCP came to terms with the new GMD leadership under Lee Teng-hui. Finally, there was the issue of the return to Chinese sovereignty of the British colony Hong Kong and the Portuguese colony Macau.

China moved swiftly to shore up diplomatic relations with both the former pro-Soviet regimes in the developing world and with the newly established nations that emerged from the breakup of the former Soviet Union. Two factors drove this haste. First, there was serious concern that because many of these new nations were now firmly anti-Communist, Taiwan might step in to establish diplomatic relations. Second, the new Central Asian states had the potential of presenting a challenge by supporting the Muslim fundamentalists within China.

The first Gulf War, in 1991, launched by the Bush administration with the support of the United Nations, offered China a chance to improve its standing as a cooperative global force and to work to overturn some of the sanctions that had been imposed after 1989. China used its role as a member of the UN Security Council to side with the United States as it built up an offensive coalition. Despite this, however, China had been, and remains, concerned about the use of force in other countries—unless it is launched by China itself against its neighbors. As a result, China abstained from the crucial UN Security Council vote to authorize force against Iraq. The resultant military actions and the massive but precise US forces shocked the Chinese leadership and its military, raising concerns that the new multipolar world that they had anticipated might be unipolar and dominated by the United States. A predictable relationship with the United States was clearly important if the CCP wanted to continue its economic reforms and draw in more foreign capital. Despite domestic opposition, Jiang Zemin sought to maintain Deng Xiaoping's legacy of a neutral or a pro-US international orientation. However, unlike in the 1980s, there was no strategic rationale to hold the relationship together; it was driven by specific interests and policies and thus liable to be buffeted by unexpected events. And indeed, it was.

Despite presidential candidate Bill Clinton's harsh rhetoric about China and its human rights violations, once Clinton became president he maintained the previous administration's policy of engagement, with the hope that closer integration into the global community would lead to domestic change in China. A major area of frustration for China was the need each year to renew its most-favored-nation (MFN) status. In 1993 President Clinton linked China's MFN status to human rights, protection of Tibetan culture, and allowing foreign broadcasts into China. However, in late May 1994 he reversed this decision and unlinked MFN status, much to China's delight.

This warming of relations was thrown off course by US support for Taiwan. In 1995 Taiwan president Lee Teng-hui was invited to visit his alma mater, Cornell University, and he wished to transit through the United States on his way to a state visit to Central America. The Chinese Foreign Ministry had been assured that no visa would be issued, but President Clinton, under pressure from Congress, relented. This increased mistrust, but also alerted the Chinese leadership to the power of Congress, having previously thought that simply dealing with the president was enough. The following year, as President Lee sought to become the first democratically elected president of Taiwan, the CCP leadership was unnerved and unsure of the US response. Although Lee was a member of the GMD, he was a Taiwan native, and many in China thought he harbored strong sentiments in favor of independence. As a warning, China launched missiles perilously close to the island, leading the United States to dispatch two aircraft carrier groups to the region. The situation revealed the limits of the possible. For Taiwan, the warning made it clear that China would firmly oppose any move to independence. For China, it was clear that under certain conditions the United States would intervene to protect Taiwan, something that perhaps the leadership in Beijing had felt the US government would be unwilling to do. For the United States, it clarified that its historical engagement with Taiwan was still a live issue and that, like it or not, the United States would have to remain involved. Things calmed down in 1997 as the growing economic relationship across the strait forged ahead.

1997 was an important year for China and for Jiang Zemin, with the return of Hong Kong to Chinese sovereignty in July and a state visit to the United States in October. Hong Kong played an important role for China as a window to the outside world, even during the height of the Maoist period. Exports were routed through the Hong Kong port; it was an important listening post for intelligence; and once China opened up, Hong Kong capital was important for mainland development. Lacking private capital, China made use of its connections with Hong Kong to encourage investment in the mainland, and throughout the 1980s and the 1990s much of Hong Kong's manufacturing base moved across the border where land was cheaper. Hong Kong investors played an important role in the early development of mainland real estate; many Hong Kong millionaires became billionaires as a result and were welcomed to join national and local branches of the CPPCC. This was safe capital because these Hong Kong billionaires were highly unlikely to challenge the CCP, especially as their accumulation of capital was dependent on the party's goodwill.

In terms of reclaiming Hong Kong, China could have shut off the water, most power, and much of the fresh food supply at any time, but the territory was far too valuable to disrupt. Problems occurred in 1982 when many fifteen-year leases had to be renegotiated and many people were unsure what would happen after 1997, when the ninety-nine-year lease on the New Territories was to expire. British prime minister Margaret Thatcher, during her 1982 visit to Beijing, took the view that Hong Kong was too valuable to China, and she expected agreement on some sort of continuation of the treaties governing Hong Kong Island and Kowloon. This reflected a lack of comprehension of the emotive role the unfair and unequal treaties played in the Chinese narrative of national humiliation at the hands of the foreigners. Deng Xiaoping had different ideas and insisted that the New Territories be returned, and without the New Territories, Hong Kong Island could not function.

In fact, Deng completely rejected the validity of the treaties that had ceded Hong Kong Island and Kowloon. In 1984 the Sino-British Declaration was agreed upon, as the clock was running down on the empire. The agreement required the local legislative council to be replaced by a provisional legislative body selected by Beijing, with businessman Tung Chee-hwa as chief executive of the Hong Kong Special Administrative Region. The principle on which the Special Administrative Region would relate to the mainland was encapsulated in the phrase "one country, two systems." Under this, China was to guarantee Hong Kong's economic and political systems for fifty years. Sovereignty was transferred on July 1, 1997, ending 156 years of colonial rule. Deng did not live to witness the handover, but Jiang Zemin was able to benefit. He praised Deng for his foresight in developing the concept of one country, two systems, and he confirmed that Hong Kong residents would administer Hong Kong. In December 1999, Macau was brought back into the fold, ending 442 years of Portuguese rule.

Now only the issue of Taiwan remained unresolved. At the Macau handover, Jiang suggested that the concept of one country, two systems, could provide a solution to the issue of Taiwan.[39] The economic relationship with Taiwan was expanding rapidly, and the Chinese leadership seemed to think that the strategy of tying the business community into the mainland economy would work with Taiwan. The hope was that the economic and business elite would see their future so closely intertwined with China that they would become lobbyists for reunification. However, Taiwan was very different from Hong Kong and there was a strong indigenous resistance to GMD rule, which had provided bedrock support to the opposition party, the Democratic Progressive Party (DPP). National sentiment and identity could trump economic interest. The Beijing leadership received a sharp shock when, in 2000, DPP leader Chen Shui-bian was elected Taiwan's president.

The second half of the 1990s was a roller coaster ride in the relationship between China and the United States. Roiled by the tensions in cross-strait relations, the two administrations worked to settle the relationship. State visits in 1997 and 1998 between President Clinton and President Jiang improved the relationship and seemed to be setting it on a steady course for the future.

Following the successful Fifteenth Party Congress, President Jiang, in October 1997, undertook a state visit to the United States, which, despite differences over human rights, was considered a success for Jiang. He received a twenty-one-gun salute and agreed with President Clinton that summitry should form an integral part of the relationship. It was also agreed that President Clinton would visit China in 1998. Clinton announced that the ban on the export of US nuclear energy equipment to China would be lifted and military communications would be improved. Both sides confirmed their interest in China entering the WTO, although differences remained over the pace and the level of accommodation that China would have to make for this to be acceptable.

Visiting China in June 1998, President Clinton moved the relationship forward. In a speech at Peking University, he praised China's progress and expressed America's willingness to work with China, but he repeated his concern about human rights. For Clinton, certain rights were universal, such as freedom to express one's opinions, to choose one's leaders, to associate freely, and to worship freely.[40] Clinton met with actors in civil society and visited a village that had held a local election. In the 1990s, village elections had become a favorite of international NGOs, organizations, and bilateral programs. They were viewed as one bright spot for democratic progress in China. Most importantly, during his trip Clinton mentioned publicly the "three nos." Apparently he had communicated these to Jiang in the summer of 1995 and he had relayed them orally when Jiang visited the United States in 1997, but now they were made clear for all to hear. They were: no recognition of Taiwan independence, no support for two Chinas or one Taiwan and one China, and no endorsement of Taiwan's entry into any international organization for which statehood was required. This abandoned the two-decades-old policy designed to preserve the right of Taiwan's people to self-determination.[41]

The relationship was rocked again on May 7, 1999, when during the bombing of Yugoslavia by the North Atlantic Treaty Organization (NATO), US bombers accidentally struck the Chinese embassy in Belgrade, causing considerable damage and killing three reporters. The bombing had been co-ordinated by the US Central Intelligence Agency, but the CIA claimed that the wrong coordinates had been used. The event caused outrage in China and led to spontaneous demonstrations in a number of Chinese cities.[42] The demonstrations reflected the growing disillusionment and resentment of the West felt by some in China. As the downsides of reform became apparent and with the rise of corruption, inequality, and uncertainty, there was in-creased cynicism about the West's motives with respect to China. Compared to the demonstrations of 1989, those outside the US Embassy in 1999 after the Belgrade bombing showed a remarkable turnaround. Instead of setting up a Goddess of Democracy, the protestors brandished anti-US slogans and stoned the US embassy compound. The Chinese leadership had to tread care-fully not to alienate the demonstrators while at the same time maintaining its relationship with the United States.

Vice President Hu Jintao spoke on May 9, condemning the criminal con-duct of NATO and giving his support to the demonstrations as long as they did not stray to extreme or illegal conduct. Beijing authorities provided trans-portation from the university area to the protest sites to show their support, but also to keep the situation under control. To allow the steam to subside, President Clinton's apology was not broadcast for four days, and it was only on May 14 that the two countries reestablished contacts. By this time Chi-nese authorities had become concerned about the violence that was occur-ring and about the fact that some of the demonstrators were critical of Bei-jing's weak response. In August the United States made a "voluntary" payment of $4.5 million to the families of those killed and injured in the bombing, and in December a final settlement was reached under which the United States paid $28 million in compensation for damages and China paid $2.87 million for damages to the US embassy in Beijing and other diplomatic sites.

In response, some voices called for putting teeth into a genuine strategic partnership with Russia or returning to the Maoist position, with China at the head of a coalition of Third World nations. Nothing would come of these suggestions. When Yeltsin, then president of Russia, visited Beijing, he cut a forlorn figure. Again, how things had changed. Instead of dominating a Soviet empire, he came looking for aid from China. Eventually the importance of the relationship with the United States and the decision to join the WTO trumped other considerations for China.

The agreements for China's admittance to the WTO, discussed below, should have ensured a smoother relationship between the United States and China, but unexpected events still dictated the flow of the relationship. Over the longer term, as the Chinese economy boomed, differences increased over issues such as the trade deficit, the transfer of technology, and the protection of intellectual property. As it became clear to the United States that China was not becoming "more like us" and was in fact becoming a challenge to US hegemony, subsequent administrations wrestled with how to deal with the rise of China.

For the short term, George W. Bush's being sworn in as the next US president in January 2001 seemed to confirm China's worst fears. The new administration adopted a confrontational stance toward mainland China and a more sympathetic view of Taiwan. Breaking with Clinton, Bush viewed China as a strategic competitor. Two unexpected events reset the relationship, causing the new administration to revert to a position similar to that of its predecessors. It did not appear that this would be the result after the first incident, in April 2001—the collision of a US spy plane, or reconnaissance plane in US parlance, and a Chinese jetfighter, resulting in the US plane making a forced landing on Hainan Island. With the loss of Chinese life, a tense standoff ensued. The twenty-four American crew members were detained for eleven days before a resolution was reached. The Chinese side claimed that the US plane had violated Chinese airspace and sovereignty and should apologize to the Chinese people, whereas the United States refused to accept responsibility or to apologize, asserting that its plane was in international airspace. The crew and plane returned to the United States, the plane in packing crates, and the relationship hit a new low, which confirmed Chinese suspicions about the new US administration.[43]

The second major event was the Al-Qaeda attack on the World Trade Center in September 2001. In diplomatic terms, China was a major beneficiary because it was difficult for the US administration to maintain the rhetoric of China as an enemy or a threat to the United States when Al-Qaeda terrorists had flown civilian aircraft into the World Trade Center and the Pentagon. China was regarded as a positive contributor to the ensuing "War on Terror," thus placing the relationship on as good a footing as at any time since the 1980s. At the October 2001 meeting of Asia-Pacific Economic Co-operation in Shanghai, Bush stated that China and the United States stood side-by-side in combating terrorism and that the two nations could pursue constructive cooperation. China was supportive of US actions in Afghanistan, but was far more cautious about the US-led invasion of Iraq in 2003.

Jiang Zemin's Legacy

The last years of the Jiang era bequeathed two major legacies that would be crucial for China's development in the new century. The first was a fundamental shift in the nature of the CCP, welcoming private entrepreneurs to become party members. Second, at the end of 2001, China finally became a member of the WTO, leading to a further economic boom. There were challenges, however, such as the election of the DPP opposition in Taiwan, and despite the initial attempts to deal with the downsides of reform, regional and urban-rural inequality remained and corruption flourished.

When visiting Guangdong in February 2000, Jiang delivered an important speech intended both to portray himself as a great theoretician and to show that the CCP was still relevant to China's future.[44] With the traditional working class on the defensive and the rise of the new middle class and the private entrepreneurial elite, the definition of the party as the advanced representative of the proletariat was wearing thin. Jiang put forward a simple idea encapsulated as the Three Represents: the CCP was to represent the advanced social productive forces, the most advanced culture, and the fundamental interests of the majority of the people. The remainder of the year saw the unfolding of a major campaign to promote this concept, and in 2002 it was incorporated into the Party Statutes, thus situating Jiang alongside the pantheon of greats. Unlike his predecessors, however, Jiang's name was not included.

Promotion of the Three Represents portrayed the CCP as not only leading the new and dynamic areas of the economy but also leading the newly emerged technical and economic elite. This approach further distanced the CCP from exclusive reliance on the industrial proletariat it had strived to create after 1949. With the proletariat fading in the rearview mirror, the CCP claimed a broader constituency of support. It was a move in the direction of Khrushchev's idea of the party as that of the whole people. The party was not only welcoming new constituents but also was going to exercise its leadership over the rapidly developing new sectors of the economy. On July 1, at the eightieth anniversary of the party's founding, Jiang pushed the notion further. He declared that under certain circumstances, private entrepreneurs could become party members. This reversed the decision that was taken in 1989 in the wake of the demonstrations that private entrepreneurs were supporters of the students. Not surprisingly, the announcement generated howls of disapproval from the old left and the new left.

The decision to join the WTO was equally contentious, so much so that many of the details of the agreement were kept secret from the public, and Jiang, Zhu Rongji, and their close associates kept debate away from the NPC system and the government bureaucracy. WTO membership would have clear advantages because China would no longer have to deal with the whims of the US Congress over annual trading decisions, and it would help avoid rounds of antidumping accusations from the West. Instead, China's exporters would be able to access international markets under a commonly agreed-upon set of global rules, with established dispute mechanisms for infringements. Membership would also put pressure on the domestic economy to reform further in order to remain competitive. The advantage here was that the painful reforms that Jiang and Zhu wanted to pursue could be blamed on foreigners. Against the positives was the huge uncertainty about what exactly the domestic impact would be, and many were concerned that the WTO would have an adverse impact on the rural sector and the SOEs, and that the Chinese government would have to cede important levers of control.

The process leading to China's admittance to the WTO on December 11, 2001, was not entirely smooth, and the NATO bombing of Yugoslavia almost caused the Chinese leadership to postpone Premier Zhu Rongji's visit to Washington. No real progress was made during either the visit of Jiang to Washington or the reciprocal visit of Clinton to Beijing. President Clinton wrote at least three letters to Jiang in early 1998 and early 1999 expressing the hope that a decision could be reached in early 1999 and that matters could be concluded during Premier Zhu Rongji's proposed visit. In January Zhu had already told Federal Reserve chairman Alan Greenspan that China was willing to make significant concessions.[45] Indeed, given the politics in Beijing, Jiang and Zhu did offer considerable concessions, including allowing 51 percent foreign ownership for joint telecommunications ventures. During Zhu's visit the Clinton administration pushed for an even better deal, resulting in Zhu returning to China with nothing to show. When the Office of the US Trade Representative published what China was willing to offer, there was outrage in China, and Zhu was even denounced as a traitor. As noted, tensions heightened following the bombing of the Chinese embassy in Belgrade, thus putting Jiang and Zhu under unprecedented pressure at home. This did not mean that they would abandon attempts to join the WTO—this was too important for their reform program—and on November 15 the United States and China signed a bilateral agreement that marked a crucial step toward membership.

The final terms did contain concessions, but they were not as generous as those Zhu had offered in Washington. For example, foreign ownership in joint ventures could not exceed 50 percent. Progress was made on allowing foreign entities to invest in the Chinese internet, and there was a considerable reduction in key tariffs. In the 1990s Chinese tariffs were among the highest in the world; now they would be reduced from an overall average of 24.6 percent to 9.4 percent, and to 7.1 percent on US priority goods. In a major concession to US manufacturers and agricultural exporters, China agreed to relax its tight controls over trading rights and distribution services, opening up repair and maintenance sectors as well as storage and transportation. Dramatic concessions were also made in the financial and insurance sectors, agreeing to full foreign access for US banks within five years; after two years, foreign banks would be allowed to conduct local currency business with Chinese firms, and this would be extended to individuals three years later. With respect to life insurance, 50 percent ownership would be allowed (51 percent for non-life insurance), permitting wholly owned subsidiaries after two years. Last but not least, there were measures to deal with the challenges of dumping, export surges, and subsidies to SOEs, and for fifteen years after China's admission to the WTO the US would be able to retain its antidumping policy and protection against import surges. The question, of course, was whether China would fulfill these commitments; this would become the subject of considerable differences between US and Chinese administrations.

Given the disruption that these measures would cause for the Chinese economy, as well as the considerable opposition, why did Jiang Zemin and Zhu Rongji decide to push ahead so swiftly and with such determination?[46] More than ever before, China's future economic health would be intertwined with the progress of the global economy and vice versa. Basically, China had very little choice other than to join. Remaining outside would have afforded protection over the short term, but would have shut China out from the benefits of membership. First, as an outsider, China would more easily be the subject of unilateral sanctions, not only on economic issues but also on political issues. This had been impressed on the CCP leadership by the imposition of sanctions by the West following the repression of 1989. Second, China increasingly wanted to be seen as a major player on the world stage, befitting its history and rising economic development. Jiang Zemin clearly wanted China to be consulted on major global issues, and sitting outside of the premier trading organization would limit China's capacity to be involved in the global decision-making process. If China was not a member of the WTO, key decisions would be made that would have an impact on its vital interests without it having a voice.

Third, Jiang, Zhu, and their supporters concluded that without strong external disciplinary mechanisms, domestic economic reform might stall, with vested interests setting in to frustrate forward momentum. The WTO measures supported the push to increase market influences in the economy, with a particular impact on the SOEs and financial sectors. Finally, there were specific benefits that WTO entry would bring. State investment was producing diminishing returns, and by the late 1990s overall growth was beginning to slow, meaning that new sources of growth had to be tapped. Most importantly, WTO entry improved access for Chinese goods to reach major markets in Europe, Japan, and the United States, especially textiles, fashion goods, and telecommunications equipment. The "made in China" label became ubiquitous. In 1999 foreign direct investment had dropped, but WTO membership encouraged increased US and European capital to supplement that from Hong Kong and Asia. The basis was established for a twenty-first-century boom.

Party and state meetings began the preparations for entry. The Fifth Plenum of the Fifteenth CC, held in October 2000, acknowledged the need to improve competitiveness in light of China's forthcoming admittance to the WTO. The need to push on with restructuring restored Premier Zhu's position as the key economic decision maker. Policy pronouncements called for state banks to clean up their extensive bad-policy loans, and in the future they were to make loans on a more commercial basis. Clear warnings were given to the large SOEs that they would feel the impact of WTO entry and thus they had to make preparations. The plenum's focus was on the blueprint for the new Five-Year Economic Plan (2001–2005), approved at the March 2001 NPC meeting, that sought to improve competitiveness before joining the WTO. Growth was set at 7 percent, with the objective of doubling the size of the economy by 2010, a target that was easily exceeded in the post-WTO boom. The plan stressed that economic gains would feed into improvements in welfare, providing most Chinese citizens with a comfortable standard of living—a theme that was developed further at the Sixteenth Party Congress in November 2002 and by the incoming CCP leadership.

The one unexpected development was Taiwan's election of DPP member Chen Shui-bian as president, defeating the official GMD candidate. Although the Chinese leadership was aware that electoral gains at the local level raised the possibility of a transfer of power at the national level, it had not anticipated it coming so soon. Chen's victory was aided by a split in the GMD leadership, with its former secretary general running as an independent, only to see his campaign derailed by a financial corruption scandal. Both sides had learned from the tensions of 1995–1996, and the hawks were kept in check. The rhetoric from Beijing was harsh, but Beijing's actions were more calculated, waiting to see how President Chen would act. In February 2000 Beijing issued a white paper that stressed the one-China principle, claiming that anything that undermined this principle would lead to force, as would refusal to pursue a peaceful settlement.[47] Premier Zhu contributed his own harsh condemnation, commenting that anyone who promoted Taiwan independence would come to a bad end: "We will never promise to renounce the use of force."[48]

For his part, Chen Shui-bian displayed a conciliatory attitude and affirmed that he would not declare independence unless attacked by the mainland. He offered to meet China's leaders anywhere to discuss any topic, including the one-China principle. For the CCP, however, this was nonnegotiable, as there was only one China and that was the PRC. Further, Chen promised that he would not adopt former president Lee Teng-hui's state-to-state theory to govern the relationship.[49] To appease domestic concerns, Chen and his supporters noted that there was no reason to declare independence as Taiwan was already an independent, sovereign nation. Beijing responded by pursuing contacts outside of official channels while receiving delegations from other Taiwanese political parties, such as the pro-unification New Party, the GMD, and the People First Party.

Changing of the Guard: The Sixteenth Party Congress

With these major developments as the prelude, the question of succession dominated the Sixteenth Party Congress, held on November 8–14, 2002, and the Tenth NPC, held in March 2003. The meetings did not offer much new in terms of policy but they provided Jiang Zemin and Zhu Rongji an opportunity to reflect positively on their decade in power. As usual in the buildup to such an important meeting, efforts were made to keep the media on message and to prevent social protests. There were two main areas of concern. The first was the impact of the SOE layoffs. Whereas the sector had employed over 110 million people at the end of 1997, by 2001 there were 76 million employees. In the spring this had resulted in a series of demonstrations in the Northeast and in other cities. Local authorities moved swiftly to calm the unrest, using a mixture of force and attempts to redress grievances because of unpaid wages and pensions. The second area of concern was the burgeoning internet culture; new controls were put in place and certain search engines were closed down. Between May and October 2002, of the 200,000 internet cafes, 80,000 were shut down, citing operational problems and other irregularities.[50]

Jiang Zemin's political report to the Sixteenth Party Congress reaffirmed his policy priorities, calling for the party to keep up with the times. It was important that his Three Represents be accepted because they would allow entrepreneurs and members of the new middle class to join the party.[51] This would make the party more representative of the new China and would give these groups a stake in the status quo. This was a remarkable turnaround in Jiang's thinking from 1989, when he first became general secretary and stressed the crucial role of the working class and warned of the dangers that might be posed by entrepreneurs and the growing middle class.[52] Economic development was the crucial factor, and he called for people to "emancipate their minds" and to do away with ideas that hindered development as well as with regulations and practices that were detrimental. For those who were fully enjoying the benefits of the reforms, Jiang promised that a comfortable society would be created and GNP will have quadrupled by 2020.

A major issue for the congress was installation of the new leadership, the "fourth generation," which would take China into the new century. Although there were complications, this was the first and only peaceful transition of the leadership in the history of the PRC, although Jiang did retain control over the military. Hu Jintao took over as general secretary, having been proposed by Deng Xiaoping in 1992. Even though he was appointed general secretary, Hu was not designated the core of the new generation. Indeed, the period under Hu was one of consensus-building and genuine collective leadership, something that his successor Xi Jinping saw as causing stasis and avoidance of hard decisions.

Before the congress, rumors floated that Jiang Zemin was considering extending his term, something that turned out to be only partially true. In fact the congress was delayed from its intended September date to enable Jiang to visit President Bush at his Crawford, Texas, ranch and to attend the Asia-Pacific Economic Cooperation meeting in Mexico. Jiang did muddy the transition waters by retaining his position as chair of the Central Military Commission. This was justified as providing continuity and stability in foreign policy, especially when dealing with the important but often difficult relationship with the United States. But it did create confusion, and some wondered who the military listen to—the general secretary or the chair of the Central Military Commission. In September 2004 Jiang stepped down as chair and was replaced by Hu.

Despite stepping down as general secretary, Jiang retained his influence within the party apparatus. Immediately after the congress, Hu Jintao told the party that he would continue to seek instructions from Jiang on all important matters. Further, Jiang was the only departing leader to continue to receive minutes of Politburo Standing Committee meetings. The new leadership of the Standing Committee and the Politburo certainly was not of Hu's making—it was dominated by Jiang's supporters. Surprisingly, the number of members of the Standing Committee was increased from seven to nine, with five or six clearly in Jiang's camp (including the scandal-tainted Jia Qinglin). Indicating the increasing importance of domestic security, Minister of Public Security Zhou Yongkang was given a seat on the Politburo. Zhou later became the highest-level official ever to be arrested on charges of corruption.

To accommodate the concept of the Three Represents, the Party Statutes incorporated some key amendments and included the Three Represents in the preamble. The definition of the nature of the CCP was changed, as it now was the vanguard not only of the working class but also of all Chinese people and all its nationalities. With an expanded definition of who could be a member, the door was open for private entrepreneurs and the new middle class to join the party. In reality, this was already the case, as a significant number were already party members, and many had made their wealth either through party connections or through their party positions.[53]

The stage was set for the new century with the Chinese economy booming, but serious cleavages existed between the haves and the have-nots. There were still challenges for regional development: the inadequate public services in the countryside and the integration of migrants into the rapidly expanding urban areas. It would fall to Hu and the new premier, Wen Jiabao, to come to terms with these challenges, as well as to deal with China's new, prominent role in global affairs. The results were a mixed bag.

CHAPTER ELEVEN

The WTO World and China's Rise

2002–2012

★

Some regard the years under the leadership of Hu Jintao and Wen Jiabao as a time of drift, despite the economic boom that followed China's admission to the WTO. However, although there were continuities with the Jiang Zemin years, such as the ineffective railing against corruption, there were also significant divergences in policy, and certain trends were set in motion that Xi Jinping would advance further. First, Hu and Wen promoted a form of populist authoritarianism. As with all CCP leaderships, they were tough on dissenting views. But Hu and Wen had spent significant parts of their careers in the poorer parts of western China rather than in the wealthy east like Jiang Zemin and Zhu Rongji, and under the slogan "Putting the people first" they set about addressing the plight of those who had not fared so well during the reform era. Second, although economic growth accelerated, the negative impacts became more apparent and the new leadership sought to emphasize sustainability and the quality of growth. Third, Hu proved to be more orthodox in his thinking than Jiang, but he did continue the tough line on deviance.

Fourth, the reality of China's growth and its growing influence in the global economy led to a shift in Jiang Zemin's essentially pro-American position. Hu made it clear that China was willing to look beyond the United States to develop its international profile, and he sought to form alliances with countries that were not necessarily friendly with America. This process promoted the growing nationalism, as many Chinese became disillusioned with the West and were proud of China's domestic achievements. A high point in national pride was reached when China hosted the 2008 summer Olympics, and when it celebrated the sixtieth anniversary of the founding of the PRC. Disillusionment with the West sharpened after the 2008–2009 financial crisis, when influential economists and officials reassessed what could be learned from the developed countries and they began to have more confidence in their own experience.

Scientific Development and Balancing Growth

The Tenth NPC, in March 2003, completed the leadership transition and provided the outgoing premier, Zhu Rongji, with a chance to outline the successes of the previous five years.[1] The appointment of Wen Jiabao as premier and Hu Jintao as president as well as the other NPC appointments completed the first peaceful and uneventful transition of power in the history of the PRC. However, Jiang Zemin still remained as chair of the Central Military Commission. The one further wrinkle for the new leadership was the low level of support for Jiang Zemin's confidant, Zeng Qinghong, as vice president. In the NPC, four hundred withheld support, which is remarkable given the carefully controlled environment of CCP politics; this matched the low level of support Li Peng had received in the vote for premier in 1993. Zeng's poor showing was said to have angered Jiang.[2]

The delegates to the congress reflected the urban bias of the post-Mao years and the impact of Jiang's promotion of the Three Represents. In a clear structural bias, urban representation was four times that of rural representation, with one delegate for every 260,000 urban residents as opposed to one delegate for every 960,000 rural residents. Reflecting the shift in the nature of the party, workers and peasants had made up 54 percent of the delegates in the 1950s but they accounted for only 19 percent in 2003.[3] At the Second Session of the congress, in March 2004, the Constitution was revised to protect private property, and the number of delegates working in the non-state sector rose from 48 in 1998 to 118 in 2004.

The suggestions for administrative reform were far more modest than those in 1998, but two new commissions—to oversee the banking sector and asset administration—were established, along with a new food and drug administration, continuing the move toward building a regulatory state. Of symbolic significance was the change in the name of the State Development and Planning Commission to the State Development and Reform Commission.

This organization became the most powerful economic and political agency, retaining all of the powers of its predecessor.

Zhu's report suggested continuity in policy, including policy to restructure the loss-making SOEs. The new leadership did offer a few tweaks to the policy, while trying to shift the emphasis to more sustainable growth. Significantly, the first two trips taken by newly anointed General Secretary Hu Jintao were not to the developed coastal areas but to Xibaipo and Inner Mongolia. Xibaipo lies to the southwest of Beijing and it is where Mao Zedong plotted the army's final push on the capital in 1949. In his speech at Xibaipo, Hu marked out a different approach from that of his predecessor, while drawing a line of legitimacy from Mao, mentioning more than sixty times the need for "plain living and arduous struggle."[4]

Despite this intent, the transition was blown off course by an unexpected development. As the incoming leaders surveyed the challenges that lay ahead, they never thought that their first test would come from the rural health sector with the outbreak of severe acute respiratory syndrome (SARS). This new illness broke out in Guangdong province and then spread not only throughout China but also globally. The international community was not confident that China had the capacity to deal with such outbreaks effectively and honestly. Local authorities and the Guangdong authorities both tried to cover up the outbreak and its extent, and some at the central level must have been aware of the dangers even before the problem was admitted publicly.[5] The delay derived from systemic faults—such as poor coordination within the bureaucracy, and incentives that prioritized social stability over getting truthful information to the public—and the leadership chose the cover-up out of fear of inciting panic.

Later, in early 2020, General Secretary Xi Jinping was confronted with the same challenge following the outbreak of the new coronavirus, which causes the disease COVID-19, in the central Chinese city of Wuhan. The response revealed the same problems of governance: failure to regulate wet markets, a breeding ground for disease, and not reporting in a timely and honest fashion. However, once the Center was clearly aware of the challenge, Xi acted forcefully to impose draconian measures to attempt to control the spread. Perhaps too little too late for the international community.

With the NPC out of the way, Premier Wen could focus on the challenge presented by the SARS epidemic. In mid-April following a Politburo meeting the leadership began to take action. The mayor of Beijing and the minister of public health were dismissed. Madam Wu Yi, a tough administrator, was placed in charge, and Wang Qishan, who would later become vice president, was moved from Hainan to serve as acting mayor of Beijing. The new leadership appeared business-like, open, and willing to adopt modern management techniques. This created an air of optimism that there might be movement in the political realm, with increased transparency and a more aggressive role for the press. Such views were soon nipped in the bud as the press began to extoll the virtues of the party in dealing with the challenge. Constraints were put back into place. The whistle-blower who called attention to the virus, and was at first hailed as a hero, was shunned. In 2004 he was briefly detained for writing a letter to the premier calling for a reassessment of the events of 1989. The crisis did provide the new leadership with credibility to pursue its approach of focusing on social development to accompany economic growth.

In May 2003 Hu Jintao unveiled his own approach to streamlining and improving SOE performance. At the Sixteenth Party Congress in 2002, Jiang Zemin had called for diversification of ownership, while still referring to SOEs as the pillar of the national economy. A major concern was the corruption and speculation that had resulted from the selling off and management buyouts of the smaller SOEs; some estimates place the loss of state assets at $41 billion. Hu's proposal was to separate ownership and management and, for the SOEs that were dispersed, to centralize management across a range of ministries under a new central State-owned Assets and Supervision Administration Commission (SASAC), with counterparts at the lower levels of government. The SASAC was established in June 2003 and initially oversaw 196 of the largest SOEs, with combined assets of $834 billion. The objective remained the creation of a small number of thirty to fifty major players that would be modeled after the South Korean *chaebols* and thus would be able to compete in the global economy. Over time the number under SASAC supervision was reduced, with only ninety-six remaining as of June 2020.

The October 2003 party plenum adopted a decision on the socialist market economy that appeared to level the playing field between the state sector, the non-state sector, and the foreign sectors of the economy.[6] Although the SOE sector was still referred to as the mainstay of the economy, the decision stated that all players would enjoy equal rights, legal status, and rights of development. The goal was the creation of a "unified, open and orderly modern market system." In practice, to this day this has never been the case.

The power and sense of entitlement of the SOE sector is strong, and its monopolistic or quasi-monopolistic position in the economy has made some SOEs extremely profitable.[7] The former chief of Sinopec has referred to the SOEs as "the eldest son of the Republic," arguing that if they did not enjoy a monopoly, then who would?[8] This was a theme that had been promoted in the official press, citing the "most honored place" of the SOEs.[9] The SOEs form a core component of the CCP's patronage system, with the CEO, party secretary, and chairs of the boards of the largest enterprises appointed by the party's Central Organization Department. In the revolving door of CCP politics, a large percentage of provincial governors and vice governors have spent some of their careers working in the SOE sector.[10]

The profitability of the SOEs led to the question of who should benefit from the profits, given that, after all, they were "owned by the whole people." In April–May 2005 the role of the SASAC was strengthened, with new regulations that prohibited management buyouts of large SOEs. As with related measures, this revealed the statist thrust to policy, and in December 2006 the State Council announced that state capital would exert total control in seven strategic industries: armaments, oil and petrochemicals, civil aviation, power, coal, shipping, and telecommunications. This thrust had been signaled earlier—for example, in September 2006 when the Ministry of Commerce was given greater powers to block foreign purchases of Chinese companies. The vice minister justified this by claiming that the objective of the foreign companies was to eliminate competition and monopolize the domestic market.

The question of who should control the SOE profits attained a sense of urgency as the Hu–Wen leadership sought to expand social welfare programs. The funds were significant, with the 152 SOEs under SASAC control earning 1 trillion yuan in profits in 2007—around 4 percent of GDP. The Ministry of Finance sought greater control over these profits, claiming that it had a broader mandate on how to disburse funds than did the SASAC, which either retained the profits or merely reinvested them in the enterprises.[11] In September 2007 the SASAC was granted a revenue stream but in return it received a lower share of profits than it had been pushing for. The SOEs were to turn over 5 to 10 percent of their profits; to sweeten the pill, the corporate income tax was reduced from 33 percent to 25 percent. Revealing the power of the SOEs both as corporations and as political players, during the next several years they failed to turn over the minimum of 5 percent, and they only averaged about 2 percent. In 2013 the decision was made that by 2020 the SOEs would turn over 30 percent of their profits in the form of dividends, most of which the Ministry of Finance would allocate for social welfare.

While grappling with the SOE sector, the leadership also decided to shift away from rapid economic growth to "scientific development" in order to balance growth with equity and to deal with the environmental consequences of uncontrolled development. The breakneck speed of growth had exacerbated the inequalities between the hinterland and the coastal areas, which received most of the foreign direct investment and were better positioned for export-led growth. Despite the "Develop the West" initiative, the inland provinces were falling behind. Expansive growth also strained China's resources and energy, leading to a significant rise in imports. As things settled down in 2004, Hu and Wen recognized that the overheating economy, racing along at 10 percent, had to be tamed. The investment boom that had followed China's joining the WTO led to the building of many trophy projects, which in turn led to corruption. Inflation was increasing as input prices rose due to the pressure on resources and energy. Measures to cool the economy, such as raising interest rates and curtailing large projects, had little effect, but the global financial crisis of 2008–2009 did temporarily calm things down.

In preparing the new five-year program for 2006–2010, the October 2005 plenum codified Hu Jintao's approach, promulgating a concept of "scientific development" based on a people-centered approach. This continued the shift from extensive to intensive growth.[12] Although the party saw the next few years as a potential golden period for development, it did warn that there would be serious challenges in the next five years—including pressure on resources and the environment, blind investments, and poor regional coordination. It highlighted the weaknesses of the scientific and research sectors and called for a strengthening of China's independent innovation capabilities. The latter, drawn together under the slogan "Made in China 2025," has been a key theme of the leadership under Xi Jinping.

The Three-Dimensional Rural Problem

Wen Jiabao was particularly concerned about the challenges in rural China, which were expressed in the slogan "Three-dimensional rural problem." The three dimensions were peasants, the countryside, and agriculture. Unrest in the countryside caused by high fees and levies and illegal, or questionable, land seizures brought the issue of rural policy back to the center of policy making. Premier Wen introduced a number of specific measures to redress the complaints, which culminated in 2006 with talk of building a "new socialist countryside." In a symbolic gesture, in 2004 the CC and the State Council revived the tradition that the first document of the year would cover rural issues. The 2006 document laid out in stark terms the problems: "At present, agricultural and rural development are still arduously crawling uphill, basic infrastructure is weak, rural social service development is backward, and the contradictions of a widening urban–rural income gap remain stark."[13] One of Wen's key advisers on rural affairs stated that agriculture and rural savings had fueled the boom in the cities and the coastal regions, but now it was time for the money to be redirected to the countryside.[14]

The first measure was to break up the system of subsidies going through the grain procurement bureaus. These bureaus were kept afloat by loans from the Agricultural Development Bank, and the loans were to be repaid after the grain was sold. The bureaus controlled about 80 percent of the wholesale grain trade and 50 percent of the retail grain trade, employing over one million people. The state obsession with grain self-sufficiency placed the procurement bureaus in a powerful position, and they often exploited this to force the state to pump in more money. The problem was that very few subsidies were passed along to the farmers. In Anhui province, for example, the bureaus received 4 billion yuan annually, but only 400 million yuan reached the farmers. Not surprisingly, corruption was rife, with officials buying at low, government-set prices and selling at the higher market prices. In June 2003 the government announced that the subsidies would be paid directly to the farmers, who would be free to make their own decisions about what to plant, and the farmers would receive the subsidies regardless of whether the market slumped. The state grain procurement bureaus, no longer underpinned by their preferential loans, now had to compete with private merchants, and many bureaucrats were laid off as a result.

The second major move was to eliminate illegal fees and levies. All levies were converted into taxes, and subsequently the agricultural taxes were abolished entirely. Local governments strapped for cash were very inventive in terms of the types of fees that they would charge.[15] In 2004 Wen called for the agricultural tax to be decreased by at least 1 percent per year and to be abolished completely within five years. This was an extraordinary shift to remove a tax that had existed for over 2,000 years and had been a core component of local funding. By early 2005, twenty-two provinces had abolished the agricultural tax, and in 2006 the tax was abolished completely. Interestingly, this did not seem to have a significant impact on farmers' overall incomes.[16] It did affect some provinces' income. Although the overall share of the tax in the fiscal budget was small (less than 2 percent), in some provinces it was important. In Anhui it accounted for 12.1 percent, and in Henan, 11.3 percent. Consequently, the government provided support to those provinces where the agricultural tax had exceeded 5 percent.

These measures and other proposals were pulled together in 2006 under the slogan "building a new socialist countryside." The intention was to maintain the farmers' incomes through gains in agricultural productivity and improvements in the quality of village governance. An instruction went out for governments at all levels to regard rural issues as their top priority. The policy package also called for eliminating the restrictions on labor migration, eradicating discrimination against migrants, and increasing investment in education, health, and infrastructure. Grain and livestock subsidies and price supports were to be regularized to boost income.

Following this, the third major initiative pursued by Wen Jiabao was to reduce the illegal land seizures by local governments and to seek to raise revenue by converting the land into development land. This conversion allowed local governments to reap huge windfall profits that were not passed on to the farmers whose land had been taken. With other avenues for revenue closing off, revenue had to come from somewhere, and land conversion offered the potential for huge government extractions and personal gain. The loophole allowing this exploitation is the stipulation in the Constitution that all land in the countryside is collectively owned. The problem is that there is no clear definition of what is the collective and thus who represents the collective interest. In some cases it is considered the natural village, in others it is considered the administrative village, while in yet others it is considered the township. This legitimized the appropriation of land by higher-level authorities.

Those villages in Guangdong province that retained control over collective land thrived, attracting outside investment and setting up cooperative economic entities to divide up the benefits among all registered villagers.[17] In Yantian village this enabled the locals to amass unprecedented wealth. At its peak the village was home to 400 foreign-invested enterprises, employing 80,000 migrant laborers and producing wealth for the 3,500 registered residents. From the village collective, each household received about 50,000 yuan, and this was supplemented by income from their own business ventures.[18]

The old village of Yantian.

Yantian in 2019.

In September 2006 an urgent notice was issued to control land supply, stating that local leaders would be penalized if they did not investigate illegal land sales. Moreover, they would be prosecuted if they sold land below its minimum market price. Major cities were being surrounded by golf courses, development zones, and other trophy projects, with the surge in fixed-asset investment coming from land transactions. In the following month the State Council authorized the Ministry of Land Resources to supervise and overhaul land use by local governments. Nine regional bureaus operated under a national office.

In 2007 the Ministry of Land Resources noted that in some cities in west and central China almost 80 percent of new land projects were illegal. In January 2006, as reported in the *People's Daily*, Wen had already criticized the illegal seizures of land intended to raise public funds, and he called on all levels of government to take this issue seriously. At a Politburo meeting on January 27, Hu Jintao took up the theme and urged resolution of the major contradictions and problems faced in the countryside. Failure to rise to this challenge would prevent China from building a relatively prosperous society. This did lead to some action; in early 2008 the Ministry of Land Resources announced that some 3,000 people had been disciplined and 530 had incurred criminal penalties.[19]

However, the speculation did not stop, and in the first half of 2008, there were 25,231 cases of illegal land use reported nationwide.[20] Determining how much authority to give farmers over the land they worked was tricky; the words "privatization" and "sale" were taboo because all rural land was supposed to be owned collectively. The idea of providing farmers with ownership rights rather than use rights was opposed by a wide range of critics. Those on the left felt that private ownership had no place in a socialist economy. Some reformers feared that if farmers owned their land, they might be tricked into selling it cheaply, thereby depriving themselves of their best guarantee against hardship.

As a result, the new CCP regulations released in October 2008 were rather unclear. They permitted farmers to lease their contracted farmland or to transfer their land-use rights to make farming more efficient by increasing scale and allowing agribusinesses to develop. This was viewed as a crucial element in reaching the goal of doubling farmers' incomes by 2020. However, the regulations did not imply that land could be bought and sold. Collective ownership of land was maintained, and farmers were only permitted to "sublet, lease, swap, and transfer" land rights. Furthermore, such actions

Migrant work in a wealthy village.

were not to change land use; this provision was meant to put an end to large amounts of rural land being converted to urban use.[21]

The new leadership made a start at coming to grips with the rural challenges, but the regulations remained unclear and left much room for local officials to continue to exploit for personal gain. As with the reforms of the SOEs, the key challenges persisted, and these early measures did not deal with them effectively. One area where progress was made was in the provision of social welfare guarantees for rural dwellers and migrants who had moved to the cities in search of work.

People-Centered Welfare

Whereas the welfare reforms under Jiang Zemin and Zhu Rongji had focused on shoring up support systems for urban China, Hu and Wen shifted the focus to the countryside and the migrant community. Some view the Hu–Wen years as a lost decade and the shift to collective leadership as no leadership, but this was not the case with respect to social policy. Policy stressed a people-centered approach to build a harmonious society. This centered on supporting those who had not thrived during the reform era, underscored by an emphasis on the need to maintain social stability. The alarm bell had rung with the outbreak of SARS—which led to the realization that unexpected events could threaten the entire system. Hu and Wen moved away from the idea prevalent throughout the 1990s that a rising tide would lift all boats, having seen that in some areas the state would have to step in. A more coherent policy framework was developed based on identification of the vulnerable groups, such as the rural poor and the migrant communities, which were then provided with targeted support. Policy was gradually shifting from short-term safety nets to a more integrated, comprehensive system. Greater guarantees were given to the rural population, and welfare structures were developed to help the huge number of urban migrants who had left their rural homes.

The system was to become more inclusive because it was based on the notion of citizenship rather than place of birth or residence. However, considerable differences remained between the services for town and country and between the migrants and the official urban inhabitants. Inequality was rising. The Gini coefficient—a key indicator of social inequality—had increased from 0.33 in 1978 to 0.49 in 2005. In one generation, China had shifted from being one of the most egalitarian countries in Asia to one of the least equal. Wealth had become highly concentrated, and in June 2005 the National Statistical Bureau reported that the top 10 percent of the population controlled 45 percent of the wealth. Those at the bottom of the ladder only shared 1.4 percent of the wealth. Disposable income of the richest cohort was 1.8 times that of poorer Chinese. The urban–rural income ratio had also increased to about 3:1, one of the highest discrepancies in the world. The gap was most pronounced in the poorer regions. It was 2.26:1 in Shanghai, but it was 4.34:1 in the poor southwest province of Guizhou. In the rural areas, neonatal mortality per 1,000 live births was twice that in urban China and infant mortality per 1,000 live births was three times as high. Surveys in late 2005 found that medical costs, including medicine, amounted to 7.85 percent of urban annual disposable income versus 20.98 percent in the rural areas.[22] The structural inequality in access to education and health care had to be addressed as it was preventing or reducing opportunities for many of China's youth.

Addressing these inequalities was all the more important for a political party that still called itself Communist and stressed the socialist nature of its system. The clear inequities could have fueled opposition, and they did draw criticism from both the old left and the new left. Much of the inequality resulted from conscious policy choices, which was increasingly pointed out in published articles. The trenchant criticism came not only from voices outside the party but also from the key State Council think tank, the Development Research Center. Its 2005 report asserted that health-care reforms had failed the rural poor, and it blamed the government for ignoring its responsibility to provide this important public good.[23]

Beginning in 2002 the government stepped up experimentation with rural pensions; in 2003 a major push was launched to extend coverage of rural cooperative medical insurance; in 2006 agricultural taxes were abolished; in 2007 rural residents no longer were expected to pay miscellaneous school fees, and free compulsory education was introduced for rural children; and also in 2007 the leadership began extending minimum living support payments to all those eligible in rural China.[24] These measures were popular with the recipients. Our 2007 survey shows that just over 50 percent of the respondents felt that the new medical-insurance scheme could protect them from the consequences of major illnesses, with some 70 percent noting that they would enroll in the scheme in the following year. Only 5 percent responded that they would not enroll again.

The Hu–Wen social policy agenda was pulled together at the October 2006 party plenum that highlighted the slogan "building a harmonious society." The plenum was remarkable for its focus on the social challenges, while still stressing that economic development remained the core of work. This provided content to the slogan that Hu Jintao had first raised in 2004. It reaffirmed the commitment to improving life in the rural areas, moderating the impact of economic growth on the environment, and providing more opportunities for disgruntled citizens to provide feedback.

Importantly, the plenum communiqué recognized the need for the party to come to grips with the expanding moral vacuum in China. Explanations based on Marxist theory and references to the socialist character of China's development bore little resemblance to the lives that most citizens were leading in an increasingly tough socioeconomic environment. The party called for a socialist core value system that would lay the moral and ideological foundations to underpin the policies for the harmonious society. In addition to the stress on Marxism, a "socialist sense of honor and disgrace" was to be developed, a concept that Hu had first raised in March.[25] This guidance would help citizens distinguish right from wrong. Hu was not willing to cede the moral high ground to a revival of neo-Confucianism. This challenge of providing a credible party-sponsored belief system persists to the present day, with the continued emphasis on Marxism combined with elements of Confucianism and nationalism all rolled into Xi Jinping's slogan of the China Dream.

One potential source of disruption to social stability was the massive number of migrants who had moved into the cities and who faced an uncertain future. Among them were second-generation migrants who had never experienced full rural life but who were not accepted as true city residents. During the 1980s and 1990s, policy initiatives had already sought to unlink employment from household registration status.[26] In particular, this favored those with much sought-after skills and higher education by facilitating the transfer of registration. Hu Jintao and Wen Jiabao engineered a shift as their policies sought to decouple welfare services and benefits from household registration. This was designed to help the rural poor and the migrants. The prior notion that migrants did not need welfare support because the land they worked in their home villages provided insurance was no longer tenable. Many migrants, together with their families, were now permanent fixtures in the towns, and many no longer had any land back in the village. Up until 2002–2003, household registration reforms mainly benefited investors and those who were well educated; this reflected the more elitist thrust of Jiang Zemin and Zhu Rongji's policy. The Hu–Wen leadership refocused the policy on providing training and social welfare coverage for migrant workers.

During 2002–2003, measures were introduced to improve the lot of migrant workers, even though, in theory, they had already been brought into pension schemes in 1999. In June 2002 it was announced that migrant workers should be able to take out industrial injury insurance; in November 2002 migrants were declared to be a part of the working class, which was an important improvement in their status; in January 2003 the State Council confirmed that migrants should be accorded equal treatment with urban residents when applying for work, and urban education departments had to recognize schools for migrant children and provide them with equal education; and in 2006 the State Council set up a joint committee to coordinate rural migration affairs across different ministries.

Momentum was maintained when the NPC adopted the national Social Insurance Law, which went into effect July 1, 2011. The law also promoted steps to reduce, and perhaps eventually eliminate, the distinctions between administrative units and the urban–rural divide. This was the first law that combined urban as well as rural residents working in all enterprises with five mandatory types of insurance: pensions, basic medical insurance, unemployment insurance (these three are paid for by employer and employee), work-related injury, and maternity insurance (these two are paid for by the employer). The law sought to free up labor mobility by allowing individuals to transfer the first three types of insurance should they relocate elsewhere for work. Especially important was the provision that medical insurance could be paid for in one city but the service could be claimed in another. Initially pensions were to be managed at the provincial level, with the intention of eventually moving to a nationwide scheme.[27]

While the party paid attention to redressing the inequalities and social welfare challenges as a means to ensure social stability, the other equally important step was to exert stronger control over society to prevent the spread of dangerous views. This entailed strengthening the capacity of the party as a ruling entity rather than as a revolutionary, mobilizing organization.

Keeping the Lid on Social Tensions

The impact of SARS and the way it was handled led to some optimism about the possibility for revisiting political reform. Despite occasional nods in this direction by Premier Wen Jiabao, such hopes were soon deflated. Instead of political reform, what Hu Jintao offered was administrative tightening, stricter control over society, and attempts to reassert the authority of the party. Insofar as there were reforms, they focused on promoting inner-party democracy.

At the September 2004 party plenum, Jiang Zemin stepped down from his final leadership position as chair of the Central Military Commission, turning the post over to Hu Jintao. At the same plenum, for the first time discussion of governing capacity was placed at the center of the deliberations. In the run-up to the plenum, articles appeared in the official press outlining the challenges the party faced and the poor quality of many officials, especially at the local levels. One senior official noted that the party faced a dual challenge: promoting reform and opening-up, while "consolidating its ruling status."[28]

The plenum's decision rang all the usual bells and credited the party with having been chosen to rule by both history and the people, a refrain that would be repeated by the Xi Jinping leadership. Ignoring the Great Leap Forward and the Cultural Revolution, the decision praised the party for delivering decent living standards. However, it did sound a warning not only about the problems of the capabilities of some officials and their illegal actions but also that "it is not easy for a proletarian political party to seize power, and still less easy for it to hold onto power, especially over a long period." In a time of peace, it was necessary to think of danger. As a practical guide, little was offered beyond the slogans of Deng Xiaoping Thought, the Three Represents, building a harmonious socialist society, and so forth. The plenum did reconfirm the commitment to global integration to maintain an "independent foreign policy of peace."[29] One goal for the new millennium was to Sinicize Marxism and render it timely and popular, something that Mao Zedong had supposedly completed in the previous century and a project that Xi Jinping would later claim to have completed.

More revealing was Hu Jintao's unpublished speech to the plenum. Many of those who were aware of the speech were shocked by the harshness of his tone, a toughness that he had already displayed in his time in Tibet. Hu was no closet liberal. Mindful perhaps of the fate of Hu Yaobang and Zhao Ziyang in the eighties, he attacked the spread of bourgeois liberalization promoted by foreign and domestic groups. His solution was a crackdown that followed the plenum. He referred to party members who advocated political reform as creators of turmoil. Although the context is unclear, he praised Cuba and North Korea for their control over ideology and the flow of information, despite their "temporary" economic problems, claiming that they had always adhered to a sound political line.

The sense of threat that the party felt was demonstrated by the January 2005 launch of an eighteen-month major Campaign to Maintain the Advanced Nature of the Party to outline and reinforce the norms to which individual party members were expected to conform. Party members' lack of discipline and decline in morals had been clear for some time. An unannounced decision, made at the Sixteenth Party Congress in 2002, led to careful experimentation.[30] Although the campaign highlighted Jiang Zemin's Three Represents, Hu clearly intended to use the campaign to inculcate his own ideas among party members and through this to consolidate his own power as the head of the party. The campaign revived Liu Shaoqi's notion of self-cultivation, for which Liu had been criticized during the Cultural Revolution because of its Confucian ethos. The objective was to strengthen socialist ideology and the leading role of the party. During the study period, members were judged on their performance as a basis for deciding whether they should continue with their work.

Showing how much the world had changed, the campaign was greeted with cynicism and with so many jokes that the party had to send out a directive insisting that party members only use the full name of the campaign and not abbreviations that could easily be turned into puns. One enterprising group set up a website, where the appropriate self-criticisms for officials at different levels could be downloaded for a fee. All the busy officials had to do was to put their names in the correct place and personalize the details where necessary; many officials were annoyed that the campaign detracted from the priority work of economic development. Responding to criticism, Vice President Zeng Qinghong claimed that the campaign would raise the quality of party organizations so they could better serve the people.[31]

The leadership were unnerved by the prospect that society might slip out of their control, and by the continuing corruption. This led to a tougher political atmosphere in the following period. Playing into this was the outcome of the "colored revolutions" in Central Asia that had led to the overthrow of authoritarian regimes. This was deeply disturbing to the party leadership and raised concerns that an emerging civil society could provide a catalyst for change. Foreign foundations came under greater scrutiny; those funded by Washington were interpreted as being behind the fall of the pro-Beijing authoritarian regime in Kyrgyzstan and the upheaval in Uzbekistan. At a Politburo meeting, Hu Jintao called on state security and police officials to raise their vigilance against "underground organizations as well as NGOs."[32] This led to "interviews" with Chinese NGOs that received foreign funding and with the Chinese staff of international NGOs, as the Ministry of Foreign Affairs established a new unit to manage, review, and oversee the work of foreign NGOs.

More controls on society followed. Restraints on reporting in the media were noticeably tightened and more topics were placed on the banned list. The Propaganda Department was particularly aggressive, and a number of public intellectuals were referred to in terms that had only been rarely used since the Cultural Revolution. Some were specifically referred to as counterrevolutionaries. Neoliberalism came in for special criticism, even though economic policy had moved significantly in that direction.

The new media and the internet remained a headache for the CCP, and so more regulations were introduced to try to gain party oversight and control. In June 2005 all Chinese websites and bloggers were required by the end of the month to register with the authorities the real names of all persons involved or run the risk of being closed down. Further regulations tightened a noose around cyberspace. On September 25 the State Council Information Office and the Ministry of Information Industry issued joint rules on administering news information on the internet and banning its use to either incite unlawful assembly or carry out activities on behalf of illegal civil organizations. In addition to banning and punishing, the party also employed an army of people to post positive comments and to drive debate in cyberspace—these people were called the "50-cent party."

The fact that the CCP would not tolerate any independent organizing was signaled clearly by its response to the online promulgation of Charter '08 to mark the December 10 anniversary of the Universal Declaration of Human Rights. The document called for an end to authoritarian one-party rule and, in its place, presented a vision for a rights-based society. The inspiration for the Chinese document was the Czech Charter '77, which appealed for freedom from Soviet dominance and rule by the Communist Party. The rapid spread of Charter '08 on the internet both within China and overseas confirmed party concerns about the potentially damaging role of the new media. The authorities moved swiftly and arrested two key figures; others were placed under house arrest and still others faced interrogation. One of the key organizers, Liu Xiaobo, was sentenced to eleven years in prison in December 2009. In 2010 he was awarded the Nobel Peace Prize, but in 2017 he died of liver cancer while under detention. The charter produced a mixed response among the socially engaged community. Some felt that the time was not ripe for such a charter, while others felt it was too abstract and did not pay sufficient attention to the plight of marginalized and vulnerable groups.

However, Charter '08 marked a turning point in the relationship between activist intellectuals, lawyers, and professionals and the party.[33] An alternative approach to the charter was distilled in the April 2010 Citizens' Commitment Pledge, which called on people to behave as citizens and in both private and public to adhere to basic principles to transform China. Importantly, there was a call to adhere to the rule of law and to protect those rights guaranteed in the Chinese Constitution and in Chinese laws.[34] The pledge approach led to the launch in May 2012 of the New China Citizens' Movement, which was subsequently crushed.

The other key concern for the leadership was the continuation of the high levels of corruption, and again popular campaigns and high-court politics became entwined. Just before the Sixth Plenum, held in October 2006,

Shanghai party secretary Chen Liangyu was dismissed on charges of corruption. He was also a rival to Hu Jintao and had clashed with Wen Jiabao over the reorientation of economic policy. Again, an accusation of corruption was the weapon of choice in elite politics. Chen's fall came as a result of a security fund scandal that had been developing in Shanghai for several years. When the head of the Municipal Labor and Social Security Bureau was dismissed in August 2006 for lending money from the fund to projects to which he had a personal connection, the writing was on the wall for Chen. Chen was seen as part of an informal Shanghai gang, headed by Jiang Zemin, although it was said that Jiang agreed with his removal. In the run-up to the National Party Congress set for 2007, Hu's position was strengthened further by the death of Politburo Standing Committee member Huang Ju (one of Jiang Zemin's associates) in June 2007 and the pending retirement of Jia Qinglin, whose time serving in Beijing and Xiamen had been blighted with alleged involvement in major corrupt activities.

The need to be seen as grappling with corruption was important—an online opinion poll carried out by a state-managed website just before the March 2009 NPC session discovered that 75.5 percent of the respondents ranked corruption and cleaner government as their number one concern.[35] Since the beginning of the reforms, party leaders had railed against the blight of corruption, but they had been unable to stem its growth. Hu Jintao was no more successful in these efforts. In addition to the land seizures noted above, real estate speculation was a major area of corruption. In early June 2006, Beijing's vice mayor in charge of overseeing construction at the venues for the Olympic games was suddenly dismissed when it was revealed that he had been taking kickbacks from land sales. If this had not warned Chen Liangyu, he should have taken notice of Hu's warnings to the Politburo at the end of June when Hu condemned corruption for eroding the party's standing. In late August the Politburo dusted off old regulations from 1997 that required all officials to provide details (internally, not publicly of course) of their personal financial affairs.

The press was full of exposés revealing to the public the extent of corruption, and the nation's top auditor warned that looting and misuse of government-held property were destroying the value of many assets and constituted the nation's most serious threat. The annual report of the National Audit Bureau suggested that no central government ministry or organization was immune to malpractice. Public cynicism was increased by rumors of the involvement of senior officials and their families, including Premier Wen

Jiabao's wife, who was alleged to be involved in setting policy in the jewelry business, and his son, who was also thought to have questionable business dealings.[36]

Despite the attention and scrutiny, the problems continued. The June 2009 audit report to the NPC revealed that 26.77 billion yuan of embezzled public funds had been recovered, making one wonder just how much remained hidden. Some cases were quite spectacular. In 2009 the former head of Sinopec, the oil and gas conglomerate, was said to have taken bribes amounting to 196 million yuan and had shared the same mistress with the party secretary of Qingdao city. Together, before being caught, the three had set up a string of businesses in Hong Kong, Shenzhen, and Qingdao. Given this situation and public dissatisfaction, it is not surprising that upon taking power Xi Jinping made the control of corruption his number one priority.

Power Consolidation, Crises, and Games

The Seventeenth Party Congress, held on October 15–21, 2007, and the Tenth NPC session, held in March 2008, were high points for the Hu–Wen leadership because they consolidated the leaders' positions and policy approaches.[37] However, shortly thereafter it was buffeted by a series of unexpected crises. The ship was eventually righted by the summer Olympics and the ceremonies for the sixtieth anniversary of CCP rule. By this time the politics of succession was already setting in.

The party congress showcased a Hu Jintao who was clearly in charge, but not everything was going his way, and his populist policies were tempered by those who favored a primary focus on economic growth rather than redistribution. Hu's report stressed, in no uncertain terms, the centrality of, and the need to persist with, reform and opening-up. It might seem strange that after almost three decades such a strong reaffirmation was still necessary. Reform and opening-up were defined as the crucial choice that would decide China's destiny and rejuvenate the nation. The old left and the new left had strongly criticized the negative impacts of reform, and prior to the congress there had been heated debates about the future direction of reform—so it was clear why the reaffirmation was needed. Hu's own slogans of a harmonious society and people-centered development had been seized upon by those concerned about the increasing inequality and weak social justice to criticize the outcomes of the reforms. Neoliberalism came in for particular attack, with claims that it was undermining the party and changing the nature of socialism.[38] In contrast, defenders of the reforms argued that the problems, including corruption, came from insufficient, not excessive, reform.

Hu's report downplayed his slogan of building a harmonious society, although it was adopted in the revised statutes.[39] Instead, pride of place was given to the scientific outlook on development. Adoption in the statutes was a strong positive for Hu as it was only at the end of his second term as general secretary that Jiang Zemin's concept of the Three Represents was included. On this basis, Hu was doing well. Importantly, the concept of the scientific outlook on development had economic development at its core, and it called on the party to consider development as the top priority in governing and rejuvenating the country. In a break with the past, the only specific economic target noted by Hu was a shift from quadrupling GDP by 2020 to quadrupling GDP per capita, evincing confidence in the continued growth potential of the Chinese economy. However, Hu followed this with the imperative of people-centered development, maintaining his emphasis that future development had to be more balanced and sustainable.

As usual, anyone expecting movement on political reform was disappointed. Much fuss was made about the more open atmosphere at the congress, and Hu mentioned democracy, usually socialist democracy, multiple times, although little indication was given about what this might mean in practice. Similarly, inner-party democracy was limited—there were more candidates for positions on the CC, but genuine choice was restricted by the needs for functional representation from the regions, central agencies, and the military. For the leadership, the main intention was to improve debate and information flows within the party. There was a push for better feedback loops on the performance of party officials, including modern management techniques, such as 360-degree review and more canvassing of the public. Such measures were designed to improve performance while not opening up to greater responsiveness to society. The CCP confirmed that it still did not trust government organs and society to carry out the party's will.

The elected leadership provided Hu with a more favorable leadership for the tasks for the following five years. The one surprise was the elevation of Xi Jinping to the Politburo Standing Committee, even though he had not served on the previous Politburo. In a nod toward institutionalization, the functional positions for the members of the Politburo and its Standing Committee remained consistent, and the retirement age of 68 was retained. The one supporter of Jiang Zemin on the Standing Committee who survived was

Jia Qinglin, who was heavily compromised by his alleged engagement in corruption scandals while working in Xiamen and Beijing.

The elevation of Xi Jinping from his position as Shanghai party secretary took most observers by surprise, and the listing of his name above that of Li Keqiang in the hierarchy suggested that he would be the next CCP general secretary. Rumors circulated that Li Keqiang was Hu Jintao's preferred candidate, given their earlier experiences together in the Communist Youth League. Hu was successful in placing two close associates to head crucial party bodies: the powerful Organization Department, which would help with future appointments, and the General Office, which oversaw key appointments and administrative matters. Xi was put in charge of the Secretariat but, suggesting Hu's wariness, its scope of work was narrowed.

Before the congress Xi Jinping had received a very high approval rating in informal soundings of CC members. He was acceptable to different interest groups within the party and, as a son of one of the founders of the PRC, he was clearly viewed as a safe pair of hands who would not rock the boat. He ticked other important boxes. He had extensive administrative experience in the provinces and a brief six-month stint running Shanghai after replacing the disgraced Chen Liangyu, which he survived without being tainted with the whiff of corruption. He had connections in the military and, unlike Hu Jintao and Jiang Zemin, he had worked in the military; and he was not clearly identified with any specific faction. His rise was also a part of the rehabilitation of the princelings, children of senior CCP officials from prior generations. When complaints about them were at a peak during the 1990s, these princelings did not fare well. For instance, in the elections for the Fifteenth Party Congress in 1997, Xi received the lowest number of votes to become an alternate member of the CC. After the Seventeenth Congress, Xi took on increasingly high-profile roles, overseeing the final preparations for the summer Olympics and the festivities for the sixtieth anniversary of CCP rule.

Xi's elevation indicated that Li Keqiang would take over as premier of the State Council, and this was effectively confirmed at the Eleventh NPC, held on March 5–15, 2008. The occasion provided Premier Wen with the opportunity to reflect on progress over the last five years, touting achievements such as the completion of the Qinghai-Tibet Railway and the Three Gorges Dam, a pet project of Li Peng that had created considerable debate. For the rest, his report reaffirmed the reform objectives, including pushing ahead with SOE reform. A prime concern was calming down economic growth to prevent overheating, but this would change dramatically by the end of the year as the economy was blown off course.

The post-congress leadership had expected to enjoy a successful Olympics, the celebration of thirty years of reform, and celebration of the sixtieth anniversary of the founding of the PRC. Instead it was knocked off its stride by a series of unexpected domestic and international disasters. Riots in Tibet in March 2008 unsettled the leadership and brought unwanted international attention. Snowstorms in January and February devastated twenty-one provinces and caused about $21 billion in economic losses. The massive May 2008 earthquake in Wenchuan, Sichuan province, produced international sympathy, led to an outpouring of national support, and enhanced the reputation of the military as it took on a major role in providing relief and reconstruction. The fact that so many buildings collapsed and had not been provided with earthquake protection pointed the finger at local officials who had skimped on construction work and had diverted funds.[40]

Compounding these crises was the impact of the global financial crisis of 2008–2009, which threatened to undermine the policies of the leadership just as it was preparing for the major celebrations. The crisis, which originated in the United States, had two overriding consequences. The first was an immediate the shift in economic policy. The second consequence was long-term and fed into the growing disillusionment with the United States as an economy to aspire to. The US financial mismanagement tarnished the image of a neoliberal market economy and convinced Chinese leaders that their own statist approach was more suitable for China's situation. Whereas after the NPC meeting the leadership was focused on calming down the economy and managing inflation, by October there had been a complete reversal in economic policy.[41] A slowdown in growth had been expected, but nothing as dramatic as what occurred. Factors slowing the growth were the completion of the many construction projects related to the Olympics, the closing of many factories in the north of China to improve air quality, and the Olympics themselves, which brought much of the country to a halt. Growth during the third quarter of 2009 was the lowest in five years.

The immediate response was to rerun the playbook from the 1997–1998 Asian financial crisis and launch a massive stimulus program. In November a 4-trillion-yuan ($570 billion) package was announced, and Wen Jiabao urged local governments not to hold back. At the March 2009 NPC session, Wen pledged to speed up delivery of funds and stated that more funding could be made available if necessary. The funds were to be spent over two years and were to cover ten major areas, including rural infrastructure, low-income housing, transportation, water, and electricity. The headline figure needs further unpacking, as the central government was providing less than one-half of the total amount. The expectation was that local governments and others would provide the remainder. It was unclear how many of the projects and how much of the funding from the localities were new; many existing projects might simply have been shifted onto a different budget. Some critics worried about corruption and others worried about local governments pursuing wasteful trophy projects. No self-respecting local official was going to miss out on this financial bonanza, whether or not the projects were good ones.

The stimulus package did not help shift the reforms in the direction desired by Hu and Wen. They had already concluded that, moving forward, the economic reform model that had been so successful to date had to be adjusted. The two main drivers of growth had been state investment and foreign trade, but there was a limit to how much those could be further expanded. Investment accounted for about 40 percent of GDP, and the profile for foreign trade resembled that of a small island economy rather than that of a large continental economy. Consumption accounted for an extremely low 35 percent. Up until the present, the CCP leadership has sought to boost domestic demand to become the principal driver of economic growth. For Hu and Wen, with the global economy slowing, it was important to promote policies that boosted consumption while preserving macroeconomic stability. The stimulus package pushed back the timing of this shift. Although the massive injection of funds did produce a V-shaped recession in China, and economic growth in 2009 was a respectable 8.7 percent, consumption was not boosted. Concerns that easy credit would lead to inflation meant that in January 2010 the leadership started to tighten monetary policy and to exert more control over lending. Longer-term challenges due to the stimulus were becoming apparent, with overcapacity in the SOE sector and many enterprises using the loose credit to prevent the necessary reforms. A common phrase was "the state advances and the private retreats."

Dealing with these legacies led Premier Wen to comment that 2010 was the "most complicated" year in terms of managing the economy. The stimulus package not only helped to revive the SOEs, but also raised fears of inflation, and misallocation of resources, and it contributed to yet another real estate bubble. The state was accumulating wealth at a much faster rate. So much for balanced, sustainable growth! Consequently, Hu Jintao began to speak about inclusive growth, and this was included in the Twelfth Five-Year Program, for 2010–2015, which was approved at the March 2011 NPC session. The priorities in the program revealed how little progress had been made on key questions of balancing and moderating growth. To some extent, this can be attributed to the impact of the stimulus plan, but it was also due to resistance from vested interests in the state-sponsored sector. Again, quantitative targets were absent except for the GDP growth target set for 7 percent, the economy had grown at an average of 10 percent during the previous five years. Domestic consumption was designated to be the primary driver of economic growth, which itself was to be more equitable. The Hu–Wen concern for expanding welfare was reaffirmed, while $600 billion was set aside for investment in priority economic areas. In terms of sustainability, measures were to be stepped up to manage the environment and a 15 percent reduction in energy intensity was called for. As with previous plans, the policies would straddle the appointment of the new leadership to try to ensure a smooth transition and continuity. However, two unexpected events made the transition far from smooth.

The Arab Spring began in December 2010 and gave rise to a range of pro-democracy uprisings across the Middle East and North Africa; this alerted the CCP leadership to the disturbances that China's rising unrest might produce. The reforms had created an increasingly diverse and sophisticated citizenry that was using social media to promote heterodox ideas and that was more willing to take to the streets to protest. The limited institutional mechanisms to redress grievances contributed to the increase in street protests.[42] The Chinese Academy of Governance reported that the number of protests doubled between 2006 and 2010, reaching 180,000 in 2010, amounting to almost 6,000 protests per province, or some 16 protests per day.[43] Few, if any, presented a systemic challenge. Most were focused on specific abuses and were local in nature, and very few led to political unrest. Although not presenting an immediate challenge to the state, they were unlikely to go away, meaning that the threat of instability was always present.[44] Indeed, protest spread to the new urban middle classes, who were concerned about quality-of-life issues.

The traditional response was to step up repression, and because local officials were expected to maintain social stability, this did lead to harsh crackdowns in some areas. Gradually the budget for domestic security exceeded that of the formal military, and there was a large expansion of both the people's armed police and thugs hired by local governments to break up disputes. Such responses increased the likelihood of collective action, with local authorities seeking to nip the protests in the bud or to repress them once they began, but also trying to buy off trouble wherever possible.

A more imaginative approach was announced by Hu Jintao with his promotion of social management. At a September 2010 Politburo meeting that was convened to discuss the new forms of conflict, Hu proposed strengthening and innovating social management. This led to an upsurge in publications on the theme in early 2011, and Hu elaborated on the concept in a number of speeches. It was clear that the party and government alone could no longer deal with all the needs of the diversified society, and that they would have to call on social organizations, the traditional mass organizations, and the public and private sectors to share the burden. This was not to be taken as recognition of the legitimacy of a civil society or an autonomous realm. A service-oriented government would reduce conflicts. In addition, these organizations were to operate under the leadership of the party so as to strengthen the party's ability to oversee society and manage sudden outbursts of anger and discord. For the first time, a section on social management was included in the program for social and economic development presented at the March 2011 NPC meeting.[45]

Responsible Stakeholders or New Kids on the Block?

As we have seen, the terrorist attacks of September 11, 2001, in the United States, and the invasion of Iraq benefited China by improving its relations with the United States and giving the country time and space to develop its external relations. By the midpoint of the Hu–Wen era, China was playing an increasingly important role in the global economy, and its needs for resources and energy were resulting in the development of a wider range of relationships, whereas its export-led growth was creating trade tensions with the United States and others. Frictions with Japan and Taiwan continued off and on, while the noisy neighbor, North Korea, became increasingly troublesome with its development of nuclear weapons.

By 2005, American officials were comfortable with the habit of describing the relationship with China as being the best ever. Superficially, this may have been true, but ever since the dismemberment of the Soviet Union there clearly was no solid underpinning to the relationship, and there were deep disagreements about how to interpret the rise of China. In the United States, debate began to intensify. Should the policies of engagement continue, in the hope that China would become an amenable player with a liberalizing economy and polity? Or should its practices be challenged more vigorously? Was the United States' China policy based on the "Starbucks fallacy," as Jim Mann suggested, or had the two economies become, as Niall Ferguson phrased it, a "Chimerica" by having become so complementary?[46] By 2009 Ferguson had ditched his nomenclature because he felt that the Chinese authorities were no longer willing to underwrite US debt and were deeply concerned about American financial management and wasteful ways.

After initial concern over President Bush's harsh rhetoric, the administration became generally popular in China and frictions were kept to a minimum, despite the rising trade and investment issues—issues that have only intensified in recent years. Some American politicians blamed Chinese practices for the large trade imbalances, and in part this is true. The picture is more complicated because much of China's exports are intermediate and semi-finished products that were imported from other countries to be processed in China and then shipped out again—so there is a significant amount of double-counting. Further, the crude figures omit domestic value-added, and many of the exports are by US companies producing in China, such as Apple. Recalculation on this basis significantly reduces the figure for the trade imbalance. Apple iPhone production provides a good example. The iPhone is designed in the United States, but it is assembled in and exported from China. China's contribution to the value is only about $20 per phone, a value-added ratio of 4 percent—but in the US trade figures, it is assessed at some $500.[47] This issue became, and remains, a political problem for the United States.

Reflecting the generally good atmosphere, in April 2006 General Secretary Hu Jintao, using the title "president," visited America, marking the fifth US-China presidential meeting in two years. Despite the best-laid plans, things did not go smoothly. Gaffes included a well-known Falun Gong activist interrupting the proceedings at the White House, and the announcement by the official hosts of the "anthem of the Republic of China"—that is, the anthem of Taiwan, not the mainland. This did not go down well in China, where many online commentators saw it as a deliberate snub rather than simple American incompetence. Although the relationship was not unduly disrupted, US officials did begin to describe the relationship as "complex," a more realistic judgment of the state of affairs. Hu's visit made it clear that China would not change its behavior simply to satisfy the US national interest.

President Bush had already indicated his wish for a positive relationship in his February 2003 speech at Tsinghua University when he announced that America welcomed "the emergence of a strong and peaceful and prosperous China." Not all in the United States agreed, however, and many in China were skeptical, viewing US bases in traditional places such as Japan and South Korea as well as in Afghanistan and Central Asia not only as "hedging" but as something approaching containment. The administration continued its courtship to woo China into the global community, and in December 2005 Deputy Secretary of State Robert Zoellick defended engagement and encouraged China to become a "responsible stakeholder." The hope remained that China would work with the United States and others to sustain, adapt, and advance the peaceful international system that had driven China's economic growth. When Zoellick became head of the World Bank in July 2007, he appointed a Chinese economist from Peking University, Justin Yifu Lin, to become chief economist.

When Barack Obama moved into his new role as US president in January 2009, attitudes in Beijing were shifting and it was clear that Hu Jintao did not necessarily share Jiang Zemin's pro-US position. In part this was natural as China's international relations were now far more complex and its national interest did not always coincide with that of America. The Olympics and the celebrations for the sixtieth anniversary of the founding of the PRC boosted national pride, which had been growing since the mid-1990s. Phrases such as "rejuvenation of the Chinese nation" were scattered throughout the press, and the US-induced global financial crisis led many to reject Western institutions as inadequate models for China's future path. With criticisms rising in the West about China's trade practices, some Chinese saw the elements of the global order structured in a way to prevent the economic practices that had aided China's growth. China's quick rebound from the financial crisis confirmed this perspective and allowed it to be assertive in terms of what it sought from the relationship with the United States. Beijing no longer considered itself the junior partner and was not willing to allow the United States to dictate the terms of the relationship. As one well-known Chinese professor put it: "We are business partners who share material interests rather than common values."[48] However, even the material interests would eventually come into conflict.

While President Obama sought to build on the positive legacy bequeathed by the Bush administration, the relationship became even more complex. This led the Obama administration to describe the relationship it hoped for as a "positive, cooperative, and comprehensive one." This phrasing indicated that the relationship was now multifaceted and that no single issue would dominate matters. Finding the correct balance was difficult—witness the criticism Secretary of State Hillary Clinton faced for not having paid enough attention to human rights during her May 2009 visit to China. In 2010 the relationship between China and the United States suffered its first serious tests, when the United States sold arms to Taiwan, and when President Obama met with the Dalai Lama. Although China vociferously expressed its contempt for these US actions, clearly it did not wish to undermine the relationship. However, it would not yield on questions of currency and trade.

In addition to the traditional tensions in the relationship, such as human rights and Taiwan, the economic and trade dimensions were increasingly moving to center stage. Despite the omnipresence of McDonalds and Starbucks in China, not all were happy and some US businesses began to complain about hidden barriers to entry into the Chinese market, piracy, and forced transfers of technology. It was becoming clear that China's entry into the WTO was not going to resolve these challenges. In 1980 the United States had run a trade surplus with China of $2.7 billion; this had now reversed dramatically, and according to US official figures, the trade deficit was $266 billion in 2008, three times the US deficit with Japan. This ongoing problem in the relationship will be dealt with in more detail in Chapter 12.

The two countries did work more cooperatively on the issue of the nuclearization of the Korean peninsula, although even here there were differences in policy priorities. Nuclear tests by North Korea in October 2006 and May 2009 placed China in an awkward position. China's peace treaty with North Korea has never been rescinded, and it commits China to support North Korea in the case of war. That this circumstance would arise is unlikely, but the treaty is still embarrassing because the countries are no longer "as close as lips and teeth." The tensions not only helped the relationship between the United States and China but also helped China and Japan find some common ground. China was congratulated for its role in the Six-Party Talks—the participants were China, Japan, North Korea, Russia, South Korea, and the United States—and it also had the most influence over the North. For example, 70 percent of North Korea's energy needs are met by China. However, if it had not known this already, it soon discovered how difficult it is to deal with the regime.

China's patience was tested in November 2009 when North Korea announced that it had finished reprocessing its spent nuclear fuel for use in a bomb, and it used this development to push for a break in the Six-Party Talks and to deal with the United States directly.[49] This was the last thing China wanted, as its core interests differed from those of the United States. Like South Korea, China is worried about the potential consequences of regime collapse in North Korea, and it has opposed excessive sanctions that might cause the regime to fall, which would bring chaos to China and US troops to its border. This is another legacy from the past that continues to the present.

The last enduring legacy is the issue of cross-strait relations. The tensions in the relationship while Chen Shui-bian was president, in 2000–2008, eased considerably once the GMD returned to power with Ma Ying-jeou as president. Direct flights across the strait began, trade and investment expanded, and tourism took off. This did not mean that China would completely let up its pressure on Taiwan, but a diplomatic truce did seem to be operating. China allowed Taiwan to send a delegation to the World Health Assembly in May 2009; this was the first time China had agreed to allow Taiwan to send a delegation to any UN activity. The high point of interaction came under the new PRC administration when Xi Jinping met with Ma Ying-jeou in Singapore in November 2015. However, the thaw would not be extended once the DPP regained the presidency. Indeed, Ma had received considerable criticism in Taiwan for giving away too much to the mainland.

China's newfound wealth and its need for resources made it a much more active player on the world stage, even though it lacked a coherent strategy. In September 2007 China established the world's largest sovereign wealth fund, the China Investment Corporation (CIC), launched with special bonds issued by the Ministry of Finance. This enabled it to acquire $200 billion of the nation's foreign exchange reserves, dwarfing Singapore's Temasek ($139 billion). Its primary objective was to provide better returns to the state than US Treasury bonds, and in 2007 it took stakes in Blackstone and Morgan Stanley to enhance its financial acumen. The CIC does not operate as an independent financial institution, and any major activity must be approved by China's political leadership, but it has become a major player in China's overseas resource acquisitions.

A Wrinkle in Succession Planning: The Purge of Bo Xilai

Although Xi Jinping had been marked as Hu Jintao's successor at the Seventeenth Party Congress and had taken over important party affairs, the carefully prepared succession did not go according to plan. Xi did take on the position of general secretary at the Eighteenth Party Congress in November 2012, but this was preceded by an unexpected crisis within the party, leading to the disgrace of a key rival. Once again the weak institutionalization of the CCP's governing mechanisms was exposed. However, the struggle against Bo Xilai involved more than individuals sparring for power. It represented different visions for China's future and different approaches to politics.

Like Xi Jinping, Bo Xilai was a princeling, one of those who felt that the trials and tribulations of their parents had given them the right to take over the mantle of leadership. Unlike Xi, Bo was charismatic, extroverted, and willing to be bold in experimentation. Having served in Liaoning province and as minister of commerce, he was promoted to the Politburo in 2007 and sent to Chongqing municipality, in southwest China, as party secretary. His time in Chongqing rocked the traditional establishment as he seemed to launch a public campaign to be promoted through his actions. The purge of Bo Xilai was distinct from the purges of Chen Xitong by Jiang Zemin and Chen Liangyu by Hu Jintao, because even though they were power struggles, neither had a genuine policy program to challenge the status quo. In contrast, Bo Xilai did.[50]

Bo Xilai's policies in Chongqing had a strong populist flavor that appealed to the new left and the neo-Maoist groups, which had recently become more prominent.[51] One prominent member of the new left went to work for him, and another described his policies as "socialism 3.0."[52] The policies were packaged together in what was referred to as the Chongqing model.[53] The program produced impressive economic growth by relying heavily on state investment. There was nothing new in this; it was the same model pursued by most cities to generate growth.[54] What was different was the combination of this with aggressive policies to reduce crime, serve those who had been disadvantaged, and revive cultural aspects of the revolutionary tradition, such as the singing of "red songs."

Chongqing was notorious for its organized crime, and Bo began his rule with a campaign to attack it. He was joined by his chief of police, whom he had brought with him from Liaoning province. Almost 6,000 were arrested during the campaign, including businesspeople, police, and government officials. The campaign was generally popular, but some were not so enamored, suggesting that it had ignored the legal process, had engaged in torture to extract confessions, and had been used to eliminate political foes. Bo's second strategy was to build support among those who had not profited from the reforms, by introducing a set of welfare changes that addressed the major challenges of rising inequality and the rural–urban divide. He directed significant funding to providing housing for low-income residents, including migrant workers. Experiments were pioneered in Chongqing to allow rural residents to obtain urban residence permits so they would have better access to education and welfare facilities. Bo's populist stance was also enhanced by his promotion of "red culture." This included the singing of patriotic songs, showing revolutionary operas on television, and even encouraging students to work on farms, as had been done during the Cultural Revolution. Bo and his team would send out text messages to mobile phone users in the municipality, which were often quotes from Chairman Mao Zedong.

For a while this approach seemed successful. Bo might have expected to take over the security portfolio in the Standing Committee from Zhou Yongkang, with whom he enjoyed close ties. His high-profile actions seemed to be reaping benefits, and in 2010 *Time* magazine included him in its "World's 100 Most Influential People" issue.[55] A number of high-profile visitors came to pay homage—including not only Zhou Yongkang but also Xi Jinping, who praised Chongqing's achievements.

Despite these initiatives, Bo's colleagues were concerned about his ambitions and they distrusted him. The leaders in Beijing divorced themselves from Bo's achievements in Chongqing, and it is noteworthy that when he was removed, the Chongqing mayor, who had worked closely with him, was retained. The focus of the party attack did not touch his policies and the model, but instead focused on corruption and abuse of power. This focus was pursued to undermine his support and to rein in those who wanted to push his model nationally. His fall from grace is an amazing story of palace politics and intrigue, involving not only corruption but also murder, attempts at a cover-up, and a flight to a US consulate.[56] The trouble for Bo began in November 2011 when his wife was accused of the murder of a British businessman. Things really fell apart in February 2012, when his chief of police sought asylum in the US consulate in Chengdu, perhaps bringing incriminating materials with him.

A decision on Bo's dismissal was taken at a March 7 meeting of the Politburo Standing Committee, during which the lone dissenting voice was Zhou Yongkang, Bo's close associate and security czar. Thus, it is not surprising that, following Bo's dismissal, slowly but surely investigations of Zhou Yongkang and his associates also began. The first inklings of trouble were provided by Premier Wen Jiabao at the press conference to conclude the March 2012 NPC session. Wen referred to the "pernicious influences" that lingered from the Cultural Revolution and called on the leadership in Chongqing to reflect on the process of reform and what the case of Bo's chief of police meant.[57] The general-secretary-in-waiting, Xi Jinping, chipped in during a speech to the Central Party School. He asked members to preserve the purity of the party and he criticized those who sought to split the party. In what would become a theme of his leadership, he called for party members to behave humbly.[58]

In April Bo was suspended from the Politburo and CC while investigations into "serious disciplinary violations" were conducted. In late September 2012 he was expelled from the party for discipline violations that included not only his time in Chongqing but also his work in Liaoning and while at the Ministry of Commerce. This led to protests from his neo-left supporters, and he still remained popular among many in Chongqing. As a result, the party shut down the main leftist website and scrubbed pro-Bo articles from the internet. In September 2013 Bo was sentenced to life imprisonment, having been found guilty of taking $3.3 million in bribes and abuse of power. Nothing was said about his policies and the Chongqing model. Bo's judgment on his sentence was that it was something "even the lousiest TV drama scriptwriter wouldn't create."[59]

The need to clean house had two major policy impacts. First, the leadership took its eyes off the economy as it slowed in 2012, and second, the leadership-in-waiting did not have a chance to float its own policy priorities in the run-up to the transition. In contrast, Hu Jintao and Wen Jiabao were able to send a clear indication of their wish to shift to a more sustainable development model. Thus, as the Eighteenth Party Congress approached, it was not clear what direction the new leadership would take. Xi Jinping, who had played by the rules and had maintained a low profile in public without rocking the boat, soon emerged as a stronger leader than anyone had expected. Ironically, central to his leadership were many of the approaches pursued by Bo Xilai. Xi Jinping began his leadership with an attack on corruption, he showed compassion for those who had been left behind, and he promoted certain practices from the Cultural Revolution, while clamping down on critical views of CCP history. A full policy program was unveiled at the Third Plenum of the Eighteenth CC in November 2013.

CHAPTER TWELVE

Creating the China Dream

2012–2021

★

The carefully planned leadership transition for the Eighteenth Party Congress was seriously disrupted by the fallout from the arrest of Bo Xilai. No one knew what to expect from Xi Jinping as general secretary, since he had played his cards close to his chest over the five years since his appointment as heir apparent in 2007. He had overseen the Olympics and the celebrations for the sixtieth anniversary of the establishment of the PRC, but in meetings with foreigners he seemed bland and noncommittal. Since the death of Deng Xiaoping in February 1997, each succeeding leader enjoyed a reduced level of authority as the system settled into collective leadership. Yet Xi dramatically reversed this trend in an assertive manner that took many by surprise. Seen as an appointment of the lowest common denominator of acceptability, he accumulated power swiftly and dominated the political discourse.

As Xi Jinping viewed the economic, social, and political terrain, it seemed riven with problems. There was the aftermath of Bo's arrest, corruption was still rampant, and social protests and modest challenges to CCP rule continued. In 2012, politics appeared frozen, with economic and institutional reforms seemingly frustrated by the vested interests that dominated the CCP.[1] Consequently, Xi clearly felt that the challenges facing China were so severe that drastic measures were required. Politics had to take priority over economics, but also there remained the need for a fundamental shift in the development strategy. To meet his objectives, it would be crucial to have a party that was disciplined and unified, in order to push through the next phase of reforms. At a simplistic level, Xi's overriding objective was to maintain CCP rule, but this does not tell us very much. In significant respects Xi broke with the existing norms and rules that saw senior party officials dividing power among themselves and sustaining elite stability through a balance of power among the different groups.

Xi Jinping has proceeded to concentrate power not only at the center but also around his own person in a way that has not been seen since Deng Xiaoping and perhaps even since Mao Zedong. The challenges to maintain stable economic growth and to cement China's position within the global and regional communities were daunting. Domestically, China had to avoid the "middle-income trap." China's leaders clearly felt that the economic development model that had proved successful in the past was no longer suitable as the nation sought to shift to consumer-led growth and higher-quality production. The growth model had created serious environmental pollution, not only for air quality but also, and even more importantly, for water and soil. In addition, during the reform years, 1978 to the present, China went from having one of the lowest levels of inequality in Asia to having one of the highest. Additionally, there was the awaiting challenge of integrating several hundred million people into new and old urban environments. Externally, Xi and the new leaders of the "fifth generation" would have to be clear about the nation's place in the world and how to deal with other nations that were concerned about China's rise, best personified by President Trump's actions after his election in 2016. Whether its leaders acknowledge it or not, China's increasing economic power and associated influence mean that it is involved in the internal affairs of other countries in significant ways. Finally, the unexpected challenge brought by COVID-19 not only increased international scrutiny of China's practices but also caused a major economic challenge just as the party was preparing to celebrate key economic achievements, such as doubling the size of the economy between 2010 and 2020.

As with his predecessors, Xi Jinping does not trust the state or society to carry out his policies, and it is debatable to what extent he trusts the local party apparatus. He wanted to recreate the party in his image and to use it to promote his policies. To rebuild credibility after the Hu Jintao–Wen Jiabao years and the Bo Xilai affair, Xi promoted a simple image of the CCP that stressed modesty and simplicity. This was accompanied by an attempt to provide overall meaning for China's future, captured in the slogan "The China Dream to rejuvenate the nation." This does not mean that Marxism was forgotten, and the party continued Hu Jintao's attempts to foster support for the official ideology.

Assuming Power: Party and NPC Meetings

Xi Jinping's first task was to consolidate power within the party leadership; policy initiatives would come later. The Eighteenth Party Congress was delayed until November 8–14, 2012, and the speech by the outgoing general secretary, Hu Jintao, seemed to suggest business as usual, with little new offered either in his speech or in Wen Jiabao's speech at the NPC in March 2013. Hu Jintao's report on behalf of the outgoing leadership was more cautious than his speech in 2007.[2] He recounted a number of successes but reiterated warnings for the new leadership that had been aired in recent years. This included the unbalanced and unsustainable nature of the development model together with the environmental constraints. Hu stressed the threat that corruption could pose to the continued health of the party, a facet of work that Xi Jinping seized upon as his first target for action. Hu did not offer much hope for a shift in the dominance of the state-owned sector in the economy, calling for its consolidation and enhancing its vitality. This seemed to contrast with the pro-market predilection of Li Keqiang, who would become premier in March 2013. The report did include a section on political reform, but offered little beyond platitudes and the need to put in place a "healthy mechanism" for local self-governance.

Before the congress, rumors swirled about how many members would be included on the Politburo Standing Committee, and in fact the number was reduced from nine to seven. Five new members were promoted, as were fifteen new members of the twenty-five-person Politburo. Clearly, factional ties, age, and years of experience were more important than policy preferences. Thus, the five new members of the Standing Committee were the most senior members of the outgoing Politburo. This had the advantage for Xi Jinping that all of them would have to retire within five years. Further, together with the reduction in the number of Standing Committee members to seven, it meant that those with more liberal views on political and administrative reform were excluded.

This new leadership structure contained both advantages and disadvantages for Xi. The fact that not one but two former general secretaries were looking over his shoulder could have complicated his decision making. However, this situation allowed Xi to play the associates off against each other. One sign of Xi's emerging strength was that he immediately took over as chair of the Central Military Commission. Hu, unlike Deng Xiaoping and Jiang Zemin, was unable to hold on to this powerful position for an interim period. As with the previous leadership turnover in 2002–2003, it appeared as if the heirs apparent were anointed as the core leaders of the sixth generation. Sun Zhengcai, Chongqing party secretary, was being lined up to become the next general secretary, with Hu Chunhua, the Guangdong party secretary, as the next premier. For Sun, things ended badly.

The Twelfth NPC, in March 2013, completed the leadership transition, appointing Li Keqiang as Wen Jiabao's replacement as premier and Xi replacing Hu as president. The meeting proposed a more limited administrative restructuring and provided the first glimmers of future policy direction. Administratively, there was a tidying up of unresolved issues, the most noteworthy being the breakup of the independent power of the ministries of Railways and Energy. The Ministry of Railways was folded into the Ministry of Transport and Energy was absorbed by the National Energy Commission, which paved the way for impending moves against corruption in these powerful agencies. Addressing popular concerns about product quality, food safety was raised to the ministerial level, after having been downgraded in 2008 following a number of scandals and the execution of its former head on corruption charges.

Wen Jiabao reiterated the same policy objectives that had laced his speeches during the previous ten years, indicating just how difficult it is to shift the Chinese economy and to push back the vested interests.[3] Once again Wen called for shifting to consumption as the main driver of growth to develop a more sustainable economic model. He repeated his and Hu's phrase that current development was "unbalanced, uncoordinated, and unsustainable." The era of super growth was over, and he called for growth in 2013 of 7.5 percent—and it came in as 7.7 percent. The need for better health care and the need to deal with pollution were stressed, and these concerns were reflected in the budget. Spending on social welfare was boosted 28 percent, and spending for the environment was increased by 18.8 percent. Finally, and importantly, Wen signaled that reform of the financial sector was back on the agenda, with measures to improve financial markets, reform interest rates, and base currency levels on market rates. The hope of the reformers was to use the financial sector to push ahead reforms in the real economy by liberalizing interest rates and moving capital to those sectors of the economy that produce jobs and operate with higher productivity.

As the NPC concluded, the new leadership duo, Xi and Li, gave a brief indication of their policy preferences. Xi raised his slogan of the China Dream and called for the great rejuvenation of the Chinese nation by following the

"Chinese road." Xi represented those who were confident in the path the nation had taken, especially since the global financial crisis of 2008–2009, and he would not be told by outsiders what was best for China. This became a hallmark of his rule. This view went hand in hand with Xi's more strident and nationalistic approach. When Premier Li Keqiang met with the press at the end of the congress, he noted that there was no alternative to reform. In fact, he identified reform with the destiny of the nation. Unlike Hu Jintao at the party congress, Li proposed a greater role for the market, a stronger push against corruption, and more attention to environmental degradation. A more liberal approach was proposed for the economy, but unity was to be maintained by promoting nationalism and by a tough approach toward the political environment. Despite the promulgation of a strong reform document in November 2013, pushing ahead with a more market-based set of reforms proved difficult, and it seemed that Xi and Li were singing from different song sheets when it came to the reform and the role of the state-owned sector.

Charting a New Path?

Whereas some key components of Xi's policy preferences—such as the need to combat corruption and to show more concern for those not so fortunate—had been developed under Hu and Wen, Xi drove ahead far more forcibly than any of his colleagues might have expected. It is evident that the majority of the party leadership felt that Xi was trustworthy and that he would ensure continued party rule and maintain its preeminent position, while restoring party credibility and support among the population at large. It was up to Xi and the new leadership to find a new basis for legitimacy that combined both traditional mechanisms and new methods.

Xi Jinping clearly decided that for the party to remain in charge, he had to regain control over the apparatus and to prioritize political challenges over the continued restructuring of the economy. Ideally he would have liked the anticorruption campaign and economic reform to proceed together. Cleaning up the image of the CCP was crucial if the party was to retain its grip on power. However, the centralization of power had a negative effect, with many complaining of paralysis within the government and party, as some local officials decided it was safer to do nothing than to approve investment or other decisions that might subsequently lead to accusations of misuse of power.

The reform proposals presented at the Third Plenum of the Eighteenth CC in November 2013 were wide-ranging and provided a major statement of reform intent that promised progress in politics, economics, and international affairs to complete the China Dream. Sixty tasks were put forward.[4] The problem, of course, is that in outlining so many tasks, local leaders and members of the central bureaucracy could pick and choose which ones to focus on and which ones to ignore, so that in the end there was no focus on any of them. The decision of the plenum reaffirmed the leadership's view that the old economic model had run its course and that consumption was now the main driver of growth. Liu Shijin, a former vice minister of the State Council Development Research Center, commented: "The end has come to the period of purely 'quantitative expansion' and of extensive cultivation for meagre returns." What is most remarkable about the priorities is that many are identical to those put forward in 2002–2003 when Hu Jintao and Wen Jiabao assumed power. This is indicative that it is difficult to engineer a transition, and this has continued to be the case.

To maintain more sustainable growth, the plenum called for a lower growth rate, more judicious use of the market, and a stepped-up program of urbanization. Growth thereafter came in at the lowest levels since 2009 and has continued to moderate. To encourage people to adjust to the lower rate of growth, it was dubbed the "new normal." The decisive role of the market was highlighted with the announcement that the prices of water, oil, gas, electricity, transportation, and telecommunications all would be set by the market. The increasing emphasis on the positive role of the market can be seen in the sequential five-year plans—culminating in the Twelfth Five-Year Plan, for 2011–2015, which gave "full play to the socialist mechanism as well as the market in terms of allocating resources." In March 2013 Premier Li Keqiang stated that "the market is the creator of social wealth and the wellspring of self-sustaining economic development."[5]

This notwithstanding, the document contained a clear emphasis on the role of SOEs and state direction of economic development, an approach akin to state capitalism, although the Chinese leadership refers to it as "socialism with Chinese characteristics," and more recently has referred to it as "supply-side economic reforms." The main elements are cutting excess capacity, especially in steel production (Chinese exports have roiled global markets and upset President Trump); closing down some of the "zombie" SOEs, but subsidizing a smaller number of favored and often inefficient industries; and tax breaks for new industries, such as electric vehicles and eco-friendly agriculture. The current Chinese leadership has certainly developed an industrial policy designed to ensure that the party retains control over key sectors of the domestic economy and has greater influence over investment outside of China, an approach that has strengthened over time. The new leadership maintained the view that any reform of the SOE sector should result, not in wholesale privatization, but instead in the development of national champions, along the lines of the industries in Japan and South Korea, to contribute more effectively to the CCP's political standing. This followed the path established by former Premier Zhu Rongji, who in the 1990s sought to establish a stronger industrial policy and state oversight combined with promotion of stronger market forces.

An earlier policy move to solidify the dominance of the SOE sector was the launch in 2006 of "indigenous innovation," focusing on industries such as new-energy vehicles, high-end equipment manufacturing, biotechnology, and information technology. State dominance over the domestic economy is also reflected in Chinese overseas investment. These strategic industries and pillars were essential to the "going out" strategy to increase overseas investments and to expand Chinese enterprises globally. The state clearly intends to play a major role in Chinese overseas investment and to more effectively control the buying sprees and mergers and acquisitions of the preceding years.

One of the most dramatic announcements was further relaxation of the family planning program. Although Mao Zedong had believed in the more the merrier, to outnumber the citizens of the capitalist nations, Deng Xiaoping had seen the population explosion as a threat to economic progress. An elaborate system of family planning agencies was established that reached down to the villages, with the performance of local officials monitored in terms of their ability to keep within the population quotas. Change was strongly resisted by the family planning agencies, which issued dire warnings about the economic consequences whenever reform was mooted. The waning influence of the family planning commission system was signaled at the March 2013 NPC meeting when that commission was merged with the Ministry of Health to form a new National Health and Family Planning Commission. Policy was relaxed to allow couples to have a second child if either partner was a single child, and it was relaxed even further in 2015 for all to be able to have a second child. The driving factor for this change is the aging of Chinese society—it will become the first major nation to grow old before it grows rich. In 2019 about 12.6 percent of the population was over the age of sixty-five; the UN has predicted that the figure would reach over

17 percent by 2030. This has caused declining dependency ratios, with only 2.8 young for each elderly person and with a projection of 1.3 young for each elderly person by 2050.[6] The financial burden on future generations from a shrinking population and ballooning numbers of elderly will be a significant drain on the economy and on families. The specifics of implementation and timing were left to local administrations. However, it can cost 32,000 yuan a year to raise a child in Shanghai, just above the average total disposable income, and therefore far fewer couples have taken advantage of this new policy than was predicted by the government. In 2017, when the full effect should have been felt, there was an actual drop in the birth rate compared to the previous year. This has led the leadership to promote slogans such as "have children for the country" to increase birth rates.[7] Maternity leave is being increased, together with cash incentives and tax breaks, with some provinces providing more generous support. Clearly, it was easier to enforce the policy of having fewer children than it has been to encourage parents to have more children.

The plenum decision was far more reserved on reform of the household registration system, which forms the basis for the unequal treatment of migrants and their families with respect to welfare services in urban China. For a number of years, reformers had pushed for changes and even abolition of the system, but despite progress, many cities still put up roadblocks to a shift in status, in part fearing the additional costs. The decision did identify the binary structure of city and country as a primary barrier to effective urban development. Despite this, the concern of booming megalopolises meant that the focus was on the development of small and medium-sized cities. The system was to be kept in place and decisions would be left to the localities, which would evaluate their ability to absorb migrant workers and their families.

Urbanization was presented as a major factor that would facilitate future growth, boost consumption, and smooth out the inequalities of service provision. To accelerate urban development, the plenum decision announced that local governments would be allowed to experiment with a range of financing mechanisms, including property taxes and the issuance of government bonds. Diversifying financing avenues was also seen as a way to reduce land protests because much financing had been derived from the conversion of rural land for construction, often with inadequate compensation for the dispossessed farmers. Consequently, in a dramatic shift, farmers were to be allowed to trade their land rights and thus were afforded more protection against exploitation by local government officials. Their property rights were to be strengthened and they could use shareholding systems to serve as collateral.

Following the plenum, in March 2014 the government issued its ambitious "National New Urbanization Plan (2014–2020)," which focused on the development of small and medium-sized cities, estimating that 60 percent of the population would live in cities by 2020.[8] The plan had four main objectives: to allow migrants to become genuine city dwellers, to optimize urban layout, to make urban living more sustainable, and to integrate the rural and urban areas. Environmental quality certainly had to be improved. An official study revealed that in 2014 only 16 out of 161 cities that had been expected to commit to new air quality standards had complied, and the quality of groundwater in nearly 60 percent of the cities was poor or very poor. Thus, local government commitment was vital but difficult to ensure.

The most important administrative initiative was the establishment of two new central agencies: the National Security Commission and the Central Leading Group on Comprehensively Deepening Reform. It is no surprise that Xi Jinping was appointed to head both of them. The National Security Commission has the remit to deal not only with global challenges but also with domestic security, and it brought together in one body those who dealt with traditional and nontraditional security issues, including terrorism, financial turmoil, cyber security, food safety, and environmental challenges. Externally, there had been coordination challenges among different branches of the services and the civilian leadership. With an increasing global footprint and the potential for conflicts in areas such as the South China Sea, coordination was viewed as crucial. The establishment of the commission and the appointment of Xi to chair it attested to Xi's growing authority within the new leadership. Jiang Zemin had tried at least twice to establish such a commission, but he had been thwarted by institutional resistance and concerns that it might place too much power in the hands of one individual. Xi clearly was not bothered by this concern, and he was able to justify his dominance by referencing incidents in previous decades when decision-making had suffered from poor coordination.

Simultaneously taking the lead over the new body to push ahead with reform exemplified both Xi's confidence as the key leader and his determination to take ownership of the reform program. Xi Jinping broke with Hu Jintao's more consensual, collective decision-making approach to leadership, clearly feeling that this had led to slow progress when the situation demanded a swift response.[9]

Consolidating Power

From the outset, the new leadership exuded much greater confidence than the prior leadership had shown during the previous ten years. Xi Jinping moved quickly to consolidate his power and to strengthen his position, leading to his coronation at the Nineteenth Party Congress, held on October 18–24, 2017. He was not only appointed chair of the Central Military Commission, placing him simultaneously at the head of the party, state, and army. In addition, as noted, he was named in November 2013 to head the two new bodies that were created to drive reform: the Central Leading Group for Comprehensively Deepening Reform and the National Security Commission.

In the run-up to the Nineteenth Party Congress, Xi's power as the pre-eminent leader, which enabled him to dominate policy making and personnel appointments, was consolidated by five pivotal events. First, in October 2016 Xi was named as the core of the party leadership, with a steady stream of military and civilian leaders all pledging support. This is an important designation in CCP terminology, indicating his dominance within the political hierarchy, placing him in a direct line of leadership following Mao Zedong, Deng Xiaoping, and Jiang Zemin. His predecessor, Hu Jintao, had not been awarded this appellation. Although there is still adherence to collective leadership, decisions cannot go forward if the core does not agree, and Xi, as the core, can initiate policies on his own. This marks a step back from the more collective decision-making style that marked the Hu Jintao and Wen Jiabao years (2002–2012) to one with a preeminent leader at the core—as "chairman of everything."

Second, in January 2017 the Chinese press published comments by Xi Jinping at the October 2016 plenum accusing five senior members of the party of engaging in political conspiracies.[10] This went beyond the earlier accusations that the five were "greedy financially" and "corrupt in their lifestyles." The group included Bo Xilai and his supporter and former Jiang Zemin associate, Zhou Yongkang, and one other, who was said to be close to Hu Jintao. The other two were key military leaders. The publication of these comments served as a warning to others in the party who might think of challenging Xi, and they were an expression of his confidence in the strength of his position. Third, the NPC meeting in March 2017 was noteworthy for the dominance of Xi, rather than Premier Li Keqiang, over the proceedings. The NPC is a government meeting but the CCP received some thirty mentions, more than at any time since the reforms began in the late 1970s. Xi himself was mentioned eight times, and the core was mentioned eleven times.[11] Economic objectives featured less prominently than in previous reports, reflecting Xi's preference for party dominance over state and society.

Fourth, in the immediate buildup to the congress Xi consolidated his position by removing rivals and promoting allies. The most noticeable target was Sun Zhengcai, who was removed as Chongqing party secretary and was replaced by Xi associate Chen Min'er. Sun had been considered a potential future general secretary. This was the latest case where a potential rival was removed on the grounds of corruption. In May 2018 Sun was sentenced to life imprisonment for having admitted to taking $27 million in bribes. Earlier, in May 2017, another Xi acolyte was promoted from the position of acting mayor of Beijing to party secretary of Beijing. Finally, these moves paved the way for Xi to change the State Constitution to allow the president to remain in his position for more than two five-year terms. There is no limitation on how long the general secretary may serve, but it had become the norm that the leadership of party and state would serve two terms.

Using Power: It's the Politics, Stupid

The new leadership under Xi Jinping immediately sought to restore the party's credibility and to curb the lavish lifestyles that some within the party were enjoying. This was accompanied by an even more concerted attempt than that of Xi's predecessors to exert control over a wayward state apparatus and an even more wayward society, producing the toughest political atmosphere in many years. Surveying the legacy he inherited, Xi must have felt that such drastic measures were necessary to ensure the survival of the CCP. The key question arises whether these are actions by a strong administration or are they actions deriving from fears that things are slipping out of control. The answer is a mixture of both. Xi is an extremely self-assured leader who moved quickly to consolidate his rule; yet a party that must rail incessantly against Western values would suggest that many still aspire to such values—thus, the need to present a positive alternative under the slogan of the China Dream. Unfortunately, like many such slogans in China, the slogan has become subject to exploitation and abuse. The range of products advertised under the China Dream motif quickly grew as businesses rushed to make money off the slogan.

On assuming power, Xi launched a movement for officials to practice more frugal behavior—which he encapsulated in the slogan "four dishes and a soup"—as well as to implement the strongest campaign in recent memory against corruption within party and government ranks. Pictures were shown of General Secretary Xi sitting down in a simple restaurant eating Chinese buns and of him strolling in the winter smog, without a face mask, to press home his common touch. Thereafter, the restaurant's business began to boom. An attack was launched against the wasteful "three public expenditures": overseas trips, banquets and excessive pomp and ceremonies, and vehicles. Lavish official banquets were banned, as was serving expensive alcohol. Officials worked around these new restrictions by inviting a business leader who would pay for the meal.[12] Regulations were also issued on the size of offices

Promoting frugality, Xi Jinping dines at a steamed dumpling shop in Beijing, 2013.

for officials at different levels. In many organizations, this resulted in the frantic and expensive rebuilding of walls to conform to the measurements before the inspection teams came to check.

In 2013 some 20,000 officials were punished for breaking these new regulations, with 5,000 punished for the misuse of official cars and 900 punished for celebrating too elaborately.[13] The measures did show some initial changes in behavior. In 2013, central government spending on the three public expenditures dropped by 35 percent and hospitality at the provincial level dropped by 26 percent. There were unexpected results, with one report suggesting that one-third of the local liquor vendors of the fiery Maotai drink, which is essential to any self-respecting banquet, in Maotai Village, Guizhou province, had gone bankrupt.[14] Overseas training for government officials was cut, in part because Xi Jinping claimed that there was no longer anything to learn from overseas programs, and also because many local governments had turned such programs into "educational tourism." These cuts were accompanied by strict controls over the number of days an official could spend overseas. Given that universities in China are public institutions, this regulation extended to the deans of schools, making it difficult for them to attend international conferences. Realizing the constraints this placed on academic exchanges and the need to promote Chinese institutions and values internationally, the regulation was later relaxed.

The length and persistence of the campaign against corruption caught most observers by surprise. The movement was to catch "tigers and flies"—that is, senior officials as well as those at the grassroots. Later the targets also included "foxes"—citizens who had fled overseas with their ill-gotten gains. Over four years, the Sky Net campaign returned 5,000 individuals. Among the 1,335 individuals who had fled abroad in 2018, party members numbered 307, netting a total of $519 million. The highest-profile fox was the Chinese head of Interpol, who was brought back in September 2018 and, in January 2020, was sentenced to thirteen years in prison. Another colorful phrase is "naked officials," referring to officials who remain in China while their families relocate abroad. Regulations were introduced in 2014 barring any such officials from promotion.

Some felt that the campaign was merely a ploy to remove political opponents, a view reinforced by the removal and subsequent charges against Bo Xilai, which had paved the way for Xi's ascendency. This perspective seemed to be confirmed with the capture of the biggest tiger—Zhou Yongkang, the only member of the Politburo Standing Committee to defend Bo. In a familiar pattern, the noose was slowly tightened around Zhou as former colleagues in the oil and gas industry were rounded up. During his final decade in power, Zhou had overseen the security system in China, giving him access to important information on party leaders, leading many to view him as untouchable. In June 2015, however, he was sentenced to life imprisonment on charges of corruption, abuse of power, and the intentional sharing of state secrets. Zhou was the first member of the Standing Committee to be arrested on corruption charges since the founding of the PRC.

Nevertheless, it is clear that Xi and his close supporter and childhood friend, Wang Qishan, who have led the anticorruption campaign, wanted to use the slogan "catching tigers and flies" to broaden the movement beyond a factional struggle. In discussions, Wang had spoken of how disgusted he was by the behavior of colleagues, and some claimed that he was in an ideal position to lead the charge because he had no children of his own. Despite the initial sense that, similar to previous efforts, the campaign would soon wind down, the numbers increased over time, rising from 172,000 cases in 2013 to a peak of 621,000 cases in 2018, before dropping to 485,000 in 2019. In the first half of 2020, thirteen provincial or ministerial officials were charged, along with forty senior staff of state-owned enterprises. [15]

Xi and Wang view the campaign as crucial to ensure that the CCP will function effectively and to restore public faith in the party. The problems are not only with the party but also with the administration more generally. Thus, in 2018 the National Supervisory Commission was created to facilitate going after officials in a range of organizations who were not party members. The goal is to capitalize on the momentum to attack corrupt behavior among the elite of those who are not necessarily factional enemies.

The campaign has proved popular, but many citizens remain suspicious. In surveys of what citizens think about government performance under Hu and Wen, dealing with corruption always ranked as the area of work with which they were the most dissatisfied.[16] Given the regular exposure in the press of spectacular cases of corruption, it is not surprising that this is a major concern. Under Xi Jinping, popular perceptions have improved slightly. In a 2016 survey, 10.1 percent thought that government and government officials were extremely honest (up from 2.6 percent in 2011), while 4.4 percent thought they were extremely dishonest (down from 8.4 percent in 2011). The strength of the campaign pursued by Xi Jinping and Wang Qishan has impacted citizens' views of the government's determination to deal with corruption. During the initial years, the percentage of respondents who felt that the government was strongly committed to fighting corruption rose to 31.9 percent (in 2014). However, perhaps indicating that people were tiring of the campaign, the figure dropped to 26.6 percent in 2016 and still 20 percent felt that corruption had increased. Although perceptions are changing, large percentages still see corruption as part and parcel of life, suggesting that should the pressure be lifted, there is a potential for a return to previous practices.[17]

The fear that society is moving away from subservience to party dictates has led Xi Jinping to pursue measures to reassert control even more ardently than his predecessors. This has been heightened by recognition that the next phase of the reforms will be more difficult to implement because of opposition from vested interests—state monopolies and real estate and energy industries that benefit from close connections to local governments and central ministries. Official publications refer to powerful vested interests that obstruct measures they do not like.[18] Rather than relying on society and the media to provide oversight and to monitor errant behavior, the party under Xi has tightened control and rejected any show of independence.

Therefore, mechanisms have been developed to strengthen oversight. Xi has made it clear that complete obedience to the party is expected not only from party members but also from members of society at large. Given, of course, Xi's dominance of the party, in practice this means absolute obedience to Xi. There have been new regulations to tighten control over new social media, vehicles for expression have been limited, and human rights lawyers have been persecuted. Xi and his colleagues share the same apprehension about social media as did the previous administrations. In September 2013 they announced that social media users who posted comments considered slanderous could face a prison sentence if the posting received 5,000 hits or was reposted over 500 times. Of course, the party would decide what was slanderous. Worried about the reliability of their own media, in December 2013 it was announced that when Chinese reporters wanted to renew their press cards, they would have to take an exam to ensure that they had the correct ideological predisposition.

"Document Number Nine," issued and circulated by the CC Office in April 2013, made the tough stance clear and shocked the intellectual community. In one of the most conservative documents issued during the years of reform, the document outlines seven topics that should not be discussed.[19] The document is interesting in that it reveals the streams of thought circulating in Chinese intellectual circles. First, those who promoted "Western constitutional democracy" were slated for negating the features of the Chinese socialist system. Claims of universal values shook the party's ideological and theoretical foundations. Promotion of civil society undermined the social basis of the ruling party, and the promotion of neoliberalism was viewed as an attempt to change the basic economic system. Not surprisingly, press freedom was rejected. Finally, anyone who questioned the policy of reform and opening-up denied the party's line and principles. Resorting to a common refrain, Western influence was blamed for many of the ills with which China was wrestling. The document criticized Western embassies, consulates, and NGOs for spreading Western values and cultivating anti-government forces. Outsiders used dissidents and human rights activists to promote their objectives, and the self-immolations in Tibet and the unrest in Xinjiang were the result of outside manipulation. Clearly, the CCP remains incapable of accepting responsibility for the outcomes of its own actions.

The document was followed by action. In February 2016 when visiting three top media institutions, taking a page out of Mao Zedong's book Xi stated that editors and reporters must pledge absolute loyalty to the CCP and closely follow its leadership in "thought, politics, and action."[20] In December 2016 Xi delivered a similar message to the nation's schools and universities, claiming that adherence to party leadership was essential and that universities should be built into "strongholds that adhere to party leadership."[21] Inspectors were sent to China's top universities to ensure that teachers were not making "improper" remarks in class. There was special scrutiny in the humanities and the social sciences, with reading lists reviewed and works in foreign languages often dropped or translated into Chinese to facilitate scrutiny.

As a child of one of the founders of the PRC, Xi is proud of the achievements of the CCP and he has criticized those who have sought to undermine the party's image or to separate out the years of Mao Zedong's rule from those of the reform era. This has led to a clampdown on critical research and a promotion of publications that minimize the damage caused by movements such as the Great Leap Forward. There have been attacks on domestic and international historians who have promoted historical nihilism—which is to say, those who have not followed the official account of Chinese party history. It was a chill that had not been felt for many, many years. In August 2018 the chill turned to frost with the announcement of a campaign to instill patriotism among intellectuals, which would unleash an "unremitting struggle" to "strengthen unity" through study sessions to truly understand Xi Jinping's philosophy.[22]

In 2016 China introduced two pieces of legislation to deal with the not-for-profit sector, one of which placed tougher restrictions on foreign NGOs operating in China, and the second of which, the Charity Law, sought to direct the flow of new, domestic wealth to CCP priorities. The law governing foreign NGOs, which became effective on January 1, 2017, provided clarity and also established tighter regulations. The law followed the spirit of the National Security Law of July 1, 2015, which states that "all necessary measures" must be taken to protect the country from hostile elements. Most importantly, registration was placed under the remit of the Ministry of Public Security, highlighting security concerns. The areas in which foreign NGOs could work were spelled out, and fund-raising within China was prohibited. In contrast, the Charity Law of September 1, 2016, revealed that the party was coming to terms with the enormous wealth that the reforms had helped to create but it had to be clear about where that wealth might be directed. Registration for organizations was eased and public fund-raising was allowed, but the areas for which support was encouraged were limited to those such as poverty relief, care for the elderly and orphans, disaster relief, and promotion of education, science, culture, and sports. Those considered reliable can engage in "charitable activities that represent the core values of socialism and promote the traditional morals of the Chinese nation."[23] Thus, registration was eased, but subsequently direction was tightened and party control was enhanced.[24]

The crackdown on social activism continued and intensified. Two organizations were singled out for special attention. The first was the New Citizens' Movement, founded by Xu Zhiyong. Xu began his career as a lawyer, representing plaintiffs who had been affected in a tainted milk scandal. He moved on to deal with broader questions about social justice and transparency. As the name of the group indicates, it wanted to promote the idea of citizens who enjoyed rights and worked according to the slogan "freedom, justice, love."[25] The group seized on the anticorruption campaign to call for officials' assets to be made public. In 2012–2013 it organized a number of small protests that worried the authorities—such as a program of citizens' meals, where people were encouraged to get together in an environment of equality to engage in spirited discussions. As a result, Xu Zhiyong was arrested and sentenced to four years in prison for "gathering a crowd to disturb public order." A related movement was that of human rights lawyers who defended people attacked during political campaigns as well as followers of the Falun Gong spiritual movement. By July 9, 2015, more than 200 had been detained, with many given jail terms, suspended sentences, or placed under house arrest. The perceived threat to the system was that these movements and lawyers were justifying their actions in terms of China's own laws and Constitution. The use of the law to punish these activists, perhaps taking a page out of Singapore's book, followed the example of lawyer Chen Guangcheng, who had sought to defend those abused by the system. In 2006 Chen was sentenced for "damaging property and organizing a disturbance to disturb traffic." Chen is blind.

On paper, there was a greater commitment to the rule of law. The decision of the October 2014 plenum pulled together certain measures for the courts that had been put forward with the five-year plan.[26] For example, in November 2013, detailed recommendations were issued to prevent wrongful arrests: judges were to presume innocence until suspects were actually proven guilty, collusion with the police was discouraged, and evidence obtained through torture or sleep deprivation was to be dismissed. Similarly, Xi commented on the need to govern in line with the Constitution, which, as we have seen, led some to try to hold the CCP to its commitments. The phrase "governing the nation in accordance with the Constitution" was included in the plenum decision. However, although individual party members might be more easily held accountable in civil courts, there was no intention that the party as an institution would be subject to oversight. Those who promoted constitutionalism were swiftly silenced. The decision did suggest certain future reforms, such as preventing local officials from interfering in legal cases and not deciding the outcomes of legal cases in advance. However, neither the law nor the Constitution was to provide an independent check on the party: party leadership was the most vital fundamental guarantee for the socialist rule of law. The Constitution enshrines the leading role of the party, and the plenum decision makes this clear, noting that "the leadership of the party and socialist rule of law are identical."

The leadership has taken a much tougher line on the issue of the northwestern province of Xinjiang. The leadership is intent on crushing any independent Uighur identity once and for all. Two things have driven this harsher approach. First, Xinjiang is a crucial artery for the corridor of the Belt and Road Initiative (BRI) through Central Asia. Second, there is a fear that independence activity in Xinjiang may link up with groups across the border. Policy has focused on expanding the Han population in Xinjiang to the point where one-half of the population of 24 million are Han Chinese. Two academics have suggested that since multiracial states have failed elsewhere in the world, China should push more vigorously to integrate the minorities to create a single race. Ethnic group identity is to be diluted.[27] This view has been accompanied by the construction of "unity villages" for Uighurs and Han to live together and the promotion of interracial marriages.[28] However, outbreaks of violence shifted the attitude of the leaders in Beijing to push a harder line.

The possibility for a harsher response was set by Xi Jinping following his 2014 visit to Xinjiang when, in addition to calling for development and integration, he called for a "people's war on terror" to combat separatism, terrorism, and religious extremism and said that "absolutely no mercy should be shown." Xi had reacted strongly to three terrorist attacks in the spring. This led to abandoning the long-held belief that economic investment and growth would develop the problem away. A campaign of mass reeducation was required.

In 2016 the party secretary of Tibet was moved to Xinjiang, and he brought with him the tougher practices he had implemented in Tibet. Beginning in 2017, reports began to surface about reeducation camps in the province. UN experts and other outside observers have claimed that some one million Uighurs have been detained in these camps. A trove of 400 pages of Chinese documents was leaked to the *New York Times* detailing the crackdown.[29] Not surprisingly, the Chinese authorities have taken a different tack, with a Foreign Ministry spokesperson dismissing outside interference in internal affairs, claiming that China's treatment of the Uighurs was no different from that of other countries fighting extremism.[30] The Chinese defense was that the camps are not internment camps but instead places that provide opportunities for vocational training, and that far from destroying traditional culture, they are promoting it. At first the government had denied the existence of the camps, before foreign reporting forced China to acknowledge them and local Xinjiang legislation was revised to permit local governments to "educate and transform" people influenced by "extremism" at "vocational training centers."[31] The ideological education the Uighurs received would purge extremist thoughts and permit them to return to their families with unsullied minds. Part of the training is classes on spoken and written Chinese. The CCP hopes that assimilation, repression, and eradication of local culture will resolve the problems. This seems unlikely and may even increase the challenge over time.

To provide cohesion across society, in addition to promotion of the China Dream to rejuvenate the nation, Xi Jinping offers a mixed strategy of relying on traditional support, evoking Chinese tradition, and reinforcing the explanatory power of Marxism. In contrast to Jiang Zemin who, in his Three Represents, had expanded the definition of who the CCP represented, on May Day 2013 Xi reaffirmed the CCP commitment to the proletariat. For Xi, the party is the "pioneer of the working class," and its goal is to consolidate its "class base among the workers"[32]—surely a difficult task, given the retrenchment of the SOE sector and a workforce spread across new sectors of the economy that are more diverse than the traditional industries. To highlight what he saw as attempts by the West to undermine the system, Xi, in another gesture reminiscent of the past, resurrected the phrase "peaceful evolution"—a term rarely heard from senior party leaders since the aftermath of the 1989 demonstrations.[33]

With the talk of moral decay, the loss of faith in Marxism, and the lingering influence of what is termed Western liberal values, the leadership turned to a selective interpretation of traditional culture, especially Confucianism, to bolster the appeal to socialism and to portray the CCP—not the GMD on Taiwan—as the true descendent of the imperial past. Xi Jinping's claim that the CCP is the genuine successor to China's glorious past is remarkable. When the CCP took power in 1949, and especially during the Cultural Revolution, the CCP portrayed itself as representing a radical break with the past. However, Xi Jinping is not the first leader to trace this heritage, and it echoes the populism promoted by Hu Jintao and Wen Jiabao and even the ideas of Liu Shaoqi, for which he was soundly punished. Xi has been more explicit, noting that together with other philosophies and cultures, Confucianism was "taking shape and growing within China" and that such philosophies were "spiritual experiences, rational thinking, and cultural achievements of the nation while it strived to build its identity."[34]

Although the ideology of Marxism-Leninism seems ill-suited to explain the rapidly evolving landscape that Chinese citizens inhabit, the leadership has stressed the importance of Marxism as a guide to action for party members. In December 2013, Xi ordered all party members to study Marxist philosophy, as the Marxist theories, especially historical materialism, still had a "strong vitality and serve as powerful arms of thought for guiding Communists to make progress."[35] On the ninety-fifth anniversary of the founding of the CCP, Xi called on party members not to "betray or abandon" Marxism.[36] This was part of the effort to shift party members away from their obsession with GDP growth and with amassing individual wealth. Marxism was confirmed as a compulsory course in all academic institutions, and all media organizations were instructed to train their journalists in the Marxist concepts that dictated their role. On the two-hundredth anniversary of Marx's birth, in May 2018, Xi Jinping called for treating Marxism as a spiritual pursuit.

All the same, rather than providing a critical lens through which to view society and its development, Marxism has been used to reinforce obedience to the party and its policies. The stress on Marxism's relevance had at least one unintended effect on a group of students who took Xi seriously and used Marxist analysis to understand the state of society. On some university campuses, students organized Marxist societies to run social activities for workers and night classes to teach migrant workers about their rights. Some moved further to mobilize workers in support of their rights, and in August 2018 more than fifty students were arrested for helping workers at a factory in the southern city of Shenzhen. This led to a crackdown on such activist societies: Nanjing University refused to register a society, others have been harassed, and the president of Peking University was moved to a new position and the party secretary demoted to the less powerful position of president. In a scathing comment about university officials, one student commented: "They want students to focus on studying Marxism, not to practice it or fight for its cause. When we do that, it causes too many problems for them."[37] The lack of tolerance was evident when on December 26, 2018, the student head of the Peking University Marxist Society, on his way to join a celebration for the 125th anniversary of Mao Zedong's birth, was grabbed by plainclothes police.[38]

Finally, the promotion of nationalism has accompanied the revival of traditional culture to bolster regime legitimacy. This trend, which began earlier under Hu and Wen, was picked up following the global financial crisis of 2008–2009, and it has been strengthened under Xi Jinping. Declaring that any criticism of party policy is unpatriotic has been key to this process. This has also been accompanied by a more assertive posture over territorial issues.

Hail to the Chief

Xi Jinping entered the Nineteenth Party Congress, held in October 2017, in a position of great strength within the party, and not surprisingly he dominated the proceedings. Clearly, the party was now being reshaped to conform

Xi Jinping at the Nineteenth Party Congress.

to his vision of China's future. Marking an end to the era of Deng Xiaoping, he traced a line of continuity from Chinese history through to a vision of what the nation would look like in 2050. The new leadership did include representation from other groups within the party, but it was clearly focused around Xi Jinping as the core and was distinct from the model of collective leadership that had been epitomized by the Hu Jintao–Wen Jiabao leadership.

In his political report, Xi Jinping linked his China Dream of national rejuvenation to the original mission of the CCP, which was to bring happiness to the Chinese people and relieve the nation from its national humiliation at the hands of foreigners. He noted the importance of never forgetting why one started, because then "you can accomplish your mission."[39] Xi has rejected the division of the history of the PRC into two periods, one under Mao Zedong and one during the era of reform, and sees his leadership as building on the legacies of the past. This stress on historical legitimacy and continuity was reinforced when, following the congress, he took the members of the Politburo Standing Committee to visit the two sites of the 1921 founding congress of the CCP. Further, drawing the line of continuity with the past, his report stressed that China's socialist culture was derived from its "fine traditional culture, which was born of the Chinese civilization and nurtured over more than 5,000 years."

Looking forward, Xi made it clear that China is now in a new historical era, and he added to his core contribution to the CCP canon the phrase

"Socialism with Chinese characteristics for a new era." This called for a prosperous society to be built by 2050, which would realize socialist modernization and rejuvenation of the nation; have strong confidence in the chosen
path; deal with the contradiction between unbalanced and inadequate development and the people's needs for a better life; develop the rule of law;
and implement a strong military under party control. Externally, this incorporated the previous calls for a new type of international relations that would
build a shared future for humankind.

All of this had to take place under CCP leadership; otherwise rejuvenation would be mere wishful thinking. Even ensuring that state power belonged to the people was dependent on following the party leadership. Even
though each leader has stressed the leading role of the party, Xi Jinping has
been more forceful in reasserting control over all sectors and reversing some
of his predecessors' relaxation of control. This is reflected in the new statutes, with the incorporation of the phrase "party, government, military,
people and intellectuals, whether north, south, east or west, the party leads
in everything." This makes it difficult to see how the people will genuinely
control the state or local governments or how businesses will be able to conduct effective work free of party interference.

Moving forward, Xi outlined a three-phase timeline to becoming a prosperous society. By 2020, the objective was to be a moderately prosperous society, doubling the size of the economy from 2010. The period 2020–2035
would be used to achieve socialist modernization. China would become a
global leader in innovation, with an expanding middle-income group living
in a better environment. By 2050 China would become a "great, modern socialist country" that will be "prosperous, strong, democratic, culturally advanced, harmonious, and beautiful." Externally, China's overall strength will
make it a global leader.

On the whole, Xi has applied certain informal norms, balancing different
streams within the party, but he has ensured that he is clearly *primus inter
pares*. At the First Plenum for the new Central Committee, held on October 18–24, 2017, five of the seven members of the Politburo Standing
Committee retired and were replaced, as required, by members drawn from
the Politburo. Before the congress there had been discussion as to whether
Xi's close associate and leader of the anticorruption campaign, Wang Qishan,
would retire. He did retire, but given his knowledge of and the importance
of Sino-US relations, at the March 2018 NPC meeting he was appointed
vice president of the PRC. The five new members of the Standing Committee

showed some balance: two were close associates of Xi, two were close to Hu Jintao, and one had been close to Jiang Zemin. This was wise of Xi, and the end result was unity, with Xi as the clear core. Most importantly, unlike at previous such meetings, no clear successor was chosen who might replace Xi in 2022, raising the possibility that Xi might seek to extend the period of his formal leadership. At the March 2018 NPC session, this was given even greater credence when the two-term limit on the presidency of the PRC was lifted.

There were fifteen open posts to fill on the Politburo, and the majority of newcomers were close Xi associates, some of whom would be eligible for promotion to the Politburo Standing Committee in 2022. Xi's dominance was also reflected in changes to the new Party Statutes. His contribution to the CCP lexicon of "Xi Jinping Thought on Socialism with Chinese Characteristics for a New Era" is important in two respects. First, it places Xi alongside Mao Zedong as the only leader to have his name included in the statutes while still in a formal position. Deng had effectively retired when his thought was added, and the names of Jiang Zemin and Hu Jintao have not been attached to their theoretical contributions. Second, while it builds on the notion of socialism with Chinese characteristics, it clearly marks China under Xi as having entered a new era, one for which Xi will define the evolution of Marxism to suit the current Chinese situation. This ability to redefine ideology to suit the priorities of the new leadership was underscored by the reaffirmation that China was still in the primary stage of socialism. The new statutes also incorporated the BRI. Xi's dominance within the new leadership was affirmed at the new Politburo's first meeting when the members pledged loyalty to Xi as "leader"—an appellation that in the past had been used only for Mao and Deng.

Party dominance of economic policy making and Xi's overall authority was confirmed at the Thirteenth NPC, held on March 5–20, 2018, marking the further eclipse of the State Council and Premier Li Keqiang. A series of party meetings at the end of December 2018 and the February 2018 plenum outlined priorities for the next year.[40] As usual, every effort was made to ensure that the economy looked good for the forthcoming congress, and in fact the economic planners were very successful in delivering an economy with stable growth and an SOE sector that was reviving. The "three battles" for the future were outlined as reducing financial risk, fighting poverty (Xi had called for the eradication of poverty in the rural areas by 2020), and improving the physical environment.

The NPC followed the economic policies with an emphasis on quality of growth over quantity. The main business was yet another attempt to overhaul the administrative structure. Eight ministerial units and seven vice-ministerial units were cut, and the overall thrust was to effectively centralize administration under party control to ensure that Xi's policies could be implemented. This was emphasized by the new vice premier, Liu He, who stated that the key question of governance was to strengthen party leadership and satisfy Xi Jinping's "important demands."[41] Given the financial turmoil of 2015–2016, attention was focused on tightening up the financial sector. To this end, the Banking Commission and the Insurance Regulatory Commission were merged, the People's Bank was given additional powers to formulate monetary policy and to enforce financial and banking regulations, and earlier a new Financial Stability and Development Commission was established.

Li Keqiang was reappointed as premier, but with his powers very much diminished by the elevation of Liu He and changing the status of the Leading Group for Comprehensive Deepening Reform to a commission. A competent, technocratic leadership was put in place to oversee the economy and the financial sector, but with Xi still clearly calling the shots, and party control was strengthened over the state sector. One important example was that the three state bodies covering minority affairs, religion, and overseas Chinese were brought under the leadership of the CCP's United Front Work Department. Oversight of the civil service, press, media, and film were all brought under party control. Four of the central leading groups that Xi had set up were raised to the level of commissions, and they covered the overall reform program, cyberspace, financial and economic matters, and foreign affairs. Ideas earlier in the reform era of trying to separate government from party have clearly been abandoned, confirming mistrust of the government apparatus and society to bend to Xi's will on policy questions.

The new head of the NPC, Li Zhanshu, a Xi associate, was fulsome in his praise: Xi was the "core of the party, military commander, the people's leader, the helmsman for a new era in socialism with Chinese characteristics, and the people's guide."[42] The use of the word "helmsman" is important, as this term had always been reserved for Mao Zedong. In December 2019 the Politburo went further—not only praising Xi Jinping for his long-term vision but also using the phrase "people's leader," another phrase traditionally reserved for Mao Zedong.[43] The State Constitution was revised to eliminate the two-term limit for the president and the vice president. The official reasoning was that this brought it into line with party rules, which have no limits on the tenure of the general secretary. Most have interpreted the move as indicating Xi's intention to stay on in a position of formal power beyond his two terms. Not surprisingly, his thought was incorporated into the revised preamble of the Constitution.

Party and state meetings consolidated Xi Jinping's primacy within the leadership, while cementing elite unity. This cleared the way for Xi to push ahead with his own agenda, unhindered by others. There are two problems associated with this. First, his policy program, beyond reasserting control of the party and eradicating corruption, was unclear. Greater clarity for the economy was provided at the fifth plenum, which met in October 2020. Second, there is no one else to blame if things go wrong, and China has had problems in the past with overcentralized and personalized rule. Xi Jinping clearly rejects Deng Xiaoping's intention to avoid this and to allow more flexibility and local initiative in favor of highly personalized and centralized rule.

After the two congresses, forward momentum was shaken by three major setbacks: the slowing of the economy, the pushback from the international community because of China's growing influence, and the eruption of the massive demonstrations in Hong Kong. These three challenges were exacerbated by the unexpected outbreak in late 2019 of the new coronavirus that causes COVID-19. The spread of the virus caused the slowing economy to stall temporarily, paused the Hong Kong demonstrations, and heightened the international community's concerns about China's transparency and responsibility as the virus spread beyond China to infect most parts of the world. China's response exposed flaws in the heavily centralized system of governance, because lower administrative levels were hesitant to report bad information and many waited for guidance from Xi Jinping on how to respond. The same faults were evident as with the outbreak of SARS in 2002–2003: failure to effectively regulate wet markets; attempts to silence those sounding the alarm; unclear reporting lines to Beijing; failure to report bad news promptly so that countermeasures could minimize damage; and mistrust of official pronouncements among many citizens. Once the central leadership became aware of the severity of the problem, Xi Jinping ordered an aggressive response of quarantine and other measures to try to contain the spread of the disease. Now the strength of the system came to the fore—an entire hospital was built in just a few days, and tens of millions prevented from traveling in order to reduce spread of the virus. The Chinese propaganda system shifted into high gear, extolling the party's effective response under

Xi's leadership in comparison with the faltering efforts to control the virus in other countries such as the United States. This propaganda has proved effective. The initial outrage that many Chinese citizens expressed online was replaced by greater support for the government as foreign governments criticized China for its behavior.[44]

Ironically, part of the impetus for the international pushback to China's policies was caused by China's prior, limited increase in transparency about its objectives. Domestically, articulation of "Made in China 2025" is intended to make China the "master of its own technologies," entailing self-sufficiency in important advanced industries. This created concern among foreign governments and businesses about the extent to which China is favoring its own businesses and tilting the playing field unfairly against them. China was seen as prioritizing its own companies in domestic markets, while providing generous subsidies for its companies that are competing internationally. To address international concerns, it is noteworthy that the phrase "Made in China 2025" was not mentioned at the March 2019 NPC meeting. In addition, the meeting passed a new law that prohibits the forced transfer of technology. Foreign concerns have not been limited to the United States. In September 2018 the commerce ministers of the United States, Japan, and the European Union issued a harsh condemnation of Chinese business practices. While not referring to China by name, the critique of non-market-oriented policies, unfair competitive conditions, and harmful subsidy practices were directed at the Chinese government.[45]

Internationally, China's more assertive policy on territorial questions has raised concerns, thus bringing the BRI into the spotlight. While China portrays the BRI as a benign program of much-needed investment in infrastructure throughout the region, the US administration sees more sinister objectives, with a Chinese system evolving to parallel the post–World War II global architecture. China's regional trade arrangements are seen as a challenge to the WTO, and its regional financing vehicles are seen as a challenge to the World Bank.[46] The one comparable organization China has not yet developed is a lender of last resort to match the International Monetary Fund.

Economic Slowdown: Tariffs or Structural Impediment

Some have attributed the economic slowdown to the imposition of trade tariffs by the Trump administration, but the slowdown began long before this and instead has been caused by structural factors. Policy still favors the SOE sector, yet it is the non-state sector that is providing the impetus that the economy needs. The non-state sector contributes 60 percent of GDP growth, 90 percent of new jobs, and 50 percent of fiscal revenue, but receives only 11 percent of funding. The state sector receives at least 80 percent of funding at preferential rates.

Beyond this, the impact of those factors that contributed to China's spectacular growth are either exhausted or are declining.[47] Government resource allocation has become more market-based, but as noted above, this process requires further progress. The shift from near isolation of the Chinese economy to extensive global integration following entry into the WTO provided a massive boost, but the most important impacts have already been felt. Importantly, hundreds of millions of workers shifted from laboring in low-productivity agriculture to more productive work in the growing economy. And China experienced a demographic dividend with a young workforce coming of age just when China was integrating globally and needed a large workforce. Now, because of the impact of the family planning policies of the 1990s and beyond, the Chinese population is aging rapidly and faces rising pension expenses and health-care burdens for the elderly.

With these rising pressures, perhaps not surprisingly the celebration of forty years of reform at the end of 2018 and the Central Economic Work Conference, held on December 19–21, 2018, revealed how little had been completed in terms of implementing the wide-ranging reform aspirations proposed in December 2013. Of the ten major policy initiatives, only two showed progress (labor and innovation), four showed little change (fiscal affairs, trade, environment, and the financial system), and four had been backsliding (land, cross-border investment, competition, and SOE reform).[48] The work conference responded to external pressures, especially President Trump's tariff policies. The internal and external challenges gave reformers hope that Xi Jinping's speech celebrating the fortieth anniversary of reform, on December 18, 2018, would revive progress and outline the future path.[49] Instead Xi Jinping chose to hunker down, offering praise for what had gone before but offering little idea of what to expect in the future.

Continuing his view that the achievements under Mao Zedong should not be separated from those of the reform era, Xi credited Mao with all that followed, claiming that Mao set down "the political premise and institutional foundations for all development and progress in contemporary China." His disastrous policies that had been criticized in earlier party pronouncements were referred to as "explorations" that had provided the basis for the era of socialism with Chinese characteristics. Not surprisingly, those expecting a bold statement of reform intent were disappointed. Xi strongly defended the Chinese model of development and claimed that its success meant that no one was in a position to tell China what to do. China would reform only what the party deemed it necessary to reform and nothing else—a clear response to external pressures and the Trump administration. As discussed below, Xi would yield significant ground in the Phase One trade agreement of January 15, 2020. Despite its growing power and influence, Xi was at pains to stress that China was not a threat to the global order and instead promoted the "shared future of mankind," including world peace, and saw itself as a "defender of the international order." Xi took the opportunity to restate the party's centrality, pointing out that all its achievements were derived from its centralized and united leadership. Indeed, party dominance over the economy was a key feature of the Central Economic Work Conference held immediately following Xi's speech.[50]

The centrality of the party's role in ensuring all that was good was reinforced at the seventieth anniversary of the founding of the PRC, on October 1, 2019. Xi's official comments were brief, simply noting that no force could shake China's foundations, but a policy paper and publication of an earlier speech stressed the centrality of the party. Most notable was the call for a strong, unified party leadership to prevent the nation from "crumbling."[51] Obsessed with the collapse of the Soviet party, Xi commented to the new CC members: "When the Communist Party of the Soviet Union had 200,000 members, it seized power. When it had 2 million members, it defeated Hitler. When it had almost 20 million members, it lost power."[52] The CCP leadership remains haunted by this collapse, and on a number of occasions Xi has lamented how no one had stood up to defend the party.

The task of delivering on key economic goals was not helped by the onset of the COVID-19 pandemic over the winter of 2019–2020 with its unpredictable spread. With the country shutting down just around the Chinese Lunar Year, domestic demand collapsed as travel was curtailed and citizens went into lockdown. International demand fell, disrupting supply and production chains. The Chinese economy contracted 6.8 percent in the first quarter of 2020, but growth revived to 4.0 percent in the third quarter, which would produce an annual growth rate of around 0.7 percent. This is respectable given the circumstances, but well below original projections. Still, the economic achievement over the decade remains remarkable.

Navigating the World as a Global Power

The unprecedented level of China's integration into the global economy and energy markets, its accumulation of huge foreign reserves, and its role in climate change have forced fundamental changes in what was formerly its low-profile international position. National pride in its economic achievements and disillusionment with the West as a model led the Xi Jinping leadership to become more assertive about its economic role. Xi is certainly more ambitious in the international arena than his predecessor Hu Jintao was, and his policy to pursue rejuvenation of the Chinese nation projects his vision. Deng Xiaoping's doctrine of "hiding one's capabilities and biding one's time"—that is, keeping a low profile and not claiming leadership—has been replaced by Xi's desire to adopt a more active international role. The CCP is willing to step up global leadership in those areas from which the United States has withdrawn, redressing the relationship with the United States and with the Asian region. At a December 2014 Politburo session, Xi noted that China was now embarking on a "new round of opening to the world," emphasizing that China would no longer take a passive role in global economic governance. He stated: "We cannot be a bystander but must be a participant, a leader."

China has been more explicit about its aims, and this has caused disquiet in a number of countries in the region and in the West. At the Nineteenth Party Congress, held on October 2017, Xi announced that by 2050 China would be a "global leader in terms of composite strength and international influence," and in June 2018 he proposed the notion of "foreign policy with Chinese characteristics." This brought the BRI into the spotlight, with China claiming that it is contributing to and building on existing structures, while providing much-needed finance for infrastructure.

How to deal with and assimilate China's rise has created considerable concern. Clearly, China's economic rise will change geopolitics; there is already a divergence of views about how threatening this might be to traditional US dominance and agenda setting and whether relations between the United States and China have reached a "tipping point."[53] For the first time in several centuries, the largest economy in the world will not be Western, and the world might come under a leadership that does not share the consensual values and political structures of the West. This has led some US analysts to suggest that policy should shift from engaging China to being more confrontational and even to constrain its rise.[54] Certainly, this was the conclusion

China today as seen by Beijing, including the nine-dash line and Taiwan.

that the Trump administration reached. However, also for the first time, the world's largest economy will not enjoy the highest living standards, and moving forward it still faces considerable challenges. This gives more succor to those who wish to continue engagement under the belief that it will result in China's conforming to most global norms and practices, while accepting that there will be a shift from "strategic cooperation" to "strategic competition."[55] Yet others have warned of a new cycle of the "Thucydides trap," whereby a rising power creates concern and unease in the dominant power, providing the possibility for unanticipated conflict.[56]

In addition, a potentially dangerous bifurcation is emerging between an economic Asia where China is the central player and a security Asia that is dependent on US military power.[57] President Trump's decision to abandon the Trans-Pacific Partnership (TPP), which excludes China but ties together other key nations in the Asia-Pacific, has severed a potential valuable link for the United States between economics and security. This raises the question of whether China's leaders will seek to redefine regional and perhaps global trade and investment norms. This may not be as easy for China's new leaders to achieve as some have assumed. Certainly, the US abandonment of the TPP and its not joining the Asia Infrastructure Investment Bank (AIIB), a decision taken by the Obama administration, heralds a decline in US influence in Asia that cannot be replaced by increased military spending. However, this does not mean that China will automatically fill the gap. With respect to trade, the TPP reached a general agreement on the standards and rules that would be adopted for a diverse range of economies and included regulations for labor and environmental standards. The China-promoted Regional Comprehensive Economic Partnership, which excludes the United States, does not have such an integrated approach and allows members flexibility to choose which commitments to adopt. Importantly, it will not help with the market for services, which is growing rapidly in Asia but remains heavily protected in much of the region. Further, despite its relative decline, the United States retains a stronger network of alliances than China. That said, China is improving its ties with the Philippines and with Thailand, while dominating the Kampuchean and Lao economies and putting Myanmar in an increasingly difficult position. Yet this and China's actions in the South China Sea have caused concern within the region, with one observer claiming that China is using up its "great reserves of goodwill" and sacrificing long-term objectives and global interests for short-term objectives.[58]

Powerful countries shape the world, and whether they like it or not, China's leaders will be forced to take a more proactive stance not only on questions of territorial sovereignty but also on reserve currencies, banking and financial regulations, trade and investment agreements, climate discussions, the provision of global public goods, and so forth. This will present a huge challenge for the leadership, as it has not had extensive experience with negotiations in many of these areas. It will have to come to terms with the fact that the country is a major player and the global community will expect clearer explanations of policy intent. The need to focus on its increasingly demanding global role may draw its attention away from the necessary focus on the domestic agenda.

Defining a Role in Asia

Much of China's foreign policy is rooted in the Asia region, yet in the past, at the conceptual level, the CCP rarely articulated a strategy to guide its actions. Historically, Taiwan has been the focus of China's major sovereignty challenge, but China has disputed claims with most of its neighbors, including Russia, India, and Vietnam, and it has fought a border war with each of them. China also has territorial disputes with Japan and a number of Southeast Asian neighbors over the demarcation of territorial boundaries in the South China Sea. This includes the disputed territory that China situates within its "nine-dash line" of control within the South China Sea. In recent years its growing investment and trade relations have altered this somewhat passive approach, with the exception of sovereignty claims, and the CCP is developing a more coherent policy with respect to Asia.

In 2013, Foreign Minister Wang Yi signaled a shift indicating that more attention would be paid to the Asian region and that a "community of common destiny" could be created.[59] The approach entails carrots and sticks. The carrot is the range of investments that China is developing in the region. This includes the BRI and establishment of the AIIB, which are meant to facilitate Chinese export of its domestic capacity (steel, cement, and so forth) to the region, but also to tie nations throughout the region into China's sphere of influence. The stick relates to questions of sovereignty and China's more aggressive moves in the South China Sea and the East China Sea that have created concern among countries such as Japan and Vietnam and escalated security tensions with the United States.

China's leaders have been at pains to stress that their economic rise will not come at the expense of other countries in the region. In June 2014 Xi Jinping reiterated that China's foreign policy was peaceful in nature and that China retained a policy of noninterference in the internal affairs of other countries. In the previous May, at the Conference on Interaction and Confidence Building in Asia, which excluded the United States and Japan, Xi provided a fuller articulation of a "new security concept" for a "common, comprehensive, cooperative, and sustainable security strategy for Asia." He stressed that security should be mutually beneficial and that, to be sustainable, it should be based on economic development, with no country seeking to dominate regional security affairs. In a dig at the United States, Xi commented that a "military alliance that is targeted at a third party is not conducive to common regional security." The problem, of course, is that China's proposal of noninterference rings hollow when China itself is such a major player in the economies of many of its neighbors and it still aggressively asserts its territorial claims in the South and East China Seas.

The major game changer is the promotion of the BRI (originally called "One Belt, One Road"). Put into motion during Xi's trip in September–October 2013 to Kazakhstan and Indonesia, it is the signature component of his attempts to develop China's global standing. Although it is one of his highest priorities, and certainly the increased investment in infrastructure is welcome, it is difficult to define clearly its scope and the precise role of the funding agencies. Formally, it covers sixty-five countries, with one-third of global GDP and 60 percent of the world's population. Despite the creation of the Silk Road Fund and the existence of the AIIB, most funding comes through the China Development Bank and the Export-Import Bank. It has been named one of three major national strategies and enjoys an entire chapter in the 2015–2020 five-year plan. Importantly, and somewhat surprisingly, pursuit of the BRI was incorporated into the statutes adopted at the Nineteenth Party Congress in October 2017. Prior to this, in May 2017 twenty-eight heads of state visited Beijing to lobby to be part of the initiative.[60] However, significant Chinese investment has brought challenges as well as benefits.

To date, most of the overseas lending has not gone to the countries defined as a part of the BRI; its main destinations are Europe, the United States, Australia, and Canada. Being along the Belt and Road has not yet delivered more investment than is received in other parts of the developing world.[61] The key question is whether Chinese enterprises will engage in risky projects despite the stated intent that such projects must be financially viable.

Given that Xi Jinping's reputation is tied to the success of this program, and with the party reasserting control over major outbound investment, riskier projects may be taken on to meet political objectives.

Clearly, there is a geopolitical objective to the BRI and the drive to create and maintain secure energy supplies, but it also has explicit objectives to help with China's domestic economic challenges and to offer an opportunity to take on a global role and provide an alternative to the TPP and US actions.[62] The massive investment in the Pakistan corridor has a strategic intent, binding with a traditional ally and making sure that it keeps a distance from the United States and its regional ally, India. Chinese investments have also been criticized as a new form of colonialism. Malaysian prime minister Mahathir canceled Chinese funding projects and warned of a new version of colonialism, although later he claimed that he was not referring to China.[63] The US administration has been especially concerned that China is using debt-trap diplomacy to promote its regional strategic interests. For instance, defaults have occurred in Africa, and questions of sovereignty have been raised in Myanmar. A prime case occurred with the port that China financed and built in Sri Lanka. The Sri Lankan government was unable to meet debt repayments and its debt was restructured in December 2017, with 70 percent of the port leased and operations turned over to China for a period of ninety-nine years. The United States has expressed concern that the port could become a Chinese naval base, but the Sri Lankan authorities maintain that it will only be available for civilian use.

There is a clear domestic rationale for the BRI, and it will form part of China's strategy to reduce regional inequality by focusing significant funds on provinces such as Xinjiang. By tying in the Central Asian nations, Beijing hopes that this will reduce support for independence movements within the Islamic communities in the Northwest. The stimulus package that was introduced in 2008–2009 did keep the economy afloat, but it also produced enormous production overcapacity that can be exported to the infrastructure projects along the Belt and Road. Finally, the administration hopes that its dominance in key sectors funded for the project will help China set industry standards that will form a part of China's Made in China 2025 strategy.[64]

The success or failure of the BRI will be a game changer or a game breaker in terms of global politics and whether targets such as controlling climate change and environmental degradation can be met. The challenges and problems confronting development of the BRI are reasonably clear. As noted, the association of the BRI with General Secretary Xi might encourage investors to take on projects that are riskier than can be justified by the economic potential. The question arises as to whether there are enough financially feasible projects to go around. The problem of contributing to China's debt is raised by the fact that many of the core countries have poor credit ratings and are not stable political environments. Last but not least, the question also arises as to whether Russia will accept the growing influence of China in what it has traditionally viewed as its own backyard. This has led China to encourage Russia's participation and to strengthen ties, especially against the United States.

The international pushback meant that the April 2019 BRI Forum was a less boastful affair. Xi Jinping's address exhibited a more sober attitude, seeking to confront such accusations as creating debt traps, the transparency and sustainability of projects, and responsible financing.[65]

The major challenge testing China's capacity for leadership is wrestling with North Korea's nuclear ambitions. President Trump made clear his view that China had not done enough to curb North Korea's nuclear development and that China's leadership of the Six-Party Talks had not yielded progress, a view not shared by all those working on the talks at the time. The US capacity to pressure North Korea is not strong, nor is its capacity to push China. Thus, in a surprising move, President Trump shifted from hurling threats and abuse at North Korea's leader, Kim Jong-un, to meeting with him in Singapore in June 2018 to try to strike a deal. The supposed agreement appeared to call for complete denuclearization of the Korean peninsula in return for guarantees of security for the North. Despite this, it is unclear what, if any, procedures would be in place to move forward, and mistrust grew on both sides; President Trump walked away from the second meeting in Vietnam in February 2019. North Korea is a de facto nuclear state, and despite the summits, it is not clear that it would really accept any agreement that would require disarmament. This is dangerous for China. If North Korea retains its nuclear weapons, what is there to stop other nations in the region from developing them as well?

Dealing with an Unpredictable American President

China's development has had dramatic consequences for its relationship with the United States. With the Cold War ended, there is no long-term durability underpinning the relationship, making it vulnerable to sudden events.

Even under President Obama, the relationship was marked by mistrust and differing interpretations of the same events. While the United States saw China's renewed assertiveness in the South China Sea as a challenge to international waters and its allies, China saw the United States as mobilizing allies to constrain its development. Eventually it looked as if Obama and Xi Jinping were moving toward common ground. A decent working relationship provided an opportunity to emphasize common interests, such as dealing with North Korea and climate change, while outlining clear differences on other issues, such as cyber security and China's wish for an end to US arms sales to Taiwan.

The US approach was summed up by Secretary of State John Kerry when he termed the constructive relationship a "new model that would be shaped by better cooperation and shared challenges." In particular, Kerry was concerned about avoiding the "trap of strategic rivalry."[66] The high point in the relationship came with an agreement on climate change. The United States and China account for 40 percent of the world's greenhouse gases, with China taking over as the largest emitter of carbon gases in 2009. In September 2016, on the eve of the G-20 summit in Hangzhou, the two presidents announced that they had agreed to sign the Paris Climate Agreement later in the year. Both sides hailed this as a significant example of what cooperation could achieve, despite differences on other issues. After his election, President Trump announced US withdrawal from the agreement.

Initially it appeared that President Trump, despite harsh campaign rhetoric, would maintain the momentum, and he seemed to form a positive relationship with Xi Jinping. Many Chinese expressed the view that, as a businessman, Trump would appreciate a good deal. They were mistaken. In the past it had been the Chinese leadership that set challenges for incoming US presidents, but this time President Trump provided China with a challenge that China had never encountered before—a president who was inconsistent on many issues but who was willing to take tough actions to pressure other countries to meet his demands. Tariffs were President Trump's weapon of choice to try to force other countries to bend to his will. What began as a dispute over trade and business practices by 2019 had expanded to such a wide range of differences that some wondered whether the two countries were on the brink of a new Cold War and the two economies might decouple.

US attitudes toward China had been shifting for some time. Although some in the US administration were opposed to President Trump's imposing tariffs on Chinese exports in order to try to force a change, there was an increasing unwillingness to accept Chinese business practices and actions in other fields. Even though businesses and governments might have been willing to accept China's statist economic and industrial policies when it first entered the WTO, once China became a major economic global player, many felt that it had to fully implement the changes to which it had agreed at entry. The earlier expectation was that over time reforms would bring China into conformity with global trading practices and that, perhaps, China would even embark on meaningful political reforms. Further, the crackdown in China on religion and other organizations as well as the clampdowns in universities furthered negative attitudes toward China and increased worries about how China might use its newfound wealth and power.

Thus, although the most obvious example of the differences between the two countries was the issue of trade imbalance, underlying this was a deeper concern about the nature of the relationship. The US National Defense Strategy, of December 2017, clearly articulated the US view that China, together with Russia, was a strategic competitor. It accused China of using "predatory economics to intimidate its neighbors," and claimed that together with Russia, China was shaping a "world consistent with their authoritarian model—gaining veto authority over other nations' economic, diplomatic, and security decisions." The overall objective for China was to reorder the Indo-Pacific to its advantage and to displace the United States, thus facilitating its future global preeminence.[67] Vice President Pence, using the platform of the Hudson Institute, outlined across-the-board disagreements with China in the toughest statement of the relationship since the normalization of relations in 1979. While acknowledging the close personal relationship that Trump had sought to develop with President Xi, Pence cited a long list of Chinese malpractices that had adversely affected the relationship. He echoed the hope that after entering the WTO, China would develop in a positive direction, but this hope had gone unfulfilled: "Instead China has chosen economic aggression, which has in turn emboldened its growing military." The turn had been away from increasing freedoms to control and repression.

For a president who has shown inconsistency, the one area where he has always been consistent is trade and the meaning of trade imbalances. He linked Chinese practices to the loss of manufacturing and jobs in the United States since China joined the WTO. However, the number of manufacturing jobs in the United States had been declining since 1952. In September 2019 Trump claimed that the theory that China's entry into the WTO would lead to liberalization of the economy "has been tested and proven completely wrong."[68]

In principle, only Congress has the ability to impose tariffs on other countries, but the Trump administration has used a national security clause to allow him to place tariffs on goods from China and other countries. The Trump administration's intention was to encourage consumers to buy American goods by making imports more expensive and claiming that it would be China that footed the bill, not the US consumers. Few agreed. By September 2019 the United States had imposed tariffs on over $360 billion of Chinese goods, with China retaliating with tariffs on $110 billion of US goods. Set against this, it should be noted that in the past US investment in China was more strategic, forming a key component of many companies' global production chains, whereas many Chinese investments in the United States have been expensive trophy purchases in real estate and entertainment.

While retreat might have been politically dangerous for him, Xi Jinping still took steps to satisfy the United States. In part, the slowing economy—around 6 percent growth in 2019—meant extra pressure was unwelcome, but more importantly there were growing concerns that the United States was intent on decoupling in certain fields. Restrictions on China's access to US financial markets would be especially damaging.

First, in late December 2018 the NPC published a draft of a new integrated foreign investment law. The objective was to relax market access and accelerate foreign investment in telecommunications, education, health care, and culture. Addressing concerns of foreign investors, the law promises equal treatment in areas such as government procurement. Given that the problem is often with lower-level administrative units acting to protect their own industries, the draft law prohibits government departments and officials from using their administrative powers to force technology transfers.[69]

Second, China has been at pains to stress that its rise is not a threat to others. On April 1, 2019, Xi moved to allay fears by publishing a speech he had delivered six years earlier in which he pointed out that the West was resilient and that it would enjoy long-term advantages in the economic, scientific, and military fields, and that the future with the United States would encompass long-term cooperation and struggle. So that party comrades would not be too disheartened to read this news, they should strive to make socialism better than capitalism, something that Xi was sure would come to pass.[70]

Third, on January 15, 2020, China and the United States signed the Phase One Economic and Trade Agreement, which caused President Trump to announce at Davos, "America is winning like never before," but he added that the relationship with China was the best ever.[71] At face value, it seems that China conceded considerable ground and the United States gave up little. The tariffs are for the most part in place, but China notes one hundred times that it "shall" make commitments whereas the United States noted only five times that it would do so.[72] The most obvious benefit for China is its removal from the US Treasury list of currency manipulators. Why did Xi Jinping sign off on the agreement? It provides some breathing space while the leadership deals with other challenges in the economy. Also, China was already undertaking a number of the measures agreed to, and even with the best will in the world, it is unlikely that China can import the range of goods proposed. If China did meet the objectives, it would seriously upset other important trading partners. Perhaps most importantly, China wants to buy time to refocus its trading relations to offset what it sees as the inevitable decline of US trade and investment. Phase Two will be much tougher to negotiate, with China less likely to yield because negotiations will cover crucial areas such as the role of SOEs domestically and externally, and industrial policy.

President Trump's criticism of China increased dramatically as the number of infections and deaths from COVID-19 rose in the United States. Despite having complimented Xi in January 2020 and noting China's transparency, as critics turned on the Trump administration for its slow, incoherent response to the pandemic, the president sought to deflect blame by launching scathing attacks on China, even referring to the disease as the "Chinese virus." At the end of May 2020 Trump announced a range of new measures to "punish" China for its behavior: denying visas to certain Chinese students who were deemed a potential security threat, increasing the scrutiny of Chinese companies listed on US markets, a ban on investing in companies linked to the military, and rolling back special preferences for Hong Kong. Last but not least, President Trump announced that the United States would withdraw from the World Health Organization, which he criticized repeatedly for being pro-China. China has sought to push back by increasing its support for the WHO as well as offering help to other countries under stress.

The Challenge of Hong Kong

What appeared to be protests about a narrow topic of extradition of criminals burgeoned over the spring and into 2020 and turned into a movement that called for democratic and other reforms in the Hong Kong Special

Administrative Region. The Hong Kong government had moved to introduce an extradition bill that would allow criminals sought in other jurisdictions to be extradited. This would have meant that people could be extradited
from Hong Kong to face the nontransparent and unfair Chinese legal
system. In 2015 five booksellers had disappeared from Hong Kong; they
later turned up in Chinese custody and were forced to utter scripted confessions. Protests began on March 31 calling for the extradition bill to be withdrawn, something that the Hong Kong authorities initially refused. The
chief executive suspended the bill on June 15, said it was dead on July 9, and
finally withdrew it on September 4. By then, however, it was too late. The
demonstrations increased and so had the demonstrators' demands. On
June 16, an extraordinary number of Hong Kong citizens turned out to
demonstrate. Clearly, sentiments went beyond the question of extradition,
and four more demands were added: the chief executive should step down; an
inquiry should be launched into police brutality; those arrested should be
released; and there should be greater democratic freedoms. Underpinning this is a general sense in Hong Kong that the "one country, two systems" agreement, which guarantees Hong Kong's way of life until 2047,
was being eroded as Beijing chipped away at freedoms and at Hong Kong
identity.

The demonstrations of 2014, known as the Umbrella Movement, had developed because the reforms Beijing had proposed to the electoral system in
Hong Kong fell far short of local demands. Only one-half of the seats in the
legislature are directly elected and the chief executive is selected by a small
pro-Beijing group on the Election Committee. During the movement, Chinese officials signaled that the Sino-British Joint Declaration of 1994, which
effectively enshrined the principle of one country, two systems, was no
longer valid. This shifting attitude toward the agreement on Hong Kong's
autonomy was clearly signaled in 2017 when China's Ministry of Foreign Affairs stated that the Joint Declaration was a historical document with no
current practical significance.[73] That position was reiterated by Beijing's Hong
Kong liaison office in 2020. However, the document is a legally valid agreement that was deposited with the United Nations in 1985, and according to
British authorities it remains in force. Such measures and statements challenged Hong Kong's identity and created uncertainty about how long the
leadership in Beijing would remain committed to the fifty-year process.
While Hong Kongers stressed the two systems, mainlanders tended to emphasize the one country.

The scale of the 2019 demonstrations took both the Hong Kong authorities and Beijing by surprise, and their responses badly misjudged the situation. Beijing's strategy has been to stress that Hong Kong's future is tied to that of the mainland and all will enjoy economic growth. This may be true for the tycoons, but it is not the case for many young people who are faced with unaffordable housing and dismal job prospects. For Hong Kong citizens, identity has trumped the claim of economic prosperity offered by Beijing Just like it thought regarding Tibet and Xinjiang, and even Taiwan, the CCP leadership thinks that such problems can be erased by means of economic development. The initial response in Beijing was to impose censorship on reporting about the demonstrations in the mainland, but as they continued and spread, the propaganda network moved to present scenes of chaos and violence. The party resorted to its usual defense that the situation was created by a handful of instigators and that foreign forces—the United Kingdom, the United States, and Taiwan—were behind the movement, a view echoed by supporters in Hong Kong. By the end of 2019, the demonstrations were becoming more violent, and even though Beijing had not intervened directly, in October Xi Jinping warned that any attempt to divide China would result in "bodies smashed and bones ground to powder."[74]

The onset of COVID-19 brought a temporary halt to demonstrations and gave Beijing the opportunity to consider its response. The question of how to deal with Hong Kong monopolized discussions at the CCP Fourth Plenum, held on October 28–31, 2019, and this set in train a series of actions.[75] One clear outcome was that Beijing was determined to exert greater control over Hong Kong through the Basic Law and the principle of one country, two systems. Patriotic education was stepped up, and there was greater oversight of the appointment not only of the chief executive but also of other senior officials, who would be evaluated on the basis of their patriotism. The offices overseeing Hong Kong were reorganized, and in January and February 2020 the heads of the Hong Kong liaison office and the Beijing-based Hong Kong–Macau Affairs Office were replaced by officials known to be close to Xi Jinping.

At the May 2020 NPC meeting, the authorities in Beijing signaled that they had given up on Hong Kong passing a National Security Law and passed legislation to draft it themselves. The action was portrayed in part as necessary to defend against hostile actions by foreign agencies. The prosed legislation is tougher than that which failed in Hong Kong in 2003 and criminalizes subversion, separation, terrorism, and foreign interference. Despite pronouncements that this would not affect Hong Kong's freedoms, it provides Beijing with increased license to intervene in Hong Kong. Certainly, many in Hong Kong did not agree with these platitudes and the comments of their chief executive, and demonstrations briefly commenced again. The principle of "one country" was clearly prioritized as the foundation for the implementation of the "two systems." It is highly unlikely that the divisions can be healed. Beijing's policy of one country, two systems, has failed, and whether Hong Kong will continue to be a major business and financial center in the future is unsure. In July 2020 the US administration withdraw the special preference accorded to Hong Kong in response to the new legislation, which may have an adverse impact on the local economy, a risk that Beijing appears willing to take. One unintended consequence of the demonstrations and Beijing's response was the rise in support for Taiwan's president, Tsai Ing-wen, and she was reelected in January 2020.

In addition to the failure of policy toward Hong Kong, the hope for reunification with Taiwan is dimmer than ever before. China's economic and trade practices have incited strong opposition not just from the United States but also from other major trading partners. The much heralded win-win of the BRI has met pushback with concerns about China's economic dominance and the unsustainable debt levels in some recipient countries. Not surprisingly, in September 2019 Xi Jinping sounded a warning note to young officials at the Central Party School in Beijing. He painted a picture of a party surrounded by challenges both internal and external, and he used the term "struggle" a reported fifty-six times. Leading officials had to train themselves in the art of struggle to overcome difficulties in development, social stability, foreign relations, and national defense.[76]

Looking to the Future

In preparing for the hundredth anniversary of the founding of the CCP, significant challenges remain to achieving Xi Jinping's China Dream of national rejuvenation, a question we will return to in the Conclusion. None of the challenges will necessarily undermine party rule, but they are significant. Xi is demonstrably a much stronger leader and more confident than his predecessors, and he has fashioned a party and state apparatus in his image. However, there are clear internal and external challenges. Can the slowing of the economy, which is at its lowest rate of growth since 1990, be halted without resorting to the old playbook of pumping out state investment? Can vested interests be shunted aside to allow investment and resources to flow to the more productive sectors of the economy? Will China be able to resist external pressures to change its domestic business practice and its trade policies?

Certainly, Xi Jinping exudes confidence and has rebuilt the system to strengthen his preeminent position. He views China as at least the equal of the United States and has launched a more assertive form of international diplomacy. The starting point is the perception that the United States is in relative decline and consequently would not confront China militarily as China seeks to expand its influence in the region. The CCP is now willing to step up to global leadership in those areas from which it feels the United States has withdrawn. The June 2018 Central Conference on Work Relating to Foreign Affairs confirmed the burial of Deng Xiaoping's adage of "hiding one's capabilities and biding one's time," in favor of a more assertive diplomacy. The meeting also affirmed Xi Jinping's grip over the foreign policy establishment with foreign policy officials reminded that first and foremost they were party members.[77]

China's response to the increasing pressure from the United States and other nations was dealt with at the CCP's fifth plenum, which was held October 26–29, 2020.[78] The CCP presented its vision for the future. There were three key components: the promotion of Xi Jinping's theory of "dual circulation," the outline of a new five-year plan that was a first step in realizing a longer range vision by 2035. This was the first time that such a linkage had been made since 1995 and began to fill some of the details of the long-term objectives outlined at the Nineteenth Party Congress.

Dual circulation encapsulates how the Xi administration intends to manage globalization for the national benefit. If enacted fully, it would have major ramifications for the global economy. The "first circulation" contends that China will shift away from reliance on global integration; the "second circulation" emphasizes reliance on domestic consumption and technological upgrading. The approach is driven by Beijing's analysis that even with a Biden administration, tensions with the United States, including tensions over trade, and the pressure to relocate manufacturing chains will endure, and that some decoupling of the two economies will continue. Last, but not least, China is concerned that overreliance on trade can expose the country to risks should other countries hold China to ransom. China's biggest fear concerns the need to import semiconductors, which are crucial to its hopes for technological advancement. Although dual circulation will impact global business and trade, the outcome might not be as severe as might be expected. Foreign multinationals are still heavily committed to the China market, integrated manufacturing systems are not so easy to relocate, and China needs access to global financial markets to meet its ambitious developmental goals.

Contrary to the view that China might not reach its stated goals for 2020, the plenum announced that it had indeed attained the status of a "moderately prosperous society." The sketch of the new five-year plan was light on details because these would be filled in at the spring 2021 NPC meeting. Yet again, the need to boost domestic consumption was stressed, requiring raising wages, weaving together a more integrated social safety net, and expanding economic opportunities in the countryside. Strengthening the domestic economy was paramount, and this was to be achieved through improving the quality of production and productivity. The plan stressed the need for technological independence so that China could become a major player in the areas of manufacturing, cyber, and the digital economy. The need for self-reliance in science and technology was stressed more strongly than in the previous plan.

Importantly and unusually, the plan was presented as part of a fifteen-year project that would culminate in 2035 with China attaining "socialist modernity." China was expected to become a mid-level developed country, equivalent to that of South Korea currently. This would result in almost doubling the ranks of the middle class, while the inequality between urban and rural China would be significantly reduced. China's citizens would enjoy working in a green economy while living in an improved environment. This progress would enable China to enhance its soft power and allow it to play a more active role in reform of the global economic system. Although mention of the market in allocating resources is retained, it is clear that the more statist approach of recent years will dominate. For example, the role of government, rather than that of the market, in promoting science, technology, and innovation is stressed.

Finally, the plenum and the long-range plan give us clues as to how Xi Jinping sees his own future. With no successor in sight, the introduction of the long-range vision suggests that Xi intends to dominate the policy landscape until at least 2035 by which time he will be 82 years of age. Clearly, this is Xi's future to shape.

Conclusion

LEGACIES FROM THE PAST,

CHALLENGES FOR THE FUTURE

★

The experiences of the revolutionary struggle are varied, and once the CCP had consolidated its power, they influenced the practice of rule. Some legacies have had an enduring impact into the Xi Jinping years, determining how the CCP sees the world and how it governs. These legacies have been supplemented by practices developed after the establishment of the PRC. These have operated sometimes in tandem, and sometimes in conflict. The idea of the united front has been evoked whenever the party focused on economic development and needed domestic support from people who were not members of the CCP or from overseas Chinese, including those on Taiwan. On other occasions when politics became radicalized, the CCP was more likely to rely on mobilization of the masses. Ideology and adherence to the correct political line were the main weapons of inner-party struggle during the years of Mao Zedong's dominance, but gradually accusations of corruption became the primary means to discredit and purge political opponents.

Party Dominance of State and Society

Although there are eight other "democratic" political parties in the PRC, the CCP is the only one that matters. Unchallenged by other organizations or significant religious or social groupings at the national level, the party presents itself as the sole authority, with the right to interpret the past and lay

435

out the policies for the future. It also claims to be infallible. The experiences before 1949 reinforced its hegemonic position within society. As we have seen, the party lost effective contact with the proletariat after the defeat of 1927, but it still claimed the right to lead the revolution and to act on behalf of the working class. Although the party increasingly drew recruits from the peasantry, it is difficult to call it a peasant party in terms of the interests it promoted.[1] It did eradicate the landlords and implement policies of rent reduction and tax elimination at various times, but on coming to power the party soon took away the land from the peasantry for the benefit of the state. The autonomy of the party from social forces or classes in the revolutionary struggle allowed the more controlling and authoritarian impulses to dominate after 1949. Even though some observers have teased out the proto-democratic elements of CCP practices before 1949 and its willingness to collaborate with others, as seen during the two periods of the united front, an authoritarian thrust was always present in the drive to consolidate party power and take the national stage.

On assuming power, the CCP's self-identification as the representative of the progressive forces in the Chinese revolution began to diminish. For many, the revolution was experienced as the replacement of "one form of domination with another," rather than any form of personal liberation.[2] Studying the revolution in Raoyang on the North China plain, Edward Friedman and his colleagues conclude that as the CCP strengthened its rule, aspects of the socialist dynamic and structures produced brutal outcomes. Seeds planted during the revolutionary struggle included a security force whose objective was to arbitrarily crush those denounced as counterrevolutionary, and an interpretation of socialism that portrayed all accumulated wealth as derived from exploitation and therefore something the party-state could take control of, even in an extreme and arbitrary manner, and even against its own society.[3] These tendencies meant that the party could act in the name of the proletariat without the inconvenience of having a strong proletariat to counter it. As a result, the form of political representation is Leninist in nature, an extreme form of trustee relationship.

The absolute leadership of the CCP was enshrined by Deng Xiaoping early in the reform period; the goal was to prevent critiques of the Cultural Revolution, which had led party intellectuals to question the CCP's role and relationship to society. In March 1979 Deng called for adherence to the four cardinal principles, which indicated there would be limits to how far the reforms could push against the current structure of effective single-party rule.[4] The preeminence of the party and the strengthening of its role over state and society have persisted to the present. In the view of one well-placed Peking University professor, "socialism with Chinese characteristics" under Xi Jinping simply meant CCP leadership.[5]

The party has never accepted autonomous activity outside of its sphere of control that might challenge its power, and it has continually sought to control as much of state and society as feasible. Party cells exist throughout society and operate not only in government organizations and SOEs but also in private businesses and nongovernmental organizations. The party reinforces its authority in newly developing sectors, such as the high-tech sector, where initially it had only weak control. In the technology hub of Hangzhou, the home to Alibaba, the local government designated officials to work with one hundred local companies.[6]

The party will recruit those elements it deems important to prevent a rival organization from developing, and it will seek to destroy those that it views as a threat. This has meant that recruitment can be surprisingly flexible for a party of "workers and peasants." Before 1949, attitudes toward the rich peasantry and their role varied depending on the level of policy radicalization, as did the perception of patriotic intellectuals. Landlords and the gentry were nearly always a target. In the 1950s the eradication of landlords and capitalists was soon followed by the elimination of small-scale businesses. By the end of the 1990s Jiang Zemin fought to create space under the Three Represents for private entrepreneurs to join the party, because they had become an important driver of economic development. The crushing of autonomous student and workers' organizations in 1989 is the most visible example of the repression, other targets were the China Democratic Party, the Charter '08 movement, and by the mid-2010s, human rights lawyers.

It is also important to recognize that party members play a key role in policy implementation. Although the CCP has set up an elaborate state bureaucratic structure, it relies on party organizations and individual members to achieve certain policy objectives.[7] Campaigns and mobilization are run through the party network, not through the state apparatus. While the lowest level of government administration in the countryside is the township, party organizations and membership penetrate into the village.

The Importance of History

The "correct" recounting of history is a crucial element in the CCP's claim to legitimacy, and that version of history is carefully nurtured, promoted, and disseminated. In October 2019, as the seventieth anniversary of the founding of the PRC approached, the screening of the war epic *The Eight Hundred* was canceled at the Shanghai International Film Festival. The reason: in depicting the fall of Shanghai to Japanese invaders in 1937, the film more accurately portrayed the role of the Nationalists in the battle, and it showed their flag. This ran counter to the official, patriotic narrative of the CCP's role in defeating the Japanese. One former PLA general was quoted as saying that the film "glorifies the fighting of the Nationalist Party, which seriously violates history." Such deviation from historical materialism is not to be encouraged.[8]

Xi Jinping is the latest leader who has taken to heart Orwell's adage, "Who controls the past controls the future. Who controls the present controls the past."[9] Xi's campaign against historical nihilism sought to eliminate all writing that challenges official party history.[10] Even though official history has not remained constant as new leaders have come to power and old leaders have been purged or have faded away, control over narrative has been an essential element of the CCP's claims to be China's legitimate ruler. The most recent historical housecleaning began with the investigation of the liberal magazine *Chinese Annals* (*Yanhuang chunqiu*), which had published articles exploring alternative views of the party's past. In July 2016 the editorial board was forced to resign and the magazine was taken over by Xi loyalists. Mentions of the tumultuous events of the Cultural Revolution have been deleted from new middle-school history textbooks, and official publications have taken to referring to the period as one of "arduous exploration and achievement in development" rather than as "a period of massive political upheaval, social turmoil, and violence."[11]

A crucial component of Mao Zedong's legitimacy derived from the narrative he told of China's fall at the hands of the imperialists, the rapacious landlords, and the comprador bourgeoisie—and China's redemption when the CCP saved the country from dismemberment and ruin. Xi Jinping's narrative follows a similar theme intended to complete the unfinished objective of fulfilling the China Dream of rejuvenating the Chinese nation. Just as Xi's narrative forms a crucial element in his claims to legitimate rule, adoption of the 1945 Resolution on Party History places Mao at the center of all that was correct in the revolutionary struggle. In contrast, Mao's enemies, foreigners, and the GMD were portrayed as having been responsible for all that had gone wrong. The resolution contributed to building a unified party based on a common conception of its history. Failure to accept the official history indicated a lack of loyalty and, even worse, opposition.

The party's 1951 publication *Thirty Years of the Communist Party* was intended to cement the CCP's legitimacy in the eyes of the entire nation. All nations build foundational myths and the CCP is no different; its many myths range from the iconic Long March to defeating the Japanese and the GMD to save the nation. The CCP had just seized power and was dealing with a dislocated economy, dangerous levels of inflation, continued pockets of opposition, the existence of the GMD on Taiwan, and entry into the Korean War. But a top priority was to create an official history for the people. The Politburo charged Liu Shaoqi, aided by Mao's close associate Hu Qiaomu, with reviewing the history. Production was so important that Liu Shaoqi sent a letter to senior leaders, including Mao Zedong, asking them to reply within twenty-four hours.[12] And reply they did. Mao had never forgiven Zhang Guotao for challenging his leadership and thus he suggested— or perhaps more correctly, instructed—that "treacherous" be added to Zhang Guotao's name because of his betrayal. Mao also stated that despite initial drafts that referred to Chen Duxiu as a "propagandist of Marxism and party founder," Chen was not a good Marxist. Mao Zedong was mentioned 118 times, and eighteen of his works were cited.

Thus was constructed for the nation an official history that placed Mao at the center and made it clear that any challenge to this history would be taken as an attack on the legitimacy not only of the party but of the nation itself. Subsequently the CCP created an entire structure of party schools and research institutes dedicated to promulgation of the official history.

Mao Zedong's death in 1976 and the arrest of the "Gang of Four" required creating a new history that would detach the "bad" Mao from the "good" to ensure that party credibility remained. No easy task, as Mao was both the Lenin and the Stalin of the CCP. Although critical of Mao's role, the new history stressed two aspects. Mao Zedong Thought and CCP policies were presented as a collective product before the personality cult began to destroy inner-party democracy. The achievements were not Mao's alone, and many of his former disgraced and dead comrades were restored to their rightful place in history. Second, the excesses were blamed on those, such as Lin Biao and Jiang Qing, who sought to exploit the situation to promote their own positions.[13] Thus the failings were not Mao's alone. This was the party's attempt to preserve its own legitimacy and to keep Mao as the standard-bearer of the revolution, while acknowledging the chaos and disaster unleashed by Mao in his later years—from which many of those now ruling China had suffered.

As the CCP has regained confidence under Xi Jinping, memories of the disasters of the Great Leap Forward and the Cultural Revolution have faded and many Chinese alive today are not clear on the details, and official history has backed away from the 1981 resolution. The distinction between a good and a bad Mao has been blurred. Xi Jinping has warned historians not to dwell on a divide between the years before 1978 and those of "reform and opening-up." There are not two Chinas under CCP rule, but just one narrative of struggle and success.

As with any regime that takes so seriously the control of history, language, and thought, China is vulnerable to subversion and critique by allegory, as in the case leading up to the Cultural Revolution of the drama *Hai Rui Dismissed from Office*. Official language is prey to jokes and puns. Authorities were concerned that such wordplays could cause chaos and in November 2014 felt it necessary to ban such linguistic tricks in order not to mislead the public, especially children. There is also a question about which histories Chinese people want to read. I am frequently asked to bring books to China with alternative perspectives on CCP history or on CCP individuals, or with salacious dealings of the elite. The Hong Kong booksellers were a great market for this, which is presumably why five publishers disappeared in 2015, later to turn up in the custody of the mainland authorities. This was a clear warning to others not to peddle stories or accounts of CCP history that do not follow the official narrative. I remember vividly in 1998, when the atmosphere was more relaxed, visiting the old CCP revolutionary base in Yan'an. Inside the compound where Mao Zedong had hunkered down after the Long March, the books on sale reflected the current party line, with titles such as *Mao Zedong Enters Yan'an*, whereas outside, under the counter, cheery entrepreneurs peddled a different history that told of Mao's sexual prowess, the inner secrets of palace intrigue in Beijing, and unofficial biographies of national leaders. A good example of the market versus the plan.

Clandestine Work and Military Struggle

Before 1949 much CCP activity took place underground, operating in uncertainty, and enduring protracted warfare. The cell structure that the party adopted was designed to protect its members against the ever-present dangers of discovery and betrayal. If one party member was discovered, he or she would inform on as few other comrades as possible. This structure created a culture of secrecy and suspicion within the party and of groups outside of direct party control. In addition, the party came to power after a brutal struggle against the Japanese invaders and the civil war with the GMD. Not surprisingly, the party was militarized, a language of war described movements, inner-party struggle was vicious, and serious internal divisions were not tolerated. The nature of the struggle meant that military support is the key to power for any CCP leader, as is respect for the military as an institution.

This heritage created an especially violent language that was combined with the inability to accept criticism of the core concepts. Harsh rhetoric and even violence were deemed acceptable when dealing with critics—not only those who attacked the party from without but also often critics from within. The concept of loyal opposition was rejected. The need to cleanse people's souls and bring them to accept the truth as defined by the party leadership at any particular time led to virulent campaigns of denouncement and criticism.

The seeds were sown from the late 1920s as the party absorbed the methods of inner-party struggle learned from Moscow, but they blossomed in Yan'an during the Rectification Campaign. Wang Shiwei was one of the last intellectuals who fled to Yan'an but retained the ethos of the May Fourth tradition. Wang was disturbed by the hypocrisy he observed among the party elite, and he spoke his mind. This ran counter to Mao's drive for party unity to prepare for the coming struggles. The style of criticism to which Wang was subjected formed the prototype for later movements, which culminated in the vicious denunciations during the Cultural Revolution. It is no coincidence that Chen Boda, who orchestrated the criticism of Wang Shiwei, was a crucial figure behind the violent rhetoric of the Cultural Revolution. In 1971, once the leadership moved to restore order to the chaotic situation, Chen fell victim to his own style of politics, and he was denounced as an ultra-leftist and a "sham Marxist."[14] The CCP promoted this style of criticism, which formed the prototype for post-1949 political struggle not only during the Cultural Revolution but also in the 1980s with the brief campaigns against bourgeois liberalization. The vehemence of language still pervades critiques by the party of those both within and outside the country. The last British governor of Hong Kong was notably denounced as a "whore for a thousand generations."

The protracted struggle had important consequences for the role of the military in the political system and the esteem in which it is held. We have seen the importance of the military in the years after the collapse of the Qing dynasty, and it was only after the CCP developed its own military force that it was able to create zones of safety to develop its policies. Despite the presence of bandits among its ranks, it was distinct from other roving groups or warlord armies in that, for the most part, the army was loyal to the party. This was enforced by a system of political commissars that was copied from the Soviet Red Army.

Mao's rise to the summit of party power was backed by support from the military commanders, and in the CCP any aspiring leader must court military approval to consolidate party leadership. For many in China, especially in the South, the first signs of the party were the military contingents that came down to take over from the retreating GMD; they occupied factories and carried out land reform, leading to the description of the regime as one of military conquest.[15] This should not be taken to mean that the CCP was or is a military party; the dictum remains "the party controls the gun," but the military has served as a model for societal behavior in campaigns and is a crucial institution of support for the top leadership. On taking power, the new general secretary usually begins with a reshuffle of the military leadership to bring in supporters, the most recent example being Xi Jinping. The relationship was weakened under Jiang Zemin and Hu Jintao, but it was reaffirmed when Xi Jinping came to power. Xi had the military connections from his father and he had worked in the military as a political secretary earlier in his career.

For Mao Zedong, the military embodied his principles of revolution, hard work, plain living, and sacrifice for the common good—characteristics that he often felt were lacking in society. This led to individual soldiers or units being featured as models for others to emulate—such as the plain-living soldier Lei Feng, darning his wool socks and doing good deeds for others. In the early 1960s when Mao feared he was losing control of the party, a campaign was launched in the PLA to study Mao's Thought. Lei Feng was again promoted for study after the arrest of the "Gang of Four" following the Cultural Revolution and once again after the military had been called in to put down the student-led demonstrations in 1989. The message is simple: be a cog in the wheel, behave loyally and unquestioningly, and serve the party faithfully.

One important legacy is the holding of multiple roles within the party and the military apparatus. This was true not only for Mao and Deng Xiaoping but also for others. Holding multiple positions has declined progressively, except in the case of the general secretary, who is expected to serve as the chair of the Central Military Commission. However, the dual functionality of the PLA has persisted. The PLA not only serves as defender from external threats but also has a strong voice in policy concerning Taiwan and the United States. Domestically, the military has a key role in disaster relief and in crushing threats to party rule. Mao and other leaders called in the PLA to restore order from the chaos that he had unleashed during the Cultural Revolution. While this was well-received by many, Deng Xiaoping's use of the military to restore order in 1989 received a more mixed reception. Some members of the military were worried that its reputation among the people had been tarnished by the brutality of clearing the center of Beijing during the night of June 3–4. Some PLA leaders felt that they took the blame for cleaning up a crisis that should have been resolved by the civilian leadership.

The more positive reputation of the military is enhanced by its role in dealing with domestic natural emergencies, such as floods and earthquakes. Because China does not have an effective emergency management system or a national first-responders network, the PLA has taken on a major role with emergency relief and initial response. Only the PLA has the necessary organizational capacity to mobilize quickly to deal with these events. This was seen clearly with the terrible flooding of 2005, the ice storms of 2008, and the massive earthquake that struck Wenchuan, Sichuan province, in May 2008.

The Indigenous Nature of the Chinese Revolution

We have seen that the CCP might owe not only its survival but its very existence to Soviet support, and that post-1949 it initially adopted Soviet structures, the PRC is quite distinct from the baggage-train governments brought to power in Central and Eastern Europe following World War II. The fact that the Communists developed policies and practices in a number of base areas before the onset of the civil war and their military victory meant that they did have alternative policy choices to turn to once Mao Zedong and those around him began to question the appropriateness of Soviet-style state-building in the mid-1950s. The CCP had a set of leaders who were confident in their own abilities to govern without outside advice. Once Stalin had passed from the scene, Mao clearly felt that he was the elder statesman of the socialist camp, and although initially he continued to pay limited deference to the Soviet Union under Khrushchev, he was not afraid to break with the Soviets once he felt that their advice ran counter to China's own interests.

This independence has allowed for a degree of pragmatism in policy making, and when combined with the notion of Chinese exceptionalism it permitted the CCP to avoid the fate of the Soviet Union and the CPSU. Contrary to the expectations of many, the CCP has been adaptable and flexible, traits that are not normally associated with a Leninist regime. This flexibility extends to the ideological realm, where phrases such as "socialism with Chinese characteristics" means that socialism is whatever the CCP says it is at any given moment.

CCP historians stress the independent nature of the Chinese revolution, and that the success of the revolution was indivisible from the adaptation of Marxism-Leninism that took place under Mao and then gave rise to Sinification. This enabled the CCP to show greater flexibility in policy choice than was the case in those regimes that fell more squarely within the Soviet orbit and were integrated into the Soviet production structures. Xi Jinping has cast himself in this tradition, providing the Sinification of Marxism for the new era, and clearly placing himself on the same plane as Mao Zedong. When combined with the narrative about the years of humiliation at the hands of the foreigners, this has provided a platform for a strident nationalism that, on occasion, can tip over into xenophobia. We have seen already the blame that is placed on foreigners for developments that run counter to the wishes of the CCP leadership. Such nationalism also contributes to the antiforeign sentiment that can burst out at any time.

Following the demonstrations of 1989, the CCP led a determined campaign of patriotic education, especially for the youth. When accompanied by the spectacular economic growth that began in the 1990s and boomed once China entered the WTO, this led to a rise in nationalist sentiment in the Chinese press, in online forums, and in much of the Chinese public. Naturally the patriotic education campaign focused on Japan, China's old enemy, and the United States, China's new rival. The textbooks and other materials used for teaching have been particularly critical of these two nations, and there have been a number of anti-Japanese demonstrations and boycotts. Online denunciations of and demonization of foreign countries that are believed to be frustrating China's rise are especially virulent. The use of nationalism to mobilize domestic support has played further into the CCP's rejection of patriotic or loyal opposition, with criticism seen as antination or even pro-foreigners. The "Gang of Four" labeled Deng Xiaoping a traitor for his proposals on foreign trade; Premier Zhu Rongji and the former head of the People's Bank of China were similarly denounced by the old left and the new left.

The assertion of China's success and the mistreatment of the nation at foreign hands has led to more aggressive Chinese diplomats who are not afraid to criticize the countries within which they are posted. This is a new generation of diplomatic "wolf warriors," who appeal to Chinese nationalists.[16] Eschewing diplomatic language, they aggressively dispute comments they deem to be anti-China and often using pithy statements on Facebook and Twitter, both of which are banned in China. The approach was given a seal of approval by China's foreign minister in May 2020 when he noted that China would push back against "deliberate insults" and "resolutely defend our national honor and dignity."[17] As China came under criticism internationally for its handling of the outbreak and spread of COVID-19, a number of its diplomats hit back, accusing foreign governments of incompetence and defending China's own actions. While the style of diplomacy has met with approval among nationalist circles, others within the diplomatic community and international affairs academic community have expressed caution. They have warned that this more aggressive response may play well at home but is damaging China's reputation globally.[18] Certainly, it has produced negative reactions from a number of governments—including those friendly toward China, such as Venezuela.

The indigenous nature of the revolution not only has permitted the CCP greater flexibility with domestic policy but also has informed its global stance. Unlike the regimes in Eastern and Central Europe, the CCP came to rely on its self-told history of humiliation at the hands of foreigners to enhance its legitimacy. This provides the CCP with a commanding narrative independent of the Soviet Union. China's leaders have been obsessed with the collapse of the Soviet Union and the CPSU, and Xi Jinping is no exception. Shortly after his appointment, Xi asked why the Soviets collapsed, and in answering he stated that it was because they wavered in defending their ideals and convictions. "In the end nobody was a real man, nobody came out to resist."[19] Drawing on China's own traditions facilitates a strong case for Chinese exceptionalism, underpins the promotion of pride in the party's achievements, and is a source of nationalist sentiment. This inheritance necessitates maintaining territorial integrity, a territory that is based on the late Qing dynasty and is the most expansive in Chinese history. It defines Tibet and Xinjiang as integral parts of China and justifies its claims that Taiwan must be reunited with the mainland.

Techniques of Rule

The revolutionary struggle produced an optimism about what could be achieved through willpower, which created a form of voluntarism in Mao Zedong's thinking. This was especially clear during the GLF with the conviction that human endeavor could overcome objective barriers to development. Underpinning this optimism are certain practices common to CCP policy implementation: the mass line, mass mobilization, and a campaign style of politics. One other inheritance from the revolutionary struggle is the use of the united front to reach out to those who are not CCP members but who are critical to advancing the CCP's agenda.

As with other socialist systems, the CCP sought to change the nature of the human beings under its rule. Mao's thought contains a strong emphasis on participation, albeit not the kind of democratic participation one might think of in the West. For Mao, it was not enough for the masses merely to accept a policy passively; they were expected to display their support in public ways—such as joining movements to criticize bourgeois liberalization, joining in anti-Japanese actions, and participating in the implementation of policy through application of the mass line and the campaign style of politics. Mao described the mass line as the "Marxist theory of knowledge." Although a distinct break with Chinese traditional practice, it does have roots in the Leninist notion of democratic centralism. Application of the mass line combines the advantages of centralized control over policy with the benefits derived from consultation not only with those working at the grassroots within the party but also with the masses at large.

Use of the term "masses" is significant because there is no intention that individuals should participate as citizens. The masses are undifferentiated, as are "the people," and the CCP claims to represent them in their entirety. Being defined as a member of the people is crucial, especially during campaigns. When those who are considered part of the people make mistakes, they can be saved through reeducation and small-group study. As Mao Zedong noted, the most important questions for the revolution are "Who are our enemies? Who are our friends?"[20] The problem is that there is no fixed definition of who constitutes the people, and regardless, it changes over time depending on the circumstances. Standing outside of the people can expose one to attacks and persecution.[21]

When confronted with unfavorable external criticism, a common CCP response is that the Chinese people (or masses) are offended. The CCP thus claims to represent the views of the entire 1.4 billion Chinese people.[22]

During the period of guerrilla warfare, it was essential to create a close bond between the party-army and the peasantry that was to provide support. In a time of danger and scarcity, it was important that no resource be wasted and that all positive factors were mobilized to ensure CCP survival and success in the war against Japan. Mao believed in the malleability of people and that education, including theory and practice, could transform the character of members of different social classes. People would undergo this transformation through a process of criticism and self-criticism. The idea was that people could come to truly believe in the CCP goals without subjecting them to the bloody purges that had marked the attempts at transformation in the Soviet Union.

This approach was retained after power was seized to attempt to complete the transformation of the old society into the new socialist society. On several occasions Xi Jinping has reemphasized the value of the mass line and the process of self-cultivation. For Mao, "In all practical work of our Party, all correct leadership is necessarily 'from the masses to the masses.' This means: take the ideas of the masses (scattered and unsystematic ideas) and concentrate them (through study turn them into concentrated and systematic ideas), then go to the masses and propagate them and explain these ideas until the masses embrace them as their own, hold fast to them and translate them into action and test the correctness of these ideas in such action. . . . Such is the Marxist theory of knowledge."[23]

This might imply that the role of the Party Center is akin to a processing plant synthesizing views that bubble up from below. However, this was never the intention, and while it does suggest information gathering, the party decides what information is to be gathered and what is then to be disseminated for acceptance by the masses. Once the process is complete, dissent would mean that a person was not only anti-party but also anti-masses. The idea of the mass line and the accompanying campaign style of policy implementation has been taken as evidence of Mao's populism and voluntarism. Natural barriers, obstacles, and objective economic laws could be swept aside by human willpower. This is best reflected in Mao's retelling of the traditional folktale about the foolish old man who moved the mountains. In Mao's rendering, the twin mountains were imperialism and feudalism, which were suppressing the Chinese people and could be destroyed by sheer willpower.[24]

However, Mao was not anti-leadership, especially his own, despite what might have appeared to be the case when he launched the Cultural Revolution. For example, when confronted with the call of the Shanghai People's Commune to abolish "heads" (leaders), Mao denounced the idea as "extreme anarchy" and "most reactionary."[25] This did not stop the campaign style of politics and the excesses that were produced, such as Mao's revolutionary optimism regarding the speed of collectivization and the GLF. Why did other leaders follow him in seeking to achieve such seemingly unrealistic objectives? It was not simply a matter of fear of persecution, although that was real. When I asked party members who lived through this period, they explained that Mao had been right in the past when the odds were seemingly stacked against the CCP, and while they may have had reservations, they felt that he should be given the chance to show his correct analysis once again. Deng Xiaoping certainly shared the view that faster was better.

Mao saw the mass line and campaigns as a mechanism for keeping a check on bureaucratic excesses and preventing the revolution from becoming routine. Mao feared that corruption would creep in and the leaders would become divorced from the interests of those being led. Yet over time the approach of campaign politics and the mass line became formulaic and destructive, and no longer served as mechanisms for policy implementation. In fact, soon after Mao's death when the economic reforms began in earnest, the CCP newspaper, the *People's Daily*, criticized this approach to policy formulation and implementation, blaming the faults on the idealist conception of history. The idea that heroes, not the masses, made history was promoted, with the result that the views of the masses were suppressed rather than incorporated. The people had become "materials and instruments for carrying out the 'superior's' will."[26] The superior was, of course, Mao Zedong. The mass campaign approach to policy implementation was effectively curtailed after 1978 by Deng Xiaoping, but the notion of gaining popular support through mobilization and the propaganda apparatus has not disappeared. We have witnessed a shift from mass campaigns to managed campaigns.[27]

After 1949, before Mao's radical interventions, it seemed that the CCP would continue its united front policy to encourage a broad coalition of interests, including private entrepreneurs, public intellectuals, and those who had joined the eight other political parties, to participate in rule making. Institutionally, this was expressed in the system of people's political consultative conferences that included those with the kinds of skills that the CCP required to realize its ambitions. With the dismantling of the private sector and the Anti-Rightist Campaign of the mid-1950s, this was quickly abused and then decimated during the years of the Cultural Revolution, while the other parties went into political limbo.

Once the reforms began in earnest after 1978, the united front approach was resurrected to attract technicians, engineers, and intellectuals to work with the CCP. Later the broad coalition was extended to include private entrepreneurs, and representation of these groups in the political consultative committees was revived, eventually even within the CCP. Similarly, the definition of "the people" was expanded as wide as possible. In 2019 the chair of the CPPCC stressed the importance of its work and called on members engaged in united front work to "befriend and guide" non-Communist intellectuals and members of the new social stratum.[28] Externally, the approach is used to connect with ethnic Chinese (overseas Chinese, in CCP parlance) and through related organizations, such as the Chinese People's Association for Friendship with Foreign Countries, to build platforms for global support of its interests and policies. These activities have raised serious concerns about CCP influence overseas, especially in Australia and New Zealand.[29] The CCP has been striving to enhance its global footprint—setting up television stations in London, Washington, D.C., and Nairobi; placing paid advertisements in foreign newspapers; and having Chinese diplomats overseas take to Facebook and Twitter.

Diverse Legacies and Micropolitics

The CCP was successful where it was good at micropolitics and either where its officials came from within the local community or where they integrated the interests of that community with the dictates of the Party Center. We have seen how the party had to deal with bandits, secret societies, local elites, and a variety of other forces as it tried to establish footholds in urban and rural China. Central directives had to be adapted to local conditions. Support was always conditional and had to be fought for and worked hard for in order to be retained. In the Shanxi-Chahar-Hebei (Jin-Cha-Ji) Border Region, the local party devised policies and a management approach that co-opted the local elite into the power structure, thus preventing their outright opposition.

The converse problem has been locals dominating government decision making for the benefit of their community and ignoring or not fully implementing central policy. In the 1980s one heard numerous complaints that local officials in Guangdong did not listen to central directives and even that they spoke in Cantonese at meetings in order to block out the officials sent from Beijing. In certain provinces this problem led to public spats between officials who saw their role as representing the locality and those who tried to impose central discipline. Often this was best represented in a conflict between the governor of the province and the party secretary, who usually came from outside the province.[30] Therefore, the Central Organization Department rotates officials on a regular basis to try to break up local alliances. Xi Jinping has certainly made sure that appointees are loyal to his agenda.

For many years CCP historians painted an idealized picture of the CCP and its operations, portraying them as acting as the champion of the dispossessed. As we have seen, reality was dramatically different. In the Jiangxi Soviet, when the party tried to implement a land policy based on abstract ideological categories or on dictates from outside, it was not successful. Gaining and mobilizing support was difficult and required a lengthy learning process and constant adjustments and flexibility: "The CCP was successful in putting down local roots only where it showed flexibility in adapting policy to local circumstances, where initially it was good at micro-politics. By contrast, attempts to transform local environments to conform with predetermined ideology were unsuccessful."[31]

What this meant was that the Chinese revolution, especially in the countryside, was made up of a series of different revolutions.[32] This provided the CCP with an array of policy experiences to choose from. When the post-Mao leadership wanted to move away from the radicalism of Mao's later years, there were other experiences they could turn to. For example, in the Shanxi-Chahar-Hebei Border Region, Peng Zhen had operated a program of village elections; in other areas, policy closely resembled the agricultural responsibility system that was crucial during the post-1978 period.

This willingness to experiment in accordance with the realities of different areas was a hallmark of reform experimentation under Deng Xiaoping, which accounts for its flexibility and adaptability.[33] The reform period also restored the pre-1949 regional hierarchy of the economy. As we have seen, the Maoist policies ignored the coastal and more cosmopolitan areas of China and sent industry to the inland regions. Once reforms began, the situation changed and Guangdong province rose from being one of the poorest provinces in China to being one of most affluent.

Despite this, the hand of the Center still weighs heavily, and immediately after 1949 the positive lessons were forgotten as the myths of the CCP's rise to power came to be believed and local variations were forgotten. The authoritarian impulses that had always been present in the construction of the border regions before 1949 crowded out the more populist and proto-democratic elements of the regions. The tendency to "cut with one knife" rather than allow variation was even apparent early in the post-1978 rural reform period. In 1979 only 0.02 percent of the production teams had adopted the household responsibility system; by the end of 1983 the percentage had risen to 97.8.[34] Such expansion was not the result of spontaneous actions by farmers to dismantle the collective agricultural structures; it was forced from above. In grain-producing areas, such as Heilongjiang in the Northeast where large-scale, mechanized farming would have made sense, the evolving co-operatives were forced to break up and focus on household-based farming, irrespective of the farmers' wishes. The comparative advantage of specific regions was ignored.[35]

This struggle between local adaptation and central imposition continues to this day and is evident in the attempts by Xi Jinping to centralize greater control in Beijing. Given the background to his assumption of power, one might understand Xi Jinping's drive to centralize power. The arrests of Bo Xilai and Zhou Yongkang, the pervasive corruption, and the fact that society and local governments were often pursuing their own interests at the expense of the collective appear to indicate a system that is slipping out of control. Xi's approach to governance is a stark contrast to that of Deng Xiaoping and Jiang Zemin. The latter accepted the need for greater flexibility and decentralization in what amounted to a softer form of authoritarian rule. Much of the dynamism came from local experimentation and societal initiatives. The breakup of the communes and the return to household farming was initially resisted by the Center, the explosive growth of the township and village enterprises was not foreseen by the leadership, and the rise of the private sector as a major generator of growth and employment was resisted until Jiang Zemin bestowed legitimacy on it toward the end of the last century. Even now, although the private sector enjoys higher productivity, it is still disfavored in contrast to the SOE sector. As in the past, when the economy has faced difficulties, Xi has loosened constraints on the private sector in the hope that it will help the party through a difficult period.

However, this hardly amounts to a long-term commitment to the private sector.

By contrast, Xi Jinping has sought to concentrate as much power as possible at the Center, with party-led small groups taking over decision-making authority from the state administration. The consequence has been to concentrate more power in his own hands, epitomized by his decision to abolish the term limits for the PRC presidency. Under his leadership, control over domestic and international economic activity has been centralized, with an industrial policy that clearly favors the SOE sector at home and abroad. Externally this is clear with the BRI, and certain high-profile acquisitions by the Chinese private sector have been criticized and ordered to be sold. With restrictions on capital flows, these companies have been forced to cover outstanding overseas debt by selling assets. The private actors have been portrayed as overpaying for trophy projects that aroused criticism overseas, despite initial CCP encouragement. Going global will continue to be a strategy, but with the state enterprises as the dominant players and supported by financial institutions such as the China Development Bank.

Domestically, the trend has been evident in the booming high-tech sector. In interviews, people at several of the newer, successful high-tech startups referred to the pressure they were under to allow the local party apparatus a voice in their activities. In a pattern that has been repeated in other fields, when the state has lacked capacity, development has been outsourced to the private sector, but only for the party to seek to regain control once the sector has matured and grown in significance. Thus, the role of party groups within the sector has been strengthened, the CCP has taken seats on their boards, the state has assumed a stake in the companies, and there is now stronger oversight of investments and acquisitions.

One enduring legacy is the belief in the primacy of the collective. The CCP's system is based on the concept of methodological collectivism, which posits that any individual will get more out of belonging to the collective than from acting alone.[36] The CCP has always put priority on the collective over individual will, and thus has been able to exert its control over society. After the CCP took power in 1949, peasants soon were reorganized into agricultural producers' collectives and then communes, the workplace became the main focus of activity in the urban areas, and for those not in the workplace the local neighborhood committee became the locus of the party-state oversight. In the years after 1956 the party heightened its intrusion into individual lives to an unprecedented extent and drove policy through collective and communal organizations. This resulted in disaster and forced the party to withdraw its overbearing presence. As the old collectives were dismantled during the reform period, the party sought to find new forms of collectivity.[37] Rather than allowing people to interact individually with government and the market, the party has tried to find organizations that can take over collective service and provision. This is more difficult to achieve as there is a greater variety among the new communities. For example, in the wealthier gated communities (supposedly now with their gates removed) there may be a communal space but these communities are privatized realms, and the government has found it more difficult to infiltrate them. The government and the party have been more successful in the poorer, more run-down neighborhoods.[38] Urban governance has thus become more complex, with roles performed by a mix of actors from the public and private sector.

Challenges for the Future

The CCP experience to date has been remarkable in terms of both gaining power against incredible odds and reviving from the devastation wrought by the GLF and the Cultural Revolution. Despite many predictions to the contrary, it has survived and thrived as an institution during the forty-plus years of reform to deliver a nation that is a major global player economically and increasingly so politically. For international business, China is an important market and a key part of global production chains. China's seat on the UN Security Council gives it a powerful global voice, should it wish to use it. Not surprisingly, this success has made the Chinese leadership proud of its economic and political model, and now the leadership is far less willing to be told by outsiders how it should regulate its economy, value its currency, or manage its internal affairs. Despite this, China has not yet achieved the wealth and power that have been its goal for more than a hundred years. The CCP has brought the nation close, but considerable challenges remain.

The easy parts of the reforms have been completed, and the remaining parts will be more difficult and will test the core of party power. The barriers to forward momentum are both internal and external and cover the political, economic, and global outreach. It does not mean that the China Dream cannot be realized, but hard work and accommodation will be necessary. Can the institutions be developed to facilitate competition and innovation to help China move beyond the middle-income trap? Can vested interests be overcome to enable investments to flow to the more productive

parts of the economy rather than to the less efficient SOEs? Can the CCP
deal with the environmental consequences of its growth model? On the political front, is the concentration of power in the hands of the "chairman of
everything" what China needs at its current stage of development? Can China
develop the institutions necessary to provide transparency of government action and feedback loops for its citizens? On the global front, will China
become a responsible stakeholder that helps set global norms and a key pro-
vider and guardian of global public goods?

Externally, success depends not only on the general health of the global
economy but also on how other countries interpret and respond to China's
growth and rising influence. Increasingly the international community
has concluded that, in part, China's success derives from unfair competition, dumping of products, and forced transfers of technology. The Trump
administration's imposition of tariffs and tough negotiating stance is the
clearest evidence of the concerns of the global community. While a Biden
administration may be more stable and predictable, it is likely to be just
as tough on Chinese business and trade practices. It is more likely to seek
to build coalitions of the willing and aggrieved to put joint pressure on
China.

It is clear that the 2008–2009 financial crisis contributed to the disillusionment with the West—economically, financially, and politically—
reaffirming the view that the Chinese approach to development was the
correct one.[39] Some former Chinese officials have said that they knew a day
of reckoning would come with the United States. They might not have foreseen President Trump's tariff attack, but they had realized that China would
face pushback as its role in the global economy became more important. As
a result, the country needed to prepare the ground to decouple from the US
economy to the greatest extent possible. This lies behind the Made-in-China
2025 policy, which seeks to ensure that domestic companies dominate high-
tech and strategic industries crucial for the nation's development. It also
explains why Xi Jinping was willing to agree to the January 2020 trade agreement, which on the surface does not seem to be in China's interest. Signing
was intended to buy China time to significantly reduce its dependence on
US trade.

Internally, there are challenges, such as maintaining a sufficient growth
rate and expanding a consumption-driven economy with alternatives put in
place to substitute gradually for proactive fiscal spending. In 2019 growth
was stimulated by means of a different approach—a $281 billion fiscal stim-

ulus composed of tax cuts for businesses and households. This was a temporary measure, similar to the limited stimulus measures taken to help the
economy recover from COVID-19.

Some of the immediate policy challenges stem from the legacies of the
Hu Jintao–Wen Jiabao era and from policies that have only been partially or
poorly implemented. Despite the promotion by Hu and Wen of a service-
oriented government, key challenges were only addressed indirectly. Concern has risen about the rising levels of inequality, the depth of corruption,
and the trade-off between economic growth and environmental degradation.
Yet there are deeper trends that must also be dealt with to ensure future momentum. The CCP leadership needs to come to grips with structural issues,
but the reform program, especially since China entered the WTO in 2001,
has created strong vested interests that wish to maintain the status quo.[40]
This includes many in the state-owned sector, a key source of patronage for
the CCP as well as for central and local officials and their families. With
the reforms of the 1980s, it was easier to see who would benefit, as was the
case in the 1990s when Deng Xiaoping launched a free-for-all to exploit state
resources to get rich. The current proposed economic reforms will hurt the
interests of those who once benefited, while the current anticorruption campaign will cause those local officials on whom Xi Jinping must rely to be
cautious and often inactive.

Despite Xi's attempts to recentralize power, the reforms have redefined
the social structure and are changing the distribution of power between state
and society. Chinese society has become more complex in terms of both
structure and attitudes. The rising middle class in urban China is concerned
about quality-of-life issues. Will the CCP develop sufficiently representative institutions, mechanisms, and feedback loops to accommodate their demands? This challenge has increased because of the rise of social media, but
the CCP has been more successful than anyone would have predicted in limiting the potential of social media for disruption and in using it to the advantage of the regime. However, this rapidly advancing field exposes the
weakness of the CCP's traditional system of information management. The
CCP prefers to channel information flows vertically, limiting the horizontal
flow of information, which is challenged by the rapid flow of information
through texts, tweets, blogs, and such. The old practice of treating citizens
as children who need to be spoon-fed information and closely monitoring
the news they receive is no longer viable. China's citizens are now part of
the global information community, tracking and trading information online.

This may not be an insurmountable problem if the regime delivers on other important issues such as the environment and economic growth.

Performance Legitimacy

As belief in Marxism-Leninism declines as a source of its legitimacy, the CCP loses its power to explain development by relying on its "supernatural ability" to divine current and future trends. Instead, better-informed citizens begin to judge performance on more earthly criteria. Two key areas are managing the environment and the economy.

The phenomenal economic growth has created enormous environmental damage and placed tremendous strains on the supply of natural resources, especially water. In addition to the pace of economic growth and the increased urbanization, there are two long-term legacies from Mao Zedong's approach to development. The first is the Marxist disregard for the environment and the privileging of production over all other factors. Mao saw nature as something to be conquered and tamed, favoring the rapid exploitation of natural resources to build up a heavy industrial base.[41] This was accompanied by the policy of low pricing for water, coal, and other inputs. Lights were left on and water taps were left running. The fact that the property supposedly belonged to the people through state ownership meant that no one actually owned it or took care of it. Furthermore, it was impossible to find toilet paper in any public lavatory. The property was there to be used as a free good and it was plundered for personal use.

The love of grandiose projects that display party and state power has continued in the post-Mao era. The two most glaring examples are the construction of the Three Gorges Dam on the Yangzi and the massive project to divert river waters hundreds of miles from the south to the north. The latter is a technical fix to a problem that could instead be ameliorated through pricing and other policy measures. Costing almost $100 billion, it will supply roughly one-third of Beijing's water supply, but its sustainability is unclear and little attention has been paid to the communities where the rivers will be drained. Yet this project appeals to the engineering instincts of many in the Chinese leadership. In many locales, the party has built lavish symbols of its power. When I asked one set of local officials why they had built such a massive monument to house their headquarters and whether it was a good use of public funds, they were taken aback. They eventually replied, "Of course, as it was the party that had brought the wealth to the people."

A second legacy is Mao's promotion from the mid-1950s of a large population as a key driver of economic growth, which aggravated China's already difficult ratios of resources to population. China's water resources are only about one-third of the world's average per capita, forests cover one-eighth of the global average, and croplands are about one-third of the world's average. The damage has occurred at low levels of development, and despite the government undertaking serious measures to mitigate the impacts, pollution will continue to grow as the population becomes wealthier and urbanization continues apace.[42] The phrase "green at home, black abroad" has become common, indicating that while the CCP is trying to deal with the environmental damage at home, it is exporting its dirty industries.

Air quality, water pollution, and unsafe food affect all—poor or rich, urban or rural—and the leadership recognizes clearly the severity of the challenge. Economic costs are also high, now exceeding 1 trillion yuan per year, exclusive of increased health costs and premature deaths. One study has suggested that people in South China will live more than five years longer than those in the North.[43] With an endless list of environmental woes, the total cost of pollution and environmental degradation may be as high as 6 percent of GDP. Given these problems, it is not surprising that environmental protests have been growing in China and activists have taken advantage of party concerns and legal reforms, such as the 2014 amendments to the Environmental Protection Law.[44]

Given the economic success to date, it may seem strange that a level of nervousness about the future trajectory has been displayed not only by the current leadership but also by the Hu Jintao and Wen Jiabao leadership; they have recognized that fundamental change is necessary. There is a consensus that the economic model that has served China so well in the past must undergo fundamental changes to maintain the economic momentum. Many of the key factors that explain China's phenomenal success have run their course and will not provide the same contribution in the future.[45] The two key drivers of growth, state investment and international trade, have reached their limits. They will remain important, but they cannot contribute more. It is difficult to further increase the level of state investment, and the various stimulus programs have led to mounting debts in the state-owned sector that eventually will need to be paid. Similarly, foreign trade will not increase. As the "factory of the world" moves to another destination, China will have to develop higher-quality production. The easier gains of investment in transport—witness the massive development of high-speed rail (and high-level corruption) and housing that were promoted after the financial crisis of 2008–2009—have almost run their course.[46] This leaves consumption as the principal driver of future growth. This is not to deny that consumption has increased significantly but its contribution to GDP increased only by around 2 percent between 2009 and 2019. This did represent about one-quarter of global consumption growth. The fact that the current reform priorities differ little from those proposed by Hu and Wen in 2002–2003 reveals how difficult it is to engineer such a fundamental shift.

The days of high-level growth, much of which was catch-up growth, are now over. This is accepted by the leaders, who have progressively lowered forecasts for growth rates to about 6 percent. This may overestimate the real economy and make certain assumptions about growth that may be difficult to fulfill. A longer-term challenge will be whether the temporary break in global supply chains causes international businesses to look elsewhere for future production. The China market will remain attractive to foreign businesses, but concerns have been raised about overreliance on production of key goods such as medical supplies.

Despite the party's continual first response of pumping in more stimulus, the returns have been declining with each round. In turn, this has created dramatic increases in debt—which, while not regime-threatening given that they are domestic and China maintains large foreign reserves, will place future pressure on the economy and the capacities of local governments. Growth rates have slowed, and the main question is whether the nadir has been reached. If the real growth rates are lower than the official figures, which is most likely, the severity of the debt level will be heightened. The economies of Japan, the Republic of Korea, and Taiwan all slowed down after decades of high-level growth at a similar level of above $13,000 per capita income purchasing power parity (PPP), never again to be significantly revived.[47] China's per capita income PPP by 2018 was around $15,000, according to the World Bank.

Thus, growth will remain at a lower level, but just how much it slows will depend on whether total factor productivity (TFP) can be raised. The demographic dividend that helped drive growth once the reforms began has ended because of the decline of the active labor force. This decline and the aging of the population will weigh heavily on the future budget. In addition, there are problems of diminishing returns in many economic sectors that are characterized by overcapacity, due in large part to the stimulus package launched to help China through the global financial crisis. Future

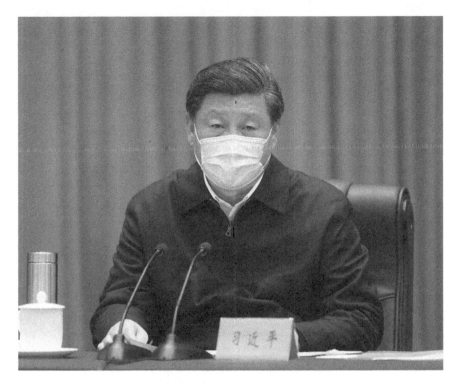

The "China Dream" challenged.

growth will depend on raising TFP and directing investment in capital stock toward more productive assets.[48] This requires a move from state allocation to market intermediation; without this, growth could fall significantly.

Searching for Deeper Legitimacy

These economic factors present a challenge to the future of the CCP if its rule is tied to performance legitimacy. Although the leadership has never abandoned its professed faith in Marxism-Leninism and Mao Zedong Thought, it has recognized that ideology is insufficient in the eyes of many. With these traditional mechanisms of legitimacy eroding, the CCP has resorted to nationalism and claims that it is the rightful inheritor of Chinese tradition. Vice President Wang Qishan has stated that the party's legitimacy is derived from its history and is determined by popular support—legitimacy depends on whether the people are happy, satisfied, and supportive of party work.[49] For most observers, maintaining successful economic growth is essential to continued CCP rule. Narratives of history are a questionable source of legitimacy and face continual contestation. Nonetheless, the CCP works hard to control the historical narrative, including criticizing those who have suggested dividing the history of the PRC into two periods and threatening those who reject Mao Zedong and Mao Zedong Thought with "serious political consequences." All of which may be a distraction from the real focus needed to maintain its legitimacy—performance.

The sources of legitimacy are fragile, but citizen support and trust in the regime have not declined significantly. Of course, support is distinct from legitimacy, and support can erode more easily. Surveys taken between 2003 and 2016 reveal high levels of satisfaction with the central government, mirroring other surveys covering levels of trust and so forth. The surveys suggest that the majority of citizens view abuses as local aberrations rather than stemming from party policies.[50] The surveys indicate three main findings: respondents "disaggregate" the state; satisfaction has, on the whole, risen since the surveys began in 2003; and satisfaction has risen most noticeably for the poorest in the rural areas and those in the hinterland. Citizens express high levels of satisfaction with the central government (over 90 percent in 2016, with 31 percent extremely satisfied), but such support declines at each lower level of government (70 percent at the level of the village, township and street committee, with 13 percent extremely satisfied). These levels of satisfaction mark a considerable improvement since the beginning of the Hu–Wen leadership, when only 43.6 percent of the respondents were satisfied with the lowest level of government. The findings suggest that Chinese citizens are responding to the government's attempts to rebalance economic growth along regional lines and to establish a basic social safety net for the country's most vulnerable residents. Countering the notion that challenges to the regime may come from the poorer marginalized communities, we find that satisfaction has improved most significantly for the lowest-income households in rural China and within the poorer regions. This may provide a deeper form of performance legitimacy that is not based on economic growth alone.

The decline in satisfaction as the government gets closer to the people is understandable, not only because of the daily propaganda that seeks to boost Xi Jinping's standing but also because local government is required to supply the overwhelming majority of public goods. In Chinese history, there is a notion of honest officials working at higher levels who would redress local wrongs if only they knew the facts. This is well-captured in the movie *Qiu Ju*, in which a poor rural woman goes to ever-higher levels of government to seek justice for her husband, who was beaten by the local village head. Needless to say, she does not receive the justice she feels he deserves, and the film underscores how personal connections override any notion of the rule of law. This is also reflected on the streets by the large number of petitioners who flock to the capital in search of justice for local abuses. Local governments often send thugs to return the petitioners to their home base so that criticism of their performance will not reach the ears at higher levels.

The Challenge of Governance

To achieve its objectives, the CCP will have to complete the transition of governing structures from those that oversaw a Communist state and a planned economy to those that can manage a modern, market-influenced economy. To add to this, the party will have to develop the kinds of institutions that can accommodate a pluralized and knowledgeable society. There is a relationship between institutional development and sustainable growth. A comparison of the World Bank governance indicators with income per capita reveals that countries with higher incomes have better governance indicators. There is a strong empirical relationship between the quality of institutions and economic growth.[51] Some have pondered whether China might follow the development trajectory of its East Asian tiger neighbors. Successful development in Taiwan and Korea is attributed to the nature of their institutions and state interventions. These provided a policy framework for competition, growth, and exports. Countries such as China and Vietnam have good institutions for their current levels of economic growth, and consequently they have been able to attract high levels of foreign direct investment. As incomes rise, however, it becomes more difficult for authoritarian regimes to maintain growth, because at this juncture the economic system needs political and economic institutions that promote competition, innovation, and growth of productivity rather than simply accumulating increasing amounts of capital. This is the core institutional challenge for the CCP in the next decade. However, the differences with Taiwan and South Korea are so significant that it raises questions as to whether this is the correct comparison. In addition to the structure of their economies and their more vibrant civil societies, both were in the sphere of influence of the United States, which supported moves toward liberalization and democratization. The CCP is far less likely to release its grip over the economy and society.

The challenges of governance extend much farther than effective management of the economy. Most of the problems confronting the CCP are linked to the challenges of governance—poor implementation at the local level of good national regulations, illegal transfers of land by local administrations, lack of transparency in the government or in the corporate sector, and so on. These government failures were revealed clearly with the initial response to the outbreak of COVID-19. Furthermore, the party must devise the institutions and framework that can enable the Chinese people to develop a moral framework to guide the relationships between the party-state, society, and the individual and within which individuals can pursue their own goals. What Xi Jinping has been offering to date has been the restoration of party prestige through the campaign against corruption and calls for officials to adopt a simple lifestyle. This is a top-down approach, punishing dissenters and preventing a more open press and an informed public. A major problem for the CCP is that it is difficult, perhaps impossible, to open a national dialogue about what kind of society the people want. Many fear that removal of the CCP would be destabilizing, a view promoted by the party.

Some outside observers have argued that inevitably China will move in the direction of a more open and democratic political system.[52] Others have predicted collapse unless China moves in this direction.[53] Although China has become more open, it has not become democratic. This is not to say that there has been no political reform, but the core features of the Leninist party-state remain essentially unchanged. What happens if China does not change? Can a system with increased market influences combined with an authoritarian political structure provide a more enduring system than merely being a transitional form? Such questions have led to studies of the resilience of the authoritarian system and the nature of consultations that exist.[54] These findings suggest that China's political evolution might not follow the path of other industrial and postindustrial societies.

Indeed, numerous factors caution against anticipating a democratic transition. Ever since the purge of Zhao Ziyang following the 1989 demonstrations, political reform has remained a divisive issue among the party leadership, and with no clarity about what the ultimate objective might be, despite the continual references to building socialist democracy and the rule of law. Second, the party elite fear that opening up too wide might open floodgates that will lead to a collapse of the CCP, such as occurred to the CPSU. Any such opening, in their view, would be seized upon by hostile foreign forces to bring down the party. With legitimacy to a large extent dependent on economic growth, a democratic opening is viewed as potentially destabilizing and thus harmful to the economy. The fusion of political power at the local level creates strong vested interests against moving ahead with reform and "traps" the transition.[55] The experience of Taiwan, however, counters the argument that Chinese traditional culture cannot accommodate democracy. Perhaps China is a-democratic rather than antidemocratic.[56]

Despite the daily demonstrations, today there is little pressure from below to push the CCP to undertake significant changes, and satisfaction levels remain high. Unlike in the Soviet Union, the reforms have created a substantial group of people who are invested in the current system. The overseers of the declining but powerful state sector of the economy, the rising middle class, and the private sector titans are products of party policy, and they are not willing to rock the boat as long as they continue to derive benefits from the current system. The close relationship between many private entrepreneurs and the party reinforces this unwillingness to seek fundamental change, as does the fear of potential retribution by those who struggle to make ends meet in the informal urban economy or on the land in the remote areas.

Further, civil society is weak in China and there are no alternative social institutions such as the church around which opposition could coalesce. This is not to say that religion is not widespread in China, with perhaps as many as 400 million believers, including more than 200 million Buddhists.[57] The revival of religion has caused concern. Xi Jinping has reemphasized that party members cannot practice religion, and he has denounced religion as "spiritual anesthesia." For society, the tightening of control intensified after 2016 when General Secretary Xi called for the Sinification of religion. Apart from Buddhism (even though it came from India) and local folk religion, other belief systems are viewed as foreign constructs that might clash with the values of the CCP. This has resulted in the destruction of Protestant churches as illegal constructions, the repression of believers in Xinjiang, and even the banning of displays of Christmas symbols by some local authorities. In Henan province it has been reported that churches were instructed to replace the Ten Commandments with quotes by Xi Jinping![58]

The most powerful social institution is the clan, but clans are local in nature, and even though they protect their own interests and may frustrate central policy, they are not a threat to higher levels of administration. The clans or lineages themselves are exclusive organizations, and outsiders do not benefit from any advantages that communal organizing might bring. In many places the head of the clan is also the local party secretary—so is the party controlling the clan? or are the interests of the clan and its values invading the local party apparatus? The answer is both.

There are similar situations in other parts of the society. For many migrants in urban areas, one of the most important social organizations is the locality from where they came, which by definition is exclusionary. For the new middle class, many of whom live in gated compounds, their primary social organization might be their local neighborhood, and any protests they might be involved in tend to be about immediate local problems.[59] The CCP has been very successful in ensuring the continuation of such a cellular society. The main challenge has come from industrial labor and critical intellectuals, but they have rarely formed a bond like that of Solidarity in Poland. As we have seen, once organizations threaten to expand horizontally across party-defined structures, they are quickly eliminated. Having eliminated any possible alternative to the CCP, the party claims that without the party, there would be chaos. If the CCP can continue to grow the economy while developing greater protection of property rights, enforcing stricter anticorruption measures, and providing greater consumer protection, it might become the first titular Communist movement to co-opt the middle class in a political transition. However, we have seen how unreliable predictions can be.

The CCP has been poor at institutionalizing ruling structures, and succession has been a continual problem. Mao removed his chosen heirs and Deng removed the first two heirs he had selected. Xi Jinping came to power only after the very public removal of rival princeling Bo Xilai. Xi's decision to extend the term of the presidency of the PRC indicates that he may wish to continue beyond the expected two terms. This pushes the challenge of succession farther into the future, and the lack of an obvious successor means that when succession comes, it could be all the more destabilizing.

Although the number of protests has increased and the party pays special attention to such threats, the CCP has been the most vulnerable when the elite has fallen out, not when it has been threatened by pressures from below. This was the case both before 1949 and subsequently during the Cultural Revolution and during the divisions over how to deal with the student-led demonstrations of 1989. Hence, Xi Jinping stresses party unity and loyalty above all. An unforeseen crisis such as serious divisions within the elite over the future development strategy or an economic meltdown could erode the CCP's capacity to maintain order. Despite its strong demeanor, the party and its structures are factional and therefore subject to rapid breakdown. The recentralization of power under Xi and the attempts to eradicate Western thought and unconventional ideas certainly indicate that these are far more widespread than the party admits, and the party clearly fears their influence.

None of this means that achieving the China Dream of rejuvenation of the nation is impossible, but it will require luck and skillful policy making. The record on trying to predict the future of authoritarian regimes has not been very good; few predicted the sudden fall of the Soviet Union, and even fewer saw the rapid expansion of the 1989 protests in China, let alone the collapse of the Qing dynasty. The future of the CCP is uncertain and open to a range of possible scenarios.[60] The most attractive development for the West would be for the Chinese leadership to respond to the increasing diversity in society and the rising protests to broker an accommodation with society. This would entail a reform-inclined section of the elite to break with the current system and form a new social compact. The possibility might have existed in 1989 had Zhao Ziyang overcome his opponents within the CCP leadership. However, it is difficult to see what would cause the current elite to willingly reject the existing beneficial system. The fear of disintegration and uncertainty about what might follow argues against this. Before the financial crisis of 2008–2009, the leadership was interested in exploring alternatives, such as the "third way" under UK prime minister Tony Blair, or the social democracy in Northern Europe. Social democracy remains of interest to reform-minded party members in China. A more unpredictable outcome would be the Yeltsin scenario—chaotic pluralization with democracy not entrenched and the elite and their families continuing to benefit from their political connections to privatize public wealth. The era under Yeltsin in Russia is regularly held up by the CCP leadership as the worst sort of outcome it might face if the reforms move too quickly and undermine the CCP's ruling capacity. During the Yeltsin era the Chinese press delighted in running articles about former Soviet establishment intellectuals who had fallen on hard times.

The most likely scenario over the short to medium term would be a continued fluctuation between soft and hard authoritarianism, making bold initiatives improbable. This would include shifting between the relatively flexible and decentralized approach to governance pursued by Xi Jinping's predecessors and the heavier-handed centralized approach of Xi himself.

Perhaps some within the party might be able to enable the shift back to a softer form of authoritarianism. The party will continue to take over decision-making authority from the state administration, and national industrial polices will continue, as will dominance of the state sector in external initiatives such as the BRI. This will ensure that the party elite will continue to reap the benefits of China's expanded global engagement. The leadership is confident in its model of development and will continue to promote it overseas and through international organizations. It is clear that the Chinese leadership anticipates continued conflict with the United States. As a result, it is preparing for a time when there is less interdependency in economic and financial engagement. China will need access to global financial markets for a considerable time to come, but it is preparing to release itself from reliance on trade with the United States and to develop its own capabilities in high-tech and artificial intelligence. To manage the internal threats, strong repression of alternate organizing will be accompanied by policies of redistribution and continued increases in investment in social policies and poverty alleviation, which have proven popular.

Political transitions are rare, and there is no reason to expect China to follow its East Asian neighbors in South Korea and Taiwan and develop into a robust democracy. Enthusiasm for the third wave of democratic expansion has receded, and the focus has shifted from theories of transition to those of resilience.[61] Transition rarely occurs during a period of economic growth; it is more likely to occur in a system under stress. The emergence of an illiberal democracy would be quite plausible in a period of economic stress.[62] Such an outcome could resemble some of the post-Soviet Central Asian states or Russia under Putin, where authoritarian practices remain strong. There would be a dominant executive with a weak legislature and a fragmented civil society overseen by a strong domestic security apparatus and military. The leadership would stress the dangers of social chaos to keep the middle class supportive and a stronger nationalism to cement patriotic cohesion. Relations with the United States and neighbors such as Japan and Taiwan would remain contentious, and they would be exploited to cement patriotic support. This scenario is not encouraging, but it is a quite likely future for China if the CPP falls.

NOTES

ACKNOWLEDGMENTS

ILLUSTRATION CREDITS

INDEX

Notes

Introduction

1. Yangyang Zhang, "Party People: What Kind of Students Join the CCP?" *Sixth Tone*, June 12, 2018, sixthtone.com/news/1002438/party-people-what-kind-of-students-join-the ccp%3F.
2. For a brilliant study of the varied role of the party at the subnational level, see Daniel Koss, *Where the Party Rules: The Rank and File of China's Communist State* (Cambridge: Cambridge University Press, 2018).
3. Elizabeth J. Perry's study of the revolutionary fulcrum in Anyuan, Jiangxi province, looks at how Mao Zedong and his colleagues used rituals and other practices to promote the revolutionary movement. See her *Anyuan: Mining China's Revolutionary Tradition* (Berkeley: University of California Press, 2012).
4. Official CCP histories date the Cultural Revolution from 1966 to 1976, incorporating the destruction of the early phase, the death of Mao Zedong, and the arrest of his widow and closest supporters. In this work, I use a shorter time frame, 1966 to 1969, that covers the early years before rebuilding began.
5. Quoted in Gao Hua, *How the Red Sun Rose: The Origins and Development of the Yan'an Rectification Movement, 1930–1945* (Hong Kong: The Chinese University Press, 2018), 9.
6. The "Three Represents" were Jiang's attempt to adapt the party to the more complex and affluent society over which the CCP was presiding. They called for the CCP to represent the advanced social productive forces, the most advanced culture, and the fundamental interests of all the people.
7. Adrian Wan, "Chinese Academy of Social Sciences Is 'Infiltrated by Foreign Forces': Anti-graft Official," *South China Morning Post*, June 15, 2014.
8. "HNA Is Victim of Conspiracy against China: Co-Chairman," *Bloomberg News*, February 7, 2018.
9. Charles Tilly, *European Revolutions, 1492–1992* (Oxford: Blackwell, 1993).

1. The End of the Empire

1. Jonathan Porter, *Imperial China, 1350–1900* (Lanham, MD: Rowman and Littlefield, 2016), 2.

2. Moss Roberts, trans., *Three Kingdoms: A Historical Novel,* attributed to Luo Guanzhong, abridged ed. (Berkeley: University of California Press, 2014), 3.

3. Peter Perdue, "The Expansion of the Qing Dynasty of China and Zunghar Mongol State," in *Oxford Research Encyclopedia,* https://oxfordre.com /asianhistory/view/10.1093/acrefore/9780190277727.001.0001/acrefore -9780190277727-e-7.

4. Mark C. Elliott, *The Manchu Way: The Eight Banners and Ethnic Identity in Late Imperial China* (Stanford, CA: Stanford University Press, 2001).

5. Between 1980 and 1984, China established three zones (Shantou, Shenzhen, and Zhuhai) in Guangdong province to take advantage of their proximity to Hong Kong and Macau, and one zone (Xiamen) in Fujian province to take advantage of possible engagement with Taiwan.

6. Reuters, March 2, 2007.

7. John Powers, *The Buddha Party: How the People's Republic of China Works to Define and Control Tibetan Buddhism* (Oxford: Oxford University Press, 2016).

8. "China Steps Up Discredited Attempts to Control Dalai Lama's Succession," *International Campaign for Tibet,* September 12, 2019, https://savetibet .org/china-steps-up-discredited-attempts-to-control-dalai-lamas-succession/.

9. Xu Youwei and Philip Billingsey, "Heroes, Martyrs, and Villains in 1930s Shaanbei: Liu Zhidan and His 'Bandit Policy,'" *Modern China* 44, no. 3 (May 2018): 247.

10. Ho Ping-ti, *Studies on the Population of China, 1368–1953* (Cambridge, MA: Harvard University Press, 1959), 270.

11. Youngmin Kim, *A History of Chinese Political Thought* (Cambridge: Polity Press, 2018), 200.

12. On the growing militarism of China in the twentieth century, see the excellent studies by Hans J. van de Ven, *War and Nationalism in China, 1925–1945* (London: RoutledgeCurzon, 2003); *China at War: Triumph and Tragedy in the Emergence of the New China* (Cambridge, MA: Harvard University Press, 2018).

13. Etienne Balazs, *Chinese Civilization and Bureaucracy: Variations on a Theme* (New Haven, CT: Yale University Press, 1977); Mark Elvin, *The Pattern of the Chinese Past* (Stanford, CA: Stanford University Press, 1973).

14. Elvin, *Pattern of the Chinese Past,* 298–315.

15. This is best captured in the work of the "California School." Representative works are Bin R. Wong, *China Transformed: Historical Change and the Limits of European Experience* (Ithaca, NY: Cornell University Press, 1997); Kenneth Pomeranz, *The Great Divergence: Europe, China and the Making of the Modern World Economy* (Princeton, NJ: Princeton University Press, 2000). A tremendous sweeping overview of China's economic development can be found in Robert Von Glahn, *The Economic History of China: From Antiquity to the Nineteenth Century* (Cambridge: Cambridge University Press, 2016); chap. 9 argues persuasively that domestic crises and uprisings, together with external challenges, were particularly relevant.

16. This economic depression is referred to as the "Daoguang Depression" (1820–1850), a period when a growing population faced deflation and stagnant or declining wages. The family-based agricultural system of production also hampered innovation and technological advance.

17. Von Glahn, *Economic History of China*, 349.

18. The White Lotus Rebellion was set off by the Qing suppression of perceived religious dissidents in western Hubei. Its spread and the subsequent military actions took an enormous toll on the state treasury.

19. A good review is Ramon H. Myers, "How Did the Chinese Economy Develop? A Review Article," *Journal of Asian Studies* 50, no. 3 (August 1991): 604–628.

20. Jonathan D. Spence, *God's Chinese Son: The Taiping Heavenly Kingdom of Hong Xiuquan* (New York: W. W. Norton, 1996).

21. Joseph Levenson, *Confucian China and Its Modern Fate* (Berkeley: University of California Press, 1965).

22. Porter, *Imperial China, 1350–1900*, 269.

23. On the inroads made by Buddhism, see E. Zürcher, *The Buddhist Conquest of China: The Spread and Adaptation of Buddhism in Early Medieval China*, 3rd ed. (Leiden: Brill, 2007).

24. Kim, *History of Chinese Political Thought*, 12.

25. In his speech commemorating the 2,565th anniversary of the birth of Confucius.

26. Karl August Wittfogel, *Oriental Despotism: A Comparative Study of Total Power* (New Haven, CT: Yale University Press, 1957).

27. Carol Lee Hamrin and Timothy Cheek, eds., *China's Establishment Intellectuals* (Armonk, NY: M. E. Sharpe, 1986).

28. Tony Saich and Biliang Hu, *Chinese Village, Global Market: New Collectives and Rural Development* (New York: Palgrave Macmillan, 2012).

29. Jürgen Habermas, *The Structural Transformation of the Public Sphere: An Inquiry into a Category of Bourgeois Society* (Cambridge, MA: Polity Press, 1989). William T. Rowe's analysis of Hankou provides an important contribution on the development of a public sphere. See his "The Public Sphere in Modern China," *Modern China* 16, no. 3 (July 1990): 309–329.

30. Frederic Wakeman, "The Civil Society and Public Sphere Debate: Western Reflections on Chinese Political Culture," *Modern China* 19, no. 2 (April 1993): 108–138.

31. Emperor Qianlong's Letter to King George III, 1793, academics.wellesley .edu/Polisci/wj/China/208/READINGS/Qianlong.html. This is taken from E. Backhouse and J. O. P. Bland, *Annals and Memoirs of the Court of Peking (from the 16th to the 20th Century)* (Boston: Houghton Mifflin, 1914).

32. Benjamin I. Schwartz, *In Search of Wealth and Power: Yen Fu and the West* (Cambridge, MA: Belknap Press of Harvard University Press, 1964), 42.

33. Odd Arne Westad, *Restless Empire: China and the World since 1750* (New York: Basic Books, 2012), 127. This is the best and most accessible account of China's engagement with the outside world.

34. An interesting early discussion of this question is Simon de Beaufort, *Yellow Earth, Green Jade: Constants in Chinese Political Mores* (Cambridge, MA: Center for International Affairs, Harvard University, 1978).

35. David Bray, *Social Space and Governance in Urban China: The Danwei System from Origins to Urban Reform* (Stanford, CA: Stanford University Press, 2005).

36. Officially, the electronic system is intended to rebuild trust after the paper system that was seriously undermined during the reform years. Aiming to monitor honesty in government affairs, commercial integrity, societal integrity, and judicial credibility, it was intended to become fully operational in 2020.

37. Simina Mistreanu, "Life inside China's Social Credit Laboratory," *Foreign Policy*, April 3, 2018.

2. Origins, Alliance, and Failure, 1920–1930

1. Liu was a faithful supporter of Mao until his purge and humiliation during the Cultural Revolution. Li headed the party between 1928 and 1930 and oversaw a series of disastrous uprisings.

2. The Autumn Harvest Uprising of 1927, which is considered to be the origin of the CCP military, was launched from this region. Elizabeth J. Perry provides a wonderful account of the region in her *Anyuan: Mining China's Revolutionary Tradition* (Berkeley: University of California Press, 2012).

3. Hans J. van de Ven, *From Friend to Comrade: The Founding of the Chinese Communist Party, 1920–1927* (Berkeley: University of California Press, 1991); Tony Saich, with a contribution by Benjamin Yang, *The Rise to Power of the Chinese Communist Party: Documents and Analysis* (Armonk, NY: M. E. Sharpe, 1996).

4. The best account of the early days of women's engagement and influence in the Communist movement remains Christina K. Gilmartin, *Engendering the Chinese Revolution: Radical Women, Communist Politics, and Mass Movements in the 1920s* (Berkeley: University of California Press, 1995).

5. Michael Y. L. Luk, *The Origins of Chinese Bolshevism: An Ideology in the Making, 1920–1928* (Oxford: Oxford University Press, 1990), 16.

6. In December 1920, Li Dazhao was writing about his conversion to Marxism, and in May and September 1920, Chen Duxiu was stressing the importance of the working class and the idea that class struggle would bring about the realization of socialism in China and resolve the social problems faced by the nation.

7. Sow-Theng Leong, *Sino-Soviet Relations: The First Phase, 1917–1920* (Canberra: Australian National University Press, 1971).

8. No original documentation exists to support this view; it originated from a speech by Gao Yihan at Li Dazhao's memorial service in 1927. Ishikawa Yoshihiro, *The Formation of the Chinese Communist Party* (New York: Columbia University Press, 2013), 101–103.

9. Voitinsky had worked in the United States. Sneevliet had worked in the Dutch labor movement and the anticolonial movement in the Dutch East Indies.

10. As the first formal envoy to China, he arrived with his wife and two assistants. Although approved by the Comintern, he led a delegation of Bolshevik party members, under the auspices of the Far East Bureau Party Branch.

11. Voitinsky's reports of June and August 1920 in *RKP(B), Komintern und die national-revolutionäre Bewegung in China, Dokumente* (Russian Communist Party (Bolshevik) (RCP [B]), the Comintern and the National-Revolutionary Movement in China, Documents), vol. 1: 1920–1925 (Paderborn: F. Schöningh, 1996), docs. 1 and 2. We know he met with future party luminaries, Li Dazhao, Chen Duxiu, and other influential thinkers, as well as important political figures, such as the southern warlord Chen Jiongming and Sun Yat-sen.

12. Tony Saich, *The Origins of the First United Front in China: The Role of Sneevliet (Alias Maring)*, 2 vols. (Leiden: Brill, 1991); and Saich, *Finding Allies and Making Revolution: The Early Years of the Chinese Communist Party* (Leiden: Brill, 2020).

13. Interview with Luo Zhanglong, summer 1987.

14. Perry, *Anyuan*, 52, 90.

15. For example, the October 1921 report by Lidin refers to the isolation of the "small intellectual group" from the workers. *RKP(B), Komintern und die national-revolutionäre Bewegung*, vol. 1, doc. 21.

16. Sneevliet was aware of problems with Sun and complained about his focus on a military solution to the detriment of developing party and propaganda work. Initially he was willing to downplay these issues so that his ideas would be accepted. But as he began to work with Sun more closely, his frustration grew, even leading him to suggest that further support for Sun should be withheld.

17. Chen Duxiu, April 6, 1922, "Letter to G. Voitinsky," in *The Second and Third Party Congresses* (Beijing: Zhongguo shehui kexue chubanshe, 1985), 36. By June, Chen's views had mellowed somewhat, but he still rejected the idea of a united front. Nevertheless, he expressed his hope that Sun Yat-sen would "temporarily follow the same road as us." Chen Duxiu, June 30, 1922, "Letter to Voitinsky," in *Second and Third Party Congresses*, 55.

18. Chen Duxiu, "Report to the Comintern," June 30, 1922 [1997], in *Selected Documents on the Communist International, the Russian Communist Party (Bolshevik), and the Chinese Revolution, 1917–1925*, ed. No. 1 Research Office of the CC Central Party History Office, vol. 2 (Beijing: Beijing tushuguan

chubanshe, 1997), 304–310; Chen Duxiu, "Report to the Third Party Congress," June 1922, translated in Saich, *Origins*, 2:572–577.

19. Perry, *Anyuan*, 9, 65–73.

20. Luo Zhanglong, "Professor Luo Zhanglong Discusses the Major Strike of 'February 7,'" *Dangshi yanjiu ziliao* (Research Materials on Party History), no. 4 (1983): 254.

21. Bukharin was a leader of the ECCI, becoming chair in 1926. He was also a member of the China Committee.

22. For the version of the resolution that Sneevliet brought back to China, see Saich, *Origins*, 2:565–567.

23. Handwritten letter in English from Zhang Guotao to Voitinsky and Musin, November 16, 1923. Copy in author's possession.

24. This was in Moscow in 1930 when he was defending himself against charges of counterrevolutionary behavior. Quoted in Lydia Holubnychy, *Michael Borodin and the Chinese Revolution, 1923–1925* (New York: Columbia University, East Asia Institute, 1979), 376a–377.

25. S. A. Smith, *A Road Is Made: Communism in Shanghai, 1920–1927* (Honolulu: University of Hawai'i Press, 2000), 55; *RKP(B), Komintern und die national-revolutionäre Bewegung*, vol. 1, doc. 111, February 16, 1924, pp. 454–529.

26. Letter of January 25, 1924, to Karakhan, in *RKP(B), Komintern und die national-revolutionäre Bewegung*, vol. 1, doc. 107, p. 438.

27. Letter to Raskol'nikov, December 16, 1924, in *RKP(B), Komintern und die national-revolutionäre* Bewegung, vol. 1, doc. 133, pp. 603–607.

28. The resolutions of the congress, January 1925, are translated in Saich, *The Rise to Power*, 129–152.

29. Smith, *A Road Is Made*, 89–107.

30. Perry, *Anyuan*, 115–127.

31. Perry, *Anyuan*, 125–127.

32. Smith, *A Road Is Made*, 111.

33. Saich, *The Rise to Power*, 161–162.

34. For the evolution of Stalin's views, see Alexander Pantsov, *The Bolsheviks and the Chinese Revolution, 1919–1927* (Honolulu: University of Hawai'i Press, 2000), 84–98.

35. Letter to Karakhan, April 22, 1925, in *RKP(B), Komintern und die national-revolutionäre Bewegung*, vol. 1, doc. 147.

36. Report dated February 20, 1926, to the ECCI, quoted in Smith, *A Road Is Made*, 114.

37. Letter from Voitinsky to Chen Duxiu, Moscow, April 24, 1926, in *KPdSU(B), Komintern und die national-revolutionäre Bewegung in China, Dokumente* (RCP[B] The Comintern and the National-Revolutionary Movement in China, Documents), vol. 2, 1926–1927, ed. Mechthild Leutner and M. L. Titarenko (Paderborn: F. Schöningh, 1998), pt. 1, doc. 42, pp. 276–281.

38. C. Martin Wilbur and Julie Lien-ying How, *Missionaries of Revolution: Soviet Advisors and Nationalist China, 1920–1927* (Cambridge, MA: Harvard University Press, 1989), 258–261.

39. See the two reports by Stepanov, in Wilbur and How, *Missionaries of Revolution*, docs. 50 and 51, pp. 703–706.

40. Jane Degras, ed., *The Communist International, 1919–1943: Documents* (Oxford: Oxford University Press, 1960), 2:277–279.

41. Radek first put forward this idea in his theses of June 22, 1926; in Leutner and Titarenko, *KPdSU(B), Komintern und die national-revolutionäre Bewegung in China, Dokumente*, vol. 2, pt. 1, doc. 62, pp. 373–378.

42. Notes of Meeting of the Politburo of the RCP(B), April 29, 1926, in *KPdSU(B)*, vol. 2, pt. 1, doc. 47, pp. 297–298.

43. See the record of discussions between Voitinsky and Gu Mengyu in Guangzhou (August 31, 1926), noting how widespread this had become, in *KPdSU(B)*, vol. 2, pt. 1, doc. 89, pp. 490–492. For Borodin's comments, see his letter to Karakhan, May 30, 1926, in *KPdSU(B)*, vol. 2, pt. 1, doc. 55, pp. 335–348.

44. Telegram to the Bureau of the Delegation of the RCP(B) at the ECCI, July 1, 1926, in *KPdSU(B)*, vol. 2, pt. 1, doc. 64, pp. 380–386.

45. For the key documentation, see Saich, *The Rise to Power*, 169–297.

46. Elizabeth J. Perry, *Patrolling the Revolution: Worker Militias, Citizenship, and the Modern Chinese State* (Lanham, MD: Rowman and Littlefield, 2005).

47. Protocol of the RCP(B) meeting on March 31, 1927, in Leutner and Titarenko, *KPdSU(B), Komintern und die national-revolutionäre Bewegung in China, Dokumente*, vol. 2, pt. 2, doc. 183, pp. 884–887.

48. In Shanghai the number of CCP members dropped from about 8,000 to only 1,200. Patricia Stranahan, *Underground: The Shanghai Communist Party and the Politics of Survival, 1927–1937* (Lanham, MD: Rowman and Littlefield, 1998), 37.

49. The Resolution of the Eighth Plenum of the ECCI, in Degras, *The Communist International*, 2:384–390.

50. The key documents from the Fifth Party Congress, April–May 1927, are translated in Saich, *The Rise to Power*, 228–359.

51. Alexander V. Pantsov, with Steven I. Levine, *Mao: The Real Story* (New York: Simon and Schuster, 2012), 228.

52. Xenia Joukoff Eudin and Robert C. North, *Soviet Russia and the East, 1920–1927: A Documentary Survey* (Stanford, CA: Stanford University Press, 1964), 303–304; Robert C. North and Xenia J. Eudin, *M. N. Roy's Mission to China: The Communist-Kuomintang Split of 1927* (Berkeley: University of California Press, 1963), 107.

53. *Pravda*, September 30, 1927, quoted in Pantsov, *The Bolsheviks*, 155–156.

54. Alexander Pantsov and Gregor Benton, "Did Trotsky Oppose Entering the Guomindang 'From the First'?," *Republican China* 19, no. 2 (April 1994): 52–66.

55. The translation of key documents can be found in Saich, *The Rise to Power*, 341–386.
56. "Letter from the ECCI to the CC of the CCP," in *Gongchan guoji you guan Zhongguo geming de wenxian ziliao* (Materials of the Comintern concerning the Chinese Revolution), ed. Chinese Academy of Social Sciences, Modern History Research Institute, Translation Office (Beijing: Zhongguo shehui kexue chubanshe, 1982), 2:1–18.
57. Alexander M. Grigoriev, "The Far Eastern Bureau of the ECCI in China, 1929–1931," in *The Chinese Revolution in the 1920s: Triumph and Disaster*, ed. Mechthild Leutner et al. (London: RoutledgeCurzon, 2002), 156–165.
58. Grigoriev, "Far Eastern Bureau," 163–164.
59. On the early rural movement, see Roy Hofheinz Jr., *The Broken Wave: The Chinese Communist Movement, 1922–1928* (Cambridge, MA: Harvard University Press, 1977); and the excellent study by Fernando Galbiati, *P'eng P'ai and the Hai-Lu-Feng Soviet* (Stanford, CA: Stanford University Press, 1985).
60. Translated in Stuart R. Schram, ed., *Mao's Road to Power: Revolutionary Writings, 1912–1949*, vol. 2, *National Revolution and Social Revolution, December 1920–June 1927* (Armonk, NY: M. E. Sharpe, 1994), 429–464.
61. Mao arrived in the area in October 1929, but he moved out in January 1930 to look for opportunities in southern Jiangxi and western Fujian. For a wonderful account that provides not only a detailed historical account but also a deep investigation into the socioeconomic structures and their influence on the practice of local CCP rule, see Stephen C. Averill, *Revolution in the Highlands: China's Jinggangshan Base Area* (Lanham, MD: Rowman and Littlefield, 2006).
62. Saich, *The Rise to Power*, 483.

3. Wanderings in the Wilderness, 1930–1940

1. Stephen C. Averill, *Revolution in the Highlands: China's Jinggangshan Base Area* (Lanham, MD: Rowman and Littlefield, 2006), 407–410.
2. Stephen C. Averill, "The Origins of the Futian Incident," in *New Perspectives on the Chinese Communist Revolution*, ed. Tony Saich and Hans van de Ven (Armonk, NY: M. E. Sharpe, 1995), 79–115; Ch'en Yung-fa, "The Futian Incident and the Anti-Bolshevik League: The 'Terror' in the CCP Revolution," *Republican China* 19, no. 2 (April 1994): 1–54.
3. Violent rhetoric to denounce enemies in the party had become the norm, but the military clashes between local Communist forces and those allied with Mao were the first armed conflicts among CCP forces that I have been able to locate.
4. There are different views regarding what "A.B." stood for. One dominant view is that it stands for Anti-Bolshevik, but it is more likely that it stood for the different levels of membership at the provincial and district levels. See

Alexander Pantsov, with Steven I. Levine, *Mao: The Real Story* (New York: Simon and Schuster, 2012), 240.

5. Those put to death included dozens of regimental commanders. Gao Hua, *How the Red Sun Rose: The Origins and Development of the Yan'an Rectification Movement, 1930–1945* (Hong Kong: Chinese University Press, 2018), 20; Averill, "Origins of the Futian Incident," 104–105.

6. Averill, "Origins of the Futian Incident," 108.

7. Patricia Stranahan, *Underground: The Shanghai Communist Party and the Politics of Survival, 1927–1937* (Lanham, MD: Rowman and Littlefield, 1998), chap. 3.

8. There are different interpretations about what he was doing in Hankou. Pantsov and Averill, following Zhang Guotao's memoirs, state that he was preparing an assassination attempt on Chiang Kai-shek. A more mundane explanation is that he was checking on supply lines along the Yangzi between Shanghai and the Jiangxi Soviet. Frederic E. Wakeman Jr., *Policing Shanghai, 1927–1937* (Berkeley: University of California Press, 1995), 151–161.

9. This was justified by an October 1928 CC circular that called for any "rebels and turncoats" to be put to death.

10. This is argued perceptively by Stranahan, *Underground,* chap. 3.

11. Telegram, December 29, 1931, translated in Warren Kuo, *Analytical History of the Chinese Communist Party* (Taibei: Institute of International Relations, 1968), bk. 2, 413–414.

12. Pantsov, with Levine, *Mao: The Real Story,* 261.

13. For translations, see Tony Saich, with a contribution by Benjamin Yang, *The Rise to Power of the Chinese Communist Party: Documents and Analysis* (Armonk, NY: M. E. Sharpe, 1996), 552–558.

14. "The First All-China Soviet Congress Draft Land Law," in *Liuda yilai— dangnei mimi wenjian* (Since the Sixth Party Congress: Secret Inner Party Documents), ed. CCP CC Central Secretariat (Beijing: Renmin chubanshe, 1981), 1:181–183.

15. For an example of Luo Ming's writings and the resolution, see Saich, *The Rise to Power,* 596–602.

16. The troops had called for a truce and a military alliance with the Red Army against Japan and Chiang Kai-shek.

17. The key documents are translated in Saich, *The Rise to Power,* 607–627.

18. Pantsov, with Levine, *Mao: The Real Story,* 271.

19. Otto Braun, *A Comintern Agent in China, 1932–1939* (Stanford, CA: Stanford University Press, 1982), 76–79.

20. Later Chen Yi would serve as mayor of Shanghai and as China's foreign minister.

21. For a positive, lively account, see Harrison E. Salisbury, *The Long March: The Untold Story* (New York: Harper and Row, 1985). For a more critical account, see Sun Shuyun, *The Long March: The True History of Communist China's*

Founding Myth (New York: Doubleday 2006), 145. The best academic analysis remains Benjamin Yang, *From Revolution to Politics: Chinese Communism on the Long March* (Boulder, CO: Westview Press, 1990).

22. The longer document is translated in Jerome Ch'en, "Resolutions of the Tsunyi Conference," *China Quarterly*, no. 40 (December 1965): 1–38. The shorter, more pointed document, from February 28, 1935, is translated in Saich, *The Rise to Power*, 640–643.

23. Chang Kuo-t'ao, *The Rise to Power of the Chinese Communist Party, 1928–1938* (Lawrence: University of Kansas Press, 1972), 2:409.

24. "Report to the Conference of Activists among the 'Party Center' Ranks," June 6, 1936, translated in Saich, *The Rise to Power*, 748–755.

25. Salisbury, *The Long March*, 286.

26. Hans J. van de Ven, *China at War: Triumph and Tragedy in the Emergence of the New China* (Cambridge, MA: Harvard University Press, 2018), 5.

27. A party veteran told me that she had returned to Yan'an. When I pointed out that this was the first time she had been there following her flight, she replied, placing her hand on her heart, that you never simply *went* to Yan'an but always *went home* to Yan'an, as it was indeed the spiritual center.

28. Interviews conducted with David Apter, in David E. Apter and Tony Saich, *Revolutionary Discourse in Mao's Republic* (Cambridge, MA: Harvard University Press, 1994), esp. 144–170.

29. Mark Selden, "The Guerrilla Movement in Northwest China: The Origins of the Shensi-Kansu-Ninghsia Border Region," pt. 1, *China Quarterly*, no. 28 (October–November 1966): 63–81, and pt. 2, *China Quarterly*, no. 29 (January–March 1967): 61–81.

30. Interview, Beijing, June 21, 1988.

31. It is difficult to verify such tales, but the brutality of inner-party conflicts was also recounted by several other participants. Interview, Beijing, June 21, 1988.

32. In the post-Mao era, rumors swirled about the true cause of Liu's death. Some argue that he was sent by Mao to a battle that would almost certainly end in his death. The most extreme told to me was that one of Mao's own troops had taken him out during the battle.

33. Hans J. van de Ven, *War and Nationalism in China: 1925–1945* (London: RoutledgeCurzon, 2003), 146.

34. Kui-Kwong Shum, *The Chinese Communists' Road to Power: The Anti-Japanese National United Front, 1935–1945* (Oxford: Oxford University Press, 1988), 19.

35. "Message to Compatriots on Resistance to Japan to Save the Nation," August 1, 1935, translated in Saich, *The Rise to Power*, 692–698.

36. For Dimitrov's comments, see *KPdSU (B), Komintern und China, Dokumente*, vol. 4, *1931–1937*, pt. 2 (CPSU [B], Comintern and China: Documents, vol. 4, 1931–1937, part 2) (Berlin: Lit Verlag, 2006), doc. 375, pp. 1286–1290. It is marked secret. The telegram from the ECCI Secretariat to the CCP CC, in ibid., doc. 380, pp. 1294–1298.

37. Steve Tsang makes excellent use of Chiang's diary at the Hoover Institution and the Presidential Archives on Taiwan to argue that Chiang was not forced to agree to a united front with the Communists at this time and that he had indeed been preparing to resist Japan. See Steve Tsang, "Chiang Kai-shek's 'Secret Deal' at Xian and the Start of the Sino-Japanese War," *Palgrave Communications*, no. 1 (2015), https://doi.org/10.1057/palcomms .2014.3.

38. Yang Kuisong uses this delay to argue that the CCP decided to resolve the standoff without Stalin's input, in *Xi'an Shibian Xintan: Zhang Xueliang yu Zhonggong guanxi zhi yanjiu* (New Exploration of the Xi'an Incident: Research on the Relationship between Zhang Xueliang and the CCP) (Saratoga, CA: Dongda tushu gongsi, 1995), 322–332.

39. Tsang, "Chiang Kai-shek's 'Secret Deal,'" 6.

40. Parks M. Coble, *Facing Japan: Chinese Politics and Japanese Imperialism, 1931–1937* (Cambridge, MA: Council on East Asian Studies, Harvard University, 1991). On the response of the Shanghai CCP, see Stranahan, *Underground*, chaps. 4 and 5.

41. Organizations such as the Leftist League, the Film League, and the Red Trade Unions. See Stranahan, *Underground*, 154–172.

42. Stranahan, *Underground*, 184.

43. Gao, *How the Red Sun Rose*, 132–134.

44. Shum, *The Chinese Communists' Road to Power*, 114. Wang Ming arrived by plane, but Mao was afraid of flying.

45. Translated in Saich, *The Rise to Power*, 802–812.

46. The resolution also approved the expulsion of Zhang Guotao from the party. See "Decision of the Presidium of the ECCI," September 1938, in *Zhonggong zhongyang wenjian xuanji, neibu ben* (Selection of CCP Central Documents, Internal Volume), ed. Central Archives (Beijing: Zhonggong zhongyang dangxiao chubanshe, 1986), 10:571–576. Wang Jiaxiang had lobbied on Mao's behalf in Moscow.

47. Mao Zedong, "The Role of the Chinese Communist Party in the National War," in *Selected Works of Mao Tse-Tung* (Peking: Foreign Languages Press, 1967), 2:259–260.

48. Shum, *The Chinese Communists' Road to Power*, 149; and Lyman P. van Slyke, *Enemies and Friends: The United Front in Chinese Communist History* (Stanford, CA: Stanford University Press, 1967), 96–97.

4. Victories at Last, 1940–1948

1. See Gregor Benton's superb studies, *Mountain Fires: The Red Army's Three-Year War in South China, 1934–1938* (Berkeley: University of California Press, 1992), and "Under Arms and Umbrellas: Perspectives on Chinese Communism in Defeat," in *New Perspectives on the Chinese Communist Revolution*, ed. Tony Saich and Hans van de Ven (Armonk, NY: M. E. Sharpe, 1995), 116–143.

2. Benton, *Mountain Fires*, 125.

3. Gregor Benton, *New Fourth Army: Communist Resistance along the Yangtze and the Hual, 1938–1941* (Berkeley: University of California Press, 1999). An earlier study that is broader in scope is Yung-fa Chen, *Making Revolution: The Communist Movement in Eastern and Central China, 1937–1945* (Berkeley: University of California Press, 1986).

4. Benton, *Mountain Fires*, 433.

5. Benton, *New Fourth Army*, 458–459.

6. The January 19, 1940, directive is translated in Tony Saich with a contribution by Benjamin Yang, *The Rise to Power of the Chinese Communist Party: Documents and Analysis* (Armonk, NY: M. E. Sharpe, 1996), 945–946.

7. Mao Zedong, "Freely Expand the Anti-Japanese Forces and Resist the Onslaught of the Anti-Communist Diehards," May 4, 1940, in *Selected Works of Mao Tse-Tung* (Peking: Foreign Languages Press, 1967), 2:431–436. For Xiang Ying's reply, see "Xiang Ying's Telegram in Reply to the Party Center concerning the Party Center's Directive on the Tactics for the NFA," May 12, 1940, in Central Party School, ed., *Zhonggong dangshi jiaoxue ziliao* (Reference Materials for Teaching Party History) (Beijing: Renmin chubanshe, 1979), 2:296.

8. This was the largest major campaign waged by Communist troops, lasting for two and a half months at the end of 1940.

9. "Telegram from Zhu De, Peng Dehuai, Ye Ting, and Xiang Ying to He Yingqin and Bai Chongxi on Saving and Protecting the General Situation," November 9, 1940, translated in Saich, *The Rise to Power*, 947. He Yingqin and Bai Chongxi were senior GMD military commanders.

10. *New China Daily*, January 18, 1941, translated in Saich, *The Rise to Power*, 950–954.

11. These two documents—"Central Directive on the Southern Anhui Incident," January 18, 1941, and "Decision of the Party Center on the Mistakes of Xiang Ying and Yuan Guoping," January 1941—are translated in Saich, *The Rise to Power*, 954–958.

12. Rana Mitter, *Forgotten Ally: China's World War II, 1937–1945* (Boston: Houghton Mifflin Harcourt, 2013), 215.

13. "CCP Declaration on the War in the Pacific," December 9, 1941, translated in Saich, *The Rise to Power*, 965–966.

14. Both are translated in Stuart R. Schram, ed., *Mao's Road to Power: Revolutionary Writings, 1912–1949*, vol. 7, *New Democracy, 1939–1941* (Armonk, NY: M. E. Sharpe, 2005), the former at 244–254, the latter at 330–369.

15. The Shanxi-Chahar-Hebei Border Region was established in January 1938 and was the only other border region besides the Shaan-Gan-Ning to be recognized by Chiang Kai-shek's government. The headquarters of the ERA moved to the Taihang area of Shanxi-Hebei-Shandong-Henan in October 1937. It was formally proclaimed on July 7, 1941, but was never truly unified.

16. Lyman van Slyke, "The Chinese Communist Movement during the Sino-Japanese War, 1937–1945," in *The Cambridge History of China*, vol. 13, *Republican China, 1912–1949*, ed. John K. Fairbank and Albert Feuerwerker (Cambridge: Cambridge University Press, 1986), pt. 2, 652.

17. Carl Dorris, "Peasant Mobilization in North China and the Origins of Yenan Communism," *China Quarterly*, no. 68 (December 1976): 697–719.

18. Lyman P. van Slyke, *Enemies and Friends: The United Front in Chinese Communist History* (Stanford, CA: Stanford University Press, 1967), 142–153. Van Slyke suggests that the concept was put forward as a counter to the GMD stress on constitutional rule.

19. Key passages of the report are translated in Saich, *The Rise to Power*, 1011–1038. Peng Zhen was a strong supporter of Mao Zedong in Yan'an, but he was dismissed as the mayor of Beijing as the first major victim of the Cultural Revolution.

20. Fang Chengxiang and Huang Zhao'an, eds., *Shaan-Gan-Ning bianqu gemingshi* (The Revolutionary History of the Shaan-Gan-Ning Border Region) (Xi'an: Shaanxi shifan daxue chubanshe, 1991), 225–226.

21. Kathleen Hartford, "Step by Step: Reform, Resistance and Revolution in Chin-Ch'a-Chi Border Region, 1937–1945" (PhD diss., Stanford University, 1980).

22. Peter Schran, *Guerrilla Economy: The Development of the Shensi-Kansu-Ninghsia Border Region, 1937–1945* (Albany: SUNY Press, 1976), chap. 7.

23. Editorial and Writing Group of the Finance and Economics Department of the Shaanxi-Gansu-Ningxia Border Region and the Shaanxi Provincial Archives, ed., *KangRi shiqi Shaan-Gan-Ningbiabqu caizheng jingji shiliao zhaibian* (Extracts of Materials concerning Finance and Economics in the Shaan-Gan-Ning Border Region during the Anti-Japanese War) (Shaanxi: Renmin chubanshe, 1981), 6:40, 44–45.

24. Mitter, *Forgotten Ally*, 195; Jay Taylor, *The Generalissimo: Chiang Kai-shek and the Struggle for Modern China* (Cambridge, MA: Belknap Press of Harvard University Press, 2009), 171.

25. Lyman P. Van Slyke, "The Chinese Communist Movement during the Sino-Japanese War, 1937–1945," in *The Nationalist Era in China, 1927–1949*, ed. Lloyd E. Eastman et al. (Cambridge: Cambridge University Press, 1991), 253.

26. Yung-fa Chen, "The Blooming Poppy under the Red Sun: The Yan'an Way and the Opium Trade," in Saich and van de Ven, *New Perspectives*, 263–298.

27. Crack troops, simple administration, down to the village, rent and interest reduction, cooperative movement, production movement, and the popular education movement are described well in Mark Selden, *The Yenan Way in Revolutionary China* (Cambridge, MA: Harvard University Press, 1971), chap. 8.

28. Selden, *The Yenan Way*, 215–216.

29. "Decision of the CC on Land Policy in the Anti-Japanese Base Areas," in *Kangzhan yilai zhongyao wenjian huiji, 1937–42* (Collection of Important

Documents since the War of Resistance, 1937–1942), ed. Central Secretariat Committee ([Yan'an]: Zhongyang weiyuanhui shujichu, 1942), 188–192.

30. The meeting covered other important topics that supported Mao's preeminence in the party, such as his "correct" view of party history, especially his criticisms of Wang Ming. It was a crucial step on his road to supreme power.

31. Chen, "The Blooming Poppy under the Red Sun."

32. Although not covered in the official histories, party historians have noted that it was an open secret, although one officer who dared to publish this was arrested.

33. Peter Vladimirov, *The Vladimirov Diaries: Yenan, 1942–1945* (Garden City, NY: Doubleday, 1975), entries for May 22 and 29, 1942. For a list of the institutions, see the appendix in David E. Apter and Tony Saich, *Revolutionary Discourse in Mao's Republic* (Cambridge, MA: Harvard University Press, 1994), 335–336.

34. "On Policy," in *Selected Works of Mao Tse-Tung*, 2:441–442.

35. "Reform Our Studies," May 5, 1941, translated in Saich, *The Rise to Power*, 1001–1006. On the importance of this speech, see Raymond F. Wylie, *The Emergence of Maoism: Mao Tse-tung, Ch'en Po-ta and the Search for Chinese Theory, 1935–1945* (Stanford, CA: Stanford University Press, 1980), 151–154.

36. As early as mid-1937 Liu Shaoqi had bitterly criticized this tendency with respect to work in the white areas.

37. Subjectivism meant not applying Marxism-Leninism properly to China's situation and remaining dogmatic in work; sectarianism meant putting individual interests above those of the party; and formalism was a stereotyped, bureaucratic way of writing. In practice, what they meant was not following Mao Zedong.

38. Apter and Saich, *Revolutionary Discourse*, 14–15.

39. Apter and Saich, *Revolutionary Discourse*, 109.

40. His two key articles are "Statesmen, Artists" (February 17, 1942) and "The Wild Lily" (March 13 and 27, 1942). In the post-Mao years, the history and events around Wang Shiwei and his fate were excavated by some writers in China. The best example is Dai Qing, *Wang Shiwei and "Wild Lilies": Rectification and Purges in the Chinese Communist Party, 1942–44* (Armonk, NY: M. E. Sharpe, 1994). His case also attracted the interest of writers in the West. See Timothy Cheek, "The Fading of Wild Lilies: Wang Shiwei and Mao Zedong's *Yan'an Talks* in the First CPC Rectification Movement," *Australian Journal of Chinese Affairs*, no. 11 (January 1984): 25–58.

41. Bonnie S. McDougall, *Mao Zedong's "Talks at the Yan'an Conference on Literature and Art": A Translation of the 1943 Text with Commentary*, Michigan Papers in Chinese Studies, no. 39 (Ann Arbor: University of Michigan, 1980). The speeches were not published until October 19, 1943, perhaps attesting to resistance to the message.

42. Interview, Wen Jize, Beijing, July 1988.

43. Wen Jize, "Diary of Struggle," entries for June 28 and June 29, 1942, translated in Saich, *The Rise to Power*, 1113–1122.

44. Saich, *The Rise to Power*, 1122.

45. One of Wang's original pieces had the title of Wild Lily with Chen suggesting that the Wild Lily was not as beautiful as Wang supposed.

46. Zhou Enlai, "On the Relations between the Chinese Communist Party and the Kuomintang from 1924 to 1926" (spring 1943), and "On the Sixth Congress of the Party" (April 3–4, 1944), in *Selected Works of Zhou Enlai* (Beijing: Foreign Languages Press, 1981), 1:130–143, 177–210.

47. Wang Ming, *Mao's Betrayal* (Moscow: Progress, 1979), 61–62.

48. Party History Materials and Research Department of the Central Party Archives, "Wang Ming during Yan'an Rectification," *Dangshi tongxun* (Bulletin on Party History), no. 7 (1987), 11.

49. Wang, *Mao's Betrayal*, 145.

50. Apter and Saich, *Revolutionary Discourse*, 171.

51. Discussion with Li Rui, Los Angeles, 1993.

52. Kang Sheng, "Rescue Those Who Have Lost Their Footing," July 15, 1943, translated in John Byron and Robert Pack, *The Claws of the Dragon: Kang Sheng, the Evil Genius behind Mao and His Legacy of Terror in People's China* (New York: Simon and Schuster, 1992), 179. See also "Abstract of Kang Sheng's Report to a Training Class," in Dai Qing, *Wang Shiwei.*

53. "Summary by Comrade Gao Gang at the Senior Cadres Meeting of the Northwest Bureau," January 14, 1943. Copy available at the Bureau of Investigation Archives, Taibei.

54. "Liquidate Menshevik Thought in the Party," July 6, 1943, in Boyd Compton, trans., *Mao's China: Party Reform Documents, 1942–44* (Seattle: University of Washington Press, 1966), 255–268.

55. Tony Saich, "Writing or Rewriting History? The Construction of the Maoist Resolution on Party History," in Saich and van de Ven, *New Perspectives*, 299–338.

56. "Resolution of the CCP CC on Certain Historical Questions," April 20, 1945, in *Liuda yilai—dangnei mimi wenjian* (Since the Sixth Party Congress: Secret Inner Party Documents), ed. CCP Central Secretariat (Beijing: Renmin chubanshe, 1981), 1:1179–1200.

57. "Directive of the CC on Diplomatic Work," August 18, 1944, translated in Saich, *The Rise to Power*, 1211–1215.

58. Mao Zedong, "On Coalition Government," April 24, 1945, published in *Jiefangshe* (Liberation Society), May 1945.

59. Mao Zedong, "Speech to the Seventh Party Congress," April 24, 1945, in *Long Live Mao Zedong Thought* (n.p.: February 1967), 62–82.

60. Constitution [Statutes] of the CCP, June 11, 1945, in Conrad Brandt, Benjamin Schwartz, and John K. Fairbank, *A Documentary History of Chinese Communism* (Cambridge, MA: Harvard University Press, 1952), 422–439; Liu Shaoqi, "Report on the Revision of the Party Constitution," May 14,

1945, in *Three Essays on Party-Building* (Beijing: Foreign Languages Press, 1980), 163–300.

61. Odd Arne Westad, *Decisive Encounters: The Chinese Civil War, 1946–1950* (Stanford, CA: Stanford University Press, 2003), 7–8. My thinking on this period has been deeply influenced by Westad's writings.

62. Lloyd Eastman, *Seeds of Destruction: China in War and Revolution, 1937–1949* (Stanford, CA: Stanford University Press, 1984); James C. Hsiung and Steven I. Levine, eds., *China's Bitter Victory: The War with Japan, 1937–1945* (Armonk, NY: M. E. Sharpe, 1992).

63. In addition to Westad, Suzanne Pepper focuses on the GMD's incompetence during the 1946–1947 period. See her *Civil War in China: The Political Struggle, 1945–1949*, 2nd ed. (Lanham, MD: Rowman and Littlefield, 1999).

64. Westad, *Decisive Encounters*, 35

65. This was noted in an August 20 message. Taylor, *The Generalissimo*, 317.

66. Steven I. Levine, *Anvil of Victory: The Communist Revolution in Manchuria, 1945–1948* (New York: Columbia University Press, 1987).

67. "Directive of the CC concerning Swiftly Occupying the Northeast and Controlling the Vast Countryside," August 29, 1945, translated in Saich, *The Rise to Power*, 1269–1270. In addition to the three northeastern provinces, the directive noted that they could also make progress in Jehol (Rehe) and Chahar as they were not included in the treaty. Jehol was located north of the Great Wall to the west of Manchuria and to the east of Mongolia. Its capital was the summer imperial resort, Chengde. Chahar covered what is now eastern Inner Mongolia.

68. On Chiang's crucial mistakes, see Westad, *Decisive Encounters*, 9.

69. Odd Arne Westad, *Cold War and Revolution: Soviet-American Rivalry and the Origins of the Chinese Civil War, 1944–1946* (New York: Columbia University Press, 1993), 125–126.

70. "Directive of the Northeast Bureau on Evacuating Large Cities," November 26, 1945, translated in Saich, *The Rise to Power*, 1270–1272.

71. Westad, *Decisive Encounters*, 35.

72. Niu Jun, *From Yan'an to the World: The Origin and Development of Chinese Communist Foreign Policy* (Norwalk, CT: EastBridge, 2005), 210–219.

73. "Directive of the CC on the Current Situation and Tasks," February 1, 1946, translated in Saich, *The Rise to Power*, 1277–1280.

74. Westad, *Decisive Encounters*, 61.

75. "A Three Months' Summary," in *Selected Works of Mao Tse-tung*, 4:113–118.

76. "Strategy for the Second Year of the War," September 1, 1947, in *Selected Works of Mao Tse-tung*, 4:141–146.

77. Hans J. van de Ven, *China at War: Triumph and Tragedy in the Emergence of the New China* (Cambridge, MA: Harvard University Press, 2018), 244–255.

78. For a harrowing account of the siege, see Frank Dikötter, *The Tragedy of Liberation: A History of the Chinese Revolution, 1945–1957* (London: Bloomsbury, 2013), 3–8.

79. Westad, *Decisive Encounters,* 205–211.
80. Westad, *Decisive Encounters,* 113.
81. It seems the CCP leadership harbored suspicions that Stalin wanted to argue for a divided China, split at the Yangzi. Westad, *Decisive Encounters,* 217–218.

5. The Chinese Communist Revolution

1. Richard Pipes, *Three "Whys" of the Russian Revolution* (New York: Vintage Press, 1997).
2. Theda Skocpol, *States and Social Revolutions: A Comparative Analysis of France, Russia, and China* (Cambridge: Cambridge University Press, 1979); Barrington Moore, *Social Origins of Dictatorship and Democracy: Lord and Peasant in the Making of the Modern World* (Boston: Beacon Press, 1966).
3. On resistance to Japan, see Chalmers A. Johnson, *Peasant Nationalism and Communist Power: The Emergence of Revolutionary China, 1937–1945* (Stanford, CA: Stanford University Press, 1962); on social/peasant mobilization, see Lucien Bianco, *The Origins of the Chinese Revolution, 1915–1949* (Stanford, CA: Stanford University Press, 1971); on organization, see Tetsuya Kataoka, *Resistance and Revolution in China: The Communists and the Second United Front* (Berkeley: University of California Press, 1974).
4. Benjamin I. Schwartz, *Chinese Communism and the Rise of Mao* (Cambridge, MA: Harvard University Press, 1951); Stuart R. Schram, *Mao Tse-tung,* rev. ed. (Baltimore: Penguin Books,1967); Schram, *The Thought of Mao Tse-tung* (Cambridge: Cambridge University Press, 1989).
5. Mark Selden, *The Yenan Way in Revolutionary China* (Cambridge, MA: Harvard University Press, 1971), republished, with a new preface and epilogue, as *China in Revolution: The Yenan Way Revisited* (Armonk, NY: M. E. Sharpe, 1995).
6. Kathleen Hartford and Stephen M. Goldstein, eds., *Single Sparks: China's Rural Revolutions* (Armonk, NY: M. E. Sharpe, 1989); Tony Saich and Hans van de Ven, eds., *New Perspectives on the Chinese Communist Revolution* (Armonk, NY: M. E. Sharpe, 1995).
7. David E. Apter and Tony Saich, *Revolutionary Discourse in Mao's China* (Cambridge, MA: Harvard University Press, 1994); Elizabeth J. Perry, *Anyuan: Mining China's Revolutionary Tradition* (Berkeley: University of California Press, 2012).
8. John Dunn, "Conclusion," in Saich and van de Ven, *New Perspectives,* 389.
9. For a brilliant account of the global footprint of Maoism, see Julia Lovell, *Maoism: A Global History* (London: Bodley Head, 2019).
10. Jack Goldstone, "Revolution," in *The Oxford Companion to Comparative Politics,* ed. Joel Krieger (Oxford: Oxford University Press, 2013), 315.
11. Elizabeth J. Perry, *Rebels and Revolutionaries in North China, 1845–1945* (Stanford, CA: Stanford University Press, 1980).

12. Goldstone, "Revolution," 317.
13. Skocpol, *States and Social Revolutions,* 41.
14. Moore, *Social Origins,* esp. chap. 4.
15. On storytelling and symbolism in revolutionary movements, see Eric Selbin, *Revolution, Rebellion, Resistance: The Power of Story* (New York: Zed Books, 2010).
16. Robert Carver North, *Moscow and the Chinese Communists* (Stanford, CA: Stanford University Press, 1953). Not surprisingly, the most vehement account of the CCP as being little more than a Soviet stooge is by Chiang Kai-shek, *Soviet Russia in China: A Summing Up at Seventy* (New York: Farrar, Straus and Cudahy, 1957).
17. Schwartz, *Chinese Communism.*
18. Arif Dirlik, *The Origins of Chinese Communism* (Oxford: Oxford University Press, 1989).
19. Hans J. van de Ven, *From Friend to Comrade: The Founding of the Chinese Communist Party, 1920–1927* (Berkeley: University of California Press, 1991).
20. Tony Saich, *Finding Allies and Making Revolution: The Early Years of the Chinese Communist Party* (Leiden: Brill, 2020).
21. Harold R. Isaacs, *The Tragedy of the Chinese Revolution,* 2nd rev. ed. (Stanford, CA: Stanford University Press, 1961); Conrad Brandt, *Stalin's Failure in China, 1924–1927* (Cambridge, MA: Harvard University Press, 1958).
22. Alexander Pantsov, *The Bolsheviks and the Chinese Revolution, 1919–1927* (Honolulu: University of Hawai'i Press, 2000), 149–150; Alexander Pantsov and Gregor Benton, "Did Trotsky Oppose Entering the Guomindang 'From the First'?," *Republican China* 19, no. 2 (April 1994): 52–66.
23. Joseph W. Esherick, "Ten Theses on the Chinese Revolution," *Modern China* 21, no. 1 (January 1995): 51.
24. Frederick C. Teiwes with Warren Sun, "From a Leninist to a Charismatic Party: The CCP's Changing Leadership, 1937–1945," in Saich and van de Ven, *New Perspectives,* 341–350.
25. Xinhua "Full Text: Xi Jinping in Military Parade Speech Vows China Will 'Never Seek Hegemony, Expansion,'" https://www.scmp.com/news/china /policies-politics/article/1854943/full-text-xi-jinping-military-parade-speech -vows-china.
26. Lucien Bianco, "Peasant Responses to CCP Mobilization Policies, 1937– 1945," in Saich and van de Ven, *New Perspectives,* 177.
27. Jay Taylor, *The Generalissimo: Chiang Kai-shek and the Struggle for Modern China* (Cambridge, MA: Belknap Press of Harvard University Press, 2009), 169.
28. Rana Mitter, *Forgotten Ally: China's World War II, 1937–1945* (Boston: Houghton Mifflin Harcourt, 2013), 189.
29. Mitter, *Forgotten Ally,* 5.
30. Hans J. van de Ven, *China at War: Triumph and Tragedy in the Emergence of the New China* (Cambridge, MA: Harvard University Press, 2018), 8.

31. Bianco, "Peasant Responses."

32. Eric R. Wolf, *Peasant Wars of the Twentieth Century* (New York: Harper and Row, 1969); Joel S. Migdal, *Peasant, Politics, and Revolution: Pressures toward Political and Social Change in the Third World* (Princeton, NJ: Princeton University Press, 1974); Theda Skocpol, "What Makes Peasants Revolutionary?," *Comparative Politics* 14, no. 3 (April 1982): 351–375. The classic moral economy argument is James C. Scott, *The Moral Economy of the Peasant: Rebellion and Subsistence in Southeast Asia* (New Haven, CT: Yale University Press, 1976). The most enthusiastic moral economy argument applied to China is Ralph Thaxton, *China Turned Rightside Up: Revolutionary Legitimacy in the Peasant World* (New Haven, CT: Yale University Press, 1983).

33. See his argumentation in Bianco, *Origins of the Chinese Revolution*, 155, 202.

34. Mark Selden, "Yan'an Communism Reconsidered," *Modern China* 21, no. 1 (January 1995): 22.

35. Selden, "Yan'an Communism Reconsidered," 28.

36. Hartford and Goldstein, "Introduction: Perspectives on the Chinese Communist Revolution," in Hartford and Goldstein, *Single Sparks,* 33.

37. "Report of the Shanghai Locality," May 1924, translated in Tony Saich with a contribution by Benjamin Yang, *The Rise to Power of the Chinese Communist Party: Documents and Analysis* (Armonk, NY: M. E. Sharpe, 1996), 127.

38. Saich, *The Rise to Power,* il.

39. "Instruction of the CC concerning Urban Work," June 5, 1944, translated in Saich, *The Rise to Power,* 1157–1164.

40. Liang Shangxian, *Guomindang yu Guangdong nongmin yundong* (The GMD and the Guangdong Peasant Movement) (Guangzhou: Guangdong renmin chubanshe, 2004), 8.

41. Yuan Gao, "Revolutionary Rural Politics: The Peasant Movement in Guangdong and Its Social-Historical Background, 1922–1926," *Modern China* 42, no. 2 (March 2016): 182.

42. Bianco, "Peasant Responses," 177. On the experience of the peasantry and the CCP in the twentieth century, see Lucien Bianco, *Peasants without the Party: Grass-Root Movements in Twentieth Century China* (Armonk, NY: M. E. Sharpe, 2001).

43. Yung-fa Chen shows how important material incentives were in eastern China for bringing the peasantry into the struggle against Japan. See his *Making Revolution: The Communist Movement in Eastern and Central China, 1937–1945* (Berkeley: University of California Press, 1986).

44. Steven I. Levine, *Anvil of Victory: The Communist Revolution in Manchuria, 1945–1949* (New York: Columbia University Press, 1987).

45. Pauline B. Keating, *Two Revolutions: Village Reconstruction and the Cooperative Movement in Northern Shaanxi, 1934–1945* (Stanford, CA: Stanford University Press, 1997).

46. "Public Letter," June 16, 1934, translated in Saich, *The Rise to Power,* 583–585.

47. Discussion with Li Rui, Los Angeles, 1993.

48. Van de Ven, *From Friend to Comrade*.
49. This point is made by Esherick in "Ten Theses," 62.
50. Saich, *The Rise to Power*, liv.
51. Zhang Ruxin, "Summary of Thought Reform at the Central Research Institute since Rectification," *Jiefang ribao* (Liberation Daily), October 31, 1942.
52. John King Fairbank, *The Great Chinese Revolution, 1800–1985* (New York: Harper and Row, 1986), 226.
53. Teiwes with Sun, "From a Leninist to a Charismatic Party," 347.
54. Parks M. Coble, *Chinese Capitalists and Japan's New Order: The Occupied Lower Yangzi, 1937–1945* (Berkeley: University of California Press, 2003).
55. Lloyd E. Eastman provides the best analysis of the GMD in power, and of why it could not maintain power, in *The Abortive Revolution: China under Nationalist Rule, 1927–1937* (Cambridge, MA: Harvard University Press, 1974) and *Seeds of Destruction: Nationalist China in War and Revolution, 1937–1949* (Stanford, CA: Stanford University Press, 1984).
56. Eastman, *The Abortive Revolution*, 5–7.
57. Eastman, *Seeds of Destruction*, 203–210.
58. Guy S. Alitto, "Rural Reconstruction during the Nanking Decade: Confucian Collectivism in Shantung," *China Quarterly*, no. 66 (June 1976): 213.
59. Parks M. Coble, *Facing Japan: Chinese Politics and Japanese Imperialism, 1931–1937* (Cambridge, MA: Council on East Asian Studies, Harvard University, 1991).
60. A complex and more sympathetic Chiang Kai-shek emerges in Taylor's excellent biography, *The Generalissimo*.
61. On five major mistakes made by the GMD in 1945–1948 that turned a possibly favorable situation into a disaster, see Odd Arne Westad, *Decisive Encounters: The Chinese Civil War, 1946–1950* (Stanford, CA: Stanford University Press, 2003), 8–10.
62. His views resulted in his difficult relationship with the GMD, but he did serve as the ambassador to the United States from 1938 to 1942. On Hu's thought and influence, see Jerome B. Grieder, *Hu Shih and the Chinese Renaissance: Liberalism in the Chinese Revolution, 1917–1937* (Cambridge, MA: Harvard University Press, 1970).
63. This debate is covered insightfully in Maurice J. Meisner, *Li Ta-chao and the Origins of Chinese Marxism* (Cambridge, MA: Harvard University Press, 1967).
64. Esherick, "Ten Theses," 54.
65. Westad, *Decisive Encounters*, 9, 197, 199.

6. Consolidating the Revolution, 1948–1956

1. It is commonly recounted that he said this when he stood on the rostrum of the Forbidden City on October 1, 1949, but he said it instead on September 21, 1949, at the first meeting of the Chinese People's Political Consultative Conference (CPPCC).

2. The most critical account that the period was not a golden age is in Frank Dikötter, *The Tragedy of Liberation: A History of the Chinese Revolution, 1945–1957* (London: Bloomsbury, 2013). See also Julia C. Strauss, "Morality, Coercion and State Building by Campaign in the Early PRC: Regime Consolidation and After, 1949–1956," *China Quarterly,* no. 188 (December 2006): 891–912.

3. Su Shaozhi, "Marxism in China: 1949–1989," in *Marxism and Reform in China* (Nottingham: Spokesman, 1993), 33–34. Su was the head of the Institute of Marxism-Leninism-Mao Zedong Thought under the Chinese Academy of Social Sciences (CASS) before the student-led demonstrations of 1989. Similar views were expressed by CASS vice president Yu Guangyuan, in *From the "Theory of New Democracy" to "The Theory of the Primary Stage of Socialism"* (Beijing: Renmin chubanshe, 1996). These essays were written in 1988.

4. János Kornai, *The Socialist System: The Political Economy of Communism* (Princeton, NJ: Princeton University Press, 1992).

5. Odd Arne Westad, *Decisive Encounter: The Chinese Civil War, 1946–1950* (Stanford, CA: Stanford University Press, 2003), 260–261.

6. Mao Zedong, "Circular of the CCP CC on the September Meeting," October 10, 1948, in *Selected Works of Mao Tse-Tung* (Peking: Foreign Languages Press, 1967), 4:69–276.

7. "On Strengthening the Party Committee System," in *Selected Works of Mao Tse-Tung,* 4:267–268.

8. "Resolution of the CCP CC concerning the Convocation of Party Congresses and Conferences at All Levels," September 1948, translated in Tony Saich with a contribution by Benjamin Yang, *The Rise to Power of the Chinese Communist Party: Documents and Analysis* (Armonk, NY: M. E. Sharpe, 1996), 1323–1326.

9. Zhang Wentian, "Outline of Basic Policies concerning the Structure of the Economy in the Northeast and Its Economic Construction," September 15, 1948, translated in Saich, *The Rise to Power,* 1351–1364.

10. Mao Zedong, "On the People's Democratic Dictatorship," June 30, 1949, in Conrad Brandt, Benjamin Schwartz, and John King Fairbank, *A Documentary History of Chinese Communism* (Cambridge, MA: Harvard University Press, 1952), 449–461.

11. In 1947 Inner Mongolia became the first autonomous region carved out of part of the former Manchuria. In theory, an autonomous region should enjoy greater powers to suit the special circumstances of the area. In practice this has been very limited, but it does allow more flexibility for certain social policies.

12. Jeremey Brown and Paul G. Pickowicz, eds., *Dilemmas of Victory: The Early Years of the People's Republic of China* (Cambridge, MA: Harvard University Press, 2007); Jeremy Brown and Mathew D. Johnson, eds., *Maoism at the Grassroots: Everyday Life in China's Era of High Socialism* (Cambridge, MA: Harvard University Press, 2015).

13. Perhaps 712,000 were executed during the Campaign to Suppress Counter-revolutionaries. Felix Wemheuer, *A Social History of Maoist China: Conflict and Change, 1949–1976* (Cambridge: Cambridge University Press, 2019), 67.

14. Julia C. Strauss, "Paternalist Terror: The Campaign to Suppress Counter-revolutionaries and Regime Consolidation in the People's Republic of China, 1950–1953," *Comparative Studies in Society and History* 44, no. 1 (January 2002): 82.

15. "Directive of the CCP CC on Settling Accounts, Rent Reduction, and the Land Question," May 4, 1946, translated in Saich, *The Rise to Power,* 1280–1285.

16. Tanaka Kyoko, "The Civil War and Radicalization of Chinese Communist Agrarian Policy, 1945–1947," *Papers on Far Eastern History,* no. 8 (September 1973): 70–114.

17. Ch'en Yung-fa, "Civil War, Mao Zedong and the Land Revolution: Incorrect Assessment of Political Intrigue," *Dalu zazhi* (Mainland Magazine), vol. 92, no. 1 (1996), 14; Hans J. van de Ven, *China at War: Triumph and Tragedy in the Emergence of the New China* (Cambridge, MA: Harvard University Press, 2018), 238–243.

18. The law is translated in Saich, *The Rise to Power,* 1295–1298.

19. Liu Shaoqi's report to the CC, August 4, 1947, translated in Saich, *The Rise to Power,* 1287–1295.

20. Mao Zedong, "The Present Situation and Our Tasks," December 25, 1947, in *Selected Works of Mao Tse-Tung,* 4:157–176.

21. See the two telegrams from February 3 and 6. The first, to Liu Shaoqi, is in *Selected Works of Mao Tse-Tung,* 4:193–194; the second, to Li Jingquan and Xi Zhongxun, is in Central Archives, ed., *Zhonggong zhongyang wenjian xuanji (neibu ben)* (Selection of CCP Central Documents, Internal Volume) (Beijing: Zhonggong zhongyang chubanshe, 1987), 14:21–22.

22. Those foreigners who observed the process wrote favorably. The classic account is William Hinton, *Fanshen: A Documentary of Revolution in a Chinese Village* (New York: Vintage, 1966).

23. *The Agrarian Reform Law of the People's Republic of China, Together with Other Relevant Documents* (Peking: Foreign Languages Press, 1950), 1–18.

24. Liu Shaoqi, "On the Agrarian Reform Law," June 14, 1950, in *The Agrarian Reform Law,* 78.

25. One *mu* is one-sixth of an acre.

26. Andrew G. Walder points out that other nations in East Asia underwent land reform without the attendant violence. See his *China under Mao: A Revolution Derailed* (Cambridge, MA: Harvard University Press, 2015), 51.

27. Tony Saich and Biliang Hu, *Chinese Village, Global Market: New Collectives and Rural Development* (New York: Palgrave Macmillan, 2012), 32–33. It is worth pointing out that every single party secretary in the village has been from the Deng lineage.

28. Dikötter, *The Tragedy of Liberation,* 76–79.

29. Walder, *China under Mao*, 52.
30. Frederick Teiwes, *Politics and Purges in China: Rectification and the Decline of Party Norms, 1950–1965*, 2nd ed. (Armonk, NY: M. E. Sharpe, 1993). For a higher figure, see Dikötter, *The Tragedy of Liberation*, 83.
31. Mao Zedong, "Don't Hit Out in All Directions," June 6, 1950, in *Selected Works of Mao Tse-Tung* (Peking: Foreign Languages Press, 1977), 5:33–36.
32. Yang Kuisong, "Reconsidering the Campaign to Suppress Counterrevolutionaries," *China Quarterly*, no. 193 (March 2008): 103.
33. Dikötter, *The Tragedy of Liberation*, 85.
34. "CCP CC Directive on the Suppression of Counterrevolutionary Activities," October 10, 1950, in Central Literature Research Office of the CCP, *Jianguo yilai zhongyao wenxian xuanbian* (Selected Important Documents since the Founding of the Nation) (Beijing: Zhongyang wenxian chubanshe, 1992), 1:421–423. The two best accounts of this campaign are Strauss, "Paternalist Terror," 80–105, and Yang, "Reconsidering the Campaign," 102–121.
35. Yang, "Reconsidering the Campaign," 107–109.
36. "Regulations of the PRC on the Punishment of Counterrevolutionaries," *People's Daily*, February 22, 1951.
37. Yang, "Reconsidering the Campaign," 110.
38. Mao Zedong, "On the Correct Handling of Contradictions among the People (Reading Text)," February 27, 1957, in *Mao zhuxi wenxian sanshipian* (Thirty Texts by Chairman Mao) (Beijing: Beijing teshu gangchang xuanchuan qinwuzi, n.d.), 97. Interestingly, this figure does not appear in the official version published in the *People's Daily*, June 19, 1957.
39. Dikötter, *The Tragedy of Liberation*, 100.
40. Michael M. Sheng, "Mao Zedong and the Three-Anti Campaign (November 1951 to April 1952): A Revisionist Interpretation," *Twentieth-Century China* 32, no. 1 (2006): 56–80. The impact on the business community at the local city level is discussed in Ezra Vogel, *Canton under Communism: Programs and Politics in a Provincial Capital, 1949–1968* (Cambridge, MA: Harvard University Press, 1969); and Kenneth Lieberthal, *Revolution and Tradition in Tientsin, 1949–1952* (Stanford, CA: Stanford University Press, 1980).
41. Sheng, "Mao Zedong and the Three-Anti Campaign," 58. For Mao's support, see "Report Forwarded from the Center on Instructions on the Report of Gao Gang on the Three-Anti Campaign," November 20, 1951, in *Jianguo yilai Mao Zedong wengao* (Manuscripts of Mao Zedong since the Founding of the Nation) (Beijing: Zhongyang wenxian chubanshe, 1988), 2:513–514.
42. Mao Zedong, "The Central Committee on Publishing the Notice on 'The Resolution of the Central Committee of the Chinese Communist Party on Implementing the Streamlining of Administration, Increasing Production, Saving Costs, Opposing Corruption, Opposing Waste, and Fighting against Bureaucratism' as Well as Mao Zedong's Criticisms and Modifications of

the Draft Resolution," in *Jianguo yilai Mao Zedong wengao* (Manuscripts of Mao Zedong), 2:532.

43. Dikötter, *The Tragedy of Liberation*, 159–163.

44. Many adopted a strategy of spreading the risk by sending some of their family to the Chinese diaspora while others remained in China to protect assets and wait and see. Siu-lun Wong, *Emigrant Entrepreneurs: Shanghai Industrialists in Hong Kong* (Hong Kong: Hong Kong University Press, 1988).

45. Dikötter, *The Tragedy of Liberation*, 171.

46. Chang-tai Hung, "The Anti-Unity Sect Campaign and Mass Mobilization in the Early People's Republic of China," *China Quarterly*, no. 202 (June 2010): 400–420.

47. Neil J. Diamant, *Revolutionizing the Family: Politics, Love and Divorce in Urban and Rural China, 1949–1968* (Berkeley: University of California Press, 2000).

48. Elizabeth J. Perry, "Masters of the Country? Shanghai Workers in the Early People's Republic," in Brown and Pickowicz, *Dilemmas of Victory*, 59–79.

49. Tiejun Cheng and Mark Selden, "The Construction of Spatial Hierarchies: China's *Hukou* and *Danwei* Systems," in *New Perspectives on State Socialism in China*, ed. Timothy Cheek and Tony Saich (Armonk, NY: M. E. Sharpe, 1997), 45.

50. Li Feilong, "Village Society Migration before Reform and Opening: Based on an Analysis from the Perspective of State and Society," *Tianfu xinlun* (Tianfu New Ideas), no. 2 (2011): 94–98.

51. Andrew G. Walder, *Communist Neo-Traditionalism: Work and Authority in Chinese Industry* (Berkeley: University of California Press, 1986).

52. "On the People's Democratic Dictatorship," June 30, 1949, in *Selected Works of Mao Tse-Tung*, 4:411–424.

53. Deborah A. Kaple, *Dream of a Red Factory: The Legacy of High Stalinism in China* (Oxford: Oxford University Press, 1994).

54. Niu Jun, "The Origins of the Sino-Soviet Alliance," in *Brothers in Arms: The Rise and Fall of the Sino-Soviet Alliance, 1945–1963*, ed. Odd Arne Westad (Washington, DC: Woodrow Wilson Press, and Stanford, CA: Stanford University Press, 1998), 47–89.

55. "Report to the CPSU CC Politburo, July 4, 1949," in Westad, *Brothers in Arms*, 301–313. Liu and the group secretly arrived in Moscow on June 26 and left on August 14, arriving back in Beijing on August 29, together with the first 220 Soviet advisers.

56. Westad, *Brothers in Arms*, 311.

57. Chen Jian, *China's Road to the Korean War: The Making of the Sino-American Confrontation* (New York: Columbia University Press, 1994); Sergei Goncharov, John W. Lewis, and Xue Litai, *Uncertain Partners: Stalin, Mao, and the Korean War* (Stanford, CA: Stanford University Press, 1993); Zhihua Shen, *Mao, Stalin and the Korean War: Trilateral Communist Relations in the 1950s* (London: Routledge, 2012); Kathryn Weathersby, "Stalin, Mao, and the End of the Korean War," in Westad, *Brothers in Arms*, 90–116.

58. Kathryn Weathersby, "New Findings on the Korean War," *CWIHP Bulletin*, no. 3 (1993): 14–16.
59. Shen, *Mao, Stalin and the Korean War*, 85–87.
60. Westad, *Decisive Encounter*, 319–320; Yang Kuisong, "Introduction," in Shen, *Mao, Stalin and the Korean War*, 3.
61. Quoted in Yang, "Introduction," 15.
62. Alexander V. Pantsov, with Steven I. Levine, *Mao: The Real Story* (New York: Simon and Schuster, 2012), 384.
63. One of the worst examples was the promotion of the pseudo-science of the Soviet scientist Lysenko, which dominated Chinese science between 1949 and 1956. Lysenko argued against genetics and rejected popular views on natural selection.
64. "The Party's General Line for the Transition Period," August 1953, in *Selected Works of Mao Tse-Tung*, 5:102.
65. Liu Jianhui and Wang Hongxu, "The Origins of the General Line for the Transition Period and of the Acceleration of the Chinese Socialist Transformation in Summer 1955," *China Quarterly*, no. 187 (September 2006): 724–725.
66. Two of the first phrases I learned while shopping in Beijing in the 1970s were "We don't have it" and "We've sold out."
67. Walder, *China under Mao*, 86; see 82–99 for an excellent overview of the socialist economy.
68. Kenneth G. Lieberthal, *Governing China: From Revolution through Reform* (New York: W. W. Norton, 1995), 99.
69. The system of ration coupons continued well into the 1990s. When traveling outside of Beijing in 1976, we ran into a problem trying to order a meal in a local restaurant. Our grain coupons were only valid for Beijing; we had not applied for nationally valid coupons. The manager was very apologetic but said he could not provide us with any food as he did not have the necessary authority. When I suggested that it was not good "propaganda" to let foreigners go hungry, we struck a deal that we would pay a supplement for the rice we ate. At the time, only six cities were open to legal visits by foreigners and a travel permit was required, with the specific dates of travel designated.
70. Saich and Hu, *Chinese Village, Global Market*, 33–39.
71. For villages in North China, see Edward Friedman, Paul G. Pickowicz, and Mark Selden, with Kay A. Johnson, *Chinese Village, Socialist State* (New Haven, CT: Yale University Press, 1991), 273.
72. Liu and Wang, "The Origins of the General Line," 728. One *jin* is the equivalent of 1 pound.
73. The best account of this period is Frederick C. Teiwes and Warren Sun, eds., *The Politics of Agricultural Cooperativization in China: Mao, Deng Zihui, and the "High Tide" of 1955* (Armonk, NY: M. E. Sharpe, 1993).
74. "On the Cooperative Transformation of Agriculture," July 31, 1955, in *Selected Works of Mao Tse-Tung*, 5:28.

75. "The Debate on the Cooperative Transformation of Agriculture and the Current Class Struggle," October 11, 1955, in *Selected Works of Mao Tse-Tung,* 5:211–234.

76. This account is based on Frederick C. Teiwes, *Politics at Mao's Court: Gao Gang and Party Factionalism in the Early 1950s* (Armonk, NY: M. E. Sharpe, 1990).

77. Pantsov, with Levine, *Mao: The Real Story,* 393–395.

78. Zhou Enlai, in his speech to a February 1954 plenum, stated that Gao had claimed that the party was a product of the army in order to drive a wedge between those who had worked in the white areas and those who served in the Red Army. Gao used this to claim that the "cadres of the white areas are now attempting to seize power." "Comrade Zhou Enlai's Speech Outline at the Discussion Meeting on the Gao Gang Question," February 1954, quoted in Teiwes, *Politics at Mao's Court,* 241.

79. Deng Xiaoping, "Report on the Gao Gang, Rao Shushi Anti-Party Alliance," March 21, 1955, translated in Teiwes, *Politics at Mao's Court,* 254–276.

80. These same dangers existed in the post-Mao era—Deng Xiaoping in the 1980s jettisoned two of his chosen successors, Hu Yaobang and Zhao Ziyang.

81. Walder, *China under Mao,* 336–337.

7. Radicalizing the Revolution, 1956–1969

1. The terms "revolutionary modernizer" and "managerial modernizer" are those of John H. Kautsky, *The Political Consequences of Modernization* (New York: John Wiley and Sons, 1972).

2. Elizabeth J. Perry, *Patrolling the Revolution: Worker Militias, Citizenship and the Modern State* (Lanham, MD: Rowman and Littlefield, 2006), 2ff.

3. For elite politics, see Roderick MacFarquhar, *The Origins of the Cultural Revolution,* vol. 1, *Contradictions among the People, 1956–1957;* vol. 2, *The Great Leap Forward, 1958–1960;* vol. 3, *The Coming of the Cataclysm, 1961–1966* (New York: Columbia University Press, 1974, 1983, 1997). Frederick C. Teiwes and Warren Sun have made excellent use of newly available materials. See Teiwes and Sun, *"China's Road to Disaster": Mao, Central Politicians, and Provincial Leaders in the Unfolding of the Great Leap Forward, 1955–1959* (Armonk, NY: M. E. Sharpe, 1999); and Teiwes and Sun, *The Tragedy of Lin Biao: Riding the Tiger during the Cultural Revolution, 1966–1971* (London: Hurst, 1996).

4. Frederick C. Teiwes with Warren Sun, "The Politics of an 'Un-Maoist' Interlude: The Case of Opposing Rash Advance, 1956–1957," in *New Perspectives on State Socialism in China,* ed. Timothy Cheek and Tony Saich (Armonk, NY: M. E. Sharpe, 1997), 151–190.

5. MacFarquhar, *Origins of the Cultural Revolution,* 1:125.

6. Liu Shaoqi, *The Political Report of the Central Committee of the Communist Party of China to the Eighth National Congress of the Communist Party of China, Delivered on September 15, 1956* (Peking: Foreign Languages Press, 1956).

7. "On the Historical Experience of the Proletarian Dictatorship," *People's Daily*, April 5, 1956.

8. Mao Zedong, "On the Ten Major Relationships," in *Mao Tsetung Unrehearsed: Talks and Letters, 1966–1971*, ed. Stuart R. Schram (Harmondsworth: Penguin, 1974), 6–83. Mao's speech from May 2 has not been published in full, but its main contents can be found in Lu Dingyi, "Let a Hundred Flowers Bloom, Let a Hundred Schools Contend," *People's Daily*, June 13, 1956.

9. Zhou Enlai speaking to the CPPCC. This is the body that includes many who are not party members but whose skills are useful to the party.

10. "On the Correct Handling of Contradictions among the People," February 27, 1957, *People's Daily*, June 19, 1957. His speaking notes are in *The Secret Speeches of Chairman Mao: From the Hundred Flowers to the Great Leap Forward*, ed. Roderick MacFarquhar, Timothy Cheek, and Eugene Wu (Cambridge, MA: Council on East Asian Studies, Harvard University, 1989), 131–190. The speaking notes ramble more than the sanitized official version.

11. MacFarquhar, *Origins of the Cultural Revolution*, 1:192–196.

12. MacFarquhar, *Origins of the Cultural Revolution*, 1:177–183.

13. Merle Goldman, *Literary Dissent in Communist China* (Cambridge, MA: Harvard University Press, 1967), chap. 7.

14. Mei Zhi, Hu's wife and fellow author, was also arrested. She was released in 1961. During the Cultural Revolution, the two were sent to a prison camp in Sichuan; Hu was rehabilitated in 1981.

15. Andrew G. Walder, *China under Mao: A Revolution Derailed* (Cambridge, MA: Harvard University Press, 2015), 139–148.

16. Li Zhisui, *The Private Life of Chairman Mao: The Memoirs of Mao's Personal Physician* (New York: Random House, 1994), 200.

17. Yen-lin Chung, "The Witch-Hunting Vanguard: The Central Secretariat's Roles and Activities in the Anti-Rightist Campaign," *China Quarterly*, no. 206 (June 2011): 391–411.

18. Frederick C. Teiwes, "Establishment and Consolidation of the New Regime," in *The Cambridge History of China*, vol. 14, *The People's Republic*, pt. 1, *The Emergence of Revolutionary China, 1949–1965*, ed. Roderick MacFarquhar and John King Fairbank (Cambridge: Cambridge University Press, 1987), 140.

19. Elizabeth J. Perry, "Shanghai's Strike Wave of 1957," in Cheek and Saich, *New Perspectives*, 234–261.

20. On Chen's economic thought, see Nicholas R. Lardy and Kenneth Lieberthal, eds., *Chen Yün's Strategy for China's Development: A Non-Maoist Alternative*

(Armonk, NY: M. E. Sharpe, 1983); David M. Bachman, *Chen Yün and the Chinese Political System* (Berkeley: Institute of East Asian Studies, University of California, 1985).

21. For the elite politics, see MacFarquhar, *Origins of the Cultural Revolution*, vol. 2. For the broader consequences, see Jasper Becker, *Hungry Ghosts: Mao's Secret Famine* (New York: Free Press, 1996); Frank Dikötter, *Mao's Great Famine: The History of China's Most Devastating Catastrophe*; and the excellent Yang Jisheng, *Tombstone: The Great Chinese Famine, 1958–1962* (New York: Farrar, Straus and Giroux, 2012). Having worked as a journalist before becoming an independent writer, he could never have written such a critical study had he remained in government employ. He is one of only a very few Chinese historians to have written critically about the CCP's official narrative.

22. Mao Zedong, *A Critique of Soviet Economics*, trans. Moss Roberts (New York: Monthly Review Press, 1977). This work contains Mao's comments on Stalin's 1951 work, *Economic Problems of Socialism in the U.S.S.R.* (New York: International Publishers, 1952), and on *Political Economy: A Textbook*, ed. K. V. Ostrovityanov et al. (Moscow: State Publishing House of Political Literature, 1954).

23. The Forty Articles fed into the Twelve-Year Agricultural Program.

24. Tony Saich and Biliang Hu, *Chinese Village, Global Market: New Collectives and Rural Development* (New York: Palgrave Macmillan, 2012), 38.

25. Walder, *China under Mao*, 155.

26. Felix Wemheuer, *A Social History of Maoist China: Conflict and Change, 1949–1976* (Cambridge: Cambridge University Press, 2019), 152–154.

27. The best account of the information that was available is contained in Yang, *Tombstone*.

28. MacFarquhar, *Origins of the Cultural Revolution*, 2:187–251; Teiwes and Sun, "*China's Road to Disaster.*" For recollections by one of the key participants, see Li Rui, *A True Record of the Lushan Plenum* (Zhengzhou: Henan renmin chubanshe, 1999), and Li Rui, "Lessons from the Lushan Plenum," in *Chinese Law and Government* 29, no. 5 (September–October 1996): 1–96, ed. Tony Saich and Nancy Hearst. Li Rui was serving as a secretary to Mao at the time and was denounced following the Lushan Plenum as one of Peng Dehuai's supporters.

29. MacFarquhar, *Origins of the Cultural Revolution*, 2:202–203. Peng had disagreed with Mao in the pre-1949 period, and Mao was not one to forgive and forget.

30. *The Case of Peng Teh-huai, 1956–68* (Hong Kong: Union Research Institute, 1968), 7–13.

31. "Speech at the Lushan Conference," in Schram, *Mao Tsetung Unrehearsed*, 137, 139.

32. Yang, *Tombstone*, 385–386.

33. Walder, *China under Mao*, 173.

34. The most prominent example is the series of articles written by the mathematician Sun Jingxian, who calculates that fewer than three million deaths from nutritional deficiencies is realistic.

35. Walder, *China under Mao*, 169.

36. Odd Arne Westad, ed., *Brothers in Arms: The Rise and Fall of the Sino-Soviet Alliance, 1945–1963* (Stanford, CA: Stanford University Press, 1998); Lorenz M. Lüthi, *The Sino-Soviet Split: Cold War in the Communist World* (Princeton, NJ: Princeton University Press, 2008); Zhihua Shen and Yafeng Xia, *Mao and the Sino-Soviet Partnership, 1945–1959* (Lanham, MD: Lexington Books, 2015).

37. Deborah A. Kaple, "Soviet Advisors in China in the 1950s," in Westad, *Brothers in Arms*, 117–140.

38. Shen and Xia, *Mao and the Sino-Soviet Partnership*, chap. 8.

39. Translated in Michael Schoenhals, "Mao Zedong: Speeches at the 1957 'Moscow Conference,'" *Journal of Communist Studies* 2, no. 2 (1986): 106–126. China did not officially publish Mao's speeches until 1992.

40. Shen and Xia, *Mao and the Sino-Soviet Partnership*, chap. 7.

41. When I arrived as a student at Nanjing University in early 1977, one of the first things we were taken to see was the impressive bridge across the Yangzi, which was proudly presented as having been designed and built solely by the Chinese. The Chinese had left one other pillar in the river, which they declared had been built by the Soviets.

42. MacFarquhar, *Origins of the Cultural Revolution*, 3:353–364.

43. Editorial Departments of the *People's Daily* and *Red Flag*, *On Khrushchev's Phony Communism and Its Historical Lessons for the World: Comment on the Open Letter of the Central Committee of the CPSU (IX)* (Peking: Foreign Languages Press, 1964).

44. *On Khrushchev's Phony Communism*.

45. The best account is MacFarquhar, *Origins of the Cultural Revolution*, vol. 3. Frank Dikötter follows MacFarquhar's outline of the political flow, but adds considerably by providing much local detail and describing the movements' effects on individuals. See Frank Dikötter, *The Cultural Revolution: A People's History, 1962–1976* (London: Bloomsbury, 2016), 3–50.

46. Dali L. Yang, "Surviving the Great Leap Famine: The Struggle over Rural Policy, 1958–1962," in Cheek and Saich, *New Perspectives*, 262–302; Dali L. Yang, *Calamity and Reform in China: State, Rural Society, and Institutional Change since the Great Leap Famine* (Stanford, CA: Stanford University Press, 1996).

47. "Urgent Directive regarding Current Policy Issues in the Rural People's Communes," Central Literature Research Office of the CCP, *Jianguo yilai zhongyao wenxian xuanbian* (Selected Important Documents since the Founding of the Nation) (Beijing: Zhongyang wenxian chubanshe, 1996), 13:662.

48. Office of the Agricultural Committee, ed., *Nongye jihua zhongyao wejian huibian (1958–1981)* (Collection of Important Documents on Agricultural

Collectivization, 1958–1981) (Beijing: Zhonggong zhongyang dangxiao chu-banshe, 1981), 2:455–469, 474–491.

49. Teiwes and Sun, *"China's Road to Disaster,"* 217–221.

50. Yang, "Surviving the Great Leap Famine."

51. MacFarquhar, *Origins of the Cultural Revolution,* 3:137–181; Yang, *Tombstone,* 499–505.

52. Yang, *Tombstone,* 502.

53. Yang, *Tombstone,* 502–503; MacFarquhar, *Origins of the Cultural Revolution,* 3:166–68.

54. Yang, *Tombstone,* 503.

55. Yang, *Tombstone,* 507.

56. Schram, *Mao Tsetung Unrehearsed,* 189.

57. Richard Baum and Frederick C. Teiwes, *Ssu-Ch'ing: The Socialist Education Movement of 1962–1966* (Berkeley: Center for Chinese Studies, University of California, 1968); Richard Baum, *Prelude to Revolution: Mao, the Party and the Peasant Question, 1962–1966* (New York: Columbia University Press, 1975).

58. Walder, *China under Mao,* 189.

59. Mao told this to American journalist Edgar Snow. See Snow, *China's Long Revolution* (London: Pelican Books, 1974), 26. However, MacFarquhar writes that, in fact, Mao had decided to remove Liu some months before and named the date in January so that he appeared reactive to Liu's unacceptable conduct of the Socialist Education Campaign. See MacFarquhar, *Origins of the Cultural Revolution,* 3:432.

60. Zhou Enlai added the word "departments" to mitigate the impact. MacFarquhar, *Origins of the Cultural Revolution,* 3:428.

61. Andrew G. Walder, "Factional Conflict at Beijing University, 1966–1968," *China Quarterly,* no. 188 (2006): 1023–1047.

62. "Speech at the Tenth Plenum of the Eighth Central Committee," September 24, 1962, in Schram, *Mao Tsetung Unrehearsed,* 195.

63. "Talks with Mao Yuan-hsin," July 5, 1964, in Schram, *Mao Tsetung Unrehearsed,* 243.

64. On Deng Tuo, see Timothy Cheek, *Propaganda and Culture in Mao's China: Deng Tuo and the Intelligentsia* (Oxford: Clarendon Press, 1997). On Wu Han, see Mary G. Mazur, *Wu Han, Historian: Son of China's Times* (Lanham, MD: Lexington Books, 2009). Deng Tuo committed suicide in 1966, Wu Han died in prison in 1969, and Liao Moshi died of natural causes in 1990.

65. This apt phrase is from Roderick MacFarquhar and Michael Schoenhals, *Mao's Last Revolution* (Cambridge, MA: Belknap Press of Harvard University Press, 2006), 27.

66. Zhang, Yao, and Jiang would be denounced after Mao's death as the "Gang of Four," together with Shanghai activist Wang Hongwen. Lin died in 1971, following an alleged "coup d'état."

67. "A Reappraisal of 'Hai Rui Dismissed from Office,'" *Beijing Review* 22, no. 10, March 9, 1979, 27.

68. Official Chinese accounts now date the Cultural Revolution from 1966 to 1976 to include the death of Lin Biao and the arrest of the "Gang of Four." Originally it was defined as lasting from 1966 to 1969, when rebuilding party and state structures began after the destructive phase. I prefer this latter dating.

69. The best account through to 1976 is MacFarquhar and Schoenhals, *Mao's Last Revolution*. The best account of the local struggles is Andrew G. Walder, *Fractured Rebellion: The Beijing Red Guard Movement* (Cambridge, MA: Harvard University Press, 2009).

70. Walder, *China under Mao*, 335, 341.

71. MacFarquhar and Schoenhals, *Mao's Last Revolution*, 12.

72. MacFarquhar and Schoenhals, *Mao's Last Revolution*, 11.

73. For details of the process, see MacFarquhar, *Origins of the Cultural Revolution*, 3:456–459.

74. MacFarquhar, *Origins of the Cultural Revolution*, 3:458–459.

75. Peng Zhen, Luo Ruiqing, Lu Dingyi, and Yang Shangkun. Luo was dismissed as PLA chief of staff; Yang was dismissed as head of the General Office, which controlled the flow of information to the senior party organs.

76. "Circular of the CC of the Communist Party of China on the Great Proletarian Cultural Revolution," May 16, 1966, *Peking Review*, no. 21, May 19, 1967, 6–9. It was not published until one year after its approval (*People's Daily*, May 17, 1967), but its content was widely disseminated at the time of its approval.

77. MacFarquhar and Schoenhals, *Mao's Last Revolution*, 41.

78. MacFarquhar and Schoenhals, *Mao's Last Revolution*, 95–98.

79. Walder, *China under Mao*, 203–204.

80. Yin Hongbiao, "The Cultural Revolution's 'First Marxist-Leninist Big Character Poster,'" *Ershiyi shiji shuangye kan* (Twenty-First Century Bimonthly), no. 36 (August 1996), 37–45.

81. MacFarquhar and Schoenhals, *Mao's Last Revolution*, 55. As the pendulum swung against the "radicals," in 1983 Nie was sentenced to seventeen years in prison, having been detained in 1978, but was released later on medical parole. She died in September 2019.

82. "Talk to Leaders of the Centre," July 21, 1966, in Schram, *Mao Tsetung Unrehearsed*, 253. Beiyang refers to the army under Yuan Shikai after the fall of the Qing dynasty.

83. MacFarquhar and Schoenhals, *Mao's Last Revolution*, 84–85; Walder, "Factional Conflict at Beijing University," 1023–1047; Walder, *Fractured Rebellion*, chap. 2, 28–58, and chap. 3, which deals with the fissures that came to the surface once the work teams were withdrawn.

84. "Bombard the Headquarters—My First Big-Character Poster," August 5, 1966, *Peking Review*, no. 33, November 3, 1967, 5.

85. *Decision of the Central Committee of the Chinese Communist Party concerning the Great Proletarian Cultural Revolution* (Peking: Foreign Languages Press, 1966), 1–13.
86. MacFarquhar and Schoenhals, *Mao's Last Revolution*, 117; see chap. 7, "Red Terror," 117–135, for more graphic details. For a concrete account of the impact, see Nien Cheng, *Life and Death in Shanghai* (New York: Grove Press, 1986).
87. MacFarquhar and Schoenhals, *Mao's Last Revolution*, 110.
88. Dikötter, *The Cultural Revolution*, 114.
89. Rae Yang, *Spiders: A Memoir* (Berkeley: University of California Press, 1997), 163.
90. Liu did not acknowledge this in two further self-criticisms in April and July 1967. MacFarquhar and Schoenhals, *Mao's Last Revolution*, 136–138, 146.
91. Mao Zedong, "Talk at the Central Work Conference," October 25, 1966, in Schram, *Mao Tsetung Unrehearsed*, 270–274.
92. Walder, *China under Mao*, 231–232.
93. "Talks at Three Meetings with Comrades Chang Ch'un-ch'iao and Yao Wen-yüan," February 1967, in Schram, *Mao Tsetung Unrehearsed*, 277–279.
94. On the history of the revolutionary committees and membership of the provincial-level committees, see Anthony J. Saich, "The Revolutionary Committee, 1967–1978" (MSc. thesis, School of Oriental and African Studies, University of London, June 1978).
95. MacFarquhar and Schoenhals, *Mao's Last Revolution*, 253–259; Walder, *China under Mao*, 271–77.
96. Michael Schoenhals, "The Central Case Examination Group, 1966–79," *China Quarterly*, no. 145 (1996): 87–111.
97. Andrew G. Walder suggests a total death rate for the Cultural Revolution of between 1.1 and 1.6 million, with a further 22 to 30 million victims. See his "Rebellion and Repression in China, 1966–1971," *Social Science History* 38, no. 3–4 (Fall–Winter 2014): 513–539.
98. MacFarquhar and Schoenhals, *Mao's Last Revolution*, 258–259. On cannibalism, see Zheng Yi, *Scarlet Memorial: Tales of Cannibalism in Modern China*, trans. T. P. Synn (Boulder, CO: Westview, 1996).
99. Andrew G. Walder and Yang Su, "The Cultural Revolution in the Countryside: Scope, Timing and Human Impact," *China Quarterly*, no. 173 (March 2003): 77.
100. "Decision of the CC of the Chinese Communist Party, the State Council and the Military Affairs Committee of the CC and the Cultural Revolution Group of the CC, concerning the Resolute Support of the PLA for the Revolutionary Masses of the Left," in *Chinese Communist Party Documents of the Great Proletarian Cultural Revolution, 1966–1967* (Hong Kong: Union Research Institute, 1968), 195.
101. MacFarquhar and Schoenhals, *Mao's Last Revolution*, 176.
102. He made this remark in December 1970 during a breakfast with American journalist Edgar Snow.

103. Shaoguang Wang, *Failure of Charisma: The Cultural Revolution in Wuhan* (Oxford: Oxford University Press, 1995).

104. Wang was a member of the CCRG; Xie became chair of the Beijing Municipal Revolutionary Committee in 1967 and a member of the Politburo in 1969. He died in 1972.

105. MacFarquhar and Schoenhals, *Mao's Last Revolution*, 214.

106. Walder, *China under Mao*, 253.

107. John Gittings, "Stifling the Students," *Far Eastern Economic Review* 61, no. 35 (August 29, 1968). 377–378.

108. Gregor Benton and Alan Hunter, eds., *Wild Lily, Prairie Fire: China's Road to Democracy, Yan'an to Tian'anmen, 1942–1989* (Princeton, NJ: Princeton University Press, 1995), 124–134. The key author was Yang Xiguang, a nineteen-year-old high school senior. The genesis of the group and its demise is covered in Yiching Wu, "The Great Retreat and Its Discontents: Re-Examining the Shengwulian Episode in the Cultural Revolution," *China Journal*, no. 72 (July 2014): 1–28.

109. Constantine C. Menges, *China: The Gathering Threat* (Nashville, TN: Thomas Nelson, 2005), 54; Benton and Hunter, *Wild Lily, Prairie Fire*, 134.

110. Wu, "The Great Retreat," 24.

111. "Communique of the Enlarged 12th Plenary Session of the Eighth Central Committee of the Communist Party of China," October 31, 1968, *Peking Review*, vol. 11, no. 44, supplement, v–vii.

8. Charting a Way Forward, 1969–1981

1. These were set up in late 1968 and took their name from Mao Zedong's directive of May 7, 1966, to Lin Biao.

2. Yang Jiang, *Six Chapters from My Life "Downunder,"* trans. Howard Goldblatt (Seattle: University of Washington Press, 1984), 53. This is a wonderful tongue-in-cheek account of two years spent at a May Seventh Cadre school. When I was a student in China and we did our stint of open-door schooling in the countryside in 1977, the peasants had to be bribed with extra rations to take on the inconvenience of a bunch of students and teachers, who were a burden and knew nothing about farming. However, we were lucky as one of the German students had grown up on a farm and knew how to plow a straight furrow with a tractor.

3. Frederick C. Teiwes and Warren Sun, *The Tragedy of Lin Biao: Riding the Tiger during the Cultural Revolution, 1966–1971* (Honolulu: University of Hawai'i Press, 1996). This remains the best account of Lin's spectacular rise and even more spectacular fall.

4. While these denunciations continued, Liu was suffering from diabetes and not given proper care, suffering horribly before passing away from pneumonia on November 12, 1967.

5. Lin Biao, *Report to the Ninth National Congress of the Communist Party of China* (Peking: Foreign Languages Press, 1969). This report was delivered on April 1 and adopted on April 14, 1969.

6. Tony Saich, *China: Politics and Government* (New York: St. Martin's, 1981), 153–154.

7. Of the first secretaries, 69 percent were from the military, representing 57 percent of all secretaries. Teiwes and Sun, *Tragedy of Lin Biao*, 128.

8. Teiwes and Sun, *Tragedy of Lin Biao*, 141–142.

9. Roderick MacFarquhar and Michael Schoenhals, *Mao's Last Revolution* (Cambridge, MA: Belknap Press of Harvard University Press, 2006), 328–332; and especially Teiwes and Sun, *Tragedy of Lin Biao*, 134–151.

10. Of the various explanations put forward, this is deemed the most plausible by Teiwes and Sun, *Tragedy of Lin Biao*, 148–149.

11. The letter was released to party members on September 14, 1971. *Zhongfa*, no. 57, marked top secret, in *The Lin Piao Affair: Power Politics and Military Coup*, ed. Michael Y. M. Kau (White Plains, NY: International Arts and Science Press, 1975), 68.

12. *Zhongfa*, no. 25, 1972, quoted in MacFarquhar and Schoenhals, *Mao's Last Revolution*, 355.

13. Indeed, his daughter Lin Doudou claimed this was the case, and she went to Premier Zhou Enlai to report their flight. She was clearly a daughter more influenced by the Cultural Revolution and the denunciation of errant relatives than by traditional notions of filial piety.

14. "Struggle to Smash Lin-Ch'en Anti-Party Cliques Counterrevolutionary Coup," pts. 2–3, in Kau, *The Lin Piao Affair*, 89–90, 98.

15. Li Zhisui, *The Private Life of Chairman Mao: The Memoirs of Mao's Personal Physician* (New York: Random House, 1994), 542.

16. Lyle J. Goldstein, "Return to Zhenbao Island: Who Started Shooting and Why It Matters," *China Quarterly*, no. 168 (December 2001): 985–997.

17. MacFarquhar and Schoenhals, *Mao's Last Revolution*, 308–323.

18. Two of the memoirs by the participants are Richard Nixon, *RN: The Memoirs of Richard Nixon* (London: Book Club Associates, 1978); Henry Kissinger, *White House Years* (Boston: Little, Brown, 1979). Good journalistic accounts are James Mann, *About Face: A History of America's Curious Relationship with China from Nixon to Clinton* (New York: Alfred Knopf, 1999); Patrick Tyler, *A Great Wall: Six Presidents and China: An Investigative History* (New York: Public Affairs, 1999).

19. Odd Arne Westad, *Restless Empire: China and the World since 1750* (New York: Basic Books, 2012), 368–369.

20. William Burr, ed., *The Kissinger Transcripts: The Top Secret Talks with Beijing and Moscow* (New York: New Press, 1999), 61.

21. Andrew G. Walder, *China under Mao: A Revolution Derailed* (Cambridge, MA: Harvard University Press, 2015), 294.

22. A wonderful analysis and collection is Yang Jian, *Underground Literature during the Cultural Revolution* (Beijing: Zhaohua chubanshe, 1993).

23. Anita Chan, Stanley Rosen, and Jonathan Unger, eds., *On Socialist Democracy and the Chinese Legal System: The Li Yizhe Debates* (Armonk, NY: M. E. Sharpe, 1985). The name was drawn from the characters of the family names of each of the three authors.

24. MacFarquhar and Schoenhals, *Mao's Last Revolution,* 354–355.

25. Zhou Enlai, "Report to the Tenth National Congress of the Communist Party of China," delivered on August 24 and adopted on August 28, 1973, in *The Tenth National Congress of the Communist Party of China (Documents)* (Peking: Foreign Languages Press, 1973), 1–31. It seems that it was Zhang Chunqiao who had drafted the report with Mao's approval, although Zhang denied he had written it. MacFarquhar and Schoenhals, *Mao's Last Revolution,* 361.

26. Wang Hongwen, "Report on the Revision of the Party Constitution," delivered on August 24 and adopted on August 28, 1973, in *The Tenth National Congress,* 39–58.

27. Conversations when I was a student in Nanjing.

28. Thierry Pairault, "Industrial Strategy (January 1975–June 1979): In Search of New Policies for Industrial Growth," in *China's New Development Strategy,* ed. Jack Gray and Gordon White (London: Academic Press, 1982), 120–121.

29. *People's Daily,* July 28, August 15, and September 11, 1975.

30. Zhou Enlai, "Report on the Work of the Government," January 13, 1975, in *Documents of the First Session of the Fourth National People's Congress of the People's Republic of China* (Peking: Foreign Languages Press, 1975), 45–65.

31. "Report on the Revision of the Constitution," delivered January 13 and accepted January 17, 1975, in *Documents of the First Session,* 37.

32. MacFarquhar and Schoenhals, *Mao's Last Revolution,* 381.

33. Ezra Vogel, *Deng Xiaoping and the Transformation of China* (Cambridge, MA: Belknap Press of Harvard University Press, 2011), 122–140.

34. In mid-1975, Mao had allowed Deng some space in these sectors to spread his message. Vogel, *Deng Xiaoping,* 174–177.

35. MacFarquhar and Schoenhals, *Mao's Last Revolution,* 401–402.

36. I remember reading such materials while I was studying in Beijing in 1976. This was one method to spread a contrary message within a highly controlled political environment. Another method was to exaggerate the extent of Mao's mystical powers, such that people would recognize the folly. Unfortunately, too many people believed the fantastic claims.

37. *People's Daily,* February 9, 1975.

38. *Peking Review* 18, no. 9, February 28, 1975, 5.

39. Yao Wenyuan, "On the Social Basis of the Lin Piao Anti-Party Clique," *Peking Review* 18, no. 10, March 7, 1975, 5–10.

40. Zhang Chunqiao, "On Exercising All-Round Dictatorship over the Bourgeoisie," *Peking Review* 18, no. 14, April 4, 1975, 5–11.

41. This process is traced in detail in Frederick C. Teiwes and Warren Sun, *The End of the Maoist Era: Chinese Politics during the Twilight of the Cultural*

Revolution, 1972–1976 (London: Routledge 2007), 363–399; MacFarquhar and Schoenhals, *Mao's Last Revolution*, 404–412; and Vogel, *Deng Xiaoping*, 140–151.

42. MacFarquhar and Schoenhals, *Mao's Last Revolution*, 397–399.
43. *People's Daily*, March 10, 1976.
44. *People's Daily*, March 23, 1976. During the Cultural Revolution, Deng was criticized for using the phrase "It does not matter whether the cat is white or black; if it catches mice, it is a good cat."
45. Sebastian Heilman, *Nanking 1976: Spontane Massenbewegungen im Gefolge der Kulturrevolution—Eine Regionalstudie* (Nanjing 1976: Spontaneous Mass Movements in the Wake of the Cultural Revolution—A Regional Study) (Bochum: Brockmeyer, 1990). In early 1977, when I was studying in Nanjing, some students would recount proudly that they had been at the forefront of the demonstrations.
46. *People's Daily*, August 24 and 27, 1976.
47. *People's Daily*, December 30, 1976; *Red Flag*, no. 1 (1977).
48. I was studying in Beijing at this time. September 9 was a school holiday commemorating the day Mao had penned the calligraphy for our school, and some other students and I had bicycled to Tiananmen Square for the day off.
49. The phrase appeared in a joint editorial in *People's Daily, Liberation Army Daily*, and *Red Flag* on September 16.
50. I was a student in Beijing at the time, and we foreign students were approached one evening in our dormitory by the official who oversaw us and he asked us whether we had heard any rumors. He informed us that when we heard them on the BBC World Service, we should take them seriously but we should not tell the Chinese students as they were not yet prepared to receive the news.
51. One of the first to make the claim was Raymond Lotta, ed., *And Mao Makes 5: Mao Tsetung's Last Great Battle* (Chicago: Banner Press, 1978). The book contains translations of a number of key articles.
52. "Resolution on Certain Questions in the History of our Party since the Founding of the People's Republic of China," June 27, 1981, *Beijing Review* 24, no. 27, July 6, 1981, 10–39.
53. Tony Saich, "Party Building since Mao—A Question of Style?," in *China's Changed Road to Development*, ed. Neville Maxwell and Bruce McFarlane (Oxford: Pergamon Press, 1984), 149–167.
54. Gordon White, "The New Course in Chinese Development Strategy: Context, Problems and Prospects," in Gray and White, *China's New Development Strategy*, 6.
55. After the GLF, China stopped providing comprehensive economic data until the reforms were introduced. For more detail on these statistics, see Michel Korzec and Tony Saich, "The Chinese Economy: New Light on Old Questions," *Amsterdam Asia Studies*, no. 28 (1983): 7–8. Walder, *China under Mao*,

320–328, provides a useful summary and comparative perspectives that paint a similar picture.

56. Frank Dikötter, *The Cultural Revolution: A People's History, 1962–1976* (London: Bloomsbury, 2016), 266.

57. Korzec and Saich, "The Chinese Economy," 8.

58. This was in my student days in Beijing. Following a major aftershock in November, we were repeatedly told that the tents given to us to live in were graciously provided by Chairman Hua for our comfort. In 1977, while studying at Nanjing University, at a lecture I attended, it was claimed that the "Gang of Four" had deliberately lowered the figures regarding the strength of the earthquake to ensure that China would not need to accept international aid.

59. Nicholas R. Lardy and Kenneth Lieberthal, eds., *Chen Yun's Strategy for China's Development: A Non-Maoist Alternative* (Armonk, NY: M. E. Sharpe, 1983), xi.

60. Frederick C. Teiwes and Warren Sun, "China's New Economic Policy under Hua Guofeng: Party Consensus and Party Myths," *China Journal*, no. 66 (July 2011): 1–23.

61. Tony Saich, *Governance and Politics of China*, 2nd ed. (New York: Palgrave Macmillan, 2004), 54.

62. As Teiwes and Sun clearly show ("China's New Economic Policy," 2), this was somewhat unfair to Hua and only argued later as an accusation. As late as September 1979, Deng Xiaoping made similar comments, even adding that the party's "mistakes came from not insisting on Chairman Mao's line."

63. Hua Guofeng, "Political Report to the 11th National Congress of the Communist Party of China," *Peking Review* 20, no. 35, August 26, 1977, 23–57.

64. Richard Baum, *Burying Mao: Chinese Politics in the Age of Deng Xiaoping* (Princeton, NJ: Princeton University Press, 1994), 43. This is the best general analysis of elite politics of the period and should be read in conjunction with Vogel, *Deng Xiaoping*.

65. *People's Daily*, October 25, 1976.

66. I was listening to the speeches in the square at the time.

67. For Hua's report, see *Peking Review* 20, no. 35, August 26, 1977, 23–57. For the new Statutes, Ye's report, and Deng's closing comments, see *Peking Review* 20, no. 36, September 2, 1977, 16–22, 23–37, and 38–39, respectively.

68. "Practice Is the Sole Criterion for Testing Truth," *Guangming Daily*, May 11, 1978.

69. *People's Daily*, June 24, 1978.

70. On the controversy, see Michaels Schoenhals, "The 1978 Truth Criterion Controversy," *China Quarterly*, no. 126 (June 1991): 243–268.

71. Baum, *Burying Mao*, 62–63; Roderick MacFarquhar, "The Succession to Mao and the End of Maoism, 1969–82," in *The Politics of China, 1949–1989*, ed. Roderick MacFarquhar (Cambridge: Cambridge University Press, 1993), 319–321.

72. In interviews, some of Chen's supporters claimed that at a meeting in April 1990, he criticized Deng for unleashing the trends that culminated in the 1989 student-led demonstrations. A speech by Chen, published in the *People's Daily* on July 17, 1987, stresses the need for leaders to listen to different opinions.

73. *People's Daily,* December 24, 1978; Tony Saich, "New Directions in Politics and Government," in Gray and White, *China's New Development Strategy,* 20–22.

74. *Peking Review* 21, no. 52, December 29, 1978, 15.

75. In fact, Hu Yaobang had headed the department from December 1977, providing Deng with strong input on personnel decisions. I am grateful to Ezra Vogel for pointing this out to me.

76. Interview with the influential economic reformer Yu Guangyuan, summer 1986.

77. Warren Sun and Frederick C. Teiwes, *Paradoxes of Post-Mao Rural Reform: Initial Steps toward a New Chinese Countryside, 1976–1981* (London: Routledge, 2016).

78. Kate Xiao Zhou, *How the Farmers Changed China: Power of the People* (Boulder, CO: Westview Press, 1996); David Zweig, *Freeing China's Farmers: Rural Restructuring in the Reform Era* (Armonk, NY: M. E. Sharpe, 1997), 12–15 and chap. 2.

79. Tony Saich, "The Reform Decade in China: The Limits to Revolution from Above," in *The Reform Decade in China: From Hope to Dismay,* ed. Marta Dassù and Tony Saich (London: Kegan Paul International in association with Centro Studi di Politica Internazionale, 1992), 22.

80. "Written Judgment of the Special Court under the Supreme People's Court of the People's Republic of China," January 23, 1981, *Peking Review* 24, no 5, February 2, 1981, 13–24.

81. Baum, *Burying Mao,* 116–117. As we have seen, there is little evidence that he vigorously opposed Deng's return, and his approach to the economy was aligned with that of Deng.

82. For the communiqué, see *Peking Review* 24, no. 27, July 6, 1981, 6–8.

83. Baum, *Burying Mao,* 135.

84. For the full text of the resolution, see *Peking Review* 24, no. 27, July 6, 1981, 10–39.

85. "Reform of the System of Party and State Leadership," August 18, 1980, *in Selected Works of Deng Xiaoping, 1975–1982* (Beijing: Foreign Languages Press, 1983), 304.

86. Kjeld Erik Brødsgaard, "The Democracy Movement in China, 1978–1979: Opposition Movements, Wall Poster Campaigns, and Underground Journals," *Asian Survey* 21, no. 7 (1981): 747–774.

87. For a selection of the poetry, see David S. G. Goodman, ed., *Beijing Street Voices: The Poetry and Politics of China's Democracy Movement* (London: Marion Boyers, 1981).

88. *New York Times,* November 27, 1978, A1; John Fraser, *The Chinese: Portrait of a People* (New York: Summit Books, 1980), 244–247.
89. On Deng's role during this period, see Vogel, *Deng Xiaoping,* 249–265.
90. Baum, *Burying Mao,* 70–71.
91. Wei Jingsheng, "The Fifth Modernization: Democracy," in *The Courage to Stand Alone: Letters from Prison and Other Writings,* trans. Kristina M. Torgeson (New York: Viking, 1997), 199–212.
92. Personal communication from participants at the conference. Li would be the first to indirectly criticize Mao in the press, Su was head of the Institute of Marxism-Leninism-Mao Zedong Thought at the Chinese Academy of Social Sciences, Yan was head of its Institute of Politics, and Yu became its vice president. Su and Yan were exiled following the student-led protests of 1989. On the theory conference, see Merle Goldman, "Hu Yaobang's Intellectual Network and the Theory Conference of 1979," *China Quarterly,* no. 126 (June 1991): 219–242.
93. "Uphold the Four Cardinal Principles," March 30, 1979, cpcchina.chinadaily .com.cn/2010-10/15/content_13918193.htm.
94. "Historical Experience of Our Path of Development," *Zhonggong yanjiu* (Research on the CCP) 15, no. 9 (September 1981): 108–177.
95. Even in the 1980s, in discussions with Liao, he was still concerned about the need for more substantive change.
96. Tony Saich, "Modernization and Participation in the People's Republic of China," in *China: Modernization in the 1980s,* ed. Joseph Y. S. Cheng (Hong Kong: Chinese University Press, 1989).
97. Lü Cheng and Zhu Gu, "Conscientiously Safeguard the People's Democratic Rights," *Hongqi* (Red Flag), no. 17 (1980), 9–11, 4.
98. Baum, *Burying Mao,* 107–110; Andrew Nathan, *Chinese Democracy* (New York: Alfred A. Knopf, 1985), chap. 10.
99. Saich, "Reform Decade in China," 27–33.
100. Westad, *Restless Empire,* 369.
101. *The Guardian,* January 30, 1979.
102. Discussions with former executives of China Central Television.

9. Reform, Rebellion, and Restoration, 1982–1993

1. Richard Baum, *Burying Mao: Chinese Politics in the Age of Deng Xiaoping* (Princeton, NJ: Princeton University Press, 1994), 111.
2. Information from friends who were involved in the production.
3. "On Opposing Wrong Ideological Tendencies," March 27, 1981, https:// dengxiaopingworks.wordpress.com/2013/02/25/on-opposing-wrong -ideological-tendencies/.
4. *Beijing Review* 26, no. 42, October 1983, 1; Tony Saich, "Party Consolidation and Spiritual Pollution in the People's Republic of China," *Communist Affairs* 3, no. 3 (July 1984): 283–289.

5. Ezra F. Vogel, *Deng Xiaoping and the Transformation of China* (Cambridge, MA: Belknap Press of Harvard University Press, 2011), 447.

6. Chen Yun, "Speech at the National Conference of the CCP," *People's Daily*, September 24, 1985; Chen Yun, "Combating Corrosive Ideology," *Beijing Review* 28, no. 41, October 14, 1985, 15–16.

7. *Beijing Review* 24, no. 17, April 27, 1981, 15–23.

8. "Create a New Situation in All Fields of Socialist Modernization: Report to the Twelfth Congress of the Communist Party of China," September 1, 1982, *Beijing Review* 25, no. 37, September 13, 1982, 11–40. The term "socialist spiritual civilization" was used first by Ye Jianying in his National Day speech of October 1, 1979.

9. "Opening Speech at the Twelfth National Congress of the CPC," September 1, 1982, in *Selected Works of Deng Xiaoping (1975–1982)* (Beijing: Foreign Languages Press, 1984), 394–397.

10. Tony Saich, "Party Building since Mao—A Question of Style?," in *China's Changed Road to Development*, ed. Neville Maxwell and Bruce McFarlane (Oxford: Pergamon Press, 1984), 149–168.

11. Tony Saich, "The Fourth Constitution of the People's Republic of China," *Review of Socialist Law* 9, no. 2 (1983): 113–124, and my translation of the Constitution on 183–208.

12. Hu Sheng, "On the Revision of the Constitution," *Beijing Review* 25, no. 18, May 3, 1982, 17.

13. Merle Goldman, *Sowing the Seeds of Democracy in China: Political Reform in the Deng Xiaoping Era* (Cambridge, MA: Harvard University Press, 1994), 117–120.

14. Saich, "Party Building since Mao," 282–289.

15. "Decision on Reform of the Economic Structure," *Beijing Review* 27, no. 44, November 4, 1984, i–xvi.

16. In the 1950s Liu had been labeled a rightist, and in 1987 he was expelled from the party. Mark Harrison, trans., *A Translation of "The Second Kind of Loyalty"* (Adelaide: University of Adelaide, 1989); Liu's memoir, *A Higher Kind of Loyalty* (New York: Random House, 1990).

17. On the activities of the group under Zhao Ziyang, see Wu Guoguang, *Zhao Ziyang yu zhengzhi gaige* (Zhao Ziyang and Political Reform) (Hong Kong: Taipingyang shiji yanjiusuo, 1997).

18. *Issues and Studies* 23, no. 6 (June 1987): 17.

19. Cheng Hsiang, "News from Beidaihe," *Wen Wei Po*, August 8, 1986.

20. "The Resolution of the CCP Central Committee with regard to the Guiding Principles of the Construction of a Socialist Spiritual Civilization," September 28, 1986, *Beijing Review* 29, no. 40, October 6, 1986, i–viii.

21. Robin Munro, "Political Reform, Student Demonstrations and the Conservative Backlash," in *Reforming the Revolution: China in Transition*, ed. Robert Benewick and Paul Wingrove (Basingstoke: Macmillan Education, 1988).

22. Baum, *Burying Mao*, 206–207.

23. Deng had been contemplating Hu's dismissal from at least as early as May 1986. Vogel, *Deng Xiaoping*, 579.

24. Central Document Number 1, January 6, 1987, in *Chinese Law and Government* 21, no. 1 (Spring 1988): 18–21.

25. Central Document Number 3, January 17, 1987, in *Chinese Law and Government* 21, no. 1 (Spring 1988): 24–28. This was based on comments by Bo Yibo to the enlarged Politburo meeting.

26. "Radical or Moderate Democracy," in *Xinquanweizhuyi: Dui gaige lilun gangling de lunzheng* (Neo-Authoritarianism: A Debate on the Theoretical Program of Reform), ed. Liu Jun and Li Lin (Beijing: Beijing jingji xueyuan chubanshe, 1989); Wu Jiaxiang, "Democratization through Marketization," *Shijie jingji daobao* (World Economic Herald), April 10, 1989.

27. Interviews with Su Shaozhi and Yan Jiaqi, summer of 1986. Both fled into exile in the summer of 1989.

28. "Advance along the Road of Socialism with Chinese Characteristics," *Beijing Review* 30, no. 45, November 9–15, 1987, 9–15.

29. "Speech at a Meeting of Propaganda, Theoretical, Press and Party School Cadres," May 13, 1987, in *Summary of World Broadcasts: The Far East* (hereafter cited as *SWB:FE*), 8617 (July 11, 1987), National Library of Australia online. That the talk was not released until July is indicative of the continued resistance.

30. Tony Saich, "The Chinese Communist Party at the Thirteenth National Congress: Policies and Prospects for Reform," in *Political and Social Changes in Taiwan and Mainland China*, ed. King-yuh Chang (Taipei: Institute of International Relations, 1989), 74–107; Saich, "The Thirteenth Congress of the Chinese Communist Party: An Agenda for Reform?," *Journal of Communist Studies* 4, no. 2 (June 1988): 203–208.

31. Su Shaozhi, one of those credited with this idea, told me that what he had said was that China was not even in the initial stage of socialism.

32. Interviews with members of the Institute of Politics and Law, Jiangsu Provincial Academy of Social Sciences, and the Institute of Marxism-Leninism and Mao Zedong Thought, CASS, June 1988.

33. "On Separating Party and Government—Part of a Speech at the Preparatory Meeting for the Seventh Plenary Session of the Twelfth Central Committee," *People's Daily*, November 26, 1987, 1. The meeting was held on October 14, 1987.

34. *Beijing Review* 31, no. 17, April 25–May 1, 1988, 18–43.

35. Zhao Ziyang, *Prisoner of the State: The Secret Journal of Premier Zhao Ziyang* (New York: Simon and Schuster, 2009), 233.

36. Baum, *Burying Mao*, 233–239.

37. I was in China at this time, and when I mentioned to a friend that the price of a bar of soap seemed to be about the same, he replied yes, but the bar was one-third smaller.

38. This account of the 1989 demonstrations is based on personal observations while I was in Beijing; and also Saich, "The Rise and Fall of the Beijing

People's Movement," *Australian Journal of Chinese Affairs*, no. 24 (July 1990): 181–208; Saich, "When Worlds Collide: The Beijing People's Movement of 1989," in *The Chinese People's Movement: Perspectives on Spring 1989*, ed. Tony Saich (Armonk, NY: M. E. Sharpe, 1990), 25–49.

39. Woei Lien Chong, "Present Worries of Chinese Democrats: Notes on Fang Lizhi, Liu Binyan and the Film 'River Elegy,'" *China Information* 3, no. 4 (Spring 1989): 1–20.

40. Fang had denounced the Chinese government as a modern form of feudalism, and in one speech he pointed out that since the end of World War II there had been no successful socialist country. Vogel, *Deng Xiaoping*, 577.

41. Woei Lien Chong, "Petitioners, Popperians, and Hunger Strikers: The Uncoordinated Efforts of the 1989 Chinese Democratic Movement," in Saich, *The Chinese People's Movement*, 106–125; Shen Tong, with Marianne Yen, *Almost a Revolution: The Story of a Student's Journey from Boyhood to Leadership in Tiananmen Square* (Boston: Houghton Mifflin Harcourt, 1990).

42. At a meeting at his home to which he had invited a number of leaders, excluding one of Zhao's top aides, Deng stressed the need for a tough response. See the entries in Li Peng's diary for April 23, 24, and 25. *Li Peng liusi riji* (Li Peng's June 4 Diary), copy in the Fairbank Collection, Fung Library, Harvard University; *The Critical Moment: Li Peng Diaries* (N.p.: West Point Publishing House, 2010).

43. The meeting was attended by five members of the Politburo Standing Committee and President Yang Shangkun, who provided the link to the military. The decision was also taken to effectively replace Zhao with Jiang Zemin as general secretary because Deng had praised his handling of the Shanghai demonstrations in 1986. *Li Peng's June 4 Diary*, May 17, 1989, and Zhao, *Prisoner of the State*, 27–28.

44. Brook provides the most careful account of the military actions and suggests that 478 died and 920 were wounded. Timothy Brook, *Quelling the People: The Military Suppression of the Beijing Democracy Movement* (Oxford: Oxford University Press, 1992), 161 and 151–169.

45. Vogel, *Deng Xiaoping*, 625–626.

46. *Beijing Review* 32, no. 28, July 10–16, 1989, 14–17.

47. See Bao Pu, ed., *The Last Secret: The Final Documents from the June Fourth Crackdown* (Hong Kong: Xin shiji chubanshe, 2019), esp. Nathan's introduction; Andrew J. Nathan, "The New Tiananmen Papers: Inside the Secret Meeting that Changed China," *Foreign Affairs*, 98, no. 4 (July / August 2019).

48. *Beijing Review* 32, no. 27, July 3–9, 1989, 9–10.

49. Yang Jisheng, "Zhao Ziyang's Speech in His Own Defense at the Fourth Plenary Session of the 13th Central Committee of the Chinese Communist Party," in *Chinese Law and Government* 38, no. 3 (May–June 2005): 51–68; Zhao, *Prisoner of the State*, 3–49.

50. Baum, *Burying Mao,* 295–296; Zhang Liang, comp., *The Tiananmen Papers,* ed. Andrew J. Nathan and Perry Link (New York: Public Affairs, 2001), 260–261, 308–314.

51. The *People's Daily,* June 24, 1989, ran extracts of Deng's comments on the four cardinal principles.

52. "On Opposing Bourgeois Liberalization," *Qiushi* (Seeking Truth), no. 3, February 15, 1990.

53. "Patriotism and the Mission of China's Intellectuals," *People's Daily,* May 4, 1990.

54. "Several Questions concerning Journalistic Work—An Outline of a Speech at a Study Class on Journalistic Work," *Qiushi* (Seeking Truth), no. 5, March 1, 1990. The speech was delivered on November 28, 1989.

55. "Speech at the Meeting in Celebration of the 40th Anniversary of the Founding of the People's Republic of China," September 29, 1989, *Beijing Review* 32, no. 41 (October 9–15, 1989): 11–24.

56. "CPC Vows to End Corruption," *Beijing Review* 32, no. 32 (August 7–13, 1989): 5.

57. "Li Describes SEZs as Part of Nation's Major Reform Plan," *China Daily,* February 10, 1990, 1.

58. Jiang Zemin, "Building Socialism the Chinese Way," *Beijing Review* 34, no. 27 (July 8–14, 1991): 14–31.

59. Tony Saich, "Peaceful Evolution with Chinese Characteristics," in *China Briefing, 1992,* ed. William A. Joseph (Boulder, CO: Westview Press, 1993), 12–15.

60. Information from an informed source in Beijing.

61. Gao Di, "The Question of the Soviet Coup," August 30, 1991. Author's personal copy.

62. Gu Xin and David Kelly, "New Conservatism: Ideological Program of a New Elite," in *China's Quiet Revolution: New Interactions between State and Society,* ed. David S. G. Goodman and Beverley Hooper (Melbourne: Longman Cheshire, 1993), 219–233.

63. "Realistic Responses and Strategic Choices for China after the Soviet Upheaval," September 9, 1991, *Chinese Law and Government* 29, no. 2 (1996).

64. Chen Yepin, "Have Both the Ability and Political Integrity, with Political Integrity as the Main Aspect—Comments on the Criteria for Selecting and Promoting Cadres," *People's Daily,* September 1, 1991. Chen, no relative, was close to Chen Yun.

65. The speech was at a rally on October 9, 1991, translated in *SWB:FE,* 1200, C1/1–4.

66. Suisheng Zhao, "Deng Xiaoping's Southern Tour: Elite Politics in Post-Tiananmen China," *Asian Survey* 33, no. 8 (August 1993): 739–756; Vogel, *Deng Xiaoping,* 664–684. Deng and his entourage left Beijing without informing any party leaders.

67. The full text of the document is in the Hong Kong magazine *Zhengming*, April 1, 1992, 23–27.

68. "Excerpts from Talks Given in Wuchang, Shenzhen, Zhuhai and Shanghai, January 18–February 21, 1992," https://dengxiaopingworks.wordpress.com/2013/03/18/excerpts-from-talks-given-in-wuchang-shenzhen-zhuhai-and-shanghai.

69. Tony Saich, "The Fourteenth Party Congress: A Programme for Authoritarian Rule," *China Quarterly*, no. 132 (December 1992): 1136–1160.

70. Zhao, "Deng Xiaoping's Southern Tour," 755.

71. Xinhua, March 11, 1992.

72. For Li's unamended report, see *SWB:FE* 1336, C1/1–12. For the politics that went into writing it, see *Zhengming*, April 1, 1992.

73. Baum, *Burying Mao*, 350.

74. "Deng and Chen Lines of Battle on the Eve of the 14th Party Congress," *Zhengming*, October 1992, 6–8. In addition to his cautious nature, Chen was well aware of the damage that Mao Zedong's haste in the late 1950s had caused and the problems that the excessive foreign imports had caused in the late 1970s.

75. "Speed Up the Pace of Reform, the Open Door and Modernization Construction in Order to Strive for Even Greater Victories for the Cause of Socialism with Chinese Characteristics," *People's Daily*, October 12, 1992, 1–3.

76. Deng had begun to use the phrase as early as June 1984. Vogel, *Deng Xiaoping*, 465.

77. *People's Daily*, overseas edition, October 10, 1992.

78. Apparently Chen had put forward two other priorities for the congress: two of his close supporters should not step down (they did); and Shenzhen must not become a model for the whole country (it did).

10. Renewed Reform and the Roots of Wealth, 1993–2002

1. Joseph Fewsmith, *China since Tiananmen: From Deng Xiaoping to Hu Jintao*, 2nd ed. (Cambridge: Cambridge University Press, 2008), 165–170 and throughout for an excellent analysis of this period.

2. Barry Naughton, *Growing out of the Plan: Chinese Economic Reform, 1978–1993* (Cambridge: Cambridge University Press, 1995); Yingyi Qian, *How Reform Worked in China: The Transition from Plan to Market* (Cambridge, MA: MIT Press, 2017).

3. Barry Naughton, "The Chinese Economy: Fifty Years into the Transformation," in *China Briefing, 2000: The Continuing Transformation*, ed. Tyrene White (Armonk, NY: M. E. Sharpe, 2000).

4. "Decision of the Communist Party of China Central Committee on Certain Issues concerning the Establishment of a Socialist Market Economic Structure," November 22, 1993, *Beijing Review* 36, no. 47, November 22–28, 1993, 12–31.

5. Ezra F. Vogel, *One Step Ahead in China: Guangdong under Reform* (Cambridge, MA: Harvard University Press, 1989).

6. Dali L. Yang, "Reform and the Restructuring of Central-Local Relations," in *China Deconstructs: Politics, Trade and Regionalism*, ed. David S. G. Goodman and Gerald Segal (London: Routledge, 1994), 74.

7. Gerald Segal, "China's Changing Shape," *Foreign Affairs* 73, no. 3, May–June 1994, 43–58; Shaoguang Wang, "The Rise of the Regions: Fiscal Reform and the Decline of Central State Capacity in China," in *The Waning of the Communist State: Economic Origins of Political Decline in China and Hungary*, ed. Andrew G. Walder (Berkeley: University of California Press, 1995), 87–113.

8. Tony Saich, "The Blind Man and the Elephant: Analysing the Local State in China," in *East Asian Capitalism: Conflicts, Growth and Crisis*, ed. Luigi Tomba (Milan: Fondazione Guangiacomo Feltrinelli, 2002), 75–100.

9. Fewsmith, *China since Tiananmen*, 168–169.

10. Fewsmith, *China since Tiananmen*, 168.

11. Fewsmith, *China since Tiananmen*, 165.

12. In a wonderful study, Sebastian Veg coins the phrase "grassroots intellectuals" for those who eschew the symbiotic relationship between intellectuals and the party-state. See his *Minjian: The Rise of China's Grassroots Intellectuals* (New York: Columbia University Press, 2019).

13. Wang Shuo, "The Dealers," in *Wang Shuo xiequ xiaoshuo xuan* (Selected Comic Fiction of Wang Shuo) (Beijing: Zuojia chubanshe, 1990), 59.

14. Wen Hui, *Shanghai Baby* (London: Robinson, 2002), 90.

15. Veg, *Minjian*, chap. 2.

16. Athar Hussain et al., *Urban Poverty in the PRC: Measurement Patterns and Policies* (Geneva: International Labour Organization, 2003).

17. Marc J. Blecher, "Hegemony and Workers' Politics in China," *China Quarterly*, no. 170 (June 2002): 283–303.

18. In my discussions with laid-off workers, I found a sense of inevitability rather than resistance as they realized that the old-style industries were finished. Their hopes were that the reforms would provide better job opportunities for their children.

19. "Human Rights in China Press Report," July 16, 1997; "Troubled Sleep in China," *Economist*, July 24, 1997.

20. "People's Republic of China: Summary of Amnesty International Concerns," February 1998, AI Index: ASA, amnesty.org/download/Documents/144000 /asa/70021999.en.pdf.

21. Ma Licheng and Ling Zhijun, *Jiaofeng* (Crossing Swords) (Beijing: Jinri chubanshe, 1998).

22. Ian Johnson, *Wild Grass: Three Stories of Change in Modern China* (New York: Vintage Books, 2004); David Ownby, *Falun Gong and the Future of China* (Oxford: Oxford University Press, 2008). One party member told me that what frightened him the most was the discipline of the Falun Gong. When

its members ended their silent protest, not a piece of trash was left behind. Not something one would normally see with large Chinese crowds.

23. Wen Jieming et al., eds., *Yu Zongshuji tanxin* (Heart-to-Heart Talks with the General Secretary) (Beijing: Zhongguo shehui kexue chubanshe, 1996).

24. Information from those present. Many Chinese leaders were drawn from technicians trained at Tsinghua, which is regarded as China's MIT, whereas Peking University is seen as China's Harvard.

25. I was present at the event.

26. For the Fifteenth Party Congress, see Richard Baum, "The Fifteenth National Party Congress: Jiang Takes Command," *China Quarterly*, no. 153 (March 1998): 141–156.

27. Jiang Zemin, "Hold High the Great Banner of Deng Xiaoping Theory for an All-Round Advancement of the Cause of Building Socialism with Chinese Characteristics into the 21st Century," *Beijing Review* 40, no. 6, October 6–12, 1997, 10–37.

28. World Bank, *China's Management of Enterprise Assets: The State as Shareholder* (Washington, DC: World Bank, 1997), 1.

29. United Nations Development Programme, *China Human Development Report: Human Development and Poverty Alleviation, 1997* (Beijing: UNDP, 1998), 65.

30. *Chaebols* are the large industrial conglomerates that are powerful drivers of the South Korean economy. Often family run, they incorporate diversified affiliates. In China, the key difference is that such industrial organizations are state-run rather than run by families or individuals.

31. Baum, "Fifteenth National Party Congress," 149–150.

32. Nicholas R. Lardy, "China and the Asian Contagion," *Foreign Affairs* 77, no. 4, July/August 1998, 86.

33. Tony Saich, *Providing Public Goods in Transitional China* (New York: Palgrave Macmillan, 2008); Saich, "The Politics of Welfare Policy: Towards Social Citizenship?," in *Handbook of Welfare in China*, ed. Beatriz Carrillo et al. (Cheltenham: Edward Elgar, 2017), 81–97.

34. Blecher, "Hegemony and Workers' Politics"; Willliam Hurst, *The Chinese Worker after Socialism* (Cambridge: Cambridge University Press, 2009).

35. Li Cheng, "China in 1999: Seeking Common Ground at a Time of Tension and Conflict," *Asian Survey* 40, no. 1 (January–February 2000): 122.

36. Hu Angang, *Zhongguo fazhan qianying* (Prospects for China's Development) (Hangzhou: Zhejiang renmin chubanshe, 1999), 35–36.

37. *Wall Street Journal*, November 23, 2001.

38. See David Shambaugh's comments on "The Other Tiananmen Papers," July 8, 2019, http://www.chinafile.com/conversation/other-tiananmen -papers.

39. *People's Daily* (overseas edition), December 20, 1999, 1.

40. Speech at Peking University, June 29, 1998, http://news.bbc.co.uk/2/hi/asia -pacific/122320.stm.

41. Nancy Bernkopf Tucker, "Dangerous Liaisons: China, Taiwan, Hong Kong, and the United States at the Turn of the Century," in White, *China Briefing*, 251.

42. The Chinese had seen the films of US precision bombing in the Iraq war, and no one I spoke with could believe that the Belgrade bombing was an accident.

43. Joseph Y. S. Cheng and King-Lun Ngok, "The 2001 'Spy Plane' Incident Revisited: The Chinese Perspective," *Journal of Chinese Political Science* 9, no. 1 (March 2004): 63–83.

44. *People's Daily*, February 26, 2000, 1.

45. Fewsmith, *China since Tiananmen*, 215–217.

46. Tony Saich, "China's WTO Gamble: Some Political and Social Questions," *Harvard Asia Pacific Review* 6, no. 1 (Spring 2002): 10–15.

47. "PRC White Paper—The One-China Principle and the Taiwan Issue," February 21, 2000, www.taiwandocuments.org/white.htm.

48. "Taiwan Independence in Whatever Form Unacceptable," *Beijing Review* 43, no. 13, March 27, 2000, 6.

49. Chen Shui-bian's inauguration speech, May 20, 2000, ken_davies.tripod .com/inaugural.html.

50. Dali L. Yang, "China in 2002: Leadership Transition and the Political Economy of Governance," *Asian Survey* 43, no. 1 (January–February 2003): 30.

51. "Full Text of Jiang Zemin Report at 16th Party Congress on November 8, 2002," https://www.fmprc.gov.cn/mfa_eng/topics_665678/3698_665962 /t18872.shtml.

52. Joseph Fewsmith, "The Sixteenth National Party Congress: The Succession That Didn't Happen," *China Quarterly*, no. 173 (March 2003), 3–6.

53. Bruce Dickson, *Red Capitalists in China: The Chinese Communist Party, Private Entrepreneurs, and Political Change* (New York: Cambridge University Press, 2003).

11. The WTO World and China's Rise, 2002–2012

1. "Report on the Work of the Government," March 5, 2003, http://www.npc .gov.cn/zgrdw/englishnpc/Special_11_5/2010-03/03/content_1690622.htm.

2. Jean-Pierre Cabestan, "The 10th National People's Congress and After: Moving towards a New Authoritarianism—Both Elitist and Consultative?," *China Perspectives*, 2003, https://journals.openedition.org/chinaperspectives /272.

3. Hu Angang, quoted in *South China Morning Post*, April 21, 2003, A5.

4. Erik Eckholm, "China's New Leader Works to Set Himself Apart," *New York Times*, January 12, 2003.

5. Tony Saich, "Is SARS China's Chernobyl or Much Ado about Nothing?," in *SARS in China: Prelude to Pandemic?*, ed. Arthur Kleinman and James L. Watson (Stanford, CA: Stanford University Press, 2006), 71–104.

6. Xinhua News Agency, October 21, 2003.
7. Duan Peijun and Tony Saich, "Reforming China's Monopolies," Harvard Kennedy School Faculty Research Working Paper Series, RWP 14-023, May 2014.
8. "As the Eldest Son of the Republic, Who We Do Not Monopolize, Will Monopolize," *South China Daily* online, August 3, 2009, http://opinion .nfdaily.cn/content/2009-08-03/content-5472399.htm.
9. For example, Du Feijing and Liao Wengen, "The Commitment of the Eldest Son of the Republic," *People's Daily*, December 2, 2008.
10. Kjeld-Erik Brødsgaard, "State-Owned Enterprises and Elite Circulation," Background Brief no. 858 (Singapore: East Asian Institute, 2013).
11. Barry Naughton, "SASAC and Rising Corporate Power in China," *China Leadership Monitor*, no. 24, 2008.
12. Xinhua News Agency, October 11 and 18, 2005.
13. BBC Monitoring International Reports, Financial Times Information, ACC-NO: A200602248-1031B-GNW.
14. "Building a New Socialist Countryside Is an Urgent Immediate Task of China: Official," Xinhua News Agency, February 22, 2006.
15. Visiting one farming household in Sichuan, we counted almost 120 different fees that the household had to pay.
16. Xiaxin Wang and Yan Shen, "The Effect of China's Agricultural Tax Abolition on Rural Families' Incomes and Production," *China Economic Review* 29 (June 2014): 185–199.
17. Him Chung and Jonathan Unger, "The Guangdong Model of Urbanization: Collective Village Land and the Making of a New Middle Class," *China Perspectives*, no. 3 (2013): 33–41; Tony Saich and Biliang Hu, *Chinese Village, Global Market: New Collectives and Rural Development* (New York: Palgrave Macmillan, 2012).
18. In addition to the payout from the village-level cooperative, each individual also received a payout from their own hamlet collective. Saich and Hu, *Chinese Village, Global Market*, 81–89.
19. "China Punishes Thousands in Crackdown on Illegal Land Transfers, April 15, 2008," *Jurist*, https:www.jurist.org/news/2008/04/china-punishes -thouands-in-crackdown/.
20. Reuters, October 20, 2008.
21. *Caijing*, October 20, 2008.
22. Based on our surveys. From 2003 to 2016, we analyzed regular surveys of about 4,000 respondents regarding their levels of satisfaction with government provision of services. Seven sites were chosen based on their geographic locations, average income, and populations. See, for example, Tony Saich, "The Quality of Governance in China: The Citizens' View," *CDDR Working Papers* (Center on Democracy, Development, and the Rule of Law, Stanford), no. 129, April 2013.
23. "Evaluation and Suggestions on Reform of the Chinese Medical Health System (Abstract and Key Points)," July 29, 2005, http://www.sina.com.cn.

24. Tony Saich, *Providing Public Goods in Transitional China* (New York: Palgrave Macmillan, 2008), 90–97.

25. "Communiqué of the Sixth Plenum of the Sixteenth Central Committee," October 11, 2006, Xinhua News Agency, October 18, 2006.

26. All citizens are registered at their place of birth, as either rural or non-rural. The designation determines the benefits to which they are entitled.

27. "Social Insurance Law of the People's Republic of China," October 28, 2010, https://www.cecc.gov/resources/legal-provisions/social-insurance-law-of-the-peoples-republic-of-china

28. Yu Yunyao, executive vice president of the Central Party School, quoted by Xinhua News Agency, September 16, 2004.

29. "CCPCC Decision on the Enhancement of the Party's Governance Capability," Xinhua News Agency, September 26, 2004.

30. Joseph Fewsmith, "CCP Launches Campaign to Maintain the Advanced Nature of Party Members," *China Leadership Monitor*, no. 13, Winter 2005, 3–4.

31. "Zeng Qinghong on the Correct Way of Waging the Campaign to Preserve the Advanced Nature of the CCP," Xinhua News Agency, May 25, 2005.

32. Willy Lam, "Hu's Recent Crackdown on Political Dissent," *China Brief* 13, no. 5, June 7, 2005, http://www.freechina.net/2005/comment/00074.htm.

33. See the insightful discussion in Sebastian Veg, *Minjian: The Rise of China's Grassroots Intellectuals* (New York: Columbia University Press, 2019), 192–199.

34. In addition to Veg, *Minjian*, see Eva Pils, *China's Human Rights Lawyers: Advocacy and Resistance* (London: Routledge, 2015), 232.

35. *Chinanews.com*, reported in *Asia Times*, March 26, 2009.

36. Xia Wensi, "Scandals concerning Wen Jiabao's Wife and Son," *Kaifang* (Open Magazine) (Hong Kong), no. 6, June 2006, 16–18.

37. Tony Saich, *Governance and Politics of China*, 3rd ed. (Basingstoke: Palgrave Macmillan, 2011), 102–105; Joseph Fewsmith, "The 17th Party Congress: Informal Politics and Formal Institutions," and Alice L. Miller, "China's New Party Leadership," both in *China Leadership Monitor*, no. 23, Winter 2008.

38. Liu Guoguang, "On Certain Issues in Teaching and Researching Economies," *Jingji yanjiu* (Economics Research), no. 10 (October 2002): 4–11. Liu had been at the forefront of the economic reforms in the 1980s but later became embittered as he was passed over for the kind of promotion he felt he deserved. Thereafter he was an outspoken critic of organizations such as the Ford Foundation, from which he had received funding for his early research.

39. Hu Jintao, "Hold High the Great Banner of Socialism with Chinese Characteristics and Strive for New Victories in Building a Moderately Prosperous Society in All Respects," October 15, 2007, http://www.bjreview.com.cn/document/txt/2007-11/20/content_86325.htm.

40. This was covered briefly in the media, but again as the situation stabilized any such discussion was forbidden. During the height of concern and limited transparency, I was invited to participate in an international group to review

what had happened. It was soon made clear that we could not look at anything that had occurred before the quake, i.e., corruption and shoddy buildings ("bean-curd" dwellings), and we could only examine disaster relief. The group went nowhere, I never saw a draft of any report but I did receive a plaque for my non-efforts.

41. Barry Naughton, "The Scramble to Maintain Growth," *China Leadership Monitor*, no. 27, Winter 2009.

42. Yongshun Cai, *Collective Resistance in China: Why Popular Protests Succeed or Fail* (Stanford, CA: Stanford University Press, 2010); Yao Li, *Playing by the Informal Rules: Why the Chinese Regime Remains Stable despite Rising Protests* (Cambridge: Cambridge University Press, 2019).

43. Tony Saich, "China's Domestic Governing Capacity: Prospects and Challenges," in *Assessing China's Power*, ed. Jae Ho Chun (New York: Palgrave Macmillan, 2015).

44. Jae Ho Chung, Hongyi Lai, and Ming Xia, "Mounting Challenges to Governance in China: Surveying Collective Protestors, Religious Sects and Criminal Organizations," *China Journal*, no. 56 (2006): 1–31.

45. "Outline of the 12th Five-Year Plan for China's Economic and Social Development," http://news.sina.com.cn/c/2011-03-17/055622129864.shtml.

46. For the "Starbucks fallacy," see Jim Mann, *The China Fantasy: How Our Leaders Explain Away Chinese Repression* (London: Viking, 2007), chap. 3. For "Chimerica," see Niall Ferguson, "'Chimerica' and the Global Asset Market Boom," *International Finance* 10, no. 3 (December 2007): 215–239.

47. Lawrence J. Lau et al., "Estimates of U.S.-China Trade Balances in Terms of Domestic Value-Added," October 2006, Working Paper No. 295, Stanford King Center for Global Development, https://kingcenter.stanford.edu/publications/estimates-u-s-china-trade-balances-terms-domestic-value-added. For a later analysis, see Lawrence J. Lau, "The U.S.-China Deficit Isn't as Bad as Trump Says," *Dallas News*, April 6, 2017, https://www.dallasnews.com/opinion/commentary/2017/04/06/the-u-s-china-trade-deficit-isn-t-as-bad-as-trump-says/.

48. Yan Xuetong, quoted in the *Wall Street Journal*, November 9, 2009.

49. *South China Morning Post*, November 4, 2009.

50. Joseph Fewsmith, "Bo Xilai and Reform: What Will Be the Impact of His Removal?," *China Leadership Monitor*, no. 38, Summer 2012.

51. For an excellent study of the revival of neo-Maoist influence in Chinese society and politics, see Jude D. Blanchette, *China's New Red Guards: The Return of Radicalism and the Rebirth of Mao Zedong* (New York: Oxford University Press, 2019).

52. Tsinghua University professor Cui Zhiyuan went to work for him, and Hong Kong academic Wang Shaoguang praised the model. See http://www.aisixiang.com/data/38896.html.

53. For a positive appraisal, see Kevin Lu, "The Chongqing Model Worked: Bo Xilai Might Be a Crook, but He Was Actually Pretty Good at His Job,"

Foreign Policy (August 8, 2012), https://foreignpolicy.com/2012/08/08/the
-chongqing-model-worked/.

54. Yasheng Huang, *Capitalism with Chinese Characteristics: Entrepreneurship and the State* (Cambridge: Cambridge University Press, 2008).

55. *Time*, April 29, 2010.

56. John Garnaut, *The Rise and Fall of the House of Bo* (Melbourne: Penguin, 2013).

57. *People's Daily*, March 15, 2012.

58. "Do a Good Job in Every Aspect of Work in Maintaining the Party's Purity in a Down-to-Earth Manner," *Qiushi* (Seeking Truth), March 13, 2012, www.qstheory.cn/qsgcyi/201203/t2012315_145649.htm.

59. Reuters, September 23, 2013.

12. Creating the China Dream, 2012–2021

1. Carl Minzer, "China after the Reform Era," *Journal of Democracy* 26, no. 3 (July 2015): 129–143.

2. "Full Text of Hu Jintao's Report at the 18th Party Congress," November 8, 2012, and published November 19, 2012, en.people.cn/90785/8024777.html. Xi Jinping played a major role in the drafting of the speech.

3. Wen Jiabao, "Report on the Work of the Government," delivered at the First Session of the Twelfth National People's Congress, March 5, 2013, www .bjreview.com.cn/pdf/2013/government_work_report_2013.pdf.

4. "Decision of the Central Committee of the Communist Party of China on Some Major Issues concerning Comprehensively Deepening the Reform," November 12, 2013, www.china.org.cn/china/third_plenary_session/2014 -01/16/content_31212602.htm.

5. David Barboza and Christ Buckley, "China Plans to Reduce the State's Role in the Economy," *New York Times*, March 24, 2013.

6. In 2050, the median age in China is projected to be 50.7 years of age. America will be 42.7 and India 38.1.

7. "Having Children Is a Family Matter but also a National Matter," *People's Daily*, August 6, 2018. Some have even suggested a three-child policy or abandoning the limits entirely.

8. At www.gov.cn/zhengce/2014-03/16/content_260075.htm.

9. Chinese colleagues told me that Xi felt that too much time and energy was wasted building consensus, leading to decisions based on the lowest common denominator.

10. "Chinese President Accuses Fallen Top Officials of 'Political Conspiracies,'" *South China Morning Post*, January 2, 2017.

11. "Words Count: Chinese State of the Nation Speech All About the Party," *China Real Time Report, Wall Street Journal*, March 5, 2017.

12. At one meeting, leaders of an organization agonized over whether they should invite me to a meal in an outside restaurant. Given that they were entertaining a foreigner, some thought it would be acceptable, but others

argued that a posting on social media would be bad publicity and thus the decision was made to eat in their own canteen: a five-star kitchen.

13. Reuters, December 2, 2013.
14. *The Atlantic*, November 8, 2013.
15. Of those accused of corruption in 2019, almost 19,000 cases were turned over to the procuracy, double the number from the previous year. Shi Yu, "In Data: China's Fight against Corruption in Poverty Alleviation," *CGTN*, August 9, 2020, news.cgtn.com/news/2020-08-09/in-data-China-s-fight -against-corruption-in-poverty-alleviation-S080gC70Q0/index.htm/.
16. Tony Saich, "How Chinese Citizens View the Quality of Governance under Xi Jinping," *Journal of Chinese Governance* 1, no. 1 (2016): 1–20.
17. Saich, "How Chinese Citizens View the Quality of Governance."
18. Xinhua News Agency, November 4, 2013; "Whither Goes the Anti-Graft Drive," *China Daily*, September 1, 2014.
19. Copy in my personal possession and available at http://www.chinafile.com /document-9-chinafile-translation.
20. "Xi Jinping Asks for 'Absolute Loyalty' from Chinese State Media," *Guardian*, February 19, 2016.
21. "Xi Calls for Strengthened Ideological Work in Colleges," *China Daily*, December 9, 2016, http://www.chinadaily.com.cn/china/2016-12/09/content _27617203.htm.
22. "China Launches 'Patriotic Struggle' Campaign Targeting Intellectuals," https://www.rfa.org/english/news/china/campaign-08032018104859.html /ampRFA?__twitter_impression=true.
23. Article 5 of the Nonprofit Law, https://www.cof.org/content/nonprofit-law -china.
24. Tony Saich, "How Do China's New Rich Give Back?," in *The China Questions: Critical Insights into a Rising Power*, ed. Jennifer Rudolph and Michael Szonyi (Cambridge, MA: Harvard University Press, 2018), 148–154.
25. Sebastian Veg, *Minjian: The Rise of China's Grassroots Intellectuals* (New York: Columbia University Press, 2019), 196.
26. "Communiqué of the 4th Plenary Session of the 18th Central Committee of the CCP, October 23, 2014," http://www.china.org.cn/china/fourth_plenary _session/2014-12/02/content_34208801.htm; "CCP Central Committee Decision concerning Some Major Questions in Comprehensively Moving Governing the Country according to the Law Forward," October 30, 2014, https://chinacopyrightandmedia.wordpress.com/2014/10/28/ccp-central -committee-decision-concerning-some-major-questions-in-comprehensively -moving-governing-the-country-according-to-the-law-forward/.
27. Hu Angang and Hu Lianhe, "Second Generation Ethnic Minority Policies: Promoting Organic Ethnic Blending and Prosperity," *Xinjiang shifan daxue xuebao: Zhexue shehui kexue bao* (Journal of Xinjiang Normal University: Philosophy and Social Sciences) 32, no. 5 (2011): 1–12.
28. An excellent overview and analysis is Christian Shepherd, "Fear and Oppression in Xinjiang: China's War on Uighur Culture," *Financial Times*

Magazine, September 12, 2019. See also James Leibold, "Hu the Uniter: Hu Lianhe and the Radical Turn in China's Xinjiang Policy," October 10, 2018, *China Brief* 18, no. 16, https://jamestown.org/program/hu-the-uniter-hu-lianhe-and-the-radical-turn-in-chinas-xinjiang-policy/.

29. Austin Ramzy and Chris Buckley, "'Absolutely No Mercy': Leaked Files Expose How China Organized Mass Detentions of Muslims," *New York Times,* November 16, 2019, https://www.nytimes.com/interactive/2019/11/16/world/asia/china-xinjiang-documents.html.

30. "China Slams US 'Lies' about Treatment of Uygurs in Xinjiang Region," *South China Morning Post,* September 9, 2019, https://www.scmp.com/news/china/diplomacy/article/3026402/china-slams-us-lies-about-treatment-uygurs-xinjiang-region. This defense had already been raised in August 2018 at the UN Committee on the Elimination of Racial Discrimination.

31. "China Changes Law to Recognize 'Re-education Camps' in Xinjiang," *South China Morning Post,* October 10, 2018.

32. *People's Daily,* May 3, 2013.

33. Lance Gore, "Deciphering the Two Abrupt Turns of the Xi Jinping Regime," Background Brief no. 890 (Singapore: East Asian Institute, 2014), 4.

34. Charles Horner, "China's Democratic Future: The Movement's Next Hundred Years," *Claremont Review of Books* (Fall 2019).

35. Xinhuanet, December 4, 2013.

36. Lucy Hornby, "Xi Jinping Pledges Return to Marxist Roots for China's Communists," *Financial Times,* July 1, 2016.

37. "In China, the Communist Party's Latest, Unlikely Target: Young Marxists," National Public Radio, November 21, 2018, https://www.npr.org/2018/11/21/669509554/in-china-the-communist-partys-latest-unlikely-target-young-marxists.

38. *South China Morning Post,* December 26, 2018.

39. "Full Text of Xi Jinping's Report at 19th CPC Congress: Secure a Decisive Victory in Building a Moderately Prosperous Society in All Respects and Strive for the Great Success of Socialism with Chinese Characteristics for a New Era," October 18, 2017, www.xinhuanet.com/english/special/2017-11/03/c_136725942.htm.

40. "CCP Center Resolution on Deepening Reform of Party and State Institutions," March 5, 2018, http://english.www.gov.cn/policies/latest_releases/2018/03/05/content_281476067521228.htm.

41. *People's Daily,* March 13, 2018.

42. *People's Daily,* March 20, 2018.

43. *Wall Street Journal,* December 28, 2019.

44. Wei Shan and Juan Chen, "The COVID-19 Pandemic and Political (Dis)Satisfaction: Tracing Public Opinions in China Using Social Media Data," *East Asia Institute Background Briefs,* no. 1529, May 7, 2020.

45. "Joint Statement on Trilateral Meeting of the Trade Ministers of the United States, Japan and the European Union," September 25, 2018, http://ustr.gov

/about-us/policy-offices/press-office/press-releases/2018/september/joint
-statement-trilateral.

46. In November 2020 fifteen nations accounting for one-third of the global
economy signed the Regional Comprehensive Economic Partnership, an
agreement promoted by China. The US was not included, and in 2017 it had
already withdrawn from the Trans-Pacific Partnership, which was seen as a
way to stem China's influence in trade.

47. Richard N. Cooper, "Can China's High Growth Continue?," in Rudolph
and Szonyi, *The China Questions*, 119–125.

48. These policy areas are tracked by Dan Rosen, together with the Asia Society
Policy Institute. See chinadashboard.asiasociety.org.

49. Full text accessed at Transcend Media Service, from Xinhua, https://www
.transcend.org/tms/2018/12/xi-jinpings-speech-on-40th-anniversary-of
-chinas-reforms-opening-up-full-text/.

50. Xinhuawang, December 21, 2018.

51. "China Needs Strong Leadership or Will 'Crumble,' Policy Paper Says,"
Reuters, September 27, 2019, https://www.reuters.com/article/us-china
-anniversary-politics/china-needs-strong-leadership-or-will-crumble-policy
-paper-says-idUSKBN1WC0BX.

52. "Promotion of the New Great Project of Party Building Must Be Consistent," *Qiushi* (Seeking Truth), October 2, 2019. The speech was originally
delivered on January 5, 2018, to new CC members and other leaders, but it
was published on the occasion of the seventieth anniversary.

53. David M. Lampton, "A Tipping Point in US-China Relations Is Upon Us,"
speech at the conference "China Reform: Opportunities and Challenges,"
May 6–7, 2015, dated May 11, 2015, http://www.uscnpm.com/model_item
.html?action=view&table=article&id=15789.

54. Robert D. Blackwill and Ashley J. Tellis, "Revising US Grand Strategy
toward China," Council on Foreign Relations, Special Report No. 72
(March 2015).

55. Kevin Rudd, "US-China 21: The Future of U.S.-China Relations under Xi
Jinping—Toward a New Framework of Constructive Realism for a Common
Purpose" (Harvard Kennedy School, April 2015); Rudd, "The Avoidable
War: Reflections on U.S.-China Relations and the End of Strategic Engage-
ment," Asia Society Policy Institute, 2019.

56. Graham T. Allison, *Destined for War: Can America and China Escape the
Thucydides Trap?* (Boston: Houghton Mifflin Harcourt, 2017).

57. Evan A. Feigenbaum and Robert A. Manning, "A Tale of Two Asias," *Foreign Policy*, October 31, 2012.

58. Kishore Mahbubani, "ASEAN Still Critical Catalyst for China's Future,"
East Asian Forum, October–December 2016.

59. See, for example, "Foreign Minister Calls on China, ASEAN to Enhance
Political Trust," July 25, 2016, http://english.www.gov.cn/state_council
/ministries/2016/07/25/content_281475401180259.htm.

60. "China Is About to Hold a Giant Meeting on Spending Billions to Reshape the World," CNBC, May 10, 2017, http://www.cnbc.com/2017/05/10/china-is -about-to-hold-a-giant-meeting-on-spending-billions-to-reshape-the-world.html.

61. David Dollar, "Yes, China Is Investing Globally—But Not So Much in Its Belt and Road Initiative," May 8, 2017, https://www.brookings.edu/blog /order-from-chaos/2017/05/08/yes-china-is-investing-globally-but-not-so -much-in-its-belt-and-road-initiative/.

62. Among various pieces, see Justin Yifu Lin, "China's Silk Road Vision," *Project Syndicate,* January 21, 2016, https://www.project-syndicate.org /onpoint/china-maritime-silk-road-economic-belt-by-justin-yifu-lin-2016 -01?barrier=accesspaylog.

63. "Malaysia's Mahathir Warns Against 'New Colonialism' during China Visit," Bloomberg News, August 20, 2018. He canceled a $20 billion east-coast rail link and a natural gas pipeline that he called "unfair deals" negoti-ated by his predecessor.

64. Peter Cai, "Understanding China's Belt and Road Initiative," March 22, 2017, https://www.lowyinstitute.org/publications/understanding-belt-and -road-initiative.

65. It still drew a large number of attendees, and thirty-seven leaders signed the joint communiqué. For highlights of Xi's speech of April 26, 2019, see https://news.cgtn.com/news/3d3d674e32636a4d34457a6333566d54/index .html; "List of Deliverables of the Second Belt and Road Forum for Interna-tional Cooperation," April 27, 2019, https://www.fmprc.gov.cn/mfa_eng /zxxx_662805/t1658767.shtml.

66. John Kerry, "U.S. Pacific for Asia-Pacific Engagement," August 13, 2014, https://2009-2017.state.gov/secretary/remarks/2014/08/230597.htm.

67. "Summary of the 2018 National Defense Strategy of the United States of America: Sharpening the American Military's Competitive Edge," Jan-uary 2018, https://dod.defense.gov/Portals/1/Documents/pubs/2018 -National-Defense-Strategy-Summary.pdf.

68. "Remarks by President Trump to the 73rd and 74th Sessions of the United Nations General Assembly," September 25, 2018: https://www.whitehouse .gov/briefings-statements/remarks-president-trump-73rd-session-united -nations-general-assembly-new-york-ny/; and https://www.whitehouse.gov /briefings-statements/remarks-president-trump-74th-session-united-nations -general-assembly-new-york-ny.

69. Zhong Nan, "China, US See Fresh Progress in Bilateral Trade Discussions," *China Daily,* December 28, 2018.

70. *Qiushi* (Seeking Truth), April 1, 2019, http://www.qstheory.cn/dukan/qs /2019-04/01/c_11224307480.htm.

71. Cnn.com/2020/01/21/politics/Donald-trump-davos-speech-climate-change /index-html; "Remarks by President Trump in Press Conference, Davos Switzerland, January 22, 2020," whitehouse.gov/briefings-statements /remarks-president-trump-press-conference-davos-switzerland/.

72. Agreement accessed at wto.gov/default/files/files/agreeemnts/phase%20 one%20agreement/Economic_And_Trade_Agreement_Between_The _United_States_And_China_Text.pdf.

73. "China Says Sino-British Joint Declaration on Hong Kong No Longer Had Meaning," Reuters, June 30, 2017.

74. BBC newsfeed, October 14, 2019.

75. Tony Cheung et al., "How Beijing Plans to Use Powers Contained in Basic Law to Tighten Control over Hong Kong," *South China Morning Post*, November 1, 2019, https://www.scmp.com/news/china/politics/article/3036003 /how-beijing-plans-use-powers-contained-basic-law-tighten.

76. "Xi Jinping's Important Speech at the Opening of the Training Course for Young and Middle-Aged Cadres at the Central Party School (National School of Administration)," September 3, 2019, xinhuanet.com/politics/2019 -09/03/c_1124956081.htm.

77. "Xi Urges Breaking New Ground in Major Country Diplomacy with Chinese Characteristics," *Xinhua*, June 24, 2018, xinhuanet.com/English/2018 -06/24/c_1372769.htm.

78. "Proposals of the CCP CC on Formulating the Fourteenth Five-Year Plan for National Economic and Social Development and the Long-Term Goals for 2035," moe.gov.cn/s78/A01/s4562/gfwzx.zcwj/202011/t20201104_498258 .html.

Conclusion

1. See the collection of essays in Lucien Bianco, *Peasants without the Party: Grass-Roots Movements in Twentieth-Century China* (Armonk, NY: M. E. Sharpe, 2001).

2. Joseph W. Esherick, "Ten Theses on the Chinese Revolution," *Modern China* 21, no. 1 (January 1995): 49.

3. Edward Friedman, Paul G. Pickowicz, and Mark Selden, with Kay Ann Johnson, *Chinese Village, Socialist State* (New Haven, CT: Yale University Press, 1991).

4. The principles are: upholding socialism, upholding the people's democratic dictatorship, upholding the leadership of the party, and upholding Marxism-Leninism and Mao Zedong Thought.

5. "Jiang Shigong on Philosophy and History: Interpreting the 'Xi Jinping Era' through Xi's Report to the Nineteenth National Congress of the CCP," May 11, 2018, https://www.thechinastory.org/cot/jiang-shigong-on-philosophy-and -history-interpreting-the-xi-jinping-era-through-xis-report-to-the-nineteenth -national-congress-of-the-ccp/. Translated by David Ownby and analyzed by David Ownby and Timothy Cheek. The original Chinese was published in the journal *Kaifang shidai* (Open Times) (January 2018).

6. "China to Send State Officials to 100 Private Firms Including Alibaba," Reuters, September 24, 2019.

7. Daniel Koss demonstrates how in provinces with greater party penetration, adherence to the former one-child policy and tax collection are better than in provinces with lower figures for party membership. See Koss, *Where the Party Rules: The Rank and File of China's Communist State* (Cambridge: Cambridge University Press, 2018), esp. chaps. 3 and 4.

8. Patrick Brzeski, "Chinese Industry on Edge after 'Depressing' Censorship of Shanghai Festival's Opening Film," *Hollywood Reporter,* June 14, 2019. Following revisions and editing, the film was released and received an enthusiastic response from audiences.

9. George Orwell, *1984,* updated ed. (New York: Chelsea House, 2007).

10. Pamela Kyle Crossley, "Xi's China Is Steamrolling Its Own History," *Foreign Policy,* January 29, 2019. On the revival of the influence of "neo-Maoism" on the reassessment of history, see Jude D. Blanchette, *China's New Red Guards: The Return of Radicalism and the Rebirth of Mao Zedong* (New York: Oxford University Press, 2019).

11. Mandy Zuo, "Controversy over Chinese Textbook's Cultural Revolution Chapter as State Publisher Denies Censorship," *South China Morning Post,* January 11, 2018. See also Jules Zhao Liu and Prynne Yan Liu, "The Maoist Historiographical Legacy in China: A Foucauldian Study on the Relation between History and Politics," unpublished paper.

12. Central Party Literature Research Office and Central Archives, eds., *Jianguo yilai Liu Shaoqi wengao* (Works of Liu Shaoqi since the Founding of the Nation) (Beijing: Zhongyang wenxian chubanshe, 1998), 3:491.

13. "Resolution on Certain Questions in the History of Our Party since the Founding of the People's Republic of China," June 27, 1981, https://www .marxists.org/subject/china/documents/cpc/history/01.htm.

14. Kang Sheng, the shadowy coordinator of the CCP's security apparatus, played an important role in the persecutions in Yan'an and again during the Cultural Revolution. He died before retribution could be sought.

15. David Shambaugh writes, "It is essential to view the CCP's victory as an armed seizure of power following protracted military campaigns." Shambaugh, "Building the Party-State in China, 1949–1965: Bringing the Soldier Back In," in *New Perspectives on State Socialism in China,* ed. Timothy Cheek and Tony Saich (Armonk, NY: M. E. Sharpe, 1997), 127.

16. The name is taken from the series of movies, the first debuting in 2015, which feature a Rambo-type figure who battles against foreign enemies. The movies have been huge box office hits in China.

17. See cnn.com/2020/05/28/asia/china-wolf-warrior-diplomacy-intl-hnk/index .html. The previous year Wang had called for Chinese diplomats to adopt a more assertive approach.

18. "Too Soon, Too Loud: Chinese Foreign Policy Advisors Tell 'Wolf Warrior' Diplomats to Tone It Down," *South China Morning Post,* May 14, 2020.

19. Chris Buckley, "Vows of Change in China Belie Private Warning," *New York Times,* February 14, 2013.

20. Mao Zedong, "Analysis of the Classes in Chinese Society," March 1926, in *Selected Works of Mao Tse-Tung* (Peking: Foreign Languages Press, 1967), 1:13.

21. An illuminating discussion is Michael Schoenhals, "Demonising Discourse in Mao Zedong's China: People vs Non-People," *Totalitarian Movements and Political Religions* 8, no. 3–4 (September–December 2007): 465–482.

22. In 1976, having witnessed a parade of "Gang of Four" followers heading to the execution ground, we were called in for an interrogation. The photos we had taken, we were told by the officials, had upset the Chinese people, and they demanded that we hand over our undeveloped film. Interestingly, earlier in our stay we had been told that China did not have the capacity to develop our color film, but then the official informed us that it could be developed in double-quick time. Imagine our shock that we had been lied to previously!

23. "Some Questions concerning Methods of Leadership," June 1, 1943, in *Selected Works of Mao Tse-Tung*, 3:119.

24. "The Foolish Old Man Who Removed the Mountains," June 11, 1945, in *Selected Works of Mao Tse-Tung*, 3:271–274.

25. Mao Zedong, "Talks at Three Meetings with Comrades Chang Ch'un-ch'iao and Yao Wen-yuan," in *Mao Tse-tung Unrehearsed: Talks and Letter, 1956–71*, ed. Stuart R. Schram (Harmondsworth: Penguin Books, 1974), 277.

26. "Correctly Understand the Role of the Individual in History," *People's Daily*, July 4, 1980.

27. Elizabeth J. Perry, "From Mass Campaigns to Managed Campaigns: 'Constructing a New Socialist Countryside,'" in *Mao's Invisible Hand: The Political Foundations of Adaptive Governance in China*, ed. Sebastian Heilmann and Elizabeth J. Perry (Cambridge, MA: Harvard University Asia Center, 2011), 30–61.

28. "Top Political Advisor Calls for Enhanced Efforts in United Front Work," January 18, 2019, http://www.xinhuanet.com/english/2019-01/18/c_137755079.htm.

29. See, for example, Anne-Marie Brady, "China in Xi's 'New Era': New Zealand and the CCP's 'Magic Weapons,'" *Journal of Democracy* 29, no. 2 (April 2018): 68–75.

30. This was a problem not only in Guangdong but also in Jiangsu in the 1990s.

31. Tony Saich, "Introduction," in Tony Saich with a contribution by Benjamin Yang, *The Rise to Power of the Chinese Communist Party: Documents and Analysis* (Armonk, NY: M. E. Sharpe, 1996), xlvii.

32. Kathleen Hartford and Steven M. Goldstein, "Introduction: Perspectives on the Chinese Communist Revolution," in *Single Sparks: China's Rural Revolutions*, ed. Kathleen Hartford and Steven M. Goldstein (Armonk, NY: M. E. Sharpe, 1989).

33. Sebastian Heilmann, "Policy Experimentation in China's Economic Rise," *Studies in Comparative International Development* 43, no. 1 (Spring 2008): 1–26; Heilmann and Perry, *Mao's Invisible Hand*.

34. Yiping Huang, *Agricultural Reform in China: Getting Institutions Right* (New York: Cambridge University Press, 1998), 158.

35. Andrew Watson, "Agriculture Looks for 'Shoes That Fit': The Production Responsibility System and Its Implications," *World Development* 11, no. 8 (August 1983): 705–730.

36. David E. Apter and Tony Saich, *Revolutionary Discourse in Mao's Republic* (Cambridge, MA: Harvard University Press, 1994).

37. On this phenomenon in urban China, see David Bray, *Social Space and Governance in Urban China: The Danwei System from Origins to Reform* (Stanford, CA: Stanford University Press, 2005).

38. Luigi Tomba, *The Government Next Door: Neighborhood Politics in Urban China* (Ithaca, NY: Cornell University Press, 2014).

39. See China's Future Direction Editorial Group, ed., *Zhongguo weilai: Juji gaoceng juece yu guojia zhanlüe buju* (China's Future Direction: Uniting High-Level Policymaking and National Strategic Arrangements) (Beijing: Renmin chubanshe, 2009).

40. William H. Overholt, *China's Crisis of Success* (Cambridge: Cambridge University Press, 2018); Carl Minzer, *The End of an Era: How China's Authoritarian Revival Is Undermining Its Rise* (Oxford: Oxford University Press, 2018).

41. For a nuanced account of the interplay between mobilization and attempts at "scientific farming," see Sigrid Schmalzer, *Red Revolution, Green Revolution: Scientific Farming in Socialist China* (Chicago: University of Chicago Press, 2016).

42. Sam Geall, ed., *China and the Environment: The Green Revolution* (London: Zed Books, 2013); Judith Shapiro, *China's Environmental Challenges*, 2nd ed. (Cambridge: Polity Press, 2016).

43. Kira Matus et al., "Health Damages from Air Pollution in China," *Global Environmental Change* 22, no. 1 (February 2012): 55–66.

44. Yew Wei Lit, "Disembedding Lawful Activism in Contemporary China: The Confrontational Politics of a Green NGO's Legal Mobilization," *China Information* 32, no. 2 (July 2018): 224–243.

45. Richard N. Cooper, "Can China's High Growth Continue?," in *The China Questions: Critical Insights into a Rising Power,* ed. Jennifer Rudolph and Michael Szonyi (Cambridge, MA: Harvard University Press, 2018), 119–125.

46. Dwight H. Perkins, "Is the Chinese Economy Headed toward a Hard Landing?," in Rudolph and Szonyi, *The China Questions,* 126–132.

47. Dwight H. Perkins and Thomas G. Rawski, "Forecasting China's Economic Growth to 2025," in *China's Great Economic Transformation,* ed. Loren Brandt and Thomas G. Rawski (New York: Cambridge University Press, 2008).

48. Daniel H. Rosen, "China's Outlook—Now and in 2020," August 8, 2014, http://rhg.com/notes/chinas-outlook-now-and-in-2020.

49. Lotus Ruan, "China's Communist Party Hails Its Own Legitimacy amid Online Skepticism," *Tea Leaf Nation,* September 17, 2015, https://foreignpolicy.com/2015/09/17/china-communist-party-legitimacy-government-wang-qishan-internet/.

50. Tony Saich, "Citizens' Perception of Governance in Rural and Urban China," *Journal of Chinese Political Science* 12 (2007): 1–28; Saich, "How

China's Citizens View the Quality of Governance under Xi Jinping," *Journal of Chinese Governance* 1, no. 1 (2016): 1–20.

51. David Dollar, "What Institutions Do Asian Countries Need to Keep Growing?," *East Asia Forum,* May 31, 2015.

52. Bruce Gilley, *China's Democratic Future: How It Will Happen and Where It Will Lead* (New York: Columbia University Press, 2004); Yu Liu and Ding-ding Chen, "Why China Will Democratize," *Washington Quarterly* 35, no. 1 (2012): 41–63.

53. Gordon G. Chang, *The Coming Collapse of China* (New York: Random House, 2001); David Shambaugh, "The Coming Chinese Crackup," *Wall Street Journal,* March 6, 2015.

54. Andrew J. Nathan, "Authoritarian Resistance," *Journal of Democracy* 14, no. 1 (January 2003): 6–17; Steve Tsang, "Contextualizing the China Dream: A Reinforced Consultative Leninist Approach to Government," in *China's Many Dreams: Comparative Perspectives on China's Search for National Rejuvenation,* ed. David Kerr (Basingstoke: Palgrave Macmillan, 2015), 10–34.

55. Minxin Pei, *China's Trapped Transition: The Limits of Developmental Autocracy* (Cambridge, MA: Harvard University Press, 2006).

56. Shaohua Hu, "Confucianism and Western Democracy," in *China and Democracy: Reconsidering the Prospect for a Democratic China,* ed. Suisheng Zhao (New York: Routledge, 2000), 55–72.

57. Ian Johnson, *The Souls of China: The Return of Religion after Mao* (New York: Vintage Books, 2017).

58. "China Makes Churches Replace Ten Commandments with Xi Jinping Quotes: 'This Is What the Devil Has Always Done,'" *Christian Post,* September 17, 2019. See also Ben Halder, "Xi's Crackdown on Religion Is China's Worst in 40 Years," August 8, 2019, ozy.com/acumen/xis-crackdown-on-religion-ischinas-worst-in-40-years/95719.

59. Luigi Tomba, *The Government Next Door.*

60. Jean-Pierre Cabestan, *China Tomorrow: Democracy or Dictatorship?* (Lanham, MD: Rowman and Littlefield, 2019); Daniel C. Lynch, *China's Futures: PRC Elites Debate Economics, Politics, and Foreign Policy* (Stanford, CA: Stanford University Press, 2015); David Shambaugh, *China's Future* (Cambridge: Polity Press, 2016).

61. Samuel P. Huntington, *The Third Wave: Democratization in the Late Twentieth Century* (Norman: University of Oklahoma Press, 1991).

62. Fareed Zakaria, "The Rise of Illiberal Democracy," *Foreign Affairs,* November/December 1997, 22–43.

Acknowledgments

The idea for this book originated many years ago, when Timothy Cheek suggested that I should turn the narrative of my documentary collection of pre-1949 materials into a stand-alone book. Not having done that, it seemed a good time to write a longer history of the Chinese Communist Party as it approached its hundredth anniversary. I want to thank Kathleen McDermott at Harvard University Press for displaying faith in the project and shepherding it through the publishing process.

The endnotes reveal the debts I owe to various colleagues. I am especially grateful to my teachers David S. G. Goodman and Stuart R. Schram, who launched me on the path of inquiry about China. I benefited enormously from discussions about Chinese politics with Roderick MacFarquhar.

The specific genesis of this book derived from lengthy conversations with Arne Westad, who encouraged me to plow ahead with the project. The book benefited from the comments of three anonymous readers. In addition, Timothy Cheek, Amanda Saich, Ezra Vogel, Andrew Walder, and Arne Westad provided great feedback on earlier drafts. Sarah Gruzca provided wizardry with the illustrations, and Mark Seah helped with locating the photos. I am lucky to have access to the resources of both the Fairbank Center Library and the Harvard-Yenching Library and the support of the staff. My colleagues at the Ash Center for Democratic Governance and Innovation provide a stimulating environment for work. I would like to thank Isabelle Lewis for the maps of Republican China, the Long March, and the PRC today. As with so many works in the China field, Nancy Hearst put the bibliographic details to right and also reviewed the entire manuscript. Wendy Nelson from Westchester Publishing Services did a wonderful job with the copyediting.

Portions of Chapter 12 were first published as "What Does General Secretary Xi Jinping Dream About?," Ash Center Occasional Paper Series, Harvard Kennedy School, August 2017, 1–22.

Illustration Credits

53   Photograph by Tony Saich

66   Paul Popper/Popperfoto/Getty Images

94   World History Archive/Alamy Stock Photo

143   Wu Yinxian/Magnum Photos

216   Tiananmen Archives Collection of the Harvard-Yenching Library of the Harvard College Library, Harvard University

217   Sovfoto/Getty Images

234   © Li Zhensheng/Contact Press Images

238   Tiananmen Archives Collection of the Harvard-Yenching Library of the Harvard College Library, Harvard University

264   David King Collection. Photo © Tate

265   Photograph by Tony Saich

266   Photograph by Tony Saich

267   Tiananmen Archives Collection of the Harvard-Yenching Library of the Harvard College Library, Harvard University

268   Tiananmen Archives Collection of the Harvard-Yenching Library of the Harvard College Library, Harvard University

274   International Institute of Social History

284   Photograph by Tony Saich

288   Bettmann/Getty Images

290   Photograph by Tony Saich

309   Tiananmen Archives Collection of the Harvard-Yenching Library of the Harvard College Library, Harvard University

311   Tiananmen Archives Collection of the Harvard-Yenching Library of the Harvard College Library, Harvard University

365   *Top:* Used by permission of Bin Zhang

365   *Bottom:* Photograph by Sarah Grucza

367   Photograph by Sarah Grucza
401   Reproduced from inews.ifeng.com
411   Xinhua News Agency/Getty Images
459   Xinhua News Agency/Getty Images

Index

Note: Figures are indexed in italic.

agriculture, 24, 26, 198, 214, 227, 280, 293; agricultural taxes abolished (2006), 369; APCs (agricultural producers' cooperatives), 201–202, 215; collectivization of, 199, 272, 279, 366; communal kitchens and, 217–218; communes and, 215, 452; cooperatives, 129; decentralization of, 298; Five-Year Plans and, 209; gross value of, 270; industrial sector and, 259, 273, 275; mechanization of, 208; modernization of, 257, 279; "Oriental despotism" and, 30; recovery after GLF and, 213, 224, 225, 226; in Republican period, 65, 128; socialist, 187; Soviet planning model and, 199; "three-dimensional rural problem" and, 362–363. *See also* land reform

anarchism, 35, 44, 45, 51, 163

Anti-Rightist Campaign (1950s), 153, 211–213, 270, 282, 326, 449

Belt and Road Initiative (BRI), 25, 407, 413, 416, 422–425, 432, 452, 466

Bo Gu, 84, 86, 88–90, 95, 96, 110; Mao's leadership accepted by, 137; rivalry with Mao, 130; San Francisco Conference and, 142; war against Japan and, 111

Bolsheviks, 9, 38–39, 48, 69, 152, 158

Borodin, Mikhail, 50, 54, 56–57, 61, 158; flight from Wuhan, 69; Northern Expedition and, 62–63; on Shanghai as revolutionary center, 64

Bo Xilai, 386–389, 390, 391, 399, 402, 451, 464

Bo Yibo, 191, 192, 203, 278, 304

Braun, Otto, 88, 89, 90, 91, 95

Britain/British empire, 32–33, 38, 43, 120, 222

Bush, George W., 343, 349, 350, 356, 383, 384

Campaign to Suppress Counterrevolutionaries (1950–1953), 184, 191–192, 193, 490n13

capitalism, 21, 36, 123, 127, 229, 303, 440; socialism as transition from, 214; state capitalism, 181, 395

"capitalist roaders," 14, 225, 237, 262, 263, 265, 276

CCP (Chinese Communist Party): broadened appeal of, 122–124; changing of the guard in 21st century, 354–356; Chinese tradition and, 36; control over society, 193–195; debates on economic strategy/leadership, 208–210; demise of USSR and, 317–319; diversity within, 1–7; dominance of state and society, 435–437; emergence from wilderness, 100–102; formal and informal organization of, 7–11; founding (1921), 15; groundwork laid for (1920s), 42–45; heritage of military struggle and,

CCP (Chinese Communist Party)
(*continued*)
440–443; historical narrative control
by, 437–440; insurrections of 1920s as
policy failure, 70–73; language used by,
1, 8, 11, 441; micropolitics and, 163,
174, 449; myths about origins of, 42,
46–47; national unity after Cultural
Revolution and, 252–258; policy
response to economic hardship, 125–129;
preparation for rule, 179–184; rise to
power, 152; scientific development and,
358–362; social unrest and, 371–376,
381, 406–407; sources of legitimacy,
456–461; techniques of rule, 446–449;
unification under Mao, 127, 129–133.
See also Central Committee; civil war,
CCP-GMD; Communist revolution,
Chinese; Politburo
CCP–GMD alliance, first (1920s), 49–51,
164; after Chiang's betrayal, 67–70;
debates among communists over, 60–65;
growth of CCP fueled by, 55–57; role
of working class and, 57–61; Third
Party Congress and, 51–54
CCP–GMD alliance, second (war against
Japan), 102–107, 141–143; fragility of,
115–120; Mao's clash with Wang Ming
and, 109–114
Central Committee (CC), 8, 15, 25, 68,
79, 138; creation of PRC and, 183;
land reform and, 187; preparation for
Communist rule, 180; Secretariat and,
113
Chen Boda, 136, 234, 235, 239, 242,
243, 255; downfall of, 248, 249;
Rescue Campaign and, 137; trial of,
281
Chen Duxiu, 10, 45, 62, 67, 68, 154, 439,
472n6; at First Party Congress, 48;
GMD–CCP alliance and, 50–51, 53,
64, 65; origins of CCP and, 46, 47;
peasant movement and, 74; resignation
of, 69; Stalinist criticism of, 71; Trotsky's
influence and, 61, 139; on workers and
CCP, 164

Chen Yun, 110, 159, 214, 225, 272, 277,
279, 294, 304, 305; compromise with
Deng, 322; as critic of reforms, 291,
292, 293, 296, 312, 321; Soviet
planning model and, 213
Chiang Kai-shek, 9, 46, 55, 67, 70, 93,
101; CCP strategy to isolate, 113;
China's Destiny (1943), 139; civil war
and, 150, 151; communists in Shanghai
suppressed (1927), 66, 164; corruption
surrounding, 167; deterioration of
relationship with Soviet Union, 121;
GMD inefficiency and, 171; kidnapped
in Xi'an, 106, 116, 158, 174; legacy of
Sun Yat-sen and, 132; Northern Expedition and, 62–63, 64, 65; pursuit of
communists in Long March, 173; retreat
to Taiwan, 182; second united front
with CCP and, 112, 141; slide toward
civil war and, 147; strategy of, 87–88;
suppression campaigns of, 79, 80, 82, 83,
89; tarnished credibility of, 161–162;
war against Japan and, 103–107, 109,
114, 117–118, 161
China, imperial. *See* Qing dynasty
China, People's Republic of (PRC):
break with Soviet Union, 221–223;
as challenge to US hegemony, 349;
economic growth (1980s), 289;
establishment of, 180, 181; as global
power, 419, *420*, 421–422, 454, 466;
"golden age" of, 197–203; Olympic
Games (2008) hosted in, 379, 384, 390;
political purges in, 203–206; red-hot
economy of 1990s, 326–329; role in
Asia, 422–425; seat in UN Security
Council, 252, 453; Tibet incorporated
into, 177; US relations with, 251–252,
382–386, 412, 425–429, 432, 444,
466
civil war, CCP-GMD, 144–146, 148–151
class struggle, 14, 58, 105, 212, 214;
economic reforms and, 316; persistence
under socialism, 206; road to Cultural
Revolution and, 228, 231
Clinton, Bill, 12, 334, 344, 345, 347, 351

Comintern (Communist International), 43, 44, 46, 49, 76, 84, 130; crucial role in Chinese revolution, 156, 157, 158–159; dissolution of, 139, 159; Far Eastern Bureau, 73, 75; GMD–CCP united fronts and, 53, 58, 65, 104; influence over CCP, 73, 122; Long March and, 90–91; Second Congress (1920), 48, 50; Shanghai disaster (1927) and, 136; united front against fascism and, 158

Communist revolution, Chinese, 152–155, 173–174; GMD corruption / incompetence and, 170–173; indigenous nature of, 443–445; nationalist resistance to Japan and, 159–162; role of organization and ideology in, 167–170; as series of different revolutions, 450; socioeconomic policies and, 162–167; Soviet Russian role in, 156–159

Confucianism, 13, 24, 28, 35, 193, 409; Campaign to Criticize Lin Biao and Confucius, 256, 372; imperial system and, 34; modern mass party and, 168; neo-Confucian revival, 369; undermined by revolution, 28–32

COVID-19 outbreak (December 2019), 12, 391, 415, 431, 445; economic effects of, 418, 455; PRC government failures in response to, 359, 462; in United States, 416, 429

Cultural Revolution (1966–1969), 4, 18, 30, 136, 153, 295, 330, 372, 389; class struggle and, 228; complete dismantling of, 281; death toll of, 240–241, 500n97; efforts to safeguard gains of, 249, 254, 255, 258, 261, 262, 272; faded memories of failures of, 440; falling out among elites in, 464; idea of continual revolution and, 215; legacies of, 269–272; limits on critique of, 436; Mao cult and, 5, 139, 238, 246; Mao's attacks on the party, 221, 232; "old party" decimated in, 9; order restored by PLA, 241–244; party assessment of, 252–258; political adventurism of, 17; political campaigns

leading to, 177; recovery from, 453; Red Guards, 233, 236, 237, 238, 242, 245–246, 252, 272; reevaluation of, 278; Rescue Campaign as dress rehearsal for, 137–138; as rule through chaos, 230–241, 234; scientific community devastated by, 259; time frame of, 469n4; violent rhetoric of, 441. See also "Gang of Four"

democracy, 8, 269, 285, 337, 466; Chinese traditional culture and, 463; Goddess of Democracy statue (1989), 310, 311; inner-party, 371, 377; social democracy, 318; Western (liberal) constitutional, 173, 404–405

Democracy Wall Movement (1978–1979), 270, 283–284

Deng Xiaoping, 1, 10, 88, 211, 224, 415; Anti-Rightist Campaign and, 212, 285; break with legacy of Maoism, 277–282; brought back by Mao (1973), 255–256; conservative backlash to reforms and, 312–315; as core of second-generation leadership, 329; Cultural Revolution and, 5, 236, 239, 241, 244, 253, 504n44; death of, 335, 390; Democracy Movement and, 282–287; economic plans (1975–1976) and, 258–259; empiricism of, 1, 260; focus on the economy, 257; "Gang of Four" campaigns against, 259–264, 271, 444; legacies of, 325, 344; legacy of Mao and, 272–277; limits of reform and, 436; Long March and, 93; as managerial modernizer, 207; mass campaigns curtailed under, 448; pace of reforms and, 305; party critics of reforms and, 290–294; PLA political influence and, 296; reforms overseen by, 17, 24; retreat from GLF and, 226, 227, 229, 230; sovereignty over Hong Kong and, 346; Tiananmen Square crisis and, 306, 307, 308, 310, 312; tour of South China to revive reform, 316–324, 333

Eighth Route Army (ERA), 107, 109, 117, 119, 161; Mao's clash with Wang Ming and, 110; mobile warfare and, 111; 100 Regiments Campaign, 125

Falun Gong movement, 193, 333, 383, 407
financial crisis, global (2008–2009), 379, 394, 410, 454, 458

"Gang of Four," 7, 220, 240, 258, 277, 444, 498n66; arrest of, 266, 269, 272, 275, 283, 318, 439, 442, 499n68; campaigns against Zhou and Deng, 259–264; downfall after Mao's death, 264–268, 265–268, 282; trial of, 281
Gao Gang, 102, 138, 192, 196, 203–206
GMD [Guomindang] (Nationalist Party), 9, 14, 16, 90, 160, 438; failures and incompetence of, 170–173; flight to Taiwan, 30; Leninist structure of, 56, 170; New Life Movement, 171; Northern Expedition, 62, 163, 164, 171; peasantry and, 74–75; pro-Japanese elements within, 119–120; war against Japan and, 34, 43, 111; warlord factions and, 27; warlords and, 57. See also CCP–GMD alliance; civil war, CCP-GMD
Gorbachev, Mikhail, 305, 308, 310, 316, 317–318, 334
Great Leap Forward (GLF), 3, 168, 213, 222, 232, 249, 270, 405; backyard steel furnaces, 217, 217; commune as innovation of, 215, 216; criticized as adventurist, 278; deaths from starvation during, 4, 271; disastrous effects on economy, 220–221; economic adventurism of, 17; faded memories of failures of, 440; famine caused by, 208, 217–218; opposition to, 219; recovery from, 213, 224, 225, 226, 453; retreat from, 224–226; voluntarism of, 446
Guangzhou (Canton), city of, 24, 32, 39; early days of CCP and, 60, 64; Guangzhou Commune, 71

Hong Kong, 15, 33, 177, 328, 353; last British governor denounced, 441; mass demonstrations in, 415, 429–432; return to Chinese sovereignty, 335, 344, 345–346
Hua Guofeng, 243, 253, 264, 271, 279, 281, 289, 337; Cultural Revolution and, 263; downfall of "Gang of Four" and, 265–266, 267, 282; legacy of Mao and, 272–277, 274
Hu Jintao, 11, 22, 323, 339, 355, 394; collective leadership and, 9–10; future of economic reform and, 457, 458; legacies of, 455; on NATO bombing of Chinese embassy in Belgrade, 348; neo-Confucianism and, 30; populist authoritarianism and, 357; scientific development and, 362; social control and, 371, 373; "three-dimensional rural problem" and, 366, 368, 370; US visit of, 383
Hundred Flowers Movement, 210–213, 214, 230, 285
Hu Yaobang, 259, 280, 282, 285, 289, 296, 322, 342; death of, 307; party critics of reforms and, 291, 292; removal of, 299, 300, 301

imperialism, 44, 46, 85, 140, 190, 247, 438; nuclear weapons and, 221, 222; "social imperialism" of Soviet Union, 251, 258; US imperialism, 221, 247, 258; World War II and, 121

Japan, 189, 343, 353, 382, 466; attack on Pearl Harbor, 121; defeat in World War II, 115, 145, 187; economic slowdown in, 458; Meiji reforms, 34, 45; US military bases in, 384
Japanese invasion of China, 16, 28, 167, 326, 441; in Manchuria, 82, 84, 102–103, 114, 158; occupation of Shanghai, 108, 109, 438; Operation Ichigo (1944), 141, 161; survival of CCP and, 159–162, 172; Tanggu Truce (1933), 87, 103. See also CCP–GMD alliance, second

Jiang Qing, 231, 232, 235, 240, 242–244, 246, 250, 253, 439; Deng Xiaoping in conflict with, 258; as leader of radical group, 248; self-criticism of, 272; trial of, 13, 281. *See also* "Gang of Four"

Jiangxi Soviet (1931–1934), 26, 75, 77, 78–82, 84, 97, 164, 450; evacuation of, 116, 173; failure of, 174; highs and lows of, 85–90

Jiang Zemin, 11, 313–314, 316, 339, 354–356, 370, 398, 510n43; Deng's legacies and, 325; "Develop the West" program, 341; economic reforms and, 319, 320, 321, 334–335; legacy of, 350–354; nationalism and, 343; PLA and, 322, 340; rise to leadership, 329–330; Shanghai gang of, 329, 375; sovereignty issues and, 346–347; in Soviet Union, 317; Three Represents policy, 12, 350, 355, 358, 377, 437, 469n6; tightened control over society, 330–334; WTO membership and, 351

Kang Sheng, 110, 133, 138, 230, 243; Cultural Revolution and, 234, 235, 241; death of, 258; inner-party struggle and, 159; Rescue Campaign and, 137

Khrushchev, Nikita, 14, 209, 221–223, 232, 235, 247, 350, 443

Korea, North (DPRK), 196, 197, 372, 382, 385–386, 425, 426

Korea, South (Republic of Korea), 197, 336, 360, 384, 434, 458, 461, 466, 514n30

Korean War, 184, 190, 191, 193, 202, 439

Kuomintang. *See* GMD [Guomindang]

Land Law, 78, 86, 87, 185–186, 187

landlords, 14, 17, 71, 87, 123, 130, 162, 437; beaten and humiliated, 190; class categories and, 165, 189; execution of, 3, 190; land reform and, 187; middle peasants reclassified as, 89; sympathetic to Communist cause, 185

land reform, 115, 166, 167, 184–190, 197

"left deviation," 13, 71, 121, 138, 185

Lei Feng, 229, 293, 314, 324, 442

Lenin, Vladimir, 30, 49, 86, 130, 144, 439

Leninism, 8, 15, 16; democratic centralism, 446; economic reforms and, 312; GMD organized on lines of, 9, 170, 171; party structure and, 36, 168; political reform and, 462; struggle against imperialism and, 44. *See also* Marxism-Leninism

Li Dazhao, 45, 67, 154, 172–173, 472n6; First Party Congress and, 48; origins of CCP and, 46

Li Keqiang, 378, 392, 393, 394, 395, 413, 414

Li Lisan, 42, 52, 59, 72, 79, 83, 87, 136, 139

Lin Biao, 75–76, 205, 227, 244, 254–256, 283, 439; Campaign to Criticize Lin Biao and Confucius, 256–257; civil war and, 149, 150; Cultural Revolution and, 231, 233, 234, 236, 237, 241, 246, 268; downfall and death of, 248–252, 254, 498n66, 499n68; named as Mao's successor, 247, 255; PLA led by, 229, 233

Li Peng, 296, 305, 310, 313, 314, 323, 335, 337, 358; on anti-reform leftism, 320; legacy of Deng and, 325; special economic zones and, 316; Three Gorges Dam and, 378

Liu Shaoqi, 5, 13–14, 42, 73, 138, 224, 277, 472n1; Campaign to Suppress Counterrevolutionaries and, 191; as "capitalist roader," 276; Confucianism and, 30, 372; contacts with Soviets, 159; creation of PRC and, 179, 182; criticism of Mao and the GLF, 220, 226–229; Gao Gang's criticism of, 203; "hundred flowers" phrase and, 210, 211; land reform and, 184, 185–186, 188, 189; Mao's alliance with, 112, 130; rehabilitation of, 278; as victim of Cultural Revolution, 139, 205, 212, 239, 243–244, 247, 501n4

Long March (1934–1935), 26, 77, 86, 90–91, 93–96, 116, 137; Mao during, 94–95, 173; map of routes, 92; mythic status of, 439; pilgrimage sites associated with, 238; veterans of, 102, 161

Maoism, 37, 126, 127, 133, 177, 345, 450; global influence of, 154; high point of, 253; neo-Maoism, 387; obsession with grain production, 304, 337; relationship of art/literature to political power, 135; spontaneous mass participation in, 270

Mao Zedong, 16, 42, 156, 321, 438; campaigns against "counterrevolutionaries," 79–80; Comintern and, 159; as "core leader," 10, 115; Cultural Revolution and, 230–241, 243, 261, 268, 269, 273, 281, 282, 448; cult worship of, 5, 9; death of, 7, 17, 23, 258, 264, 439, 469n4; early days of CCP and, 52, 54, 60; "Gang of Four" and, 262, 263, *264*, 268, 283; on humiliation of China by foreigners, 33, 169; independent intellectual inquiry quashed by, 133–136; Jiangxi Soviet and, 85–86, 88; Korean War and, 196–197; land policy and, 184; leadership of the CCP, 112, 127, 129–133, 136–144, 168; Long March and, 94–95, 173; Nixon's visit to China and, 251–252, 287; permissible criticism of, 278, 293; on political power and violence, 71; on "red and expert," 259; revolutionary potential of peasantry and, 38, 56, 73–76; second united front with GMD and, 112; Sinification of Marxism and, 44, 129, 169, 372; Stalin's influence on, 206, 207; voluntarism of, 126, 179, 214, 222, 446–447; Wang Ming as rival of, 108, 109–114, 120, 130, 132–133, 139, 159, 482n30; war against Japan and, 118; Xi Jinping compared to, 413, 414; Zhang Guotao as rival of, 26, 47, 77, 96–100, 439

Mao Zedong, writings/speeches of: *Critique of Soviet Economics*, 214; "hundred flowers" speech (1957), 210–213, 214; "Introduction to *The Communist*" (1939), 122; "New Democratic Politics" (1940), 122, 123; "On the Correct Handling of Contradictions among the People" (1957), 212; "On New Democracy" (1940), 114; "On the

People's Democratic Dictatorship" (1949), 182; "On the Question of Agricultural Cooperativization" (1955), 201–202; "On the Ten Major Relationships," 210, 214, 273; Sixty Articles on Agriculture, 224

Mao Zedong Thought, 9, 11, 247, 285, 335, 459, 460

Marxism, 8, 29, 39, 154, 369, 391; Confucian revival and, 30; disregard for the environment, 456; as scientific truth, 211; Sinification of, 44, 129, 153, 169, 372, 444; theory of knowledge, 446, 447; workers' understanding of, 60; in Xi Jinping era, 409–410

Marxism-Leninism, 14, 16, 131, 180, 232, 482n37; decline as source of CCP legitimacy, 456; Mao Zedong Thought and, 247, 335

May Fourth Movement (1915–1919), 10, 39, 43, 115, 130, 314, 441; anniversary of, 307; cosmopolitanism of, 134; liberalism and, 172

nationalism, 58, 155, 331, 334, 342, 357, 466; Communism and, 162; diplomatic "wolf warriors" and, 445; patriotic education and, 444; peasant, 159; revival of traditional culture and, 410; Sun Yat-sen's principles and, 154

Nationalist Party. *See* GMD [Guomindang]

New Democracy, 134, 143, 178, 193, 210

New Fourth Army (NFA), 107, 111, 116, 117, 119, 125, 161

Nie Yuanzi, 230, 236, 237, 239, 245–246, 499n81

Nixon, Richard, 251–252, 287

Obama, Barack, 384–385, 421, 426

Opium War, First (1839–1842), 22, 27, 28, 32–33, 132, 154

Opium War, Second (1856–1860), 28, 33, 132, 154

peasantry, 63, 73–76, 128, 143, 436, 452; abandonment of cooperatives, 212;

CCP–GMD alliance (1920s) and, 164; collective structures rejected by, 225; exploited to build socialism, 214; land reform and, 186–189; middle peasants, 87, 89, 166, 186; poor peasants, 165, 167, 201; radicalism beyond party's intentions, 166; rich peasants, 89, 125, 130, 167, 189; rural collectives and, 187; support for CCP, 162, 163; toleration of private markets and, 279; wealthy peasants, 78

Peng Dehuai, 72, 80, 109, 227, 252, 277, 282, 293; criticism of GLF, 219, 249; Korean War and, 197; rehabilitation of, 278

Peng Zhen, 124, 125, 128, 147, 224, 230, 299; Campaign to Suppress Counterrevolutionaries and, 191; as critic of reforms, 291; Cultural Revolution and, 231, 233–235; "hundred flowers" phrase and, 211; rehabilitation of, 278; village elections and, 450

people's democratic dictatorship, 22, 182, 285, 295

PLA (People's Liberation Army), 26, 182, 229, 276, 340; civilian control of the military, 322; in civil war, 149, 150; Cultural Revolution and, 231–232, 240, 241–244, 443; military models for society, 442. See also Red Army

Politburo, 9, 72, 276, 377, 382; Cultural Revolution and, 231, 261; economic reforms and, 312; land policy and, 127; Mao as member of, 89; Mao's clash with Wang Ming and, 111; preparation for Communist rule, 180–181; Secretariat subordinated to, 138

proletariat, 14, 48, 58, 60, 67, 163; dictatorship of, 47, 182, 260, 295; diminished importance of, 84; isolation of, 62; mass Communist party and, 52; party's links with urban proletariat broken, 71; peasantry in relation to, 72, 74, 86; struggle against imperialism and, 123. See also working class

Qing dynasty (1644–1912), 21–24, 26–28, 32–36, 43, 154, 180, 441–442, 445, 465

Rectification Campaign (1942–1944), 122, 127, 130, 131, 144, 159, 168, 235, 441; Sinification of Marxism and, 169

Red Army, 72, 75, 86; Long March and, 91, 94; uses of, 77; in war against Japan, 103, 107. See also Eighth Route Army, Fourth Front Army; PLA (People's Liberation Army)

reforms, pro-market, 4, 289; conservative backlash and, 311–316; difficult consequences of, 339–342; maintaining of, 334–339; mixed signals of Twelfth Party Congress and, 294–305; party critics of, 289–294; Tiananmen Square crisis and, 306–308, 309, 310, 311

revisionism, 207, 230; in Soviet Union, 221, 223, 232, 247; in Yugoslavia, 14, 228

"right opportunists," 13, 65, 69, 89, 110, 120, 168, 220

Russia, post-Soviet, 422, 425, 465, 466

Russian Revolution (1917), 39, 45, 152

SARS outbreak (2002–2003), 12, 359, 368, 371, 415

Shanghai, city of, 4, 24, 32, 163, 183; CCP revival in, 108–109; communists/leftists slaughtered (1927), 55, 66, 171; demise as revolutionary center, 83–84; French Concession, 21, 47, 67; International Settlement, 39, 59, 66–67, 84; Japanese bombing of, 84; Japanese occupation of, 108, 109; labor organizing in, 58–59; origins of CCP and, 46, 47; Shanghai faction of CCP, 11; Shanghai People's Commune, 240

Sneevliet, Henk (alias Maring), 46, 50–51, 53–54, 56, 157, 158, 473n16

socialism, 182, 209, 212, 275, 301; central planning and, 303; "with Chinese characteristics," 22, 321, 335, 395, 412, 413, 418, 437, 444; civil society and, 179; class struggle under, 260; collectivization

socialism (*continued*)
and, 190, 201; contradictions in, 215,
222; democratic revolution and, 112,
123, 143; persistence of class struggle
in, 206; primary stage of, 321, 323,
336, 413; proletariat in leading role,
86; speed of progress toward, 79, 209;
as transitional form between capitalism and communism, 214; transition to, 149, 178–179, 181, 198, 204,
213, 214, 216, 224, 225
Socialist Education Movement (1962–
1965), 228, 230, 231, 233, 236, 498n59
SOEs (state-owned enterprises), 293, 320,
322, 324, 327, 338, 339, 360–362, 378,
409; CCP cells in, 437; debts of, 329,
336; inefficient, 454; Japan and South
Korea as models, 396; layoffs, 355;
policy favoring, 416–417; restructuring
of, 325, 335, 359; revived by stimulus,
380; trade agreement with United
States and, 429; WTO and, 351, 352,
353; "zombie," 395
South China Sea, 398, *420*, 421, 422,
426
Soviet Union (USSR), 16, 64, 104, 144,
463; CCP strength in Northeast and,
172; Chiang Kai-shek and, 106; China
alienated from, 36; collapse of (1989), 7,
316, 331, 344, 382, 418, 445; economic
development model of, 178, 198–199,
207; end of alliance with PRC, 221–223;
hardliners' coup (1991), 317; interest in
CCP–GMD cooperation, 145; Korean
War and, 196–197; neutrality pact with
Japan, 121; nonaggression pact with Nazi
Germany, 120; policy shifts leading up
to World War II, 120; PRC alliance
with, 195–196; PRC conflicts with, 245,
251; response to Chiang's White Terror,
67; "revisionism" in, 14; role in Chinese
Communist revolution, 156–159; "social
imperialism" of, 251, 258; troops
withdrawn from Manchuria, 146–148;
uprisings in Eastern Europe crushed
by, 210; view of socialism, 215; war

against Japan and, 145. *See also*
Bolsheviks; Russian Revolution
Stalin, Joseph, 2, 9, 67, 103, 160, 203–204,
295; accusatory language used by, 13;
CCP–GMD alliance (1920s) and, 55,
61, 64, 157; Chiang kidnapping in
Xi'an and, 106; collectivization policy,
190; criticism of, 136; death of, 221;
influence on Mao, 206, 207; interest
in CCP–GMD cooperation, 145–146,
150; Khrushchev's denunciation of,
209, 221; Korean War and, 196–197;
Mao compared to, 130, 439, 443; Mao's
criticism of, 212, 214; on peasants and
land policy, 188; reputation of, 228;
response to failure of CCP–GMD
alliance, 69; rivalry with Trotsky, 38,
61, 62, 63, 157; *Short History*, 159;
Soviet economic aid to China and,
125; Soviet industrialization and,
179
Stalinism, 15, 36, 71, 232; collectivization and, 209; inner-party struggle
and, 159
Sun Yat-sen, 9, 24, 39, 49, 54, 157;
collaboration with Soviet Russia and,
51, 56, 57; death of, 58, 61; dream of
land to the tiller, 143, 184; as founder
of GMD, 42; legacy of, 65, 132, 143;
"three people's principles" of, 154

Taiwan, 9, 15, 30, 189, 190, 344,
346–347, 349, 382; as China's major
sovereignty challenge, 422; democracy
in, 463, 466; diplomatic truce with
PRC, 386; economic development in,
461; economic slowdown in, 458; GMD
loss of power in, 354; as GMD stronghold, 177; independence movement in,
345, 354; indigenous resistance to GMD
rule, 347; US military support for,
287, 426
Three-Anti and Five-Anti Campaigns
(1951–1953), 184, 190–191, 192, 213
Three Represents policy, 12, 350, 355,
358, 372, 377, 437, 469n6

Tiananmen Square crisis (1989), 11, 288, 306–308, *309*, *311*, 313, 343, 464

Tibet, 15, 24, 25–26, 188, 190, 323, 431; Dalai Lama's influence in, 25, 26; defined as integral part of China, 445; end of autonomy for, 218; incorporated into PRC, 177; set up as autonomous region, 183; unrest in, 333, 379, 405; uprising in (1959), 218–219

Trotsky, Leon, 38, 62, 63, 64; criticism of Stalin's China policy, 157–158; on failure of CCP–GMD alliance, 70; independence of CCP supported by, 61

"Trotskyites," 13, 73, 136, 203, 249

Trump, Donald, 15, 395, 418, 421, 454; China's relationship with, 425–429; North Korea and, 425

ultra-leftism, 186–187, 241, 278, 441; Cultural Revolution and, 242, 245, 248, 249

United States, 120, 144, 146, 222, 343–344, 444, 466; Asian countries in US sphere of influence, 461–462; atomic bombings of Japan, 145; Belt and Road Initiative (BRI) and, 423; COVID-19 in, 416, 429; Deng Xiaoping's visit to, 285, 287–288; interest in CCP–GMD cooperation, 141, 142, 145, 148; in Korean War, 197; Nixon's visits to China, 251–252, 287; Al-Qaeda attack on (September 2001), 349; Taiwan issue and, 345, 347–348, 349, 426; US imperialism, 221, 247, 258; wars in Afghanistan and Iraq, 350, 382; in World War II, 121

urbanization, 194, 395, 397, 398, 456

Vietnam, 152, 191, *420*, 422, 425; Chinese invasion (1979), 285, 287–288; economic growth in, 461; US war in, 245, 287

Voitinsky, Grigori, 46–47, 53, 56, 61, 157, 158, 473n9; at Fourth CCP Congress, 57; reports to Moscow on CCP–GMD alliance, 62

Wang Dongxing, 235, 265, 276, 277, 280

Wang Hongwen, 239–240, 244, 253, 255, 256, 258, 281, 498n66

Wang Jingwei, 66, 68, 70; pro-Japanese regime of, 114, 120, 170; warlords and, 82

Wang Ming, 73, 90, 100, 117, 122; Mao's leadership accepted by, 137; reduced influence of, 129; returned students' loyalty to, 132; as returnee from Moscow, 10, 77, 81, 156, 158; rivalry with Mao, 108, 109–114, 130, 132–133, 139, 159, 482n30; second united front with GMD and, 103

warlords, 27, 39, 52, 57, 65, 93

Wei Jingsheng, 283, 284, 285, 300, 306

Wen Jiabao, 339, 356, 357, 358, 364; future of economic reform and, 457, 458; legacies of, 455; SARS epidemic and, 359; "three-dimensional rural problem" and, 362–363, 368, 370

working class, 51, 56, 108, 164, 212–213, 325, 332, 436; economic reforms and, 338; national revolution and, 59. *See also* proletariat

World Bank, 332, 384, 416, 458, 461

WTO (World Trade Organization), 325, 340, 342, 347, 427; China's entry into, 347, 349, 351, 352, 362, 385, 444, 455; China's regional trade as challenge to, 416

Xiang Ying, 80–81, 85, 91, 95, 117; death of, 119, 120; second united front with GMD and, 118

Xi Jinping, 7, 15, 22, 355, 388, 432–433, 450; centralization and, 8, 415, 452, 455, 465; China as global power and, 419; China Dream slogan, 370, 391, 393, 400, 411, 432, *459*; consolidation of power, 10–11, 392–394, 399–400; as "core leader," 10; corruption as target of, 376, 400–404, 415, 462; COVID-19 outbreak and, 359; dominance within CCP leadership, 413–416; economic slowdown and, 417–418; elevation

Xi Jinping (*continued*)
within the party, 378, 390–391; exercise of power by, 400–410; historical narrative control and, 438; Mao's legacy and, 135; Marxist ideology and, 409–410; neo-Confucianism and, 29–30; at Nineteenth Party Congress, 410–412, *411*, 419; placed on level of Mao, 11; reform policies of, 394–398; relationship with Trump, 426–429; religion in China and, 463; revisionist history and, 221; Sinification of Marxism and, 444; Victory Day celebrations and, 160
Xinjiang, 15, 24, 240, 407–408, 431, 463; CCP fear of radical Islam in, 25; defined as integral part of China, 445; "reeducation" program for Muslims, 4–5, 408; set up as autonomous region, 183; unrest in, 333, 405

Yantian village, 3, 32, 364; changes in, *365*; Great Leap Forward (GLF) in, 217–218; party control in, 202
Yao Wenyuan, 231, 232, 240, 254, 260, 281. *See also* "Gang of Four"
Ye Jianying, 71, 265, 276–277, 278, 294
Yugoslavia, 160, 197, 227; NATO bombing of, 348, 351, 352; revisionism in, 14, 228

Zhang Chunqiao, 231, 240, 242, 244, 254, 257, 258, 260, 262, 281. *See also* "Gang of Four"
Zhang Guotao, 26, 47, 73, 77, 82; expelled from CCP, 129; GMD–CCP alliance and, 49, 50, 53–54; Long March and, 94; rivalry with Mao, 26, 47, 77, 97–100, 439; Sichuan-Shaanxi Base Area established by, 83
Zhang Wentian, 90, 91, 95, 96, 110, 113
Zhang Xueliang, 104, 105, 106, 174
Zhao Ziyang, 10, 279, 280, 289, 296, 301, 304–305, 322, 342, 465; central planning criticized by, 303; party critics of reforms and, 291, 292, 313; purge of, 311, 314, 315, 316, 462; Tiananmen Square crisis and, 308, 310
Zhou Enlai, 60, 73, 84, 90, 110, 224, 256, 286; creation of PRC and, 179, 183; Cultural Revolution and, 233, 234, 235, 243, 246; death of, 258, 262; "Gang of Four" campaigns against, 260, 261, 263; Great Leap Forward (GLF) and, 215; Jiangxi Soviet and, 85, 86; Nixon's visit to China and, 251; purge of Gao Gang and, 203, 204, 494n78; second united front with GMD and, 142; support for Mao's leadership, 136–137; war against Japan and, 105, 111, 160–161
Zhou Yongkang, 356, 360, 388, 399, 402–403, 451
Zhu De, 72, 75, 80, 85, 98, 109, 286; death of, 258; end of "iron rice bowl" and, 338; Jiangxi Soviet and, 86; second united front with GMD and, 118
Zhu Rongji, 320, 326, 330, 336, 337, 370, 396, 444; industrial reform and, 327; legacy of Deng and, 325; WTO membership and, 351